American Passages

A History of the United States
VOLUME II: SINCE 1863

Brief Second Edition

EDWARD L. AYERS
University of Virginia

LEWIS L. GOULD
University of Texas at Austin, Emeritus

DAVID M. OSHINSKY
University of Texas at Austin

JEAN R. SODERLUND
Lehigh University

THOMSON
———✶———
WADSWORTH

Australia · Canada · Mexico · Singapore · Spain
United Kingdom · United States

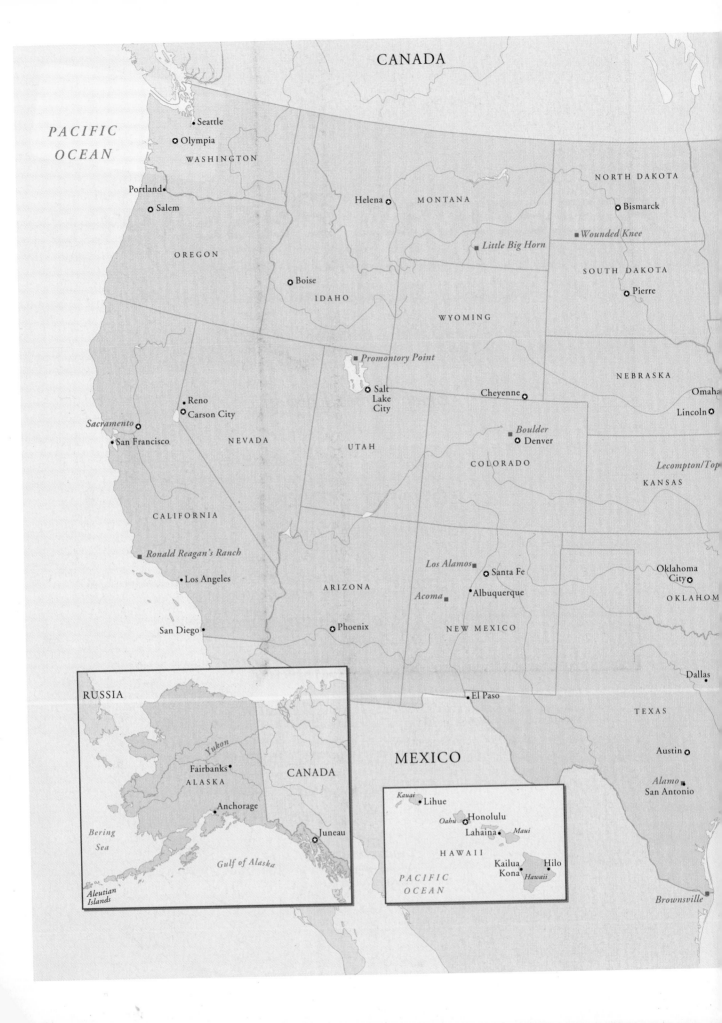

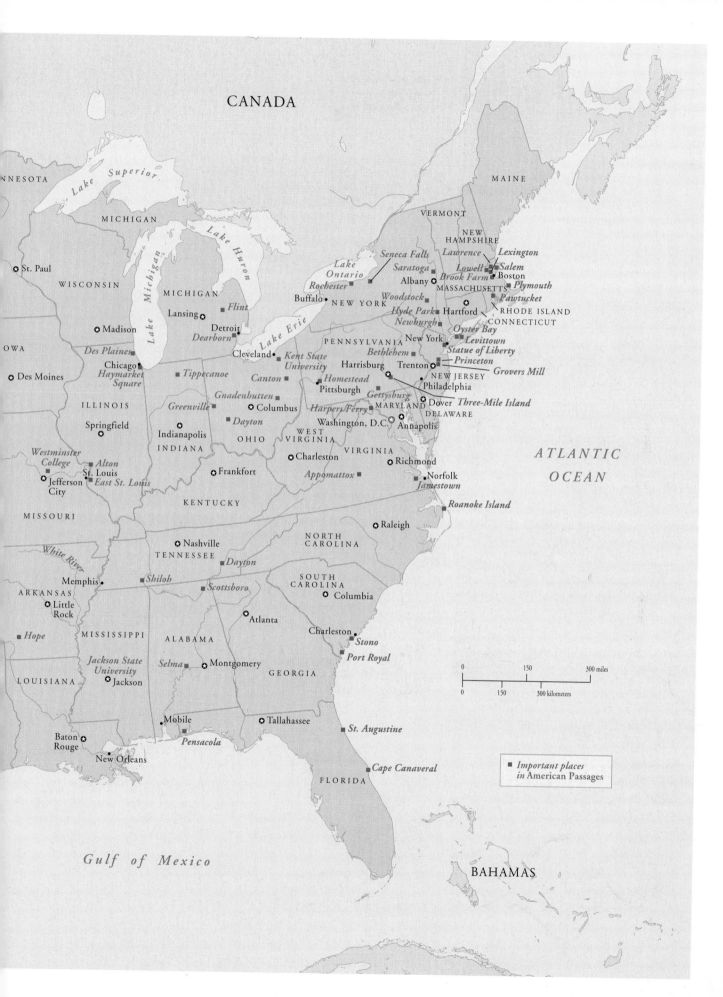

CANADA

MAINE

VERMONT

NEW HAMPSHIRE

Lake Superior

MINNESOTA

MICHIGAN

Lake Huron

Lake Michigan

MICHIGAN

WISCONSIN

• St. Paul

• Madison

IOWA

• Des Moines

Des Plaines

Chicago •
Haymarket Square

ILLINOIS

Springfield ✪

Westminster College
Alton
St. Louis •
East St. Louis
• Jefferson City

MISSOURI

White River

Memphis •

ARKANSAS

Little Rock ✪

Hope

LOUISIANA

Baton Rouge ✪

New Orleans •

Lansing ✪

Flint

Detroit •
Dearborn

Cleveland •

Tippecanoe

Greenville

Indianapolis ✪

INDIANA

Dayton

OHIO

Columbus ✪

Canton

Gnadenhutten

Pittsburgh •
Homestead

WEST VIRGINIA

Charleston ✪

Frankfort ✪

KENTUCKY

Appomattox

TENNESSEE

Nashville ✪

Dayton

Shiloh

Scottsboro

MISSISSIPPI

Jackson State University

Jackson ✪

ALABAMA

Selma • Montgomery ✪

Mobile •

Pensacola

GEORGIA

Tallahassee ✪

FLORIDA

Seneca Falls

Lake Ontario

Rochester

Buffalo •

NEW YORK

Saratoga

Albany ✪

Woodstock

Hyde Park

Newburgh

PENNSYLVANIA

Bethlehem

Harrisburg ✪

Harpers Ferry

Washington, D.C. •

MARYLAND

Richmond ✪

VIRGINIA

Annapolis ✪

Jamestown

Norfolk •

Roanoke Island

Raleigh ✪

NORTH CAROLINA

SOUTH CAROLINA

Columbia ✪

Charleston •

Stono

Port Royal

Lawrence *Lexington*

Lowell *Salem*

Brook Farm • Boston

MASSACHUSETTS *Plymouth*

Pawtucket

Hartford ✪ RHODE ISLAND

CONNECTICUT

Oyster Bay

New York • *Levittown*

Statue of Liberty

Trenton ✪ *Princeton*

NEW JERSEY *Grovers Mill*

Gettysburg

Philadelphia •

Dover ✪ *Three-Mile Island*

DELAWARE

ATLANTIC OCEAN

Lake Erie

Kent State University

Atlanta ✪

St. Augustine

Cape Canaveral

Gulf of Mexico

BAHAMAS

0   150   300 miles

0   150   300 kilometers

■ *Important places in American Passages*

THOMSON

★

WADSWORTH

Publisher: *Clark Baxter*
Senior Acquisitions Editor: *Ashley Dodge*
Senior Development Editor: *Margaret McAndrew Beasley*
Assistant Editor: *Julie Yardley*
Editorial Assistant: *Anne Gittinger*
Technology Project Manager: *Melinda Newfarmer*
Marketing Manager: *Lori Grebe-Cook*
Marketing Assistant: *Mary Ho*
Project Manager, Editorial Production: *Katy German*
Art Director: *Maria Epes*
Print/Media Buyer: *Rebecca Cross*

Permissions Editor: *Joohee Lee*
Production Service: *Orr Book Services*
Text Designer: *Lisa Buckley*
Photo Researcher: *Image Quest*
Copy Editor: *Kay Mikel*
Illustrator: *Graphic World*
Cover Designer: *Lisa Henry*
Cover Image: *Josef Scaylea/CORBIS*
Cover Printer: *Coral Graphic Services*
Compositor: *G&S Typesetters, Inc.*
Printer: *Courier-Kendallville*

Printed in the United States of America
1 2 3 4 5 6 7 08 07 06 05

For more information about our products, contact us at:
Thomson Learning Academic Resource Center
1-800-423-0563
For permission to use material from this text or product, submit a request online at http://www.thomsonrights.com.
Any additional questions about permissions can be submitted by email to thomsonrights@thomson.com.

Library of Congress Control Number: 2005 920801
ISBN 0-495-00135-X

Thomson Wadsworth
10 Davis Drive
Belmont, CA 94002-3098
USA

Asia
Thomson Learning
5 Shenton Way #01-01
UIC Building
Singapore 068808

Australia/New Zealand
Thomson Learning
102 Dodds Street
Southbank, Victoria 3006
Australia

Canada
Nelson
1120 Birchmount Road
Toronto, Ontario M1K 5G4
Canada

Europe/Middle East/Africa
Thomson Learning
High Holborn House
50/51 Bedford Row
London WC1R 4LR
United Kingdom

Latin America
Thomson Learning
Seneca, 53
Colonia Polanco
11560 Mexico D.F.
Mexico

Spain/Portugal
Paraninfo
Calle Magallanes, 25
28015 Madrid, Spain

Preface

A "Novel" Approach: Telling the Story of the American Past

In the first edition of *American Passages* we introduced a tight narrative organization that places readers directly into the story of the past, experiencing events as they unfolded for the people of that era—whether simultaneously or in a sequential chain. Judging by the responses from instructors and students who are using the text and Web resources, this approach has proven both engaging and valuable in making history make sense.

Why Story Is at the Center of Our History

History textbooks often focus on one topic at a time—politics, culture, reform, or the economy, for example. That kind of presentation, logical as it may seem, comes with a cost: it turns textbooks simply into gathered information rather than compelling stories.

People do not live one topic at a time. We experience many facets of history every day, all in the flow of time. Things happen simultaneously and in connection. We are used to the idea that our lives combine a mixture of major and minor events, of fads and movies and TV shows as well as elections, wars, and laws. The past was like that as well.

People confront surprise every day, for history seldom follows a straight line. No one could have predicted Bacon's Rebellion, John Brown's Raid, the Haymarket Riot, or the Watergate break-in. Nor could Americans have foreseen the emergence of Thomas Paine, Harriet Beecher Stowe, Henry Ford, or Martin Luther King, Jr. And who could have known on the morning of September 11, 2001, how different life would seem just that afternoon and in the days, weeks, and months that followed?

Features of *American Passages*

We highlight important parts of the stories we tell with special features, many of them new to this edition.

One suite of features emphasizes connections across chapters. Eight **"Passages"** sections, appearing regularly throughout the text, provide broad overviews that connect ideas and themes, using photographs, charts, maps and timelines to show the interrelationships of people, ideas, movements, and events. **"America and the World" maps** help set the American story in global context. The maps identify specific locations in the world and briefly explain why those places were particularly important to the United States in the years covered in each Passage section.

Web icons throughout the text alert students to the remarkable resources available on the **Companion Web Site** custom-built for *American Passages*. The site offers hundreds of documents, maps, illustrations, and multimedia selections—all organized to match the text's table of contents. Visit the companion site at http://history.wadsworth.com/ ayersbrief02.

Finally, a new set of features helps students to understand the most important points of the narrative. At the beginning of each chapter, **outlines** provide an overview of the stories they are about to read. Visually striking **timelines** portray the duration and overlap of crucial historical processes and occurrences. Along the way, **boldface glossary terms defined in the margin** ensure that students know the meaning of important people, events, organizations, and movements. At the end of each chapter, **summaries illustrated with photos and maps** tie together major points and themes. **A new set of review questions entitled "Making Connections Across Chapters"** guides students in their thinking, helping them to locate crucial issues in the stories they have just read and to anticipate the future implications of the events and changes they have just encountered.

Reviewers

The authors wish to thank the following professors who have provided useful feedback and suggestions at various stages in the writing and revising of *American Passages.*

Joseph Adams, St. Louis Community College at Meramec
Dawn Alexander, Abilene Christian University
Charles Allbee, Burlington Community College
Julius Amin, University of Dayton
Melodie Andrews, Mankato State University
Richard Baquera, El Paso Community College–Valle Verde
Robert Becker, Louisiana State University
Peter Bergstrom, Illinois State University
Blanche Brick, Blinn College
John Brooke, Tufts University
Neil Brooks, Essex Community College
Linda D. Brown, Odessa College
Colin Calloway, Dartmouth University
Milton Cantor, University of Massachusetts
Kay Carr, Southern Illinois University
Paul Chardoul, Grand Rapids Junior College
Thomas Clarkin, University of Texas, Austin
Myles Clowers, San Diego City College
William Cobb, Utah Valley State College
David Coon, Washington State University
Stacy Cordery, Monmouth College
Debbie Cottrell, Smith College
A. Glenn Crothers, Indiana University Southeast
David Cullen, Collin County Community College
Christine Daniels, Michigan State University
Amy E. Davis, University of California, Los Angeles
Ronnie Day, East Tennessee State University
Matthew Dennis, University of Oregon
Robert Downtain, Tarrant County Junior College, Northeast Campus
Robert Elam, Modesto Junior College
Rob Fink, Texas Tech University
Monte S. Finkelstein, Tallahassee Community College
Linda Foutch, Walter State Community College
Robert G. Fricke, West Valley College
Michael P. Gabriel, Kutztown University
David Hamilton, University of Kentucky
Beatriz Hardy, Coastal Carolina University
Peter M. G. Harris, Temple University
Thomas Hartshorne, Cleveland State University
Gordon E. Harvey, University of Louisiana at Monroe
Ron Hatzenbuehler, Idaho State University
Robert Hawkes, George Mason University
William L. Hewitt, West Chester University
James Houston, Oklahoma State University
Raymond Hyser, James Madison University
Lillian Jones, Santa Monica College
Jim Kluger, Pima Community College

Timothy Koerner, Oakland Community College
James Lacy, Contra Costa College
Alton Lee, University of South Dakota
Liston Leyendecker, Colorado State University
Robert Marcom, San Antonio College
Greg Massey, Freed-Hardeman
Michael Mayer, University of Montana
Randy McBee, Texas Tech University
Loyce B. Miles, Hinds Community College
Kimberly Morse, University of Texas, Austin
Augustine Nigro, Kutztown University
Elsa Nystrom, Kennesaw State
David O'Neill, Rutgers University
Elizabeth R. Osborn, Indiana University–Purdue University, Indianapolis
Betty Owens, Greenville Technical College
Mark Parillo, Kansas State University
J'Nell Pate, Tarrant County Junior College, Northeast Campus
Louis Potts, University of Missouri at Kansas City
Noel Pugach, University of New Mexico
Alice Reagan, Northern Virginia Community College
Marlette Rebhorn, Austin Community College, Rio Grande Campus
David Reimers, New York University
Hal Rothman, Wichita State University
Erik S. Schmeller, Tennessee State University
John G. Selby, Roanoke College
Ralph Shaffer, California Polytechnic University
Kenneth Smemo, Moorhead State University
Jack Smith, Great Basin College
Thaddeus Smith, Middle Tennessee State University
Phillip E. Stebbins, Pennsylvania State University
Marshall Stevenson, Ohio State University
William Stockton, Johnson County Community College
Suzanne Summers, Austin Community College
Frank Towers, Clarion University
Steve Tripp, Grand Valley State University
Daniel Usner, Cornell University
Daniel Vogt, Jackson State University
Stephen Webre, Louisiana Technical College
John C. Willis, University of the South
Harold Wilson, Old Dominion University
Nan Woodruff, Pennsylvania State University
Bertram Wyatt-Brown, University of Florida
Sherri Yeager, Chabot College
Robert Zeidel, University of Wisconsin

Acknowledgments

I would like to thank my students and colleagues at the University of Virginia who have helped me struggle with the tough questions of American history. I am grateful, too, to Katherine Pierce and Margaret Beasley for their imagination, hard work, and good advice in the creation of this book. Finally, I am very appreciative of my co-authors, who have been engaged scholars, thoughtful critics, devoted teachers, and good friends throughout the years it took us to write *American Passages*.

Edward L. Ayers

I would like to acknowledge the help of the following former students who contributed in constructive ways to the completion of the textbook: Martin Ansell, Christie Bourgeois, Thomas Clarkin, Stacy Cordery, Debbie Cottrell, Patrick Cox, Scott Harris, Byron Hulsey, Jonathan Lee, John Leffler, Mark Young, and Nancy Beck Young. Karen Gould gave indispensable support and encouragement throughout the process of writing the text. Margaret Beasley supplied patient, informed, and thorough editorial guidance for the second edition, and the authors are all in her debt for that significant contribution. I am grateful as well to the readers of my chapters who made so many useful and timely criticisms.

Lewis L. Gould

I would like to thank my colleagues and students at Rutgers for allowing me to test out an endless stream of ideas and issues relating to modern American history, and also for their thoughts on how a good college textbook should "read" and what it should contain. As always, the support and love of my family—Matt, Efrem, Ari, and Jane—was unshakable.

Above all, I must commend my co-authors and my editors for their remarkable patience and professionalism during this long collaborative process.

David M. Oshinsky

I am grateful to my husband, Rudolf Soderlund, and my family for their support throughout this project. They have provided valuable feedback on the text. Many scholars in the colonial and early national periods shared their ideas orally and through publications. I received very helpful comments from James S. Saeger, Roger D. Simon, Marianne S. Wokeck, my co-authors of this text, and the anonymous readers for the press.

Jean R. Soderlund

List of Documents

List of Maps

For animated versions of selected American Passages maps, please visit the companion web site at *http://history.wadsworth.com/ayersbrief02.*

A Guide to Using Primary Sources

Primary sources include the documents, census data, photographs, interviews, poetry, songs, cartoons, and films that historians use to write narratives of the past. *American Passages* contains examples of many types of primary sources, including a letter from an early Virginia settler, the trial of an accused Salem witch, the journals of Lewis and Clark, petitions for civil rights, presidential speeches, advertisements, posters, and political cartoons.

As students of history, how can we use these materials to understand American society and culture? Historians collect evidence from a variety of primary documents to write secondary sources, which are second-hand interpretations of events. In writing texts like *American Passages,* scholars make interpretive decisions about which primary sources to emphasize and who to believe. Many components of *American Passages*—the text narrative, document introductions, questions, maps, and timelines—are secondary sources.

Primary sources, in contrast, were created by people who witnessed past events. Sometimes individuals produced the source immediately after an event, as with a newspaper story or photograph; sometimes authors waited decades to describe their experiences, as with a Civil War soldier's memoir. In either case, primary sources allow us to view events from the perspective of a particular individual or group. First-hand documents let us step back into time to look directly at life in the 1620s, 1830s, or 1980s. Each chapter in *American Passages* contains a document, from a U.S. president or more ordinary Americans, that sheds greater light on the era. Read each document carefully, considering the questions below. As we study primary sources, we learn the job of historians: to consider various perspectives, place them within the larger historical context, and create an interpretation that is meaningful in our time.

One famous primary source is *Democracy in America* by the French nobleman, Alexis de Tocqueville, who toured the United States in the early 1830s. (See Chapter 11 for a somewhat longer version of this document.)

> . . . In America I saw the freest and most enlightened men, placed in the happiest circumstances which the world affords; it seemed to me as if a cloud habitually hung upon their brow, and I thought them serious and almost sad even in their pleasures.
>
> . . . A native of the United States clings to this world's goods as if he were certain never to die; and he is so hasty in grasping at all within his reach, that one would suppose he was constantly afraid of not living long enough to enjoy them. He clutches everything, he holds nothing fast, but soon loosens his grasp to pursue fresh gratifications. In the United States a man builds a house to spend his latter years in it, and he sells it before the roof is on; . . . If his private affairs leave him any leisure, he instantly plunges into the vortex of politics; and if at the end of a year of unremitting labor he finds he has a few days' vacation, his eager curiosity whirls him over the vast extent of the United States, and he will travel fifteen hundred miles in a few days, to shake off his happiness. Death at length overtakes him, but it is before he is weary of his bootless chase of that complete felicity which is for ever on the wing.

Questions to analyze a document:

1. **What kind of primary source is this?** This is an excerpt from Tocqueville's *Democracy in America,* a published analysis of U.S. society based on his tour in 1831–32. He covers many other topics in the two-volume work, including prisons, religion, politics, and slavery.

2. **Who created the primary source?** Knowledge that Tocqueville was a French nobleman who visited the United States for nine months is important information. He was an outsider and thus brought a different perspective than a U.S. citizen. As an outsider, was he more or less likely than an American to be biased in his description of U.S. society?

3. **Who was his intended audience?** Tocqueville wrote and published his work in French, so he intended to make his thoughts public, in France. Did he expect Americans to read his assessment of their character? How can we find out?

4. **What is his thesis?** Tocqueville's main point in this excerpt was that Americans, while free politically, found little happiness because they put so much effort into earning a living and even taking vacation! What assumptions does he make in this argument? What evidence does he offer? In general, what historical information do we learn from this excerpt?

5. **Is this document accurate?** In the early 1830s were all Americans materialistic, unhappy, and mobile? Did Tocqueville emphasize these qualities for a reason?

6. **How does the document fit into the historical context?** What events and circumstances affected Tocqueville's writing?

7. **What is the document's significance?** What was the impact of *Democracy in America* in France? In the United States? Did Tocqueville, in this excerpt, accurately capture the American national character in the 1830s? Do aspects of that national character exist today?

Brief Contents

Detailed Contents

About the Authors

EDWARD L. AYERS

Edward Ayers is the Hugh P. Kelly Professor of History and Dean of the College and Graduate School of Arts and Sciences at the University of Virginia. He was educated at the University of Tennessee and Yale University, where he received his Ph.D. in American Studies. Ayers was named National Professor of the Year by the Carnegie Foundation and the Council for the Support of Education in 2003. His most recent book, *In the Presence of Mine Enemies: War in the Heart of America, 1859–1863* (2003), won the Bancroft Prize for distinguished work on the history of the United States. *The Promise of the New South: Life After Reconstruction* (1992) won prizes for the best book on the history of American race relations and on the history of the American South. It was a finalist for both the National Book Award and the Pulitzer Prize. He is the coeditor of *The Oxford Book of the American South* (1997) and *All Over the Map: Rethinking American Regions* (1996). The World Wide Web version of "The Valley of the Shadow: Two Communities in the American Civil War" was recognized by the American Historical Association as the best aid to the teaching of history. Ayers is the author of Chapters 9–15.

LEWIS L. GOULD

Lewis Gould is the Eugene C. Barker Centennial Professor Emeritus at the University of Texas at Austin. After receiving his Ph.D. from Yale University, he began a teaching career in which he had more than ten thousand students. He was recognized for outstanding undergraduate teaching in large lecture sections of the American History survey and for his excellent graduate teaching.

Gould is a nationally recognized authority on first ladies and the presidency. His comments have appeared in numerous press accounts about presidential wives, including *The New York Times*, the *Washington Post*, and the *Los Angeles Times*. He has appeared on C-Span, The CBS Morning News, Nightline, The ABC Evening News, and a large number of nationally syndicated radio programs. He also participated in the PBS program on Lyndon Johnson and the A&E biography of Lady Bird Johnson. Among his important publications are *American First Ladies: Their Lives and Their Legacy* (2001); *1968: The Election That Changed America* (1993); *The Presidency of Theodore Roosevelt* (1991); *Lady Bird Johnson: Our Environmental First Lady* (1999); *The Modern American Presidency* (2003); and *Grand Old Party: A History of the Republicans* (2003). Gould is the author of Chapters 16–24, 31, and 32.

DAVID M. OSHINSKY

David Oshinsky received his undergraduate degree from Cornell University and his doctorate from Brandeis. He is currently Littlefield Professor of History at the University of Texas at Austin. Prior to that he taught for twenty-six years at Rutgers University, where he held the Board of Governors Chair as well as chairman of the History Department. Oshinsky is the author of four books, including *A Conspiracy So Immense: The World of Joe McCarthy* (1983), which was voted one of the year's "best books" by the New York Sunday Times Book Review, and won the Hardeman Prize for the best work about the U.S. Congress. His latest book, *Worse than Slavery: Parchman Farm and the Ordeal of Jim Crow Justice* (1996), won both the Robert Kennedy Book Award for the year's most distinguished contribution to the field of human rights and the American Bar Association's Scribes Award for distinguished legal writing.

Oshinsky is a regular contributor to scholarly journals, the Washington Post Book World, New York Sunday Times Book Review, New York Times Op-Ed page, and New York Times Sunday Magazine. He was awarded a senior fellowship by the National Endowment for the Humanities and spent 1999–2000 as a Phi Beta Kappa Visiting Scholar. Oshinsky is the author of Chapters 25–30.

JEAN R. SODERLUND

Jean Soderlund is Professor of History at Lehigh University and Co-Director of the Lawrence Henry Gipson Institute for Eighteenth-Century Studies. She received her Ph.D. from Temple University and was a post-doctoral fellow at the McNeil Center for Early American Studies at the University of Pennsylvania. Her book *Quakers and Slavery: A Divided Spirit* won the Alfred E. Driscoll Publication Prize of the New Jersey Historical Commission. Soderlund was an editor of three volumes of the Papers of William Penn (1981–1983) and co-authored *Freedom by Degrees: Emancipation in Pennsylvania and Its Aftermath* (1991).

She has written articles and chapters in books on the history of women, African Americans, Native Americans, Quakers, and the development of abolition in the British North American colonies and early United States. She is currently working on a study of the Lenape people within colonial New Jersey society. She is a council member of the McNeil Center for Early American Studies, and she served as a committee chair for the American Historical Association and the Organization of American Historians. Soderlund is the author of Chapters 1–8.

CHAPTER 15

Blood and Freedom

1863–1867

T HE CIVIL WAR ENVELOPED THE ENTIRE NATION, HOME FRONT AND battlefield alike. The outcome of a battle could win an election or trigger a riot, while events at home affected the leaders' decisions of when and where to fight. In the North the strong political opposition to Abraham Lincoln and his policies exerted a constant pressure on his conduct of the war. In the South slaves abandoned plantations and white families' hardships led soldiers to rethink their loyalties.

The outcome of the Civil War was not predetermined by the North's advantages of population and resources. Deep into the war, events could have taken radically different turns. Slavery might have survived the conflict had the Confederacy won at particular junctions or, more likely, had the United States lost the will to push the devastating war to the South's full surrender and the immediate abolition of slavery. Even with the war's end, the future course of the nation remained in doubt as Americans confronted the greatest rupture in their history.

People at War: Spring 1863

Both northerners and southerners expected the spring of 1863 to bring the climax of the Civil War. Much had been decided, organized, and mobilized over the preceding two years. Yet while generals and armies determined the result of battles, the women, slaves, workers, bureaucrats, draft dodgers, and politicians behind the lines would determine the outcome of the war.

Life in the Field

Soldiers eventually got used to the miseries of sleeping on the ground, poorly cooked food, driving rain, and endless mud. They learned to adapt to gambling, drinking, cursing, and prostitution, either by succumbing to the temptations or by steeling their resolve against them. They could toughen themselves to the intermittent mails and the arrival of bad news from home. Men recalled their initial mortification and humiliation on discovering their entire company infested with lice, a shame that turned to indifference when the sharper horror of wounds descended.

Even the most stalwart of soldiers could not adapt to the constant threat of diseases such as diarrhea, dysentery, typhoid, malaria, measles, diphtheria, and scarlet fever. As bloody as the battles were, disease killed twice as many men as died from the guns of the enemy. Many doctors of the Civil War era used the same instruments of surgery on soldier after soldier, unwittingly spreading disease and infection. After every battle, screams filled

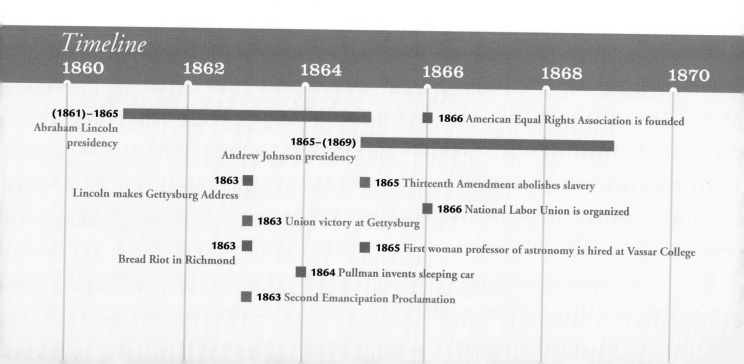

Timeline

1860	1862	1864	1866	1868	1870

(1861)–1865 Abraham Lincoln presidency

1866 American Equal Rights Association is founded

1865–(1869) Andrew Johnson presidency

1863 Lincoln makes Gettysburg Address

1865 Thirteenth Amendment abolishes slavery

1866 National Labor Union is organized

1863 Union victory at Gettysburg

1863 Bread Riot in Richmond

1865 First woman professor of astronomy is hired at Vassar College

1864 Pullman invents sleeping car

1863 Second Emancipation Proclamation

the night as surgeons sawed off legs and arms, feet and hands, often in the vain hope of stopping gangrene.

Purposes

The North fought for ideals of union and democracy; the South fought for ideals of self-determination. Yet soldiers acted courageously not only because they believed in the official political purposes for which they were fighting, but also because they wanted to be admired by the people at home, because they wanted to do their part for their comrades, because they wanted to bring the war to a quicker end, and because they grew to hate the enemy.

Many men fought alongside their brothers, uncles, and cousins. A steady stream of letters flowed back and forth between the units and the families and neighbors back home. Gossip, praise, and condemnation flourished. Any soldier who planned to return home knew that his deeds in the war would live with him the rest of his life. As a result, even fearful or halfhearted soldiers might throw themselves into battle to demonstrate their courage.

Whereas about three-fifths of Civil War soldiers were over twenty-one at the age of enlistment, the largest single group of soldiers was eighteen. For those who passed the birthdays of their late teens or early twenties on the battlefields, the transition to manhood became inseparable from the war. A soldier from Illinois proudly wrote his family that "this war has made a man of your son." To be manly meant more than the simple ability to inflict violence on the enemy. It meant pride, responsibility, loyalty, and obedience. Every battle became a test of manhood, which had to be proven every time it was challenged under fire.

Courage developed, too, out of hatred. People on both sides spread the worst stories and rumors about one another. Newspapers printed exaggerated or fabricated atrocity reports about the enemy. While many were repelled by battlefield carnage, others took satisfaction. One Confederate artillery officer admired the "severed limbs, decapitated bodies, and mutilated remains" at Fredericksburg and declared that it did "my soul good" to ride over the bodies of the federal dead. Union troops also hardened their attitudes. A Wisconsin soldier informed his fiancée that his unit wanted to fight until "we kill them all off and cleanse the country." The longer the war went on, the more people felt they had to hate one another to justify so much bloodshed.

The sermons men heard in the camps told them they were fighting on the side of the right. The Old Testament afforded rich imagery and compelling stories of violence inflicted for good causes. Many Americans believed that God enacted His will directly in human affairs. As the war ground on, the leaders, the soldiers, and the civilians of both sides came to feel that events were more than the product of human decision or even courage. Surely, they told themselves, so much suffering and sacrifice had to be for a larger purpose.

The Problems of the Confederate Government

Convinced that greedy merchants were holding supplies of flour until prices rose even higher, in the spring of 1863 poor women in Richmond broke open the stores of merchants accused of hoarding the precious staple, taking what they needed. After President Davis climbed on a wagon and threw coins at the crowd, he ordered a militia unit to prepare to fire on them. The threat of violence and of arrest, as well as the promise of free supplies, broke up the riot, but similar events occurred in several other southern cities including Atlanta, Columbus, and Augusta. No one could tell when even larger riots might erupt again. Fearing the consequences for morale, military officers in Richmond ordered the press and telegraph office to suppress news of the riot, but word of the riot soon spread.

The rioters were not the only ones who took what they needed. Confederate officers in the field forced reluctant farmers to accept whatever prices the army offered, in an increasingly devalued currency. In the spring of 1863, the Confederate government attempted to curb the worst abuses of this practice in the Impressment Act. If a farmer did not think the prices he or she received were fair, the case could be appealed before local authorities. In practice, however, this cumbersome system failed. Farmers hid their produce from officers and resented it when they were forced to sell. North Carolina's governor denounced impressments to the War Department in Richmond: "If God Almighty had yet in store another plague . . . I am sure it must have been a regiment or so of half-disciplined Confederate cavalry."

The southern government could not afford to lose civilian support. Although the absence of political parties originally appeared to be a sign of the South's consensus, that absence eventually undermined what original consensus the Confederacy had enjoyed. Jefferson Davis, without a party mechanism to discipline those who spoke out against him, could not remove enemies from office. Davis's own vice president, Alexander Stephens, became a persistent and outspoken critic of the Confederate president's "tyrannical" policies, actively undermining support for Davis and even allying with avowed enemies of Davis and his policies.

The Confederate government faced a fundamental dilemma. The whole point of secession had been to move political power closer to localities, protecting slavery in particular and self-determination in general. The government of the Confederacy, however, had to centralize power. If the armies were to be fed and clothed, if diplomats were to make a plausible case for the Confederacy's nationhood, if soldiers were to be mobilized, then the Confederate government had to exercise greater power than its creators had expected or intended. Jefferson Davis continually struggled with this tension. For every southerner who considered Davis too weak, another considered the president dangerously powerful.

The Northern Home Front

In the North the war heightened the strong differences between the Democrats and the Republicans. The Democrats won significant victories in congressional elections in the fall and winter of 1862, testifying to the depth and breadth of the opposition to Lincoln and his conduct of the war. Wealthy businessmen were eager to reestablish trade with their former southern partners, whereas Irish immigrants wanted to end the risk of the draft and competition from freed slaves. Many citizens of Ohio, Indiana, and Illinois, whose families had come from the South, wanted to renew the southern connections that had been broken by the war.

The Union passed its Conscription Act in March of 1863 because disease, wounds, and desertion had depleted the ranks of soldiers faster than they could be replaced. When drafted, a man could appear for duty, hire a substitute to fight in his place, or simply pay a fee of $300 directly to the government. Poorer communities resented the wealthy who could avoid service. Demonstrations broke out in Chicago, Pennsylvania mining towns, rural Vermont, and Boston. State and federal governments often paid bounties—signing bonuses—to those who volunteered. More than a few men took the bounties and then promptly deserted and moved to another locality to claim another bounty.

The opposition to the Lincoln government raised crucial issues. With the North claiming to fight for liberty, what limitations on freedom of speech and protest could it enforce? A Democratic congressman from Ohio, Clement Vallandigham, tested those limits in the spring of 1863. Hating both secessionists and abolitionists, Vallandigham refused to obey a general's orders to stop criticizing the Lincoln administration. He was arrested, tried before a military court, and sentenced to imprisonment for the rest of the war. Lincoln was dismayed by these events. He commuted Vallandigham's sentence, sending him to the Confederates in Tennessee, hoping to make Vallandigham appear a southern sympathizer rather than a martyr to the cause of free speech. Vallandigham quickly escaped to Canada, however, where he continued his criticisms. Ohio Democrats defiantly nominated Vallandigham for governor in the elections to be held in the fall of 1863. If things continued to go badly for the Union, who knew what kind of success a critic of Lincoln might find?

African American Soldiers

Though northern civilian and military leaders remained deeply divided and ambivalent about black freedom, it became clear to everyone that black men could be of great value to the Union. In May 1863 the War Department created the Bureau of Colored Troops. African American men from across the North rushed to enlist as soon as they heard of the new black regiments.

At first black recruits found themselves restricted to noncombat roles and a lower rate of pay: $10 a month versus the $13 a month and $3.50 clothing allowance given to white soldiers. **African American soldiers,** though eager to serve, protested that they could not

African American soldiers
Finally allowed to enlist in May 1863, African American soldiers accounted for more than one hundred eighty thousand troops and played a major role in the Union victory.

support their families on such amounts. African Americans knew, and coveted, the rights and privileges of other Americans. They wrote petitions and appealed to higher authorities, often in the language of the Declaration of Independence and the Constitution.

Black men had called for their inclusion in the U.S. Army from the beginning of the war. In the spring of 1863, the U.S. Colored Troops were formed, and more than one hundred eighty thousand African American men fought for the Union over the next two years.

Confederate officials who expected black soldiers to make reluctant or cowed fighters soon discovered otherwise. In May of 1863 two black regiments stormed a heavily fortified Confederate installation at Port Hudson, Louisiana, seven times. Soon thereafter, black soldiers found themselves on the other side of the barricades. At Milliken's Bend, Louisiana, they fought Confederates hand to hand. Northern newspapers echoed the words of praise from generals in the field: "No troops could be more determined or more daring."

Encouraged and frequently supported financially by their communities, African American men in the North went to the recruiting tables in great numbers. Frederick Douglass, the leading spokesman for black Americans, celebrated the enlistments: "Once let the black man get upon his person the brass letters, *U.S.;* let him get an eagle on his button, and a musket on his shoulder, and bullets in his pocket, and there is no power on earth which can deny that he has earned the right to citizenship in the United States." From Rhode Island to Ohio, black troops prepared to head south.

The Battlefields of Summer: 1863

Everything seemed in place for a climactic culmination of the war in the summer of 1863. The Union had almost severed the western half of the Confederacy from the eastern; the Union Army had penetrated deep into Tennessee and stood on the threshold of Georgia. On the other hand, the Confederate Army had toughened itself to its disadvantages and learned to make the most of the advantages it enjoyed.

Vicksburg and Chancellorsville

Union leaders needed all the help they could get in early 1863. Grant and Sherman remained frustrated in their goal of seizing Vicksburg; Rosecrans faced Bragg in Tennessee; Lee's army had yet to be decisively defeated despite the men, resources, and determination thrown into battle against him. Lee would face General Joseph Hooker, whom Lincoln had chosen to replace Ambrose Burnside. Throughout the spring, "Fighting Joe" Hooker energized his men and repaired some of the damage to morale and readiness inflicted at Fredericksburg. But no one knew if he would be able to handle Lee.

The northern public was especially impatient with Grant and Sherman. Grant knew the delays threatened his command. Vicksburg, heavily fortified by both geography and the Confederates, seemed most vulnerable to attack from the southeast, but to get there Grant would have to find a way to move his men across the Mississippi River without landing them in swamps. Throughout the long wet winter, Grant had tried one experiment after another, including digging canals. Nothing worked.

Grant finally decided on a bold move: he would run a flotilla of gunboats and barges past Vicksburg under the cover of night to ferry his men across the Mississippi south of the city, where the land was better. The guns of Vicksburg stood two hundred feet above the river, ready to fire down on any passing craft, but the Union men covered their ships'

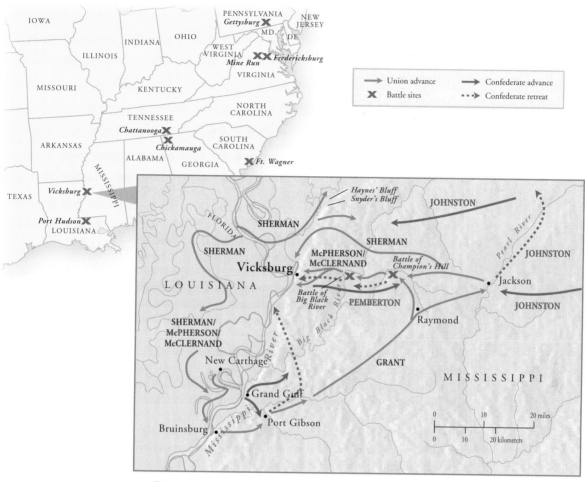

MAP 15.1 Vicksburg

After months of frustration, Ulysses S. Grant and William T. Sherman found a way to attack Vicksburg from the south and east. Following great struggle, the Union generals were able to take the city on July 4, 1863. View an animated version of this map or related maps at http://history.wadsworth.com/ayersbrief02.

boilers with sacks of grain and bales of cotton to protect them from the shelling. Most of the boats made it through. Grant had Sherman create a diversion, confusing the Confederates, and then ferried his entire army across the Mississippi. Grant's army remained vulnerable, cut off from his allies and his major supply base, but by mid-May, Grant had fought four battles, cost the South eight thousand dead and wounded, marched two hundred miles, and pinned thirty thousand Confederates within Vicksburg's fortifications.

In the same week Grant made his landing near Vicksburg, Hooker began his attack on Lee, still based in Fredericksburg. Hooker commanded a hundred thirty thousand men. Unlike Burnside, however, Hooker intended to outsmart Lee rather than try to overwhelm him with numbers. A large Union force would sweep around Lee and attack him from behind, even as another force attacked from the front. To keep from being bottled up in Fredericksburg, Lee would have to emerge from his well-entrenched defensive position. Lee met this bold move with an even bolder one. He would divide his forces and send Stonewall Jackson to attack Hooker's men from the rear, outflanking Hooker's own flanking maneuver.

On May 2 Jackson assaulted Hooker's troops near Chancellorsville. The outnumbered Confederates defeated the surprised and indecisive Hooker, achieving a major victory. Southern jubilation, though, ended the very night of this triumph, for nervous Confederate soldiers accidentally shot Stonewall Jackson while he surveyed the scene near the front lines. The surgeons removed his arm that evening and hoped that he might live.

While Jackson lay in his tent, fading in and out of consciousness, Lee managed to contain another assault on Fredericksburg and to push the Union troops away from their positions. The losses had once again been staggering—thirteen thousand casualties, roughly 22 percent of the army—but Lee had overcome a larger opponent. After the last battles quieted, however, Jackson died. His death took with it Lee's most trusted general.

Gettysburg

Despite his victory at Chancellorsville, Lee recognized that the Confederacy was in trouble. Rosecrans still threatened to break through Tennessee into Georgia, Grant clawed his way closer to Vicksburg, and the Union blockade drew an ever-tighter net around the coast. Some of his generals urged Lee to rush with his troops to Tennessee to defend the center of the Confederacy and pull Grant away from Vicksburg. But Lee decided that his most effective move would be to invade the North again, taking the pressure off Virginia and disheartening the Union. A successful strike into the North might yet persuade Britain and France to recognize the Confederacy and give heart to Peace Democrats in the North.

In early June Lee began to move up through the Shenandoah Valley into southern Pennsylvania with seventy-five thousand men. Hooker seemed confused, and when he offered his resignation to Lincoln after a minor dispute, the president quickly accepted and put General George Meade in charge. Meade had to decide how best to stop the greatest threat the Confederate Army had yet posed to the North. Washington and Baltimore lay in danger, along with the cities, towns, and farms of Pennsylvania where Confederate troops enjoyed taking food and livestock from the rich land. Free blacks and fugitive slaves were also seized and forced south into slavery.

Although Lee and his men moved unchecked across the Potomac and deep into Pennsylvania, they found themselves in a dangerous situation. Lee had permitted Jeb Stuart's cavalry, his "eyes," to range widely from the main army; as a result, the Confederates had little idea where the Union Army was or what moves it was making. For their part, Meade and his fellow officers decided to pursue Lee, but not too aggressively, looking for a likely time and place to confront the enemy.

On June 30 units from the Confederacy and the Union stumbled over one another at a small town neither side knew or cared much about: Gettysburg. On July 1 they began to struggle for the best defensive position near the town, fighting over the highest and most protected land. It appeared at first that the southerners had the better of the first day's battle, but as the smoke cleared both sides could see that late in the day the Union Army had consolidated itself on the most advantageous ground. Meade's men, after fierce fighting at the ends of their line, occupied a fishhook-shaped series of ridges and hills that permitted them to protect their flanks. The second day saw the Confederates slowly mobilize their forces for assaults on those positions and launch attacks late in the afternoon. The resulting battles in the peach orchard, the wheat field, Little Round Top, and the boulder-strewn area known as the Devil's Den proved horrific—with thirty-five thousand men dead or wounded—but left the Union in control of the high ground.

Despite the Union's superior position, Lee decided on a frontal attack the next day. The Confederates hoped their artillery would soften the middle of the Union lines. The Confederates did not realize how little damage their guns had done until well-entrenched Union troops decimated waves of an attack led by George E. Pickett. Only a few southern men made it to the stone wall that protected the northerners, and even those Confederates quickly fell. It proved a disastrous three days for the Confederacy, which lost twenty-three thousand men through death or wounds, about a third of its entire force. While the Union lost similar numbers of men, it had more to lose. The northerners and their new general had fought a defensive battle; the southern side, short on supplies and men, had gambled on an aggressive assault. Elation swept the North. "The glorious success of the Army of the Potomac has electrified all," a northerner exulted. In the wake of Chancellorsville and Lee's apparently effortless invasion of Pennsylvania, he admitted, many northerners "did not believe the enemy could be whipped."

The next morning, a thousand miles away, Vicksburg surrendered to Ulysses S. Grant. Unlike Gettysburg, where the battle had been fought in a place no one considered strategically crucial, Vicksburg held enormous tactical and psychological importance. It had

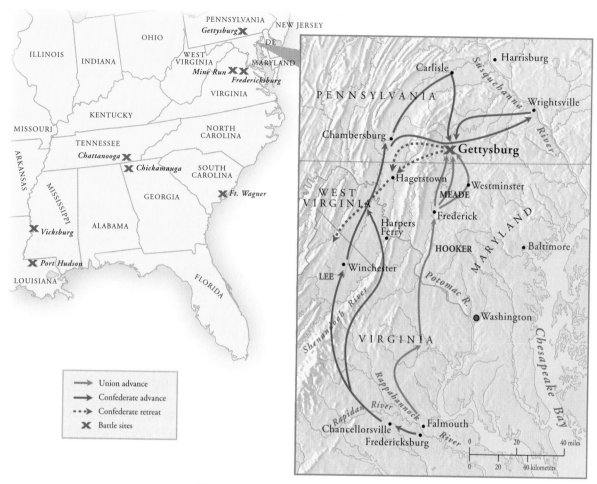

MAP 15.2 Virginia, 1863

The battle of Chancellorsville, not far from Fredericksburg, was a great victory for the Confederates. But it marked just the opening stage of a long summer of fighting that would culminate at Gettysburg two months later. In that battle, the Confederates sorely missed General Stonewall Jackson, accidentally killed by his own troops at Chancellorsville. View an animated version of this map or related maps at http://history.wadsworth.com/ayersbrief02.

been the symbol of Confederate doggedness and Union frustration. After six weeks of siege and near starvation behind the Confederate defenses, Vicksburg fell. The Mississippi River now divided the Confederacy while it tied the Union to the Gulf of Mexico.

Some southerners, including Jefferson Davis, did not perceive Gettysburg as a defeat. In their eyes, Lee and his men had pushed deep into the Union, inflicted heavy losses, and damaged northern morale without being trapped there. Northerners at the time often agreed that Gettysburg had not been a decisive Union victory, pronouncing themselves more frustrated than satisfied with Meade, who had not destroyed Lee's army despite his greater numbers. During the Confederate retreat to Virginia, the southerners found themselves caught between a swollen Potomac River and pursuing federal troops. Meade, his army exhausted and weakened, chose not to fight against the defenses Lee's men hurriedly put up against their pursuers. Meade could not know that the condition of the southern troops was even worse than his own. Fortunately for the Confederates, the river soon calmed enough that they were able to escape back into Virginia.

The New York City Draft Riots

On the very day that Lee struggled across the Potomac to safety, riots broke out in New York City. Northern working people held complicated feelings about the war. Many of those who labored in the North's factories, mines, farms, and railroads had come to the

United States in the last few years. These people, mostly Irish and Germans, volunteered in large numbers to fight for the Union cause. Between 20 and 25 percent of the Union Army were immigrants, the great majority of them volunteers.

Despite their patriotism for their adopted country, many of the immigrants viewed black Americans with dread and contempt. Urban labor organizations divided over Lincoln's election and over the response to secession. Many Catholic Irishmen, almost all of them Democrats, proclaimed that they had no quarrel with white southerners and that they resented the federal government's draft. The obvious effect of inflation on the wages of workers created strong resentments as well. Working people sneered at those men who had enough money to hire substitutes to fight in their place. Three hundred dollars, after all, constituted half a year's wage for a workingman.

Irish immigrants despaired at the losses among Irish American units in the field. When their regiments were decimated at Fredericksburg, Gettysburg, and elsewhere, Irish people began to wonder if commanders valued their lives as highly as those of the native-born. When word came, just as the draft lottery was to take place in New York City on July 11, 1863, of the twenty-three thousand men lost at Gettysburg, the fury of working people rose. On July 13 it exploded. Mobs began by assaulting draft officials, then turned their anger on any man who looked rich enough to have hired a substitute, then on pro-Lincoln newspapers and abolitionists' homes. They assaulted any African Americans they encountered on the streets, burning an orphanage, whipping men and women, and hanging victims from city lampposts. Lincoln was sickened by accounts of the riot, and a city editor despaired, "Great God! What is this nation coming to?"

The police struggled for three days to control the riot. Eventually, troops (including all-Irish units) rushed from the battlefields of Pennsylvania to aid the police. The troops fired into the rioters; more than a hundred people died and another three hundred were injured. The working people got some of what they wanted: more welfare relief, exemptions from the draft for those whose families would have no other means of support, and an exodus of black people who feared for their lives.

Ironically, a few days after the New York draft riots, scores of black troops died during a bold nighttime assault on Fort Wagner near Charleston, South Carolina. Despite the bravery of the African Americans, the assault failed. The Confederates made a point of burying the African American soldiers in a mass grave along with their white officer, Robert Gould Shaw, intending to insult him and his memory. Instead, they elevated him to a northern martyr. The *Atlantic Monthly* marked a change in northern attitudes toward black soldiers: "Through the cannon smoke of that dark night, the manhood of the colored race shines before many eyes that would not see."

Chickamauga

After Gettysburg, Vicksburg, and the New York riots in July, events slowed until September, when Union General William Rosecrans left Chattanooga, near the Georgia border, and began moving toward Atlanta. His opponent, Braxton Bragg, hoped to entice Rosecrans into dividing his forces so that they could be cut off. The armies confronted one another at Chickamauga Creek—a Cherokee name meaning "river of death." The Confederates took advantage of Union mistakes on the heavily wooded battlefield, inflicting harrowing damage and driving Rosecrans back into Chattanooga. The Union troops were trapped there, the Confederates looming over them on Lookout Mountain and Missionary Ridge, with few routes of escape and limited supplies. The northerners had gone from a position of apparent advantage to one of desperation.

Lincoln, judging Rosecrans "confused and stunned" by the battle at Chickamauga, used this opportunity to put Grant in charge of all Union armies between the Appalachian Mountains and the Mississippi River. In the fall of 1863 Grant traveled to Chattanooga, where Sherman joined him from Mississippi and Hooker came from Virginia.

The Gettysburg Address

The North's victories in the summer of 1863 aided Lincoln's popularity. The draft riots in New York City damaged the reputations of Democrats, whereas the bravery of black soldiers on the battlefields of Louisiana and South Carolina led white northerners, particularly Union soldiers, to rethink some of their prejudices. In the fall of 1863 the Republicans won major victories in Pennsylvania and Ohio. Lincoln determined to make the most of these heartening events.

When Lincoln received an invitation to speak at the dedication of the cemetery at Gettysburg on November 19, he saw it as a chance to impart a sense of direction and purpose to the Union cause. The event had not been planned with him in mind, and the president was not even the featured speaker. But Lincoln recognized that a battlefield offered the most effective backdrop for the things he wanted to say.

Burial crews had been laboring for weeks on the Gettysburg battlefield. Thousands of horse carcasses had been burned; thousands of human bodies had been hastily covered with a thin layer of soil. Pennsylvania purchased seventeen acres and hired a specialist in rural cemetery design to lay out the burial plots so that no state would be offended by the location or amount of space devoted to its fallen men. Only about a third of the reburials had taken place when Lincoln arrived; caskets remained stacked at the station.

Lincoln, contrary to legend, did not dash off his speech on the back of an envelope. He had reworked and polished it for several days. The "remarks," as the program put it, lasted three minutes. Lincoln used those minutes to maximum effect. He said virtually nothing about the details of the scene surrounding the twenty thousand people at the ceremony. Neither did he mention slavery directly. Instead, he spoke of equality as the fundamental purpose of the war. He called for a "new birth of freedom."

Lincoln was attempting to shift the purpose of the war from Union for Union's sake to Union for freedom's sake. He sought to salvage something from the deaths of the fifty thousand men at Gettysburg. Democratic newspapers rebuked Lincoln for his claim, arguing that white soldiers had "too much self-respect to declare that negroes were their equals." But other northerners accepted Lincoln's exhortation as the definition of their purpose. They might not believe that blacks deserved to be included as full participants in a government of, by, and for "the people," but they did believe that the Union fought for liberty broadly conceived. As battles and years went by, the words of the **Gettysburg Address** would gain force and resonance.

Just four days after Lincoln's speech, Grant gave the North new reason to believe its ideals might triumph. On November 23 Grant's men overwhelmed the Confederates on Lookout Mountain outside Chattanooga; two days later Union soldiers accomplished the improbable task of fighting their way up Missionary Ridge because Confederate artillery could not reach opponents coming up directly from below. The Union, now in control of Kentucky and Tennessee, had a wide and direct route into Georgia.

England and France finally determined in late 1863 that they would not try to intervene in the American war. First Britain, then France detained or sold to foreign powers warships intended for the Confederacy. The northern public, encouraged by events on the battlefield, supported Republican candidates in the congressional elections of 1863 more vigorously than had seemed possible just a few months before.

Gettysburg Address
A brief speech given by President Lincoln at the dedication of the Gettysburg Cemetery in November 1863 that declared that the Civil War was dedicated to freedom.

The Winter of Discontent: 1863–1864

The battles of the summer had been horrific. Both sides held their victories close to their hearts and brooded over their losses. The resolve and fury of summertime faded into the bitterness and bickering of winter. As the cycle rolled around again, people steeled themselves for a final push.

Politics North and South

Lincoln hoped to end the war as soon as possible, using persuasion as well as fighting to entice white southerners back into the national fold. In early December 1863, Lincoln issued his proclamation of amnesty and reconstruction. To those who would take an oath of loyalty to the Union, Lincoln promised a full pardon and the return of all property other than slaves. Though he excluded Confederate leaders and high officers from this offer, Lincoln tried to include as many white southern men as possible. As soon as 10 percent of the number of voters in 1860 had sworn their loyalty to the Union, he decreed, the southerners could begin forming new state governments. Education and apprenticeship programs would aid former slaves in the transition to full freedom. He did not provide for African American participation in the new governments of the South.

Two factors worked against acceptance of Lincoln's policy. First, northern Republicans and much of the public overestimated the extent and depth of southern Unionist sentiment after years of war and occupation. Second, even in areas under federal control such as Tennessee and Kentucky, guerrilla bands and raiders terrorized the local populations. Elections in parts of Tennessee were blocked by irregulars. "The people are warned . . . not to hold such an Election under pain of being Arrested and Carried South for trial," one observer reported. Civilians were often caught between threats. Those who failed to aid Union forces were perceived as "enemies of mankind" with "the rights due to pirates and robbers," whereas those who actively aided the federals were liable to find crops trampled, barns burned, and vigilante justice enacted by neighbors and guerrillas.

Abolitionists and their allies attacked Lincoln's reconstruction plan as far too lenient to the Rebel masters and not helpful enough for the former slaves. In the Wade-Davis bill of February 1864, Republican congressmen attempted to inflict more stringent conditions on former Confederates and offer more help to former slaves. They wanted to use the power of the national government to enforce a standard set of laws across the South and to require 50 percent, rather than 10 percent, of the population to swear the loyalty oath, an oath of past as well as future loyalty. They feared that too weak a plan of reconstruction would permit former slaveowners and Confederates to negate much of what the war might win. Congressmen and Secretary of the Treasury Salmon P. Chase worked behind the scenes in opposition to Lincoln's plan. With an eye toward the upcoming election and the need to entice Arkansas and Louisiana to rejoin the Union, Lincoln refused to sign the Wade-Davis bill.

Although Jefferson Davis did not have to worry about his own reelection in late 1863 — the Confederacy had established the presidential term at six years — he did have to worry about congressional elections. They did not go well: 41 of the new 106 representatives expressly opposed Davis and his policies, while he held only a slight majority in the Senate. Just as northern Democrats called for compromise and peace, so did some southerners. When Davis took a hands-off policy, he was criticized for doing too little. When he tried to assert more control, he found himself called "despotic" by his own vice president. Editors savaged Davis as responsible for the South's worsening fortunes: "Had the people dreamed that Mr. Davis would carry all his chronic antipathies, his bitter prejudices, his puerile partialities, and his doting favoritisms into the Presidential chair, they would never have allowed him to fill it." The Confederacy stumbled through the winter and into the spring of 1864, desperately watching for signs that the North might be losing heart.

Prisons

Early in the Civil War both sides had exchanged prisoners of war rather than spending men and resources to maintain prisons. Such arrangements worked well enough into 1863, but then things began to break down. The Confederates decreed that any former slave captured would be executed or re-enslaved, not taken prisoner. The Union, as a matter of principle, refused to participate in any exchanges so long as this policy remained in effect. Prisoners began piling up on both sides, and stories of mistreatment became more frequent and more horrifying.

Northerners became livid when they heard of the Confederate camp at Andersonville, Georgia. The camp was built early in 1864 when the Confederates decided to move prisoners from Richmond. Not only would prisoners be less likely to be rescued by northern troops moving south, but they could more easily be supplied by railroad away from the heavy fighting in Virginia. The camp, built for ten thousand men in an open, partly swampy field, soon became overcrowded; it held thirty-three thousand by August. Gangs of northern soldiers controlled daily life within the prison, routinely beating and robbing new arrivals. Of the forty-five thousand men eventually held at Andersonville, thirteen thousand died. The camp's commander, Colonel Henry Wirz, was the only Confederate official executed for war crimes after the war.

Even higher proportions died at smaller camps in North Carolina. Although Confederates held in northern prisons were better supplied, even there, death rates reached as high as 24 percent with rations often short and men reduced to eating rats. Overall, about 16 percent of northern soldiers died in prison, and 12 percent of southerners. Many in the North criticized Lincoln for refusing to reinstitute exchanges, but Lincoln would not sacrifice the former slaves. Moreover, he knew that exchanges helped the soldier-starved Confederacy more than they did the North.

Union Resolve

In March 1864 Lincoln gave new direction and purpose to the Union effort by putting Ulysses S. Grant in charge of all northern forces. Grant and Lincoln agreed that the Union had to use its superiority in materiel, manpower, and navy to attack the Confederacy on every front at once, forcing the South to decide what territory it would sacrifice. While Grant would fight in Virginia, Lincoln left **William T. Sherman** in charge in Chattanooga. Sherman would attack the young railroad center of Atlanta, cutting the Gulf South off from the Upper South. The loss of Atlanta would chop the Confederacy into pieces too small to resist the northern army.

In retrospect, the events of 1864 may appear anticlimactic. The Confederates seemed to face overwhelming odds. Yet southerners recognized that everything turned around holding the northerners off until the presidential election in the North. If the southerners could inflict enough damage on the Union Army, northerners might elect someone willing

William T. Sherman
Union general under Ulysses S. Grant who took Atlanta and led the "March to the Sea."

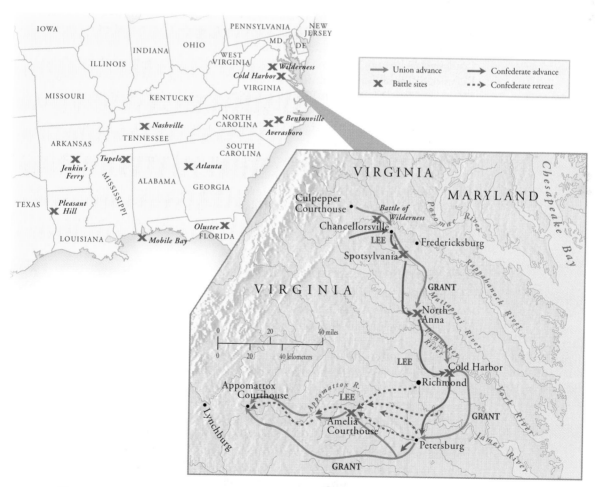

MAP 15.3 Grant Against Lee in Virginia
The two most important generals of the war confronted one another at one brutal battle after another between May 1864 and April 1865. View an animated version of this map or related maps at http://history.wadsworth.com/ayersbrief02.

to bring the war to an end through compromise. The Confederates knew, too, that the three-year terms of the most experienced veterans in the Union Army expired in 1864. More than half of those veterans chose to leave the army, even though the war was not over. They would be replaced with younger, less seasoned soldiers. The Confederates also realized that Grant, new to his command, would be confronting Robert E. Lee, who was fighting with an experienced army. All things considered, it was by no means clear in 1864 that the Union would win in Virginia or win the war.

African Americans played an increasingly large role in Union plans, and more than one hundred eighty thousand black soldiers enlisted just when the North needed them most. By the spring of 1864, the means of recruitment, training, and pay for these soldiers had become well established. The Confederates, however, refused to recognize the same rules of warfare for black soldiers that they acknowledged for whites. In April 1864, at Fort Pillow in western Tennessee, Confederate cavalry under the command of Nathan Bedford Forrest shot down black Union soldiers and their white commander who attempted to surrender.

With the election clock running, Grant set out in May 1864 to destroy Lee's army. The Battle of the Wilderness near Chancellorsville saw brutal fighting and horrible losses. Fire in the tangled woods trapped wounded men, burning them alive. Grant lost more men than Hooker had in the battle of the previous year, but whereas Hooker treated such losses as a decisive defeat and retreated, Grant pushed on.

The two armies fought again and again over the next two months in the fields of Virginia. The Confederates turned the Union Army back to the east of Richmond and rushed up the Shenandoah Valley to threaten Washington itself. While failing to take the capital, Confederate raiders "taxed" Maryland towns for thousands of dollars of greenbacks and burned the town of Chambersburg, Pennsylvania, when it refused to pay $500,000. The North repulsed the invasion and dispatched Philip Sheridan to the valley to make sure the Confederates did not regroup. With the Confederates pinned down in Petersburg, near Richmond, Pennsylvania coal miners volunteered to tunnel under the fortifications and plant explosives. Throughout July they dug; finally, at the end of the month, they detonated a charge and blew an enormous crater in the Confederate lines. The attack that followed the explosion, however, failed. Union soldiers piled into the crater, where the rallying Confederates trapped them.

Fortunately for Lincoln, things were going better farther south. Throughout June and July, Sherman pushed relentlessly through north Georgia toward Atlanta. By the end of July, the southern army had fallen back into Atlanta, preparing to defend it from siege. It seemed only a matter of time before the Union triumphed. But how much time? After rapidly advancing, federal troops slowed as they closed on Atlanta, and many feared that Sherman was "on the eve of disaster."

The Northern Election of 1864

The president had to fight off challenges even within his own party. Some Republicans considered Lincoln too radical; others considered him too cautious. Through adroit use of patronage, however, Lincoln managed to win renomination in June. The Republican party tried to broaden its appeal to Democrats by nominating **Andrew Johnson,** a former Democrat from Tennessee, to the vice presidency.

In the meantime, the Democrats confidently moved forward. They knew that in the eyes of his critics Lincoln had caused the war, trampled on constitutional rights, consolidated too much power, and refused to end the war when he had a chance. The Democrats intended to take full advantage of such criticisms, especially by nominating George McClellan as their candidate. McClellan demonstrated that a person could oppose Lincoln's political purposes of the war without being a coward or a traitor. McClellan and the Democrats portrayed themselves as the truly national party, for they were determined to restore the United States to its prewar unity and grandeur. McClellan said he would end the war if the South would reenter the Union—bringing slavery with it. It was a bargain that appealed to many in the North.

Just when it appeared that the Democrats would unseat Lincoln, however, news from the battlefield changed everything. Sherman swung around Atlanta and began destroying

Andrew Johnson
The seventeenth president of the United States (1865-1869); he succeeded the assassinated Abraham Lincoln.

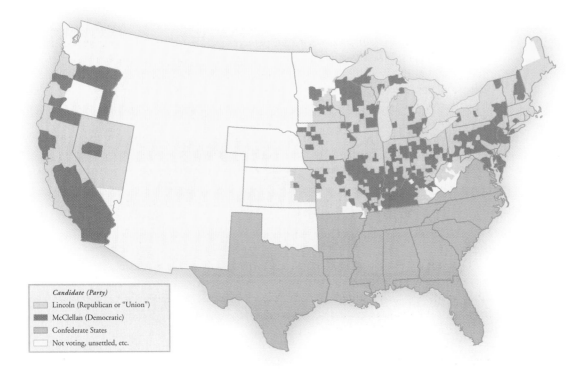

MAP 15.4 The Election of 1864

Though Lincoln won easily in the electoral college vote, he faced strong opposition throughout much of the North from George McClellan, who claimed 45 percent of the popular vote. With the popular vote so close, in many states the outcome hinged on the votes of soldiers. Compare the distribution of votes for Lincoln in 1864 and 1860 (see Map 13.2) and note the areas where Lincoln gained and lost support.

the railroads that made the small city an important junction. The Confederates, afraid they would be encircled and trapped within the city, set much of Atlanta on fire and abandoned it. Sherman and his army marched into the city on September 2. Two weeks later, Phillip Sheridan attacked the Confederates in the Shenandoah Valley, systematically destroying the valley's ability to support the southern army again.

Even with these military victories, Lincoln won only 55 percent of the popular vote. Contrary to expectations, Lincoln carried the large majority of the armies' votes. In their letters, soldiers who identified themselves as Democrats rejected McClellan. A Vermont soldier who described himself as "a McClellan man clear to the bone" would not accept "peace by surrendering to the rebels"; instead "he would let his bones manure the soil of Virginia." Lincoln did much better in the electoral college, sweeping every state except three. The Republicans also elected heavy majorities to both houses of Congress and elected the governor and legislative majorities in all states except New Jersey, Delaware, and Kentucky. Lincoln believed the election validated the strength of republican government: "We can not have a free government without elections; and if the rebellion could force us to forego, or postpone a national election, it might fairly claim to have already conquered and ruined us."

The March to the Sea

Jefferson Davis traveled through the Lower South after the fall of Atlanta, exhorting citizens to remain defiant. A week after Lincoln's election, Sherman set out across Georgia, provisioning his army along the way, taking the war to the southern people themselves. Such a march would be as much a demonstration of northern power as a military maneuver: "If we can march a well-appointed army right through [Confederate] territory," Sherman argued, "it is a demonstration to the world, foreign and domestic, that we have a power which Davis cannot resist." The triumphant army of sixty thousand made its way across the state

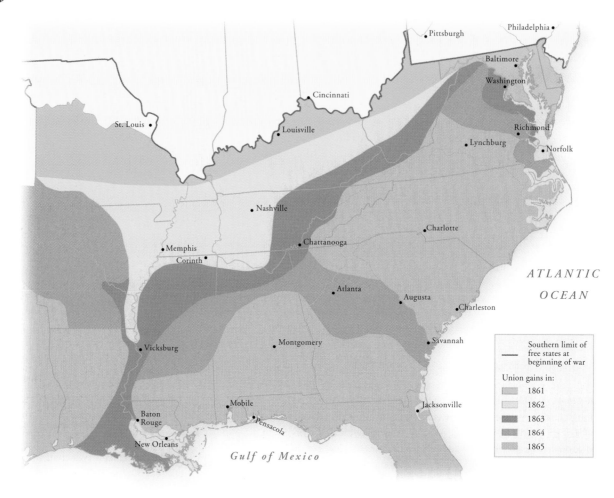

MAP 15.5 The Territory of War

The Confederacy managed to protect large parts of its interior throughout the war, but the Union increasingly controlled the crucial rivers, rail lines, and ports. View an animated version of this map or related maps at http://history.wadsworth.com/ayersbrief02.

throughout the fall of 1864. Large numbers of deserters from both sides, fugitive slaves, and outlaws took advantage of the situation to inflict widespread destruction and panic. Sherman arrived at Savannah on December 21. "I beg to present to you, as a Christmas gift, the city of Savannah," Sherman buoyantly telegraphed Lincoln. Contrasting with the devastation of the South, the president's annual message to Congress outlined a portrait of a North gaining strength with "more men now than we had when the war began. . . . We are gaining strength, and may, if need be, maintain the contest indefinitely."

From War to Reconstruction: 1865–1867

As the war ground to a halt in early 1865, Americans had to wonder if they remembered how to share a country with their former enemies. They had to wonder, too, how different the country would be with African Americans no longer as slaves. Of all the changes the United States had ever seen, **emancipation** stood as the most profound.

War's Climax

Events moved quickly at the beginning of 1865. In January, Sherman issued **Special Field Order 15,** which reserved land in coastal South Carolina, Georgia, and Florida for former slaves. Those who settled on the land would receive forty-acre plots. Four days later, the

emancipation
The ending of slavery, initiated in the Emancipation Proclamation of 1863 but not accomplished in many places until the Confederate surrender in 1865.

Special Field Order 15
Issued by William T. Sherman in January of 1865, this order reserved land in coastal South Carolina, Georgia, and Florida for former slaves. Those who settled on the land would receive forty-acre plots.

Republicans in Congress passed the **Thirteenth Amendment,** abolishing slavery forever. Antislavery activists, black and white, packed the galleries and the House floor. Observers embraced, wept, and cheered. A Congressman wrote his wife that "we can now look other nations in the face without shame."

At the beginning of February, Sherman's troops began to march north into the Carolinas. Columbia, South Carolina, burned to the ground. Growing numbers of Confederate soldiers deserted from their armies. Lincoln met with Confederate officials at Hampton Roads on board the steamship *River Queen* to try to bring the war to an end, offering slave-owners compensation for their freed slaves if the southerners would immediately cease the war. Jefferson Davis refused to submit to the "disgrace of surrender."

At the beginning of March, Lincoln was inaugurated for his second term. Rather than gloating at the impending victory on the battlefield, Lincoln called for his fellow citizens to "bind up the nation's wounds." That same month, Congress created the Bureau of Refugees, Freedmen, and Abandoned Lands to ease the transition from slavery to freedom. Nine days later, the Confederate government, after hotly debating whether to recruit slaves to fight as soldiers if their owners agreed, finally decided to do so after Lee, desperate for men, supported the measure.

Appomattox and Assassination

The Confederates' slave recruitment law did not have time to convert slaves to soldiers, however, for Grant soon began his final assault on Confederate troops in Virginia. Petersburg fell on April 2, and Richmond the next day. Lee hoped to lead his army to the train station at **Appomattox** Court House to resupply them, but on April 9 Grant intercepted Lee's men just short of their destination. Lee, with nowhere else to go and no ally to come to his aid, surrendered.

A number of Confederate armies had yet to surrender, and Jefferson Davis had yet to be captured, but it was clear that the war had ended. Cities and towns across the North erupted in celebration and relief as crowds filled the streets to sing, embrace, fire salutes, and wave the flag. Southerners began to straggle home. Two days later, Lincoln addressed a Washington audience about what would come next for the freedmen. He admitted that northerners differed "as to the mode, manner, and means of Reconstruction" and that the white South was "disorganized and discordant."

Lincoln did not live to take part in the planning, for he was assassinated on April 14 by **John Wilkes Booth,** a well-known actor and southern sympathizer. Booth attacked Lincoln while the president sat with Mrs. Lincoln at Ford's Theater in Washington, shooting him in the back of the head and then leaping to the stage. Lincoln never recovered consciousness; he died early the next morning. After a long and frantic search, Booth was captured and killed in a burning barn.

Thirteenth Amendment
Passed in 1865, this constitutional amendment abolished slavery.

©CORBIS

This picture of Lincoln, taken four days before his assassination, shows the toll four years of war had taken on the fifty-six-year-old president.

Appomattox
The small Virginia village that served as the site of surrender of Confederate forces under Robert E. Lee to Ulysses S. Grant on April 9, 1865, generally recognized as bringing the Civil War to an end.

John Wilkes Booth
An actor and southern sympathizer who assassinated Abraham Lincoln on April 14, 1865.

The Costs and Consequences of the War

The North lost almost 365,000 men to death and disease in the Civil War, and the South lost 260,000. Another 277,000 northerners were wounded, along with 195,000 southerners. Black Americans lost 37,000 men in the Union Army and another 10,000 men, women, and children in the contraband camps. Widows and orphans, black and white, northern and southern, faced decades of struggling without a male breadwinner. Many people found their emotional lives shattered by the war. Alcohol, drug abuse, crime, and violence became widespread problems.

The southern economy fell to its knees. Major southern cities had been reduced to ash. Railroads had been ripped from the ground, engines and cars burned. Fields had grown up in

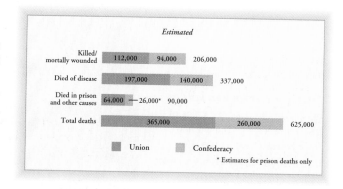

CHART 15.1 The Causes and Numbers of Civil War Deaths
Disease killed even more men than did the bullets of enemies.

Total Casualties

1863 Gettysburg
23,053
28,063

1862 Seven Days' Battles
15,849
20,614

1864 Chickamauga
16,170
18,454

1863 Chancellorsville/ second Fredericksburg
16,845
12,764

1862 Antietam
12,410
10,316

1862 Second Manassas/Chantilly
16,054
9,286

1862 Shiloh
13,047
10,694

1862 Fredricksburg
12,653
5,309

■ Union   ■ Confederacy

CHART 15.2 The Most Costly Battles
Battles exacted horrible costs from early in the war until near its very end.

weeds and brush. Farm values fell by half. Livestock, tools, barns, and fences had been stolen or destroyed by the armies of both sides. Recovery was slow. In Georgia, for example, as late as 1870 the state recorded 1 million fewer pigs, 200,000 fewer cattle, and 3 million fewer acres under cultivation than in 1860. Just as damaging in the long run, lines of credit had been severed. Before emancipation, planters had used slaves as collateral for loans. Now, without that basis, few people outside the South were willing to loan money to planters or other investors.

The Civil War did not mark a sudden turn in the northern economy, but it did accelerate processes already well under way. The nationalization of markets, the accumulation of wealth, and the dominance of larger manufacturing firms all became more marked after 1865. Greenbacks, bonds, and a national banking system regularized the flow of capital and spurred the growth of business. The Republicans passed the Department of Agriculture Act, the Morrill College Land Grant Act, the Homestead Act, and the Union Pacific Railroad Act, all using the power of the federal government to encourage settlement of the West, strengthen public education, and spur economic development.

Emancipation and the South

As the battles ground to a halt, slaves became former slaves. Some, especially the young, greeted freedom confidently, whereas others, especially the elderly, could not help but be wary of anything so strange, no matter how long and how much they had prayed for it. Some seized their freedom at the first opportunity, taking their families to Union camps or joining the army. Others celebrated when the Yankees came to their plantations, only to find that their owners and white neighbors retaliated when the soldiers left. Others bided their time. Some refused to believe the stories of freedom at all until their master or mistress called them together to announce that they were indeed no longer slaves.

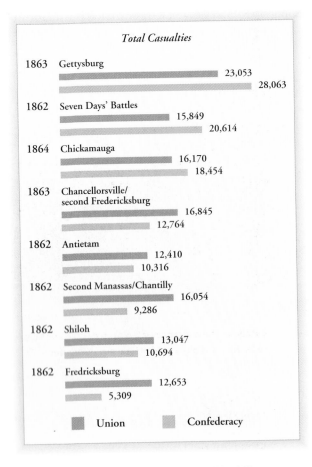

After four years of war, little remained in the besieged cities of the Confederacy. One woman from North Carolina bitterly lamented her transformation from "social queen" to "domestic drudge." African American women looked forward to working for the benefit of their own families.

Upon hearing the news, the freedpeople gathered to discuss their options. For many, the highest priority was to reunite their families. Such people set off on journeys in desperate efforts to find a husband, wife, child, or parent sold away in earlier years. For others, sheer survival was the highest priority. Freedom came in the late spring, barely in time to get crops in the ground. Some former slaves argued that their best bet was to stay where they were for the time being. They had heard rumors that the government would award them land. Between July and September of 1865, however, those dreams died. Union officers promised land to former slaves in Virginia, Louisiana, Mississippi, and South Carolina, but then Washington revoked the promises. The land would be returned to its former owners.

©Bettmann /CORBIS

Former slaveowners also responded in many different ways. Some fled to Latin America. Others tried to keep as much of slavery as they could by whipping and chaining workers to keep them from leaving. Still others offered to let former slaves stay in their cabins and work for wages. The presence of black soldiers triggered resentment and fear among former slaveowners who marked the increased independence among blacks that was encouraged by "Negro troops." One slaveowner believed "the people of the South are in very great danger . . . I tell you most seriously that the whole south is resting upon a volcano."

African Americans had no choice but to compromise with white landowners. At first, in the spring of 1865, planters insisted that the former slaves work as they had worked before emancipation, in "gangs." In return for their work, they would receive a portion of the crop, shared among all the workers. Many black people chafed at this arrangement, preferring to work as individuals or families. In such places, landowners found that they had little choice but to permit black families to take primary responsibility for a portion of land. The former slaves provided the labor and received part of the crop as a result. Planters, though reluctant to give up any control over the day-to-day work on their land, realized they had few choices. They possessed little cash to pay wage workers and had no alternative labor pool.

©North Wind Picture Archives

Black southerners took advantage of the presence of Union troops to leave the farms and plantations on which they had been held. Many set out to find family members.

The Bureau of Refugees, Freedmen, and Abandoned Lands—the **Freedmen's Bureau**—oversaw the transition from a slave economy to a wage economy. Its agents dispensed medicine, food, and clothing from the vast stores of the federal government to displaced white and black southerners. The bureau created courts to adjudicate conflicts and to draw up labor contracts between landholders and laborers. It established schools and coordinated female volunteers who came from the North to teach in them.

Although many white southerners resented and resisted the Freedmen's Bureau, it helped smooth the transition from slavery to freedom, from war to peace.

Freedmen's Bureau
A federal agency created in 1865 to supervise newly freed people. It oversaw relations between whites and blacks in the South, issued food rations, and supervised labor contracts.

Black Mobilization

Black southerners mourned the loss of Abraham Lincoln. Without his leadership, former slaves rightly worried, the forces of reaction might overwhelm their freedom. Southerners of both races watched to see what Andrew Johnson might do.

Throughout the South, former slaves and former free blacks gathered in mass meetings, Union Leagues, and conventions to announce their vision of the new order. They wanted, above all else, equality before the law and the opportunity to vote. They did not demand confiscation of land, nor did they speak extensively of economic concerns in general. Let us have our basic rights before the courts and at the ballot box, they said, and we will take care of ourselves. Such concerns and confidence reflected the perspective of the conventions' leadership: former free blacks, skilled artisans, ministers, and teachers. The great mass of southern blacks found their concerns neglected.

Black southerners agreed on the centrality of two institutions, however: the church and the school. At the very moment of freedom, they began to form their own churches. For generations, African Americans had been forced to worship alongside whites. For many ex-slaves, one of their first acts of freedom was to form their own churches. Before the war, forty-two thousand black Methodists in South Carolina attended biracial churches. By 1870, only six hundred mostly elderly blacks remained. People who owned virtually nothing somehow built churches across the South. A black church in Charleston was the first

Black Citizens of Tennessee, "Letter to the Union Convention, 1865"

In this petition by black Tennesseans to their white Unionist counterparts in the waning days of the Civil War, the themes of the Gettysburg Address receive eloquent endorsement. The fifty-nine men who signed the petition articulated the highest ideals of the American nation. There is no record of a response.

[Nashville, Tenn., January 9, 1865]
To the Union Convention of Tennessee Assembled in the Capitol at Nashville, January 9th, 1865: . . .

We claim to be men belonging to the great human family, descended from one great God, who is the common Father of all, and who bestowed on all races and tribes the priceless right of freedom. Of this right, for no offence of ours, we have long been cruelly deprived, and the common voice of the wise and good of all countries, has remonstrated against our enslavement, as one of the greatest crimes in all history.

We claim freedom, as our natural right, and ask that in harmony and cooperation with the nation at large, you should cut up by the roots the system of slavery, which is not only a wrong to us, but the source of all the evil which at present afflicts the State. For slavery, corrupt itself, corrupted nearly all, also, around it, so that it has influenced nearly all the slave States to rebel against the Federal Government, in order to set up a government of pirates under which slavery might be perpetrated. . . .

Devoted as we are to the principles of justice, of love to all men, and of equal rights on which our Government is based, and which make it the hope of the world. We know the burdens of citizenship, and are ready to bear them. We know the duties of the good citizen, and are ready to perform them cheerfully, and would ask to be put in a position in which we can discharge them more effectually. We do not ask for the privilege of citizenship, wishing to shun the obligations imposed by it.

Near 200,000 of our brethren are today performing military duty in the ranks of the Union army. Thousands of them have already died in battle, or perished by a cruel martyrdom for the sake of the Union, and we are ready and willing to sacrifice more. . . .

This is a democracy—a government of the people. It should aim to make every man, without regard to the color of his skin, the amount of his wealth, or the character of his religious faith, feel personally interested in its welfare. Every man who lives under the Government should feel that it is his property, his treasure, the bulwark and defense of himself and his family, his pearl of great price, which he must preserve, protect, and defend faithfully at all times, on all occasions, in every possible manner.

This is not a Democratic Government if a numerous, law-abiding, industrious, and useful class of citizens, born and bred on the soil, are to be treated as aliens and enemies, as an

building raised from the ruins of the city in 1865. Those churches often served as schools as well.

Andrew Johnson

In the meantime, events in Washington undermined the efforts of black southerners to build a new world for themselves. Andrew Johnson wanted to attract moderates from both the North and the South to a political party that would change as little as possible. Johnson had been selected to run for the vice presidency because he was a southerner who had remained true to the Union. As a result, both northerners and southerners distrusted Johnson. A longtime Democrat before the crisis of the Union, Johnson maintained a limited view of government. The new president's well-known disdain for the wealthy planters of the South appealed to equally disdainful Republicans in Washington. His public statements suggested a harsh peace for former slaveowners and Confederate leaders: "*Treason* is a crime, and *crime* must be punished." Unlike some Republicans, however, Johnson held little sympathy for black people or for expansion of the powers of the federal government. Johnson saw himself pursuing Lincoln's highest goal: reuniting the Union. He believed that reunification should start by winning the support of white southerners.

inferior degraded class, who must have no voice in the Government which they support, protect and defend, with all their heart, soul, mind, and body, both in peace and war. . . .

One other matter we would urge on your honorable body. At present we can have only partial protection from the courts. The testimony of twenty of the most intelligent, honorable, colored loyalists cannot convict a white traitor of a treasonable action. A white rebel might sell powder and lead to a rebel soldier in the presence of twenty colored soldiers, and yet their evidence would be worthless so far as the courts are concerned, and the rebel would escape. A colored man may have served for years faithfully in the army, and yet his testimony in court would be rejected, while that of a white man who had served in the rebel army would be received. . . .

There have been white traitors in multitudes in Tennessee, but where we ask, is the black traitor?

Can you forget how the colored man has fought at Fort Morgan, at Milliken's Bend, at Fort Pillow, before Petersburg, and your own city of Nashville?

When has the colored citizen, in this rebellion been tried and found wanting? . . .

In this great and fearful struggle of the nation with a wicked rebellion, we are anxious to perform the full measure of our duty both as citizens and soldiers to the Union cause we consecrate ourselves, and our families with all that we have on earth. Our souls burn with love for the great government of freedom and equal rights. Our white brethren have no cause for distrust as regards our fidelity, for neither death nor life, nor angels, nor principalities, nor powers, nor things present, nor things to come, nor height, nor depth, nor any other creature, shall be able to separate us from the love of the Union.

Praying that the great God, who is the common Father of us all, by whose help the land must be delivered from present evil, and before whom we must all stand at last to be judged by the rule of eternal justice, and not by passion and prejudice, may enlighten your minds and enable you to act with wisdom, justice, and magnanimity, we remain your faithful friends in all the perils and dangers which threaten our beloved country.

[59 signatures]

And many other colored citizens of Nashville

Questions to Consider

1. What did these African American men want above all else? Why?

2. Why were they ignored by the people they petitioned?

3. Did the petitioners ask for things that would benefit all black Tennesseans, or only some?

Explore additional primary sources related to this chapter on the *American Passages* Web site: http://history.wadsworth.com/ayersbrief02.

Source: *Free at Last: A Documentary History of Slavery, Freedom, and the Civil War.* Ira Berlin, et al., eds. (New York: New Press, 1992), pp. 497–505.

Johnson could hardly have been placed in a more difficult position. Congress was not in session at the time of Lincoln's death and would not be for seven months, so Johnson used the opportunity to implement his vision of reunion. In what became known as "Presidential Reconstruction," Johnson offered amnesty to former Confederates who would take an oath of loyalty to the Union, restoring their political and civil rights and immunizing them against the seizure of their property or prosecution for treason. By 1866 Johnson had granted more than seven thousand pardons to wealthy southerners and Confederate senior officers who applied individually for amnesty.

Johnson's plans for political reunion made no provisions at all for black voting. Indeed, his plan threatened to return the South to even greater national power than it had held before because the entire African American population would now be considered when the number of representatives was calculated, not merely as three-fifths of a people as before the war.

White southerners could hardly believe their good fortune. The state conventions elected in 1865 flaunted their opinions of the North. Some refused to fly the American flag, some refused to ratify the Thirteenth Amendment, some even refused to admit that secession had been illegal. Former Confederates filled important posts in state governments. Georgia elected Alexander H. Stephens, the ex-vice president of the aborted nation, to Congress. Even Johnson recognized that far from inaugurating new regimes led by Unionist yeomen, "there seems, in many of the elections something like defiance."

The North erupted in outrage when the new state governments enacted the so-called black codes, laws for the control of the former slaves. The southern white legislatures granted only the barest minimum of rights to black people: the right to marry, to hold property, to sue and be sued. Most of the laws decreed what African Americans could not do: move from one job to another, own or rent land, testify in court, practice certain occupations. When the members of Congress convened in December of 1865, they reacted as many of their constituents did—with fury. To northerners, even those inclined to deal leniently with the South, the former Confederates seemed to deny all the war had decided with this blatant attempt to retain racially based laws. And many northerners blamed Johnson.

Andrew Johnson attempted to forge a new alliance between white northerners and white southerners, callously abandoning black southerners in the process.

Johnson and the Radicals

It was not that most northerners, even most Republicans, wanted the kind of policies promoted by Radicals such as Thaddeus Stevens, who called for land to be seized from wealthy planters and given to the former slaves, or Charles Sumner, who wanted immediate and universal suffrage for blacks. But neither did they want the sort of capitulation that Johnson had tolerated. A Chicago editor spoke for his readers: "As for Negro suffrage, the mass of Union men in the Northwest do not care a great deal. What scares them is the idea that the rebels are all to be let back . . . and made a power in the government again." Moderates tried to devise plans that would be acceptable to both sides.

The moderates sought to continue the Freedmen's Bureau. The bureau was understaffed and underfunded—only about nine hundred agents covered the entire South—but it offered some measure of hope for former slaves. The bureau saw itself as a mediator between blacks and whites. Its commissioner, General Oliver Howard, advocated education as the foundation for improving living conditions and prospects for blacks. By 1869 approximately three thousand schools, serving more than a hundred fifty thousand students, reported to the bureau, and these numbers did not include the many private and church-funded schools throughout the South.

The bureau insisted on the innovation of formal contracts between laborer and landlord. Although these contracts infuriated southern white men, the bureau ended up supporting landowners as often as black laborers. The moderates also attempted to institute a Civil Rights bill to define American citizenship for all those born in the United States, thereby including blacks. Citizenship would bring with it equal protection under the laws, though the bill said nothing about black voting. The bureau struggled against strongly held prejudice. Its Mississippi commissioner despaired of a public that failed to "conceive of the Negro having any rights at all."

Republicans supported the Freedmen's Bureau and Civil Rights bills as the starting place for rebuilding the nation. But Johnson vetoed both bills, claiming that they violated the rights of the states and of white southerners who had been excluded from the decision making. Republicans closed ranks to override Johnson's veto, the first major legislation ever enacted over a presidential veto.

To prevent any future erosion of black rights, the Republicans proposed the Fourteenth Amendment, which, as eventually ratified, guaranteed citizenship to all American-born people and equal protection under the law for those citizens. The amendment decreed that any state that abridged the voting rights of any male inhabitants who were twenty-one and citizens would suffer a proportionate reduction in its congressional representation. This clause offered white southerners the choice of acceptance of black suffrage or reduced congressional representation. It also was the first constitutional amendment to use the word "male," angering feminist abolitionists who challenged the Republicans' denial of suffrage based on sex. Johnson urged the southern states to refuse to ratify the amendment, advice they promptly followed.

Throughout the second half of 1866 the North watched, appalled, as much that the Civil War had been fought for seemed to be brushed aside in the South. Not only did the southern men who met in the state conventions refuse to accept the relatively mild Fourteenth Amendment, but they made clear their determination to fight back in every way they could against further attempts to remake the South. The spring of that year saw riots in Memphis and New Orleans in which policemen and other whites brutally assaulted and killed black people and burned their homes with little or no provocation.

It was in 1866, too, that the Ku Klux Klan appeared. Founded in Tennessee, the Ku Klux Klan dedicated itself to maintaining white supremacy. The Klan dressed in costumes designed to overawe the former slaves, hiding behind their anonymity to avoid retaliation. The Klan became in effect a military wing of the Democratic party, devoting much of its energy to warning and killing white and black men who dared associate with the Republicans.

The Ku Klux Klan emerged in 1866, devoting itself to the maintenance of white supremacy in all its forms.

Johnson toured the country in the fall of 1866 to denounce the Republicans and their policies. Even his supporters saw the tour as a "thoroughly reprehensible" disaster. The voters rejected both Johnson and the Democrats, as the governorship and legislature of every northern state came under the control of the Republicans. In the next Congress, Republicans would outnumber Democrats sufficiently to override any presidential veto. The Republicans felt they held a mandate to push harder than they had before. They had only a few months, however, until their term ended in March, to decide what to do. They bitterly disagreed over the vote, land distribution, the courts, and education. Some wanted to put the South under military control for the indefinite future, whereas others sought to return things to civilian control as soon as possible. Finally, on March 2, 1867, as time was running out on the session, they passed the Reconstruction Act.

The Reconstruction Act

The Reconstruction Act placed the South under military rule. All the southern states except Tennessee, which had been readmitted to the Union after it ratified the Fourteenth Amendment, were put in five military districts. Once order had been instituted, the states would proceed to elect conventions to draw up new constitutions. The constitutions written by those conventions had to accept the Fourteenth Amendment and provide for universal manhood suffrage. Once a majority of the state's citizens and both houses of the national Congress had approved the new constitution, the state could be readmitted to the Union.

To ensure that Andrew Johnson did not undermine this plan—which soon became known as "Radical Reconstruction"—Congress sought to curb the president's power. With no threat of his veto after the 1866 elections, the Republicans could do much as they wanted. Congress decreed that it could call itself into special session. There, it limited the president's authority as commander-in-chief of the army and, in the Tenure of Office Act, prevented him from removing officials who had been confirmed by the Senate.

Johnson, characteristically, did not quietly accept such restrictions of his power. When he intentionally violated the Tenure of Office Act by removing Secretary of War Edwin Stanton in the summer of 1867, many in Congress decided that Johnson warranted **impeachment.** Matters stewed throughout the fall as the first elections under the Reconstruction Act took place in the South.

impeachment
The act of charging a public official with misconduct in office.

Reconstruction Begins

After word of the Reconstruction Act circulated in the spring and summer, both black and white men claimed leadership roles within the Republican party. Black northerners came to the South, looking for appointive and elective office. Ambitious black southerners, many of whom had been free and relatively prosperous before the Civil War, put themselves forward as the natural leaders of the race. Such men became the backbone of the Republican party in black-belt districts.

White southerners sneered at white northerners who supported the Republican cause. They called them "carpetbaggers." These men, according to the insulting name, were supposedly so devoid of connections and property in their northern homes that they could throw everything they had into a carpetbag—a cheap suitcase—and head south as soon as they read of the opportunities created by Radical Reconstruction. The majority of white northerners who became Republican leaders in the South, however, had in fact moved to the region months or years before Reconstruction began. Many had been well educated in the North before the war, and many held property in the South. Like white southerners, however, the northern-born Republicans found the postwar South a difficult place in which to prosper. Black people were no more inclined to work for low wages for white northerners than for anyone else, and southern whites often went out of their way to avoid doing business with the Yankees. As a result, when Reconstruction began, a considerable number of northerners took up the Republican cause as a way to build a political career in the South.

White southern Republicans, labeled "scalawags" by their enemies, risked being called traitors to their race and region. Few white Republicans emerged in the plantation districts, because they endured ostracism, resistance, and violence. In the upcountry districts, however, former Whigs and Unionists asserted themselves against the planters and Confederates. The Republican party became strong in the mountains of east Tennessee, western North Carolina, eastern Kentucky, north Alabama, and northern Georgia. Many whites in these districts, though unwilling to join with low-country African Americans or their white leaders, struck alliances of convenience with them. Black voters and white voters generally wanted and needed different things. Blacks, largely propertyless, called for an activist government to raise taxes to provide schools, orphanages, and hospitals. Most whites, on the other hand, owned land and called mainly for lower taxes.

Throughout the South, most whites watched, livid, as local black leaders, ministers, and Republicans mobilized black voters in enormous numbers in the fall of 1867. Membership in Union Leagues swept the region, with local leagues assisting with labor contracts and school construction as well as political activity. An Alabama league demanded recognition of black citizenship: "We claim exactly the same rights, privileges and immunities as are enjoyed by white men—we seek nothing more and will be content with nothing less." While many white Democrats boycotted the elections, the Republicans swept into the constitutional delegate positions. Although many black men voted, African American delegates made up only a relatively small part of the conventions' delegates. They held the majority in South Carolina and Louisiana, but much smaller proportions elsewhere. About half of the 265 African Americans elected as delegates to the state conventions had been free before the war, and most were ministers, artisans, farmers, and teachers. Over the next two years, these delegates would meet to write new, much more democratic, constitutions for their states.

At the very moment of the success of the southern Republicans, however, ominous signs came from the North. Republicans were dismayed at the election returns in the North in 1867, for the Democrats' power surged from coast to coast. Many white voters thought that the Radicals had gone too far in their concern with black rights and wanted officeholders to devote their energies to problems closer to home. Racism linked Democratic appeals against blacks in the Midwest with western diatribes against the Chinese. Integrated public schools and confiscation of plantation lands for former slaves were soundly defeated. The Republicans in Washington heard the message. They began scaling back their support for any further advances in Reconstruction.

Summary

War, Emancipation, and Reconstruction

The Civil War changed the United States more deeply than any other event in the nineteenth century—indeed, perhaps in all of American history. The conflict brought the deaths of more than 625,000 soldiers, the equivalent of five million people today and nearly as many as have died in all other American wars combined. Men who had been seriously wounded and disfigured would haunt the United States for generations to come, reminders of a horrific war. Children would grow up without fathers, and many young women would never find husbands.

The war, despite the blessings of Union and freedom it brought, also brought a steep price in social disorder. The Civil War saw bitter rioting in the streets in both the North and the South. It saw political parties arguing over the very future of the nation. And it saw the first assassination of a president.

The Civil War triggered a major expansion of the federal government. The demands of wartime created greenbacks, the draft, and government involvement in transportation and business. It also brought a profound shift in the balance of power among the regions. Since the founding of the nation, the South had wielded influence out of proportion to its population. One president after another owned slaves, and others did the bidding of slaveholders. After Appomattox, however, the South's political domination was broken. It would be half a century before a southern-born man was elected president.

Most important, the war brought what few Americans could have imagined at the end of 1860: the immediate emancipation of four million enslaved people. Nowhere else in the

Ill and injured men filled the ground around the surgical and hospital tents where horrifying surgery often awaited them.

Bettmann/Corbis

Riots in New York City were triggered by an impending draft lottery and by news from Gettysburg that told of heavy Union losses there. Black Americans suffered the most from the riots.

The Freedmen's Bureau, created in the spring of 1865, adjudicated conflicts between white landowners and black workers.

world had so many people become free so quickly. Yet freedom emerged from the war through a circuitous route. The war began as a war for Union, but as the deaths mounted and African Americans seized freedom at every opportunity, abolitionists and Republicans increasingly demanded that the war become a war to end slavery. Many white northerners supported emancipation because it seemed the best way to end the war. Abraham Lincoln worked desperately to keep the support of both the advocates and foes of emancipation, knowing that moving too quickly would shatter the fragile support that kept him in office. The New York City draft riots and the close state elections of 1863 demonstrated that many northerners resisted the continuation of the war and its embrace of black freedom. Only Union success on the battlefield in late 1864 permitted Lincoln's reelection. His assassination made an already confused situation far more so, ending slavery and restoring the Union without a blueprint and without leadership.

The end of the fighting saw the conflict shift in the South, as people struggled to determine what freedom would mean. For black southerners, the goal was autonomy and respect. For white northerners, the goal was to reconstruct the South in an idealized image of the North. For white southerners, the goal was the reassertion of the power they had held before the war, especially power over the black people in their midst. Such goals could not be reconciled. The era of Reconstruction would be devoted to the struggle among people determined that their vision of freedom would predominate.

Making Connections Across Chapters

LOOKING BACK

The massive Civil War brought consequences no one could have imagine beforehand, especially an emancipation of enslaved African Americans for which the nation had done little to prepare.

1. Did the Civil War have a turning point, a point beyond which it became clear that the United States would defeat the Confederacy?
2. How did emancipation become a central war aim for the Union?
3. To what extent did the Confederacy collapse from within, or was it overwhelmed from without?

LOOKING AHEAD

White southerners viewed their world with fear and dread after the Civil War. Black southerners went to work to build new lives in freedom.

1. Could white southerners have minimized the extent of freedom enjoyed by black southerners if whites had behaved differently in 1865 and 1866?
2. What did black southerners most want and need from emancipation? Did they receive that?

RECOMMENDED READINGS

Berlin, Ira, et al. *Freedom* (1985–). A rich and fascinating multivolume documentary collection.

Blight, David W. *Race and Reunion: The Civil War in American Memory* (2001). Documents the role of politics, myth, and race in shaping how the Civil War is remembered.

Donald, David. *Lincoln* (1995). Stands as the most elegant biography.

Faust, Drew Gilpin. *Mothers of Invention: Women of the Slaveholding South in the American Civil War* (1995). Offers a challenging and interesting interpretation.

Fellman, Michael. *Inside War: The Guerilla Conflict in Missouri During the American Civil War* (1989). Makes palpable the internal struggles in the border areas.

Foner, Eric. *Reconstruction: America's Unfinished Revolution, 1863–1877* (1988). A magisterial interpretation of the struggle over black freedom.

Gallagher, Gary W. *The Confederate War: How Popular Will, Nationalism, and Military Strategy Could Not Stave Off Defeat* (1997). Explores why the Confederacy could fight as long as it did.

Harris, William C. *With Charity for All: Lincoln and the Restoration of the Union* (1997). Offers a fresh assessment of Lincoln's attitudes toward the white South.

Hattaway, Herman, and Jones, Archer. *How the North Won: A Military History of the Civil War* (1983). Authoritatively describes strategy and tactics.

Litwack, Leon. *Been in the Storm So Long: The Aftermath of Slavery* (1979). Beautifully evokes the conflicting emotions and motives surrounding freedom.

Neely, Mark E., Jr. *The Union Divided: Party Conflict in the Civil War North* (2002). Examines the impact of political dissension in the North on the war effort.

Roark, James L. *Masters without Slaves: Southern Planters in the Civil War and Reconstruction* (1978). Describes the war from the perspective of those who lost the most in southern defeat.

Rose, Willie Lee. *Rehearsal for Reconstruction: The Port Royal Experiment* (1964). A classic account of the first efforts to create northern policy toward the freedpeople.

AMERICAN JOURNEY ONLINE AND ☙ INFOTRAC COLLEGE EDITION

Visit the source collections at http://ajaccess.wadsworth.com and infotrac.thomsonlearning.com and use the Search function with the following key terms to explore documents, images, audio and video clips, articles, and commentary related to the material in this chapter.

Ulysses S. Grant

African American soldiers

Vicksburg

Gettysburg Address

Appomattox

emancipation

ONLINE PRIMARY SOURCES

Here are some examples of the many primary sources related to this chapter that you will find on the *American Passages* Web site: http://history.wadsworth.com/ayersbrief02.

The Fate of Black Troops in Confederate Prisons, 1863

The Capture of Fort Pillow, 1864

Reactions to Emancipation in Virginia, 1865

The site also offers self-quizzes, exercises, and many additional resources to help you study.

Reconstruction Abandoned

1867–1877

FTER 1867 THE NATION CONTINUED TO STRUGGLE OVER THE GAINS THAT black Americans had earned during the Civil War. The battle was fought with the greatest intensity in the South where whites sought to recapture as many of the features of slavery as they could. Violence, brutality, election fraud, and economic intimidation ended the experiment in multiracial politics known as Reconstruction.

Racial prejudice was at the heart of the problem, but other circumstances hastened the abandonment of Reconstruction. Settlement of the West claimed the energies of many people, and the mid-1870s economic depression made civil rights seem less relevant. White Americans worried that the national government was becoming too powerful, and they reverted to traditional beliefs in localism and states' rights. For many in the North, the hum of industry, the spread of railroads, and the rise of cities all seemed more in tune with an era of progress than preserving the rights of former slaves. Slowly, painfully, the nation retreated from the principles for which the Civil War had been fought. In 1877 an informal sectional compromise sealed the return to white rule in the South.

Outside the political arena, industrialization transformed the economy. The completion of the two transcontinental railroads in 1869 symbolized the rapid pace of technological change. Four years later, however, the Panic of 1873 demonstrated that progress did not always move forward along an unbroken path.

A Period of Unrest

The waning of Reconstruction left African Americans and Indians further removed from the mainstream of society. As the drive to expand freedom for black Americans stalled, white dominance in the South hardened. Military defeat of the Indians confined them to reservations. Women found that their future remained subject to the wishes of a male-dominated nation. After the upheaval of the Civil War, the 1870s were a time to pause and reflect.

The Impeachment of Andrew Johnson

As President Andrew Johnson sought to block the Radical Reconstruction program, sentiment to impeach him grew among Republicans in Congress. The Republicans could do little until December 1867 when Congress reassembled, and by that time impeachment efforts had faltered. After the Senate refused to accept Johnson's dismissal of Secretary of War Edwin M. Stanton in January 1868, Johnson replaced him anyway—an act of defiance that Republicans claimed was a clear breach of the Tenure of Office Act (see Chapter 15).

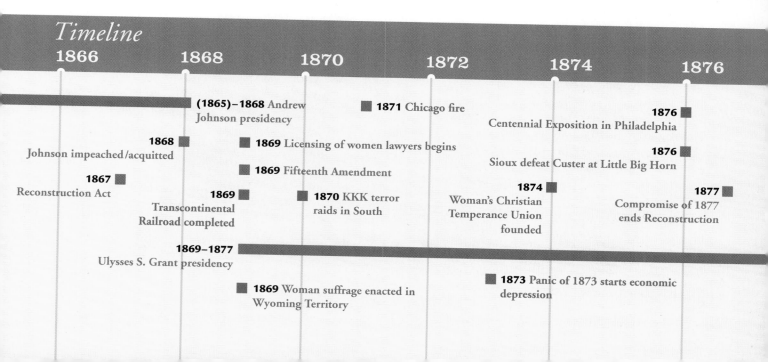

Timeline

| 1866 | 1868 | 1870 | 1872 | 1874 | 1876 |

(1865)–1868 Andrew Johnson presidency

1871 Chicago fire

Centennial Exposition in Philadelphia

1876

Johnson impeached/acquitted

1868

1869 Licensing of women lawyers begins

1876

Sioux defeat Custer at Little Big Horn

1867
Reconstruction Act

1869 Fifteenth Amendment

1874
Woman's Christian Temperance Union founded

1877
Compromise of 1877 ends Reconstruction

1869
Transcontinental Railroad completed

1870 KKK terror raids in South

1869–1877
Ulysses S. Grant presidency

1869 Woman suffrage enacted in Wyoming Territory

1873 Panic of 1873 starts economic depression

Emboldened by Johnson's action, the solidly Republican House voted for his impeachment and brought eleven charges against him. The trial got under way in March. Two months later the Senate failed to produce a two-thirds vote to convict the president. The impeachment attempt failed for several reasons. Moderate Republicans feared that if a president were impeached and convicted on political grounds a bad precedent would be set. Johnson temporarily eased obstructive tactics, and the approach of the 1868 election also made ousting him seem less urgent.

Although he was acquitted, Johnson did not become more conciliatory. His intransigence encouraged southern whites and contributed to the resistance against African American equality that marked the 1870s.

The Purchase of Alaska

In March 1867 the Russian minister to the United States hinted to Secretary of State William H. Seward that the tsarist government in St. Petersburg would respond favorably to an American offer to purchase Alaska. The Russians knew that they could not defend their northern possession against the British in Canada. The Russian diplomat and Seward worked out a treaty that was signed on March 30, 1867. The United States paid $7.2 million for Alaska. On April 9, the Senate gave its approval by a vote of 37 to 2.

Paying for the Alaska purchase required an appropriation from the House. The members did not take up the subject until July 1868, after the House had impeached the president. Faced with a *fait accompli* in that the occupation of the territory had occurred a year earlier, the House approved the money solidly on July 14, and the measure became law two weeks later.

The Election of 1868

The leading candidate for the Republican nomination was Ulysses S. Grant. His association with the Union victory gave him a popularity that transcended partisanship. In his

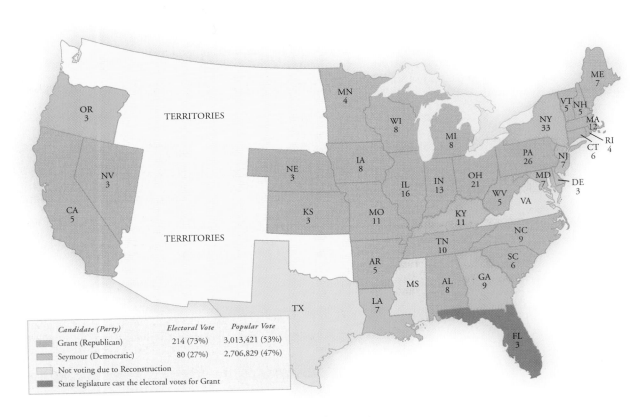

Candidate (Party)	Electoral Vote	Popular Vote
Grant (Republican)	214 (73%)	3,013,421 (53%)
Seymour (Democratic)	80 (27%)	2,706,829 (47%)
Not voting due to Reconstruction		
State legislature cast the electoral votes for Grant		

MAP 16.1 The Election of 1868

As a war hero, Ulysses S. Grant carried the Republicans to victory in this presidential election.

letter of acceptance, Grant concluded with the phrase "let us have peace" and that became the theme of his campaign. To run against Grant, the Democrats turned to the former governor of New York, Horatio Seymour. Along with his running mate, Frank Blair, Seymour made a campaign based on the philosophy of white supremacy. When the votes were counted, Grant had 53 percent and Seymour had 47 percent. In the electoral college, however, Grant had a more secure margin of 214 electoral votes to 80. The relatively close result indicated that white voters were cooling toward Reconstruction.

The Fifteenth Amendment and Woman Suffrage

After the 1868 election Republicans pushed for adoption of the Fifteenth Amendment to the Constitution, which stated that the federal and state governments could not abridge the right of a citizen to vote "on account of race, color, or previous condition of servitude." Legislative approval came in February 1869. Because the amendment reduced the legal ability of the southern states to exclude African Americans from voting, Democrats attacked it as "a step toward centralization and consolidation."

The new amendment did not assure African Americans the right to hold office, nor did it address the restrictions that northern states imposed on the right of other males to vote. These limits included literacy tests and property qualifications. State legislatures outside the South endorsed the amendment promptly, and it was ratified in 1870.

The Fifteenth Amendment ignored women. Some advocates of woman **suffrage,** such as **Susan B. Anthony,** opposed the amendment because it excluded women. She favored voting barriers for black and Asian men if women did not have the vote. Despite his earlier support for woman suffrage, Frederick Douglass now said that "this hour belongs to the negro," meaning black males. At a meeting of the Equal Rights Association in May 1869, differing views about the right strategy for achieving woman suffrage caused an open rift.

The split led to the formation of two distinct groups. The National Woman Suffrage Association (NWSA) reflected the position of Susan B. Anthony and Elizabeth Cady Stanton who believed that the Fifteenth Amendment should not be supported until it included women. The American Woman Suffrage Association (AWSA), led by Lucy Stone and Alice Stone Blackwell, endorsed the amendment and focused its suffrage efforts on the states. The new territory of Wyoming granted women the right of suffrage in 1869. The discord between the two suffrage organizations lasted for two decades, however, and slowed the progress toward reform.

suffrage
The right to vote that was extended to African American males after the Civil War.

Susan B. Anthony
Advocate of woman's suffrage and leader in the woman's rights movement along with Elizabeth Cady Stanton.

The Fifteenth Amendment

The last of the three Reconstruction amendments, the Fifteenth Amendment said that race or color could not be a reason for denying a male citizen the right to vote.

Sect. 1. The right of citizens of the United States to vote shall not be denied or abridged by the United States or by any State on account of race, color, or previous condition of servitude.

Sect. 2. The Congress shall have the power to enforce this article by appropriate legislation.

Questions to Consider

1. Was the Fifteenth Amendment a radical document, or was it a more cautious response to the problem of voting rights?

2. In what ways did the political situation of the Republicans after the war and prevailing attitudes toward women affect how the amendment was written and received?

3. Was the Fifteenth Amendment as far-reaching in its effects as the Fourteenth Amendment?

Explore additional primary sources related to this chapter on the *American Passages* Web site: http://history.wadsworth.com/ayersbrief02.

A calm and composed President Grant on the eve of his inauguration.

Grant's First Term

The new president intended to administer the government rather than promote new programs. His limited view of the presidency meant that Congress played a dominant role during his administration. As a result, the office of the presidency lost some of the authority it had acquired during the Civil War.

The new administration faced hard choices. Southern Republicans wanted help from Washington against resurgent Democrats. A growing number of northern party members questioned whether continuation of Reconstruction was wise or practical. Within the Republican ranks, party reformers wanted to limit the power of the leaders to dole out patronage. They wanted to adopt a merit system for appointing officials; this was referred to as "civil service reform." Party regulars hoped that Grant would side with them against the reformers.

At first Grant tried to avoid partisan battles. For example, in selecting his cabinet he did not follow the advice of influential Republicans but relied instead on men who shared his cautious governing style. Cabinet officers were given free rein in using merit rather than political connections to staff their departments.

In the South, the Democrats endeavored to split the Republicans. Playing down their dislike of black voters, they centered their arguments on whether former Confederates should be allowed to cast ballots. The elections in 1869 produced mixed results. Republicans did well in Mississippi and won narrowly in Texas while Democrats prevailed in Virginia and Tennessee. The latter outcomes foreshadowed an erosion of Republican electoral strength as the Democrats reestablished their power in the South.

The Railroads Meet

Throughout the 1860s, two transcontinental railroads had been laying track across the country. The Union Pacific had built westward and the Central Pacific eastward. The competing lines faced significant obstacles. The Central Pacific had crossed the heights of the Sierra Nevada mountains through rocky gorges and treacherous rivers. Several thousand Chinese laborers toiled on sheer cliffs with picks and dynamite. On the Union Pacific side, more than ten thousand construction men, many of them Irish immigrants, laid track across Nebraska and Wyoming.

On May 10, 1869, the two rail lines met at Promontory, Utah. Engine 119 of the Union Pacific stood with its cowcatcher touching the cowcatcher of the Central Pacific's Engine 60, and a gold spike was driven into the ground with a silver sledgehammer. The transcontinental lines had been built so quickly in part because of loans and subsidies from the federal government. The process by which the financing had been obtained would soon become one of the more notorious scandals of the Grant presidency.

Completion of the first transcontinental railroad in 1869 ushered in a period of railroad construction in which the nation developed one of the best and most comprehensive transportation systems in the world. It was possible to open the entire West now, and farmers pushed out onto the fertile plains of what had once been erroneously labeled "The Great American Desert." This rapid expansion raised anew the question of what should happen to the Native Americans who had been pushed westward before the Civil War and to the nomadic tribes of Plains Indians.

The completion of the transcontinental railroad at Promontory, Utah, in 1869 joined together the nation's two coasts. As the presence of photographers demonstrates, it also became an important media event.

Grant's "Peace Policy"

In its relations with Native Americans, the Grant administration pursued what became known as the "peace policy." This approach had first taken shape in the years just before Grant took office. Instead of treating the entire West as a huge Indian reservation as had

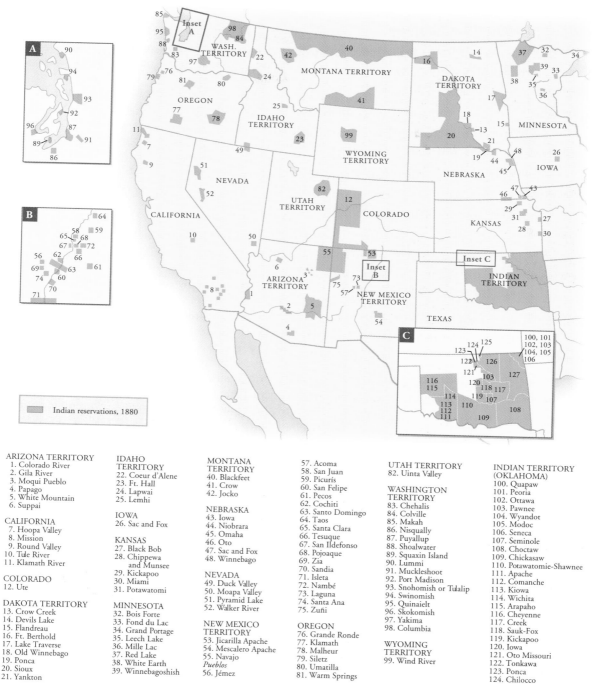

MAP 16.2 Indian Reservations in the West

Following the end of the Civil War and with the adoption of the peace policy of President Ulysses S. Grant, a network of Indian reservations spread across the West. This map shows how extensive the reservation system was.

ARIZONA TERRITORY
1. Colorado River
2. Gila River
3. Moqui Pueblo
4. Papago
5. White Mountain
6. Suppai

CALIFORNIA
7. Hoopa Valley
8. Mission
9. Round Valley
10. Tule River
11. Klamath River

COLORADO
12. Ute

DAKOTA TERRITORY
13. Crow Creek
14. Devils Lake
15. Flandreau
16. Ft. Berthold
17. Lake Traverse
18. Old Winnebago
19. Ponca
20. Sioux
21. Yankton

IDAHO TERRITORY
22. Coeur d'Alene
23. Ft. Hall
24. Lapwai
25. Lemhi

IOWA
26. Sac and Fox

KANSAS
27. Black Bob
28. Chippewa and Munsee
29. Kickapoo
30. Miami
31. Potawatomi

MINNESOTA
32. Bois Forte
33. Fond du Lac
34. Grand Portage
35. Mille Lac
36. Mille Lac
37. Red Lake
38. White Earth
39. Winnebagoshish

MONTANA TERRITORY
40. Blackfeet
41. Crow
42. Jocko

NEBRASKA
43. Iowa
44. Niobrara
45. Omaha
46. Oto
47. Sac and Fox
48. Winnebago

NEVADA
49. Duck Valley
50. Moapa Valley
51. Pyramid Lake
52. Walker River

NEW MEXICO TERRITORY
53. Jicarilla Apache
54. Mescalero Apache
55. Navajo
Pueblos
56. Jémez

57. Acoma
58. San Juan
59. Picurís
60. San Felipe
61. Pecos
62. Cochiti
63. Santo Domingo
64. Taos
65. Santa Clara
66. Tesuque
67. San Ildefonso
68. Pojoaque
69. Zia
70. Sandia
71. Isleta
72. Nambé
73. Laguna
74. Santa Ana
75. Zuñi

OREGON
76. Grande Ronde
77. Klamath
78. Malheur
79. Siletz
80. Umatilla
81. Warm Springs

UTAH TERRITORY
82. Uinta Valley

WASHINGTON TERRITORY
83. Chehalis
84. Colville
85. Makah
86. Nisqually
87. Puyallup
88. Shoalwater
89. Squaxin Island
90. Lummi
91. Muckleshoot
92. Port Madison
93. Snohomish or Tulalip
94. Swinomish
95. Quinaielt
96. Skokomish
97. Yakima
98. Columbia

WYOMING TERRITORY
99. Wind River

INDIAN TERRITORY (OKLAHOMA)
100. Quapaw
101. Peoria
102. Ottawa
103. Pawnee
104. Wyandot
105. Modoc
106. Seneca
107. Seminole
108. Choctaw
109. Chickasaw
110. Potawatomie-Shawnee
111. Apache
112. Comanche
113. Kiowa
114. Wichita
115. Arapaho
116. Cheyenne
117. Creek
118. Sauk-Fox
119. Kickapoo
120. Iowa
121. Oto Missouri
122. Tonkawa
123. Ponca
124. Chilocco
125. Kansa
126. Osage
127. Cherokee

been the case before the Civil War, the government would allocate areas to the tribes. These "reservations" would become places where Native Americans could be instructed about the cultural values and habits of white society, taught to grow crops, and paid a subsistence income until they were able to support themselves. Implementation of this program lagged, however, during 1868, and no reservations for peaceful tribes had yet been established when Grant became president.

The Peace Policy in Action

To supervise Indian policy, Grant named Jacob D. Cox as secretary of the interior. Cox, in turn, selected Ely Parker, a Seneca Indian, as commissioner of Indian affairs. The administration persuaded Congress to appropriate $2 million for Indian affairs and to set up a Board of Indian Commissioners to distribute the money.

The peace policy mixed kindness with coercion. If the Indians accepted the supervision of Christian church officials on the reservations, the government would leave them alone. Resistance to the peace policy, on the other hand, served as a reason for the U.S. Army to drive the Indians onto reservations. In its early months, the peace policy appeared to be a humane improvement over earlier practices. For the Indians, however, the new approach represented another assault on their traditional way of life. Moreover, it remained to be seen how the peace policy would fare in the face of economic and political pressures that continued white settlement generated.

An Era of Scandals

Scandals plagued the Grant administration. In the summer of 1869, two speculators, Jay Gould and Jim Fisk, sought to manipulate the market in gold. Their efforts caused a rise in the price of gold that produced financial turmoil on September 24, 1869, when investors who had contracted to sell gold at lower prices faced ruin. The government ordered the sale of its own gold supplies, and the crisis eased when the price returned to its normal level. The details of the controversy soon faded away, but the administration was embarrassed by revelations that some members of Grant's family had aided Gould and Fisk in carrying out their plan. Some critics suggested that First Lady Julia Grant had participated. Even though Grant and his wife were not implicated, the episode raised serious doubts about the ethical standards of his presidency.

To this impression of corruption the Grant administration also added a sense of confusion and incompetence. In foreign policy, there was talk of confronting Spain in an attempt to acquire Cuba. Secretary of State Hamilton Fish forestalled that potential crisis. Grant also wanted to annex the Dominican Republic (Santo Domingo). A presidential agent negotiated an annexation treaty with Santo Domingo's rulers, and the pact was sent to the Senate. Grant pushed hard for approval of the treaty, but the Senate was suspicious of the president's goals and balked at endorsing what Grant had done with the treaty.

One diplomatic area in which Grant had some success was in the resolution of American claims for maritime losses against Great Britain over the *Alabama,* one of several Confederate merchant raiding ships that had been constructed in Great Britain during the Civil War. The *Alabama* had sunk numerous Union vessels. In 1871, Secretary of State Fish negotiated a treaty that led to an amicable settlement of the issue.

Grant and the Congress

Other issues troubled Grant's relations with Congress. Congressional Republicans split on a number of economic issues. The mainstream of the party now believed that a tariff policy to "protect" American industries against foreign competition would be in the best interests of the business community, workers, and the Republican party. A minority of party members viewed the protective policy as unwise. On the currency question, eastern Republicans favored the gold standard and what was known as "hard money"; western colleagues advocated an expansion of the money supply, government use of paper money or "greenbacks," and even some reliance on silver dollars as an alternative to gold.

Equally divisive was the issue of civil service. Calls for reform in the way government employees were selected intensified. Republicans who wanted to reduce the tariff, implement the civil service, and treat the South more leniently defected from the administration and formed what they called Liberal Republican alliances with Democrats in such states as West Virginia and Missouri. In the 1870s "liberal" meant a person who favored a smaller government, lower tariffs, and an end to Reconstruction.

Grant and His Party

Faced with a series of challenges to his presidency during 1870, Grant displayed greater reliance on Republican leaders in Congress. These Republican regulars had little taste for civil service reform, lower tariffs, or an end to Reconstruction. The president's turn to traditional politicians alienated **Liberal Republicans,** and the possibility of a split in the party increased.

The president's resolve to depend more on regular Republicans strengthened after the Senate defeated his treaty with Santo Domingo. Following this episode, Grant knew that he could not work with Republican opponents of his presidency or satisfy the clamor for milder Reconstruction policies, civil service reform, and a less active national government. The Democrats could always outbid him on those issues, and courting them would only weaken the Republicans further. Failure to maintain good relations with his own party would mean political disaster.

Toward the 1870 Elections

As a result, in 1870 Grant made conciliatory gestures toward the party mainstream. When Secretary of the Interior Jacob D. Cox complained about the practice of compelling government employees to make campaign contributions, Grant dismissed him. The president nominated his attorney general, Ebenezer R. Hoar, for the Supreme Court. When the Senate rejected him, Grant decided that Hoar too should leave the cabinet. To succeed him, he chose Amos T. Akerman, a southern Republican.

In the 1870 elections, the Grant administration aligned itself with Republicans who defended Congress and the White House. Officeholders who supported Liberal Republican candidates or Democrats were removed. Despite these actions, the fall elections produced a setback for the president and his party. Liberal Republicans won in West Virginia and Missouri. Nationwide the Democrats gained forty-one seats in the House of Representatives, but the Republicans retained control. The Democrats also gained six seats in the Senate, although the Republicans still held a decisive edge in that chamber as well.

The Ku Klux Klan in the South

By the summer of 1870 reports reached Washington of growing violence in the South. Roving bands of whites calling themselves the Ku Klux Klan (see Chapter 15) were responsible for the attacks. Throughout the South the Klan repressed any challenge to white dominance.

The Klan and its offshoots, such as the Knights of the White Camellia and the White Brotherhood, acted as paramilitary agents of the Democratic party. In Tennessee a black Republican was beaten after he won an election for justice of the peace. His assailants told him "that they didn't dispute I was a very good fellow . . . but they did not intend any nigger to hold office in the United States."

The Klan would stop at nothing to eliminate its opponents. Leaders of the Republican party were hunted and killed. In an incident in Alabama, in October 1870, four blacks died in a Klan attack on an election meeting. A "negro chase" in South Carolina left thirteen blacks dead.

The Klansmen wore white robes and hoods when they attacked; their

©The Granger Collection, New York

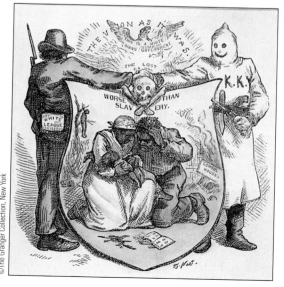

Liberal Republicans
Organization formed in 1872 by Republicans discontented with the political corruption and the policies of President Grant's first administration.

A cartoon attacks the Ku Klux Klan and the "white leagues" of the South for terrorist tactics toward the African American population. For the freed slaves, the result is "worse than slavery."

aim, they said, was to frighten their racial foes. The disguises also hid their identity. Throughout 1870, a wave of shootings and brutality swept across the South.

The Government and the Klan

During the 1870 election, Klan violence had a devastating impact on Republicans in the South. In North Carolina, Georgia, Florida, and Alabama, the Klan's terror tactics intimidated voters and demoralized the party's leadership. In county after county the night riders attacked and murdered local black leaders.

By 1871 the Republicans had less stomach for military intervention in the political affairs of the South. As an Illinois newspaper put it, "the negro is now a voter and a citizen. Let him hereafter take his chances in the battle of life." The Klan's violence, however, presented a challenge that could not be ignored. If violence could not be stopped, the Republican party in the South might simply vanish. As a result, Congress adopted legislation to curb election fraud, bribery, and coercion in elections. When these measures proved inadequate, the lawmakers passed the Ku Klux Klan Act of 1871. This legislation outlawed conspiracies to deprive voters of their civil rights and prohibited efforts to bar any citizen from holding public office. The government received expanded powers to deal with such actions through the use of federal district attorneys to override state laws and, as a last resort, through military force.

Breaking the Klan's Power

Events in the South renewed the Republicans' resolve to end the lawbreaking and violence that the Klan represented. Attorney General Akerman argued that the threat the Klan posed to democratic government amounted to war. Akerman and his solicitor general, Benjamin H. Bristow, were now part of the Department of Justice, which had been established in 1870, and they mobilized federal district attorneys and U.S. marshals to enforce prosecutions against the Klan.

During 1871, the legal offensive against the Klan went forward. In state after state indictments came down against Klan leaders. Federal troops assisted the Justice Department's work in South Carolina. The Klan was discredited as a public agent in southern politics, and its violence became more covert and less visible. Although the Klan prosecutions showed that effective federal action could force the southern states to comply with the rule of law, in the North sentiment for such stern measures was ebbing.

Scandals and Corruption: New York's Tweed Ring

The willingness to use national power that had marked the Reconstruction Era receded in part because Americans increasingly believed that politics everywhere had become hopelessly corrupt. The most celebrated example of corruption in this period was the **Tweed Ring,** which dominated New York City during the late 1860s.

Tweed Ring
The most celebrated example of political corruption in the Reconstruction Era, led by William Magear Tweed Jr.

The leader of the ring was William Magear Tweed Jr., who had risen through various city offices and by the early 1870s had won a seat in the state senate. He was closely identified with the Democratic party organization that met at a political clubhouse called Tammany Hall to plan electoral strategy. The expanding cities of the post–Civil War years offered politicians countless chances to profit from the allocation of lucrative contracts and official services. Tweed and his allies turned these new opportunities to their personal advantage.

"Boss" Tweed's power rested on the votes of the city's heavily Democratic population. Their votes were crucial if the party expected to carry the state in a presidential contest. Tammany Hall also made sure that city services and jobs were available to those who supported them at the polls. By the end of the 1860s, Tweed seemed to hold New York City's political destiny in his hands.

In fact, Tweed's moment at the top of New York politics was very brief. He came under assault from the *New York Times,* which devoted endless columns to exposing the misdeeds of the Democratic party and its leaders. More significant from a national perspective, a cartoonist named Thomas Nast used artistic skill to make Tweed an object of derision. Nast's drawings depicted Tweed as the leader of a band of criminal freebooters, a money-grabbing scoundrel, a ludicrous caricature of an official in a democratic society.

In mid-1871 a resentful member of the Tweed Ring gave city account books to a reporter. The revelation of how much had been spent on city projects stunned the population. A courthouse that had been projected to cost $250,000 came to $13 million. Within a year, Tweed had been indicted and placed on trial. He escaped conviction in his first trial but was later retried and found guilty on 204 counts. He fled the country and took refuge in Spain. Arrested there when an official recognized him from a Nast cartoon, he returned to New York a broken man and died in 1878.

For many fearful Americans, Tweed's story symbolized the decline in ethical standards that they believed had followed the Civil War. They began to think that the expanded power of the state and the extension of the franchise to all white males and many freed slaves threatened the nation's political future. "We are in danger of going the way of all Republics," said one critic of the existing system. "First freedom, then glory; when that is past, Wealth, vice, corruption."

The Liberal Republican Challenge to Grant

Restoring "higher" ethical standards was the stated purpose of the Liberal Republicans, who sought a presidential candidate to run against President Grant in the 1872 election. Their political creed included ending Reconstruction and curbing the influence of political patronage through expanded use of the merit system. The leaders of the campaign were Senator Carl Schurz, a Missouri Republican, Edwin L. Godkin, editor of *The Nation,* and Charles Francis Adams, the son of former President John Quincy Adams.

Liberal Republicans believed in smaller government. Such Republican programs as the protective tariff appalled them. Most of all, they saw Reconstruction as a failed experiment in racial democracy. As Grant's one-time secretary of the interior, Jacob D. Cox, contended: "the South can only be governed through the part of the community that embodies the intelligence and the capital." In effect, black Americans in the South would have to look to whites in that region for protection of their rights and privileges.

The Liberal Republicans lacked a national candidate with the stature to challenge Grant. Although many party leaders were unhappy with the policies of the Grant administration, few were commanding political figures. Senator Carl Schurz had been born in Germany and therefore was ineligible under the Constitution. Other presidential hopefuls included Charles Francis Adams, Senator Lyman Trumbull of Illinois, and **Horace Greeley,** the editor of the New York *Tribune.*

In May 1872, the Liberal Republicans gathered in Cincinnati. The balloting revealed that the contest lay between the colorless Adams and the well-known and eccentric Greeley. Greeley won the nomination on the sixth ballot.

The sixty-one-year-old editor was an odd choice. He favored the protective tariff, which most reformers disliked, and was indifferent to civil service reform. Once a harsh critic of the South, he had mellowed and now favored ending Reconstruction. A lifetime of passions for such offbeat remedies as vegetarianism and the use of human manure in farming made him seem a political oddball in the eyes of many Americans. "That Grant is an Ass no man can deny," said one Liberal Republican, "but better an Ass than a mischievous idiot."

Horace Greeley
Grant's opponent in the 1872 election. Seen as a political oddball in the eyes of many Americans, the sixty-one-year-old editor favored the protective tariff and was indifferent to civil service reform. He was also passionate about ideas such as vegetarianism and the use of human manure in farming.

The 1872 Election

The Republican convention renominated Grant and chose Henry Wilson of Massachusetts to be his running mate. In its platform the party stressed the continuing problem of Reconstruction. The Republican appeal urged voters to preserve what had been achieved during the Civil War.

When the Democrats held their national convention in early July, they faced a dilemma. If they failed to nominate Greeley, they had no chance of winning. Nominating him, however, would alienate southern voters. In the end the delegates accepted Greeley as their only alternative. The Liberal Republican–Democratic nominee made a vigorous campaign while Grant observed the tradition in which an incumbent president did not campaign actively.

The outcome was a decisive victory for Grant and his party. The president swamped Greeley in the popular vote and in the electoral tally. There were still enough Republicans

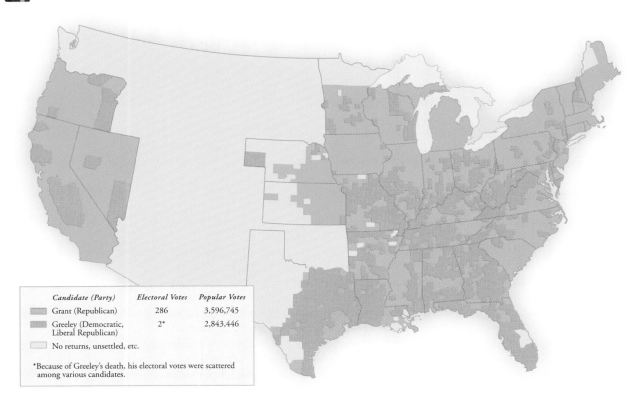

Candidate (Party)	Electoral Votes	Popular Votes
Grant (Republican)	286	3,596,745
Greeley (Democratic, Liberal Republican)	2*	2,843,446
No returns, unsettled, etc.		

*Because of Greeley's death, his electoral votes were scattered among various candidates.

MAP 16.3 The Election of 1872

The collapse of the Democrats and the Liberal Republicans made this election a landslide victory for Grant and the Republicans.

in the South to enable Grant to carry all but five of the southern states. The election marked a low point for the Democrats.

Recurrent Scandals

As the excitement of the 1872 election died down, political attention turned to sensational allegations of corruption in Congress. The first scandal concerned the efforts of the Crédit Mobilier Company (named after a French company) to purchase influence with lawmakers during the late 1860s. The directors of the Union Pacific Railroad had established Crédit Mobilier to raise money to build the transcontinental line. By paying themselves to construct the railroad, the participants in the venture made large profits and the company's shareholders did as well. The only problem was that much of the money in effect came from the federal government through loans and guarantees.

To forestall a congressional probe into the company, Crédit Mobilier's managers gave leading Republicans in Congress a chance to buy shares in the company at prices well below their actual market value. When the lawmakers sold their shares, they pocketed the difference—the equivalent of a bribe. A newspaper broke the story in late 1872, and an investigation followed. The inquiry produced a few scapegoats but cleared most of the lawmakers involved.

Another embarrassing episode occurred in February 1873. At the end of a congressional session, a last-minute maneuver gave senators and representatives a retroactive pay increase. The public denounced the action, calling it the "Salary Grab." When Congress reconvened in December 1873, repeal of the salary increase sailed through both houses in a burst of political contrition. These two incidents generated widespread calls for reducing government expenditures and rooting out corruption.

Mark Twain captured the spirit of the times in his novel *The Gilded Age.* The main character, Colonel Beriah Sellers, was an engaging confidence man who embodied the boosterism and economic looseness of the postwar years, along with the healthy amount of fraud and chicanery that accompanied the rapid growth of business. In time, the title of Twain's book came to be used as a label for the entire era between the end of Reconstruction and the start of the twentieth century. "The Gilded Age" was, however, a richer and more complex time than the stereotype of corrupt politicians and fraudulent entrepreneurs that Twain portrayed.

The Panic of 1873 and Its Consequences

The sense of national crisis deepened in September 1873 when the banking house of Jay Cooke and Company failed. The disaster was triggered by the bank's inability to market the bonds of the Northern Pacific Railroad, in which it had invested heavily. An economic downturn ensued that rivaled similar panics that had occurred in 1819, 1837, and 1857.

A hallmark of the "Great Depression," as it was then called, was declining prices for agricultural products and manufactured goods. Americans grappled with the consequences of an economy in which falling prices placed the heaviest burdens on people who were in debt or who earned their living by selling labor. An abundance of cheap unskilled labor proved a boon for capitalists who wanted to keep costs down. For the poor, however, it meant that they had little job security.

The panic occurred because of a speculative post–Civil War boom in railroad building. In 1869, railroad mileage stood at about 47,000 miles; four years later it had risen to 70,268 miles. The new railroad lines employed tens of thousands of workers and extended across a far larger geographical area than any earlier manufacturing enterprises. When large railroads such as the Northern Pacific failed because of their overexpansion and inability to pay their debts, the resulting impact rippled through society. Economic activities such as car making, steel rail production, and passenger services, which were dependent on the rail lines, declined as well. Layoffs of employees and bankruptcies of businesses followed.

The Plight of the Unemployed

Americans who were thrown out of work during the 1870s had no system of unemployment insurance to fall back on. In some cities, up to a quarter of the labor force looked for work without success. The conventional wisdom held that natural forces had to operate to restore prosperity; any form of political intervention would be futile and dangerous. When President Grant proposed that the national government generate jobs through public works, the secretary of the treasury informed him: "It is not part of the business of government to find employment for people."

Those who were out of a job during the mid-1870s could not afford such a philosophical attitude. Laborers in the Northeast mounted a campaign calling for "Work or Bread" that included large public demonstrations in major cities. The marchers asked city and state governments to sponsor projects to create parks and construct streets, thereby providing work.

Labor unrest marked the first half of the decade. Numerous and prolonged strikes occurred in 1874 and 1875. In Pennsylvania the railroads used their control of police and strikebreakers to put down the "Long Strike" of coal miners and their supporters. Twenty alleged members of a secret society called the Molly Maguires were hanged.

Distress and Protest among the Farmers

In agricultural regions, the drop in farm prices also produced discontent. The resulting decline in income meant that debts on land and equipment were a greater burden on the hard-pressed farmers.

Farmers' protests were led by the Patrons of Husbandry, also known as the Grange. Created in 1867, the nonpartisan Grange focused on complaints about the high mortgages farmers owed, the prices they had to pay to middlemen such as the operators of grain elevators, and the discrimination that they suffered at the hands of railroads.

Regulating the Railroads

The answer to the railroads' power, the angry farmers argued, lay in using the power of state governments to force the railroads to end their discriminatory practices. That meant the creation of state railroad commissions with the power to establish equitable rates and prevent unfair treatment of those who shipped agricultural products. In 1870 Illinois adopted a new state constitution that mandated that the legislature "pass laws establishing maximum rates of charges for the transportation of passengers and freight." The legislature responded a year later, giving the Illinois Railroad Commission wide powers. Neighboring states such as Iowa, Minnesota, and Wisconsin followed suit in the next several years.

The pressure for regulatory legislation affected Congress in 1873–1874. An Iowa Republican introduced legislation in the House to establish a national railroad commission. The bill passed in the House, but the Senate never acted upon it. Federal legislation would not be enacted until 1887.

The decline in consumer prices and the burden of debt on farmers and businessmen in the South and West stimulated pressure for laws to put more money in circulation. That would make debts easier to pay. The Treasury Department's decision to end the coinage of silver in 1873 aroused particular ire among southern and western advocates of inflation; they called it the "Crime of 1873." Proponents contended that an overabundance of silver in the marketplace required the move to a gold standard. By coining silver into money at a price above its market levels, the government was in effect subsidizing American silver production and cheapening the currency. Opponents of the change, however, were suspicious of the dominance of eastern bankers over financial policy.

An effort to inject a modest amount of inflation into the economy came in 1875. A currency bill cleared both houses of Congress, providing some $64 million in additional money for the financial system. President Grant considered signing the bill, but he encountered economic conservatism among eastern Republicans. Their advice led him to veto the bill in April 1875, and Congress failed to override his action.

Women in the 1870s

Amid the male-dominated political scenes that marked this period, occasional episodes reminded the nation that women were not allowed to play a direct part in public life. Susan B. Anthony sought the opportunity to address the Liberal Republican and Republican national conventions in 1872, but without success. On election day she and fifteen other women registered and voted at their polling place in Rochester, New York. Anthony and the voting officials were arrested. Her trial in federal court led to a $100 fine, which she refused to pay. Rather than giving Anthony a reason for appealing the case to a higher court, authorities did not pursue collection of the fine against her.

Another champion of woman's rights was Victoria Claflin Woodhull. A faith healer and spiritualist from Ohio, she and her sister Tennessee Claflin came to New York, where in 1870 Victoria announced her candidacy for president of the United States. In 1872 she denounced one of the nation's leading ministers, Henry Ward Beecher, for having had an affair with a member of his congregation. The exposé led to one of the most sensational public trials of the nineteenth century. The proceedings ended in a hung jury, and Victoria Woodhull and her sister fled to England to escape from public outrage.

Overcoming Barriers to Equality

For women from the middle and upper classes, the 1870s brought expanding educational opportunities. The number of women graduating from high school stood at nearly nine thousand in 1870, as compared with seven thousand men. Aware of these trends, state universities and private colleges opened their doors to women students in growing numbers. By 1872 nearly one hundred institutions of higher learning admitted women. Edward Clarke, a retired Harvard medical professor, warned in 1873 that when women expended their "limited energy" on higher education, they put their "female apparatus" at risk. Nevertheless, Cornell University began accepting women applicants in 1875.

One of the first female students at Cornell was M. Carey Thomas, who received her B.A. at Cornell in 1877. Five years later she received her Ph.D. at a German university. By the 1890s she had become the president of Bryn Mawr, a woman's college outside Philadelphia. Like other women in male-dominated institutions, she endured rudeness and indifference from her male colleagues. She later recalled that "it is a fiery ordeal to educate a lady by coeducation."

Obtaining an education did not ensure access to male-dominated professions, however. Myra Bradwell tried to become a lawyer in Illinois, but the state bar association rejected her application. She sued in federal court, and in 1873 the U.S. Supreme Court ruled that the law did not grant her the right to be admitted to the bar. That decision gave the Illinois legislature the authority to deny women the chance to practice law. In fact, in 1870 there were only five female lawyers in the entire country.

The Supreme Court also rebuffed efforts to secure woman suffrage through the courts. Virginia Minor, president of the Woman Suffrage Association in Missouri, tried to vote in the 1872 election, but the registrar of voters turned her away. She sued on the ground that the action denied her her rights as a citizen. In the case of *Minor v. Happersett* (1875) the Supreme Court ruled unanimously that suffrage was not one of the rights of citizenship because "sex has never been made one of the elements of citizenship in the United States." To achieve the right to vote, women would have to amend the Constitution or obtain the right of suffrage from the states.

The Rise of Voluntary Associations

Blocked off from politics, women created a public space of their own through voluntary associations. Notable in this process were the efforts of black churchwomen, who established missionary societies to work both in the United States and abroad. Clubs and literary societies sprang up among white women as well. In New York City women created Sorosis, a club for women only, after the New York Press Club barred women from its membership. In 1873 delegates from local Sorosis clubs formed the Association for the Advancement of Women. The New England Woman's Club, located in Boston, succeeded in the early 1870s in changing local laws to allow women to serve on the School Committee. Later the club founded the Women's Education Association to expand educational opportunities for their sex.

Despite their inability to vote, women made their presence felt in public affairs in an unexpected way in 1873. Protests against the sale and use of alcohol erupted among women in New York, Ohio, and Michigan. Women marched in the streets and demanded that saloons and liquor dealers close their establishments. They also exhorted drunkards to reform. Middle-class women went down on their knees in front of bars and smashed barrels of liquor in public. The **temperance** movement was not limited to women, but the upsurge of activity among women gave the crusade a new militance.

The Woman's Christian Temperance Union

In August 1874 a group of temperance leaders assembled at Lake Chautauqua, New York, where they called for a national meeting that developed into the Woman's Christian Temperance Union. During the next five years, temperance leagues and local organizations of the WCTU crusaded against intoxicating beverages. By the end of the 1870s a thousand unions had emerged, with an estimated twenty-six thousand members. In 1879, Frances Willard became president of the Union. Under her leadership, the WCTU went beyond its original goal of temperance and ventured into broader areas of social reform such as woman suffrage and the treatment of children.

temperance
Reducing the influence and the effect of alcoholic beverages in American life.

©The Granger Collection, New York

As women became more involved in public life after the Civil War, they found outlets for their social concerns beyond the ballot box. One of the most influential such groups was the Woman's Christian Temperance Union (WCTU). The artist evokes the imagery of the medieval Crusades to show women attacking the liquor industry and its political connections.

Women at Work

The 1870s also brought greater economic opportunities for women in sales and clerical work. The typewriter was developed in the early 1870s, and young, college-educated women were an abundant source of skilled labor to operate the new machines. By the end of the decade, 40 percent of the total number of stenographers and typists in the country were women. The developments of the 1870s laid the foundation for the growth in numbers of female office workers during the rest of the nineteenth century.

The most typical experience of American women, however, was toil. Black women in the South labored in the fields alongside their husbands who were tenant farmers or share-croppers. In the growing cities, women worked in textile factories or became domestic servants. Many urban women took in boarders; their routine was similar to that found in small hotels.

Middle-class women with domestic servants had some assistance, but they still did an incredible amount of work. Preparing food, doing laundry, keeping the house warm, and disposing of waste all required hand labor. Mary Mathews, a widowed teacher in the 1870s, "got up early every Monday morning and got my clothes all washed and boiled and in the rinsing water; then commenced my school at nine." Other days of the week passed in the same fashion for her and other women.

To assist women in performing these tasks, manuals about housework became popular in the 1870s, along with private cooking schools and college courses in home economics. Catherine Beecher collaborated with her famous sister, Harriet Beecher Stowe, in writing *The American Woman's Home* (1869). In this work, she argued "that family labor and care tend not only to good health, but to the *Highest culture of the mind.*" In the new coeducational colleges and universities, home economics programs offered instruction in operating kitchens and dining rooms in an efficient manner. Cooking schools appeared in large cities with a separate class for "plain cooks" and a "Ladies Class" for affluent women.

The ease with which divorces could be obtained in many states produced a movement to tighten the conditions under which marriages could be dissolved. Laws to limit the sale of birth control devices and restrict abortions reflected the same trend. The New York Society for the Suppression of Vice was formed in 1872 under the leadership of Anthony Comstock. It lobbied successfully for a national law barring obscene materials, including information about birth control and abortion, from the mails. Thus, while women had made some gains after the Civil War, they remained second-class citizens within the masculine political order of the Gilded Age.

Politics in the Gilded Age

After the presidential election of 1872, the North's already weakened commitment to the continuation of Reconstruction ebbed more rapidly. The Grant administration was less willing to intervene in southern politics, and the Justice Department prosecuted fewer individuals for violations of the Enforcement Acts against the Klan.

Northern support for Reconstruction had fallen away because the experiment in multiracial government appeared to have failed. Liberal Republicans and northern Democrats used racist propaganda against the political aspirations of southern blacks. White northerners found it easier to believe that the South would be better off when whites were once again dominant.

A damaging setback to African Americans' economic aspirations occurred with the failure of the Freedmen's Savings and Trust Company in Washington, D.C. Since its founding in 1865, the bank had managed the deposits of thousands of former slaves. It was supposed to provide lessons in thrift for its depositors. However, its managers sought larger returns by investing in speculative railroad projects. The Panic of 1873 caused huge losses, and the bank failed in the following year.

The Stigma of Corruption

Corruption among southern Republican governments became a favorite theme of critics of Reconstruction. There were some genuine instances of corruption, but these actions were far from widespread or typical. Moreover, the white governments that took over after Reconstruction also displayed lax political ethics and committed more serious misdeeds than their predecessors had. Nevertheless, the corruption issue gave the opponents of black political participation a perfect weapon, which they exploited fully during the 1870s.

Participation of African Americans in southern politics increased dramatically during Reconstruction, but their role in the region's public life remained limited compared to whites. Sixteen blacks served in Congress during the period, most only briefly. Many more held offices in the state legislatures, but even there, numbers were comparatively modest. In 1868, for example, the Georgia legislature had 216 members, of whom only 32 were black. One black man, P. B. S. Pinchback, served as governor in Louisiana for a little more than a month. Six African Americans held the office of lieutenant governor in the states of Louisiana, Mississippi, and South Carolina.

Two blacks served in the U.S. Senate. Hiram Revels of Mississippi became the first African American to enter the Senate. His term began in 1870 but lasted only one year. From 1875 to 1881 Blanche K. Bruce represented Mississippi for a full term. Thus, by the 1870s blacks had begun to make their presence felt in politics, but the decline of Reconstruction made that trend a short-lived one.

The Resurgence of the Democrats

The changing political situation across the nation further diminished support for Reconstruction. Hard economic times arising from the Panic of 1873 worked against the Republicans. Discontented farmers wanted the government to inflate the currency and raise prices on their crops. Factory workers wanted to see more jobs become available. The fate of African Americans in the South became a secondary concern. Accordingly, angry voters turned to the Democrats in the 1874 congressional races. The party used the issue of Republican corruption to regain control of the House of Representatives for the first time in sixteen years. The Democrats also picked up ten Senate seats.

In the South, the resurgent Democrats "redeemed," as they called it, several states from Republican dominance. They began with Texas in 1873, then took back Arkansas. Louisiana experienced the emergence of the White League, which was determined that "the niggers shall not rule over us." In September open fighting erupted in New Orleans between armed Republicans and more than three thousand White League partisans. President Grant sent in federal troops to restore calm. In Alabama the Democrats also relied on violence and murder to oust the Republicans. Some blacks who attempted to vote in the Barbour County election were shot; seven were killed and nearly seventy wounded.

The Democrats intended to use their control of the House of Representatives to roll back Reconstruction and also to prevent any further expansion of black rights. During the lame-duck congressional session of 1874–1875, Republicans enacted a path-breaking civil rights law that gave black citizens the right to sue in federal courts when they confronted discrimination in public accommodations. The law involved an additional expansion of national power; it remained to be seen how the federal courts would rule when black plaintiffs sued to enforce their rights under the new civil rights statute.

Early in 1875 the Grant administration used troops to prevent occupation of the Louisiana state capitol and illegal seizure of the state government by the Democrats in the midst of an election dispute. The action drew widespread protests from many northern Democrats and a growing number of Republicans who argued in favor of allowing the white South to handle its own affairs. Meanwhile, the Democrats used more violence to overturn Republican rule in Mississippi. Without a national consensus behind civil rights and Reconstruction, the fate of black Americans lay in the hands of white southerners who were determined to keep African Americans in economic, political, and cultural subjection.

Why Reconstruction Failed

Reconstruction failed to change American race relations because it challenged long-standing racist arrangements in both the North and the South. The Civil War had called these arrangements into question, and African Americans had acted to expand their political role and become more than passive recipients of white oppression or largesse. Then the Panic of 1873, the scandals of the Grant presidency, and waning interest in black rights caused white Americans to back away from expansion of racial justice.

To help the freed slaves overcome the effects of slavery and racial bias would have involved an expansion of national government power to an extent that went beyond political beliefs of the nineteenth century. During the two decades that followed, black Americans experienced segregation and deepening oppression. The political gains of the Reconstruction Era, especially the Fourteenth and Fifteenth Amendments, remained unfulfilled promises.

The End of Native American Resistance

While the United States was in the process of abridging its Civil War commitments to African Americans, the long struggle of Native Americans to resist white encroachment also ended. Indians' efforts to push back the wave of white encroachment failed, and after 1876 Native Americans lacked the power to determine their own destiny.

During the 1870s, easterners and new immigrants surged westward to the prairies. The newcomers competed with the Indians for space and resources. The amount of land devoted to wheat cultivation, for example, rose from nearly 21 million acres at the beginning of the decade to more than 62.5 million acres in 1880.

The cattle industry exerted further pressure on the Indians in the late 1860s. Texans returning from the Civil War drove their herds north to markets in Kansas. These cattle and others in western territories such as Wyoming, the Dakotas, and Colorado occupied space on the prairies where Indians had traditionally pursued their nomadic hunting culture.

Annihilation of the Buffalo Herds

The systematic destruction of the buffalo herds dealt the most devastating blow to the Indians. In the societies of the Plains tribes, the meat of the bison supplied food, and the hides provided shelter and clothes. Removal of these resources was calamitous, but the cultural impact was even more severe. Buffalo represented the continuity of nature and the renewal of life cycles. Destruction of the buffalo ended the Indians' capacity to resist white incursions.

The decline of the buffalo herds began during the 1860s when drought, disease, and erosion shrank the animals' habitat. Then an expanding eastern market for buffalo robes and such products as pemmican (dried buffalo meat, berries, and fat) spurred intensive hunting of buffalo. As railroads penetrated the region, hunters could transport their products to customers with relative ease. The result was virtual extermination of the buffalo. More than five million buffalo were slaughtered during the early 1870s. By the end of the nineteenth century, only a few buffalo remained alive.

A Last Stand for Custer and the Indians

During the mid-1870s, Native American tribes mounted a last, futile effort to stem the tide that was overwhelming their way of life. The renewed strife on the Plains occurred in spite of President Grant's peace policy. The churches' influence over the operation of Indian policy receded as corruption and politics again shaped the treatment of Native Americans. The tribes that retained their nomadic way of life confronted ever-increasing numbers of settlers and a hostile military.

Buffalo hunting during the years after the Civil War destroyed the vast herds that once roamed the western plains. This picture shows thousands of buffalo skulls that were later ground up into fertilizer. Meanwhile, the Plains Indians' way of life also was changed forever.

Courtesy of the Burton Historical Collection, Detroit Public Library. © 1999

Fighting erupted on the southern plains in 1874 when Comanches and Kiowas attacked wagon trains. A confrontation ensued between U.S. soldiers and Cheyennes, Kiowas, and Comanches that became known as the Red River War. The army did not win on the battlefield. Instead, the Indians' resistance collapsed because of lack of food and supplies.

In the North, the discovery of gold in the Black Hills of Dakota increased pressure on the Sioux to relinquish the area for white development. The Indians refused, and the U.S. government sent soldiers to protect the miners. The Indian leaders, **Crazy Horse** and **Sitting Bull,** rallied their followers to stop the army. Near what the Indians called the Greasy Grass (known to whites as the Little Big Horn), Colonel **George Armstrong Custer** led a force of six hundred men. With a third of his detachment, he attacked more than two thousand Sioux warriors. The result was the annihilation of Custer and his force on June 25, 1876. The Indian victory shocked the country, but it was only a momentary success. The army pursued the Indians during the months that followed, and by the end of the Grant administration, the only Indians who were able to fight actively against the army were the Apaches in the Southwest. The bad treatment that the Apaches received from the government produced sporadic clashes during the 1880s, and the army triumphed by the end of the decade.

One more tragic encounter, the Battle of Wounded Knee in 1890, lay ahead for the Plains Indians. For the most part the Grant presidency brought an end to the centuries of white–Indian warfare that had marked the history of the West in the United States.

Crazy Horse
Native American Sioux leader who defeated George Custer in battle.

Sitting Bull
Ally of Crazy Horse in the Custer battle.

George Armstrong Custer
Colonel famous for his battle at Little Big Horn against the Sioux Indians.

The Election of 1876

Several themes of late-nineteenth-century American life came together as the 1876 presidential election approached. The centennial of the Declaration of Independence offered citizens an opportunity to reflect on the nation's progress and the social issues that remained unresolved. The race question confronted leaders and citizens even as the passions and commitments of Reconstruction faded. The contest for the White House seemed unusually important as it would shape the direction of the country during the rest of the century.

The Continuing Shadow of Scandal

Toward the end of Grant's second term, political corruption continued to cast a shadow over the White House. Attention focused on the "Whiskey Ring" in the Treasury Department. The officials involved took kickbacks from liquor interests in return for not collecting federal excise taxes on whiskey. Grant had appointed a new secretary of the treasury, Benjamin H. Bristow. Grant said to Bristow: "Let no guilty man escape if it can be avoided." But when Bristow's probe discovered that the president's own secretary, Orville E. Babcock, had ties to a leader of the conspiracy, Grant allowed Babcock to avoid prosecution.

The final incident involved the secretary of war, W. W. Belknap. For some time Belknap's wife had been receiving regular cash gifts from a man who sold supplies to the army. When these financial ties were revealed, Belknap faced impeachment by a congressional committee. He resigned abruptly, and Grant accepted his hasty departure. The trail of scandal had now touched the White House, or so the president's critics argued. In the end, the most that could be laid at Grant's door was a too-trusting nature and bad judgment in some of his appointments.

Marking the Centennial

As the nation's one hundredth birthday neared, attention focused on the Centennial International Exhibition to be held in Philadelphia in May of 1876. On 285 acres of fairgrounds stood several hundred buildings and pavilions crammed with exhibits, specimens, and artifacts from thirty-seven nations. The fair opened on May 10 with two hundred thousand spectators and the entire Congress in attendance, and a welcoming address by President Grant. The crowd poured into the buildings to see what had been assembled as evidence of the advance of civilization in the United States.

For spectators the huge Corliss steam engine was a stellar attraction. Standing forty feet tall, it weighed seven hundred tons. Equally fascinating was the "harmonic telegraph" of **Alexander Graham Bell,** as the telephone was then called.

Alexander Graham Bell
His invention of the telephone at the end of the nineteenth century changed the nature of life in the United States.

For all its technological marvels, the exhibition did not do justice to the complexity of American life in the 1870s. African Americans had almost no recognition at the fair. Native American cultures were depicted as "curiosities" consisting of totem poles, tepees, and trinkets. The Woman's Pavilion stressed homemaking. The exhibit evoked a protest from Elizabeth Cady Stanton and Susan B. Anthony. On July 4, 1876, they read a "Women's Declaration of Independence" that contrasted their aspirations with the traditional attitudes toward women expressed at the fair.

Nearly ten million Americans came to the fair during its run, which ended on November 10. There they learned to eat bananas, and hot popcorn became a fad among city dwellers. Although the fair lost money, it contributed to a sense of national pride and confidence.

The Race for the White House

A key test of the nation's institutions occurred during the election of 1876. As the election year began, the Democrats were optimistic about their ability to regain power for the first time since 1860. The South would return to its usual Democratic allegiance; the Democrats could also capitalize on unhappiness with the difficult economic times in the North and Midwest.

To run as the Democratic candidate, the party selected the governor of New York, **Samuel J. Tilden.** Tilden had been an opponent of the Tweed Ring and was regarded as a political reformer. A corporate lawyer, he believed in the gold standard and governmental economy. His platform spoke of a "revival of Jeffersonian democracy" and called for "high standards of official morality."

Among the Republicans, there was some talk of a third term for President Grant. The scandals of his presidency, however, made him a political burden rather than an asset. The front-runner for the nomination was James G. Blaine of Maine, a former speaker of the House of Representatives. With the nomination seemingly in his grasp, Blaine encountered questions about his dealings with an Arkansas railroad while he was in the House. He answered the charges vigorously, but the episode raised problems about his ethics at a time when the party wanted to run a "clean" candidate against Tilden.

At the national convention Blaine took an early lead, but as the balloting continued, his candidacy lost momentum. Instead, the Republicans chose Governor **Rutherford B. Hayes** of Ohio as the nominee. Hayes had a good military record in the Civil War, and there were no questions about his honesty. The Republicans chose William A. Wheeler of New York as their candidate for vice president.

In the campaign the Democrats stressed Republican corruption and Tilden's honesty. In response, the Republicans used the Reconstruction issue, as they had in the 1868 and 1872 contests. The rhetoric invoking the Civil War became known as "waving the bloody shirt," in memory of a Republican orator who had held up a bloodstained Union tunic and urged voters to remember the sacrifices of the Men in Blue. As one Republican put it, "Soldiers, every scar you have on your heroic bodies was given to you by a Democrat."

When the election results came in, it seemed at first that Tilden had won. With most of the South in his column, the Democratic candidate had also carried New York, Connecticut, and New Jersey. Preliminary counts indicated that Tilden had won 184 electoral votes, one short of the 185 needed for victory. Hayes, on the other hand, had 165 electoral votes. Yet three southern states—Louisiana, Florida, and South Carolina—and a disputed elector in Oregon were still in doubt. They might give Hayes the White House.

Republican operatives moved to contest the outcome in the three undecided states. Telegrams to party members called for evidence of intimidation of African American voters. Honest returns from these states, the Republicans argued, would show that Hayes had carried each one. The Republicans believed that they held a trump card. In the three states that they were contesting, the Republicans could rely on federal troops to safeguard state governments that were loyal to their cause. Otherwise, Democrats could simply occupy the state capitals and count the election returns their way.

The Constitution did not specify how a contested presidential election was to be decided. With each of the states in question sending in two sets of election returns, the House of Representatives had the responsibility for electing a president if no one won a majority

Samuel J. Tilden
Governor of New York selected to run as the Democratic candidate in the 1876 presidential election. He narrowly lost what has been considered the most controversial election in American history.

Rutherford B. Hayes
Nineteenth president of the United States, he was beneficiary of the most fiercely disputed election in American history.

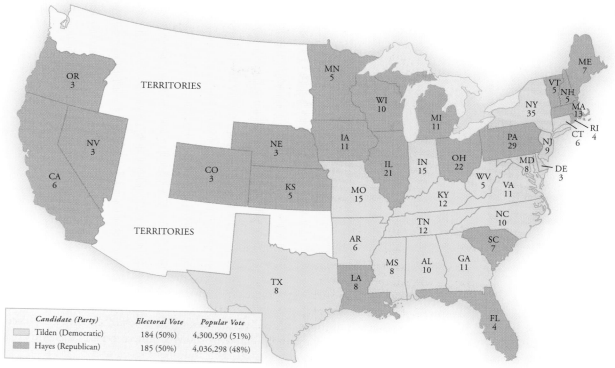

MAP 16.4 The Election of 1876

The presidential election of 1876 between Samuel J. Tilden for the Democrats and Rutherford B. Hayes for the Republicans turned on the votes of Florida, Louisiana, and South Carolina to produce the narrow one-vote victory in the electoral college for Hayes. View an animated version of this map or related maps at http://history.wadsworth.com/ayersbrief02.

in the electoral college. At the same time, the Senate had the constitutional duty to tabulate the electoral vote. With Republicans in control of the Senate and Democrats in control of the House, neither side could proceed without the support of the other.

To resolve the crisis, Congress created an electoral commission of fifteen members, ten from the House and Senate and five from the Supreme Court. As originally conceived, the panel was to have seven Republicans, seven Democrats, and a politically independent Supreme Court justice named David Davis. Then Davis was elected to the U.S. Senate by the Illinois legislature with Democratic votes in a move to defeat a Republican incumbent. Their ploy won a Senate seat but wounded Tilden's chances. Davis resigned from the commission, and a Republican justice took his place. In a series of 8 to 7 votes along straight party lines, the electoral commission accepted the Republican returns from Louisiana, Florida, and South Carolina, allocated the single disputed Oregon electoral vote to Hayes as well, and declared that Hayes had received 185 electoral votes and Tilden 184.

Despite the electoral commission's decision, the Democratic House still had to declare Hayes the winner. With the March 4, 1877, inauguration date approaching, the Democrats postponed tallying the electoral vote in an effort either to make Tilden president after March 4 or to extract concessions from the Republicans. To prevent a crisis, negotiations began among leaders from both sides to put Hayes in the White House in return for the Republicans' agreement to end Reconstruction. The discussions were complex; they involved a variety of issues such as railroad subsidies for the South. The underlying issue, however, was Reconstruction. If Hayes became president, the South wanted assurances that Republican rule would not be maintained through federal military intervention. After much maneuvering, an unwritten understanding along these lines led Congress to decide on March 2, 1877, that Rutherford B. Hayes had been elected president of the United States.

Summary

Reconstruction: A Missed Opportunity

The experiment in multiracial government and economic change in the South after the Civil War was one that people at the time and historians since have called Reconstruction. In the wake of the bitter conflict among Americans, the North sought to bring southerners back into the Union with new political guarantees for the freed slaves. Few societies have attempted such a sweeping process of social and economic transformation after strife that had cost hundreds of thousands of lives and destroyed much of the physical structure of the defeated South. That this bold endeavor failed is not surprising in light of how difficult it is to persuade people to change their long-held racial and political attitudes. What is striking are the effects on the United States that came out of this turbulent period.

By 1877, when the sentiment for Reconstruction had ebbed, the nation had added three amendments to the Constitution that ended slavery, made African Americans citizens of the country, and at least in theory guaranteed the right of men, regardless of race, to cast a vote in elections. The actual rights of black Americans would soon be restricted in a segregated nation, but the promise of the Thirteenth, Fourteenth, and Fifteenth Amendments remained in the Constitution for future generations to redeem and extend. Out of these constitutional reforms would come the modern United States.

As with any postwar period, the decade between 1867 and 1877 mixed constructive and lamentable results. The end of the fighting released economic energies that produced the construction of the transcontinental railroad, a surge of industrialization, and a re-

Reconstruction gave African Americans a real chance to serve in Congress. Robert Smalls was a congressman from South Carolina for five terms in the 1870s and 1880s.

The spread of industrialism brought new products into the home that were advertised as labor-saving devices for women. The reality was that the amount of work women did expanded as a result of the new machinery for domestic use.

HOME WASHING MACHINE & WRINGER.

HOME WASHER

DEPOT 24 CORTLANDT ST., NEW YORK.
DEPOT, 13 BARCLAY ST., NEW YORK.

newal of white settlement in the West. At the same time, Native Americans saw their way of life threatened with extinction. Political corruption infected public life, and observers lamented a general slackening of the moral tone of the nation. After economic prosperity following the war, the Panic of 1873 and the hard times that ensued tested the endurance of average Americans.

Society found that women also wanted to share some of the fruits of emancipation. Campaigns for woman suffrage got under way, only to come up against adamant male resistance. Women turned to campaigns against alcohol as another means of making a political difference. In cultural realms, these were the years of Mark Twain, William Dean Howells, Henry James, and Bret Harte—American prose stylists who looked toward the creation of a national literature. Amid the discord and clamor of a society bent on economic expansion and a return to peacetime endeavors, Americans engaged problems that would carry on to the end of the century and beyond: racial justice, industrial growth, urbanization, and the proper balance between business and government. That citizens of that generation failed to solve all their difficulties is not surprising. What this chapter reveals is that they poured their energies and imagination into the task of creating a better nation in the wake of a destructive war that shaped their lives in such a distinctive way.

Reproduced from the collections of the Library of Congress

In the dramatic 1876 election, the Democrats put forward "Honest Sam Tilden," who lost to Rutherford B. Hayes in the disputed contest.

Making Connections Across Chapters

LOOKING BACK

The working out of Reconstruction and its ultimate failure forms the key theme of Chapter 16. Since the decision not to pursue racial justice further had such long-range consequences for the United States, the substance of this chapter is central to an understanding of subsequent history.

1. How did the Republicans intend to reconstruct the South after the Civil War? What obstacles did they encounter?

2. How did the election of Ulysses S. Grant help or hinder the Reconstruction effort?

3. Why did Reconstruction not succeed in the South? What obstacles did white southerners place in the way of black voting rights?

4. What defects in the political system of the nation between 1867 and 1877 helped derail the chances of Reconstruction?

5. Which groups fully participated in making decisions about the direction of society? Which groups were either not represented or ignored?

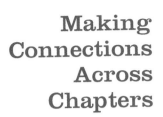

Making Connections Across Chapters

LOOKING AHEAD

The next chapter takes up the process of industrialization and its effect on the economy and society. Elements in this chapter explain the rise of industrialism and set up the treatment of this issue in Chapter 17. Let's examine a few of them now.

1. What economic changes in the 1870s undercut Reconstruction and made industrialism seem more imperative?
2. How did the political system respond to the economic downturn of the 1870s, and how did these attitudes carry forward during the rest of the nineteenth century?
3. How did the politics of the 1870s resemble modern alignments, and in what important ways were there differences?

RECOMMENDED READINGS

Edwards, Laura F. *Gendered Strife and Confusion: The Political Culture of Reconstruction* (1997). Looks at the role of women after the Civil War.

Foner, Eric. *Reconstruction: America's Unfinished Revolution, 1863–1877* (1988). An excellent treatment of the whole period, especially the decline of Reconstruction.

Perman, Michael. *Emancipation and Reconstruction, 1862–1879,* 2d ed. (2003). A good brief account of the issues and problems of Reconstruction.

Richardson, Heather Cox. *The Death of Reconstruction: Race, Labor, and Politics in the Post–Civil War North, 1865–1901* (2001). Considers how changing attitudes toward African Americans and labor undercut Reconstruction.

Simpson, Brooks D. *The Reconstruction Presidents* (1998). A treatment of Reconstruction from the perspective of the chief executives.

Smith, Jean Edward. *Grant* (2001). A full-scale, sympathetic biography of the general and president.

Summers, Mark Wahlgren. *The Era of Good Stealings* (1993). Uses the corruption issue of the 1870s to produce a political history of the decade.

Wang, Xi. *The Trial of Democracy: Black Suffrage and Northern Republicans, 1860–1910* (1997). Discusses how voting issues shaped the adoption and then the abandonment of Reconstruction.

AMERICAN JOURNEY ONLINE AND INFOTRAC COLLEGE EDITION

Visit the source collections at http://ajaccess.wadsworth.com and infotrac.thomsonlearning.com and use the Search function with the following key terms to explore documents, images, audio and video clips, articles, and commentary related to the material in this chapter.

Andrew Johnson

suffrage

temperance

Crazy Horse

George Armstrong Custer

transcontinental railroad

Reconstruction

Sitting Bull

ONLINE PRIMARY SOURCES

Here are some examples of the many primary sources related to this chapter that you will find on the *American Passages* Web site: http://history.wadsworth.com/ayersbrief02.

Elizabeth Cady Stanton on Black Suffrage, 1869

Description of the South Carolina Legislature by a "Liberal Republican," 1871

The site also offers self-quizzes, exercises, and many additional resources to help you study.

PASSAGES

1877 *to* 1909

One of the driving forces of American economic growth between 1877 and 1909 was the flow of immigrants into the United States. Their travels from Europe were often harsh and uncomfortable. These immigrants had to sleep on deck as their ship made its way across the North Atlantic.

S. S. Pennland, Steerage Deck, 1893. Museum of the City of New York. The Byron Collection. 93.1.1.18432

O WHITE AMERICANS DURING THE LATE 1870S, THE SENSE THAT THE Civil War and Reconstruction were receding into history represented a comforting illusion. African Americans knew best of all citizens how alive and painful the problem of race remained. Yet the popular belief that important forces now reshaped American life also described reality. The national journey was leaving behind an agricultural, rural, underdeveloped economy and culture and gathering speed as an industrialized nation. The transformation took decades, but its consequences proved decisive in creating the modern United States.

Industry became the way in which more and more Americans made a living during the years from the presidency of Rutherford B. Hayes (1877–1881) through the end of Theodore Roosevelt's administration in March 1909. First came the railroads, but soon followed steel, oil, machinery, telephones, and, after 1900, the automobile.

The relentless process of industrial growth drew families from the country to the city, changed the look and population of the cities themselves, and made society adapt to the pace of machinery and the factory. Business leaders Andrew Carnegie, John D. Rockefeller, and J. P. Morgan emerged as national figures. Their fellow citizens wondered about the fate of the average person in the face of such concentrated economic power.

The result of industrialism was material abundance for some and great want for many others. The ability of factories to provide cheaper standardized goods such as canned foods, sewing machines, tools, and clothes pleased those who could afford to buy them. For those left behind or shut out from society's bounty, the riches of the new system seemed a mockery. Industry knit the country together in a shared experience as consumers in a national market; it alienated others who saw their hard work bringing no fair reward for themselves.

With this first flight at Kitty Hawk, North Carolina, in 1903 the Wright brothers launched the age of aviation. Progress would be slow during the first decade of the new century, but the achievement of the Wright brothers indicated how technology was transforming lives.

Immigration into the United States changed the shape of the nation's population and instilled an even richer diversity in the society. Older residents reacted with suspicion and hostility to the influx of newcomers from southern and eastern Europe, and ethnic tensions underlay voting decisions, residence patterns, and social conflict. The immigrants filled the nation's cities, tilled and settled the western plains, and did much of the work of the industrial sector. By the first decade of the twentieth century, pressures mounted for immigration restriction.

Politics struggled to keep pace with accelerating change in the business sector. An even balance between Republicans and Democrats from 1877 to 1894 kept the national government passive and slow to react. An expansion of governmental power took place on the state level despite claims that the era favored noninvolvement in social policy. An economic depression during the 1890s destroyed the national stalemate, wounded the Democrats, and gave the Republicans a majority of the electorate. A third party, the Populists, failed meanwhile to halt the erosion of the once powerful agricultural sector.

Urbanization, 1860–1910

Class and population size	1860	1870	1880	1890	1900	1910
URBAN TERRITORY	392	663	939	1,348	1,737	2,262
Places of 1,000,000 or more	—	—	1	3	3	3
Places of 500,000–999,999	2	2	3	1	3	5
Places of 250,000–499,999	1	5	4	7	9	11
Places of 100,000–249,999	6	7	12	17	23	31
Places of 50,000–99,999	7	11	15	30	40	59
Places of 25,000–49,999	19	27	42	66	82	119
Places of 10,000–24,999	58	116	146	230	280	369
Places of 5,000–9,999	136	186	249	340	465	605
Places of 2,500–4,999	163	309	467	654	832	1,060
RURAL TERRITORY				6,490	8,931	11,830
Places of 1,000–2,499				1,603	2,128	2,717
Places under 1,000				4,887	6,803	9,113

The demand for labor swept up even young children. Here boys work in a shop in unsafe conditions with faces dulled by the toil they endured. Efforts to regulate child labor largely came to nothing before 1909.

By the end of the 1890s, the United States stepped into the arena of international politics when it acquired an empire from Spain after a war over Cuba. The heyday of imperialism did not last; the consequences of overseas expansion endured. New responsibilities in the Atlantic and Pacific meant a growth in the power of the federal government to fulfill the world role. Currents of isolationism persisted to limit foreign adventures, but the movement toward world power continued.

The nation mixed confidence and doubt as the twentieth century opened. From the small nation of 1800 had emerged a continental giant, the world's largest internal free market, and a functioning experiment in political democracy. All that bred optimism by 1900, but social crit-

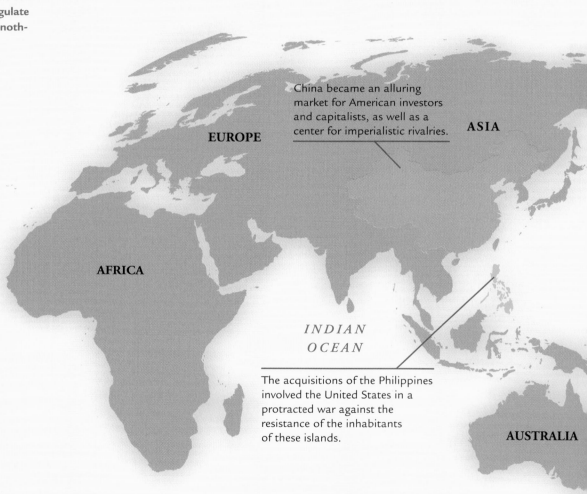

EUROPE

ASIA

China became an alluring market for American investors and capitalists, as well as a center for imperialistic rivalries.

AFRICA

INDIAN OCEAN

The acquisitions of the Philippines involved the United States in a protracted war against the resistance of the inhabitants of these islands.

AUSTRALIA

ANTARCTICA

ics pointed out the other side of the ledger. "We can feed ourselves, we are great and powerful," said a popular newspaperman in 1900, "but we have our own galling Negro problem, our rotten machine politics, our legislative bribery, our municipal corruption, our giant monopolies, our aristocracy of mere riches, any one of which is a rock on which the ship of state, unless skillfully navigated, may go to its destruction."

The indictment had merit. Too many in the United States—African Americans, Hispanics, Indians, immigrants, and women—did not share in all that the country offered. Looking back, the verdict would be that the late nineteenth century fell short of its historic duties. To Americans who lived through these times, who saw Hayes enter the White House and Roosevelt give way to William Howard Taft, it appeared that they had left the country better than they found it when they first addressed its problems during the 1870s. Their part in the American journey is the underlying theme of the four chapters that follow.

America and the World: 1877–1909

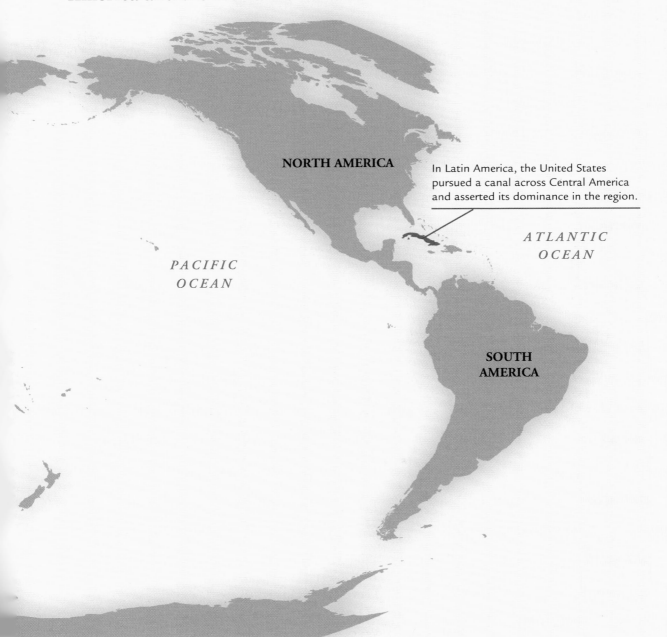

NORTH AMERICA

In Latin America, the United States pursued a canal across Central America and asserted its dominance in the region.

ATLANTIC OCEAN

PACIFIC OCEAN

SOUTH AMERICA

CHAPTER 17

The Economic Transformation of America

1877–1887

After the inauguration of Rutherford B. Hayes on March 4, 1877, national interest turned to scientific inventions, the rise of urbanization, and the growth of industry. Politics and public policy struggled with the social issues that emerged from this economic upheaval.

The agenda of social and political problems facing the nation between 1877 and 1887 was formidable. The process of industrialization transformed how Americans lived and worked together. How the American people grappled with the effects of industrial growth defined the decades between the waning of Reconstruction and the end of the nineteenth century.

Railroads and a "Locomotive People"

The railroad stood as the most visible example of the complexity that came with industrialization. One British writer noted, "The Americans are an eminently locomotive people." The completion of the transcontinental railroads signaled the energetic pace of rail development. During the 1880s the number of miles of tracks rose steadily, reaching 167,000 miles in 1890.

Creating the Railroad Network

This network of iron and steel drew the nation together as bridges and tunnels removed the obstacles posed by mountains and rivers. Another step toward unification was the establishment of a standard gauge or width for all tracks. Some railroads used the standard gauge of 4 feet 8.5 inches; others relied on tracks as much as 6 feet apart. These inconsistencies translated into higher costs. By 1880 the standard gauge dominated, with the South the principal holdout. However, on a single day in 1886, all the southern lines moved their rails to the standard gauge. To put all railroads on the same set of working times, in 1883 the railroads agreed to set up four standard time zones across the country.

Consistency streamlined the operation of the railroads. Freight was moved with greater ease through bills of lading (a statement of what was being shipped), which all lines accepted. Standard freight classifications were developed, and passenger schedules became more rational and predictable. After enactment of the **Interstate Commerce Act** (1887)

Interstate Commerce Act
Passed by Congress in 1887, this act set up an Interstate Commerce Commission (ICC), which could investigate complaints against high rates or file suit against the companies.

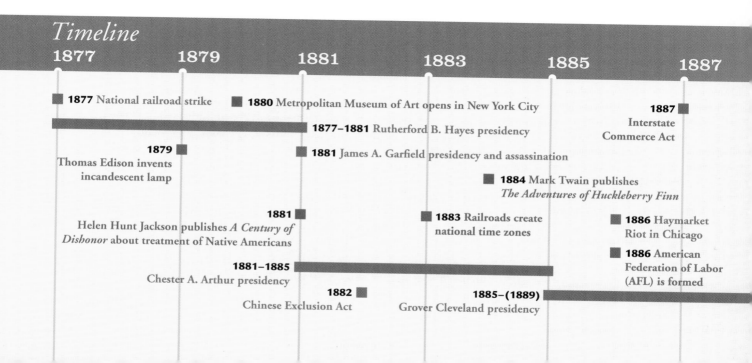

Timeline

1877 — **1879** — **1881** — **1883** — **1885** — **1887**

1877 National railroad strike

1880 Metropolitan Museum of Art opens in New York City

1877–1881 Rutherford B. Hayes presidency

1887 Interstate Commerce Act

1879 Thomas Edison invents incandescent lamp

1881 James A. Garfield presidency and assassination

1884 Mark Twain publishes *The Adventures of Huckleberry Finn*

1881 Helen Hunt Jackson publishes *A Century of Dishonor* about treatment of Native Americans

1883 Railroads create national time zones

1886 Haymarket Riot in Chicago

1886 American Federation of Labor (AFL) is formed

1881–1885 Chester A. Arthur presidency

1882 Chinese Exclusion Act

1885–(1889) Grover Cleveland presidency

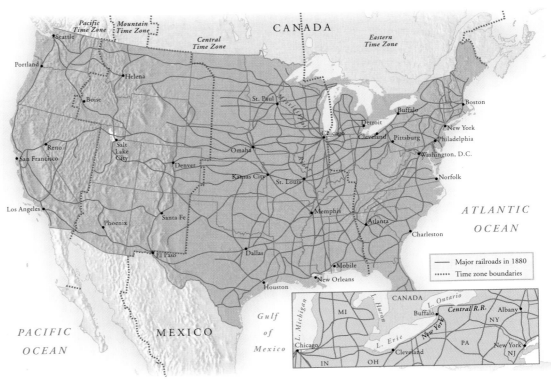

MAP 17.1 The Railroad Network

The growth of the railroad industry helped create a national market for goods and services and hastened the spread of industrialization. As railroads expanded in the 1870s and 1880s, political controversies followed in their path.

and passage of other relevant legislation during the 1890s, all railroads adopted automatic couplers, air brakes, and other safety devices.

Railroad travel also became more comfortable for passengers, and the refrigerator car preserved food and other perishables for transport to distant consumers. George Pullman pioneered the sleeping car. The railroads built huge terminals through which millions of passengers and countless tons of freight moved each day.

It took a staggering amount of money to construct the railroad system. More than $4 billion was invested by 1877. An impressive amount came from government. Total federal land grants to railroads exceeded 130 million acres, and state and local governments added another 49 million acres. Other examples of federal and state aid included loans, tax reductions, and issuing of bonds. The total amount of all such assistance approached $500 million.

By 1880 the railroad network had assumed a well-defined shape. East of the Mississippi River to the Atlantic seaboard ran four *trunk* [main line] railroads that carried goods and passengers from smaller towns connected by *feeder* [subsidiary] lines. The trunk lines were the Pennsylvania Railroad, the Erie Railroad, the New York Central Railroad, and the Baltimore and Ohio Railroad. The transcontinental lines included the Union Pacific/Central Pacific, Northern Pacific, and Southern Pacific.

Organizing the Railroad Business

Railroads were the first big business: they extended over thousands of miles and employed tens of thousands of workers. The railroads required an immense amount of equipment and facilities; no single individual could supervise it all directly.

New management systems arose to address these problems. Separate operating divisions purchased supplies, maintained track and equipment, handled freight, dealt with passengers, and transmitted information. Local superintendents took care of day-to-day matters; general superintendents resolved larger policy issues; and railroad executives made the overall decisions.

Railroads stimulated the national economy. From the late 1860s through the early 1890s, the railroads consumed more than half the nation's output of steel. Railroads also used about 20 percent of the nation's coal production.

The United States was becoming a national economic market in which similar goods and services were available to people throughout the nation. The development of a national market also encouraged the growth of big business to meet consumer demand for canned goods, ready-made clothes, and industrial machinery. Thus, the expansion of the railroads was a key element in the dramatic changes brought about by industrialization.

The Railroad as a Political Issue

Because of their economic impact, railroads became a political issue. Industry leaders believed that too much competition caused economic and political problems. To survive, a railroad needed a reliable and constant flow of freight and passengers. One strategy was to build tracks and add lines in order to gain more business. Each new line required more business to pay off the cost of building it. Railroads therefore waged a constant economic struggle for the available traffic. Cornelius Vanderbilt of the New York Central and Jay Gould of the Union Pacific, among others, were renowned for the ruthless methods they employed against their competitors. Their critics called them **robber barons.**

One obvious tactic was to lure customers with reduced prices. From 1865 to 1900 railroad rates were lowered. Some of the reduction in rates stemmed from the general deflation in prices that marked this period. Other price declines came about because the railroads and their workers found ways to move freight and passengers more efficiently.

To maintain their share of the total available business, railroads resorted to a number of secret devices. The *rebate* was a discount on published rates that was given to a favored shipper in the form of a cash payment. When faced with potentially destructive competition, the railroads engaged in price wars or tried to acquire their rivals. Railroads (and other industries) also used the *pool,* a private agreement to divide the available business in an industry or locality. Working together, the railroads hoped to maintain rates at a level that ensured profits for all members of the pool.

Attractive in theory as a means of restraining competition, in practice pools were impossible to enforce because their secrecy violated state laws against economic conspiracies. Railroad men wanted the federal government to legalize pooling through legislation, an approach that was politically unpopular because it would have endorsed price-fixing and monopolies. By the middle of the 1880s, therefore, the larger railroads moved toward consolidation as a way to deal with the problems created by too many railroads and too much competition.

Regulating the Railroads

Although rebates, pools, and consolidation made sense to the railroads, they aroused anger among those who traveled or shipped their goods by rail. Shippers who did not receive rebates regarded the tactic as unfair. Railroads often charged more for a short haul than for a longer one because fewer exchanges and stops made the long haul cheaper. Shippers claimed that this practice was further evidence of unfair tactics. Because of the advantage they gave to some shippers over others, railroad rates also served the interest of some cities such as Chicago or Kansas City to the detriment of others in the Middle West. To many observers these facts seemed to be evidence of abuses by railroad management. Added to this unease was the danger to the traveling public. In 1888 alone, some 5,200 Americans were killed while traveling or working on the railroad.

Americans debated how society should respond to the political and economic challenge that the railroads posed. The idea of government ownership of some railroads did not achieve public support. The prospect of having legislatures or courts oversee the railroads was not popular either. Instead, Americans developed a middle way between those apparent extremes.

robber barons
Railroad industry leaders such as Cornelius Vanderbilt and Jay Gould who became renowned for their ruthless methods against competitors.

The Railroad Commission

The characteristic response to such dilemmas during this period was the *regulatory commission*. Ideally, such a body, created by the state legislature, was composed of experts who decided issues of rates, finance, and service in a neutral, nonpartisan way. Railroad commissions were generally of two kinds. One variety advised railroads of possible violations and publicized information about railroad operations. The most notable example of this kind of commission was the one in Massachusetts. The second kind of railroad commission was established in Illinois in 1871. It had the power to set rates and put them into effect in 1873. Because of this authority, the Illinois model became known as the "strong" form of the railroad commission.

During the 1870s railroads challenged the authority of the state commissions. The most important case involved Illinois, and it reached the U.S. Supreme Court in 1876. The decision of *Munn v. Illinois* (1877) ruled that the state did have the power to establish a commission that could regulate railroad rates. Because Congress had not yet acted to regulate interstate commerce in railroad matters, a state could make "such rules and regulations as may be necessary for the protection of the general welfare of the people within its own jurisdiction."

Despite such successes, reservations about the effectiveness of state commissions grew. Critics complained that the railroads had too much influence over the state commissions. More important, however, the state commissions could not deal effectively with interstate railroads. In 1886, in the case of *Wabash, St. Louis, and Pacific Railway Company v. Illinois,* the Supreme Court ruled that enforcement of the Illinois law infringed on interstate commerce. It was clear that Congress needed to establish a national policy for regulating the railroads.

The Interstate Commerce Act

A number of political and economic forces combined to stimulate the demand for railroad regulation. Merchants and shippers on the East Coast wanted a government agency to ensure that they received fair treatment from the rail companies. Some railroads preferred federal regulation to the confusion of competing state commissions. Congress responded to these pressures by passing the Interstate Commerce Act in 1887. This law set up an Interstate Commerce Commission (ICC), composed of five members, that could investigate complaints of railroad misconduct or file suit against the companies. Despite a shaky start for the ICC in its first decade, commissions became a favored means of dealing with the problems of managing an industrial society. They reflected the desire of Americans to preserve the economic benefits that railroads provided while at the same time preventing the rail companies from exercising excessive economic power.

The Arrival of Big Business

The success of big business came during difficult economic times. The depression of the 1870s ebbed by 1879, but the prosperity that followed was brief. From 1881 to 1885, there was another slowdown. Two years of good times preceded another recession during 1887 and 1888. Fear of another "panic" shaped the way business leaders went about increasing the size of their enterprises.

Throughout these years, deflation brought about by increased productivity, a tight money supply, and an abundant labor force was a fact of life for businessmen. Companies with high fixed costs, such as railroads, oil, and steel, experienced intense, constant pressure to reduce competition and avoid its impact through arrangements such as pools that divided up the available business. In a few industries it even seemed possible to escape competition and achieve monopoly.

John D. Rockefeller and Standard Oil

John D. Rockefeller
Key figure in the development of the oil industry and the growth of large corporations.

The most famous example of such an industry was oil. **John D. Rockefeller** and Standard Oil became renowned as examples of monopoly power. Rockefeller had been in the oil business since the mid-1860s. From his base in Ohio, he built his company on the principle of expanding as rapidly as possible while watching costs carefully. He founded the Standard Oil Company in 1870. As Rockefeller's oil interests grew, he and his partner, Henry Flagler, used the company's size to secure rebates from the railroads. Able to assure the rail companies a dependable supply of oil to haul, they also obtained a share, or "drawback," of what their competitors paid. Despite these advantages, there were still too many producers in the industry, resulting in a glut of oil.

Through rebates, drawbacks, and price-cutting against rivals whose companies he eventually acquired, Rockefeller sought to gain control over all the supplies of oil. By the end of the 1870s, he controlled about 90 percent of the nation's oil-refining capacity. Economists call this a **horizontal integration** of the oil business.

horizontal integration
A procedure wherein a company takes over competitors to achieve control within an industry

The Emergence of the Trust

The creation of a virtual monopoly in oil triggered a political response. Under state law, Standard Oil of Ohio could not legally own stock in other oil companies or conduct its business in other states. Yet registering to do business in other states could reveal aspects of the company's business to competitors and expose it to legal challenges. In 1882, a lawyer for Rockefeller, S. T. C. Dodd, responded to these challenges by formulating a new use for an old legal device. Standard Oil became the first example of the *trust* in American business.

The forty-one stockholders of Standard Oil entered into an agreement that created a board of nine trustees. In return the board held the company's stock in trust and exercised "general supervision over the affairs of said Standard Oil Companies." The trustees could select the board of directors and set policy for all Standard Oil's subsidiaries in other states. In this way the trust escaped the restrictions of state laws everywhere. The term "trust" soon lost its legal connotation and became a general label for the rise of big business.

The trust device was used only for a brief period. In the late 1870s several states passed laws that allowed corporations to own branches in other states and hold the stock of other corporations. The "holding company" law, first enacted in New Jersey and later in Delaware, was more efficient than the trust approach. A large company simply held the stock of its subsidiaries.

In the 1888 presidential election, both major parties denounced trusts that aimed "to control arbitrarily the condition of trade among our citizens," as the Republicans put it. Fourteen states and territories passed laws to curb monopoly power. President Grover Cleveland said in 1887 that "competition is too often strangled by combinations quite prevalent at this time, and frequently called trusts." The political world seemed intent on taking at least symbolic action against large industrial combinations.

Andrew Carnegie and the Steel Industry

Almost as famous as Rockefeller was **Andrew Carnegie.** He came to the United States from Scotland in 1848 and worked first in a textile factory and then as a telegraph clerk. By 1853 he was the private secretary to Thomas A. Scott of the Pennsylvania Railroad. During the 1860s he played the stock market through investments in railroading, oil, and telegraph company securities. By 1873, however, he was focusing on the burgeoning steel industry.

In the 1870s the technology of steelmaking relied on the Bessemer process of steel production in which molten pig iron was placed in a receptacle or converter and air was blown across it to remove impurities through oxidization. The result was a flow of steel in about fifteen or twenty minutes, much faster than the earlier process in which an individual "puddler" had worked the molten iron. Eventually the open-hearth method of steelmaking supplanted the Bessemer technique. In this method the iron ore was heated up and scrap metal was then added to the mixture. The Bessemer process dominated the construction of steel rails; the open-hearth method proved better for heavy machinery, skyscraper beams, and other uses. By 1890 steel production had risen to 4,277,000 tons annually.

Carnegie became the dominant figure in steelmaking. His philosophy was simple. A steel owner should "watch the costs and the profits will take care of themselves." Between 1873 and 1889 Carnegie cut the cost of steel rail from $58 a ton to $25 a ton. He poured money into new equipment and plowed profits back into the business. Carnegie sought to

Andrew Carnegie
A major business leader in the evolution of the steel industry.

**Table 17.1
Steel Production,
1877–1887**

1877	569,618
1878	731,977
1879	935,273
1880	1,247,335
1881	1,588,314
1882	1,736,692
1883	1,673,535
1884	1,550,879
1885	1,711,920
1886	2,562,503
1887	3,339,071

Source: *The Statistical History of the United States,* p. 416.

vertical integration
A procedure wherein a company gains control of all phases of production

achieve the **vertical integration** of his steel interests; this meant controlling all the steps in the process of making steel. Carnegie therefore acquired mines to ensure that he had raw materials, boats to move ore on rivers, railroads to carry it to his mills, and a sales force to market his many products.

Carnegie's innovations in steelmaking were felt throughout the economy. The lower cost of steel spurred the mechanization of industry. As machines became more complex and more productive, machine tools were needed. In such industries as firearms, bicycles, and sewing machines, the use of machine tools spread technological innovations throughout the economy. Carnegie's and Rockefeller's managers broke work down into specific, well-defined tasks and emphasized lower costs for every aspect of the business. In that manner the innovations of Rockefeller, and especially Carnegie, typified American industry. Mass production and a continuous flow of resources into factories and of goods to consumers were part of the larger process of industrialization.

Thomas Alva Edison
The inventor of the phonograph, electric lights, and countless other products.

©The Granger Collection, New York

Here Alexander Graham Bell, the inventor of the telephone, places the first telephone call between New York and Chicago in 1892. The telephone was one of the inventions at the end of the nineteenth century that transformed how Americans communicated in business, politics, and private life.

The Pace of Invention

Inventions were a hallmark of the period. Among the devices that came into use between 1877 and 1887 were the phonograph (1877), the typewriter (1878), the cash register (1879), and the linotype in newspaper publishing (1886). The process of innovation led to such constructive changes as the twine binder, which made harvesting straw more efficient; time locks for bank vaults; and the fountain pen.

Two inventors who changed the nature of life in the United States were Alexander Graham Bell and **Thomas Alva Edison.** A Scottish immigrant from Canada, Bell wanted to transmit the human voice by electrical means. In 1876 he and his assistant, Thomas A. Watson, created a practical device for doing so: the telephone. By 1877 it was possible to make telephone calls between New York and Boston; and New Haven, Connecticut, established the first telephone exchange. Long-distance service between some cities arrived in 1884.

The most famous inventor of the time was Thomas Alva Edison. Born in 1847, Edison was a telegrapher during the Civil War. In 1876 he established the first industrial research laboratory at Menlo Park, New Jersey. In 1877 he devised the first phonograph, although it would be another decade before he perfected it commercially. More immediately rewarding was the invention of the carbon filament incandescent lamp in 1879. Edison decided to use carbonized thread in the lamp, and it glowed for more than forty-five hours.

In 1882 Edison put his invention into operation in New York City. The area covered was about a square mile, and after a year in service there were five hundred customers with more than ten thousand lamps. Edison's system, however, relied on direct electric current for power. As the distance traveled by the current increased, the amount of usable electric power decreased. One of Edison's business rivals, George Westinghouse, discovered how to use a transformer to make electricity safe at the point where the consumer needed it. This device made possible alternating current, which could transmit higher amounts of electricity.

Electricity had an immediate impact on urban transportation. The electric streetcar was invented in Germany in 1879, and Edison and others adapted it for use in the United States. **Granville T. Woods,** a black inventor, devised the "third rail" to convey electric power to the cars. Streetcars proved an efficient mode of transportation and dominated cities until the arrival of the automobile.

Granville T. Woods
A black inventor who devised the "third rail" to convey electric power to streetcars.

Americans in the Workplace

Industrialization brought many benefits to the people of the United States, but individual Americans often felt the adverse impact of these changes. They struggled to improve their lives within a society that resisted their efforts to lessen the harmful effects of industrial growth.

The labor force grew by more than 29 percent during the 1870s. One-fifth of the increase came from immigrants, and four out of every ten of these working immigrants were unskilled. Irish, Germans, British, and Scandinavians made up the bulk of the newcomers. Western states and territories hoped that the new arrivals would become farmers, but the majority found work in the cities of the Northeast and Midwest. Soon distinctive ethnic communities grew up in New York, Boston, and Philadelphia.

Skilled Workers

A key development during this period was a change in the position of skilled labor in the new industrial setting. Technology replaced craft skills with machines, and a more hierarchical system of management stripped skilled workers of much of their autonomy. The use of apprenticeship as a way of moving up in industry receded, and the workforce was divided into unskilled and semiskilled employees. All of these trends made workers more vulnerable to corporate power.

Workers resisted these changes through mutual support in times of crisis. In 1882 the Amalgamated Association of Iron and Steel Workers struck for higher pay from the owners of steel rolling mills in Pennsylvania. For five months the union held together against unified management, but finally the workers were forced to go back on the job.

Women represented another new element in the labor force. They still worked as domestic servants, but they appeared in greater numbers as teachers and office workers, and as salesclerks in the expanding department stores. Many stores preferred women, especially native-born white women. Although many immigrant women toiled as domestic servants, they also found work in the sweatshops of the textile trades. For the most part, the jobs open to women were lower paid, required fewer skills, and offered less opportunity than those open to men.

Real wages for workers increased as the prices of farm products and manufactured goods fell during the deflation that lasted until the late 1890s. The hours that employees worked declined from more than sixty-five hours a week in 1860 to under sixty by 1900. Gradual though these changes were, they represented real gains.

The Dangers of Industrialism

The desperate circumstances of many workers belied these general trends. Steelworkers put in twelve-hour days seven days a week. In the coal mines, in the factories, and on the railroads work was dangerous and deadly. From 1880 to 1900, some thirty-five thousand of the four million workers in manufacturing died in accidents each year.

Workers had almost no protection against sickness, injury, or arbitrary dismissal. If an injury occurred, the courts had decided that the liability often belonged to another worker or "fellow servant" rather than to the company that owned the factory. For a worker who was fired during an economic downturn, there were no unemployment benefits, no government programs for retraining, and little private help. Child labor reached a peak during this period. Almost 182,000 children under the age of sixteen were at work in 1880 with no health and safety restrictions to protect them.

Workers had few ways to insulate themselves from the impact of harsh working conditions. There were sporadic attempts at labor organization and strikes throughout the nineteenth century, but unions faced legal and political obstacles. The law said that a worker and his employer were equal players in the marketplace, but real equality in bargaining power rarely existed. The worker had to take what was offered; the boss set the conditions of employment.

The Rise of Unions

The workers responded to these conditions by creating labor unions. During the 1860s and 1870s, skilled craftsmen in cigar making, shoemaking, and coal mining formed unions. The National Labor Union (NLU), a coalition of trade unions, was established in 1866. In 1868, under the leadership of William Sylvis, the NLU pursued the eight-hour day and other improvements for labor. Sylvis's death in 1869 and the dominance of middle-class social reformers in the organization eroded the influence of the National Labor Union. Still, the first national labor organization provided a model for others to imitate.

Railroads were the first business to confront large-scale labor issues. The professional skills that engineers, firemen, brakemen, and others possessed made it more difficult for railroads to find replacements during a strike. Railroad workers joined unions such as the Brotherhood of Locomotive Firemen and the Brotherhood of Locomotive Engineers.

The Railroad Strike of 1877

A bitter railroad strike erupted during the summer of 1877. On July 1, in the middle of an economic depression, the major eastern railroads announced a 10 percent wage cut. Facing their second pay reduction in a year, railroad employees walked off their jobs in an unplanned protest. Strikers disrupted train traffic, and in Baltimore and Pittsburgh there were battles between strikers and state militia. A general strike spread to Chicago, St. Louis, and other large cities. Railroad unions played a relatively small part in starting these walkouts, however; during the depression their membership had declined.

The walkout of railroad employees in 1877 over low wages led to a series of strikes that convulsed the nation for several months. This painting shows the social violence that erupted when the Army was called out to help subdue the labor unrest.

The governors of the states where the riots occurred called out the militia. As violence spread, the Hayes administration sent in the army. Deaths ran into the hundreds, many more were injured. Faced with such overwhelming use of force by the government, the unrest died away rapidly. Nevertheless, the strike had touched most of the nation in some way.

The Knights of Labor

Knights of Labor
A labor organization that combined fraternal ritual, the language of Christianity, and a belief in the social equality of all citizens.

One result of the strike was increased support for a new national labor organization: the Noble and Bold Order of the **Knights of Labor.** The Knights combined fraternal ritual, the language of Christianity, and belief in the social equality of all citizens. While advancing the cause of labor through unions and strikes where necessary, the Knights wanted government to play a larger role in protecting working people. They wanted "a system adopted which will secure to the laborer the fruits of his toil." By the mid-1870s the Knights were established among coal miners in Pennsylvania. After the railroad strike, the Knights' membership grew.

The leader of the Knights was known as the grand master workman. Terence V. Powderly was elected to that post in 1879, and he soon became the first national labor figure. The Knights also grew because they had few membership requirements. Their ranks soon embraced workers from skilled craft unions, agricultural laborers in the South, and women who were new entrants into the workforce. The willingness of the Knights to include women and blacks set it apart from other unions. By 1885 the union claimed more than a hundred thousand members. Its message of working-class solidarity and mutual assistance among all producers seemed attractive to many laboring citizens.

The Knights in Decline

In 1885 the Knights conducted a strike against a railroad owned by Jay Gould. They struck his Wabash, Missouri Pacific, and other lines, and achieved a form of official recognition that allowed the Knights to represent the company's employees in relations with management. Because it appeared that the Knights had beaten Gould, their popularity exploded among workers. A second walkout was called against Gould in February 1886, but this time the strike was broken through the use of police and violence against those who had walked out.

The Haymarket Affair

Other events put labor on the defensive. On May 4, 1886, workmen in Chicago gathered in Haymarket Square to protest police conduct during a strike at a factory of the McCormick Company. As a heavy rain began to fall, the police endeavored to break up the meeting. Then a bomb exploded in the midst of the crowd. One police officer was killed; others fired into the throng. Seven policemen and two demonstrators were killed and seventy people were hurt.

Eight alleged participants in a bombing conspiracy were arrested and convicted, although none had taken part in the event itself. Four were executed, one committed suicide, and three others went to prison. The **Haymarket Affair** shocked the nation. Public support for labor's demands for an eight-hour workday and other concessions dried up.

These events did most damage to the Knights of Labor. Business leaders and conservatives blamed the Knights for the violence and unrest. The union underwent a permanent decline. To some workers, the failure of the Knights demonstrated the need for more violent action. To others, it indicated that Powderly's strategy had been wrong from the start.

Haymarket Affair
On May 4, 1886, workmen in Chicago gathered to protest police conduct during a strike at a factory of the McCormick Company.

The American Federation of Labor

One vigorous critic of the Knights of Labor was Samuel Gompers. Because a philosophy of "pure and simple unionism" had worked for his own Cigar Makers International Union, he believed that only such an approach could help labor in the long run. The son of a British cigar maker, Gompers had come to the United States in 1863. During his years of employment in the cigar trade, he decided that labor should seek concrete and limited improvements in living and working conditions and avoid political involvements.

Late in 1886 Gompers and others created the American Federation of Labor (AFL), an alliance of craft unions and skilled workers. The AFL did not try to organize the masses of industrial workers, and the union opposed immigrant labor and was cool toward the idea of black members. Nevertheless, the AFL's membership rose to more than three hundred thousand during its first ten years, and it achieved considerable benefits for its members through judicious use of strikes and negotiations with employers. Most of the men and women who worked as unskilled labor in the nation's factories and shops, however, derived little benefit from the AFL's policies.

Social Darwinism

Beginning in 1877 and continuing for a decade thereafter, many commentators praised the material accomplishments of industrialism. Because clothes were now made so cheaply, said one observer, "the very beggars in our metropolitan cities . . . wear a finer fabric than kings could boast a century ago." A more systematic justification for the existing social order was the philosophy that came to be known as **Social Darwinism.**

Charles Darwin's famous work *On the Origin of Species,* published in 1859, offered an explanation for why some species survived and others became extinct. Darwin contended that a process of "natural selection" occurs in nature that enables the "fittest" animals and plants to evolve and develop over time. Advocates of Darwin's ideas, such as the English writer Herbert Spencer, applied them to human existence. If the doctrine of "survival of the fittest" operated in the natural world, Spencer argued, it governed human affairs as well. Since capitalists and the wealthy represented the "fittest" individuals, it was folly to interfere with the "natural" process that produced them. "The law of the survival of the fittest was not made by man and cannot be abrogated by man," said William Graham Sumner, a leading exponent of this doctrine. "We can only by interfering with it produce the survival of the unfittest."

These ideas were supported in the "rags to riches" novels of Horatio Alger, a popular writer of the day. Alger's theme was that men of energy and determination (i.e., the "fittest") could triumph in the competitive system even against great odds. He wrote 106 books with such titles as *Brave and Bold* and *Paddle Your Own Canoe.* The central characters were impoverished young boys who used their natural talents to gain the support of wealthy benefactors and go on to achieve riches and success. The public consumed millions of copies of Alger's books.

Social Darwinism
A philosophy that allegedly showed how closely the social history of humans resembled Darwin's principle of "survival of the fittest." According to this theory, human social history could be understood as a struggle among races, with the strongest and the fittest invariably triumphing.

Not everyone accepted the excesses and injustices of industrialism. One of the most famous social critics of the day was Henry George. A California newspaperman, George said that the cause of the gap between the wealthy and the poor was the monopoly of land by the rich and the rents that landowners charged. He expressed his ideas in a book titled *Progress and Poverty* (1879). Rent, he wrote, was "a toll levied upon labor constantly and continuously," and the solution for this social ill was a "single tax" on rising land values. With such a tax, all other forms of taxation would be unnecessary.

Another challenge to Social Darwinism came in 1883 when a government geologist, Lester Frank Ward, published *Dynamic Sociology* in which he attacked Spencer and his followers for having left the human mind out of their philosophy. The process of evolution did not work, he wrote, because of "the unconscious forces of nature, but also through the conscious and deliberate control by man." The idea that government should not interfere with the workings of society reflected the self-interest of those who espoused it. "Those who dismiss state interference are the ones who most frequently and successfully invoke it." Ward's view of what Americans were actually doing was sound. All through this period citizens asked government at all levels to take action on matters of health, safety, and finance.

The Changing South and West

Among the most pressing concerns of the 1880s were those that focused on the South and West. In the South, issues of race, industrial development, and agricultural growth were important aspects of what was called the "New South." In the West, the vast spaces beyond the Mississippi Valley still were not fully integrated into the United States.

The Fate of Native Americans

The defeat of Custer at the Battle of the Little Big Horn in June 1876 was one of the final flurries of combat on the Great Plains. Some sporadic resistance continued. During 1877 the Nez Percé tribe in Oregon, led by Chief Joseph, resisted attempts to move them to a reservation. During four months of running battles, Joseph led his band of 650 people toward Canada, but they were beaten before they could reach safety. The Nez Percé were sent to the Indian Territory in Oklahoma, where they fell victim to disease.

©The Granger Collection, New York

Geronimo
An Apache leader who resisted white incursions until his capture in 1886.

The Apache chief Geronimo eluded capture in the Southwest and surrendered to the Army in 1886. Once in custody, he could be photographed with a rifle and menacing expression as a way of earning money from tourists.

Another famous example of Native American resistance was **Geronimo,** the Apache chief in New Mexico. With a small band of followers, he left the Arizona reservation where he had been living in 1881 and conducted raids across the Southwest. Finally, in September 1886 he was persuaded to surrender and was exiled to Florida.

As Native American resistance ebbed, the national government shaped policy for the western tribes. Many white westerners believed that the "Indian question" could be solved only when the tribes were gone. Easterners contended that Native Americans should become a part of white society through assimilation. Although the westerners had destructive motives toward the Indians whereas the easterners' policies were more benevolent, their combined efforts were devastating to Indian culture.

The Dawes Act (1887)

Congress passed the **Dawes Severalty Act** in 1887. Named after Senator Henry L. Dawes of Massachusetts, the law authorized the president to survey Native American reservations and divide them into 160-acre farms. Any Indian who adopted "habits of civilized life" be-

Dawes Act
This act distributed land to the Indians so that it could be sold to whites.

came a U.S. citizen, but most Indians did not achieve citizenship. Any surplus land left over after this process was finished could be sold to white settlers. For the reformers, this law would push the Indians toward white civilization; for the western settlers it offered a way to obtain Indian land. During the next fifty years, the total land holdings of Native Americans declined from 138 million to 47 million acres. By dividing up tribal landholdings and putting Indians at the mercy of white speculators, the Dawes Act undermined the tribal structure and culture of the Native Americans.

The Mining Frontier

One impetus for whites to develop the West lay in the mining "booms" that drew settlers to seek riches in a series of bonanzas, first of gold, later of silver, and eventually of copper. The mining camps became notorious. More than 90 percent of their inhabitants were men; most of the women were prostitutes.

During the 1870s, individual miners gradually gave way to corporations that used industrial techniques such as jets of water under high pressure to extract the metal from the ground. The ravaged land left farmers with fouled rivers and polluted fields.

In 1877 Leadville, Colorado, emerged as a major silver mining center, and Coeur d'Alene, Idaho, went through a similar process a few years later. In Butte, Montana, the development of the Anaconda Copper Mine would characterize the western mining business from the mid-1880s onward: an industrialized workforce, a company town, and bitter labor relations.

Cattle Country

White settlement on the Great Plains during the 1880s started with the cattle ranchers, who dominated the open range in Wyoming, Colorado, and Montana. After the Civil War, ranchers in Texas found that their steers had multiplied during their absence. Enterprising cattlemen drove herds north to market. Up the Chisum and Goodnight-Loving Trails came Texas longhorns to the cattle towns of Ellsworth, Dodge City, and Abilene. Unlike the mining towns, these communities were not noted for violence and vice; dance halls and bordellos for the visiting cattlemen, though plentiful at first, soon were restricted.

During the late 1870s and early 1880s, cattle raising shifted from Texas to areas nearer the railroads and the Chicago stockyards. The growth of the railroad network gave ranchers access to eastern and foreign markets. Improved breeding and slaughtering practices produced beef for consumers both in the United States and in Europe. Entrepreneurs in New York, London, and Scotland wanted to buy cattle cheaply in the West and resell them to eastern buyers at a profit. Money poured into the West and increased the number of cattle on the ranges of Montana and Wyoming.

The Life of the Cowboy

The men who worked the steers were not the glamorous "cowboys" of popular mythology. Life on a ranch was characterized by drudgery and routine. The cowboy's days were fourteen hours long. Much of what he did—riding the line, tending sick cattle, and mending fences—consisted of grinding physical labor in a harsh environment.

The cowboys reflected American diversity. One of every seven was African American. These black cowboys gained a living but were not granted social equality. Other cowboys included Hispanics and Native Americans, and they also experienced discrimination. From the Hispanic *vaqueros* and the Native Americans, other cowboys learned the techniques of breaking horses and the complex skills of managing cattle. Western development thus involved a subtle interaction of cultures that few whites understood.

The End of the Cattle Boom

The boom years in the cattle business soon ended. As the ranges became overstocked in 1885 and 1886, the prices for western cattle fell. Then came the "hard winter" of 1886–1887, during which blizzards killed thousands of cattle. Before prices rose, investors from the East and Great Britain lost all they had as the remaining stock was dumped onto an already depressed market. The cattle industry changed from a speculative, high-risk venture of part-time capitalists to a more rational, routinized business.

Ranchers in the West faced other challenges. Sheep raisers discovered that sheep could graze more economically than cattle. Range wars between cattle and sheep growers broke out. In the long run, however, sheep raising proved to be a viable business, and by 1900 there were some thirty million sheep on western ranges.

Farming on the Great Plains

During the 1880s hundreds of thousands of farmers swept onto the Great Plains. Advertising by the railroad companies painted a picture of abundant land, water, and opportunity. The reality was less hospitable.

The Homestead Act of 1862 gave farmers public land, which they could use and eventually own. In practice, the 160-acre unit of the Homestead Act was much too small for a farmer to cultivate successfully on the plains. To make a farm work, a settler had to purchase two or three times that acreage. The Homestead Act also did not give prospective farmers the money they needed to go West, file a claim, and acquire the machinery required for profitable farming.

Congress complicated the land system. Cattle ranchers persuaded lawmakers to pass the Desert Land Act (1877), which allowed individuals to obtain a provisional title to 640 acres in the West at twenty-five cents an acre. Before securing a title, they had to irrigate the land within three years and pay a dollar an acre more. This law was easily evaded.

A year later, lumber interests in the West lobbied for what became the Timber and Stone Act (1878). Directed at lands that were "unfit for cultivation," it permitted settlers to acquire up to 160 acres at $2.50 per acre. Under the act, lumber companies used false entries to gain title to valuable timber holdings.

Land and Debt

Most settlers on the Great Plains obtained their land from the railroads or land companies. Congress had granted the railroads every other 160-acre section of land along their rights of way. Large tracts of land were closed to settlement until the railroads sold the land to farmers. During the period between 1862 and 1900, land companies acquired almost one hundred million acres from railroads or the government. Other lands had been granted to eastern states to support their agricultural colleges under the Morrill Land Grant Act of 1862. These western holdings went into the hands of speculators who purchased the lands.

Most of the western settlers had to acquire their land at prices that often ranged between $5 and $10 per acre. To buy the land, the farmers borrowed from loan companies in the East and Midwest. Interest rates on the resulting mortgages were as high as 25 percent annually. As long as land values rose and crop prices remained profitable, the farmers made the needed investment. When prices fell, however, they faced economic adversity.

Fences and Water

Industrial growth and technological advances made cultivation possible on the Great Plains. Joseph Glidden of Illinois devised the practical form of barbed wire in 1873. Soon Glidden's invention came to the attention of the Washburn and Moen Company of Massachusetts, which developed a machine to produce barbed wire. By 1880 some eighty million pounds had been produced. Improved plows, the cord binder for baling hay, and grain silos also aided western farming. During the 1880s steam-powered threshers for wheat and cornhusking machines were developed.

Machines alone could not provide enough water for farming. West of the ninety-eighth meridian, which ran through the Dakotas, Nebraska, Kansas, Oklahoma, and Texas, fewer than twenty inches of rain fell annually, and most of the region lacked adequate rivers. Ordinary wells did not reach the waters far below the surface. Windmills offered a possible solution, but the high cost of drilling and installing a windmill made it too expensive for most farmers. The most practical technique was "dry farming," cultivation designed to use water that the land retained after rainfall.

Farm Life on the Plains

Life on the western farms was a grind. With little wood available, shelter often consisted of a sod house made of bricks of dirt or dried sod. To keep warm in the winter, the farmers burned buffalo chips (droppings) or dried sunflower plants. Grasshoppers ruined crops, animals trampled fields, and the weather was always uncertain.

The burdens of farmwork fell hardest on women. The child of one farm woman remembered "Bake day, mending day. A certain day for a certain thing. That's what I remember, those special days that my ma had." Amid the endless spaces of the Great Plains, women labored on small plots of land, sustained by a network of friends and neighbors. Some women achieved a degree of independence in the male-dominated West. They operated farms, taught school, ran boardinghouses, and participated in politics and cultural life.

From Territories to States

By the late 1880s some of the western territories were ready for statehood. In 1889 and 1890 Congress enacted legislation to admit the Dakotas, Montana, Washington, Idaho, and Wyoming into the Union.

Farm women on the Great Plains toiled in a harsh environment where fuel and shelter required constant attention. Buffalo chips could be burned for warmth when wood might be miles away. What this woman and her child did took place every day despite incessant wind and extremes of temperature.

During the decade from 1877 to 1887, one group of newcomers experienced danger and prejudice in the West. Chinese immigrants came to California during the 1840s and 1850s to work the gold mines. They constructed the transcontinental railroads in the 1860s. Energetic and thrifty, the Chinese soon began engaging in manufacturing enterprises and agricultural pursuits. White Californians reacted with bigotry and violence. Laws were passed to bar the Chinese from professions in which they competed successfully with whites. A movement to ban Chinese immigration gained widespread support. The Chinese Exclusion Act of 1882 barred the Chinese entry into the United States for ten years.

Ranchers and settlers had overcome natural obstacles, political difficulties, and economic problems to build new societies on the Great Plains. By the end of the 1880s, however, the process of development had created problems as farmers failed to achieve the prosperity they had anticipated. Crop prices fell, and debts became an ever-greater burden. The transition to industrialism meant pain and hardship for the West. As a result, the region was politically restive by 1887. Similar pressures were building in the South.

The New South

The presidential election of 1876 ended what remained of Reconstruction. Democrats took over state governments in South Carolina, Louisiana, and Florida. The Democrats believed that white supremacy and limited government were the basic principles of political life. The need to maintain the South as "white man's country" made the Democrats dominant among white southerners. Not all southerners became Democrats, however. Blacks voted Republican, as did whites in the southern mountain regions. Independents and others cooperated with Republicans.

The men who took over the state governments in the South after Reconstruction believed that they had "redeemed" the region from the mistaken Republican experiment in multiracial politics. Their policies, they claimed, lacked the corruption and waste characteristic of their Republican predecessors. In reality, the record of these politicians was worse than that of Reconstruction.

The Redeemers were plantation owners, Confederate officers, and aspiring capitalists who wanted to see a more urban and developed South. This coalition dominated the politics of many southern states throughout the 1880s. However, the Redeemers faced some opposition. In Virginia, the size of the public debt became a central issue, with William Mahone campaigning against using tax money to pay off out-of-state creditors. Mahone and his allies also advocated more money for public schools and other state services. These "Readjusters" attracted even many black voters. As a result, they soon faced a counterattack from the Democrats. Within a few years the Readjuster movement had been defeated, in part through the use of rigged elections and stuffed ballot boxes.

A key theme in the South during these years was embodied in the phrase "The New South." This phrase was meant to signify that the South would now welcome industrialization and economic expansion. The most famous advocate of the New South idea was an Atlanta newspaper editor named Henry Grady. The South, Grady said in 1886, would soon have "a hundred farms for every plantation, fifty homes for every palace—and a diversified industry that meets the complex needs of this complex age." All over the region there were plans to build steel mills, textile factories, and railroads.

The Industrial South

A substantial expansion of manufacturing capacity occurred in the South between 1870 and 1900. In the major cotton producing states, the amount of capital invested in manufacturing increased about tenfold between 1869 and 1889. Southern railroads expanded rapidly during the postwar period; by 1880 there were 19,430 miles of track. Other key industries grew during this decade as well.

Southern forests were cut down to satisfy the growing national demand for lumber. Almost three million board feet of yellow pine was produced in 1879. The region's ample deposits of iron ore stimulated the expansion of the iron and coal industries after the war ended. Production of iron ore rose from 397,000 tons in 1880 to almost 2 million tons twenty years later. Large amounts of coal mined in the southern Appalachian region of West Virginia and Virginia.

Before the Civil War, tobacco had been popular as something to chew, smoke in a pipe, or as a cigar. A significant change in American smoking habits occurred during the 1880s, when James Buchanan Duke began using a practical cigarette-making machine. Production costs fell rapidly, and cigarette use skyrocketed. By the end of the 1880s, Duke's company was making more than eight hundred million cigarettes annually.

The cotton textile industry also grew rapidly during this period. Increasing national demand for southern products spurred the industry. Lower labor costs made southern mills highly competitive. Women and children accounted for a high proportion of the labor force in these establishments.

Industrialism led to greater prosperity for the South, but this growth came at a high cost to those who worked in the factories and mills. Wages were often low and conditions crude. In the cotton mills an average workweek might be more than sixty hours for wages that could be as low as fifteen cents a day. Influential southerners resisted arguments against child labor, even as others tried to end the practice.

Problems of Southern Agriculture

The system of farming that evolved in the aftermath of the Civil War created serious economic problems. The central fact of southern farming between 1877 and 1887 was dependence on cotton. Although newspaper editors and publicists urged farmers to grow other crops in addition to cotton, few took this advice. Cotton growers knew that their crop rarely failed and brought a higher price per acre than any other crop.

World production of cotton was increasing, however, and prices for the South's primary crop fell between 1870 and 1885, rose somewhat at the end of the decade, and plunged again during the 1890s. Unable to increase their productivity enough to make money despite lower prices, cotton farmers became locked into a system of debt and dependence.

To make cotton growing work, farmers needed a reliable supply of cheap labor. The end of slavery meant that plantations could no longer count on having enough field hands. Whites held most of the land, whereas blacks had less land and were forced to sell their labor. The result was a system that combined **sharecropping,** tenant farming, and the "furnish merchant," who provided the farmers with the "furnish" (whatever was needed) to get them through the year.

Sharecroppers were workers who received as their wage a designated proportion of the crops they produced. The landlord or owner controlled the crop until some of it was allocated to the sharecropper. Tenant farmers, on the other hand, owned the crop until it was

sharecropping
Working land in return for a share of the crops produced instead of paying cash rent. A shortage of currency in the South made this a frequent form of land tenure, and African Americans endured it because it eliminated the labor gangs of the slavery period.

sold. They then paid to the owner of the property either cash or a fixed amount of the crop. Both tenants and "croppers" depended on a local merchant to provide the food and supplies that they needed until their harvests were completed. Southern states passed crop lien laws that gave the merchant a claim on the crop if a farmer could not make enough money to pay off his debt. Thus, the farmers in the South, both black and white, were locked in a cycle of debt in which they owed money or crops first to the landlord and then to the "furnish" merchant. In bad years the farmers did not make enough to get out of debt.

A Colonial Economy

Part of the South's problems grew out of the region's financial plight after the Civil War. The National Banking Act of 1863 required banks to have up to $50,000 in capital and to be located in a small town to get a national bank charter. Few southern communities could meet that standard, and so prospective borrowers had to compete for scarce local credit. Because national banks could not make mortgage loans, even those that opened in the South were of little help to the southern farm population. At the same time the national government followed monetary policies that promoted deflation. All of these economic elements taken together meant that the South's lack of capital worsened during the 1880s.

Southern farmers saw themselves at the mercy of a system that had been imposed upon them by northern bankers, international cotton marketing companies, and industrialism. The cotton farmers had to tolerate these conditions because there appeared to be no other way to participate in the South's burgeoning economy. By the end of the decade, however, the problems of perpetual debt were becoming acute.

Segregation

Racial segregation evolved slowly but steadily. One obstacle to this trend was the enactment of the national Civil Rights Act in 1875, which prohibited racial discrimination in public accommodations. In the *Civil Rights Cases* (1883), the Supreme Court ruled that under the Fourteenth Amendment Congress could prohibit only *state* actions that violated civil rights. It could not prohibit individual acts of racial discrimination in public places. The Court said that it was up to the states to ban discrimination, and, not surprisingly, southern states chose instead to allow and even encourage racial segregation.

During this period, segregation lacked the rigidity and legal power that it acquired later. In some southern states, for example, black citizens could use railroads and streetcars on a roughly equal basis with whites. Elsewhere in the region travel facilities were segregated.

Whatever opportunities were open to black citizens existed alongside an overall system of racial discrimination and bigotry. Black men often found their choices at the polls limited to approved white candidates, and if too many African Americans sought to cast ballots, white violence might erupt. By the end of the 1880s, growing numbers of white politicians believed that blacks should be barred from the electoral process altogether.

Thus, for African Americans in the South, the fifteen years after the end of Reconstruction began with hopeful signs but had a bleak outcome. Black families wanted to rent farms and work land for themselves. They believed that growing cotton in the delta of Mississippi gave them a chance to participate in that region's expanding economy. The area saw an influx of blacks at the end of the 1880s as African American men competed for new jobs and the opportunity to acquire land of their own. In this part of the South for a brief period there was a chance for black economic advancement. African Americans created networks of black churches and endeavored to educate their children. Booker T. Washington's leadership of the Tuskegee Institute in Alabama, which began in 1881, symbolized what education and training could do for aspiring African Americans. Growing up with no direct experience of slavery, a new generation of southern blacks demanded their legal rights. When older blacks warned of the possible consequences of such behavior, the younger generation answered that "we are now qualified, and being the equal of whites, should be treated as such."

Some African Americans preferred to get out of the South if they could. At the end of the 1870s rumors spread through the black population that Kansas offered a safer haven. During 1879 some twenty thousand blacks, known as "exodusters" because they were coming out of bondage as the children of Israel had in the Exodus, arrived in Kansas. Hundreds of thousands of other blacks left the South in these years. Their willingness to go to areas that offered less oppression and more opportunity than the South testified to the enduring optimism of black Americans.

As the end of the 1880s approached, the South produced more cotton than ever before; towns were growing throughout the region; industries had developed; and tens of thousands of black southerners had accumulated property. Yet there were danger signs. State legislatures wrote new laws to segregate first-class railroad passengers by race. Farmers who grew more cotton each year without getting ahead organized to oppose the power of merchants and railroads. Racial violence reached unprecedented levels. Although much had changed, many worried that the New South would be little better than the Old.

Life and Culture during the 1880s

According to the 1880 Census, there were 50,155,783 people in the United States in that year. More than 70 percent of them lived in "rural territory." Another 3.5 million people lived in towns and villages with fewer than 5,000 inhabitants. Of the nearly ten million households in the nation, the most common family consisted of a husband, a wife, and their three children. The father worked the family farm or at a job in an office or at the factory. The mother stayed at home and did the endless round of cleaning, cooking, sewing, and shopping that kept the home operating. The children attended schools near their home or, in less prosperous families, labored to supplement the family's income.

Their Daily Bread

The meals that Americans consumed daily were large ones. For the middle class, breakfast often included fried eggs, biscuits, wheatcakes, potatoes, and steak. The afternoon and evening meals were also quite ample. Among the upper classes, a fancy dinner might provide as many as ten or eleven courses of meats, fish, salads, and starchy foods.

Industrialism changed the way Americans ate. Vegetables and fruits were available at the twist of a can opener. In large cities fresh meats became more readily available as the Armour meat company moved beef in iced railroad cars. The saltine cracker, shipped by the National Biscuit Company and other firms, proved that packaged crackers could remain fresh and crisp. Brand names told Americans that "Uneeda" biscuit, and a portly Quaker figure appeared on containers of Quaker Oats. In 1886 an Atlanta druggist named **John Pemberton** developed a syrup from an extract of the cola nut that he mixed with carbonated water and called "Coca Cola."

John Pemberton
An Atlanta druggist who in 1886 developed a syrup from an extract of the cola nut that he mixed with carbonated water and called "Coca Cola."

Power for the Home

In the homes of city dwellers, gas and electricity provided new sources of power. Running water replaced water drawn by hand from a distant pump. Refrigeration reduced the need for daily shopping; ready-made clothing relieved housewives of the task of sewing garments for the family.

The duties of the wife were still time-consuming and tiring. However fuel was supplied, she had to prepare the meals. Despite the availability of canned fruits and vegetables, many women did their own canning and preserving. Sewing, cleaning, and household maintenance continued on a daily basis. To a large extent, the wife and mother found herself alone in the house each day as the husband went to work and the children went to school.

The Middle-Class Family

Middle- and upper-class women who could afford to hire domestic servants to perform these chores enjoyed more leisure. Smaller families also meant that women ended their child-rearing years earlier and then had more time for themselves. New magazines catered to this audience, including the *Ladies' Home Journal* in 1883 and *Good Housekeeping* in 1885. Women's clubs also spread during the 1870s and 1880s. The Young Women's Christian Association, founded in 1867, the Woman's Christian Temperance Union, established in 1874, and the Association of Collegiate Alumnae, formed in 1882, gave tangible expression to these women's desires for association and service.

The children were educated in schools that were locally controlled and designed to instill patriotism and moral values. City children attended school for some one hundred eighty to two hundred days a year. In rural areas, however, the demands of farm work often limited children's school attendance to less than one hundred days a year. Courses included arithmetic, the history of the United States, geography, reading, grammar, and spelling. In the better school systems, students received instruction in Latin and at least one other foreign language; less attention was given to the sciences. For new immigrants, the school system became a means for them to learn the values of the dominant culture.

Although only a small percentage of students attended high schools and even fewer pursued a college degree, the late nineteenth century brought rapid growth for institutions of higher learning. Wealthy businessmen created private universities such as Johns Hopkins in Baltimore (1876), the University of Chicago (1890), and Stanford in California (1891). State universities expanded in the Midwest and were created in the South. Modeled on the German educational system, these universities established academic departments and stressed research and graduate training. Higher education in the United States became increasingly professionalized as teachers had to possess graduate degrees and prove themselves through research and publication in their discipline.

Leisure in the 1880s

The cultural changes of the 1880s gave rise to new entertainments. At Chautauqua meetings (named after the lake in western New York state where the program began), held in the summer, citizens gathered for ten-week sessions, read long lists of suggested and required books and listened to lectures by scholars, prominent public figures, and artists.

Appealing to a wider audience were the circuses and Wild West shows. The first three-ring circus debuted in Manhattan in 1883, and P. T. Barnum, with his "greatest show on earth," became the entertainment equivalent to the giants of industry. During the same year, William "Buffalo Bill" Cody assembled a troupe of former Pony Express riders, stage coach robbers, and riding artists that toured the United States and Europe. In major cities, vaudeville—a form of entertainment consisting of a series of singers, comedians, and specialty acts—was a favorite of urban audiences.

Baseball was already a popular pastime. The National League, founded in 1876, entered an era of prosperity after 1880. Star players like Adrian "Cap" Anson of the Chicago White Stockings became household names. Baseball fans, known as "kranks," delighted in baiting the umpire. In the 1880s many new rules were adopted, including the three-strikes, four-balls format; overhand pitching; and substitutions of players. Sunday contests were banned, as was the sale of beer at ballparks. In 1888 Ernest L. Thayer wrote his famous poem "Casey at the Bat," and several generations of schoolchildren learned to recite how there was "no joy in Mudville" when "mighty" Casey struck out at the crucial moment.

The magazines of the day, some 3,300 in all, carried articles on every possible subject. *Atlantic Monthly, Harper's Weekly, Century, The North American Review,* and *Scribner's* dealt with scientific discoveries, literary trends, and political issues. Americans also read popular novels such as Lew Wallace's *Ben Hur* (1880). The more serious novels of the decade included *The Rise of Silas Lapham* (1885), by William Dean Howells, and *The Bostonians* (1885), by William James. Probably the most important literary work of the 1880s was *The Adventures of Huckleberry Finn,* written by Samuel L. Clemens (Mark Twain) in 1884. In it Clemens used an adventure in which a boy helps a runaway slave to create a chronicle of the nation's experience with slavery, freedom, the wonders of childhood, and the ambiguities of adult life.

Visual arts also fascinated Americans. Museums were founded in St. Louis, Detroit, and Cincinnati between 1879 and 1885, continuing a trend that had begun earlier in Boston, Philadelphia, and New York. Notable artists included Frederic Remington, who had gone west in 1880 to improve his health and arranged to accompany the army on campaigns against the Indians. His evocations of frontier life, published in *Harper's Weekly,* made him famous. Two of the most important figures of the decade were Thomas Eakins and John Singer Sargent. Eakins lived and worked in Philadelphia, and his most notable works

A Republican Defends the Protective Tariff

In the late nineteenth century the two major parties differed about the best way to promote American economic growth. Republican speakers, such as William McKinley in this Virginia speech, argued that high tariff rates would encourage domestic industry, safeguard American workers, and spread the benefits of prosperity to all sectors of society. The blend of nationalism and self-interest that Republicans advanced proved to be an important element in their party's appeal to voters.

"We do not appeal to passions; we do not appeal to baser instincts; we do not appeal to race or war prejudices. We do appeal to your own best interests, to stand by a party that stands by the people. Vote the Republican ticket, stand by the protective policy, stand by American industry, stand by that policy which believes in American work for American workmen, that believes in American wages for American laborers, that believes in American homes for American citizens. Vote to maintain that system by which you can earn enough not only to give you the comforts of life but the refinements of life; enough to educate and equip your children, who may not have been fortunate by birth, who may not have been born with a silver spoon in their mouths, enough to enable them in turn to educate and prepare their children for the great possibilities of American life. I am for America, because America is for the common people."

Questions to Consider

1. How does McKinley's speech reflect the Republican position on the protective tariff in the 1880s?

2. In what ways is he courting anti-British sentiment during these years?

3. How would a Democrat have rebutted McKinley's contentions?

4. What differences in philosophy with the Democratic party does McKinley's brand of Republicanism set forth?

Explore additional primary sources related to this chapter on the *American Passages* Web site: http://history.wadsworth.com/ayersbrief02.

Source: William McKinley, "What Protection Means to Virginia," Petersburg, Virginia, October 29, 1865, in *Speeches and Address of William McKinley* (New York: D. Appleton, 1893), p. 194.

---

included *The Swimming Hole* and *The Agnew Clinic.* Sargent became famous for portraits such as *The Daughters of Edward Boit* and *Mrs. Edward Burkhardt and Daughter Louise.*

During this era private institutions, universities, and the federal government encouraged the diffusion of scientific information. The American Association for the Advancement of Science resumed operation after the war; other scientific societies expanded after 1877 as well. From the industrial laboratories of General Electric and other corporate giants to the facilities of research universities, the United States forged a partnership between science and technology that laid the basis for future innovations.

Two symbols of the decade were the Brooklyn Bridge and the Statue of Liberty in New York. It took John A. Roebling and his son Washington Roebling twelve years to construct the longest suspension bridge in the world, but the resulting structure demonstrated what the new processes of industrialism could accomplish. The Statue of Liberty was dedicated three years later on October 28, 1886. The work of a French sculptor, Frédéric-Auguste Bartholdi, it was placed on Bedloe's Island, now called Liberty Island, at the entrance to New York Harbor. Out of the campaign to raise money came the celebrated poem by Emma Lazarus that promised the "golden door" of opportunity to Europe's "huddled masses yearning to breathe free."

Politics and Public Policy, 1877–1887

In politics, an electoral stalemate had developed after 1872. The Republicans won the presidency in 1876, 1880, and 1888; the Democrats triumphed in 1884 and 1892. Neither party controlled both houses of Congress on a regular basis. Outside the South, elections often were decided by very narrow margins.

Only men took part in elections, and most of them were whites. Those who could vote turned out at a record rate; about eight out of every ten eligible voters went to the polls. When they were not voting, Americans listened to long speeches by candidates and read about politics in the extended stories that partisan newspapers printed. Coverage of congressional deliberations was much more detailed than would be the case a century later.

Moral and religious values shaped the way that men voted. The prohibition of alcohol, the role of religious and sectarian education in the public schools, and the observance of the Sabbath were hotly contested questions. Republicans favored government intervention to support Protestant values; Democrats thought the government should keep out of such subjects.

The most prominent national issues involved the kind of money Americans used, how the government raised revenue, and who served in the government itself. On the subject of money, some Americans believed that for every dollar in circulation an equal amount of gold should be stored in the treasury or in banks. Others contended that the government should issue more money by coining silver into currency on an equal basis with gold. Debtors favored inflation, which made their loans easier to pay; creditors liked the deflation that raised the value of their dollars. Both parties struggled with the issue during the ten years after 1877.

Other major concerns were taxation and the protective tariff. There was no federal income tax; the government raised money from two main sources: excise taxes on alcohol and tobacco, and customs duties (taxes) on goods imported into the United States. The latter method, the *protective tariff,* became a hot political issue. Those who favored a tariff said that high customs duties would protect American industry, help workers, and develop the economy. Republicans championed the protective system, whereas Democrats countered that tariffs raised prices, hurt the consumer, and made government too expensive.

At bottom the argument was over the size and role of the national government. Should the government stimulate the economy, as the Republicans wanted, or allow natural forces to operate, as the Democrats advocated?

Finally, there was the question of who should serve in government. Politicians preferred the "spoils" or patronage system. Allocating government jobs to partisan supporters enabled them to strengthen their party. Critics of the patronage system called it a corrupt and inefficient way to choose government officials. They favored a *civil service* in which individuals, chosen through competitive examinations, would administer government without being subject to partisan pressure.

From Hayes to Arthur

The Republicans began the period with Rutherford B. Hayes in the White House. Hayes proved to be a capable chief executive. He pushed for civil service reform and resisted pressure from Congress to base his appointments on candidates that Congress favored. He vetoed the inflationary Bland-Allison Act (1878), which called for monthly government purchases of silver, but Congress overrode his veto.

Hayes had promised to serve only one term. To succeed him the Republicans nominated James A. Garfield of Ohio, and Chester Alan Arthur of New York was his running mate. The Democratic candidate was a former Civil War general named Winfield Scott Hancock. Garfield won by a narrow plurality in the popular vote and by a larger margin in the electoral college.

Garfield's presidency lasted only four months. On July 2, 1881, he went to the Washington railroad station to leave for a vacation. Presidents were not well guarded at this time, and a crazed assassin shot Garfield. He died on September 19, and Chester Alan Arthur became president. Arthur proved a competent chief executive. During his single term, Congress passed the Pendleton Act (1883), which created a civil service system. The act also established rules about where and how government officials could raise campaign funds. Arthur also asked Congress to consider downward revision of the tariff. They

Rutherford B. Hayes Memorial Library, Fremont, OH

President Rutherford B. Hayes conveys the aura of calm and stability that marked his presidency.

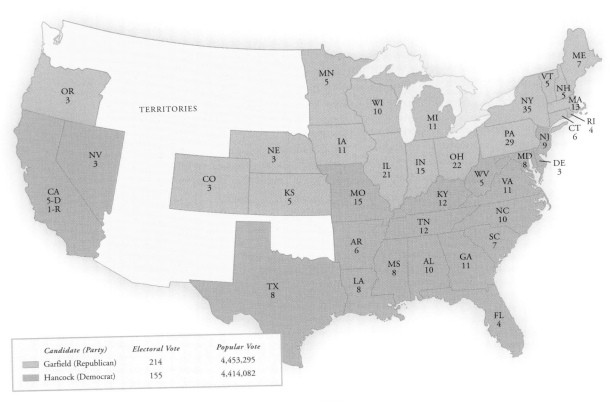

Candidate (Party)	Electoral Vote	Popular Vote
Garfield (Republican)	214	4,453,295
Hancock (Democrat)	155	4,414,082

MAP 17.2 The Election of 1880

The presidential election of 1880 underscored the evenly divided politics of that era as James A. Garfield and Winfield Scott Hancock waged a hard-fought contest that turned on the protective tariff and the legacy of the Civil War.

responded with the Mongrel Tariff of 1883 (so called because it pleased no one), which generally raised protective duties.

Blaine versus Cleveland, 1884

Despite his solid performance, Arthur was a caretaker president. In 1884 the party selected its most popular figure, James G. Blaine of Maine, to run for the presidency. Blaine had been a potential presidential candidate in 1876 and 1880, but questions had been raised about his political honesty. His enemies said that Blaine had helped railroads while he was Speaker of the House in return for money (see Chapter 16). Despite these problems, the Republicans nominated him enthusiastically.

To run against Blaine, the Democrats selected the governor of New York, Grover Cleveland. Cleveland was a lawyer in Buffalo, New York, when he was chosen to be the city's mayor in 1881. A year later he was the Democratic nominee for governor. Elected in a year when the Republicans were disunited and demoralized, Cleveland proved to be a popular state executive. The national Democrats wanted a fresh face, and the stocky Cleveland was an attractive blend of honesty, conservatism, and independence. His campaign suffered a setback when it was revealed that some years earlier he had accepted responsibility for an illegitimate child. Cleveland acknowledged his part in the episode, however, and his candor defused the issue.

Cleveland was helped by the defection of upper-class Republicans in the Northeast. These voters, calling themselves "Mugwumps" (an Indian word meaning "Big Chief"), threw their support to the Democrats. The outcome of the election was very close. Cleveland carried the South, New York, New Jersey, Connecticut, and Indiana, receiving 219 electoral votes to Blaine's 182.

Cleveland in Office

Cleveland took office on March 4, 1885. During his first term, he established that his party could govern. For the Democrats, however, Cleveland proved to be a mixed blessing. He was slow to turn Republican officeholders out of office, and he alienated many Democrats with his patronage policies. Still, Republicans made few gains in the congressional elections of 1886, and Cleveland seemed to have good prospects for a second term in 1888.

In December 1887, hoping to establish an issue for his reelection campaign, the president made the subject of tariff reform the sole issue of his annual message to Congress (known as the State of the Union message). With a surplus in the treasury, Cleveland believed that the tariff could be reduced, leading to lower prices for consumers. The Republicans' reaction to Cleveland's move was one of delight. Now the 1888 election could be fought on the issue that united the Republicans and divided the Democrats. With the stage set for the election, the stalemated politics of the 1880s slowly broke up. For the next twelve years, American politics would experience one of the most turbulent and decisive periods of change and partisan realignment in the nation's history.

Summary

The Dilemmas of Industrialism

The ten years after the end of Reconstruction left the American people aware that industrialism came with rich benefits and hard choices. The railroad network meant faster transportation as well as cheaper goods and services for all citizens. With these positive developments came fears of monopoly power and the corruption of state and national politics. Similar changes occurred with the growth of large industries in steel and oil. The evolution of big business and the rise of the trusts raised questions of whether governments needed to be made stronger to confront these new centers of power.

For working Americans, industrialization brought a new kind of workplace in which the older style of a person skilled in an individual craft disappeared. Working conditions in several key sectors of the economy became so bad that labor unions arose to enable workers to bargain together with employers. The Knights of Labor and the American Federation of Labor represented contrasting answers about how to achieve a better life for the people who felt the sharp sting of industrial change. The negative reaction of middle-class Americans to labor militancy emphasized the limits of permissible protest.

In the South and West, the decade brought the end of Native American resistance in the West, the age of the cattle boom, and the expansion of agriculture. For the South, still smarting over Reconstruction, the period meant a dependence on cotton as a cash crop, some effort at industrialization, and signs of a growing intolerance for the rights of African Americans. Farmers' protests over low crop prices and a growing burden of debt multiplied as the 1880s progressed.

The burning of the Union Depot in Pittsburgh during the Railway Strike of 1877, from *Harper's Weekly,* August 11, 1877.

©CORBIS

In national politics, these were years of even balance between the major parties. Politicians still focused on how government might be used to promote economic growth in their debates about the wisdom of the protective tariff. Some stirrings of regulatory sentiment appeared in the enactment of the Interstate Commerce Law in 1887 to oversee railroad behavior. Yet neither party had enough political clout to enact its program, and partisan alignments remained stalemated as the election of 1888 approached.

The decade saw a pause between the economic hard times of the 1870s and the equally distressed 1890s. Although few Americans shared in real prosperity, the period marked a transition from the racially based issues of Reconstruction to the problems of the new age of big business. A sense of impending change underlay much of the public sentiment of the time. Citizens asked whether the nation would manage the transformation of society into a new economy and culture that was more urbanized and industrialized. Could the United States find a way to balance the needs of the agricultural sector and the growing industrial base? These tough questions and the sense of an imminent social upheaval prepared Americans for the storms of economic depression and agrarian unrest that lay just ahead as the 1880s came to an end.

Courtesy of the author.

President Hayes redeems the South from the hands of the Democratic party in 1877. The optimism of the cartoon proved to be premature.

Making Connections Across Chapters

LOOKING BACK

The focus of Chapter 17 is on the ways that industrialism affected the United States between 1877 and 1887. The ramifications of the industrializing process would have large consequences for the subsequent course of American history. Pay particular attention to how various aspects of society responded to these new developments.

1. What conditions in the previous decade paved the way for industrialism to take hold?
2. How did cost-cutting and reducing labor expenses become a central effect of industrial growth?
3. How did the United States respond to the political problems arising from the spread of railroads?
4. In what ways was the country becoming more of a national market and economy in these years?
5. What regions of the country were left behind as industrialism grew?

LOOKING AHEAD

Chapter 18 will consider how cities developed in response to industrialism and the ways in which the South and West reacted to the changes agriculture was experiencing. Some of these shifts in thinking are anticipated in this chapter.

1. What pressures did industrialism place on farmers in the South and West?
2. How did the even balance of the political system prevent solutions to the economic changes of industrialism from being developed?
3. How did minorities fare during industrial growth?

RECOMMENDED READINGS

Ayers, Edward. *The Promise of the New South* (1992). A fine modern treatment of the South in the years after Reconstruction ended.

Calhoun, Charles W. *The Gilded Age: Essays on the Origins of Modern America* (1996). A valuable assortment of excellent essays about this period.

Chandler, Alfred D. *The Visible Hand: The Managerial Revolution in American Business* (1977). A detailed examination of how industrial growth occurred.

Cherny, Robert. *American Politics in the Gilded Age, 1868–1900* (1997). A good, brief introduction to the public life of the period.

Edwards, Rebecca. *Angels in the Machinery: Gender in American Party Politics from the Civil War to the Progressive Era* (1997). Shows that women played a much larger part in political affairs than earlier historians had realized.

Porter, Glenn. *The Rise of Big Business, 1860–1920* (1992). An excellent short introduction to the economic trends of the Gilded Age.

Saum, Lewis O. *The Popular Mood of America, 1860–1890* (1990). Considers how the nation responded to social change.

Schlereth, Thomas J. *Victorian America: Transformations in Everyday Life, 1876–1915* (1991). A good survey of the impact the changes brought by industrialism had on the lives of Americans.

Summers, Mark Wahlgren. *The Gilded Age, or The Hazard of New Functions* (1997). A lively romp through the politics and leaders of the late nineteenth century.

AMERICAN JOURNEY ONLINE AND INFOTRAC COLLEGE EDITION

Visit the source collections at http://ajaccess.wadsworth.com and infotrac.thomsonlearning.com and use the Search function with the following key terms to explore documents, images, audio and video clips, articles, and commentary related to the material in this chapter.

Rutherford B. Hayes

John D. Rockefeller

Andrew Carnegie

Alexander Graham Bell

Thomas Edison

Dawes Act

Geronimo

ONLINE PRIMARY SOURCES

Here are some examples of the many primary sources related to this chapter that you will find on the *American Passages* Web site: http://history.wadsworth.com/ayersbrief02.

The Evils of Fashionable Dress, by J. H. Kellogg, M.D., 1876

Description of Sharecropping Tenants on a Georgia Plantation, 1881

Progress and Poverty, 1879

The site also offers self-quizzes, exercises, and many additional resources to help you study.

CHAPTER 18

Urban Growth and Farm Protest

1887–1893

As the United States approached its one-hundredth birthday in 1889, its burgeoning urban population posed a growing social problem. The new metropolises were characterized by huge gaps between the rich and poor residents. Citizens sought to reconcile traditional rural values of the country with the diversity and turbulence of the cities. At the local and national level the political system struggled to adjust to the new demands of the urban population.

The farm problems that had simmered throughout the early 1880s also reached a crisis level. In the South and West angry farmers formed a fresh political organization, the People's party, to make their grievances heard. For Indians and African Americans, the 1890s brought further painful reminders of their marginal status. The end of the nineteenth century saw renewed questions about the future of the nation as it urbanized and became a world power.

The New Urban Society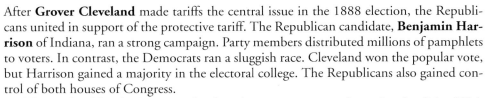

After **Grover Cleveland** made tariffs the central issue in the 1888 election, the Republicans united in support of the protective tariff. The Republican candidate, **Benjamin Harrison** of Indiana, ran a strong campaign. Party members distributed millions of pamphlets to voters. In contrast, the Democrats ran a sluggish race. Cleveland won the popular vote, but Harrison gained a majority in the electoral college. The Republicans also gained control of both houses of Congress.

The result of the election proved to have large consequences for national politics. With their hold on the executive and legislative branches, the Republicans intended to move ahead with an ambitious agenda of legislation. The Democrats were ready to challenge such initiatives in Congress and at the polls. The stalemated system that had existed since the end of Reconstruction was beginning to break down.

Sooners and Settlement Houses

During 1889 two events occurred that reflected the contrasting directions of the United States at the end of the decade. Since the 1820s the Five Civilized Tribes of Native Ameri-

Grover Cleveland
The twenty-second and twenty-fourth president of the United States, he was the first Democrat elected to the presidency after the Civil War.

Benjamin Harrison
The twenty-third president of the United States, he lost the popular vote but gained a majority of the electoral college votes in the 1888 election.

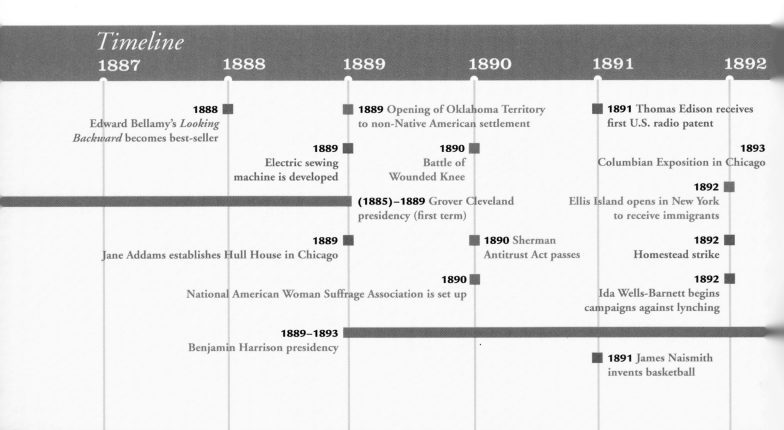

Timeline

| 1887 | 1888 | 1889 | 1890 | 1891 | 1892 |

1888 Edward Bellamy's *Looking Backward* becomes best-seller

1889 Opening of Oklahoma Territory to non-Native American settlement

1891 Thomas Edison receives first U.S. radio patent

1889 Electric sewing machine is developed

1890 Battle of Wounded Knee

1893 Columbian Exposition in Chicago

(1885)–1889 Grover Cleveland presidency (first term)

1892 Ellis Island opens in New York to receive immigrants

1889 Jane Addams establishes Hull House in Chicago

1890 Sherman Antitrust Act passes

1892 Homestead strike

1890 National American Woman Suffrage Association is set up

1892 Ida Wells-Barnett begins campaigns against lynching

1889–1893 Benjamin Harrison presidency

1891 James Naismith invents basketball

cans had lived in what is now Oklahoma. Other tribes had received land in the region after the Civil War. By the 1880s, however, pressure from white settlers to be given access to the territory proved irresistible in Congress. The Dawes Act of 1887 (see Chapter 17) completed the process of stripping the Indians of their rights. President Harrison announced that unoccupied land could be settled beginning on April 22, 1889. One hundred thousand people rushed to acquire the newly available land. Within a few hours the "Sooners," who entered the territory early, and the "Boomers" (a general name for eager settlers) had created towns and staked out farms. Other "rushes" occurred in the following four years until all the available land that the Indians had once controlled was open to white settlement.

A few months later, in August 1889, **Jane Addams** and Ellen Gates Starr founded **Hull House,** a settlement home in a Chicago neighborhood. They hoped that solutions to the troubling problems of American city life could be found in their new residence. Hull House and Addams became famous. Her personal commitment to the experiment reflected the views of many Americans that the rapid rise of large cities posed new challenges for the nation. One commentator observed that "the concentration of population in cities" was "the most remarkable social phenomenon" of the nineteenth century. Jane Addams and like-minded Americans wanted to be part of making the new cities work.

The New City

The place that Addams and Starr had chosen for their social experiment symbolized what had happened in urban America since the Civil War. In 1860, Chicago had been the nation's ninth largest city, with a population of just under 109,000. Thirty years later Chicago was the nation's second largest city, with 1,099,850 people. Through Chicago ran the major east-west railroads. To its stockyards came beef cattle from the West, to its elevators grain from the prairie, and to its lumberyards wood from the forests of Wisconsin and Minnesota. Chicago had survived the Great Fire of 1871, and from the ashes had risen the skyscrapers that gave it a distinctive skyline and the ethnic neighborhoods whose residents Hull House attempted to serve.

The Exploding Urban Population

Chicago's expansion typified the nation's rocketing urban population growth. In 1869, only nine cities had more than one hundred thousand inhabitants; in 1890, there were twenty-eight with populations of that size. Most of this urban population surge occurred in the Northeast and Middle West.

Americans moved to the cities to escape the routine of "hard work and no holidays" that dominated rural life. Immigrants from Europe remained in the large cities after they arrived. Newcomers came to large cities like Chicago and New York, worked there for months and years, and then either moved to other cities, returned to the rural areas, or went back to their home country.

The Structure of the City

After 1880 American cities grew dramatically. The horsecar gave way to cable cars in San Francisco and other hilly cities. However, cable systems were clumsy, expensive, and inefficient, and they were soon replaced by electric streetcars or the trolleys, which ran under overhead wires and moved at speeds of up to ten miles an hour. Across the nation (see Chapter 17), urban transit rapidly became electrified. To avoid traffic jams, some cities ran the streetcars on elevated tracks; others went underground to create subways. The older "walking city" soon disappeared.

As their populations shifted away from their core areas, the cities annexed their suburbs. For example, in 1889 Chicago added 133 square miles of surrounding communities. Within the core of the city, race and ethnicity determined where people lived. The more affluent residents moved as far from the center as they could. This dispersal of the population loosened the ties among the city's residents. Each class, racial, and ethnic group had fewer encounters with people in other sections of the city.

At the core of the cities, central business districts emerged. Railroads built terminals; banks and insurance companies located their main offices downtown; and department

Jane Addams
Pioneer of settlement houses in Chicago and a major reform leader.

Hull House
Founded in 1889 by Jane Addams and Ellen Gates Starr as a settlement home in a Chicago neighborhood to help solve the troubling problems of American city life.

stores anchored shopping districts. Streetcars brought customers from the suburbs to Macy's in New York, Marshall Field's in Chicago, and Filene's in Boston. In these "palaces of consumption," middle-class women spent their time in leisurely shopping for an array of attractive products. Museums, theaters, and opera houses added to the cultural resources of the industrial city.

Skyscrapers and Tenements

Two new types of structures characterized the new metropolis. Architects created the *skyscraper* as a practical solution to the need to conduct economic activities in an often compressed central business district. Architect Louis Sullivan of Chicago and others developed techniques that made it possible for buildings to rise higher than the five to ten stories that had been the upper limits of tall structures in the past. Passenger elevators, lighter walls reinforced with iron piers, and a framework of structural steel made it feasible to erect buildings with twenty to forty stories or more. The skyscrapers enabled the business district to accommodate thousands of office workers each day.

The Tenement and Its Residents

The sheer number of people who crowded into the expanding cities strained the available living space. For the middle and upper classes, apartments were a practical answer. Apartment buildings began to replace the single-family home in urban areas.

Poorer city residents lived in the *tenement houses,* six- or seven-story houses built on narrow lots. New York had twenty thousand such structures, most of them 25 feet wide and 100 feet deep, with windows only at the front and back. During the late 1870s after legislation mandated that at least some ventilation be provided, "dumbbell tenements" appeared; these had tiny, indented windows along the sides. In these buildings dozens of people were crowded into small, dark rooms. The buildings looked decent enough to a passerby, but as the novelist William Dean Howells noted, "To be in it, and not have the distance, is to inhale the stenches of the neglected street, and to catch the yet fouler and dreadfuller poverty-smell which breathes from the open doorways."

Inside the tenement or on the teeming sidewalks, urban residents strained the city's water and sanitation systems. The stench of manure, open sewers, and piled-up garbage filled their nostrils. Smoke from factories and grime from machinery was everywhere. Chicago's water systems were taxed to the limit during the 1880s, and residents of Philadelphia described their water as "not only distasteful and unwholesome for drinking, but offensive for bathing purposes."

The Need for Services

The cities expanded their facilities in order to provide better service. New York City created a system of reservoirs that brought water to the residents from surrounding rivers and lakes. Chicago faced immense difficulties in transporting water from Lake Michigan for drinking needs and providing adequate sanitation. By the end of the century, however, much progress had been made. Among other things, park building became a priority of urban machines and reformers alike. The amount of parkland in the larger cities doubled during the years from 1888 to 1898.

The New Immigration

The cities grew because people flocked to them from the countryside and from other countries. Unlike the immigrants from Northern and Western Europe who had come during the first seventy-five years of the nineteenth century, these "New Immigrants" were mainly from Southern and Eastern Europe. These Italians, Poles, Hungarians, Russian Jews, and Czechs brought with them languages, lifestyles, and customs that often clashed with those of native-born Americans or earlier immigrants. Marrying within their own ethnic group, speaking their own language, reading their own newspapers, they created distinctive, vibrant communities within the cities.

Many newcomers first saw the United States when they entered New York Harbor. They were processed at Castle Garden at the Battery in lower Manhattan. Those immigration facilities were closed in 1890 and a new, more extensive immigrant station was opened in 1892 on **Ellis Island** in New York Harbor. There the new arrivals were passed through a medical examination and questioned about their economic prospects. Sometimes even their names were changed. One often-told story was that of a German Jew confronted by an inspector who fired a volley of questions at him. When finally asked his name, the man responded in Yiddish: "Schoyn vergessen" (I forget). The inspector heard what the words sounded like and said that "Sean Ferguson" was eligible to enter the United States.

Life in the United States

They made their living any way they could. They provided the labor for city construction gangs. Some men sold fruits and vegetables from pushcarts, others worked as day laborers, and increasing numbers built their own small businesses. Italian immigrant women "finished" garments for the clothing industry.

Their cultural values and Old World experiences often dictated the jobs that men and women took. Italians preferred steady jobs that left time for family life. Greeks joined railroad gangs where they could work in the open. Jews became shopkeepers, merchants, and peddlers, the trades that had been open to them in Eastern Europe. Some nationalities, Bohemians and Slovaks, for example, allowed women to work as domestic servants; others, such as Jews, Italians, and Greeks, barred women from domestic work outside the home.

The Rise of Ethnic Communities

Ethnic neighborhoods appeared. In New York City, immigrants from Naples lived on Mott Street and Sicilians resided on Prince Street. Newcomers formed self-help societies to ease the transition for those who came after them — the Polish National Alliance, the Bohemian-American National Council, and the Hebrew Immigrant Aid Society. They built theaters and schools. Some of the newcomers moved away as they prospered; other immigrants soon replaced them.

The Nativist Reaction

As the communities of immigrants grew, prejudice and religious intolerance flared. During the 1880s the American Protective Association resolved to limit the role of Catholics in politics. These sentiments that favored "native" Americans (hence "nativist") led to calls for legislation to restrict immigration through literacy tests for entrance into the United States or quotas based on national origin.

Anti-Semitism permeated American society. In addition to the long-standing religious roots of prejudice, the struggle over the currency revived notions that Jewish financiers dominated world banking. Among academics, quasi-scientific arguments arose to justify exclusion of Jews from universities and businesses. Anti-Jewish stereotypes pervaded popular art and culture.

The Urban Political Machine

Politicians in the large cities grappled with this volatile mix of ethnicity, race, and economic class. Most cities had a mayor-council form of government in which the entire population elected the mayor, and council members represented individual districts or wards. Divided, ineffective government followed as council members traded favors and blocked legislation that hurt their districts. The urban "political machine" led by the "political boss" developed. **Boss politics** relied on the votes of the large inner-city population.

The organization began in the ward. The machine's representative in the ward got out the vote by supplying his constituents with employment, helping in an economic crisis or brush with the law, and regularly attending the weddings, funerals, and wakes of the neighborhood. A ward leader like George Washington Plunkitt in New York or John F. "Honey Fitz" Fitzgerald in Boston was the man to see when disaster threatened an urban family. "I think that there's got to be in every ward somebody that any bloke can come to — no matter what he's done — and get help," said a Boston ward leader. *"Help, you understand, none of your law and justice, but help!"*

Ellis Island
An immigration station opened in 1892 where new arrivals were passed through a medical examination and were questioned about their economic prospects.

Boss Politics
An urban "political machine" that relied for its existence on the votes of the large inner-city population. The flow of money through the machine was often based on corruption.

As the city grew, contracts were awarded to businesses to build the streets, install the sewers, lay the gas lines, and erect the trolley lines. There were abundant opportunities for politicians to decide how money was spent. Decisions about who built streets, parks, and sewer lines often depended on payoffs and graft to the boss and his associates. The flow of money, much of it based on corruption, enabled the machine to provide the social services that people wanted.

In the public's mind, the political boss stood at the top of the machine. These men rarely held office and managed affairs from behind the scenes. "Honest John" Kelly and Richard Croker of Tammany Hall in New York City were among the most famous such leaders. Their enemies depicted the bosses as unchallenged dictators. In most cases, however, the bosses were shrewd politicians who balanced factions and interest groups in a constantly shifting political scene. They represented a response to the fragmentation of the city political system because of the coming of industrialism.

Critics of the urban machine attacked its reliance on graft and corruption to sustain itself. The president of Cornell University said that cities in the United States were "the most corrupt in Christendom." Like-minded members of the middle and upper classes warred on the bosses and their machines, seeking to replace them with more efficient, economical government. The machines often defeated the campaigns of the reformers because inner-city residents appreciated what the bosses did for them. Reformers came and went; the machine was always there.

The rank-and-file residents also knew that the reformers wanted to shift power away from the lower classes. The reform programs often involved cutbacks in even the already minimal services that the poorer areas of the city received. On balance, the machines and bosses supplied reasonably good city government. Services were provided and economic opportunity expanded. Most cities had water, fire, and health services of a quality that compared with those found in the industrial nations of Western Europe.

A strong force for improving city life was the settlement houses. College-educated young women "settled" in houses in the ethnic communities to school the residents in the ways of American life. They held citizenship classes, provided training in cultural issues, and offered sports to local youth. Often settlement workers approached the ethnic neighborhood with arrogance and insensitivity. In time, some settlement workers gained a better understanding of the obstacles that the immigrants faced. Their experiences in the ghettos and streets of the cities prepared them for work in subsequent reform campaigns. At the same time, Addams and others also conveyed a strong sense of moralistic paternalism to the people they sought to serve. Despite this paternalistic attitude, the settlement house movement did soften the impact of the urban experience on the new immigrants.

A "Billion Dollar Country"

In December 1889 the first session of the Fifty-first Congress assembled in Washington. This session brought the differences between the major parties into sharp focus. To hamper the activism of the Republicans, the Democrats refused to answer their names when roll calls occurred to determine whether enough members were present to do legislative business. To break the deadlock, the Republicans elected a new Speaker of the House, the forceful and sarcastic Thomas B. Reed of Maine. Reed counted the Democrats as present even if they did not answer to the roll call. His tactic produced a working Republican majority, and the House embarked on an ambitious program of legislative action.

Sherman Antitrust Act
This legislation was passed in 1890 to curb the growth of large monopolistic corporations.

In line with their commitment to the protective tariff, the Republicans adopted the McKinley Tariff (1890), which raised customs duties. They wrote the **Sherman Antitrust Act** (1890), which declared any combination (trust) in restraint of trade illegal as a response to popular concern about the growth of big business. They passed the Sherman Silver Purchase Act (1890), which required the government to purchase 4.5 million ounces of silver each month. The Republicans also introduced a Federal Elections bill to protect African American voters in the South, but a coalition of southern and western senators, along with some urban bosses, blocked it.

By the end of the session, the Republicans believed that they had enacted a far-ranging program of constructive legislation. To their surprise, however, they found that the voters were angry at their activism. Since this was the first Congress to appropriate $1 billion,

Democrats called it the "Billion Dollar Congress." Speaker Reed responded by pointing out that the nation was a "Billion Dollar Country," but few shared his optimism.

The Diminishing Rights of Minority Groups

For African Americans, Chinese immigrants, and Native Americans, these were years when their rights were at risk from repressive forces within white society. As a result, the period produced a narrowing of the possibilities for racial minorities.

Native Americans

In the early 1890s the trends toward exclusion and segregation of racial minorities that began after Reconstruction accelerated. For Indians, the end of large-scale armed resistance to white expansion left them with few viable ways to protest the policies that destroyed their traditions and confined them to reservations or government schools. The Dawes Act (see Chapter 17) was already taking away their lands. Bowed down by despair and hopelessness, the Plains Indians were receptive to any leaders who offered them a chance to regain their lost cultural values.

The appearance of a religious movement, called the Ghost Dance, promised Plains Indians an end to white domination. If the Indians performed the rituals of the dance, said a Paiute messiah named Wovoka, the Indian dead would be reborn and the whites would vanish. Apprehensive whites saw the Ghost Dance as a portent of another Indian uprising. When the Army moved against the Sioux in December 1890, fighting occurred on Wounded Knee Creek on the Pine Ridge Reservation in South Dakota. The "battle" was no contest. The Army's machine guns cut down the Indians; they suffered 146 dead and 51 wounded, whereas Army losses were 25 killed and 39 wounded. The **Battle of Wounded Knee** was the last major chapter in the Indian wars.

Battle of Wounded Knee The last major chapter in the Indian wars, it was fought on the Pine Ridge Reservation in South Dakota.

Mexican Americans

Mexican Americans were the majority in the territory of New Mexico, and a major political issue in the Southwest was land grants that the Spanish crown had made. Lawyers acquired title to these properties in order to assemble large landholdings of their own. Hispanic residents grazed their cattle on communal lands that all ranchers shared. Anglo ranchers and settlers divided up the land with fences and sold it among themselves. Spanish Americans tried to resist this activity by forming a secret vigilante organization, *Las Gorras Blancas* (The White Caps). In 1889 they removed the fences and burned Anglo property. Thus ethnic and economic tensions led to social violence in the territory.

Chinese Immigrants

The prejudice that the 104,000 Chinese residing in the West faced became more institutionalized in the early 1890s. Congress moved to tighten the restrictions on immigration embodied in the Chinese Exclusion Act of 1882. In 1889 the Supreme Court upheld the constitutionality of such laws. In 1892 Congress extended the Chinese exclusion law for ten years, and by 1900 the number of Chinese living in the United States fell to 85,000. Most of the Chinese Americans lived in cities where they established laundries, restaurants, and other small businesses.

African Americans

The most elaborate and sustained policy of racial separation was aimed at African Americans in the South. As blacks tried to benefit from their newly acquired rights, white southerners created a caste structure to ensure their continued dominance. In the *Civil Rights* cases (see Chapter 17) the Supreme Court had ruled that the Fourteenth Amendment did not give Congress the power to prohibit discrimination by individuals, which left southern states with the opportunity to write segregation laws against their black population.

Reconstruction was widely considered to have failed by this time, and white southerners, it was argued, should deal with their black populations as they deemed best. Northern willingness to abandon the aims of the Civil War and Reconstruction was a key element in the rise of segregation. With the tacit approval of the North, the white politicians of the South devised segregation laws that covered most spheres of human activity. Blacks were barred from white railroad cars. Whites had their own hotels, parks, hospitals, and schools. Blacks had to make do with lesser facilities or do without them entirely.

Informal restrictions also shaped the everyday life of blacks. African Americans were expected to step out of the way of whites, to be respectful and deferential, and never to display resentment or anger. Courtesy titles for blacks disappeared. A young black man was a "boy" until he became old enough to be labeled "uncle." To call an African American person either "Mr." or "Mrs." would have implied a degree of individuality that the culture of segregation in the South could not tolerate.

Laws removed blacks from the political process. They could not serve on juries in judgment of whites. Although some blacks had voted in elections during the 1880s, laws were passed to make it impossible for African Americans to vote. The South took its cue from Mississippi whose constitutional convention, held in 1890, required that voters demonstrate their literacy and pay a poll tax before they could cast a ballot. An illiterate man had to qualify to vote by demonstrating that he could "understand" a provision of the state constitution when it was read to him. A poll tax had to be paid in advance and a receipt presented at the polls. In Mississippi and Louisiana the number of registered black voters fell drastically during the early 1890s.

The 1890s saw the rise of segregation in the South and an increase in violence directed against black Americans. These events often became social occasions for white southerners who gathered to see the alleged criminal receive punishment that was swift but less often sure. Members of the crowd often took home grisly souvenirs of the proceedings.

Reproduced from the collections of the Library of Congress

If legal restrictions were not sufficient to maintain white supremacy, blacks faced the constant possibility of violence. During the ten years after 1889, an average of 187 black Americans were lynched each year. Blacks convicted of crimes were often imprisoned in brutal circumstances or made to work on gangs that the state leased out to private contractors. The convict-lease system produced inmate death rates as high as 25 percent in some states.

In Louisiana, blacks decided to test an 1890 law specifying that they must ride in separate railroad cars. On June 7, 1892, **Homer A. Plessy,** who was one-eighth black, boarded a train bound from New Orleans to Covington, Louisiana. He sat in the car reserved for whites, and the conductor instructed him to move to the car for blacks. He refused and was arrested. When his case came before Judge Thomas H. Ferguson, Plessy's claim that the law violated his constitutional rights was denied. His case was then appealed to the U.S. Supreme Court.

Homer A. Plessy

In a test of an 1890 law specifying that blacks must ride in separate railroad cars, this one-eighth-black man boarded a train and sat in the car reserved for whites. When the conductor instructed him to move, he refused and was arrested.

Black leaders resisted to the extent they could with their scant resources. The remaining African American members of southern legislatures argued against discriminatory legislation, but they were easily outvoted. By the mid-1890s the South was as segregated as white leaders could make it. For most blacks the constitutional guarantees of the Fourteenth and Fifteenth Amendments existed only on paper. The fate of minorities had a low priority in a society where the values of Victorian life governed everyday existence.

A Victorian Society

In the late nineteenth century the social customs embodied in the term "Victorian" provided the context in which most white Americans lived their lives. They professed a public code of personal behavior that demanded restraint, sexual modesty, temperate habits, and hard work.

The Rules of Life

The precepts of Victorian morality applied to every aspect of daily life. Unmarried men and women were supposed to be chaperoned when they were together before marriage. A kiss resulted either in an engagement or social disgrace. Premarital sex was taboo. People married for life, mourned a dead spouse for at least a year, and showed fidelity by not re-marrying. Some people did not follow these guidelines to their full extent, but many did.

Once married, a couple was expected to engage in sexual intercourse only for the purpose of having children. The wife was considered to be naturally pure; the husband was thought to be dominated by animalistic drives. "The full force of sexual desire is seldom known to a virtuous woman," said one male writer.

In reality, women's desires did not conform to these masculine stereotypes. A survey of married women found that almost three-quarters experienced pleasure during lovemaking. Limits on the frequency of sex may have been to reduce unwanted pregnancies in a time before birth control devices became widespread.

The Moral Code

Men in Victorian society displayed the right virtues in what the age called their "character." Men in the middle and upper classes might sow their "wild oats" before marriage, but after that were expected to adhere to their marriage vows. The rising number of divorces (some 56,000 by 1900) indicated that many did not do so. Society practiced a "double standard." People looked the other way when men patronized prostitutes or had discreet sexual adventures outside marriage. When it became known that a woman followed such a course, she was disgraced.

A strict moral code also governed the raising of Victorian children. Children were required to show respect to their elders. Discussion of sex was rare. Despite the constraints placed on children's behavior, youthful high spirits found an outlet in games and play. Entertainment was centered in the home, where families assembled to play board and card games, sing around a parlor organ or piano, and, for the wealthier Americans, play croquet or lawn tennis.

A Godly Society

Religion permeated society. In 1890, there were 145 different Christian denominations with a total of nearly twenty-two million members. Families reserved the Sabbath for churchgoing, rest, and quiet. Despite fears that religious convictions were waning in the face of growing secularism, thousands responded enthusiastically to religious revivals.

By 1890, Victorian morality was challenged on several fronts. Science and the teachings of Charles Darwin had undermined traditional religious precepts. "The human soul shrinks from the thought that it is without kith or kin in all this wide universe," concluded an observer of the intellectual currents of the decade.

Sports and Leisure

While thinkers debated the impact of modern ideas on old-time religious verities, everyday Americans sought relaxation and recreation in the increasingly popular spectator sports. Among the upper and middle classes, football had emerged as second only to baseball (see Chapter 17) in its popular appeal. The first intercollegiate football game occurred between Princeton and Rutgers in 1869; the modern form of the game evolved as rules for scoring became established. Walter Camp, the unofficial coach at Yale University, devised the line of scrimmage and the requirement that a team gain five yards in three attempts in order to retain possession of the ball. Dividing the field into five-yard squares produced the "gridiron." With regular rules came also recruitment of talented athletes and intense interest in the sport among alumni. By 1890, the game held in New York City on Thanksgiving Day in which teams vied for the unofficial national championship drew crowds of up to forty thousand people.

Beyond the Gridiron

Boxing had a wider appeal for the masses. Irish American boxers dominated the sport, with **John L. Sullivan** the most famous champion. Some matches were held in secret and continued for as many as seventy-five bloody rounds. Gloves and formal rules appeared during the 1880s. Sullivan lost his heavyweight crown in 1892 to James J. "Gentleman Jim" Corbett in the first gloved title fight.

In 1891, James Naismith, an instructor at the Young Men's Christian Association Training School in Springfield, Massachusetts, wanted to develop a sport that could be played indoors during the winter. He devised an early form of basketball that soon spread across the nation.

Another popular diversion was bicycling. Before the development of the modern "safety" bicycle in the 1880s and the addition of pneumatic tires in 1889, cycling was a sport for those who could master the brakeless "ordinary" bikes with their large front wheels. But once technology put a convenient bicycle within the reach of the masses, the fad was on. Some ten million bikes were in use by 1900. Cycling led women to adopt looser garments and, according to some enthusiasts, eased childbirth. After the automobile appeared at the beginning of the twentieth century, the passion for bicycles receded.

Voices of Protest and Reform

Bicycles were not the only craze that swept the nation at the end of the 1880s. A best-selling book captured the fancy of the reading public. **Edward Bellamy,** a former reporter turned novelist, published a novel called *Looking Backward: 2000–1887* in 1888. Its main character, Julian West, had gone to sleep in 1887 and awoke in 2000. In the future he met Doctor Leete who told him how the world had changed during the 113 years he had been asleep. In the new industrial order of "Nationalism," efficiency and discipline had replaced the chaos of the late nineteenth century. Citizens served the state that in turn provided them with material rewards. Bellamy's argument made sense to many people because it offered the promise of a nation organized for a common purpose without the coercion of government.

Looking Backward sold hundreds of thousands of copies. "Nationalist" clubs sprang up to spread his doctrine. The fad ebbed quickly, but Bellamy's evocation of community and cooperative action was appealing in an increasingly competitive, capitalist society. Troubled individuals turned to their faith, to organization, and to political action to deal with their unease about the direction of the nation.

The Social Gospel

Religion offered one answer. As businesses grew, many clergymen had defended the inequalities of wealth and status that resulted. However, harsh dogma offended some of the younger members of the ministry. Walter Rauschenbusch, a Baptist clergyman in Rochester, New York, had seen firsthand the hardship and despair experienced by slum dwellers. He believed that it was necessary to "Christianize" the social order so as to bring it "into harmony with the ethical convictions which we identify with Christ."

Rauschenbusch's ideas came to be known as the *Social Gospel.* He and other ministers went into the city to preach the Gospel to poor slum dwellers. Washington Gladden spoke out from the First Congregational Church in Columbus, Ohio, and wrote a book entitled *Applied Christianity,* which was published in 1886. "The Christian moralist," he wrote, had to tell "the Christian employer" that the wage system "when it rests on competition as its sole basis is anti-social and anti-Christian." Similar doctrines were promoted within Judaism and Catholicism. The Social Gospel became a strong current in American culture.

John L. Sullivan
A famous Irish American boxing champion of the late nineteenth century.

Edward Bellamy
The author of *Looking Backward* (1888), a major protest novel.

Organized Women

Middle-class women spearheaded the reform efforts of the 1890s. The Woman's Christian Temperance Union (WCTU) expanded its role under Frances Willard, its president from 1879 to 1899. Its activities and causes now included missions to the urban poor, prison reform, and protests against male-dominated politics.

Women who had gained leisure time during the 1880s (see Chapter 17) transformed their literary and discussion clubs into groups with more ambitious agendas. In 1890 the General Federation of Women's Clubs (GFWC) was founded, with a core membership of two hundred clubs and some twenty thousand women on its rolls. The GFWC sponsored cultural and educational activities for working women and homemakers. In Chicago, women's clubs supported the Legal Aid Society and other "child-saving" endeavors.

The campaign to achieve woman suffrage had remained divided after the National Woman Suffrage Association and the American Woman Suffrage Association split. The rift was healed through the efforts of Lucy Stone Blackwell, and in 1890 the **National American Woman Suffrage Association** (NAWSA) was formed. The president was Elizabeth Cady Stanton; Susan B. Anthony succeeded her in 1892. Progress toward suffrage was slow at first. By the middle of the 1890s, only four states (Wyoming, Utah, Colorado, and Idaho) allowed women to vote. Nonetheless, NAWSA provided an important organizational foundation for future growth.

Other reform goals attracted the support of committed women. Josephine Shaw Lowell animated the Charity Organization Society (COS), which sent "friendly visitors" into urban slums to instruct residents. Homes were established for the impoverished mother and prostitute where she could obtain "Friends, Food, Shelter and a HELPING HAND." Florence Kelley of Hull House carried the ideas of the settlement movement into the more ambitious Illinois Women's Alliance in 1892. The New York City Working Women's Society protested harsh working conditions in New York in 1890; its activities led to the formation of Consumers' Leagues in other cities.

Although public opinion was not yet ready for a wide-ranging reform movement, these diverse examples of social criticism and constructive action taught lessons about the effects of industrialism that would shape the experience of the coming generation.

National American Woman Suffrage Association
This association was formed in 1890 through the efforts of Lucy Stone Blackwell, and its first president was Elizabeth Cady Stanton.

Looking Outward: Foreign Policy in the Early 1890s

Interest in the outside world was also growing. Many people thought the United States should play a larger role in world affairs. Their campaign for an expansionist foreign policy gained momentum slowly in the face of ingrained isolationism. Yet the nation could not remain aloof from a world that was becoming more competitive and interdependent.

In 1889 the United States was not a significant military or diplomatic force. The Army was small, consisting of fewer than twenty-five thousand men who served in isolated posts in the West to protect settlers. The Navy was equally insignificant. Sails and wooden vessels were the rule until the end of the 1880s when four steel ships were built. During the first Cleveland administration, additional modern ships were built, and in 1890 Congress appropriated funds for three battleships.

Overseas Markets and Foreign Policy

The Census Bureau announced the official closing of the "frontier" in 1890. As a result, some were concerned that the nation would have to expand internationally. Noting the size of the nation's industrial output, businesspeople and farmers worried about whether the home market could consume everything that factories and farms produced. Perhaps it would become necessary to gain access to overseas markets.

A quest for overseas markets did not drive American foreign policy. Official economic policy toward foreign trade was protectionist, and proponents of the protective tariff resisted efforts to lower trade barriers. Exporters lobbied for expanded foreign trade and reciprocal tariff legislation to lower foreign trade barriers, but their direct impact on policy and diplomatic decisions was less important than the general enthusiasm for a more aggressive policy that they generated.

The Roots of Imperialism

The example of other European powers engaged in a scramble for empire had a greater impact than did economic concerns. As Africa and Asia became colonies and protectorates of Great Britain, Germany, France, and other countries, Americans worried that they would be left behind. Advocates of empire said that a nation that did not expand would find itself unfit to survive in a competitive and dangerous world.

A leader in the movement for expansion was Captain Alfred T. Mahan of the U.S. Navy. Mahan's research into naval history led to his most important work, *The Influence of Seapower on History, 1660–1783,* published in 1890. More than a military historian, Mahan wanted his country to embark on the path to global greatness, and he believed that seapower was the way to achieve it. He told policy makers that the United States needed to expand its foreign commerce, construct a strong navy, and acquire overseas bases from which to operate. Of particular concern was a canal across Central America. Secretaries of the Navy from 1889 onward listened to Mahan, as did such future leaders as Senator Henry Cabot Lodge of Massachusetts and Theodore Roosevelt.

The notion of Anglo-Saxon supremacy also fed the new interest in foreign affairs. In *Our Country: Its Possible Future and Its Present Crisis* (1885), Protestant clergyman Josiah Strong contended that "God, with infinite wisdom and skill, is training the Anglo-Saxon race for an hour sure to come in the world's future." The popular author John Fiske traversed the country giving a lecture on "Manifest Destiny" that predicted "every land on the earth's surface" that was not already civilized would become "English in its language, in its religion, in political habits and traditions, and to a predominant extent in the blood of its people."

New Departures during the 1880s

American foreign policy became more activist as the new decade began (see Chapter 16). During the brief administration of James A. Garfield, Secretary of State James G. Blaine wanted to renegotiate the Clayton-Bulwer Treaty (1850) to give the United States control over any canal across Central America. Blaine hoped to create a Pan-American system that would promote stability and security in the Caribbean and South America. The end of the Garfield administration postponed any further action on Pan-Americanism for almost a decade.

The gradual movement toward an expanded foreign policy continued under Presidents Chester Arthur and Grover Cleveland. Secretary of State Frederick T. Frelinghuysen pursued treaties for trade reciprocity with nations such as Mexico, Santo Domingo, and Colombia. Frelinghuysen believed that these treaties would unite the interests of these countries with those of the United States. However, since the pacts involved concessions on the protective tariff policy, Congress declined to act on them.

Under Cleveland, the process slowed as the administration showed less enthusiasm for an expanded role around the world. Still, the size and quality of the Navy grew during the president's first term. When James G. Blaine returned to the State Department as Benjamin Harrison's secretary of state in 1889, the drive for an expansionist policy resumed.

The Pan-American Impulse

The idea of Pan-Americanism had remained alive during the 1880s, and invitations to a conference were sent out to Latin American countries in 1888. Delegates from nineteen nations gathered in Washington on October 2, 1889, for the first International American Conference. Blaine urged them to support the creation of a customs union and to work out procedures for settling their regional conflicts. Unwilling to accept what seemed to be the dominance of the United States, the conference declined to pursue these initiatives. In-

As secretary of state during the Harrison administration, James G. Blaine pursued an expansionist foreign policy that sought to develop a larger world role for the United States. One of the lasting achievements of his tenure was the Pan-American Union to promote greater unity among the nations of the Western Hemisphere.

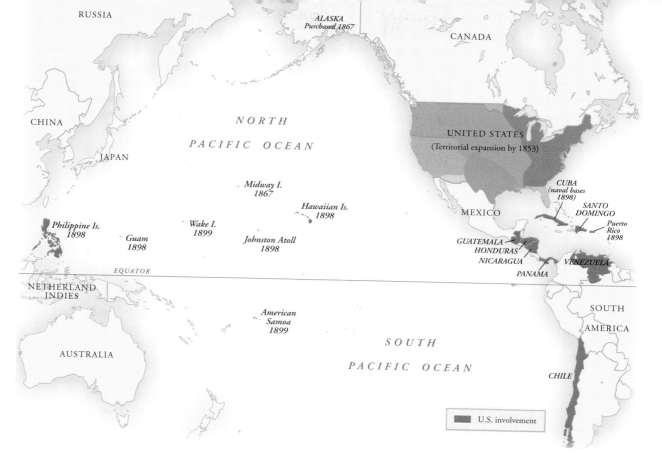

MAP 18.1 Expansion of the United States

In the late nineteenth century, the United States established a military and economic presence in the Pacific and Latin America. This map shows the areas in which the nation became involved and where new possessions in the Pacific were acquired.

stead, they established the International Bureau of the American Republics, which became the Pan-American Union in 1910. Thus, the conference laid the basis for better relations in the Western Hemisphere through the sharing of information and ideas.

Blaine's interest in improving trade with Latin America remained strong. He persuaded his Republican colleagues in Congress to include language allowing for reciprocity treaties in the McKinley Tariff Act of 1890. A number of products were placed on the free list, including sugar, molasses, coffee, and tea, with the understanding that the president could impose tariffs on such items if Latin American countries did not grant the United States similar concessions on its exports. Blaine used the reciprocity clause of the McKinley Tariff to negotiate treaties with South American countries such as Argentina, and U.S. exports increased. Republican protectionists remained cool to Blaine's idea, and the Democrats disliked reciprocity as well because it worked within the tariff system. Blaine's initiative indicated how difficult it would be to make an export-driven approach a part of the nation's trade policy.

The Harrison administration pursued a more aggressive foreign policy in two other key areas. Secretary of the Navy Benjamin F. Tracy urged Congress to appropriate money for a battle fleet. The lawmakers ultimately authorized four modern battleships. Tracy also carried out reforms within the Navy that led to more efficient weapons and a better fighting force.

The Hawaiian Involvement

The United States had long sought to exercise greater influence in Asia. Religious leaders saw China and other Asian nations as sources of potential converts. Business leaders and farmers thought of potential markets for products and crops. In the quest to enter Asia, the Hawaiian Islands seemed a logical stepping-stone. Missionaries had been working in the islands since the 1820s. Trade relations between the two countries had become stronger since the Treaty of Reciprocity, signed in 1875, which gave Hawaiian sugar and other products duty-free entry into the United States. In exchange, Hawaii agreed not to grant other countries any concessions that threatened the territorial or economic independence of the islands. Thus, Hawaii had become a virtual American protectorate. The relationship was further strengthened in 1887 when the treaty was renewed and the United States received the exclusive right to use Pearl Harbor.

Within Hawaii the white settlers and the native rulers clashed over the future of their country. The Hawaiian monarch, King Kalakua, had been inclined to accept the closer ties between the United States and his nation. He died in 1891, bringing to power his sister, Queen Liliuokalani. She believed that the white minority should not have dominant power.

Hawaiian politics became more complex after the enactment of the McKinley Tariff in 1890, which removed the duty-free status of Hawaiian sugar and granted bounties to American cane producers in Louisiana and beet sugar growers in the Rocky Mountain states. As a result, the Hawaiian sugar industry slumped. Americans in Hawaii and in the Congress called for annexation of the islands.

The Hawaiian Revolt

During 1892 the Hawaiian legislature and the queen argued over the presence and role of foreigners in the country. As the new year began, the queen dismissed the legislature and established a constitution that stripped white settlers of many of the powers they had enjoyed under the existing constitution. Proponents of annexation launched a revolt and called on the American Navy for help. The coup was successful. The queen gave in, and a provisional government was created. The United States agreed to a treaty of annexation with the pro-American rebels on February 14, 1893. It looked as if Hawaii would become a possession of the United States. Then the incoming president, Grover Cleveland, said that the treaty should not be ratified until the new administration took office.

Despite this temporary pause, the extent of American expansion during the Harrison administration was striking. The nation's ties to Latin America had been extended, and the fate of Hawaii seemed to be linked to that of the United States. In the Pacific, the United States had become one of the three participants, with Great Britain and Germany, in a protectorate over the strategic islands of Samoa. Harrison and Blaine had launched the nation on a path of expansion that would be pursued throughout the 1890s. For the moment, however, internal ferment captured the nation's attention.

The Angry Farmers

Of all the groups who found themselves at odds with the direction of American society between 1887 and 1893, the unhappy farmers of the South and West had the greatest impact on the nation. The anger of the farm sector first attracted national attention during the elections of 1890.

A Democratic Landslide

In those contests, the Republicans emphasized their achievements in the "Billion Dollar Congress." They confronted an aroused and cohesive Democratic party that took advantage of a host of grievances among voters in the Midwest. Republicans in Illinois, Wisconsin, and Iowa had pushed an agenda of social change. State legislatures passed laws to implement the prohibition of alcohol. Other measures required that schools chartered by a state teach subjects in English rather than in the languages of immigrant children. Still other laws restricted activities on the Sabbath. The Democrats realized that they could win the votes of the Catholic and German Lutheran voters who disliked these policies.

An appeal to the pocketbook strengthened the Democratic campaign. Party workers told homemakers that the McKinley tariff would raise the cost of living. The Democrats

Populist Party Platform, 1892

When the Populist party wrote its platform in 1892, Ignatius Donnelly of Minnesota composed a stinging indictment of the existing political system. His words convey some of the passions that fueled the third party movement during the early 1890s. The reference to isolating voters at the polling places alludes to the use of the secret nonpartisan ballot rather than the party-oriented ballots of the earlier years of the Gilded Age.

Preamble

The conditions which surround us best justify our cooperation; we meet in the midst of a nation brought to the verge of moral, political, and material ruin. Corruption dominates the ballot-box, the Legislatures, the Congress, and touches even the ermine of the bench. The people are demoralized; most of the States have been compelled to isolate the voters at the polling places to prevent universal intimidation and bribery. The newspapers are largely subsidized or muzzled, public opinion silenced, business prostrated, homes covered with mortgages, labor impoverished, and the land concentrating in the hands of capitalists. The urban workmen are denied the right to organize for self-protection, imported pauperized labor beats down their wages, a hireling standing army, unrecognized by our laws, is established to shoot them down, and they are rapidly degenerating into European conditions. The fruits of the toil of millions are boldly stolen to build up colossal fortunes for a few, unprecedented in the history of mankind; and the possessors of these, in turn, despise the Republic and endanger liberty. From the same prolific womb of governmental injustice we breed the two great classes—tramps and millionaires. . . .

Assembled on the anniversary of the birthday of the nation, and filled with the spirit of the grand general and chief who established our independence, we seek to restore the government of the Republic to the hands of the "plain people," with which class it originated. We assert our purposes to be identical with the purposes of the National Constitution; to form a more perfect union and establish justice, insure domestic tranquility, provide for the common defence, promote the general welfare, and secure the blessings of liberty for ourselves and our posterity. . . .

Questions to Consider

1. What issues form the basis of the complaints that the framers of the People's party are advancing?

2. What subjects from Chapters 17 and 18 are referred to in this paragraph?

3. How are Populists reacting to the rise of industrialism and the commercialization of agriculture?

4. How many of the issues mentioned here are still being debated in the United States?

Explore additional primary sources related to this chapter on the *American Passages* Web site: http://history.wadsworth.com/ayersbrief02.

---

also tapped into racial fears in the southern and border states. The results in November 1890 shocked Republicans. Their numbers in the House of Representatives dropped from 166 to 88, and the Democrats controlled 235 seats.

The Rise of the Populists

Political observers, however, noted another striking phenomenon: a new political force had appeared. Candidates identified with the Farmers Alliance, an agrarian protest group, had made impressive gains in the South and West. When the votes were counted in November 1890, the extent of farmer discontent was clear. Alliance candidates had won nine seats in the House of Representatives; they had also elected two members of the U.S. Senate. Alliance men dominated a number of southern state legislatures, and they showed strength in midwestern states such as Kansas, Nebraska, South Dakota, and Minnesota.

The crisis in southern and western agriculture had been building for decades. As productivity increased between 1865 and 1885, the prices of farm products declined. A bushel of wheat brought almost $1.20 in 1881 but just under 70 cents a bushel in 1889. Farmers had to plant more acreage to cover their costs, but the increased production that resulted further depressed crop prices.

Two other grievances were the debts that farmers owed and the costs of moving their crops to market. During the 1880s western farmers had borrowed from mortgage loan companies in the East to buy land and equipment. When farm prices declined, paying off debts became increasingly difficult. In the South, where sharecropping and farm tenancy tied many farmers to the credit that the "furnish merchants" provided, the slide in cotton prices meant that farmers' debts to the merchant increased each year. Farmers seemed trapped in a cycle of debt and dependence.

The Targets of Farm Complaints

Another villain in the eyes of the farmers was the railroad. Growers in the plains states complained that the railroads discriminated against them in favor of manufacturers and middlemen. The railroads had this power, critics said, because they corrupted the political process.

The system of money and banking also attracted the scorn of western and southern farmers. Every dollar in circulation had to have an equal amount of gold bullion behind it to keep the nation's currency on "the gold standard." Gold was stored in banks and at the U.S. Treasury. International production of gold was static and, as a result, the amount of money in circulation did not keep pace with the growth of the population. The currency became deflated as the value of the dollar appreciated. Wheat farmers on the plains or cotton growers in the South had to work harder and harder to maintain the same level of income. The thoughts of many farmers naturally turned to ways in which the currency might be inflated—that is, ways of putting more dollars into circulation.

The complaints of these farmers were genuine, but workable solutions were another matter. Farm prices were low as a result of the expanding acreage under cultivation. One long-term solution was the consolidation of small farms into larger, more efficient agricultural businesses. Such a process would occur later in the nation's history. But at the end of the nineteenth century, it ran counter to the widely held belief in the importance of small landowners to the health of a democratic society.

The problem of debt was equally complex. Farmers on the plains, for example, had purchased land whose value was expected to increase, and they now faced the ruin of their ventures. Interest rates were not as high as they believed, nor were mortgage companies as tyrannical as agrarian complaints indicated. The prevailing perception among farmers in the South and West, however, was that they were the victims of a system that took no heed of their needs or interests.

The Farmers Alliance

The campaign to improve the lives of southern and western farmers had begun during the 1870s (see Chapter 16) and slowly gathered momentum for more than a decade. The Patrons of Husbandry (the Grange) had been active between the late 1860s and the end of the 1870s when economic recovery from the Panic of 1873 eased the sense of crisis among farmers. The Farmers Alliance had been formed in Texas to stop horse thieves in Lampasas County. After some early troubles, it had emerged as the Texas Farmers Alliance in 1884. Elsewhere in the South, angry farmers had organized into alliances and associations that expressed their grievances.

The proposed solutions went through three broad stages. In the first phase the southern and western farmers looked toward cooperative action. A leader in this effort was a Texan named Charles W. Macune, who became president of the Texas Alliance in 1886. He wanted to build on local alliances to set up Alliance exchanges and cooperatives across the South. The theory was that these institutions could provide farmers with supplies and equipment at a cost below what the "furnish merchants" and local retailers charged. They would also enable the farmers to gain greater control over the marketplace. To spread the creed of the cooperatives, the Alliance relied on individual organizers or "lecturers" who fanned out across the region. Newspapers that supported the Alliance cause reprinted speeches and letters stating the complaints of agrarians and the merits of cooperation.

Cooperatives proved easier to organize than to sustain. Marketing crops at a time other than harvest season required capital because it was necessary to store the crops until prices rose. The farmers did not have the resources to make such a scheme work. It also proved difficult to obtain the lower prices sought by the cooperatives. A complex distribution system moved goods across the country, and that process had certain inherent costs no matter who controlled it. By 1889 it was evident that cooperatives alone could not solve the problems of the southern and western farmer.

The Rising Tide of Farm Protest

Although economic success eluded the Alliance between 1886 and 1890, its political power grew. The ideology of cooperative action appealed to farm families who often were isolated from one another. The Alliance meetings brought farmers together to hear speeches, enjoy entertainment, and share experiences. The Alliance thus built on shared emotion among farmers as the 1890s began.

Some members of the Alliance saw African American farmers as potential allies. The Colored Farmers' National Alliance and Cooperative Union was formed in 1886. Cooperation between the black Alliance and its white counterpart was uneasy, however. Whites were usually landowners, even if impoverished ones; blacks tended to be either tenants or farm laborers. The problem was revealed in 1891 when the Colored Alliance tried to get higher wages for cotton picking. A strike for that purpose, organized by a black leader named Ben Patterson in Lee County, Arkansas, was met with violence. Fifteen of the strikers, including Patterson, were lynched, and the Colored Alliance vanished.

A Kansas wheat harvest in the 1880s reflects the commercialization of agriculture that fueled farm protest against falling crop prices.

As the farm depression worsened during years of drought and falling crop prices, branches of the Alliance gained members in the Dakotas, Nebraska, and especially Kansas. By 1889 it was apparent that concerted national action was a logical next step. Representatives of these various organizations met at St. Louis in December 1889. Out of their deliberations came the **National Farmers' Alliance** and Industrial Union. The delegates agreed to leave out the word "white" from the organization's requirements, although state organizations in the South could continue to exclude black members. Three key northern states, Kansas and the two Dakotas, joined the national organization.

National Farmers' Alliance
This group led to the emergence of the Populist party.

The Subtreasury Plan

Charles Macune offered the most important policy proposal of the conference, the *subtreasury plan*. Macune recognized that the major problem that confronted cotton and wheat farmers was having to sell their crops at a time of the year when prices were at their lowest point. To get around this obstacle, he envisioned a system of government warehouses or subtreasuries where farmers could store their crops until prices went up. To bridge the months between storage and selling, the farmers would receive a certificate of deposit from the warehouse for 80 percent of the crop's existing market value. The charge for this service would be a 1 or 2 percent annual interest rate. Farmers would sell the crops for higher prices, repay their loans, and keep the resulting profits.

The subtreasury plan had some weaknesses. If a majority of wheat or cotton farmers waited until prices rose and then sold their crops, the market glut would force prices down again. The certificates that the farmers would have received for storing their crops at the subtreasury warehouses would represent another form of paper money. Beyond that, the idea involved a large expansion of government power in an era when suspicion of federal power was still strong. Nevertheless, to its agrarian advocates, the subtreasury seemed to be a plausible answer to the harsh conditions they confronted.

The Alliance in the 1890 Election

During the 1890 election, the protest movement poured out its energy in speeches. The Alliance attracted much attention. In Kansas it represented an entirely new third party. A candidate for Congress, Jeremiah Simpson of Kansas, attacked an aristocratic opponent known as "Prince Hal." Princes, Simpson said, "wear silk socks. I don't wear any." From that moment on he was known as "Sockless Jerry Simpson."

At a time when women took little direct part in politics, the Alliance allowed some female speakers to address audiences. One of them, Annie Diggs, came to Kansas during the 1870s. After some years in the East, she was working for a Topeka, Kansas, newspaper as the 1890 campaign got under way. Her speeches proved to be crowd-pleasers. Even more charismatic was Mary Elizabeth Lease. Her enemies changed her middle name to Ellen, which rhymed with "Yellin." She coined several phrases that became memorable parts of the agrarian cause. Kansas farmers, she said, should "raise less wheat and corn, and more hell."

The Alliance's success in the South and West led their leaders to consider mounting a third party campaign during the next presidential election. To ponder this important decision, they gathered in Ocala, Florida, in early December 1890. Their platform became known as the Ocala Demands. They included the subtreasury program, abolition of private banks, regulation of transportation facilities, and the free and unlimited coinage of silver into money at a fixed ratio to gold. The Alliance did not decide to become a third party. That issue was put off until February 1892 to allow the legislatures that had been elected with Alliance support to show what they could accomplish.

During the ensuing months cotton prices fell sharply and the Alliance lost members. Facing increasing hostility from Democrats in the South, the Alliance men looked more favorably on the idea of forming a third party. The national meeting scheduled for February 1892 appeared to present an opportunity to assemble a political party to contest the presidency. There was already a name for the new party: the People's party, or Populists.

The People's Party

The delegates met in St. Louis and quickly decided in favor of forming a third party. The Populists' first national convention would be held in Omaha, Nebraska, on a symbolic date, July 4, 1892. Their prospective candidate was Leonidas L. Polk, a North Carolinian who could bridge the gap between northern and southern Populists. But Polk died suddenly on June 11, 1892. With Polk gone, the Omaha Convention chose James B. Weaver, a long-time third party politician from Iowa. His running mate was James G. Field of Virginia.

The party's platform took a stern view of the state of the nation. It proclaimed that "We meet in the midst of a nation brought to the verge of moral, political, and material ruin. Corruption dominates the ballot box, the legislatures, the Congress, and touches even the ermine of the bench." The specific planks endorsed the subtreasury, free coinage of silver, and other reform proposals.

From the Subtreasury to Free Silver

By 1892 it was evident that Congress was not going to implement the subtreasury plan. Attention turned instead to another Populist proposal: free coinage of silver. To expand the currency, raise prices, and reduce the weight of debt on those who owed money, the best solution, Populists contended, would be to base the nation's currency on both gold and silver. If silver were coined into money at a ratio of sixteen to one with gold, there would soon be ample money in circulation.

The country needed controlled inflation. However, the market price of silver stood at more like twenty-five to one, relative to gold. A policy of free coinage would lift the price of the white metal in an artificial way. As a result, people would hoard gold, silver thus would continue to lose value, and inflation would accelerate.

The **Populist party** rejected these arguments. They maintained that "money can be created by the government in any desired quantity, out of any substance, with no basis but itself." The idea of crop supports underlying the subtreasury plan and the manipulation of the money supply that could be achieved through free coinage of silver advocated by the Populists would become common ideas during the twentieth century. But in 1892 they seemed radical to many Americans.

Populist party
Also known as the People's party, they held their first national convention on July 4, 1892. The party platform took a stern view of the state of the nation, with planks endorsing the subtreasury, free coinage of silver, and other reform proposals.

The Presidential Election of 1892

The Republicans and Democrats had watched the emergence of Populism with a mixture of bewilderment and apprehension. They sensed that something important was happening and wondered how to respond. For the moment, the familiar routines of political life went on. The elections of 1890 had left the Republicans shocked at their losses and aware that President Harrison was not a strong candidate for reelection. The alternative to Harrison was Blaine, and he made a brief run at the nomination during the spring of 1892. It was a doomed effort, however, and Harrison was unenthusiastically renominated.

The Democrats felt more confident. Their candidate was Grover Cleveland, who easily won a third nomination from his party. Although he strongly favored the gold standard, he did not stress the point. Some party leaders in the South and West saw silver as the answer to the depression and the threat of Populism. Cleveland muted his real beliefs to keep these Democrats willing to vote for him. In some western states the Democrats and the Populists struck deals and "fused" their two tickets, with Cleveland getting the electoral votes and the Populists electing state candidates.

The 1892 campaign was quiet on the surface. The political tradition at that time said that incumbent presidents should not make a formal reelection campaign. As a result, Harrison did not make speeches. That suited his challenger as well, and Cleveland stayed home too. The intense, military-style campaigning of the post–Civil War era, with the ranks of marching men parading through the streets, was passing from the scene.

Labor unrest marked the election of 1892. The most famous incident occurred in Homestead, Pennsylvania, in the company town that housed workers at Andrew Carnegie's steel mills.

The Homestead Strike

One significant event revealed the social tensions lying beneath the surface of politics. For workers at Andrew Carnegie's Homestead steel works outside Pittsburgh, Pennsylvania, the summer of 1892 was a time of misery and violence. The manager of the plant, Henry Clay Frick, cut wages and refused to negotiate with skilled workers who had unionized their craft. A strike resulted, and violence broke out when Pinkerton detectives stormed through the town of Homestead to allow strikebreakers to retake the mills. Detectives and workers died in the ensuing battle and state troops came in to restore order.

Brown Brothers

A few weeks later, an anarchist named Alexander Berkman shot and stabbed Frick. The industrialist survived his wounds, however, and the strike was broken. The walkout became a political issue that the Democrats exploited to their advantage. The **Homestead strike** seemed to many people to embody the tensions between capital and labor that industrialism had fostered.

Homestead strike
A labor uprising of workers at a steel plant in Homestead, Pennsylvania, in 1892 that was put down by military force.

The Populist Campaign

The Populists tried to make the same argument about the struggle between agriculture and capital. Weaver drew big crowds, but the Democrats in the South subjected him to personal abuse and accused the third party of promoting black rule and a return to Reconstruction. As a result, Weaver and his wife were pelted with rotten eggs and tomatoes. Other Populist campaigners attracted similar attention. Thomas E. Watson of Georgia had emerged as one of the leaders of the cause. Elected to Congress in 1890, he urged black and white farmers of the South to unite to fight their common enemy.

Democrats in the South turned weapons of intimidation and violence against their Populist foes. Watson's reelection campaign failed when the Democrats stuffed the ballot boxes. In the town of Augusta, his opponent won twice as many votes as there were registered voters. Other Populist candidates were counted out because the Democrats controlled the election machinery. When the votes were counted, the Democrats had held the South solid for Grover Cleveland.

The Election Results

On the national level, Cleveland gained a second term by a decisive margin. His plurality over Harrison was almost four hundred thousand votes, and he won in the electoral college with 277 votes to 145 for the Republicans. The Democrats also controlled both houses of Congress for the first time since before the Civil War. Weaver carried four states and won electoral votes in three additional states for a total of 22 electoral votes. His popular vote total reached just over one million.

For the moment, it appeared as if the Democrats had emerged as the majority party from the long stalemate of 1874–1890. They had captured the mood of discontent that was sweeping the country during the early 1890s. They had resisted Republican activism and an expanded role for the federal government. It remained to be seen how Cleveland would carry out the mandate to satisfy the many groups that had deserted the Republicans and appease the restless farmers who had supported Weaver and the Populists.

The "Great White City"

The American economy was in trouble at the beginning of 1893. Distracting the nation's attention from the gloomy forecasts was the prospect of a large popular spectacle that would sum up the state of civilization in the United States. The World's Columbian Exposition in Chicago commemorated Columbus's arrival in "The New World." Architect Daniel Burnham and his coworkers created a series of exhibition buildings that became known as the "Great White City." The exposition also summed up the nation's achievements.

The American Historical Association held its annual meeting in Chicago in 1893 to commemorate the exposition. There a young historian from the University of Wisconsin, Frederick Jackson Turner, offered his interpretation of how the United States had changed and the challenges it faced in the immediate future. In his paper "The Significance of the Frontier in American History," he stressed that the availability of free land and the influence of the frontier had played a significant role in the development of democracy in the United States. He inquired about what would happen to the nation now that the possibility of free land and a new life in the West was vanishing. Turner's "frontier thesis" became a powerful and controversial explanation of the way the nation had developed.

Summary

The City and the Farm

The twin problems of urbanization and the plight of rural America come together in this chapter as the cities expand and the farm belt faces a crisis. With the growth of industrialism, as outlined in Chapter 17, the towns and cities of the country swelled as residents of the rural areas and the new immigrants from Eastern Europe moved to the urban centers. As the center city and the suburbs extended beyond the old walking city of the first half of the century, transportation facilities pushed outward to provide the new population with more mobility. In the city itself, the problems of water, power, and living quarters pressed the local government for solutions. The urban machine and the city boss evolved as one means of addressing these needs.

In the farm belt of the South and West, the spread of farmland and the increased crops that followed meant that prices for farm commodities fell as production increased. With their debt burden growing and money ever harder to come by, angry farmers turned to political action for relief. The Farmers Alliance and the People's party gave voice to these sentiments and posed a threat to the two-party system. The inflationary solutions that the Populists proposed frightened middle-class Americans in the early 1890s who saw private property as under assault. As economic hard times for the nation at large ensued, the farm protest laid the groundwork for more wide-ranging social unrest.

Americans also became more conscious of their place in the world during these years. Overseas expansion seemed one means of addressing the social ills of society by finding new markets in Europe and Asia. A desire to share in the imperial sweep of Europe also motivated proponents of empire. A new Navy and a greater diplomatic role provided the foundation for more expansive initiatives during the second half of the decade.

Despite the progress and sense of optimism that pervaded many parts of society, the country still struggled with the discrimination against minorities that was so rooted in national traditions. Segregation of African Americans in the South took hold. Advocates of this racial policy pressed

©The Granger Collection, New York

The People's party used women to recruit new members and thus gave them a greater opportunity to be heard in political life. One of the most celebrated and controversial figures was Mary Elizabeth Lease of Kansas, here shown in a publicity photo for a lecturing career.

Courtesy of the author.

forward to make it a part of every phase of southern life. For Native Americans, the transition from the 1880s to the 1890s saw the end of the Indian wars that had raged since the Europeans first arrived centuries earlier. As wards of the national government, Native Americans faced economic exploitation and efforts to break down their cultural heritage.

The social progress of the period that this chapter covers left the United States still not yet a nation in a coherent and unified sense. More a collection of sections than an integrated state, the country was leaving its agrarian past for the uncertain blessings of a more industrial, more urbanized, and more international future. Troubling signs of economic difficulty in 1891 and 1892 made citizens wonder if prosperity might vanish and the hard times of the 1870s return. The next chapter describes the reality of those fears and the difference that a depression made to the bright hopes of this generation of Americans.

The tariff issue dominated the 1888 presidential election. Opponents of the tariff capitalized on ethnic tensions and anti-Chinese sentiments to depict the advocates of protection using Chinese labor to build a wall around American markets.

Making Connections Across Chapters

LOOKING BACK

The problems that urban and rural Americans faced in the period from 1887 to 1893 grew out of the achievements of industrialism during the preceding decade. This chapter discusses the consequences of rapid economic change and how Americans sought to use existing institutions to respond to these developments.

1. How did the growth of cities test the ways in which local governments operated?
2. Was the urban machine and city boss a constructive or destructive response to the ways in which life in metropolitan areas was being transformed?
3. What causes underlay the economic hard times in the South and West for the nation's farmers?
4. Why did inflation seem both necessary and appropriate to those who joined the Farmers Alliance?
5. What forces sparked interest in overseas expansion around 1890? What assumptions about the world did the cries for empire reflect?

LOOKING AHEAD

In Chapter 19 the United States will deal with the peak of farm protest during the economic depression of the 1890s. To understand what made the issues of the agrarian sector so volatile requires a good understanding of the roots of the unrest. This chapter has anticipated some of these issues.

1. What assumptions did Americans share about the role of government in this period? How do these premises differ from contemporary attitudes?
2. How well equipped was the political sector to deal with the issues that the Populists were advocating?
3. What attitudes about farm and city life in this period are still present in modern society?

RECOMMENDED READINGS

Ayers, Edward. *Southern Crossing: A History of the American South, 1877–1906* (1995). Very good on the changes in the South during the 1880s and 1890s.

Clanton, Gene. *Populism: The Humane Preference in America, 1890–1900* (1991). A sympathetic introduction to the unrest among southern and western farmers.

Crapol, Edward P. *James G. Blaine: Architect of Empire* (2000). An interpretive biography of one of the moving spirits behind American expansionism.

Cronon, William. *Nature's Metropolis: Chicago and the Great West* (1991). An interesting treatment of how Chicago grew and interacted with the region it dominated.

Duis, Perry R. *Challenging Chicago: Coping with Everyday Life, 1837–1920* (1998). An insightful book about how Americans lived their lives in the industrial cities.

McMath, Robert C. *American Populism: A Social History, 1877–1898* (1993). A thoughtful survey of the forces behind Populism.

Perman, Michael. *Struggle for Mastery: Disfranchisement in the South, 1888–1908* (2001). A thorough synthesis of the ways in which blacks were excluded from politics in the South.

Schneirov, Richard. *Labor and Urban Politics: Class Conflict and the Origins of Modern Liberalism in Chicago, 1864–1894* (1998). Examines the impact of urban industrial growth on politics in a major American city.

Sklar, Kathryn Kish. *Florence Kelley and the Nation's Work: The Rise of Women's Political Culture, 1830–1900* (1995). An excellent biography of an urban reformer in Chicago in the 1890s.

Williams, R. Hal. *Years of Decision: American Politics in the 1890s* (1993). A fine introduction to the decade.

AMERICAN JOURNEY ONLINE AND INFOTRAC COLLEGE EDITION

Visit the source collections at http://ajaccess.wadsworth.com and infotrac.thomsonlearning.com and use the Search function with the following key terms to explore documents, images, audio and video clips, articles, and commentary related to the material in this chapter.

Benjamin Harrison

Edward Bellamy

National Farmers Alliance

Jane Addams

Sherman Antitrust Act

Wounded Knee

Emily Dickinson

Homestead strike

Ida Wells-Barnett

Grover Cleveland

Ellis Island Woman

suffrage

ONLINE PRIMARY SOURCES

Here are some examples of the many primary sources related to this chapter that you will find on the *American Passages* Web site: http://history.wadsworth.com/ayersbrief02.

An act to prohibit the coming of Chinese laborers to the United States, 1888

Jane Addams, "First Days at Hull-House," 1910

Richard Croker on Tammany Hall, 1892

The site also offers self-quizzes, exercises, and many additional resources to help you study.

CHAPTER 19

Domestic Turmoil and Overseas Expansion

1893–1901

URING THE 1890S, THE SOCIAL PROBLEMS ACCUMULATING SINCE THE Civil War reached crisis proportions. An economic depression that began in 1893 sent shockwaves throughout the country. With millions out of work and faith in the institutions of the nation at a low point, the major political parties looked for solutions that would satisfy voters. In the middle part of the decade, the Republicans emerged as the majority party, with the divided Democrats in disarray and the Populists unable to transform their protest into a viable third party. The election of 1896 brought **William McKinley** to the White House.

As the condition of the economy improved at the end of the 1890s, Americans looked outward to an empire in the Caribbean and the Pacific. A war with Spain brought territorial gains and a debate about whether overseas possessions meant fundamental change. By 1900 the United States had assumed a world role.

William McKinley
The twenty-fifth president of the United States, he won by the largest majority of popular votes since 1872.

The Panic of 1893 and Its Consequences

Grover Cleveland began his second term as president on March 4, 1893. In May 1893 the weakened economy went into a collapse that became known as the Panic of 1893. The depression that followed lasted for four years.

Business had expanded during the late 1880s. In 1891 and 1892 investors turned cautious, worried about the soundness of the banking system and the stability of the currency. Banks failed as depositors pulled out their funds and hoarded cash. Individuals cut back on purchases and sought to protect their investments. Business activity slowed, workers were laid off, and businesses cut back on production.

Effects of the Depression

By the end of 1893, some six hundred banks had failed, 119 railroads were bankrupt, and an estimated fifteen thousand businesses had closed. By early January 1894, two and a half million people were unemployed.

The depression fell hardest on the average workers and their families. The expansion of industry meant that workers had become more dependent on the jobs that corporations provided. When these jobs vanished, there were no unemployment insurance payments, no government benefits, and no temporary jobs programs to bridge the gap between a living wage and poverty.

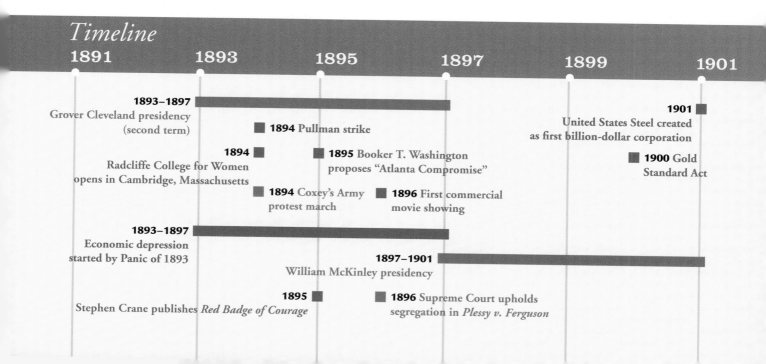

Timeline

1891   **1893**   **1895**   **1897**   **1899**   **1901**

1893–1897
Grover Cleveland presidency
(second term)

1894 Pullman strike

1901
United States Steel created
as first billion-dollar corporation

1894
Radcliffe College for Women
opens in Cambridge, Massachusetts

1895 Booker T. Washington
proposes "Atlanta Compromise"

1900 Gold
Standard Act

1894 Coxey's Army
protest march

1896 First commercial
movie showing

1893–1897
Economic depression
started by Panic of 1893

1897–1901
William McKinley presidency

1895
Stephen Crane publishes *Red Badge of Courage*

1896 Supreme Court upholds
segregation in *Plessy v. Ferguson*

States and cities endeavored to provide some relief for those out of work. Daily newspapers distributed food, clothing, and fuel to the needy. Charitable organizations coordinated volunteer efforts, but these private endeavors did not meet the needs of most of the unemployed. Most well-off Americans believed the federal government should not intervene to alleviate a depression. As a result, people slept in the parks, camped out in railroad stations, and sought food at the soup kitchens that appeared in the big cities. Angry poor people called the soup kitchens "Cleveland Cafés."

To deal with the economic slump, Cleveland proposed a simple solution: repeal of the Sherman Silver Purchase Act of 1890. That law had specified that the government buy a fixed amount of silver each month. Cleveland argued that the law produced inflation, undermined business confidence, and caused investors to take money out of the nation's gold reserve at the Treasury Department. If the amount of the reserve fell below $100 million, it would be regarded as a sign that the credit of the United States was in danger. In fact, the amount was largely a psychological issue and did not measure the nation's economic condition. To people in 1893, however, it was a crucial symbol of national confidence in the nation's credit.

In August 1893 Cleveland called a special session of Congress to repeal the Sherman Act. His own party was badly split over the issue of money. Northeastern party members believed in the gold standard with what resembled religious fervor. In the South and Far West, Democrats argued with equally passionate conviction that what the nation needed was more money in circulation through the free and unlimited coinage of silver into money at the fixed ratio to gold of 16 to 1. By asking his party to repeal the Sherman Act, Cleveland was inviting Democrats to wage war against each other.

The Special Session

Congress convened for its special session in August 1893. Over the protests of his party, Cleveland insisted that Congress repeal the Sherman Act. With the aid of Republican votes, he won the battle. The bill repealing the Sherman Act was signed into law on November 1, 1893.

Having blamed the Sherman Act for the depression, Cleveland had staked his party's political future on a turnaround in the economy. It did not come. Confidence in the dollar grew and the flow of gold out of the country eased somewhat, but as the new year approached, there was no evidence of better times ahead. More railroads failed, more businesses closed, and more people were laid off to join the millions who were already unemployed.

The Tariff Disaster

The Democrats now had to deal with the tariff issue. Their control over Congress was precarious, especially in the Senate. As a result, Senate Democrats had to write a tariff bill that in some instances raised customs rates on key products such as sugar, coal, and iron. The law fell far short of the tariff reform that the Democrats had promised in 1892.

Congress finally passed the Wilson-Gorman Tariff Act in August 1894. It reduced rates on wool, copper, and lumber, and raised duties on many other items. The measure repealed the reciprocal trade provisions of the McKinley Tariff that had aimed at opening up markets. To make up for lost revenues, the Wilson-Gorman bill added a modest tax on personal incomes. Disgusted with the outcome, Cleveland let the bill become law without his signature.

The Industrial Armies

Outside of Washington, 1894 was a year of unrest. As the hard times lingered, some of the unemployed decided to present their grievances to the nation's leaders. Those out of work wandered across the country seeking some haven where they could find a job or help. Their presence frightened the nervous middle class.

Some of the unemployed formed "Coxey's Army," uniting behind Jacob S. Coxey, a businessman from Massillon, Ohio. On Easter Sunday 1894 he left for Washington with three hundred supporters to petition for a program of road building paid for by $500 million of paper money. Coxey and his son, "Legal Tender Coxey," headed the procession, which included more than forty reporters covering the protest. Slowly and painfully, the "Commonweal Army of Christ" approached Washington.

The climax for Coxey and his followers came on May 1, 1894, when they reached Capitol Hill and tried to present their demands to Congress. Police intercepted Coxey, clubbed him, and then arrested him for trespassing and "walking on the grass." However, the spectacle of so much protest undermined the political credibility of the Cleveland administration.

The Pullman Strike

Even more devastating to the president was the major railroad strike that erupted shortly after the Coxey episode ended. **George Pullman,** the developer of the railroad sleeping car, had created a model town outside Chicago where his employees were to live. Pullman, Illinois, was often cited as an example of how a "company town" could see to every need of the worker and thus eliminate the need for unions or strikes. Employees who lived in Pullman experienced a reality that was far different from the rosy picture of life in the "model" town. The prices workers paid for services often ran 10 percent above what was charged in other communities.

When Pullman laid off employees and trimmed wages for others, he did not reduce the rents that his workers paid. As a result, in May 1894 the workers went out on strike. The strikers asked railroad workers across the nation not to handle Pullman's cars. The response from the American Railway Union (ARU) and its president, **Eugene Victor Debs,** was cautious at first. But by late June the ARU decided not to move trains that had Pullman cars attached to them.

George Pullman
Developer of the railroad sleeping car and creator of a model town outside Chicago where his employees were to live.

Eugene V. Debs was the leader of the American Railway Union that struck in sympathy with the workers in the Pullman Palace Car Company. His experience in this labor dispute helped persuade Debs to become a leader of the Socialist party.

Eugene Debs
Leader of the American Railway Union, which struck in sympathy with the workers at the Pullman Palace Car Company. This labor dispute experience helped persuade Debs to become a leader of the Socialist party.

Pullman strike
Strike by railway workers that led to nationwide unrest in 1894.

A National Railroad Strike

At its height the **Pullman strike** involved one hundred twenty-five thousand men representing twenty railroads. The commerce of the nation stalled. The ARU did not interfere with the mails lest that action arouse the opposition of the federal government. Their economic power could not match that of the railroads' General Managers' Association, which had influence with Cleveland and his attorney general, Richard Olney. On July 2, 1894, the president and the Justice Department obtained a court injunction to bar the strikers from blocking interstate commerce. Federal troops were ordered to Chicago.

Within several days violence erupted as angry mobs destroyed railroad property and equipment. "We have been brought to the ragged edge of anarchy," Olney told the press. Police and National Guard troops put down the disturbance, but the public gave Cleveland and the federal government the credit. For the moment, the president regained his popularity among conservatives in both parties.

Debs went to jail for violating the court's injunction, and the U.S. Supreme Court confirmed his sentence in *In re Debs* (1895). By doing so the Court gave businesses a potent way to stifle labor unrest. If a strike began, management could seek an injunction from a friendly federal judge, jail the union leaders, and break the strike. Union power stagnated throughout the rest of the decade.

Politically, the strike divided the Democrats once again. The governor of Illinois, John P. Altgeld, had protested Cleveland's actions. When the president overruled him, the governor resolved to oppose the administration's candidate in 1896. Across the South and West, bitterness against the president became even more intense. Hate mail flooded into the White House, warning him of death if he crossed the Mississippi River.

1894: A Realigning Election

The first chance for the voters to express themselves on the performance of the political system during the depression came in the congressional elections of 1894. The policies of the Cleveland administration had split the Democrats into factions that distrusted each other. In states where sentiment for silver was strong, the president was repudiated. For the Populists, on the other hand, these elections seemed to offer an excellent chance to establish themselves as a credible challenger to the supremacy of the two major parties.

The Republicans assailed the Democrats for failing to restore prosperity. Republican speakers urged a return to the policy of tariff protection that they had pursued under Benjamin Harrison. Party leaders, such as William McKinley, the governor of Ohio, crisscrossed the Midwest speaking to enthusiastic audiences. Soon the party was confident of victory.

The Republicans prevailed in one of the most decisive congressional elections in the nation's history. The Democrats lost 113 seats, and the Republicans regained control of the House of Representatives by a margin of 244 to 105. There were twenty-four states in which no Democrat won a federal office; six other states elected only one Democrat. In the Midwest 168 Republicans were elected to Congress, compared with 9 Democrats.

The significance of this outcome went beyond its immediate results. The stalemated politics of the late nineteenth century had ended in an election that realigned the nation's political alliances. A Republican electoral majority had arisen that would dominate American politics until 1929. Voters outside the Democratic South were inclined to support Republicans unless the party itself split. The decision foreshadowed a Republican victory in the presidential contest in 1896.

The Populist Dilemma

The Populists were almost as disappointed as the Democrats. To be sure, the total vote for the Populists had increased, but their delegation in Congress went from eleven members to seven. But by 1894 the Populists were strongly associated with the free coinage of silver. For industrial workers who had to survive on a fixed or declining income, higher prices arising from this inflationary policy held no attraction. The Populists told each other that they would do better in 1896, but they assumed that neither the Republicans nor the Democrats would adopt a free-silver position. In fact, the Populists' failure to mount a significant challenge to the major parties during the 1894 election signaled the end of their assault on the two-party system. The People's party had articulated the grievances of the agrarian United States with force and insight, but it had not proved capable of broadening its program to enlist industrial workers, owners of small businesses, and the middle class.

The Economic and Social Impact of Hard Times

The economic impact of the depression of the 1890s was profound. By 1894 the economy was operating at 80 percent of capacity. Unemployment ranged between 17 and 19 percent of the workforce.

As the amount of money in circulation dropped, the nation experienced severe deflation. In the South, for example, cotton prices fell from 8.4 cents per pound in 1892 to 4.6 cents per pound in 1894. Since a figure of 10 cents per pound was necessary to break even, southern cotton farmers faced the prospect of disaster. For people with money, their dollars bought more goods. Among those out of work and without funds, however, lower prices were little comfort. Families in the growing cities depended on wages for their livelihood, and for them the depression of the 1890s was difficult to endure.

With their husbands, fathers, and sons out of work, women joined the workforce in greater numbers during the decade. They gained employment in the expanding clerical fields, where they mastered typing and stenography. Traditional occupations such as teaching and nursing also attracted more women. In the factories, women worked in textile and clothing establishments, or they did piecework for tobacco processors and shoemakers. The earnings of these women were necessary for the survival of their families. When the male wage-earner brought home only $300 per year, and rents for a tenement dwelling were as much as $200 annually, the contributions of a daughter or wife were vital. However, the wages paid to women were as much as 40 percent below what men earned in industrial jobs.

The depression also brought young children back into the workforce. During the 1890s, the percentage of employed children between the ages of ten and fifteen rose to 18 percent, and 1,750,000 children were employed by 1900. One child worker was thirteen-year-old Fannie Harris, who told government investigators in New York that she earned $2 for the sixty hours of work she did each week in a necktie shop. When asked what she did with her money, she replied: "Gave it to my mamma." By the end of the century thirty states had passed child labor laws, but these were often ineffective.

Reshaping the Economy

In the economy as a whole, the depression brought important changes. As a result of the downturn, the number of bankrupt businesses had been growing. In railroads, for example, major systems such as the Union Pacific were in receivership. The investment banker J. P. Morgan refinanced many of these rail lines. The thirty-two railroads capitalized at over $100 million controlled nearly 80 percent of the mileage of the nation. Shippers complained that these railroads gave larger customers unfair advantages in the form of rebates. By the end of the decade there were increasing pleas from the South and Middle West to revive and strengthen the Interstate Commerce Commission.

In the 1890s "finance capitalists" like J. P. Morgan challenged the dominance of the "industrial capitalists" of the 1870s and 1880s who had built large enterprises in steel, oil, and railroads. These financiers launched a wave of corporate mergers. An average of three hundred companies a year were merged with larger firms. In New York a market for industrial stocks enabled bankers to raise capital. In the case of *U.S. v. E. C. Knight* (1895), the Supreme Court ruled that the Sherman Antitrust Act applied only to monopolies of interstate commerce and not to those solely of manufacturing. This decision made it more difficult to enforce the antitrust laws and, as a result, the government took little action against any of the mergers that occurred during the 1890s.

When the economy began to recover in 1897, the public's attention turned to the growth of large businesses and trusts. Consumers believed that it was unfair for a few men or businesses to dominate a single industry or control the price of commodities. There was, said newspaper editors, a "growing antagonism to the concentration of capital."

The Revolt against Bigness

The depression of the 1890s caused fear and apprehension across the United States. No part of the nation escaped the effects of the crisis. The accepted values of earlier generations came under scrutiny. Writers questioned whether the government should simply promote economic expansion and then allow fate to decide who prospered and who did not. For the first time many argued that government should *regulate* the economy in the interest of social justice. In discussion clubs in Wisconsin, at political rallies in Texas, and in the streets of New York and Boston, citizens wondered whether their governments at all levels should do more to promote the general welfare.

A growing number of social thinkers suggested that additional government action was necessary. In 1894 Henry Demarest Lloyd published a book entitled *Wealth against Commonwealth* that detailed what he believed the Standard Oil Company had done to monopolize the oil industry and corrupt the nation. "Monopoly cannot be content with controlling its own business. . . . Its destiny is rule or ruin, and rule is but a slower ruin." Lloyd called for public ownership "of railroads, telegraphs, and all the monopolies."

The economic hard times strengthened the resolve of the Social Gospel movement (see Chapter 18). The church, said Walter Rauschenbusch in 1893, should be the "appointed instrument for the further realization of that new society in the world about it." Other young people of the day echoed similar themes.

Women and Reform in the 1890s

In states like Illinois and New York, bands of women joined together as consumers to push for better working conditions in factories and fair treatment of employees in department stores. Social workers and charity operatives decided that better government and more enlightened policies could uplift the downtrodden. As one settlement worker put it, "I never go into a tenement without longing for a better city government."

Women's participation in the process of change was significant. Julia Lathrop and Florence Kelley worked for Governor Altgeld in Illinois improving state charitable institutions and inspecting factories. **Ida Wells Barnett** rallied African American women against lynching. Mary Church Terrell led the National Association of Colored Women, founded in 1896, in making the women's clubs in the black community a more effective force for change.

A leading voice for a new role for women was **Charlotte Perkins Gilman,** whose major work, *Women and Economics,* was published in 1898. The home, she argued, was a primitive institution that should be transformed through modern industrial practices lest it impede "the blessed currents of progress that lead and lift us all." Housework should be professionalized and homes transformed into domestic factories; women would then be free to pursue their own destinies, which could include social reform.

Ida Wells Barnett
An African American leader of an antilynching campaign.

Charlotte Perkins Gilman
An ardent advocate of feminism.

Liquor Control and Reform

The renewed emphasis on reform during the 1890s also affected the long-standing campaign to control the sale and use of alcoholic beverages. Opponents of alcohol had long sought to prohibit the sale of liquor through local and state laws. Now a new and more effective pressure group tactic appeared. In 1895 the Reverend H. H. Russell established the Anti-Saloon League in Oberlin, Ohio. Its organization relied on a network of local Protestant churches throughout the nation. They aimed to regulate saloons as tightly as possible. The League focused on a single issue, and it became a model for the kind of lobbying that would characterize reform campaigns during the first two decades of the twentieth century.

The prohibition campaigns in the South brought black and white women together in a brief alliance. In some parts of North Carolina, for example, white women organized chapters of the Woman's Christian Temperance Union (WCTU) among black women. When white volunteers did not appear, black women took over and set up their own organizations. Even as racial barriers rose in the South, women continued to work together to curb drinking until at the end of the 1890s it became politically impossible to do so.

To counter the drive for prohibition, brewers and liquor producers created lobbying groups of their own. Brewing associations appeared in battleground states such as Texas to coordinate strategies in local option elections and to get "wet" voters to the polls. Antiprohibition sentiment flourished among Irish Americans and German Americans in the cities and towns of the Northeast and Midwest. The struggles over liquor often pitted the countryside dwellers against urban residents who wanted liquor to remain available.

Reform in the Cities

Reform also appeared in the cities. In Detroit, Hazen Pingree had been elected mayor in 1889. He constructed his own political machine to pursue social justice through lower utility rates and expanded government services. That brought him into conflict with the streetcar companies and utilities that dominated Detroit politics. In Chicago, a British editor, William T. Stead, visited the city for the Columbian Exposition in 1893. What he saw in the slums led him to write *If Christ Came to Chicago* in 1894. Stead contended that the city needed a spiritual and political revival. He singled out the power of the street railway operator Charles T. Yerkes as particularly oppressive because of the high rates and poor service his companies provided. Stead's attack led to the formation of the Chicago Civic Federation, which sought to control gambling, clean up the slums, and limit the power of men like Yerkes.

By the mid-1890s these examples of urban reform sparked the creation of groups to address urban problems on a national scale. The National Municipal League came into existence in 1894. Over the next several years, reformers began to diagnose the ills of American cities and recommend solutions. "We are not unlike patients assembled in a hospital, examining together and describing to each other our sore places," said one participant at the First National Conference for Good City Government in 1894. Out of these debates came the ideas that would flourish during the Progressive Era a decade later.

Reform in the States

As the depression worsened, citizens looked to their state governments for answers and instead found political and social problems that rivaled the plight of the cities. Critics complained of corruption, political machines, and a breakdown of democracy. In Wisconsin Republican politician Robert M. La Follette built a political following by attacking the entrenched organization within his own party. Albert B. Cummins of Iowa attacked the power of railroads in his state, and Republicans in neighboring Kansas set up a Boss Busters League to challenge the party hierarchy. After his triumphs in the **Spanish-American War, Theodore Roosevelt** was elected governor of New York, where he displayed his vigorous leadership skills in publicizing the activities of large corporations and using state power to conserve natural resources.

The work of reform governors led to increased authority for these governments and greater reliance on experts and nonpartisan commissions in making decisions about public policy. Railroad commissions, public utility commissions, and investigative boards to oversee key industries were formed. By the end of the decade, however, observers believed that meaningful reform would come only when the federal government shaped national legislation to curb railroads and trusts engaged in interstate commerce.

Resistance from the Courts

Advocates of reform faced many obstacles. Among the most powerful were judges who upheld business interests in their decisions. The doctrine of *substantive due process* gave state and federal judges a way to block legislative attempts to regulate economic behavior. According to this doctrine, the due process clause of the Fourteenth Amendment did not apply only to the issue of whether the procedure used to pass a law had been fair. Judges might consider how the substance of the law affected life, liberty, and property. They could then decide whether the law was so inherently unfair that it would be unjust even if the procedures for implementing the statute were unbiased. This approach gave the judiciary the right to decide whether a law regulating business enterprise was fair to the corporation being supervised.

Judges also interpreted federal laws in ways that limited the effectiveness of efforts to curb corporate power. The same year (1895) that the Court issued the *E. C. Knight* decision, which limited the scope of the Sherman Antitrust Act, it also ruled in *Pollock v. Farmers' Loan and Trust Co.* that the income tax provisions of the Wilson-Gorman Tariff were unconstitutional.

A few jurists and lawyers, however, had doubts about this philosophy. In Massachusetts, Oliver Wendell Holmes Jr. had published a book on *The Common Law* in 1881. Holmes contended that "the life of the law has not been logic; it has been experience." By this he meant that judges should not base their rulings on abstract premises and theories but should consider the rational basis of a law in judging whether it was constitutional or not.

Conservative himself, Holmes was ready to defer to the popular will in legislative matters. If the Constitution did not prohibit a state from building a slaughterhouse or regulating an industry, his response was "God-dammit, let them build it." In Nebraska, Roscoe Pound was evolving a similar reality-based approach to legal thinking that became known as *sociological jurisprudence.* Louis D. Brandeis of Massachusetts was gaining a reputation as the "People's Lawyer" who believed that the legal system should serve small businesses and consumers as well as large corporations.

Spanish-American War
The conflict that brought the United States a world empire.

Theodore Roosevelt
The twenty-sixth president of the United States, the youngest president in the nation's history. He brought new excitement and power to the presidency as he vigorously led Congress and the American people toward progressive reforms and a strong foreign policy.

The Philosophy of Pragmatism

The philosopher William James of Harvard University evolved an explanation for what political and legal reformers were trying to do. He called it *pragmatism.* He believed that truth must demonstrate its value in the real world. To James, pragmatism meant "looking away from first things, principles, 'categories,' supposed necessities; and of looking towards last things, fruits, consequences, facts." His philosophy emphasized self-reliance and gritty reality. It appealed to a generation of reformers who sought practical solutions to the problems they saw in their communities and the nation as a whole.

Another spokesman for reform was a University of Chicago teacher and philosopher named John Dewey. In his major work, *The School and Society* (1899), Dewey contended that schools should undertake the task of preparing students to live in a complex, industrial world. The public school must do more than transmit academic knowledge for its own sake. As an institution, it should be a means of instilling democratic values and usable skills.

Literary Naturalism and Realism

During the 1890s, writers and artists turned to the world around them for inspiration and subjects. They preached the doctrine of realism, and they tried to capture the complexity of a natural world in which science, technology, and capitalism were challenging older values. William Dean Howells, a novelist, examined the impact of capitalism on workers and urban dwellers in New York City in *A Hazard of New Fortunes* (1890). **Stephen Crane** depicted the ways in which the city exploited and destroyed a young woman in *Maggie: A Girl of the Streets* (1893).

Two noteworthy practitioners of literary naturalism were Frank Norris and Theodore Dreiser. Norris wrote about California railroads in *The Octopus* (1901) and about the wheat market in Chicago in *The Pit* (1903). In Norris's Darwinian world, humanity was trapped in the impersonal grip of soulless corporations. In *Sister Carrie* (1900) Dreiser described how a small-town girl went to work in Chicago and was consumed by its temptations. These novels reached a large audience, and their depiction of characters caught in an amoral universe intensified the sentiment for reform.

By the 1890s, then, the currents that would come together as the Progressive Movement of the 1900–1920 period were already forming. Urban reformers, believers in the Social Gospel, politically active women, candidates angry with the established powers in their state's dominant party—all of these groups shared a pervasive discontent with the state of society.

African Americans and Segregation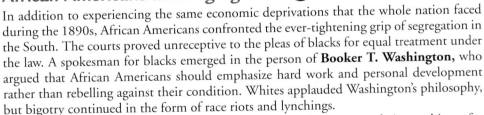

In addition to experiencing the same economic deprivations that the whole nation faced during the 1890s, African Americans confronted the ever-tightening grip of segregation in the South. The courts proved unreceptive to the pleas of blacks for equal treatment under the law. A spokesman for blacks emerged in the person of **Booker T. Washington,** who argued that African Americans should emphasize hard work and personal development rather than rebelling against their condition. Whites applauded Washington's philosophy, but bigotry continued in the form of race riots and lynchings.

Washington believed that African Americans must demonstrate their worthiness for citizenship through their own achievements. In 1895 he reached a national audience when he spoke at the Cotton States and International Exposition in Atlanta. His **Atlanta Compromise** told white America what it wanted to hear about African Americans.

"In all the things that are purely social, we can be separate as the fingers," Washington proclaimed, "yet one as the hand in all things essential to mutual progress." To his fellow blacks he said, "it is at the bottom of life we must begin" to create an economic base through hard work. Any "agitation of questions of social equality" would be "the extremest folly."

Washington's white audience gave him an enthusiastic response. Behind the scenes, Washington dominated the political lives of blacks, and even more secretly, he funded

Stephen Crane
Author of *The Red Badge of Courage.*

Booker T. Washington
A spokesman for blacks in the 1890s who argued that African Americans should emphasize hard work and personal development rather than rebelling against their conditions.

Atlanta Compromise
A program for African American acceptance of white supremacy put forth by Booker T. Washington.

Petition from the citizens of New Jersey to the U. S. Congress praying for Congress to make the act of lynching a crime in the United States, 1900

At the end of the nineteenth century, lynchings directed against blacks became a frequent occurrence in the South. Some concerned citizens in the North protested against these crimes, as this petition from individuals in New Jersey shows, but the federal government took no action against this wave of extralegal violence.

We, the undersigned petitioners, citizens of New Jersey, beg most respectfully to represent to your honorable bodies, the Senate and House of Representatives, the alarming state of the country in respect to the appalling prevalence in the Southern States, of that species of lawlessness known as lynching whereby inhabitants of that section are deprived of life without due process of law by gangs of irresponsible and wickedly disposed persons; that the victims of these barbarous outbreaks and outrages are usually members of the Negro race, and that the crimes imputed to them by their self-constituted executioners, but never proved, and for which they suffer death, have ranged all the way from petty larceny to murder; that Negroes have been hanged and shot in the South by lynching mobs on mere suspicion, or because they have incurred the odium of being politically troublesome to the community in which they resided; that human life is frightfully cheap in the South, and that a Negro's life has absolutely no value whatever there when a Southern mob scents his blood; that the local police power offers him under such circumstances no adequate protection and often times are in actual or virtual connivance with his murderers: WHEREFORE, your petitioners pray your honorable bodies to make the act of lynching a crime against

the United States, to provide for its commission the sternest pains and penalties, and to empower the President of the United States and to make it his duty to intervene whenever and wherever necessary with the armed force of the nation to prevent the commission of this atrocious crime, and to rescue any person or persons from the hands of any mob in any state of the Union, and for the better prevention of lynching your petitioners further pray your honorable bodies for the creation of a Central Detective Bureau at Washington with branch offices in various parts of the section or sections subject to this kind of lawlessness, for the purpose of collecting and transmitting information promptly to the President relative to the intentions and movements of lynching bodies, and that such information may be used in subsequent prosecuting proceedings against such individuals in the Courts of the United States for violation of the law made and provided in that behalf.

Questions to Consider

1. Why had lynching arisen in the South as an outgrowth of racial segregation?

2. What political purposes did lynching serve for believers in white supremacy?

3. What solutions did the citizens of New Jersey propose to deal with the problem?

4. Why would their ideas be difficult to enact in Congress in 1900?

Explore additional primary sources related to this chapter on the *American Passages* Web site: http://history.wadsworth.com/ayersbrief02.

Source: Petition presented to Congress, February 21, 1900, National Archives.

court challenges to segregation. In public, however, he came to symbolize an accommodation with the existing racial system.

A year later the Supreme Court put its stamp of approval on segregation. Homer A. Plessy's appeal of the Louisiana court's decision upholding segregation of railroad cars had taken four years to make its way to the Supreme Court (see Chapter 18). The Court heard oral arguments in the case in April 1896 and rendered its judgment five weeks later. By a vote of 7 to 1 in the case of ***Plessy v. Ferguson,*** the justices upheld the Louisiana law and, by implication, the principle of segregation generally. Writing for the majority, Justice Henry Billings Brown said that the Fourteenth Amendment "could not have been intended to

Plessy v. Ferguson
The 1896 Supreme Court case that approved racial segregation.

abolish distinctions based on color, or to enforce social, as distinguished from political equality, or a commingling of the two races upon terms unsatisfactory to either." In a dissenting opinion, Justice John Marshall Harlan responded that "Our Constitution is color-blind, and neither knows nor tolerates classes among citizens." This ruling determined the legal situation of African Americans for more than half a century.

As the political rights of blacks diminished, whites' attacks on them increased. During the North Carolina elections of 1898, race was a key issue that led to a Democratic victory over the Populists, Republicans, and their African American allies. Once whites had won, they turned on the black-dominated local government in Wilmington, North Carolina. Several hundred whites attacked areas where blacks lived in December 1898, killing eleven people and driving residents from their homes. Lynchings in the South continued at a rate of more than one hundred per year.

Although black Americans faced daunting obstacles in the 1890s, they made substantial progress toward improved living conditions. They founded colleges in the South, created self-help institutions in black churches, and developed pockets of well-off citizens in Washington, Boston, Baltimore, and Philadelphia. In the South black women pursued social reform in their states with impressive determination. The National Association of Colored Women, founded in 1896, sought to become, in the words of its president, Mary Church Terrell, "partners in the great firm of progress and reform."

Native Americans

In the years after the Battle of Wounded Knee (see Chapter 18), efforts to assimilate the two hundred fifty thousand Indians into the dominant culture went on. One favored method was to educate Native American children at schools either located on the reservation or many miles distant. The students were required to speak English, wear white people's clothes, and abandon their tribal ceremonies and religions. The most celebrated of these Indian schools was located in Carlisle, Pennsylvania, and was operated by Richard Henry Pratt between 1879 and 1904. "Transfer the savage-born infant to the surroundings of civilization," Pratt said, "and he will grow to possess a civilized language and habit." For many of the Indian children, however, these schools seemed more like a prison. They were malnourished, often treated cruelly, and stripped of their individuality. The goal of government policy seemed to be the extinction of the Indians' culture in the name of benevolent assimilation.

In trying to prepare Native Americans for life in mainstream society, institutions such as the Carlisle Indian School sought to take students away from tribal customs and have them emulate white practices. These pictures show a young Indian named Tom Torlino and his friends in their native clothes in 1886 and three years later in their school uniforms.

©Smithsonian Institution

©Smithsonian Institution

Foreign Policy and National Politics

Amid the political turmoil of the second Cleveland administration, foreign affairs pressed for attention. The nation stood on the verge of becoming a world power, and national leaders debated how to respond to increasing competition with powerful international rivals and the upsurge of nationalism among colonial peoples.

Diplomatic Problems: Hawaii and Venezuela

The first issue was that of Hawaii, left over from the last days of the Harrison presidency (see Chapter 18). Grover Cleveland was not convinced that the revolution that had occurred in the islands in 1893 represented the will of the Hawaiian people. Holding the treaty of annexation in limbo, he waited for the report of a special commission that he dispatched to Hawaii to investigate conditions. Believing that the native population backed Queen Liliuokalani, he refused to send the treaty to the Senate and asked instead for restoration of the native government. The revolutionary government declined to yield power, however, and in 1894 the administration granted it diplomatic recognition.

Another foreign policy crisis occurred in South America in 1894 when a dispute arose between Great Britain and Venezuela over the precise boundary line that separated Venezuela and British Guiana. In 1895 the new secretary of state, Richard Olney, sent a diplomatic note to London that asserted that the United States was "practically sovereign on this continent, and its fiat is law upon the subjects to which it confines its interposition." The British responded slowly, and when their answer finally arrived, it rejected the arguments of the Cleveland administration. The president asked Congress for the power to name a commission to decide the boundary dispute and enforce its decision. The British found themselves in a difficult position. In South Africa they were encountering problems that would eventually lead to the Boer War (1899–1902), and they had few European friends when it came to foreign policy. Accordingly they decided to arbitrate their quarrel with Venezuela through a joint Anglo-American-Venezuelan commission to resolve the dispute, and the crisis passed.

The Cuban Rebellion

The most dangerous foreign policy issue that confronted Cleveland stemmed from the revolution that Cubans launched against Spanish rule in February 1895. The beleaguered Spanish were unable to defeat the rebels in direct combat; instead, they drove the civilian population into cities and fortified areas. The "reconcentration" camps where these refugees were housed were disease-ridden and overcrowded. The architect of this harsh reconcentration policy was General Valeriano Weyler, nicknamed "The Butcher" for his cruelty to the Cubans who came under his control. These events strengthened the will of the Cuban rebels to achieve independence.

The American Stake in Cuba

The American public took a close interest in the Cuban situation. Religious denominations saw the brutality and famine of the rebellion as cause for concern and perhaps direct intervention. Sensational newspapers, known as the **yellow press,** because one of them carried a popular comic strip about "The Yellow Kid," printed numerous stories about atrocities in Cuba. **William Randolph Hearst,** publisher of the *New York Journal,* and Joseph Pulitzer of the New York *World* were the most sensational practitioners of this kind of journalism. The Cubans also established an office in New York from which their "junta" dispensed propaganda. These efforts aroused pro-Cuban sympathies among the American people.

President Cleveland tried to assist Spain in subduing the revolution through enforcement of the neutrality laws that limited shipments of arms to Cuba. He informed the Spanish that they might count on the good offices of the United States in negotiating an end to the fighting. This position suited Spain, which was following a policy of procrastination in the hope of quelling the revolt before the United States intervened. By the end of his administration, the president was trying to press Spain to make concessions to the Cubans, but he never challenged Spain's right to exercise its sovereignty over the island. Congress prodded the president toward more aggressive action, but he refused. As a result, when the end of the Cleveland administration approached early in 1897, his policy toward Cuba had failed.

yellow press (yellow journalism)
A type of journalism that stressed lurid and sensational news to boost circulation.

William Randolph Hearst
The most celebrated publisher of the yellow press.

The Election of 1896

The Cleveland administration did not recover politically from the disasters of 1894. The president's relations with the Democrats worsened. The reserves of gold were still shrinking, despite the repeal of the Sherman Silver Purchase Act in 1893. To bolster the reserves and bring in gold, the White House turned to selling government bonds. Eventually there were four bond sales that supplied needed currency for the treasury but also further alienated advocates of inflation and free silver within the president's own party. One angry Democratic senator said of the president: "I hate the ground that man walks on."

The Political Lineup

All three political parties confronted important challenges as the 1896 election approached. For the Republicans, the main task was to nominate a candidate who could lead the party to the White House. Their front-runner was William McKinley of Ohio, who had served in Congress between 1876 and 1890 and had been governor of Ohio from 1891 to 1895. He was a popular speaker and was identified with the protective tariff. With the aid of his close friend Marcus A. Hanna, an industrialist from Ohio, McKinley became the favorite for the Republican nomination. He attracted Republican voters because of his popularity within the party, his moderate record, and his abilities as a politician.

McKinley won on the first ballot at the Republican National Convention in St. Louis in June 1896. The only difficult issue was gold and silver. Eastern Republicans wanted the party to endorse the gold standard. The key plank contained that language, but it also conciliated pro-silver Republicans with a promise to seek wider international use of silver. The Republicans expected to wage a campaign centered on the tariff against a Democratic nominee burdened with the unpopularity of the Cleveland administration.

The Rise of William Jennings Bryan

The Democratic convention, however, took an unexpected turn. After the elections of 1894, the free-silver wing of the party dominated the South and West. Literature proclaiming the virtues of silver found a receptive audience. By 1896 it was clear that an articulate spokesman for the silver cause would appeal to many Democrats at their national convention.

Among the leading candidates for the nomination, however, none possessed the required excitement and devotion to silver. A young politician from Nebraska named William Jennings Bryan spoke frequently to Democrats about silver and urged leaders to think of him as a possible second choice should the convention deadlock. By the time the Democratic National Convention opened in Chicago in July 1896, there was a good deal of latent support for Bryan among the delegates.

The Cross of Gold

Bryan's chance came during the debate over whether the party platform should endorse silver. He arranged to be the final speaker on behalf of free silver. Bryan had a clear, musical voice that could be heard across the convention hall in the years before modern amplification systems. The speech he gave, entitled the "Cross of Gold," became a classic moment in American political oratory. He asked the delegates whether the party would stand "upon the side of 'the idle holders of capital,' or upon the side of the struggling masses?" His answer was simple. To those who wanted a gold standard, the Democrats would say: "You shall not press down upon the brow of labor this crown of thorns, you shall not crucify mankind upon a cross of gold."

The next day the convention nominated Bryan for president on a free-silver platform. As his running mate, it chose Arthur Sewall of Maine. Since the Democrats could not raise much in the way of campaign funds, Bryan decided to take his message to the voters in person. He prepared for an extensive nationwide campaign tour.

The Populists and the Campaign

The nomination of an outspoken advocate of free silver left the Populist party in disarray. They had delayed their national convention until after the two major parties had named their candidates. If the Republicans and Democrats picked men who endorsed the gold standard, the People's party would have the only genuine champion of free silver in the contest. Now the Populists faced a dilemma. If they failed to select Bryan as their candidate, they would be accused of depriving silver of any chance of victory. Yet if they went along with Bryan's nomination, there would be no need for their party.

The Populists wrestled with these problems at their national convention in St. Louis in late July. They ultimately decided to name Bryan as the presidential nominee, with Thomas E. Watson as their vice presidential choice instead of Sewall. The Democrats refused to accept this awkward compromise; all that Watson's nomination did was confuse the issue.

Bryan versus McKinley

Bryan set about trying to translate his popular acclaim into victory in the November election. His speaking tours were prodigious efforts. He traveled eighteen thousand miles and gave more than six hundred speeches; his audiences, estimated at a total of three million people, turned out to see "The Boy Orator of the Platte River."

To counter Bryan, the Republicans raised between $3.5 million and $4 million from fearful corporations. The Democrats charged that the Republicans and their business allies were coercing workers to vote for McKinley. Most industrial workers voted Republican because they feared the inflationary effects of free silver. Mark Hanna, who managed McKinley's campaign, used the party's substantial war chest to distribute several hundred million pamphlets to the voters. Republican speakers took to the campaign trail; party newspapers poured out information about the merits of the tariff and the gold standard.

The key to the Republican campaign was McKinley. He did not try to match Bryan's tours. Instead, he stayed home in Canton, Ohio, and let the voters come to him. As the weeks passed, more than seven hundred fifty

Ohio Historical Society Library

Candidate William McKinley meets a delegation of Italian Republicans in 1896.

thousand people stood in McKinley's yard to hear him deliver speeches about the dangers of free silver. "If free coinage of silver means a fifty-three cent dollar, then it is not an honest dollar," he said. These addresses were published daily in newspapers across the country. By mid-September the tide had turned against Bryan.

A Decisive Election

The result was the most decisive outcome since the 1872 presidential contest. McKinley had a margin of six hundred thousand popular votes and won 271 electoral votes to 176 for Bryan. Bryan ran well in the South, the plains states, and the Far West. McKinley dominated in the Northeast, the mid-Atlantic states, and the Midwest. Despite his appeals to the labor vote, Bryan ran poorly in the cities. Free silver might lead to inflation, an idea that had little appeal to workers on fixed incomes. McKinley's argument that the tariff would restore prosperity also took hold in the more industrialized areas of the country.

Candidate (Party)	Electoral Vote	Popular Vote
McKinley (Republican)	271 (61%)	7,104,779 (52%)
Bryan (Democratic, Populist)	176 (39%)	6,502,925 (48%)

MAP 19.1 Election of 1896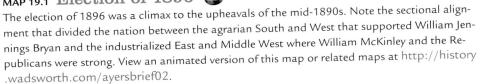
The election of 1896 was a climax to the upheavals of the mid-1890s. Note the sectional align-ment that divided the nation between the agrarian South and West that supported William Jen-nings Bryan and the industrialized East and Middle West where William McKinley and the Re-publicans were strong. View an animated version of this map or related maps at http://history.wadsworth.com/ayersbrief02.

The 1896 results confirmed the outcome of the 1894 election. The Republicans had established themselves as the nation's majority party. The South remained solidly Demo-cratic; the industrial North was Republican. By 1896 the nature of national politics was changing. The older issue of how much the government ought to promote economic ex-pansion was giving way to the new problem of whether the government should *regulate* the economy so as to relieve injustices and imbalances in the way that society worked. Bryan and the Populists had suggested that government should play a larger regulatory role. The voters had chosen instead to accept the economic nationalism of the Republicans as em-bodied in the tariff and the gold standard.

The McKinley Presidency: Achieving World Power

When Grover Cleveland left office in March 1897, he left a weakened presidency. McKin-ley revived the office during the four and a half years that followed. He improved relations with the press, which Cleveland had ignored; he traveled extensively to promote his poli-cies; and he used experts and commissions to strengthen the operation of the national government.

In domestic policy, McKinley persuaded Congress to enact the Dingley Tariff of 1897, which raised rates above those that the Wilson-Gorman Tariff contained. He also sought without success to convince European nations to agree to wider use of silver through an international agreement. As a result, when the Republicans gained secure control of both houses of Congress after the 1898 election, the Gold Standard Act of 1900 established gold as the basis of the nation's currency. The return of prosperity in the second half of 1897 also helped the administration. Gold discoveries in South Africa and Alaska inflated the currency by making more gold available.

The Road to Empire

From the beginning of his presidency, McKinley faced a growing crisis in Cuba. The administration took the position that any solution must be acceptable to the Cuban rebels. Because they would accept nothing less than the end of Spanish rule, there was little apparent basis for a negotiated settlement. During 1897, however, McKinley tried to persuade Spain to agree to a diplomatic solution. The problem was that no Spanish government could stay in power if it agreed to leave Cuba without a fight.

In the fall of 1897 the Spanish government moved toward granting the Cubans some control over their internal affairs. Foreign policy, however, was to remain in Spanish hands. The practice of moving Cubans into reconcentration camps was abandoned. However, the situation worsened during the early months of 1898. On January 12, 1898, pro-Spanish elements in Cuba rioted against the autonomy program. To monitor the situation, the White House decided to send a warship to Havana. The battleship *Maine* arrived there on January 25. Spain was pleased at this sign of normal relations, but the diplomatic problem continued. On February 1 Spain insisted that its sovereignty over Cuba must be preserved even if it meant resisting foreign intervention.

On February 9, 1898, newspapers in the United States published a letter written by the Spanish minister to the United States, Enrique Dupuy de Lôme, which the Cuban rebels had intercepted. The letter described McKinley as "weak and a bidder for the admiration of the crowd." These insulting remarks led to de Lôme's recall and resignation. De Lôme's other statements revealed that Spain was playing for time in its negotiations with Washington.

The Sinking of the *Maine*

Six days later, on February 15, the battleship *Maine* exploded in Havana harbor; 260 officers and men perished. The cause of the blast, according to modern research, was spontaneous combustion in a coal bunker. In 1898, however, the public believed that Spain had either caused an external explosion or had failed to prevent it. McKinley established a naval board of inquiry to probe the disaster. While he waited for the board's report, he made military preparations and explored unsuccessfully the idea of buying Cuba from Spain.

On March 17 a Republican senator who had visited the war, Redfield Proctor of Vermont, told the Senate that conditions in Cuba were horrible. Two days later McKinley learned that the naval board had concluded that an external explosion had caused the destruction of the *Maine.* When the report went to Congress, pressure on the president to intervene in Cuba (which would mean war) would mount.

The Last Drive for Peace

McKinley pushed Spain to agree to an armistice in the fighting or to permit American mediation that would end in Cuban independence. However, the Spanish were opposed to independence for Cuba. Still, McKinley was able to hold off Congress until Spain had another chance to consider its options. When a negative answer arrived from Spain on March 31, 1898, McKinley prepared to put the issue before Congress.

There was one last flurry of diplomatic activity. On April 9 Spain agreed, at the urging of its European friends, to suspend hostilities in Cuba. It was not an armistice, which would have meant formal recognition of the Cuban cause. The idea was for Spain to gain more time to defend Cuba against the United States. The Spanish military commander in Cuba would determine how long the cessation of the fighting would last. There was no agreement on Cuban independence from Madrid. Thus the Spanish had not yielded on the key demands of the United States.

McKinley sent his message to Congress on April 11. It requested presidential authority to end the fighting in Cuba through armed force if necessary. At the end of his message, the president mentioned that Spain had proposed to suspend hostilities, but he gave the idea little significance. Later generations would argue that Spain's acceptance of a suspension of hostilities represented a surrender to the demands of the United States. In fact, the diplomatic impasse between the two countries was unbroken.

Over the following week Congress debated the president's request for authority to intervene. To show that the United States had no selfish motives, the lawmakers adopted an amendment offered by Senator Henry M. Teller, a Colorado Democrat. The Teller Amendment stated that the United States did not intend to control Cuba or annex it. Yet Congress also declined to extend official recognition to the Cuban rebels. For McKinley, the important result was a resolution authorizing him to act. Spain immediately broke diplomatic relations with the United States; it declared war on April 24.

The War Begins

The war between the United States and Spain occurred because both sides believed their cause was just. McKinley had pursued a diplomatic solution until it became clear that Spain would not agree to a negotiated settlement. Neither of the two powers contended that the Cubans themselves should determine their own destiny. The resulting war set the United States on a path toward world power.

The war began with a stunning naval victory. On May 1, 1898, Commodore **George Dewey** and the Asiatic naval squadron inflicted a decisive defeat on the Spanish navy at Manila Bay in the Philippine Islands. The triumph at Manila Bay confronted the president with new opportunities and problems in foreign policy.

A Broadening Commitment in the Pacific

To follow up on Dewey's success, the McKinley administration dispatched troops to the Philippines. The president wanted the option of acquiring the islands as a result of the war. He thought that a port in the Philippines might be enough, but he intended to maintain flexibility.

As U.S. involvement in the Philippines increased, the fate of the Hawaiian Islands gained added importance. A treaty of annexation had been worked out during 1897, and Congress considered the pact early in 1898. It proved difficult to obtain the necessary two-thirds majority to adopt the treaty because of the opposition of southern states, whose industries competed with Hawaiian sugar. After the war began, the president and congressional leaders turned to a strategy of annexation by means of a legislative resolution that needed only a simple majority from Congress. Through presidential persuasion, the required votes for the resolution were obtained in July 1898, and Hawaii was annexed.

Meanwhile, U.S. policy toward the Philippines became a source of tension with Filipino leaders. The administration instructed army and navy officers not to have any formal dealings with the Filipinos. The buildup of military strength continued, and the ambitions of the Filipinos were seen as an obstacle to American policy rather than as a legitimate expression of nationalism.

The "Smoked Yankees" and the War with Spain

The main focus of the combat phase of the war was on Cuba. The U.S. Army numbered twenty-five thousand men, so the nation turned to volunteers to raise a larger force. Eventually about two hundred eighty thousand men saw active duty. The size of the force presented logistical problems. Soldiers complained about shortages of ammunition and supplies and the poor quality of the food rations. The press criticized the Army's performance, but by the time the fighting ended, the War Department had settled most of the snags that marked the early days of the war.

In the regular Army, an important part of the force that fought the Spanish were the four regiments composed of African American soldiers, or the **Smoked Yankees** as the Spanish troops described them. The black soldiers were ordered to move south and prepare to invade Cuba. On their way through the southern states, they encountered scorn

George Dewey
On May 1, 1898, he inflicted a decisive defeat on the Spanish Navy at Manila Bay in the Philippine Islands.

Smoked Yankees
The term used by Spanish troops to denote African American soldiers who fought in the war with Spain.

and segregation. As one black soldier put it, to whites "it mattered not if we were soldiers of the United States, and going to fight for the honor of our country . . . we were 'niggers' as they called us and treated us with contempt."

The African American soldiers did not endure such treatment quietly. Violence broke out between white and black troops in Florida, and men were killed and wounded in the exchanges of gunfire. Once the black regiments reached Cuba, their military contribution was significant.

Despite the bravery of the "Smoked Yankees," the Spanish-American War worsened the plight of African Americans. The ideology of imperialism that allowed whites to dominate Cubans and Filipinos also supported racial segregation in the South. McKinley's efforts to reconcile the whites of the North and South brought harmony at the expense of black Americans.

©The Granger Collection, New York

Because the war with Spain was fought primarily with U.S. Army regulars, African American soldiers played a large role in the nation's victory. This detachment of black troops in Cuba was part of the American advance into the island.

Victory in Cuba

In late June the U.S. Navy found the Spanish fleet in the harbor of Santiago de Cuba, and Army detachments went ashore to engage the Spanish forces holding the city. On July 1, the Army, commanded by General William R. Shafter, defeated the Spanish defenders at the Battle of San Juan Hill. Theodore Roosevelt and his volunteer regiment of Rough Riders took part in the battle. Roosevelt became a national hero on his way to the presidency, but the Rough Riders might have been defeated had it not been for the timely support they received from their black comrades.

From War to Peace

On July 3 the Navy destroyed the Spanish fleet when it tried to escape from Santiago harbor. Negotiations for an armistice began, with the French ambassador acting as intermediary. McKinley insisted that Spain relinquish Cuba and Puerto Rico and that the fate of the Philippines be discussed at the peace conference. Spain did not like these terms, but it had no choice but to accept them, which it did on August 12, 1898.

Victory had been achieved at a low cost in terms of combat deaths—only 281 officers and men. However, malaria, yellow fever, and other diseases killed more than twenty-five hundred others. A public outcry arose about the condition of the Army, and McKinley named a commission to investigate the leadership of the War Department and the way the war had been conducted. The commission's report led to reforms that enhanced the future fighting ability of the Army. The war also strengthened the power of the presidency because of McKinley's expansive use of his role as commander-in-chief of the armed forces.

The Peace Talks

The peace conference with Spain was held in Paris. McKinley appointed a commission that included several senators who would ultimately vote on any treaty that they negotiated. The president was aware that Germany and Japan had an interest in the Philippines, and he intended that the United States should retain control of the islands. Within the United States, opponents of such a policy, calling themselves **anti-imperialists,** aroused public sentiment against the administration.

To build support for his foreign policy, McKinley made effective use of the powers of his office. During October he toured the Midwest. Though billed as a nonpartisan event, McKinley's tour helped Republican candidates in the 1898 congressional contest. It also

anti-imperialists
A league created during the last two years of McKinley's first term to unite the opposition against McKinley's foreign policy.

gave the president an opportunity to state the case for a more expansive foreign policy. In a typical address, he told an Iowa audience that "we do not want to shirk a single responsibility that has been put upon us by the results of the war."

The Philippines were the most divisive issue at the peace conference. On October 25, 1898, the president's commissioners asked him for instructions. On October 28 he responded that he could see "but one plain path of duty—the acceptance of the archipelago." The peace treaty was signed on December 10, 1898. The United States gained the Philippines, Guam, and Puerto Rico. Spain gave up its claims to Cuba and received a payment of $20 million for what it had lost.

Approval of the Treaty

Opponents of imperialism tried to block acceptance of the treaty in the Senate. To win the necessary two-thirds vote, McKinley used the power of the presidency in new and creative ways. In December he went south to woo Democrats. He used patronage to persuade wavering senators and exerted pressure on the state legislatures, which elected senators. Believing that the Democrats would benefit if the issue were settled before the 1900 elections, William Jennings Bryan endorsed the treaty. That action divided the opposition at a key point. On February 6, 1899, the Treaty of Paris obtained Senate approval by a vote of 57 to 27, one more than the necessary two-thirds.

War in the Philippines

As the Senate voted, the nation knew that fighting had erupted in the Philippines between U.S. soldiers and Filipino troops. Relations between the two sides had worsened during December 1898 as it became clear that the United States did not intend to leave the islands. Although the president asserted that his nation had "no imperial designs" on the Philippines, anti-imperialists and the Filipinos were not convinced. It seemed to them that they had ousted the Spanish only to replace them with another imperial master, the United States.

After the war with Spain ended, the United States faced another conflict with Filipino nationalists. The ugly and brutal war dragged on for more than three years. This picture shows American troops after assaulting an enemy position.

The war that resulted was a difficult and controversial one. During 1899 the U.S. Army defeated the Filipinos in conventional battles. However, the Filipinos turned to guerrilla tactics. Their soldiers hit selected targets and then blended back into the population. Faced with this new threat, the U.S. Army responded by killing some Filipino prisoners and torturing others. The Army's purpose was not genocidal, but many soldiers and their officers violated the rules of war and government policy in brutal and inhumane ways. A nation that had denounced such cruel practices under the Spanish in Cuba was now accused of doing the same things in the Philippines.

The Battle over Imperialism

During the last two years of McKinley's first term, imperialism became a heated issue. An Anti-Imperialist League was created in November 1898 to unite the opposition against McKinley's foreign policy. Critics of expansionism charged that overseas possessions would damage the nation's democratic institutions. Some people used racist arguments to block the acquisition of lands where nonwhite populations lived. Others evoked moral concern about imperialism.

Advocates of empire used the ideas of Social Darwinism and Anglo-Saxon supremacy to justify the acquisition of other countries. Theodore Roosevelt, Henry Cabot Lodge of Massachusetts, and other proponents of a "large" foreign policy contended that the nation could not escape the world responsibilities that the war with Spain had brought. By 1900 the consensus was that the gains of empire should be retained and protected but not increased. Anti-imperialism had persuaded public opinion that further overseas growth would be unwise.

Other foreign policy issues emerged from the outcome of the war. The Teller Amendment blocked the annexation of Cuba, but the McKinley administration wanted to ensure that the island did not become a target of European intervention. A military government ran Cuba during 1899. As a civil government developed, the United States insisted on guarantees that Cuba would retain political and military ties with the country that had liberated it. The result of this process was the **Platt Amendment** of March 1901. Attached to an Army appropriation bill, the amendment barred an independent Cuba from allying itself with another foreign power. The United States had the right to intervene to preserve stability. Aimed at preventing what had happened in 1898, the Platt Amendment became a permanent source of Cuban–American friction.

Platt Amendment
This amendment barred an independent Cuba from allying itself with another foreign power and gave the United States the right to intervene to preserve stability.

The Open Door in China and Beyond

The acquisition of the Philippines heightened interest about the fate of China, where European powers sought to establish economic and political spheres of influence. In September 1899 the administration, through Secretary of State John Hay, issued what became known as the Open Door Notes. The messages asked European countries that were active in China to preserve trading privileges and other economic rights that gave the United States a chance to compete for markets there. The replies of the powers were noncommittal, but Hay announced in March 1900 that the other nations had accepted the U.S. position in principle.

When anti-foreign sentiment in China led to the Boxer Rebellion during the summer of 1900, an important test of the Open Door principle occurred. Secret associations known as the "Righteous and Harmonious Fists" (hence "Boxers") launched a series of attacks on westerners in China. Europeans who had taken refuge in Peking were rescued by an international force that included twenty-five hundred U.S. soldiers. President McKinley justified sending the troops into a country with which the United States was at peace as a legitimate use of his war power under the Constitution. Secretary Hay reaffirmed the U.S. commitment to the Open Door policy in a diplomatic circular to the powers that he issued on July 3, 1900. McKinley withdrew the troops rapidly after their rescue mission had been completed, but presidential authority was strengthened still further as a result.

Toward a Canal across Central America

The Spanish-American War and the expansion of American commitments in the Pacific demonstrated the need for a waterway that would link the two oceans. The McKinley administration laid the groundwork for a canal across Central America when it renegotiated the Clayton-Bulwer Treaty of 1850 with Great Britain. That document prohibited both nations from exercising exclusive control over any future waterway.

The 1900 Election

As the presidential election of 1900 approached, the signs seemed to point to McKinley's reelection. Prosperity had returned, and the conflict in the Philippines was being won. McKinley's vice president, Garret A. Hobart, died in November 1899. Theodore Roosevelt, the popular young governor of New York, became McKinley's running mate when the Republican National Convention met in Philadelphia in June 1900.

To oppose McKinley, the Democrats again turned to William Jennings Bryan. His running mate was Adlai Stevenson who had held the vice presidency under Grover Cleveland.

Bryan attacked McKinley's policies on imperialism as a threat to the nation's institutions, and he accused the Republicans of being the tools of the trusts and the business community. The Democratic candidate also renewed his pleas for a free-silver policy. The anti-imperialists did not trust Bryan, but they preferred him to McKinley.

Conforming to the custom of the day in which incumbent presidents did not make speeches, McKinley allowed Theodore Roosevelt to do most of the campaigning. McKinley increased his margin in the popular vote over what he had achieved four years earlier. The result in the electoral college was 292 for McKinley and 155 for Bryan.

McKinley's Second Term

As his second term began, McKinley gained further victories in foreign policy. Congress had set up a civilian government for the Philippines once the insurrection had ended. Enactment of the Platt Amendment further strengthened McKinley's position. On May 27, 1901, the Supreme Court ruled in the *Insular Cases* that the Philippines and Puerto Rico were properly possessions of the United States but that their inhabitants had not become citizens of the country. The decision provided legal justification for imperialism.

Meanwhile, the president was turning his attention to two major domestic issues: the growth of big business and the issue of high tariffs. By 1901 McKinley was persuaded that some action was necessary to enforce the Sherman Antitrust Act of 1890. He had also modified his earlier support for the protective tariff and now believed that reciprocal trade treaties should be adopted. Treaties that had been negotiated with France and Argentina had not yet received Senate action. McKinley intended to prod the Senate to take them up at the next session, which would convene in December 1901.

As the new century began, McKinley had revived the power of the presidency after the decades of congressional supremacy that followed the Civil War. He had expanded the size of the president's staff and begun to involve the press in the coverage of White House affairs. In many respects, McKinley was the first modern president.

The United States on the Eve of the Twentieth Century: Calls for Change

The nation saw the arrival of the twentieth century on December 31, 1900, with a mixture of confidence and apprehension. The depression of the 1890s remained a vivid memory for most citizens. The shift in attitudes toward government and its role that had occurred during the hard times led many people to advocate programs of social reform. Such people were beginning to think of themselves as "progressives" and of those who disliked change as "conservatives."

With the end of the century in sight, there was a flurry of public debate about the direction of the nation. A National Social and Political Conference took place in Buffalo, New York, in 1899. The delegates called for "equality of economic opportunity and political power" as well as equal access "to all the material and social resources needful for the living of free, righteous, happy, and complete lives." Their goals required a more activist government than had been common in the nineteenth century.

In 1900 other future advocates of change came onto the scene. After a long political battle in Wisconsin, Robert M. La Follette finally won election as governor. His agenda looked toward changes in the way the state government functioned. A devastating hurricane in Galveston, Texas, in September 1900 caused significant damage to that Texas city. Political leaders there turned to a new form of government to deal with rebuilding. Commissioners of fire, water, police, and other services replaced the older style of ward leaders. The idea of having officials tied to the workings of city departments rather than representing geographic areas would attract increasing attention after the turn of the new century.

In the academic world, a biting analysis of how Americans used the wealth that they had acquired during the process of industrialization was published. Thorstein Veblen was a professor at the University of Chicago when he wrote *The Theory of the Leisure Class* (1899). In this book he analyzed the ways in which citizens displayed their social status. "Elegant dress serves its purpose of elegance not only in that it is expensive," he wrote, "but also because it is the insignia of leisure." Veblen was a provocative critic of capitalist institutions and practices at a time when his fellow citizens worried about their impact on national life.

At both ends of the economic spectrum, Americans looked to organization to address social ills. In 1900 Italian and Jewish immigrants who worked in the clothing business in New York City united to form the International Ladies Garment Workers Union (ILGWU). The membership used the ILGWU to spread the ideas of unionism to other immigrant workers. Also in 1900 the more well-to-do business leaders of the day created the National Civic Federation (NCF). Made up of representatives from organized labor, the business community, and the public, the NCF sought to promote harmony between labor and capital.

Summary

The Mixed Blessings of Empire

Between 1893 and 1901, the United States went through one of the worst economic depressions in its history, fought a war with Spain, and acquired an overseas empire. By the time Theodore Roosevelt succeeded the slain William McKinley in September 1901, the American people had regained prosperity and assumed a world role. At the start of the new century, national leaders boasted of the confidence with which their constituents viewed the prospects for better times ahead.

The apparent sense of well-being masked deeper worries about the future. The experience of the depression caused many middle-class Americans to ask themselves whether government at all levels should play a larger role in regulating corporations and restoring the balance among the various classes of society. Later in the decade the debate over overseas expansion raised questions about whether an empire might threaten deeply held cultural values. These twin forces bred a spirit of reform that culminated in what came to be known as the Progressive Movement after 1901.

Admiral George Dewey became a favorite subject for photographs after his victory at Manila Bay in 1898. He is shown with the noted photographer Frances Benjamin Johnston on the deck of his flagship, the USS *Olympia*, in 1899.

Booker T. Washington's school at Tuskegee Institute represented the attempt by this important African American leader to train his students for their place in a segregated society. This picture shows a class at Tuskegee in the early years of the twentieth century.

In the mid-1890s the social unrest led commentators to predict that a violent revolution might be imminent. The agrarian-based People's party argued for inflationary solutions to lift farm prices and ease the burden of debt in the South and West. At the polls, however, Populism did not move beyond its sectional roots. The Republicans proved to be the big winners from the discontent with the record of President Grover Cleveland and his party. In a sweeping electoral realignment in 1894 and 1896, the Republicans became the majority party for a generation and more until another depression occurred in the 1930s.

From 1898 onward the United States expanded its presence in the Pacific and Caribbean. While citizens applauded the victory over Spain and the acquisition of the Philippine Islands, they had less stomach for protracted colonial rule over Asian and Latin American peoples. By 1901 the zest for empire had receded in favor of a gradual retreat from the commitments of the McKinley era. Cuba became an independent protectorate, and the Philippines were under a colonial government with the eventual aim of self-rule. Elements of imperial thinking warred with persistent currents of isolationist thinking in the shaping of foreign policy.

Emilio Aguinaldo, shown here with his supporters sitting in the front row, second from the right, became the leader of a nationalist rebellion against the American forces that had occupied the Philippines in 1898. Aguinaldo's capture in 1901 was a major blow against the insurgents.

In retrospect, the 1890s would seem an age of nostalgia and quaintness before the storms of the twentieth century. That impression, formed of images of horse-drawn carriages and Victorian clothes, was illusory. This chapter shows that the dilemmas to come between 1901 and 1920 were being shaped in the days of Cleveland and McKinley. Americans asked each other what the role of government should be. They pondered the part the United States should play in a world of nationalism and empires. These and other related issues made the last decades of the nineteenth century the time when the travails of the modern age impinged on Americans for good.

In 1913 at Henry Ford's plant in Highland Park, Michigan, workers assembled automobile parts on a line. This system reduced the time to produce a car, lowered cost, and enabled Ford to increase hourly wages.

Making Connections Across Chapters

LOOKING BACK

The events that dominated American life in the 1890s stemmed from problems that had been accumulating since the Civil War. The political and economic systems confronted the effects of a major depression and then the impact of world power.

1. What were the options open to government when an economic collapse occurred?
2. Why did President Grover Cleveland face the political blame for problems with business and finance that he inherited?
3. Why did the Republicans become the big winners in the politics of the 1890s?
4. How did American thinkers react to the economic downturn of the decade?
5. Should the United States have intervened in Cuba in 1898?

LOOKING AHEAD

In Chapter 20, Theodore Roosevelt will take the stage as one of the leaders of the Progressive Movement of political reform. Think about how this chapter foreshadows these developments.

1. What attitudes about the proper role of government changed during the 1890s?
2. What problems did imperialism leave to be solved after 1900?
3. In what ways, if any, did the 1890s resemble or differ from the 1990s?

RECOMMENDED READINGS

Campbell, W. Joseph. *Yellow Journalism: Puncturing the Myths, Defining the Legacies* (2001). A skeptical look at sensational journalism and the war with Spain.

Gilmore, Glenda. *Gender and Jim Crow: Women and the Politics of White Supremacy in North Carolina, 1896–1920* (1996). An excellent study of the ways in which black and white women interacted during the era of segregation.

Hoganson, Kristin L. *Fighting for American Manhood: How Gender Politics Provoked the Spanish-American and Philippine-American Wars* (1998). A provocative new study about the origins of the conflict with Spain.

Offner, John L. *An Unwanted War: The Diplomacy of the United States & Spain over Cuba, 1895–1898* (1992). Valuable for the interplay of Cubans, Spaniards, and Americans as the war drew near.

Perez, Louis A. *The War of 1898: The United States and Cuba in History and Historiography* (1998). Offers an insightful, sympathetic look at the war from a perspective that takes Cuba into account.

Schlereth, Thomas J. *Victorian America: Transformations in Everyday Life, 1876–1915* (1991). Strong on the social and cultural changes that occurred during the 1890s.

Smith, Joseph. *The Spanish-American War: Conflict in the Caribbean and the Pacific, 1845–1902* (1994). A good one-volume account of the military history of the war.

Traxel, David. *1898: The Birth of the American Century* (1998). An interpretive survey of the war with Spain and its consequences for the nation.

Williams, R. Hal. *Years of Decision: American Politics in the 1890s* (1993). The best narrative account of this important decade.

Zimmerman, Warren. *First Great Triumph: How Five Americans Made Their Country a World Power* (2002). An interesting interpretation of the origins of American imperialism.

AMERICAN JOURNEY ONLINE AND INFOTRAC COLLEGE EDITION

Visit the source collections at http://ajaccess.wadsworth.com and infotrac.thomsonlearning.com and use the Search function with the following key terms to explore documents, images, audio and video clips, articles, and commentary related to the material in this chapter.

Booker T. Washington

Atlanta Compromise

Grover Cleveland

Charlotte Perkins Gilman

Stephen Crane

Ida Wells Barnett

William McKinley

Plessy v. Ferguson

Radcliffe College

William Randolph Hearst

Spanish-American War

Pullman strike

ONLINE PRIMARY SOURCES

Here are some examples of the many primary sources related to this chapter that you will find on the *American Passages* Web site: http://history.wadsworth.com/ayersbrief02.

Eugene Debs addresses the American Railway Union, 1894

Carl Schurz against American Imperialism, 1899

The site also offers self-quizzes, exercises, and many additional resources to help you study.

CHAPTER 20

Theodore Roosevelt and Progressive Reform

1901–1909

O N SEPTEMBER 6, 1901, PRESIDENT WILLIAM MCKINLEY WAS SHOT during a public reception in Buffalo, New York. A week later he died and Vice President Theodore Roosevelt became president. The eight years that followed were a time of political change that has come to be known as the Progressive Era. Responding to the social and economic impact of industrialism, Americans endeavored to reshape their nation to curb the power of large businesses, improve conditions for the consumer, and reform the political parties.

In the process Americans confronted new issues. Citizens argued about whether government should regulate the economy. The political party became a major source of contention. Its critics contended that the intense partisanship of the late nineteenth century had weakened democracy. Power should be shifted away from the parties and toward the individual voter. Other advocates of change clamored for more voter participation in the electoral system. This would be accomplished by broadening the ability of citizens to propose laws, choose candidates, and overturn judicial decisions. The issues that Americans debated at the turn of the twentieth century would dominate the agenda of domestic policy for decades to come.

The Age of Theodore Roosevelt

At forty-two, Theodore Roosevelt was the youngest man to become president. He was already famous as an author, hunter, naturalist, soldier, and politician. During the war with Spain, he raised a volunteer regiment called the Rough Riders and led them on a dangerous charge in Cuba toward fortified Spanish positions on Kettle Hill. Victory made him a national hero, and he won the governorship of New York in 1898. When he publicized corporate abuses in his state, Republican leaders pushed his name for the vice presidency in 1900 to get him out of their way. To the chagrin of party insiders, McKinley's murder thrust Roosevelt into the political spotlight.

Roosevelt pledged to continue McKinley's policies. From his first days in office, however, the youthful and vigorous Roosevelt made news in ways that no previous president had done. He changed the official name of the president's residence to the White House. His large family—he had six children—captivated the nation. His second wife, Edith Roosevelt, played a more visible cultural role as First Lady. The president's oldest daughter, Alice Lee, made her debut in the White House, kept a pet snake, and drove around

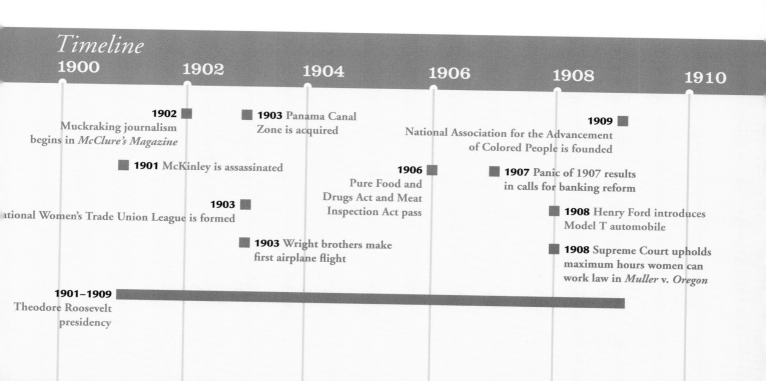

Washington in fast cars. "I can be President of the United States or I can control Alice," Roosevelt told friends. "I cannot possibly do both."

The Roosevelt Agenda

Roosevelt wanted to make the government "the most efficient instrument" to help the American people. As long as the Constitution did not prohibit executive action, the president should stretch the limits of what was possible. "I did not usurp power," he wrote later, "but I did greatly broaden the use of executive power."

The nation watched him in fascination. When Roosevelt was "in the neighborhood," said a reporter, the public could "no more look the other way than a small boy can turn his head from a circus parade followed by a steam calliope." Like a preacher in church, Roosevelt called the White House his "bully pulpit," using it to give sermons to the country about morality and duty.

The new president wanted to limit the power of big business in order to avoid pressure for more radical reforms from the Democrats or Socialists. He believed that the nation had to protect its natural resources. Before 1912, he saw the Republican party as the best means to implement his agenda. As a result, he did not challenge the party's leaders on the protective tariff. He cooperated with the conservative Republicans who dominated Congress during his first term. But after 1905, his relations with Capitol Hill worsened.

Theodore Roosevelt was the first celebrity president. The spread of newspapers and the emergence of motion pictures made it possible for Americans to follow the nation's leader with greater attention than they had during the nineteenth century. By using the power of his office, Roosevelt strengthened the presidency to meet future challenges.

The United States at the Outset of the Twentieth Century

In 1901 Americans balanced confidence about the future in a new century with worries about the direction in which their society was moving. There were ample reasons for national pride. The population stood at seventy-six million, up from sixty-three million ten years earlier. Immigrants accelerated the growth of the population. There were 449,000 new arrivals in 1900, 688,000 in 1902, and more than 1.1 million in 1906. Israel Zangwill wrote a famous play, *The Melting Pot,* which celebrated the United States as "God's Crucible, the great melting pot where all the races of Europe are melting and reforming!" The phrase "melting pot" came into widespread use in describing American society.

A Longer Life Span

People lived longer in 1900, a trend that accelerated throughout the century. Life expectancy for white men rose from forty-seven years in 1901 to almost fifty-four years in 1920. For white women, the increase was from around fifty-one years in 1901 to almost fifty-five years in 1920. Life expectancy for members of minority groups rose from thirty-five years in 1901 to just over forty-five years in 1920.

The population was young in 1900. The median age was twenty-three; it rose to just over twenty-five by 1920. The death rate for the entire population was seventeen per thousand in 1900. It fell to thirteen per thousand by 1920. For infants in the Progressive Era, the prospects were less encouraging. In 1915, the first year for which there are accurate numbers, almost sixty-one deaths were recorded for every ten thousand births. The situation worsened during the next several years, and the infant mortality rate reached more than sixty-eight deaths per ten thousand births in 1921. For nonwhite babies the picture was even worse, with almost one hundred six deaths per ten thousand live births in 1915.

Children at Work

The problem of child labor that had developed during the late nineteenth century persisted. In 1900 more than 1,750,000 children between the ages of ten and fifteen worked in the labor force. An example of the situation for these child laborers was the case of Sadie Frowne, an immigrant girl from Poland, who went to work in a sweatshop in New York City's garment district before she was fifteen. She made $4 a week and reported that "the

**Table 20.1
Immigration into
the United States,
1901–1909**

1901	487,918
1902	687,743
1903	857,046
1904	812,870
1905	1,026,499
1906	1,100,735
1907	1,285,349
1908	782,870
1909	751,786

Source: *The Statistical History of the United States* (1965), p. 56.

machines go like mad all day, because the faster you work the more money you get." Abolishing child labor became a major goal of reform campaigns after 1900.

Changes in the Family

In families whose children did not have to work, child rearing became more organized and systematic. Kindergartens became popular: there were five thousand in 1900 and nearly nine thousand twenty years later. The federal government held conferences on child rearing and issued booklets about infant care. Improved methods of contraception led to smaller families. In 1900 the average mother had 3.566 children compared with 7 children in 1800.

The status of women also changed after 1900. Divorce became easier and more common. There were fifty-six thousand divorces in 1900, and one hundred thousand in 1914. Other women delayed marriage to attend college. Yet opportunities for women to enter law, medicine, or higher education remained limited. In 1920 fewer than 1.5 percent of all attorneys were women. In 1910 there were only nine thousand women doctors, about 6 percent of all physicians. Restrictive policies on admissions to medical schools and barriers to staff positions at hospitals posed obstacles to women who sought to become doctors. Nursing and social work were more accessible to women, but they still faced condescension from men.

Women at Work

Women in factories, mills, and garment sweatshops also saw little improvement in their condition as the new century began. Their workday was ten hours long, and six- and seven-day weeks were common. Labor unions regarded women as competitors for jobs held by men. Women set up their own unions, such as the **National Women's Trade Union League,** established in 1903. They formed the backbone of the International Ladies Garment Workers Union (ILGWU), which led strikes in New York City in 1910 and 1911.

National Women's Trade Union League
A feminist labor organization.

Social trends slowly altered the status of women. Their clothes became less confining and cumbersome. Women began to show their ankles and arms in public. Some more daring young women, such as Alice Roosevelt, smoked in public; others used cosmetics openly. In dance halls and restaurants, young people danced the turkey trot and the bunny hug to the rhythms of ragtime.

The institution of marriage felt the effects of these changes. Marriage ceremonies used the word "obey" less frequently. Women asked more of their husbands, including companionship and sexual pleasure. In 1913, Congress designated Mother's Day as a national holiday. Throughout the Progressive Era, politicians and reformers debated how the government might safeguard the family.

A Nation of Consumers

In 1900 seventy-six million people in the United States owned twenty-one million horses. Some forecasters said that the automobile would replace the horse, but in 1903 only a little more than eleven thousand cars were sold. During the next decade, however, Henry Ford created the Model T. Ford's goal was to use mass production techniques to build an automobile that could be sold in large numbers. By 1908 the Model T was ready for distribution, priced at about $850. Sales increased rapidly as Ford steadily reduced the car's price. The mass-produced automobile was a key element in the evolution of the consumer society during the Progressive Era.

Standardized food products also gained popular acceptance. For example, Asa Candler's Coca-Cola (see Chapter 17) became available throughout the country when the parent company licensed bottling plants everywhere. In 1912 Procter and Gamble introduced Crisco, a vegetable shortening, as a way of selling its cottonseed oil. The company

Sponsorship of car racing provided a means for automobile manufacturers such as Henry Ford to publicize their new vehicles. Ford is standing next to the racer that is driven by Barney Oldfield, one of the first of the famous race drivers.

From the Collections of the Henry Ford Museum & Greenfield Village

used marketing campaigns in popular periodicals, held "Crisco teas" at which club women could try out their own recipes, and created cooking schools to spread awareness of the new product. Other famous brands, such as Kellogg's Corn Flakes, Uneeda Biscuit, and Kodak cameras, relied on mass advertising, billboards, and mail flyers to instill popular desire for these new and convenient consumer goods.

The Role of Advertising

Advertising became a central feature of American culture. Advertising agencies shaped the content of product information. Men were urged to buy Gillette razors because "You Ought to Shave Every Morning." The Kodak camera was an essential part of the Christmas season as "your family historian." To master these markets, advertisers surveyed potential purchasers. Agencies tracked customers through reports from salespeople, mail surveys, and questionnaires printed in magazines. Their goal was "to develop what may be called the mathematics of advertising."

The Example of Sears

Sears, Roebuck & Company was a leader in consumer marketing. Founded in 1893, the company was the brainchild of Richard Warren Sears. Beginning with mail-order watches, Sears expanded to general merchandise that was sold in a catalogue published annually. He cut prices for desirable products such as sewing machines and cream separators and soon produced record sales. Sears promised low prices, guarantees of any products and parts, and the opportunity to order merchandise without prepaying.

Americans increasingly thought of themselves as the nation of consumers that people like Sears envisioned. In many respects, the United States occupied an enviable position. National income stood at $17 billion; the average American's annual per capita income of $227 was the highest in the world. Innovations promised further abundance to a prosperous population.

Despite these positive trends, citizens worried about the nation's future. The growth of big business, the spread of labor organizations, the decline of the individual in a bureaucratic society—all these trends prompted fear that older values and attitudes were under assault. The early twentieth century saw a renewed debate about the purpose and accomplishments of the United States.

Race Relations in the Roosevelt Era

On October 16, 1901, Booker T. Washington dined with President Roosevelt and his family at the White House. The evening meal was social, but the purpose of Washington's visit was political. Since he had emerged as a leading spokesman for African Americans during the 1890s (see Chapter 19), Washington had built a political machine among black Republicans in the South. He came to the White House to discuss the new president's nominations for patronage positions in the South. When southern newspapers learned that a black man had eaten with the president, they were furious. A Tennessee editor called the occasion "the most damnable outrage that has ever been perpetrated by any citizen of the United States."

Roosevelt saw himself as a friend of African Americans, but he moved cautiously on race during his first term. Between 1901 and 1905 he defended black appointees to post offices and customs houses who were under attack in the South. He also resisted attempts by "Lily-White" Republicans to remove blacks from the party in the South. After 1905, however, he criticized African Americans when blacks did not inform southern authorities where accused black criminals might be found. When black soldiers were falsely charged with attempting to kill white residents of Brownsville, Texas, in August 1906, the president discharged their units without a hearing.

Black Life in the Early Twentieth Century

For the majority of African Americans in the era of Theodore Roosevelt, segregation was an ever-present fact of life. "Don't monkey with white supremacy," warned a Mississippi newspaper, "it is loaded with determination, gun-powder, and dynamite." Eight days after Washington and Roosevelt sat down to dinner, a black man named **"Bill" Morris** was burned at the stake in Balltown, Louisiana. He had allegedly robbed and raped a white

Bill Morris
A black man burned at the stake in Balltown, Louisiana, for allegedly robbing and raping a white woman; no trial was held.

W. E. B. Du Bois on What Blacks Felt during the Age of Roosevelt, 1903

After the Egyptian and Indian, the Greek and Roman, the Teuton and Mongolian, the Negro is a sort of seventh son, born with a veil, and gifted with second-sight in this American world—a world which yields him no true self-consciousness, but only lets him see himself through the revelation of the other world. It is a peculiar sensation, this double-consciousness, this sense of always looking at oneself through the eyes of others, of measuring one's soul by the tape of a world that looks on in amused contempt and pity. One ever feels his twoness—an American, a Negro; two souls, two thoughts, two unreconciled strivings; two warring ideals in one dark body, whose dogged strength alone keeps it from being torn asunder.

The history of the American Negro is the history of this strife, this longing to attain self-conscious manhood, to merge his double self into a better and truer self. In this merging he wishes neither of the older selves to be lost. He would not Africanize America, for America has too much to teach the world and Africa. He would not bleach his Negro soul in a flood of white Americanism, for he knows that Negro blood has a message for the world. He simply wishes to make it possible for a man to be both a Negro and an American, without being cursed and spit upon by his fellows, without having the doors of opportunity closed roughly in his face.

Questions to Consider

1. What problems in American race relations at the start of the twentieth century would have led Du Bois to his conclusions about the nature of black life in the United States?

2. What does Du Bois mean in the phrase "a world looks on in amused contempt and pity" about the strivings of black people at that time?

3. How would white society have responded to the argument that Du Bois was making?

4. How does this quotation explain Du Bois's differences with Booker T. Washington?

Explore additional primary sources related to this chapter on the *American Passages* Web site: http://history.wadsworth.com/ayersbrief02.

Source: W. E. B. Du Bois, *The Souls of Black Folk* (1903).

---

woman. Apprehended by a mob, Morris was "taken back to the scene of his crime." No trial occurred. Instead, "pine knots and pine straw were heaped about him and over this kerosene was poured and the whole set on fire." Between seventy and eighty black citizens of the United States were lynched during each year of Roosevelt's presidency.

Social and economic inequality were the lot of African Americans as well. Conditions had worsened since the passage of segregation laws in the South during the 1880s and 1890s (see Chapters 18 and 19). Nine million southern blacks lived in rural poverty. Black wage workers received much less per day and per hour than their white counterparts in the same trade. Other black men were industrial or agricultural peasants, virtual slaves who received only food and a place to sleep for their labor.

The system of segregation affected blacks in every aspect of their existence. "The white man is the boss," said one man. "You got to talk to him like he is the boss." Facilities for the races were supposed to be "separate but equal," but this was rarely the case in practice.

Exclusion from Politics

Blacks no longer voted in significant numbers. The white primary barred black voters from elections that selected Democratic party candidates. In the one-party South, this meant that African Americans had no voice in the political contests that really mattered. They retained some role in the Republican party because their votes helped to choose the delegates to the national convention. For the most part, however, the bitter comment of one African American politician summed up the situation: "The Negro's status in Southern politics is dark as Hell and smells like cheese."

When he dined with Theodore Roosevelt, Booker T. Washington demonstrated to other African Americans that he could deliver the support of white politicians. To keep the president's friendship and to obtain money from wealthy whites, Washington had to accept the existence of segregation and the system it represented. Washington was doing what he had proposed in his speech in Atlanta in 1895 (see Chapter 19). By the time Roosevelt became president, more militant blacks were saying that Washington's methods had failed.

The Stirrings of Militant Protest

W. E. B. Du Bois
Initially a supporter of Booker T. Washington's education policy, he later criticized Washington's methods as having "practically accepted the alleged inferiority of the Negro."

Their leader was **W. E. B. Du Bois,** who had received a doctoral degree from Harvard and who taught sociology at Atlanta University, a black institution. After initially supporting Washington's policy, Du Bois decided that blacks had to confront segregation. In *The Souls of Black Folk* (1903), Du Bois criticized Washington's methods as having "practically accepted the alleged inferiority of the Negro."

In June 1905 Du Bois led a delegation of twenty-nine blacks to Niagara Falls, New York, where they issued a call for political and social rights. The meeting denied that "the Negro-American assents to inferiority, is submissive under oppression and apologetic before insult." The Niagara Conference aroused Booker T. Washington's intense opposition, but it laid the basis for more lasting protests about the worsening situation of African Americans.

Roosevelt and the Modern Presidency: The First Term

Early in his first term Roosevelt launched a dramatic attack on consolidated economic power. On February 19, 1902, the Department of Justice announced that it was filing suit under the Sherman Antitrust Act (1890) against the Northern Securities Company. That firm, created in late 1901, merged major railroads in the Northwest. The key leaders in assembling this large company were James J. Hill and E. H. Harriman; their financing came from **J. P. Morgan.** Opposition to the merger came from states across which the company would operate, most notably in Minnesota. Farmers and business operators in the upper Midwest feared that a giant railroad would raise rates and limit their profits. They urged their governors to file suit against the new company in federal court.

J. P. Morgan
He purchased Carnegie Steel Company in 1901 for $480 million from Andrew Carnegie, creating United States Steel, which controlled 60 percent of the steel industry's productive capacity.

The creation of the Northern Securities Company was part of the trend toward larger economic units that had begun during the 1890s (see Chapter 19). A highly publicized case was that of the United States Steel Company. The steel merger symbolized bigness in business in the same way that the railroad combine did.

At the turn of the century the Carnegie Steel Company dominated the industry, producing finished steel products at a lower unit cost than its rivals. For J. P. Morgan and the steel companies that he represented, Carnegie's power raised the possibility that competing firms might go bankrupt. The logical answer, Morgan concluded, was to buy out Carnegie and create a steel company that could control the entire industry. Morgan sent an aide to see Carnegie. "If Andy wants to sell, I'll buy," said Morgan. "Go and find his price."

Morgan's agent, Charles M. Schwab, found Carnegie on the golf course. Carnegie sent his answer a day later. In a penciled note, he told Morgan that the price was $480 million. Morgan paused and responded: "I accept this price." The merger was made public on March 3, 1901, the day before William McKinley began his second term. The half-billion dollars that Carnegie received for his holding was a staggering sum in an era when there was no federal income tax, no capital gains tax, and low inflation.

The Challenge of United States Steel

The new company, United States Steel, was capitalized at $1.4 billion. It controlled 60 percent of the steel industry's productive capacity. Smaller steel companies would have to compete with the vertical integration Carnegie had achieved with the company that Morgan had acquired. Workers in steel now faced a powerful employer that could fix wage levels in any way it chose. The prospect worried outside observers.

Theodore Roosevelt worried too. He saw the forces that led to business consolidation as the logical outcome of economic development, but he did not believe that the federal government should passively stand by. The large corporations, Roosevelt decided, should not be destroyed. Firms that were socially beneficial should be encouraged; those that misbehaved should be regulated. At first Roosevelt thought that publicizing the activities of corporations would be enough regulation. He soon concluded that he must establish the power of the federal government to intervene in the economy. The Northern Securities Company was unpopular, so the president acted.

Controlling the Trusts

In 1904 the Supreme Court agreed with Roosevelt when the government won its case against the Northern Securities Company. By a 5 to 4 margin the justices ruled that the railroad company violated the Sherman Act. The case reestablished the power of the national government to use the Sherman Act, which had been called into question in the 1895 case of *U.S. v. E. C. Knight.* The American public saw Roosevelt as a **trustbuster** who was willing to curb the power of big business.

trustbusters
Term applied to Theodore Roosevelt's efforts to enforce the Sherman Act.

The Square Deal in the Coal Strike

The nation also applauded when Roosevelt intervened to end a strike in the coal industry during the autumn of 1902. The one hundred forty thousand members of the United Mine Workers walked off their jobs in the anthracite (hard coal) fields of Pennsylvania. The miners asked for a pay hike and for the railroads and coal operators to recognize their union in bargaining talks. As the walkout stretched into autumn, fears grew of coal shortages during the winter. If the voters were cold in November, the Republicans faced political losses in the 1902 congressional elections. Yet neither side in the walkout seemed prepared to yield to the other.

In early October Roosevelt brought both sides to the White House. He urged the workers and owners to settle. The union's president, John Mitchell, said that arbitration was acceptable, but the mine owners refused. Roosevelt responded that he might bring in the Army to mine coal. Facing that threat, J. P. Morgan and Elihu Root worked out a deal in which a presidential commission was set up to look into the strike. The panel granted the miners a 10 percent pay increase, but the union was not recognized. In 1894 Grover Cleveland had used federal troops to break the Pullman strike (see Chapter 19). Now Roosevelt wielded presidential power to treat capital and labor on an equal basis. Roosevelt called his approach the **Square Deal.**

Roosevelt's record and his popularity limited Republican losses in the congressional elections. During the session of Congress that began in December 1902, Roosevelt endorsed the Elkins Act, which would outlaw the rebates railroads gave to favored customers. Roosevelt also called for a law to create a Department of Commerce. One of the agencies of this new department would be a Bureau of Corporations, which would publicize corporate records. Other laws strengthened the power of the Justice Department to pursue antitrust cases. Roosevelt now had the weapons he sought to distinguish between businesses that he deemed socially good and those that behaved improperly.

Square Deal
Roosevelt's approach to treating capital and labor on an equal basis.

Roosevelt and Foreign Policy

Theodore Roosevelt wanted to complete the work left over from the Spanish-American War and make the United States a force in world affairs. Because the world was increasingly dangerous, military preparedness was a key goal. "There is a homely adage which runs," the president said, "'Speak softly and carry a big stick; you will go far.'" By 1905 he had added ten battleships to the Navy and improved its gunnery. But except in the Philippines, where the guerrilla war sputtered on, during his presidency Roosevelt sent no American forces into armed combat.

He did act vigorously in places where the power of the United States was dominant. In 1902 Germany and Great Britain used their navies to collect debts that Venezuela owed them; Roosevelt sent the U.S. Navy into the region to limit foreign involvement there. Similar problems with the Dominican Republic and its debts two years later led him to pronounce the **Roosevelt Corollary,** which he believed was a natural extension of the Monroe Doctrine. In his annual message in 1904, he said that "chronic wrongdoing or impotence" of Latin American nations in paying their debts might lead the United States "to the exercise of an international police power."

Roosevelt also sought better relations with Great Britain. A possible flashpoint between Washington and London was the boundary between Alaska and Canada. Discoveries of gold

Roosevelt Corollary
Roosevelt's extension of the Monroe Doctrine to Latin American States and the the right to supervise their behavior.

Roosevelt's backing for the Panamanian Revolution and the subsequent construction of the Panama Canal gave cartoonists an ideal subject. This one depicts Roosevelt personally shoveling out the locks that became "The Path Between the Seas."

in the Yukon region attracted rival miners and speculators. Roosevelt believed that Canada had no valid claims to the disputed territory of islands and inlets that provided access to the goldfields. He used his influence with the British to gain a reluctant Canadian acceptance of an Anglo-Canadian-American commission to settle the problem. That body, in turn, gave the United States most of what it wanted in late 1903.

The acquisition of the Panama Canal Zone led to the most heated controversy of Roosevelt's foreign policy. The United States had wanted to see a waterway built across Central America for decades, but disease, mud, and the jungle defeated all construction efforts. The most ambitious project collapsed during the 1880s.

In 1901 the McKinley administration negotiated with the British for the right to build a Central American canal that all nations could use freely. In the Hay-Pauncefote Treaty, Great Britain gave up its rights to participate in a canal project. Congress then decided in 1902 that the best route lay across Panama. Secretary of State John Hay opened talks with Colombia, of which Panama was then a part. In 1903 Hay and a Colombian diplomat concluded the Hay-Herrán Convention. There would be a six-mile-wide canal zone, under American control, with a ninety-nine year lease. The Colombians would receive a $10 million payment and $250,000 per year in rent. The U.S. Senate quickly ratified the pact.

Colombia was less cooperative. The Colombian Senate believed that the treaty infringed on their country's sovereignty, and the lawmakers wanted more money from the United States. Roosevelt was outraged. Within Panama, opponents of Colombia rule plotted revolution. Lawyers for the New Panama Canal Company lobbied for American intervention if a rebellion broke out. The uprising occurred in November 1903 amid strong signals that Washington supported the revolution. The presence of the cruiser USS *Nashville* and other American vessels discouraged the Colombians from putting down the rebellion.

In November 1903 discussions with the representative of Panama, a Frenchman named Philippe Bunau-Varilla, led to drafting of the Hay-Bunau-Varilla Treaty. The new pact created a ten-mile-wide zone across Panama in exchange for the $10 million payment and the $250,000 annual rent. Within the Canal Zone, the United States could act as a sovereign nation. Construction of the canal proceeded slowly until Roosevelt put the U.S. Army in charge in 1907. Then work moved ahead efficiently.

It cost more than $350 million to build the Panama Canal, and almost six thousand workers died of disease and accidents during the decade of construction. The official opening took place on August 15, 1914. Theodore Roosevelt regarded the canal as the greatest achievement of his presidency. Roosevelt's infringement on Colombian sovereignty produced hard feelings in Latin America, however. Years later the Wilson administration signed a treaty with Colombia that gave it $25 million more, accompanied by an expression of "sincere regret" about what had happened. An angry Roosevelt prevented the Senate from acting on the new treaty during his lifetime. After he died in 1919, the government agreed to another new treaty in 1921 that paid Colombia the money without an apology.

The Election of 1904

Roosevelt's domestic and foreign policy triumphs made him a unanimous choice for the Republican presidential nomination in 1904. The Democrats turned to Alton B. Parker, a very dull, conservative New York state judge. Despite last-minute Democratic charges that big business was behind the Roosevelt campaign, Roosevelt received more than 56 per-

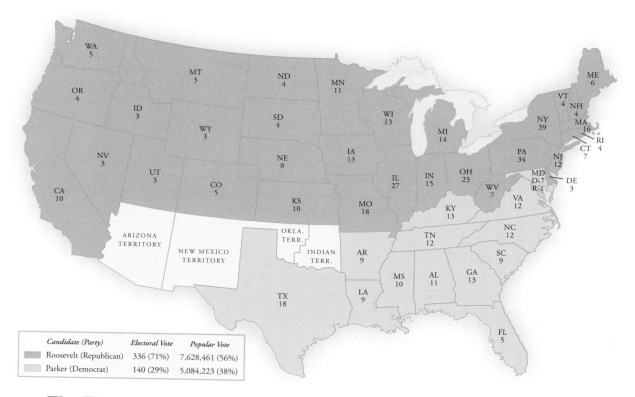

MAP 20.1 The Election of 1904

In this presidential contest, Theodore Roosevelt won the first landslide victory of the twentieth century over his Democratic rival, Alton B. Parker. As the returns came in, Roosevelt announced that he would not be a candidate for another term in 1908.

cent of the vote, compared with Parker's 38 percent. The Socialist party and its candidate Eugene V. Debs received a small number of votes. Roosevelt's 336 electoral votes were the most that any presidential candidate had ever won up to that time. It was an electoral landslide. The number of Americans who voted, however, was more than four hundred thousand below the 1900 figure. Popular participation in elections would drop further in subsequent elections as interest in politics declined.

On the night that he was elected president in his own right, Roosevelt made a dramatic statement. He said that the three years he had already served represented his first term as president. Accordingly, he promised that he would not be a candidate for another term in 1908. By respecting the third-term tradition, he hoped to allay fears that he would use his popularity to remain president for life. He planned to embark on a campaign of reform without being accused of personal ambition to stay in office.

In his 1904 annual message, Roosevelt asked Congress to strengthen the power of the **Interstate Commerce Commission** to regulate the railroads. He contended that the power of the federal government should be used to make the whole society more just and equitable. With his gift for understanding where public opinion was going, Roosevelt had caught the spirit of change that came to be called the Progressive Movement. In his second term he put the power of the modern presidency behind the new agenda for reform.

Interstate Commerce Commission

Passage of the Hepburn Act in 1906 gave this commission the power to establish maximum rates and to review the accounts and records of the railroads.

Progressive Campaigns to Reform the Nation

The efforts to improve American life had gotten under way during the 1890s (see Chapter 19) but achieved national significance in the years just after 1904. Responding to the growth of cities, the problems of industrialism, and fears about the nation's future, the American people launched movements to clean up politics and society.

Consumers and Reformers

Progressivism occurred during a time of relative economic prosperity. A sense of well-being allowed middle-class citizens to address the social and economic problems that had emerged during the depression of the 1890s. Rising prices aroused popular concern about the high cost of living. Critics of the Republicans' protective tariff policies charged that customs duties added to inflation. Equally strong were fears of the effects of business consolidation on the smaller companies for which so many people worked.

When Americans focused on the products they bought and used, they listened when investigative reporters said that patent medicines were unsafe. The discovery that meatpacking plants and other food processors tolerated unsafe conditions led to federal regulation in 1906. Pure food and pure drugs were so necessary, reformers argued, that businesses would have to accept more government intrusion than ever.

The Currents of Reform

As the problems of industrialism and urban growth emerged, a coalition of groups proposed fresh answers. Diversity of goals and approach was the striking feature of early twentieth-century reform. Nonetheless, shared assumptions united most people who called themselves progressives.

During the years before World War I in 1914, men and women believed that human nature was basically good and could be made better. The human environment could be reshaped, reformers contended. They also said that government at all levels could promote a better society, and the state had a duty to relieve the ills that confronted the nation as a result of industrial growth.

Differing Methods of Reform

The question of how best to accomplish such goals gave rise to two different approaches within progressive reform. One answer for the problems of democracy was more democracy. Proposals for a *direct primary* to allow voters to choose the candidates of their political parties became popular. The selection of U.S. senators should be taken away from state legislatures and given to the people. The voters themselves should have the right to vote on public issues in *referenda,* to propose laws in *initiatives,* and to remove or *recall* officials or judges whose decisions offended majority sentiment in a city or state.

Another strand of progressivism focused on producing greater order and efficiency in public life. Efforts were made to improve the structure of cities and states. The commission form of city government did away with elected aldermen from local wards and replaced them with officials who were chosen in citywide elections and assigned to a specific department such as utilities, transit, or housing. Regulatory agencies such as the Federal Trade Commission and the Interstate Commerce Commission, staffed with experts on the industries they supervised, would see that the marketplace operated in an orderly way without partisan influences.

The Ambiguities of Progressivism

Some reformers sought programs that emphasized social control of groups and individuals. Prohibition of the use of alcohol, restriction of immigration into the United States, and efforts to shift political power in cities away from the poor and unorganized reflected a desire to compel correct behavior or restrict democracy to native-born white Americans and the "respectable" classes. These coercive aspects of reform became less attractive to later generations.

Despite these failings, progressivism made constructive changes. The regulatory agencies, direct primaries, and other programs did not wipe out all the existing injustices, but they did soften the impact of an industrial social order. The principle that government was responsible for the general welfare of the nation also became well established.

The Muckrakers

Important figures in progressive reform were a group of journalists who exposed corruption and weaknesses in American society. They published their revelations in numerous monthly and weekly magazines. New printing techniques made these periodicals economical and profitable, and the more than two thousand daily newspapers gave reporters expanding opportunities to probe for scandals and scoops.

The Impact of *McClure's Magazine*

Samuel S. McClure, publisher of *McClure's Magazine,* helped launch the popular literature of exposure. By 1902 his monthly journal had attracted a wide middle-class audience for its appealing blend of fact and fiction. McClure had larger ambitions, however. He wanted the magazine to address the major issues of the day. He decided that the rise of big business and trusts provided the "great theme" he sought. He sent one of his star reporters, **Ida Tarbell,** to look into "the greatest of them all—the Standard Oil Company." With Tarbell's articles ready to run in the autumn of 1902, McClure decided to expand on an article that another reporter, Lincoln Steffens, had written about municipal corruption in St. Louis. That essay, "Tweed Days in St. Louis," led to a series on city government in the magazine that was published under the title "The Shame of the Cities" (1904). The January 1903 issue of *McClure's* carried articles by Tarbell and Steffens. McClure had found a format that attracted national attention.

Ida Tarbell
A preeminent female crusading journalist.

Where McClure had led, other magazines soon followed. Samuel Hopkins Adams exposed fraud in patent medicines; his series contributed to the passage of the Pure Food and Drugs Act in 1906. Ray Stannard Baker wrote about unethical railroad practices; his revelations assisted President Roosevelt in his campaign for regulation. For almost five years, the popular press echoed with disclosures of this nature.

The End of Muckraking

In April 1906 Theodore Roosevelt used the label "muckrakers" referring to investigative journalists. He was comparing them to a character in John Bunyan's *Pilgrim's Progress* who spent all his time raking the muck on the floor and therefore could not see heaven above him. The label stuck. **Muckraking** seemed to symbolize a style of reporting that emphasized only the negative. By 1907 popular interest in muckraking waned. While it lasted, however, muckraking supported the view of many reformers that once the facts of an evil situation were revealed, the political system would move to correct them.

muckraking
The name given to investigative reporters in the early 1900s.

Women and Progressive Reform

Women were the crucial foot soldiers of progressive reform; they were responsible for the success of these campaigns. The settlement house movement (see Chapter 18) continued to attract young women who were interested in social service. Jane Addams of Hull House in Chicago remained in the forefront of the movement. Other women joined Addams to promote urban-oriented reforms. Florence Kelley guided the National Consumers League. Julia Lathrop supported child labor legislation and in 1912 became the first director of the federal Children's Bureau. In New York Lillian Wald used the Henry Street Settlement as a base for work to improve conditions for women and children. Not all settlement house workers were women, but these institutions gave female reformers a supportive environment and a foundation on which to base their role in society.

Women also figured importantly in the conservation movement. In garden clubs and women's improvement clubs, they criticized the spread of billboards, dirty streets, and neglected parks. Women joined the Audubon Society, the Women's National Rivers and Harbors Congress, and the Sierra Club. They saved species of birds from extinction, fought against dams and destructive logging in the West, and campaigned for more national parks.

The Continuing Fight for Woman Suffrage

The lack of the right to vote frustrated women, and the campaign for woman suffrage became a central concern. Giving women the ballot, said suffrage leaders, would be a "tool with which to build a better nation." To reach that goal, however, the movement had to overcome substantial problems. In Congress, southern Democrats opposed suffrage because it might lead to votes for African Americans. Liquor interests feared that suffrage would help the prohibitionists. Within the suffrage campaign, fund-raising problems and organizational disarray limited the effectiveness of the drive for votes.

By 1910 it was evident that the strategy of pursuing a constitutional amendment at the federal level had stalled. Suffragists turned to the states where they devoted themselves to organizing campaigns that appealed to a majority of male voters. The result was a string of victories in the western states of Washington (1910), California (1911), Oregon (1912), Arizona (1912), Kansas (1912), Montana (1914), and Nevada (1914).

Reform in the Cities

Progressive reformers made their first important impact in the nation's cities. Two Ohio mayors, Samuel "Golden Rule" Jones of Toledo (1897–1903) and Tom L. Johnson of Cleveland (1901–1909), sought to produce changes in the way their cities functioned. Johnson lowered streetcar fares and introduced an electric lighting plan to show how rates could be kept low. Jones instituted municipal ownership of the trolley system, provided higher wages for city employees than private industry did, and founded free kindergartens. In Jersey City, the reformers George L. Record and Mark Fagan offered an East Coast variety of municipal uplift.

More typical of urban reform across the country were efforts to change the structure of city government itself. After Galveston, Texas, adopted the commission idea in 1900 (see Chapter 19), the "Galveston Idea" attracted national attention. Refined in Des Moines, Iowa, in 1908, commission government was in place in 160 cities by 1911.

Soon, however, the commission form gave way to the "city manager" idea. Under this arrangement the city council named a nonpartisan executive who was trained to administer the city under policies that the council specified. The plan promised efficiency, cost-cutting, and reduced partisan influence. Smaller and medium-sized municipalities began instituting the city manager form around 1908.

Urban reform achieved positive results in many cities. The consequences were not always constructive, however. Stressing the interest of the city as a whole did not always translate into fair treatment for the less advantaged and less powerful. In the case of the cities, as in other aspects of progressivism, efficiency and democratic values were not easy to reconcile.

Reform in the States

As urban reformers tried to improve their cities, they often confronted barriers within state government. The constitutions of many states restricted the capacity of a city government to manage its own taxes, regulate its public utilities, or supervise the moral behavior of its citizens. When progressives looked at their problems on the state level, they detected patterns of corruption and business influence that resembled those they had fought locally. Strong political organizations in many states stood in the way of the goals of reform. Reformers charged that the political party, tied to business interests, prevented meaningful improvements in state government.

At the state level, progressives favored the initiative and referendum. Allowing the people to propose laws or to vote on laws that had been enacted gave less authority to established political figures and institutions. The initiative and referendum first appeared in South Dakota in 1898. By 1915, twenty-one states had some form of these progressive procedures.

The direct primary spread across most of the nation by 1916; the recall was largely confined to a small number of western states. The primary was popular because it took the power to make nominations out of the hands of party leaders. The recall was more controversial. Angry conservatives charged that an election to remove a judge threatened the independence of the judiciary as a whole.

Increasing Regulatory Power

Greater emphasis on the regulatory power of state government accompanied these procedural reforms. Progressives strengthened the authority of existing state railroad commissions and created new commissions to oversee public utilities and insurance companies. These bodies, which would rely on experts in the field, seemed preferable to the whims of partisan lawmaking.

State government attracted popular and effective leaders during the twenty years after 1900. Theodore Roosevelt was a forceful executive for New York during his one term as governor. Also in New York, Charles Evans Hughes became famous for his probe of insurance companies, which gained him the governorship in 1906. Woodrow Wilson, elected governor of New Jersey in 1910, limited the power of corporations in that state.

La Follette of Wisconsin

The leading symbol of state reform was **Robert M. La Follette** of Wisconsin. During his two terms as governor, from 1901 to 1905, he established the direct primary, regulated Wisconsin's railroads, and levied higher taxes on corporations. He forged a close relationship between the state government and faculty members at the University of Wisconsin who advised him about policy. This reliance on academic experts was called "the Wisconsin Idea."

Robert La Follette
Progressive governor and senator from Wisconsin.

Progressivism as a National Force

By 1905 progressivism was moving onto the national stage. Corporations were interstate in character; only Washington could regulate them effectively. To solve the problems of political parties, the Constitution had to be changed. To create a more moral society, progressives contended, the national government had to grant women the vote, regulate the consumption of alcohol, and limit immigration into the United States.

With growth came problems. Where should the balance be struck between the goal of a more democratic society and that of greater efficiency? Efficiency required organization, expertise, and compulsion. Decision making should be left to the experts who knew how to regulate a railroad or a public utility. But that process enabled a well-organized interest group or lobbying campaign to exercise significant influence and sometimes corrupt the system. During this period, professional organizations such as the American Medical Association, the National Association of Manufacturers, and the National Civic Federation played a large role. Advocates of social justice organized their own lobbying groups, including the National Child Labor Committee, the National Conservation Association, and the National Consumers League.

Reproduced from the collections of the Library of Congress

Robert La Follette personified the reform energy of progressivism in his speeches to crowds in Wisconsin and across the nation.

The Problems of Reform

The changes that sought to make the political process more democratic sometimes had unexpected results. Well-funded pressure groups could employ the ballot to pursue an issue such as lower taxes or to attack an unpopular idea or group. The initiative could also reduce the electorate to deciding such issues as how long the lunch hour of a fire department might last. The direct primary did not mean that good candidates replaced bad candidates. A wealthy but less qualified candidate could circumvent the party and achieve success in the primary.

The direct election of U.S. senators, mandated through the Seventeenth Amendment in 1913, took the power of choice away from the state legislatures and gave it to the voters in each state. It meant that candidates had to raise larger amounts of money for their campaigns. Meanwhile, lobbying groups simply found new channels for improper influence. One unexpected consequence of these changes was the declining popular interest in voting that became evident in the 1904 presidential election and in later contests. Political parties, for all their weaknesses, had mobilized voters to come to the ballot box. The progressives never found a replacement for that function of the parties.

During the spring of 1905, however, reform was still fresh. Advocates of change believed that limited and gradual measures could improve society. With Roosevelt in the White House, they had a president who also believed that moderate reform was necessary. He pushed for national progressive legislation, and the result was a series of turbulent battles during his second term.

Roosevelt and the Modern Presidency: The Second Term

In the four years after he was elected in his own right, Theodore Roosevelt traveled widely to promote his programs, built up the bureaucratic machinery of the national government, and pushed Congress to consider a wide range of social problems. The president attracted bright young men to Washington to join him, and under Roosevelt the nation's capital became the focus of news and controversy.

Railroad Regulation and the Hepburn Act

Roosevelt began his reform campaign with railroad regulation. Strong constituencies supported the proposal. Customers of railroads in the South and West complained that rates were too high. Shippers and politicians maintained that the federal government, not the railroads themselves, should determine whether a rate was fair. To do that, the Interstate Commerce Commission (ICC) should have the power to review railroad rates to ensure that they were reasonable.

Presidential power had to be used to achieve Roosevelt's goal. The Department of Justice launched well-publicized probes of railroad practices to find out whether railroads were still giving rebates in violation of the 1903 Elkins Act. Roosevelt dangled the threat of revising the tariff to sway Republican leaders in the House to favor his approach. He shared information about railroad misdeeds with sympathetic reporters. When the rail companies started their own public relations effort, it backfired because the public did not believe the railroad claims.

Getting a bill that the White House wanted through Congress was not easy. Matters went smoothly in the House. The Hepburn bill, named after William P. Hepburn of Iowa, to give the ICC greater authority over railroads and their practices, was passed in February 1906 by a vote of 346 to 7. The Senate was the main obstacle. A long struggle ensued between Roosevelt and the conservative Republican leader, Nelson W. Aldrich of Rhode Island. The issue was whether the courts should have broad power to review the ICC's rulings. The Senate won some victories on the issue, but Roosevelt obtained what he most wanted. The Hepburn Act was passed in late June 1906. The ICC now had the power to establish maximum rates and to review the accounts and records of the railroads.

The Expansion of Regulation

There was more to Roosevelt's regulatory program than railroads. The public was worried about the condition of the food and drugs that Americans consumed. Led by Dr. Harvey Wiley of the Department of Agriculture, the government conducted experiments on the purity of food, and the findings revealed that adulterations and toxic chemicals made many food products unsafe. By early 1906 the clamor for reform had led to the introduction of a bill in Congress to restrict the sale of impure or adulterated food and drugs. The measure was passed by the Senate, but stalled in the House of Representatives.

During the winter of 1906, thousands of Americans read *The Jungle,* a novel about the meatpacking industry in Chicago. Written by a young Socialist named **Upton Sinclair,** the book depicted shocking conditions in the meatpacking plants. The public ignored Sinclair's political message, but they were outraged that dirt and filth endangered their meat supply.

President Roosevelt was outraged as well. The White House supported an amendment to the Agricultural Appropriation Act of 1906 that set up a federal program for meat in-

Upton Sinclair
A writer whose novel *The Jungle* exposed abuses in the meatpacking industry.

spection. The meatpacking industry tried to water down the bill, but the law represented a significant advance in regulatory power.

The controversy over meat inspection cleared the way for House action on the Pure Food Act. The Pure Food and Drugs Act was passed on June 30, 1906. A happy president called the three regulatory laws passed during that year's congressional session "a noteworthy advance in the policy of securing Federal supervision and control over corporations."

To achieve that control, Roosevelt sought to use the Bureau of Corporations to supervise companies that the White House deemed socially responsible. Having decided which businesses and corporate leaders met his standards of morality in the marketplace, he made private agreements with International Harvester and United States Steel. In return for letting the government examine their financial records, these companies would not be subjected to antitrust prosecutions. Firms that Roosevelt disliked, including Standard Oil, would be disciplined by federal lawsuits.

Roosevelt and World Politics

Roosevelt matched his activism in domestic policy with equal energy in the conduct of foreign affairs. He broadened the nation's activities in Asia and Europe and tried to educate the American people to accept the nation's new role as a world power. The result was a significant expansion of the power of the presidency in foreign affairs. The most notable achievement for Roosevelt was his part in bringing an end to the fighting between Russia and Japan.

Early in 1904 war broke out between Russia and Japan. Roosevelt sympathized with Japan because he regarded the Russians as a threat to the Open Door policy in China. As the Japanese won a series of decisive victories, however, the president concluded that a negotiated settlement would best serve the interests of the United States.

Though victorious on the battlefield, Japan was financially exhausted. In April 1905 Japan and Russia invited Roosevelt to mediate. Roosevelt summoned the combatants to a peace conference to be held at Portsmouth, New Hampshire, in August. The president's efforts as a peacemaker bore fruit when the two nations agreed to end the conflict; the Treaty of Portsmouth was signed in September 1905. Meanwhile the Roosevelt administration recognized the supremacy of Japan over its neighbor, Korea. In turn, Japan pledged that it had no aggressive designs on the Philippines.

The Algeciras Conference

In Europe, Roosevelt sought to reduce the growing tension between Germany and the other major powers, France and Great Britain. Roosevelt sympathized with Britain and France, but he wanted to persuade Germany and its leader, Kaiser Wilhelm II, to be reasonable in its international conduct. During 1905 the Germans made a major issue of French dominance of Morocco. The Kaiser wanted a conference to determine Morocco's status. Roosevelt convinced Britain and France to accept a conference rather than go to war over the fate of the North African country. The president expanded the international role of the United States when he sent delegates to the Algeciras Conference. The resulting settlement was a victory for France and its allies, but Roosevelt had for the moment staved off a European war.

The Gentlemen's Agreement

Later in 1906 the lingering problems in Japanese–American relations flared up again. Japan resented the nativist immigration policies of the United States. On the West Coast the increasing number of Japanese workers and residents intensified nativist and racist sentiments among whites. The San Francisco school board segregated children of Japanese ancestry, and Japan reacted angrily. Washington and Tokyo eventually worked out the "Gentlemen's Agreement" of 1907. The order of the school board was revoked, and Japan agreed to limit the number of immigrants who left that country for the United States.

The Great White Fleet

To increase funding for the Navy, Roosevelt sent the American Navy's "Great White Fleet" on a round-the-world tour from 1907 to 1909. When the vessels stopped in Japan in October 1908, the reception was enthusiastic and friendly. A month later the two nations negotiated the Root-Takahira Agreement, which called for the Open Door in China, the independence of that country, and preservation of the status quo in the Pacific.

When he left office in March 1909, Roosevelt expressed pride that the United States was "at absolute peace" with the rest of the world. The president had been an effective diplomat. His policy in the Caribbean had reaffirmed the supremacy of the United States and made possible the construction of the Panama Canal. In Asia he had done his best with the limited power available to him. Roosevelt's involvement in Europe had been positive, but it had not addressed the interlocking alliance systems that would lead to war in 1914.

Labor and Socialists Challenge Roosevelt

As the congressional elections of 1906 approached, the Republican party was still dominant. Some voters were turning away from the Republicans, however, and the Democrats had a new asset to help them against the Republicans: organized labor. The American Federation of Labor (AFL) had a membership of nearly 1.7 million by 1904. Its leaders hoped for legislation to limit the power of state and federal courts to block strikes through injunctions. When Republicans in Congress rejected such a program, the leader of the union, Samuel Gompers, called for the defeat of Republican candidates who were "hostile or indifferent to the just demands of labor."

In addition to the opposition of the AFL, Roosevelt worried about the growing power of the Socialist party and the most radical wing of the labor movement, the Industrial Workers of the World. Founded in 1905, the IWW, or as they were nicknamed "Wobblies," called for the overthrow of capitalism. The Socialist party, under the leadership of Eugene V. Debs, also gained strength at the polls. In 1904 Debs won some four hundred thousand votes. The threat of socialism, with its attacks on private property, disturbed the president. During the 1906 election campaign, he sent out members of his cabinet to attack the IWW as violent and dangerous.

The 1906 Elections

The Republicans lost twenty-six seats in the elections, revealing that they had significant problems. The protective tariff divided the party. Midwesterners wanted lower duties, whereas Republicans in the East would tolerate no tariff revision. Roosevelt's regulatory policies alienated party conservatives too. During the late nineteenth century, Republicans had used government power to promote economic growth, but they were less enthusiastic when Roosevelt regulated railroads, watched over the quality of food products, and attacked large corporations.

©The Granger Collection, New York

In the South women labored in the cotton mills of the region for long hours at low pay. Although in *Muller v. Oregon* the Supreme Court upheld the principle that a state could limit the hours women worked, the decision had little effect in North Carolina where these women worked in the spinning room of the White Oak Cotton Mill in Greensboro.

Problems with the Supreme Court

One barrier to reform was the Supreme Court. In the case of *Lochner v. New York* (1905), for example, the Court struck down a New York law that limited the hours employees could work in a bakery. It ruled that the law infringed on the right of the bakers under the Fourteenth Amendment to get the best reward for their labor. Sometimes the justices made an exception. In the 1908 case of **Muller v. Oregon,** they upheld an Oregon statute that limited the hours women could work. In other decisions, however, the Court invalidated the Employers Liabilities Act of 1906 and curbed the power of labor unions in the Danbury Hatters case.

Muller v. Oregon
Case in which the Supreme Court upheld limits on working hours for women.

Roosevelt and Conservation

Roosevelt's campaign for the conservation of natural resources also reflected his presidential activism. He created refuges for wild birds, preserved the Grand Canyon against intrusion from development, and set aside national parks. During his first term he worked for passage of the Newlands Reclamation Act (1902), which established a system of irrigation reservoirs in the West that was financed through the sale of public lands. The idea was to increase the amount of land available for agriculture and to preserve the rural way of life. Over the long term, however, the Newlands Act helped large farming corporations more than it did small landowners.

Roosevelt worked closely with **Gifford Pinchot** of the United States Forestry Service to formulate conservation policy. Neither man thought that natural resources should be locked up and saved for some indefinite future use. Instead, they should be managed by trained experts from the federal government. For Roosevelt and Pinchot, conservation did not mean that large corporations should be excluded from developing such resources. Conservationists who were convinced that the wilderness should be preserved rather than developed opposed the Roosevelt-Pinchot policy. Small landowners and stock growers in the West also disliked federal bureaucrats who favored big business in conservation matters.

Gifford Pinchot
He worked closely with Roosevelt to formulate a conservation policy that involved managing natural resources, not locking them up for indefinite future use.

Roosevelt had alerted the American people to a serious national problem. He raised important issues about the future of timber, water, wildlife, and mineral resources. He created national parks and established 4 national game preserves, 51 bird reservations, and 150 national forests. He could be proud of the National Monuments Act (1906) and the Governors Conference on Conservation (1908).

His policies did not, however, resemble modern environmental ideas. They required a high degree of control by the federal government and the cooperation of large corporations. In the West there was much resentment of programs that Washington had devised without much local support.

Deteriorating Race Relations

During his second term, Roosevelt showed less sympathy for the plight of African Americans than he had as a candidate for the presidency. He made no public statement about a 1906 race riot in Atlanta, Georgia, in which four blacks were killed and many others injured. Later that year he discharged without a hearing or trial the African American soldiers who were falsely accused of shooting up Brownsville, Texas, in 1906.

The situation of African Americans worsened. In August 1908 whites rioted against blacks in Springfield, Illinois; two blacks were lynched. A tide of bigotry swept the nation. In 1909 prominent white reformers such as Oswald Garrison Villard (grandson of the abolitionist William Lloyd Garrison), Mary White Ovington, and William E. Walling met with W. E. B. Du Bois, Ida Wells Barnett, and other blacks to form the **National Association for the Advancement of Colored People.** They sought an end to segregation, voting rights for blacks, and equal education for all children.

National Association for the Advancement of Colored People (NAACP)
An organization that fights against racial injustice.

Roosevelt's Last Years of Power

Roosevelt remained popular with the American people during the waning years of his administration. Among conservative Republicans, however, unhappiness with the president mounted. On Capitol Hill, party members in the House and Senate balked at Roosevelt's assertiveness. When problems in the banking industry led to the Panic of 1907, Roosevelt's Republican opponents blamed the economic troubles on his regulatory policies. To stem the danger to banks, Roosevelt agreed to let United States Steel acquire the Tennessee Coal and Iron Company.

The issue of Roosevelt's successor became a central problem for Republicans. Hoping to see his progressive policies carried on, the president decided to support his secretary of war, William Howard Taft. Roosevelt's resolve was confirmed when the secretary's major opponent, Senator

"WILL YOU PLEASE HUSH?"
From the *Herald* (New York)

By W. A. Rogers. From the *Herald*, New York

A cartoon attacks Roosevelt's antibusiness policies as a cause of the Panic of 1907.

Joseph B. Foraker of Ohio, attacked the president for his discharge of the soldiers who had been accused in the Brownsville shooting episode. By early 1907 Roosevelt had become the real campaign manager of Taft's drive to win the Republican nomination.

During early 1908 Roosevelt endorsed more sweeping regulation of corporations, a tax on inheritances of great wealth, and compensation laws for workers. Congressional Republicans reacted coolly to these proposals, and relations between the White House and Capitol Hill worsened throughout 1908. Meanwhile, Taft advanced toward the Republican nomination at the national convention in June.

His selection came on the first ballot. In their platform the Republicans promised to revise the protective tariff at a special session of Congress shortly after the new president was inaugurated. Given the divisions among Republicans over the issue, it would not be easy to reach agreement on a new tariff law.

The 1908 Presidential Election

The Democrats nominated William Jennings Bryan for the third time and were optimistic about his chances. In the early days of the campaign, Bryan ran well. Then Roosevelt threw his support behind Taft in a series of public statements. The Republicans won again: Taft garnered 321 electoral votes to Bryan's 162. The election was marked by ticket-splitting in which voters cast ballots for Taft for president and Democrats for other offices. The partisan allegiances and loyalties of the late nineteenth century were breaking down.

Roosevelt had picked Taft as his successor because he was convinced that Taft would carry on with his reform policies. Shortly after the election, however, tensions developed between Roosevelt and his political heir. Battles between Roosevelt and Congress flared as inauguration day approached.

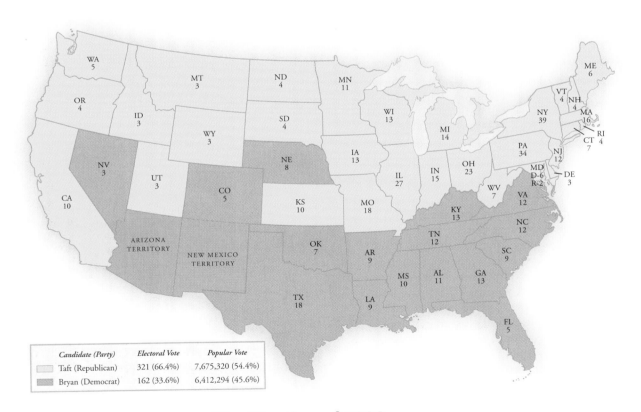

Candidate (Party)	Electoral Vote	Popular Vote
Taft (Republican)	321 (66.4%)	7,675,320 (54.4%)
Bryan (Democrat)	162 (33.6%)	6,412,294 (45.6%)

MAP 20.2 The Election of 1908

Theodore Roosevelt's hand-picked successor, William Howard Taft, defeated William Jennings Bryan, who was making his third run for the White House. Soon Taft and Roosevelt, who had once been close friends, would split with disastrous results for the Republican party.

Summary

Roosevelt and Reform

One of the hallmarks of American life in the twentieth century was the emergence of the strong presidency as the active agent of the federal government. William McKinley had done much to launch the modern American presidency, and between 1901 and 1909 Theodore Roosevelt captured the public imagination with his energy and personal charisma. In domestic affairs he argued that the chief executive should be a kind of guardian or "steward" of the national welfare. To that end, he expanded the role of Washington in regulating big business and the economy. He also embarked on conservation crusades to protect natural resources. Opposition within his own Republican party arose because of the new departure that Roosevelt was making about what presidents should be doing.

©The Granger Collection, New York

As for world affairs, Roosevelt saw the president as playing a much greater role as chief diplomat for the nation. He expanded the military, had the United States take part in international conferences, and projected American power with such enterprises as sending the "Great White Fleet" of the Navy around the globe. Traditional isolationism did not disappear because of Roosevelt's initiatives, but Americans became more accustomed to participating in international affairs as a result. In a world of rivalries among the great powers, Roosevelt believed that his country must be prepared to fight to defend its interests.

Much of Roosevelt's success came because he was so attuned to the desire for change that permeated the country in the first decade of the twentieth century. Americans sought to make their government at all levels both more efficient and more democratic. Regulatory agencies were designed to curb business excesses through the use of trained experts. Sometimes these bodies became too close to the industry they were supposed to oversee. For the most part, such groups as the Interstate Commerce Commission and the Bureau of Corporations provided a check on corporate power.

The muckrakers became famous as investigative journalists. One of the most celebrated was Ida Tarbell, who explored how Standard Oil became such a powerful economic force.

Reformers believed, as this cartoon from 1912 shows, that adoption of the direct primary would limit the power of political bosses and enable the electorate to make its voice heard with great effectiveness. It turned out, however, that direct primaries also favored candidates with money rather than just those with good ideas.

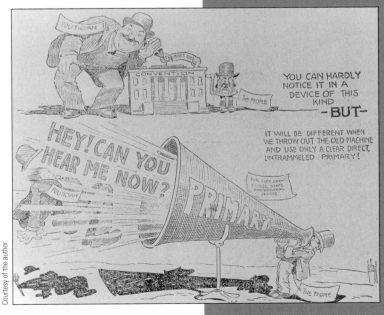
Courtesy of the author.

479

In 1908 William Jennings Bryan made his third unsuccessful run for the White House. The "boy orator" of 1896 had less hair and more flesh, but he retained his capacity to enthrall Democratic voters.

©The Granger Collection, New York

The progressives also believed that the cure for the ills of democracy was more democracy. They advanced such notions as the direct election of senators by the people, the initiative, referendum, and recall, and the direct primary in choosing candidates. Woman suffrage was another central reform idea. Left out of reform in this era were African Americans, Hispanics, and Asians who were seen as not yet ready to have the privileges of middle-class whites. This myopia limited what progressivism could do to improve the nation as a whole. Not all the crusades on which reformers embarked now seem appropriate. Prohibition of alcohol offers one such example. But the generation that cheered Theodore Roosevelt tried to make their society better. In the questions they posed and the answers they devised lay many of the debates about the nature of government and the proper means of social change that still shape contemporary thinking a century later. In that sense, Theodore Roosevelt and the Progressive Era cast a long shadow into the future.

Making Connections Across Chapters

LOOKING BACK

Much of what Theodore Roosevelt tried to do as president built on ideas and attitudes that were advanced during the 1890s and discussed in Chapter 19. In analyzing this chapter, you should be aware of how such events as the Panic of 1893, the election of 1896, and the Spanish-American War influenced the way issues were framed after 1900.

1. How did the experience of the 1890s shape the way Theodore Roosevelt approached the presidency?
2. What obstacles did the Republican party pose to Roosevelt's program in the White House?
3. Was Roosevelt a progressive or a conservative in his approach to government?
4. Why did conservation seem so important during the early twentieth century?
5. In your judgment, what made Roosevelt so popular?

LOOKING AHEAD

For all his accomplishments, Roosevelt left some problems for his political successors and the society to solve. In Chapter 21, with William Howard Taft and Woodrow Wilson, you'll see how the mixed legacy of Roosevelt shaped how society responded to these very different national leaders.

1. Did Roosevelt strengthen or weaken the Republican party during his presidency?
2. What problems do you see with Roosevelt's love of executive power and presidential discretion?
3. Was accepting big business as an accomplished fact the only way to deal with the problem of large corporations?
4. Was the United States ready to be a world power as Roosevelt envisioned?

RECOMMENDED READINGS

Cooper, John Milton Jr. *The Pivotal Decades: The United States, 1900–1920* (1990). Offers a thoughtful and well-informed account of the first two decades of the new century.

Cordery, Stacy. *Theodore Roosevelt: In the Vanguard of the Modern* (2002). A new brief biography of Roosevelt that provides a good look at his historical impact.

Dalton, Kathleen. *Theodore Roosevelt: A Strenuous Life* (2002). A full biography that examines the psychological and family influences on Roosevelt's career.

Diner, Steven J. *A Very Different Age: Americans of the Progressive Era* (1998). An interpretive synthesis that emphasizes social and economic issues.

Gould, Lewis L. *Reform and Regulation: American Politics from Roosevelt to Wilson* (1996). Covers the politics of the era.

Gould, Lewis L. *The Presidency of Theodore Roosevelt* (1991). Reviews the president's achievements in office.

Graham, Sara Hunter. *Woman Suffrage and the New Democracy* (1996). A crisp, thoughtful examination of the evolution of woman suffrage as a progressive movement.

Milkis, Sidney M., and Mileur, Jerome M., eds. *Progressivism and the New Democracy* (1999). An interesting collection of essays on the impact of progressive reforms.

Naylor, Natalie, Brinkley, Douglas, and Gable, John, eds. *Theodore Roosevelt: Many-Sided American* (1992). A group of essays on the many aspects of Roosevelt's life.

Tilchin, William. *Theodore Roosevelt and the British Empire* (1997). A good brief introduction to Roosevelt as a world figure.

AMERICAN JOURNEY ONLINE AND INFOTRAC COLLEGE EDITION

Visit the source collections at http://ajaccess.wadsworth.com and infotrac.thomsonlearning.com and use the Search function with the following key terms to explore documents, images, audio and video clips, articles, and commentary related to the material in this chapter.

Theodore Roosevelt

Ida Tarbell

muckraking

National Women's Trade Union League

Muller v. Oregon

Model T

J. P. Morgan

Upton Sinclair

NAACP

ONLINE PRIMARY SOURCES

Here are some examples of the many primary sources related to this chapter that you will find on the *American Passages* Web site: http://history.wadsworth.com/ayersbrief02.

Our Forests and National Parks, by John Muir, 1901

W.E.B. DuBois, Of Mr. Booker T. Washington and Others, 1903

The Threat of Food and Drug Adulteration, 1905

The site also offers self-quizzes, exercises, and many additional resources to help you study.

1909 *to* 1933

PROGRESS SEEMED EVERYWHERE IN 1909. AVIATORS CROSSED THE English Channel for the first time, wireless communication linked ships at sea with their destinations; at home Americans took to the open road in their new Ford automobiles. In such a heady climate of advancing technology and growing economic abundance, writers spoke of an end of war as nations talked out their disputes at the conference table rather than settling them on the battlefield. The path of history seemed well lit and clear toward a bright future of hope and peace.

The Stock Market Crash of October 1929 ended the ebullient optimism of the 1920s about the future of the American economy and the promise of wealth for millions. The entertainment newspaper *Variety* caught the mood of disillusion that anticipated the Great Depression with its sarcastic headline the day after the averages had tumbled.

Twenty-four years later, in the winter of 1933, the United States lay in the grip of a severe economic depression. Banks had closed, unemployment had soared, and the homeless and destitute roamed the land. Newspapers and magazines ran articles that speculated on whether democracy had failed. To a minority of Americans, the opposing ideologies of communism and fascism seemed alluring. As the nation faced the prospect of a potential social revolution, its citizens looked back with nostalgia to the early years of the century and wondered what had happened to destroy that optimistic and confident world.

The outbreak of a world war in the summer of 1914 did the most to unhinge the sense of progress that then permeated the United States. If advanced nations could ravage each other on European battlefields, who could any longer believe in the perfectibility of humanity? Americans first tried to stay out of the conflict, but by 1917 they entered the war on the side of France and Great Britain.

In less than two years, the experience of World War I accelerated trends toward a more powerful federal government, a more bureaucratic society, and a nation in which large corporations exercised an even greater role. At the same time, the bitter national and ideological conflicts of Europe spilled over into American life. Racial, ethnic, and sectional tensions produced social unrest and group hatreds that raged between 1917 and 1933.

During the war, however, some aspects of prewar reform reached completion. Women gained the vote in 1920 after three generations of struggle. Their ballots did not transform national politics in the years that followed, but their presence in the process ended centuries of a male monopoly of the elective system. The war years also achieved the temperance dream of a national prohibition of alcohol. Despite this reform success, the nation remained divided over its attitude toward liquor, a condition that raised problems for enforcing the new constitutional amendment.

In the aftermath of World War I, Americans rushed forward to embrace the new world of consumer goods and economic affluence. Automobiles, appliances, and installment buying reshaped attitudes about frugality and the future. The spread of mass media and big-time sports brought shared cultural experiences to many Americans. The decade seemed vibrant with the wailing of jazz, the roar of the metropolis, and the excitement of flaming youth.

Not all Americans shared in the prosperity or endorsed the headlong embrace of the modern world. Farmers never experienced the prosperity of the decade, and they encountered economic downturns sooner than did their city counterparts. Rural values remained strong even when transplanted to an urban setting. Some dislocated citizens sought the missing sense of community in the Ku Klux Klan, which promised ritual, controversy, and social change in equal measure. Many Americans found that

©Bettmann/CORBIS

The rise of the Ku Klux Klan reflected the cultural tensions that accompanied the end of the First World War. The hooded order attained nationwide popularity before its own excesses discredited it and its leaders. This illustration shows the union of the cross and the American flag that made the Klan such a potent symbol of intolerance.

The dramatic flight of Charles Lindbergh across the Atlantic alone in 1927 symbolized the promise of technology for the 1920s. "The Lone Eagle" became a popular celebrity, and thousands flocked to see him and his plane, *The Spirit of St. Louis*, when he traveled around the country after his epic adventure.

Reproduced from the collections of the Library of Congress

fundamentalist religious denominations spoke to their spiritual needs in ways that the modernist churches did not. Strains between city and country values showed themselves in politics in the 1928 presidential election when the urban, Catholic background of Democrat Al Smith turned many in his party toward the Republican nominee, Herbert Hoover.

Throughout the 1920s, the confidence that the economy would move ever upward sustained people even when they lacked wealth themselves. By the end of the decade, however, the prosperity that consumers had built and that corporations relished began to totter. Poor distribution of income, corporate excesses, weaknesses in the banking

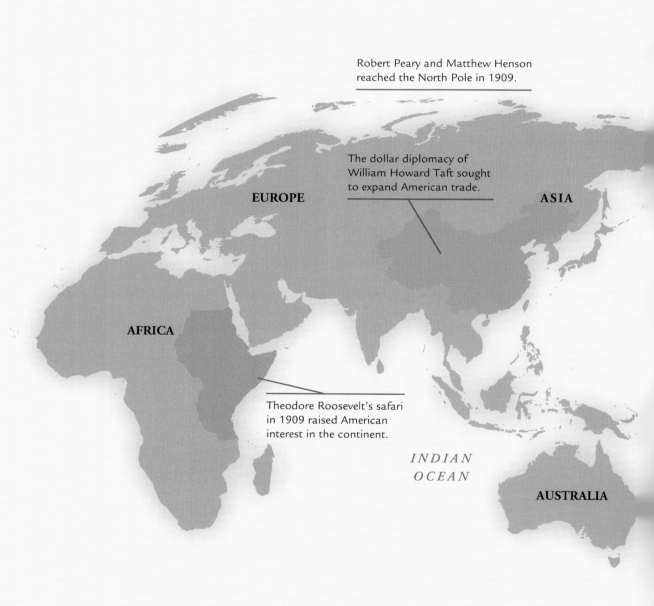

Robert Peary and Matthew Henson reached the North Pole in 1909.

The dollar diplomacy of William Howard Taft sought to expand American trade.

EUROPE

ASIA

AFRICA

Theodore Roosevelt's safari in 1909 raised American interest in the continent.

INDIAN OCEAN

AUSTRALIA

ANTARCTICA

structure, and mounting problems with international finance led to a stock market crash in 1929 and the Great Depression that grew steadily worse during the early 1930s.

A generation raised on the prospect of burgeoning prosperity found itself confronted with want, destitution, and despair. Organized charity seemed inadequate to the task of relief, and government at all levels also failed to address the economic problems in effective ways. By the winter of 1932, the nation experienced a tightening spiral of gloom and fear. The sunny days of progressivism and reform were only a grotesque echo of an age that had disappeared. In the American passage, the early 1930s seemed as close as any citizen wished to get to the valley of the shadow.

America and the World: 1909–1933

Henry Ford began assembly line process of making automobiles.

NORTH AMERICA

Theodore Roosevelt helped spread American influence into Asia and Latin America.

PACIFIC OCEAN

ATLANTIC OCEAN

After acquiring the Canal Zone, the United States began work on the waterway to connect the Pacific and the Atlantic.

SOUTH AMERICA

Progressivism at Its Height

1909–1914

WHEN THEODORE ROOSEVELT LEFT THE PRESIDENCY IN MARCH 1909, progressivism entered a phase of partisan upheaval. Under **William Howard Taft,** the Republicans split apart. The Democrats moved toward a more active role for the national government. The Socialists mounted a vigorous challenge from the left. For five years it seemed as though the party system might fragment into more consistent ideological alignments.

Political ferment also revealed the tensions among reformers. Campaigns for **woman suffrage,** the prohibition of alcohol, restriction of immigration, and social justice created new coalitions. In the process, progressivism provoked a conservative reaction that limited the possibilities for reform.

The social and economic forces that were producing a consumer society also gathered strength during this period. **Henry Ford**'s low-priced automobile gained greater popularity, and other products of industrialism attracted more customers. Women found more opportunities for employment.

Beyond the nation's borders, international strains in Europe and revolutions in Latin America and Asia made foreign policy more of a national concern than it had been since the war with Spain. Still, the outbreak of fighting in Europe during the summer of 1914 came as a shock. World War I did not resolve the crisis in which progressivism found itself. Instead, it added new complexity to an already turbulent period.

William Howard Taft
The twenty-seventh president of the United States, who split with Theodore Roosevelt once in office.

woman suffrage
Women achieved the right to vote in 1919–1920 after an intense struggle in Congress.

Henry Ford
An automaker who developed the assembly line and low-priced automobiles.

Taft's Presidency

Soon after William Howard Taft took the oath of office, Theodore Roosevelt left for his hunting safari in Africa. A celebrity as an ex-president, Roosevelt found that his activities were news, even across the ocean. The issues of regulation, social justice, and corporate power with which he had struggled were also on the agenda for his successor.

Taft came to the White House facing complex problems. Republican conservatives expected him to slow the movement toward reform. Party progressives, on the other hand, wanted the new president to expand Roosevelt's legacy. The Republicans had promised in their 1908 platform to revise the tariff but had not specified which direction the alterations would take. Protectionists who wanted no changes and reformers who sought lower rates waited to see what Taft would do.

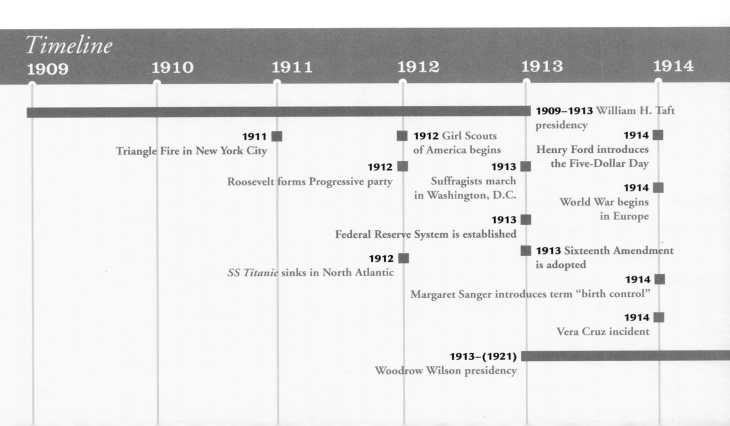

Timeline

| 1909 | 1910 | 1911 | 1912 | 1913 | 1914 |

1909–1913 William H. Taft presidency

1911 Triangle Fire in New York City

1912 Girl Scouts of America begins

1914 Henry Ford introduces the Five-Dollar Day

1912 Roosevelt forms Progressive party

1913 Suffragists march in Washington, D.C.

1914 World War begins in Europe

1913 Federal Reserve System is established

1913 Sixteenth Amendment is adopted

1912 SS *Titanic* sinks in North Atlantic

1914 Margaret Sanger introduces term "birth control"

1914 Vera Cruz incident

1913–(1921) Woodrow Wilson presidency

Taft had been a lawyer and a federal judge before heading the Philippine Commission in 1900. He proved to be an adept colonial administrator, but Roosevelt summoned him back to the United States in 1904 to serve as secretary of war. During Roosevelt's presidency, Taft acted as troubleshooter for the administration. It was widely believed that the two men agreed on almost all issues. As a result, Roosevelt looked forward to a continuation of his policies under the new president.

A Conservative President

Roosevelt had miscalculated. Taft did not agree with the expansive view of presidential power that Roosevelt had advanced. He believed that the president should act within the strict letter of the law and the constitutional boundaries of his office. Such a philosophy was bound to disappoint Roosevelt and the progressive Republicans.

Taft had other political problems as president. He lacked Roosevelt's sense of public relations. He quarreled with the press and often delayed writing speeches until the last minute. The success he had enjoyed as a speaker during the 1908 campaign was soon forgotten as he failed to sway audiences. Taft also depended on the advice of his wife, Helen Herron Taft, in political matters, but during the spring of 1909 she had a serious illness that deprived him of her emotional support.

The Dilemma of the Tariff

In revising the tariff, Taft confronted the consequences of Roosevelt's postponement of the issue. Tensions had grown among Republicans about whether rates were too high. Progressive Republicans favored reductions in customs duties; conservatives felt that high rates were justified.

To maintain Republican unity in Congress, Taft supported the reelection of conservative Joseph G. Cannon as Speaker of the House. If Taft challenged the speaker, who enjoyed the support of a majority of House Republicans, Cannon could easily stall action on the tariff program.

Once Congress assembled in March 1909, Taft sent it a message asking for a new tariff law. In April the House passed a tariff bill that lowered rates on sugar, iron, and lumber and placed coal and cattle hides on the free list. The measure was named the Payne bill after its author, Sereno B. Payne, chairman of the Ways and Means Committee. The bill passed the House.

The bill then went to the Senate, where the Republican leader, Nelson Aldrich of Rhode Island, was regarded as a virtual dictator. In fact, Aldrich's position was much more vulnerable than it seemed. Among the Senate Republicans were seven to ten midwesterners who wanted to see lower tariffs and limits on Aldrich's power. On the other side of the debate, senators from the East and Far West insisted that goods from their states must be protected against foreign competition. The result was that Aldrich did not have a majority of votes for the Payne bill.

To obtain the votes that he needed, Aldrich had the Senate Finance Committee write a bill with eight hundred amendments, half of which raised rates back toward those of the Dingley Tariff. Senate progressives were infuriated, saying that the public expected lower tariffs. The quarrels over the bill on the Senate floor damaged Republican unity. The Aldrich version finally cleared the Senate in early July by a vote of 45 to 34. Ten Republicans voted against Aldrich.

The Political Consequences

As a House-Senate conference committee hammered out the final version of the bill, both sides looked to Taft for support. The president used his leverage to obtain some concessions, such as lower duties on gloves, lumber, and cattle hides, but he failed to obtain reductions on wool, cotton, and industrial products. Convinced that he had gained all he could, Taft signed the Payne-Aldrich Tariff when it was passed in early August 1909.

Taft endorsed the new tariff during a tour of the Midwest in September. Speaking at Winona, Minnesota, he called the law "the best tariff bill that the Republican party ever passed." Conservatives applauded his remarks while progressives fumed because he had not praised their fight for lower rates. Republican harmony thus took a beating throughout the autumn of 1909.

The Battle over Conservation

To make matters worse for the president, he found himself engaged in a battle that threatened to disrupt his friendship with Theodore Roosevelt. Federal government control of natural resources had been one of Roosevelt's favorite policies. His principal aide in this program had been Chief Forester Gifford Pinchot. Taft disliked Pinchot and doubted whether the policies Roosevelt had pursued were legal. The new secretary of the interior, Richard A. Ballinger, also had little use for Pinchot. The president and Ballinger intended to pursue conservation policies that conformed to existing laws. When Ballinger began to open lands for development that Pinchot had closed off to settlers and businesses, Pinchot accused him of acting as an agent for a syndicate trying to sell valuable coal lands in Alaska. After looking into the charges, Taft sided with Ballinger.

Pinchot then wrote a letter of protest that a senator released to the public. Taft thereupon fired Pinchot for insubordination. In the ensuing controversy, a congressional probe revealed that Taft and Ballinger had not done what Pinchot had charged, but the political damage led to Ballinger's resignation in 1911.

The political consequences were significant. Taft seemed to be attacking a key Roosevelt policy. Roosevelt, still on safari in Africa, received letters saying that Taft was betraying him. Roosevelt supporters talked of restoring him to the presidency in 1912.

The congressional session of the spring of 1910 added to Taft's problems. Progressive Republicans in the House saw Speaker Cannon's reputation as a dictator as a liability for the congressional elections to be held that fall. In March, House members curtailed Cannon's power. Because Taft had supported the speaker, the episode was viewed as a rebuke to the president as well. Taft insisted that Republicans should be loyal to his administration or risk reprisals when they sought White House approval of appointments or legislation. This policy increased the tension between the president and Congress.

At the end of the session Taft adopted a more conciliatory tone. Greater harmony led to enactment of additional progressive legislation. The Mann-Elkins Act broadened the power of the Interstate Commerce Commission beyond that provided by the Hepburn Act (1906). The measure gave the ICC more authority to block railroads from charging higher rates for short hauls, gave it additional power to set rates, and compelled the railroads to justify rate increases. Other legislation included increased appropriations for the Navy. Progressives applauded a postal savings law that encouraged private citizens to use federal banks located in post offices as a means of encouraging thrift. Unhappily for Taft, progressive Republicans maintained that these results were achieved in spite of the president rather than because of his support.

Roosevelt's Return

Meanwhile, Theodore Roosevelt had returned to the United States. As he came home, Pinchot and others filled his ears with Taft's alleged misdeeds. Roosevelt decided that it was up to him to get the Republican party back on the right course. He received a tumultuous welcome when his ship entered New York Harbor. A crowd of one hundred thousand people cheered him as he rode up the streets, and his popularity seemed as strong as ever.

At first Roosevelt refrained from public quarrels with the president. The two men met in late June but did not discuss the issues

Table 21.1
Party Strength in Congress, 1894–1918

Congress	Year Elected	Republicans	Democrats	Other
SENATE				
Fifty-fourth	(1894)	43	39	6
Fifty-fifth	(1896)	47	34	7
Fifty-sixth	(1898)	53	26	8
Fifty-seventh	(1900)	55	31	4
Fifty-eighth	(1902)	57	33	
Fifty-ninth	(1904)	57	33	
Sixtieth	(1906)	61	31	
Sixty-first	(1908)	61	31	
Sixty-second	(1910)	51	41	
Sixty-third	(1912)	44	51	1
Sixty-fourth	(1914)	40	56	
Sixty-fifth	(1916)	42	53	
Sixty-sixth	(1918)	49	47	
HOUSE				
Fifty-fourth	(1894)	244	105	7
Fifty-fifth	(1896)	204	113	40
Fifty-sixth	(1898)	185	163	9
Fifty-seventh	(1900)	197	151	9
Fifty-eighth	(1902)	208	178	
Fifty-ninth	(1904)	250	136	
Sixtieth	(1906)	222	164	
Sixty-first	(1908)	219	172	
Sixty-second	(1910)	161	228	
Sixty-third	(1912)	127	291	17
Sixty-fourth	(1914)	196	230	9
Sixty-fifth	(1916)	210	216	6
Sixty-sixth	(1918)	240	190	

Source: The information in this table is derived from *The Statistical History of the United States* (Stamford, CT: Fairfield Publishers, 1965).

that separated them. Meanwhile, the Republicans' internal warfare intensified. Taft used his appointment power against the Middle Western progressives in his party; their candidates were not nominated for positions in the federal government. Taft went even further, trying to organize loyal Republicans against reform leaders. These moves failed, and the president's inability to rally support within his own party emphasized his weakness as a leader.

Roosevelt and the New Nationalism

New Nationalism
Roosevelt's far-reaching program that called for a strong federal government to stabilize the economy, protect the weak, and restore social harmony.

Roosevelt sharpened the dispute in a series of speeches during the summer of 1910. He called his program the **New Nationalism.** In doing so he drew in part upon the ideas of Herbert Croly, whose book *The Promise of American Life* had been published in 1909. Croly urged political leaders to advocate a "New Nationalism" that accepted the growth of big business and supplied strong presidential leadership. This message was a natural for Roosevelt. In a speech at Osawatomie, Kansas, he said that "The New Nationalism regards the executive power as the steward of the public welfare." The "rules of the game" should be "changed so as to work for a more substantial equality of opportunity and reward for equally good service." He meant that there should be an income tax, inheritance taxes on large fortunes, workmen's compensation laws, and legislation to protect child labor.

The congressional elections of 1910 hurt both the progressives and the conservatives in the Republican party. The Democrats gained control of the House of Representatives; in the Senate, the Republicans dropped ten seats. They still had a ten-seat majority, but the progressive Republicans often voted with the Democrats. After years of being the opposition party, the Democrats looked forward to the presidential election of 1912. For Roosevelt, the elections proved a major setback. He told friends that he would not oppose Taft in 1912.

Progressive Victories

Between 1910 and 1913 the spirit of progressivism reached its high-water mark. The reformers seemed to have public opinion behind them, and for a brief interval it appeared that conservatives in both parties were on the defensive. This did not prove to be the case in the long run, but in the short term the forces of reform pushed forward.

Woman Suffrage

A leading example of this trend was the campaign for woman suffrage. In April 1910 the National American Woman Suffrage Association (NAWSA) presented Congress with a petition that more than four hundred thousand people had signed. The document asked for a constitutional amendment allowing women to vote. Although Congress refused to act, one suffrage worker, surprised by the size of the petition, said that her cause "is actually fashionable now."

The petition reflected NAWSA's new vitality. Under the leadership of Anna Howard Shaw, the organization's membership had grown. In states like Washington (1910), California (1911), and Arizona, Kansas, and Oregon (1912), woman suffrage triumphed. However, referenda to give women the vote failed in Ohio, Wisconsin, and Michigan.

Alice Paul
A main figure in the radical wing of the woman's suffrage movement in the early twentieth century.

Woodrow Wilson
The twenty-eighth president of the United States, he was an advocate for the New Freedom and the League of Nations.

Alice Paul became the main figure of the radical wing of the suffrage movement. She had fought for the vote in England, and now she wanted to apply the same militant tactics of picketing and civil disobedience to the United States. For a few years Paul and her allies worked on NAWSA's congressional committee. In March 1913, a day before **Woodrow Wilson** became president, they staged a well-publicized suffrage parade in Washington. Frustrated at what she saw as the cautious tactics of NAWSA, Paul and Lucy Burns left the organization in early 1914 to form the Congressional Union.

Significant obstacles to suffrage remained. The liquor industry feared that women who voted would support Prohibition. White southerners worried that woman suffrage might lead to suffrage for African Americans. Men saw their dominance threatened if women took part in politics. To counter these arguments, NAWSA stressed that female voting would lead to a purer and more honest politics. They also played down the argument that women should have equal political rights. Instead, they contended that woman suffrage would offset the votes of immigrants and racial minorities in large cities. Between 1910 and 1914 momentum for suffrage increased.

Prohibition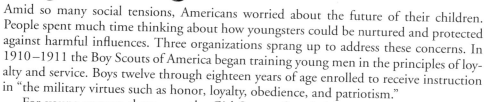

The drive to restrict the use and sale of alcohol also gained increasing support after 1910. The Anti-Saloon League had established a dominant position among prohibitionist organizations since its founding during the 1890s (see Chapter 19). The league sought to limit the power of the liquor industry to sell its product to the public. The first step in its strategy involved elections to give voters in a county or state the "local option" to ban the sale of alcohol. The plan was by a series of such elections to widen gradually the area that dry forces controlled. By 1906, impatient with the slowness of the local option method, the league shifted its emphasis to statewide elections to achieve dry dominance.

Oklahoma adopted **Prohibition** in 1907. By 1914 eight other states had banned the sale of alcohol. Militant prohibitionists (they were called "drys"; antiprohibitionists were "wets") found the state-by-state process discouraging. The presence of a wet state next to a dry one encouraged drinkers to cross the border to ease their thirst. In 1913 prohibitionists in Congress passed the Webb-Kenyon Act, which outlawed the shipment of alcohol into dry states. The Anti-Saloon League's next goal was a constitutional amendment to ban the sale of alcohol everywhere in the United States.

Prohibition
An effort to ban the sale of alcohol; it was achieved in 1919.

Restriction of Immigration

The effort to restrict immigration into the United States also accelerated during these years. The flow of newcomers from southern and eastern Europe remained large. There were more than one million immigrants in 1910, nearly two million in 1913, and over a million more in 1914, before the outbreak of World War I.

Ethnic and cultural tensions erupted. Protestants wanted to keep out Catholic and Jewish newcomers. Labor unions feared that immigrants would become strikebreakers. Prejudice against the Chinese and Japanese fed nativist sentiments on the West Coast. By 1913 a bill to impose a literacy test on immigrants passed both houses of Congress. President Taft vetoed the measure, and Congress was unable to override the veto. Despite this setback, sentiment for immigration restriction spread after the war began.

Progressivism and the Immigrant

Progressive reform offered some support to nativist and racist feelings. Businesses favored a loose immigration policy. Opposition to allowing further immigration was portrayed as a way to help workers already in the United States. A feeling that cultures from Southern and Eastern Europe threatened traditional values led some progressives to endorse restriction.

A tragic incident in Atlanta, Georgia, in 1913 underlined the tensions that accompanied the drive to restrict immigration. When a young factory worker, Mary Phagan, was murdered, suspicion fell on her superintendent, Leo Frank, a Jew whose parents had come from Russia. Frank was innocent, but he became the victim of anti-Semitism and fear of outsiders and was convicted and sentenced to death. After the governor of Georgia commuted his sentence, a mob abducted and lynched him in August 1915.

Saving the Children

Amid so many social tensions, Americans worried about the future of their children. People spent much time thinking about how youngsters could be nurtured and protected against harmful influences. Three organizations sprang up to address these concerns. In 1910–1911 the Boy Scouts of America began training young men in the principles of loyalty and service. Boys twelve through eighteen years of age enrolled to receive instruction in "the military virtues such as honor, loyalty, obedience, and patriotism."

For young women there were the Girl Scouts, founded in 1912, and the Campfire Girls, founded in the same year. These two groups prepared American girls for future domestic responsibilities. With the constructive activities that the Girl Scouts, Campfire Girls, and Boy Scouts supplied, delinquency and crime among the young would be reduced, or so their advocates maintained. In the process, members would learn the values that middle-class society cherished.

The struggle against child labor overshadowed all the other drives to improve the condition of children. In 1910 some two hundred thousand youngsters below the age of twelve labored in mills and factories. Attempts to limit child labor in textile firms in the South brought meager results. In 1912 the reformers succeeded in establishing a Children's Bureau within the federal government, but Congress failed to pass any legislation that directly addressed the child labor problem.

Despite the many obstacles that progressive reformers faced, there was a sense that the nation was making genuine progress on social issues. William Allen White, a Kansas newspaper editor, recalled that "All over the land in a score of states and more, young men in both parties were taking leadership by attacking things as they were in that day." Women, too, experienced feeling a sense of possibility that infused middle-class reform during the years before World War I.

Labor Protest in a Changing Workplace

Despite this sense of progress, conflict prevailed in the relations between labor and capital. There were many strikes, and bitter struggles between workers and employers took place. Unlike White's middle-class colleagues, American laborers measured their progress in violent and bloody confrontations against harsh conditions in the workplace.

Changes in the Corporation

Unrest grew out of changes in the way that men and women worked. As industrialization spread, factories and businesses grew. A business such as the Amoskeag Company textile mills in Manchester, New Hampshire, dominated the lives of its seventeen thousand employees with an elaborate system of welfare programs and company organizations.

The nature of these large corporations was changing as well. The need to develop new products at a regular rate led such corporations as DuPont and General Electric to emulate the example set by German firms. They created industrial laboratories where research and development could go on steadily. General Electric set up links to universities that allowed scientists and engineers on their faculties to address the needs of the corporations in their research. The ties between business and education helped propel economic growth for the rest of the century.

New Rules for the Workplace

Within the large factories, relationships between employers and workers became more structured and routinized. The informal dominance that the foreman had exercised during the nineteenth century often gave way to bureaucratic practices. To control costs and ensure steady production, companies set up procedures for regular reporting on expenditures, centralization of purchasing and maintenance, and measurement of worker productivity. The goal, according to one engineering advisor, was "the establishment of standards everywhere."

Out of these innovations came a new way to run the factory and workplace. This technique, known as *scientific management,* was developed by Frederick Winslow Taylor. As a mechanical engineer in the steel industry, Taylor became convinced that careful study of how each individual task was conducted would lead to a more efficient workplace. Once the maximum amount of time necessary to do a specific job was established, workers could be instructed on how to complete the task without any wasted motion. Stopwatches measured the speed of work down to the split second.

As a concept, Taylorism enjoyed great popularity among businesspeople. Although most employers did not adopt all of Taylor's ideas, the principle of managing factories and shops systematically took hold. The core of scientific management was to reduce all jobs to a set of simple steps that required little skill, but workers resented practices that made them perform repetitive, routine movements all day long. "We object to being reduced to a scientific formula," said one machinist.

The Limits of Paternalism

Whereas scientific management viewed workers in a detached and bloodless way, some corporations revived the tradition of paternalism in the form of welfare and incentive programs for their employees. Lunchrooms and toilet areas were cleaned up, recreational facilities established, and plans set up for pensions and profit sharing. National Cash Register of Dayton, Ohio, was a leader in the field, along with H. J. Heinz Company, the Amoskeag Mills, and Remington Typewriter.

Despite these efforts, the situation for most American workers showed only marginal improvement. Businesses used a variety of techniques to block unions and prevent workers from improving their condition. The National Association of Manufacturers (NAM) pushed for laws to outlaw the union shop (mandating membership in a union to work in the plant) in favor of what was called the "open shop" in which unions were not allowed. Blacklists of pro-union employees were circulated, and new workers often had to sign contracts that barred workers from joining a union. (Because they reduced the power of workers below that of a "yellow dog," these became known as "yellow dog" contracts.) When strikes occurred, employers used nonunion labor (strikers called them "scabs") to end the walkouts. Court injunctions limited the ability of strikers to picket and organize. Violent clashes between workers and police accompanied many strikes.

Unorganized Workers

The working classes in the cities faced the ravages of inflation during the early years of the century. Although wages rose over the levels of the 1890s, prices accelerated at a faster rate. These workers also encountered difficult and often dangerous conditions in their factories and sweatshops. Many laborers turned to unions. In New York City and Philadelphia from 1909 to 1911, the International Ladies Garment Workers Union organized workers within the shirtwaist manufacturing business. Twenty thousand women strikers took their grievances into the streets to demonstrate their solidarity. They managed to wrest some concessions from their employers in the form of union shops and improved working conditions.

Many manufacturers forced their employees to work in deplorable conditions with poor ventilation, dirt and filth, and danger to the lives of those who labored. In March 1911 a fire erupted at the Triangle Shirtwaist Company on New York City's Lower East Side. As the workers fled the flames, they found locked doors and no fire escape routes. The conflagration claimed 146 lives. Many women were killed when they jumped to the pavement below. The **Triangle Shirtwaist Fire** spurred reform efforts among politicians in the New York legislature.

Varieties of Labor Protest

Labor unions gained members between 1900 and 1914. The American Federation of Labor, led by Samuel Gompers, had several million members, but its craft unions discouraged organization among industrial workers. Women employees received little support from Gompers and his allies. Thus, the majority of workers remained out of the union movement.

The Industrial Workers of the World (IWW) appealed to the unskilled masses. Its ultimate goal was still a social revolution that would sweep away industrial capitalism. To the IWW's leadership, violent strikes seemed the best way to promote industrial warfare.

Triangle Shirtwaist Fire
A tragic fire at the Triangle Shirtwaist Company in which dozens of female workers perished.

The tragedy of the Triangle Shirtwaist Fire in New York City resulted in the deaths of dozens of women who labored in that sweatshop. Rescue workers lay out the corpses from the disaster.

Strikes in Lawrence and Ludlow

The IWW gained national attention when a strike erupted in the textile mills of Lawrence, Massachusetts, in mid-January 1912. After the textile companies announced substantial wage reductions, the workers walked out. "Better to starve fighting than to starve working," they said. The children of strikers were sent to live in other cities, a tactic that publicized the walkout and swayed public opinion to the workers' cause. On March 1 the companies granted them a pay hike. Women strikers were key participants in the victory. As one of their songs put it, they sought "bread and roses" by which they meant a living wage and a life with hope.

Another controversial strike occurred in Colorado. The United Mine Workers struck against the Colorado Fuel and Iron Company in September 1913. The workers complained about low wages and company camps with brutal guards. John D. Rockefeller, who controlled the coal company, asked the governor to call in the National Guard to maintain order. Confrontations between soldiers and miners ended in the "Ludlow Massacre" of April 1914 in which troops fired on miners in a tent city at Ludlow. Five strikers and one soldier were shot, and two women and eleven children died in the flames that broke out in the tents. Federal inquiries followed, and the workers obtained some concessions.

Changes in the workplace during the progressive period had benefited employers far more than workers. Some social legislation had been enacted to protect the worker from the effects of industrial accidents, and the length of the working day had been reduced somewhat. Compared with Great Britain or Germany, however, the United States still did not provide social insurance when a worker became unemployed, pension benefits for old age, or equal bargaining power on the job.

Dollar Diplomacy

dollar diplomacy
A phrase used to describe Secretary of State Philander C. Knox's foreign policy under President Taft, which focused on expanding American investments abroad, especially in Latin America and China.

While the nation grappled with problems arising from the struggle between business and labor, its role overseas revealed the continuing effects of the expansion that began under McKinley and Roosevelt. In foreign affairs, William Howard Taft and his secretary of state, Philander C. Knox, adopted the policy of **dollar diplomacy** in their relations with Latin America and Asia. They believed that peace and stability increased when U.S. corporations traded and invested in underdeveloped areas of the world. Instead of military force, the ties of finance and capital would instruct countries in the wise conduct of their affairs.

Latin America seemed to offer an ideal location for applying the principles of dollar diplomacy. No European countries challenged the supremacy of the United States in that region. In 1909 Taft and Knox induced bankers to loan money to Honduras to prevent British investors from achieving undue influence there. In 1911 they compelled the government of Nicaragua to accept another loan from U.S. investors. Unfortunately, some Nicaraguans regarded the scheme as an intrusion in their affairs, and they rebelled against the government that had made the deal. The Taft administration sent Marines to Nicaragua to restore order, and the resulting U.S. military presence continued for several decades.

Taft and Knox also tried to apply dollar diplomacy to China. The government wanted American capitalists to support a railroad in China, first to develop the country and then to offset further intrusion by Japan. Knox envisioned that a syndicate of nations would lend China money to purchase existing railroads in Manchuria. The plan collapsed when the British, Russians, and Japanese rejected the idea in early 1910. The Knox initiative sparked resentment in Japan, and relations between that country and the United States remained tense.

A foreign policy problem closer to home emerged in 1911. Porfirio Díaz had ruled Mexico for almost forty years. He had attracted American investment because he had maintained apparent calm and stability within his nation. In fact, however, his dictatorial rule bred discontent that eventually erupted in a revolution. Francisco I. Madero, the leader of the revolution, came to power hoping to transform the nation. But he aroused the opposition of conservative forces, including the military, large landowners, and the Roman Catholic Church. Shortly before Taft's term ended in 1913, Madero was overthrown and murdered.

Republican Discord and Democratic Opportunity

Following the Republican losses in the elections of 1910, Taft and Roosevelt worked out an uneasy agreement not to attack each other during the first half of 1911. Republican progressives still looked for an alternative to Taft in 1912. To placate the progressives, Taft eased Ballinger out of the cabinet and named two supporters of Roosevelt as secretary of the interior and secretary of war. Roosevelt told friends that he would not be a candidate in 1912.

Taft in Trouble

Taft's troubles with Congress persisted. He negotiated a trade agreement with Canada that was based on reciprocal concessions on tariffs. Neither the Democrats nor the progressive Republicans liked Canadian Reciprocity because it lowered import duties on products that affected their districts. Taft pushed the agreement through Congress, but then Canadian voters rejected the government that had supported it.

Then the president's fragile friendship with Roosevelt collapsed. Unlike his predecessor, Taft believed in greater business competition; he was more vigorous in "busting" the trusts than Roosevelt had been. In October 1911 the Department of Justice filed an antitrust suit against United States Steel. One of the practices that violated the law, according to the indictment, was the company's acquisition of the Tennessee Coal and Iron Company during the Panic of 1907 (see Chapter 20). Since Roosevelt had approved the merger, the indictment amounted to a public criticism of his presidency. Roosevelt was furious, and he listened eagerly to friends who told him that he should run against Taft. By the early part of the year, he had decided to do so.

The Struggle between Roosevelt and Taft

Throughout the spring of 1912 the two former friends waged a bitter battle for the Republican nomination. For the first time, a few states held primary elections to choose delegates to the Republican convention. Roosevelt attracted a majority of these voters. Taft ran strongly among party regulars, who selected their delegates in tightly controlled nominating conventions. As the Republican National Convention opened in Chicago, neither man had a clear majority. The Republican National Committee, which Taft controlled, gave the president 235 of the disputed delegates and left Roosevelt with only 19. When the national convention upheld what the national committee had done, Roosevelt knew that he would not have the votes to become the Republican nominee.

Summoning his followers to leave the convention, Roosevelt denounced Taft's "theft" of delegates and promised that he would fight on. For the next two months Roosevelt prepared to run as a third party candidate. At the first convention of the Progressive party in August 1912, Roosevelt put forward a

Harper's Weekly May 4, 1912

A cartoon lampoons Theodore Roosevelt's ambitions for a third term in 1912.

very progressive platform that embodied the New Nationalism he had been advocating since 1910. The party sought more government regulation of big business, minimum wages and maximum hours for workers, government pension programs, and the end of child labor. Roosevelt told reporters that he was "as fit as a bull moose." Cartoonists quickly made the animal the symbol of Roosevelt's crusade.

The Democratic Opportunity

The Democrats watched with astonishment and glee as the Republicans split apart. To exploit the disarray of their opponents, they needed a credible presidential candidate of their own. One attractive newcomer was the governor of New Jersey, Woodrow Wilson, who had carried that staunchly Republican state by a sizable majority. Soon there was talk of Wilson as a potential candidate for the Democrats.

Woodrow Wilson was fifty-six years old in 1912. Born in Virginia, he grew up in the South and shared its racial views. He attended Princeton University and earned a doctorate in history and political science at Johns Hopkins University. He joined the Princeton faculty in 1890 and became president of the university in 1902. After initial successes, he ran into resistance from more conservative alumni and faculty when he opposed class distinctions among the Princeton student body. He resigned from the Princeton presidency in 1910. New Jersey Democrats urged Wilson to run for state office. Long interested in a career that might take him to the White House, he won the New Jersey governorship in his first try at elective office.

The Democrats selected Woodrow Wilson to oppose Roosevelt and Taft in 1912. Seated in the chair, Wilson talks to supporters at a rally.

The Wilson Candidacy

Wilson had been a conservative Democrat for much of his life. The experience of his Princeton presidency led him toward progressivism. His candidacy scared some Democrats who preferred the safer and less inspiring leadership of the Speaker of the House, James Beauchamp "Champ" Clark of Missouri. Wilson, Clark, and several other Democratic hopefuls fought for the nomination in primaries and state conventions.

When the national convention met in Baltimore in late June, no candidate was in sight of the two-thirds majority needed for the nomination. Clark was the closest to having a simple majority of the delegates. In a series of ballots, the convention was deadlocked. After Clark failed to get the needed two-thirds, Wilson gained strength as an acceptable national candidate. He won on the forty-sixth ballot. With the Republicans split between Roosevelt and Taft, prospects seemed excellent for a Democratic victory in 1912.

The Socialist Challenge

There was a fourth serious candidate in the 1912 presidential race. Once again the Socialist party selected Eugene V. Debs as its candidate. Debs had run in every election since 1900, and his total vote had increased each time. A popular speaker who loved the rigors of campaigning, Debs took his "Red Special" across the country. "Comrades," Debs cried, "this is our year."

Socialism gained followers because the party spoke to the grievances of the agricultural and working poor. In an era when their doctrines were not linked to a foreign nation and did not imply totalitarian methods, Socialists seemed to present a tolerable alternative to the major parties. Disputes within their ranks over whether to pursue reform at the ballot box or through more violent means prevented the party from offering a united front. Moreover, since he had little chance of winning, Debs did not have to frame programs with a view to carrying them out in office.

Creation of the Progressive Party

President Taft decided to observe the custom that an incumbent president did not campaign for reelection. Since he expected to lose badly and the Republicans were short of money, it was a wise choice. Many conservative Republicans decided to support Wilson in order to retain control of their party and keep Roosevelt out of the presidency.

Roosevelt campaigned with his usual energy and excitement, and he attracted many reformers to his cause. The Progressive party held its national convention in Chicago during August. The atmosphere mixed the fervor of a revival meeting with the backroom bargaining of a traditional political conclave. Roosevelt told the delegates that "our cause is based on the eternal principle of righteousness, and even though we who now lead may for the time fail, in the end the cause itself shall triumph."

To woo the white South, the delegates excluded African Americans from the convention. Roosevelt defended the protective tariff and attacked reciprocity with Canada. The main financial support for the new party came from wealthy newspaper publishers and corporate executives. At its core, however, the Progressive party's endorsement of expanded social justice legislation made it more forward-looking than either the Republicans or the Democrats. The party supported woman suffrage, limits on child labor, and a system of "social insurance."

The centerpiece of Roosevelt's New Nationalism was the proposal for an "administrative commission" that would "maintain permanent, active supervision over industrial corporations engaged in interstate commerce." This would enable Roosevelt to continue his policy of distinguishing between "good trusts" that served the public interest and "bad trusts" that harmed the public. The judgment of what constituted a good or bad trust would be up to Roosevelt and his administration.

Enacting Roosevelt's program thus would involve a broadening of national authority and an expansion of the bureaucratic machinery of the federal government. The role of the president would also be expanded to ensure that the public's rights were protected. To that extent, Roosevelt's position in 1912 looked forward to the regulatory and welfare state that emerged later in the twentieth century.

Woodrow Wilson and the New Freedom

As Roosevelt laid out his program, Wilson decided that he would have to campaign as actively as his major rival. Wilson told the voters that only a Democratic president could govern effectively with the Democratic Congress that was certain to be elected. He then offered a program of his own to counter Roosevelt's New Nationalism. He called it the New Freedom.

As Roosevelt began his campaign, Wilson consulted with **Louis D. Brandeis,** a prominent Boston lawyer and reformist thinker. Brandeis believed that big business was inefficient economically and dangerous to democracy. He laid out his critique of bigness and the role of finance capitalism in a book titled *Other People's Money,* which was published in 1914. He told Wilson that the issue Roosevelt was raising could be met with a simple question: shall we have regulated competition or regulated monopoly? Wilson should emphasize the need for greater competition to control monopoly and call for stricter enforcement of the antitrust laws.

As for social justice, Wilson said that he supported the goals of eliminating child labor, improving wages for women, and expanding benefits for employees, but he questioned whether the federal government should supply these benefits. In that way he appealed to progressives but also prevented southern Democrats from opposing him as an enemy of states' rights (and segregation). The New Freedom was, like most campaign slogans, broad and vague.

Louis Brandeis
A prominent Boston lawyer and reformist thinker who was a consultant to Wilson during his campaign for election in 1912.

Wilson Victorious

The 1912 election was turbulent down to election day. During a speaking engagement in Milwaukee, Wisconsin, Roosevelt was shot, yet he finished his talk while the bullet was still embedded in the copy of his speech he carried in his pocket. The incident aroused sympathy for Roosevelt but did not change the outcome. Wilson received 435 electoral

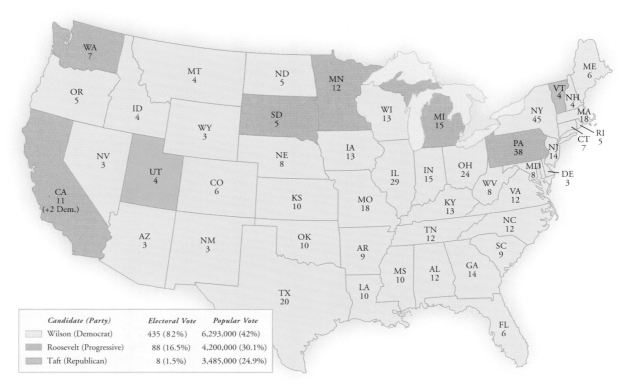

MAP 21.1 The Election of 1912

Because Democrat Woodrow Wilson faced a divided opposition in the presidential election of 1912, the result was a landslide victory in the electoral vote. Theodore Roosevelt's Progressive party ran second, and William Howard Taft's Republicans were a distant third.

votes to 88 for Roosevelt and 8 for Taft. The Democrats swept Congress. Nevertheless, Wilson was a minority president. He received about 42 percent of the popular vote. Eugene Debs won just over nine hundred thousand popular votes, or 6 percent of the total, and Roosevelt and Taft divided the rest. It was now up to Woodrow Wilson to prove that the Democratic party could govern the nation.

Wilson's Presidency

Because of the domestic achievements of his first term and his advocacy of the League of Nations in his second, Woodrow Wilson became one of the most important political leaders of the early twentieth century. He strengthened the power of the presidency, increased the regulatory role of the national government, and led the nation to play a greater part in international affairs. Even more than Roosevelt, he had the capacity to articulate national values in effective and moving language.

With these strong qualities came important limitations. Before he became president, Wilson had suffered a series of small strokes that increased his natural stubbornness. Although he often called for open government, he kept his decisions to himself and consulted only a few friends about his policies. His righteousness caused his political enemies to develop an intense dislike of his methods and tactics. However, when the tide of events ran with Wilson, as they did during his first term, he was a powerful leader.

Launching the New Freedom Program

Wilson lost no time in demonstrating his intention to be a strong president. In his inaugural address on March 4, 1913, he spoke eloquently of the negative aspects of industrial-

The Social Cost of Industrialism

Woodrow Wilson's first inaugural address on March 4, 1913, offered an eloquent statement of how a major national progressive saw the nation's task in dealing with the social cost of industrialism and rapid change.

We see that in many things that life is very great. It is incomparably great in its material aspects, in its body of wealth, in the diversity and sweep of its energy, in the industries which have been conceived and built up by the genius of individual men and the limitless enterprise of groups of men.

It is great, also very great, in its moral force. Nowhere else in the world have noble men and women exhibited in more striking forms the beauty and the energy of sympathy and helpfulness and counsel in their efforts to rectify wrong, alleviate suffering, and set the weak in the way of strength and hope. We have built up, moreover, a great system of government which has stood through a long age as in many respects a model for those who seek to set liberty upon foundations that will endure against fortuitous change, against storm and accident. Our life contains every great thing, and contains it in rich abundance.

But the evil has come with the good, and much fine gold has been corroded. With riches has come inexcusable waste. We have squandered a great part of what we might have used, and have not stopped to conserve the exceeding bounty of nature, without which our genius for enterprise would have been worthless and impotent, scorning to be careful, shamefully prodigal as well as admirably efficient. We have been proud of our industrial achievements, but we have not hitherto stopped thoughtfully enough to count the human cost, the cost of lives snuffed out, of energies overtaxed and broken, the fearful physical and spiritual cost to the men and women and children upon whom the dead weight and burden of it has fallen pitilessly the years through. The groans and agony of it all had not reached our ears, the solemn, moving undertone of our life, coming up out of the mines and factories, and out of every home where the struggle had its intimate and familiar seat. With the great Government went many deep secret things which we too long delayed to look into and scrutinize with candid, fearless eyes. The great Government we loved has too often been made use of for private and selfish purposes, and those who had used it had forgotten the people.

Questions to Consider

1. What view of an industrial society does Woodrow Wilson advance in his inaugural address?

2. To what extent does he defend the achievements of American society?

3. Where has the nation fallen short in its treatment of those affected by the rapid growth of business?

4. What is Wilson's view of the current state of national politics and the influence of lobbying on the government?

Explore additional primary sources related to this chapter on the *American Passages* Web site: http://history.wadsworth.com/ayersbrief02.

Source: *Woodrow Wilson's First Inaugural Address*, March 4, 1913.

ism. There was "the human cost, the cost of lives snuffed out, of energies overtaxed and broken, the fearful physical and spiritual cost to the men and women and children upon whom the dead weight and burden of it all has fallen pitilessly the years through."

To implement his program, Wilson first asked Congress to take up the issue of the tariff. To dramatize the problem, he decided to deliver his message to Congress in person. No president had done so since Jefferson had abandoned the practice in 1801, but presidential appearances before Congress became more common once Wilson resumed the technique.

In the speech itself, Wilson urged the House and Senate to reduce import duties. The Democratic House responded with a measure to lower tariffs, named after Oscar W. Underwood, the chairman of the Ways and Means Committee. The Underwood bill cut duties on raw wool, sugar, cotton goods, and silks. To compensate for the revenue that would be lost, the new tariff imposed a small tax on annual incomes over $4,000 with rates increasing for those who made more than $20,000 a year. Progressives had secured ratification of the **Sixteenth Amendment** in February 1913, which made the income tax constitutional.

Sixteenth Amendment
Ratified in 1913, this amendment made an income tax constitutional.

When Woodrow Wilson came to Congress to speak on behalf of tariff reform in 1913, he broke a century and more of tradition that presidents did not deliver their messages in person. His innovation became commonplace in the years that followed.

William Jennings Bryan
Named secretary of state by Wilson, he pursued world peace through arbitration treaties.

Democrats worried about what would happen when the Underwood bill reached the Senate. The Democrats were relatively unified, however, and pressure from large corporations for higher rates had eased. Only smaller businesses, fearing foreign competition, pushed hard for tariff protection. President Wilson added his voice on May 26, when he publicly denounced the "industrious" and "insidious" lobby that was trying to weaken the drive for tariff reform. The Democrats in the Senate stuck together, lowered the duties that the House had set, and passed the bill in August by a vote of 44 to 37. The conference committee's version of the bill passed both houses, and Wilson signed the Underwood Tariff into law on October 3, 1913.

The Federal Reserve System

Building on his momentum with the tariff, during June 1913 Wilson turned to reform of the nation's banking system. A modern economy could not function efficiently without a central bank with the capacity to control the currency, meet the monetary needs of different sections of the country, and ensure that the money supply was adequate to the demands of the growing economy. The issue became whether private banking interests or the national government should be in charge of the central bank.

Before Wilson was elected, the National Monetary Commission, headed by Nelson Aldrich, had offered the idea of a system of reserve banks that private bankers would supervise. Wilson initially favored this approach until Secretary of State **William Jennings Bryan** insisted that the federal government must be supreme over the reserve banks. At the urging of Louis Brandeis, Wilson accepted Bryan's ideas, and in a message to Congress on June 23, 1913, he said that the new system "must be public, not private, must be vested in the Government itself."

It took six months to get a banking bill through Congress. Wilson had to appease southern and western Democrats, who sought to expand the credit available to farmers and to outlaw the practice known as interlocking directorates, in which banking officials served as directors of banks with which they competed. The president withstood criticism from the banking community itself and used patronage and persuasion to win over potential opponents among Democrats in the Senate.

Congress completed its action in mid-December, and Wilson signed the Federal Reserve Act on December 27. This act established the Federal Reserve Board, whose members the president appointed, and created a structure consisting of twelve reserve banks located in different parts of the country. The Federal Reserve had the power to determine the amount of money in circulation, to expand or contract credit as needed, and to respond to some degree to changes in the business cycle.

Wilson and the Trusts

Wilson had now gone a good distance toward fulfilling his campaign pledges to reduce the tariff, reform the banking system, and deal with the problem of trusts. Early in 1914 the president asked Congress to consider trusts in a constructive spirit. Some of the legislation passed in that year followed the principles that Wilson had outlined in his campaign. The Clayton Antitrust Act (1914) endeavored to spell out precisely the business practices that restricted competition and then prohibit them.

As time passed, however, the president's thinking shifted. He came to favor the creation of a Trade Commission that would respond to business practices as they evolved, an idea that resembled what Theodore Roosevelt had proposed in 1912. The Federal Trade

Commission was established during the fall of 1914. A delighted Wilson said that he had almost completed the program he had promised in his 1912 presidential campaign.

Wilson and the Progressive Agenda

The president's statements left many progressives disappointed. They wanted the Democratic administration to push for social justice legislation. Wilson did not yet believe that Washington should support the demands of progressive interest groups. He also worried about the precedent that might be set by a government that used power to address specific social issues. Such a policy might lead to attacks on racial segregation in the South, and Wilson supported segregation.

When supporters of woman suffrage sought Wilson's backing in 1913 and 1914, he turned them down. He also opposed federal aid for rural credits, restrictions on child labor through congressional action, and Prohibition. Court decisions had subjected organized labor to the workings of the antitrust laws, and the unions wanted that policy changed through legislation. Again, Wilson declined to act. Worsening economic conditions during the spring and summer of 1914 reinforced Wilson's belief that his administration should remain conservative on social issues. He tried to reassure businesses that the administration was friendly toward them. These gestures did not appease the Republicans or their business supporters, however.

Social and Cultural Change during the Wilson Years

While politicians worked out Wilson's New Freedom programs during 1913 and 1914, social and cultural transformations accelerated. Americans with a literary or artistic bent turned to the ideas of European thinkers, who emphasized greater freedom for the individual in an uncertain world. Some of these principles came to be defined as *modernism*. In the days just before World War I, a sense of optimism and possibility filled the air.

Automobiles for a Mass Market

When Wilson went to his inauguration on March 4, 1913, he drove in an automobile. This action symbolized the vast changes that were making the people of the United States more mobile in their daily lives and more eager for the consumer products of an industrial society. In particular, the innovations in both production and marketing of Henry Ford (see Chapter 20) were bringing cars within the reach of the average middle-class American.

If Ford wanted to fulfill his dream of building "a motor car for the great multitude," he had to devise a means of producing cars continually and in even greater quantities. He borrowed the concept of the assembly line from the meatpacking industry, and his engineers adapted it to making cars. The Ford plant in Highland Park, Michigan, featured a large belt, fed by smaller belts, that brought the chassis of the car and its windshields, tanks, batteries, and other parts together in a smoothly functioning operation. At first it took the workforce ninety-three minutes to turn out a single Model T. By 1920 the cars were coming off the line at the rate of one per minute.

On January 5, 1914, Ford proclaimed that he would pay his workers $5 for an eight-hour day. The announcement was headline news across the country. Ford was not a serious economic thinker, but he understood that people needed to earn enough money in wages to be able to afford the cars he was making. He realized that he could make more money by selling large numbers of low-priced vehicles than he could by selling a few expensive cars.

The Five-Dollar Day program was also designed to head off potential unrest among Ford workers. Absenteeism and high turnover among employees hampered production schedules. In addition, unhappiness among workers might lead to the organization of unions. To offset these trends, the new program aimed at sharing profits in a way that would keep workers at their jobs.

The Growing Use of Electricity

Another sign of progress was the spreading reliance on electricity. Average annual use of electricity doubled during the twenty years after 1912. New products offered homemakers the chance to ease the dull routines of domestic work. General Electric introduced the Radiant Toaster in 1912, which promised "Crisp, Delicious, Golden-Brown Toast on the Breakfast Table." The Hoover Suction Sweeper would "Sweep With Electricity for 3¢ a Week." Newer stoves and washing machines also came into use.

Other technological developments were still in their early stages. The Wright brothers had made the first power flight in 1903, but aviation began in earnest five years later. Harriet Quimby of the United States was the first woman to fly a plane across the English Channel. Meanwhile, the use of wireless telegraphy in marine navigation expanded. The disaster of the *Titanic,* which hit an iceberg in April 1912 and sank with the loss of hundreds of passengers, underlined the need for reliable radio communications for all vessels. Congress enacted a bill mandating the Navy to promote radio usage.

Artistic and Social Ferment

Artistic and cultural ferment accompanied the peak years of progressivism. In 1913 the International Exhibit of Modern Art took place at the 69th Regiment Armory in New York City. Quickly dubbed "The Armory Show," it displayed the works of such European painters as Pablo Picasso and Henri Matisse. The modernist paintings offended many critics who attacked them in vicious terms. Marcel Duchamp's work *Nude Descending a Staircase* was labeled "an explosion in a shingle factory." Yet the public flocked to see the paintings, and American artists were stimulated and challenged to adopt the new forms of expression.

The period also produced innovative literary figures. Reporters and novelists clustered in New York's Greenwich Village. Among them were Max Eastman, publisher of *The Masses,* a magazine that assailed conventional values and the established political system; Eugene O'Neill, a playwright; and John Reed, a radical journalist. Outside of New York, Theodore Dreiser was continuing a literary career that included *The Financier* (1912), a novel depicting a ruthless tycoon; Sherwood Anderson was a short-story author who criticized middle-class life in the nation's heartland.

Among the influential writers of the day was Walter Lippmann, a Harvard-educated commentator and social critic, who published *A Preface to Politics* (1913) and *Drift and Mastery* (1914). Lippmann sympathized with the New Nationalism of Theodore Roosevelt and was one of the cofounders, with Herbert Croly, of *The New Republic,* soon a leading journal of political opinion and cultural commentary. Another important critical voice was H. L. Mencken, editor of *Smart Set,* a New York magazine; he assailed the cultural provincialism of much of American culture.

Women, too, sought to share the freedoms that men enjoyed. In 1912 women in Greenwich Village founded a club called Heterodoxy whose only demand was that its members should "not be orthodox" in their views. In their discussions and in the public meetings they sponsored, they called their doctrine "feminism."

Cultural changes occurred even for women who did not call themselves feminists. Women's skirts had become several inches shorter since the beginning of the century. Bobbed hair became fashionable, and more women smoked openly in public. When movie stars like Mary Pickford became famous, the use of cosmetics spread. The "flapper," an image associated with the 1920s, actually made her appearance at about this time.

Greater freedom for women in the Progressive Era brought them into places previously reserved for men. These four women are drinking in the bar of a New York hotel.

©Bettmann/CORBIS

Americans at Play

The ways in which Americans used their leisure time reflected a trend toward mass entertainment. Boxing was still a major sport. When Arthur John **"Jack" Johnson** became the first African American heavyweight champion in 1908, the public clamored for a "white hope" to reclaim the title. Johnson defeated each of his white challengers in the ring, but he had to flee the country when the government accused him of transporting women across state lines for immoral purposes.

The early years of the twentieth century brought baseball to new heights of popularity. The two professional leagues had emerged, and the World Series had become an annual fall ritual. It was a time of few home runs because of the "dead ball" (wrapped and made in such a way as to make it less resilient). Nevertheless, the public avidly absorbed the ample news coverage that baseball received.

Jack Johnson
The first African American heavyweight boxing champion, taking the title in 1908.

Motion Pictures and the Vaudeville Stage

Motion pictures and vaudeville competed for Americans' entertainment dollars. In elaborate vaudeville houses, audiences saw such stars as Fanny Brice, Al Jolson, and Sophie Tucker. By the time Wilson became president, however, motion pictures offered a challenge to the dominance of vaudeville. Movies were evolving from short features into real stories of an hour or more in length. The places where patrons saw films were upgraded, while the price of admission remained reasonable. In the darkness viewers followed the feats of the acrobatic Douglas Fairbanks Sr. or the winsome beauty of Mary Pickford. Within a decade, the movies would emerge as the mass entertainment medium of the nation.

New Freedom Diplomacy

Throughout the Progressive Era, the focus of national attention was on domestic political and economic concerns. The newspapers carried full coverage of international news, but Americans were isolated from the tensions of world affairs by two vast oceans. Americans allowed their elected leaders to conduct foreign policy as long as the general policies of isolation and noninvolvement with Europe were observed.

Woodrow Wilson and the World

Woodrow Wilson came to the presidency without any experience in foreign policy. Nevertheless, he had definite ideas about how the nation should behave in world affairs. During his first eighteen months in the White House, Wilson applied his precepts to diplomatic problems in Asia and Latin America.

The president appointed William Jennings Bryan as secretary of state, but he never allowed Bryan to have a significant role in shaping policy. Bryan spent some of his time making speeches about public issues and promoting international treaties of conciliation. Many countries signed these treaties before the war broke out in 1914; they provided for a "cooling-off" period before countries could begin fighting. Though a noble gesture, these documents had no practical effect.

Wilson's closest advisor on foreign policy was Edward M. House of Texas. House conducted foreign missions for Wilson before and during World War I. As for the rest of the diplomatic corps, Wilson allowed Bryan to select "deserving Democrats" to replace Republican ambassadors and ministers. The quality of American diplomacy suffered in the process.

Wilsonian Ideas in Practice

In foreign affairs, Woodrow Wilson believed that the United States should set an example for the world. "Morality and not expediency is the thing that must guide us," he said in 1913. The Wilson administration encouraged American business to seek markets overseas but to do so in a way that did not resemble the "dollar diplomacy" of the Taft years.

In Asia the Wilson administration stepped back from Taft's commitments, instructing American bankers to withdraw from the Chinese railroad consortium that Taft and Knox had sponsored. The United States also recognized the Republic of China, which had come into power following the 1911 revolution that ousted the Manchu dynasty. Wilson and the Democrats put the Philippine Islands on the road toward independence, but their efforts to counter the rise of Japanese influence in Asia proved less successful.

Wilson wanted his policy toward Latin America to be less intrusive and dominant than Roosevelt's had been. To that end, he worked out a treaty with Colombia that apologized for Roosevelt's actions in 1903–1904. The pact outraged the former president, and the Senate did not approve the treaty while Wilson was in office. Better relations with Latin America did not, in the president's mind, mean accepting governments that offended his moral values. That principle led him into the kinds of intervention that he would have preferred to avoid. He kept troops in Nicaragua and extracted further concessions from that country. Other military detachments went to Cuba, Haiti, and the Dominican Republic.

Mexican Involvement

Victoriano Huerta
The Mexican general who presented a problem to President Wilson.

The most controversial episode in foreign affairs that confronted Wilson was the revolution in Mexico. The Madero government, which had taken over from Porfirio Díaz in 1911, was ousted just before Wilson was inaugurated in March 1913. The man who toppled Francisco Madero was General **Victoriano Huerta.** Although most European nations quickly recognized Huerta's government, the United States did not. Wilson instead threw the weight of the United States behind Venustiano Carranza, a rebel against the Huerta government, but his offers of cooperation were not accepted. The president's policy eventually resulted in an armed confrontation in April 1914.

To block the flow of munitions into Mexico, Wilson had sent the Navy to patrol the Gulf of Mexico. Sailors from the USS *Dolphin* went ashore at Tampico on April 9, and Mexican authorities arrested them. Released quickly and without further incident, they returned to their ship. The admiral on the scene nonetheless demanded that the Mexican authorities apologize and make a twenty-one-gun salute to the American flag. Huerta's government replied that the Mexican flag should be saluted.

The president went to Congress for authority to use force and ordered troops to occupy the port of Vera Cruz. Heavy fighting erupted in which more than one hundred Mexicans and nineteen Americans died. The reaction in Mexico was immediate and unanimous: all the warring parties denounced the United States.

At this point Wilson drew back and allowed Argentina, Brazil, and Chile to act as mediators. The negotiations that followed led to the evacuation of Vera Cruz on November 14. Dependent on outside funds to pay his army, Huerta left office when his money ran out in July 1914. Carranza took power, and Wilson promptly recognized his government.

Hispanics in the Southwest

One of the lasting effects of the revolutionary upheavals in Mexico was an increase in the flow of immigrants from that country into the United States after 1910. Although many immigrants returned to Mexico after working in the United States for several months, some thirty-five thousand to seventy-five thousand stayed on each year. The dictatorial regime of Porfirio Díaz impelled political dissidents and impoverished peasants to travel north of the Rio Grande. Once the revolution began in 1911, the ensuing turbulence and violence drove more Mexicans toward the border. Throughout these years the spread of irrigation agriculture, railroads, and mining in the Southwest increased the demand for inexpensive labor.

The newcomers from south of the border found work in the sugar beet fields of Colorado, the agricultural valleys of south Texas and southern California, and the towns of Arizona and New Mexico. Other Hispanics labored for daily wages in Los Angeles, El Paso, and San Antonio. Their wages were low, sometimes under $1.25 per day.

Major centers of Hispanic life emerged in the southwestern cities. Ethnic communities sponsored mutual aid societies and established Spanish language newspapers. Religious prejudice remained strong, however, and segregation and poverty limited the opportunities open to Mexican Americans.

The international tension between Mexico and the Wilson administration led to periodic "brown scares" along the border. Anglo residents feared vague conspiracies to reclaim land lost by Mexico during the nineteenth century. By 1915 a violent cultural conflict that claimed hundreds of lives was in progress in south Texas. As a result of these struggles, Mexican Americans lost much of the land they had held in the area. Nevertheless, Hispanics had achieved the basis for a greater presence in the United States during the twentieth century.

World War I

By 1914 the major European nations were in a state of barely repressed tension. For several decades, a system of interlocking alliances tied nations together. If one country found itself at war with another, all the other powers could easily be drawn into the struggle. On one side stood Germany. Its powerful industries and efficient army made it a source of worry to its neighbors. The Germans wanted to attain the international respect they believed to be their rightful due. They had built up a large navy that had fueled tensions with Great Britain. Their leader, Kaiser Wilhelm II, had erratic dreams of world influence that

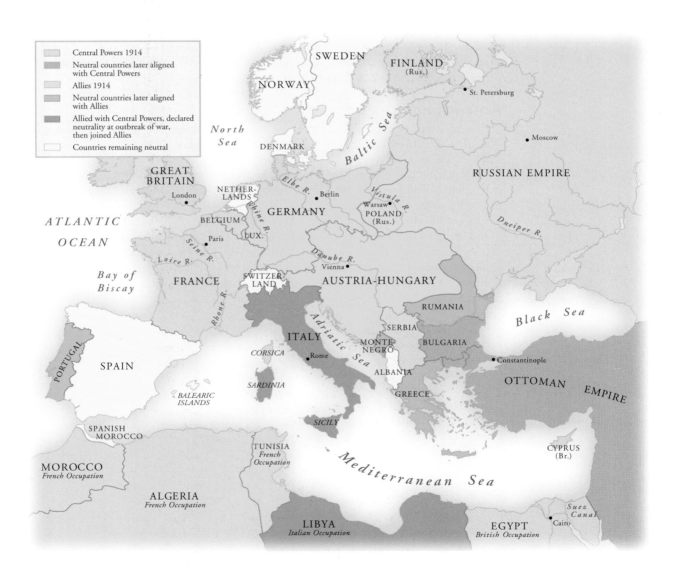

MAP 21.2 Europe on the Eve of World War I

In the summer of 1914, when the First World War erupted, Germany and Austria-Hungary dominated the center of the European land mass. France, Great Britain, and Russia counterbalanced the Central Powers. Once the fighting began, the system of alliances drew most of Europe into the conflict.

his generals and admirals adapted for their own expansionist purposes. The Germans had treaty links to the sprawling and turbulent nations of Austria-Hungary and the even more ramshackle regime of the Ottoman Turks. Italy had been part of the so-called **Triple Alliance** with Germany and Austria-Hungary, but these ties were frayed by 1914.

Against the Germans stood the French, the Russians, and, if the Germans attacked France, the British. The Russian Empire was in decay, the French feared another defeat at the hands of Germany, and the British worried about German naval strength. By 1914 all the powers had elaborate plans for mobilization in the event of a general crisis. Once these timetables went into effect, the relentless pressure of military events would frustrate efforts at a diplomatic resolution.

Triple Alliance
An alliance between Italy, Germany, and Austria-Hungary whose ties were frayed in 1914.

The Road to World War

World War I began in the Balkans. On June 28, 1914, the Austrian archduke, **Franz Ferdinand,** and his wife were murdered in the town of Sarajevo in Bosnia, a province of the Austro-Hungarian Empire. The Austrians soon learned that the killer was paid by the Serbians. The Austrians made harsh demands on Serbia that would have left that nation defenseless. The Germans supported their Austrian allies, with the result that the Russians came to the defense of the Serbs. Soon all the European countries were drawn into the conflict. By early August of 1914, Germany, Austria-Hungary, and Turkey, known as the Central Powers, were fighting against Great Britain, France, and Russia, now called the Allies. Italy remained neutral for the time being.

Franz Ferdinand
An Austrian archduke murdered along with his wife in Sarajevo, Bosnia. Austria's response to the dual murder led to the beginnings of World War I.

America and the European War

The sudden outbreak of fighting in Europe surprised Americans. It had been a century since there had been a major war involving all the major European countries. Surely, the conventional wisdom of the day said, the self-restraint and wisdom of the great nations made a destructive war unlikely. So when the armies marched, Americans were shocked. A member of Congress observed that "[t]his dreadful conflict of nations came to most of us like lightning out of a clear sky."

The world war came at a time of emotional distress for Wilson. His wife, Ellen, died of the effects of Bright's disease on August 6, 1914. This personal loss devastated the president who occupied himself in dealing with the war. On the domestic political scene, the Democrats were expected to encounter serious losses in the congressional elections. Until war broke out, it seemed as if politics might be returning to something resembling its normal patterns.

Summary

Progressivism at Its Height

This chapter examines the important five years from the time Theodore Roosevelt left the presidency until the First World War broke out in Europe during the summer of 1914. The Republican split between Theodore Roosevelt and William Howard Taft opened the way for Woodrow Wilson to win the presidency in 1912. That result in turn produced the domestic reform program that Wilson called the New Freedom. Progressivism thus went through several different phases during this brief period from the New Nationalism of Roosevelt to the governmental activism that Wilson embraced after 1914.

In the process, the contradictions in the reform movement emerged. Should government power be used, as Wilson suggested, to restore competitive balance in the economy without the need for constant regulation? Or, as Roosevelt argued, should the government become bigger to provide consistent supervision of the marketplace? Differences also surfaced over whether society should pursue social justice by doing more for those less fortunate in the nation. As these battles were waged, some of the energy and purpose of reformers ebbed as conservatism made a comeback over such issues as labor's rights and higher taxes.

In the cultural realm, currents of modern thought appeared to question older Victorian values. Women became freer in their relationships with men, artists took a skeptical look at the ills of society, and race relations changed as African Americans moved out of the South. In the years before the World War, optimism about the future of humanity pervaded the United States. Some even talked of an end to war and strife among nations.

The economy took the first steps toward the consumer culture

Immigration into the United States between 1900 and 1914 was not solely a European experience. Overcoming the obstacles of the Chinese Exclusion Act of 1882, these Chinese young men wait to go through the immigration process.

Henry Ford's cheap and efficient car became very popular during the first decade of the new century. This photograph gives a good sense of the simplicity and durability of the Model T.

Reproduced from the collections of the Library of Congress

One of the more controversial episodes of Wilson's early foreign policy was the intervention in Mexico in 1914. Marines march through the streets of Vera Cruz to carry out the president's pressure on the Mexicans.

of the 1920s. Henry Ford's Model T car was priced to appeal to many more Americans. In addition, if the spirit of his $5 a day salary for his employees was followed, customers would also have the money to buy one. Motion pictures became the fastest growing form of popular entertainment, and visionaries spoke of making the new medium of radio available to the masses.

In foreign affairs, the United States sought greater world influence without overseas involvement. The nation remained dominant in Latin America, though the revolution in Mexico underscored how complex the role of foreign policy might become. For all of the problems of Mexico, Haiti, and Nicaragua in this period, the country saw little to worry about from the world at large. Protected by oceans from the tensions of the European countries, the United States could, so the thinking went, follow its own destiny without the mistakes of the old world on the other side of the Atlantic. That comfortable assumption disappeared once the guns of August fired in 1914 and the first great modern world war broke out. After that happened, progressivism and the United States would never be the same.

Making Connections Across Chapters

LOOKING BACK

The Taft-Roosevelt split that devastated the Republicans had its origins amid the issues discussed in the previous chapter. The basis for the division had been created during the last years of Roosevelt's presidency.

1. Was Theodore Roosevelt as good a politician as he thought he was?
2. How did Roosevelt and Taft differ in their view of what a president should do?
3. How did the New Nationalism represent a culmination of Roosevelt's political philosophy as president?

LOOKING AHEAD

The next chapter considers what happened when progressives encountered the effects of the war that raged in Europe beginning in 1914. The outbreak of the conflict called into question the progressive conviction that human beings were basically good. When the United States entered the war in April 1917, some reforms were pushed forward and some progressive issues suffered. The international problems that came out of World War I set the pattern for future disputes in the Middle East and Asia.

1. How did Woodrow Wilson view the role of the United States in the world and especially in Latin America?
2. What view of human nature did the reformers have, and why did the outbreak of World War I prove such a shock?
3. How much of a world power was the United States in 1914?
4. Why did Americans believe they could stay out of European quarrels?
5. What kind of model of presidential leadership did Woodrow Wilson offer to the Democrats?

RECOMMENDED READINGS

Batchelor, Robert. *The 1900s (American Popular Culture Through History)* (2002). A brisk look at the way Americans lived and entertained themselves at the start of the twentieth century.

Chambers, John Whiteclay II. *The Tyranny of Change: America in the Progressive Era, 1890–1920* (1992). Considers the Taft and Wilson years in the context of reform.

Clements, Kendrick. *The Presidency of Woodrow Wilson* (1992). Provides a crisp, informed look at Wilson in office.

Gilmore, Glenda E., ed. *Who Were the Progressives?* (2002). A thoughtful collection of essays about how historians have viewed early twentieth-century reformers.

Margulies, Herbert F. *Reconciliation and Revival: James R. Mann and the House Republicans in the Wilson Era* (1996). Supplies a good guide to the politics of the Taft-Wilson years.

Miller, Char. *Gifford Pinchot and the Making of Modern Environmentalism* (2001). Places one of the leaders of the progressive conservation movement in a broader context.

Rodgers, Daniel T. *Atlantic Crossings: Social Politics in a Progressive Age* (1998). Looks at the international aspects of reform.

Sanders, Elizabeth. *Roots of Reform: Farmers, Workers, and the American State, 1877–1917* (1999). Provides insights into how reform legislation fared in Congress.

Stansell, Christine. *American Moderns: Bohemian New York and the Creation of a New Century* (2000). Discusses how New York City and Greenwich Village affected cultural change.

Unger, Nancy. *Fighting Bob La Follette: The Righteous Reformer* (2000). A biography of the Wisconsin senator who challenged Roosevelt for progressive leadership.

AMERICAN JOURNEY ONLINE AND INFOTRAC COLLEGE EDITION

Visit the source collections at http://ajaccess.wadsworth.com and infotrac.thomsonlearning.com and use the Search function with the following key terms to explore documents, images, audio and video clips, articles, and commentary related to the material in this chapter.

William Howard Taft

Triangle Shirtwaist

Alice Paul

woman suffrage

Woodrow Wilson

Prohibition

Henry Ford

vaudeville

ONLINE PRIMARY SOURCES

Here are some examples of the many primary sources related to this chapter that you will find on the *American Passages* Web site: http://history.wadsworth.com/ayersbrief02.

William Allen White, The Growth of Democracy in America, 1910

Votes for Women a Practical Necessity, ca. 1912

A Brief for the Palmer-Owen Child Labor Bill, 1914

The site also offers self-quizzes, exercises, and many additional resources to help you study.

CHAPTER 22

The Impact of World War I

1914 – 1921

The first impulse of Americans was to keep the European war as far away as possible. That effort proved futile. Events in Europe influenced domestic politics, altered the progressive movement, and changed the fortunes of women, African Americans, and Socialists. U.S. entry into the war in April 1917 transformed the country in even more striking fashion.

The most important result was the end of the era of progressive reform. World War I brought several campaigns for social change, most notably Prohibition and woman suffrage, to national success. Yet by the time these results occurred, the movement for reform had lost popular support and political momentum. When Woodrow Wilson left the White House on March 4, 1921, he gave way to Warren G. Harding, who promised a return to older values. Thus, the war that began in Eastern Europe in the summer of 1914 shattered the feelings of confidence and optimism about the future that white Americans had held since the end of the war with Spain in 1898.

Staying Neutral in a World Conflict

President Wilson stated official U.S. policy toward the war in August 1914 when he asked his fellow citizens to "be neutral in fact as well as in name" and "impartial in thought as well as in action." Wilson himself had more sympathy for the Allies than he had for Germany and its wartime partners. In conducting foreign policy, however, he was as evenhanded toward the two sides as any president could have been.

The War and National Politics

The initial results of Wilson's neutrality decision came in national politics. Going into the congressional elections of 1914, the Republicans anticipated regaining some of the seats in the House and Senate that they had lost in 1912. Roosevelt's Progressive party had weakened, and many of its members had returned to the Republican fold. The party resumed its familiar charge that the Democrats had produced economic hard times. In the 1914 elections the Democrats emphasized how President Wilson had kept the nation at peace. This use of the neutrality issue helped the Democrats limit Republican gains. The Republicans picked up sixty-nine seats in the House, but the Democrats retained control. In the Senate, the president's party actually added five seats.

The 1914 election results suggested that the issue of peace and war held potential benefits for the president in 1916. As Wilson looked toward reelection, he decided to form a coalition of southern and western voters united on a platform of peace and reform. To

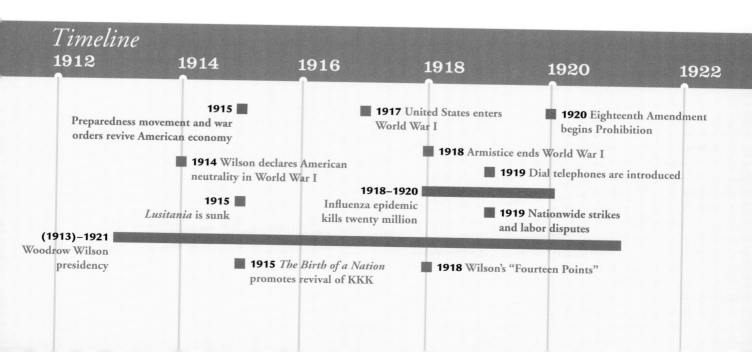

Timeline

| 1912 | 1914 | 1916 | 1918 | 1920 | 1922 |

1915 Preparedness movement and war orders revive American economy

1917 United States enters World War I

1920 Eighteenth Amendment begins Prohibition

1914 Wilson declares American neutrality in World War I

1918 Armistice ends World War I

1919 Dial telephones are introduced

1915 *Lusitania* is sunk

1918–1920 Influenza epidemic kills twenty million

1919 Nationwide strikes and labor disputes

(1913)–1921 Woodrow Wilson presidency

1915 *The Birth of a Nation* promotes revival of KKK

1918 Wilson's "Fourteen Points"

do so, the president had to pay attention to the interest groups—union workers, farmers, and woman suffrage advocates—that he had rebuffed between 1913 and 1915. If the war stimulated the economy, the combination of peace, prosperity, and reform might give the president a chance at reelection.

The Dilemma of Neutrality

Circumstances dictated that the United States would lean more toward the British and French than toward the Germans. Traditional historical and cultural ties produced widespread identification with the Allied cause. Economic links with Great Britain were also strong, and they intensified as the war progressed. Meanwhile, trade with Germany virtually ceased because of the British blockade.

The Germans did have strong support in the United States. The more than five million German Americans represented a sizable bloc of votes, and the three-million-plus Irish Americans hated England and cheered for its enemies. Germany conducted an expensive propaganda campaign paid for with money directed through the German-dominated brewing industry.

The British matched German expenditures on propaganda. They also relied on their cultural ties with the upper classes and opinion makers in the Northeast to set forth the British case in magazines and newspapers. Despite the deluge of speakers and pamphlets from both sides, the national consensus was that the United States should stay out of Europe's quarrels.

The Course of the War and American Public Opinion

It was the way the Germans waged the war that did the greatest damage to their cause with Americans. In the opening days of the fighting, the German army violated Belgium's neutrality, crossing that nation's borders to invade France. This breach of its treaty obligation indicated that Germany's word could not be trusted. Confronted with a British naval blockade, Germany turned to a new weapon, the submarine, early in 1915. In contrast to surface ships, the submarine relied on surprise attacks based on its ability to submerge. Passengers on torpedoed ships were left to drown.

Germany declared that enemy vessels would be sunk on sight, a policy many Americans regarded as a violation of the civilized rules of war. Use of the submarine put Germany in direct conflict with the United States, the leading neutral country. The strategy thus risked a wider war for Germany without the promise of victory.

The *Lusitania* Crisis

In response to the German announcement of the submarine campaign, President Wilson said that Germany would be held to "strict accountability" for any damage to the United States. Washington had to decide whether to insist on the rights of Americans to travel freely on Allied ships regardless of the danger or warn U.S. citizens to avoid such risks and stay home.

Lusitania
A British liner hit by a German torpedo in May of 1915. Among the nearly twelve hundred passengers who died were 128 Americans.

The problem became a shocking reality on May 7, 1915, when a German submarine fired a torpedo into the British liner **Lusitania** off the Irish coast. The huge vessel sank quickly, with an immense loss of life. Among the nearly 1,200 passengers who died were 128 Americans. Some Americans, such as Theodore Roosevelt, suggested that the United States should consider going to war with Germany over the sinking of the *Lusitania*.

Public opinion, however, held that the country should not enter the conflict. President Wilson was applauded when he said, three days after the *Lusitania* incident, that "there is such a thing as a man being too proud to fight. There is such a thing as a nation being so right that it does not need to convince others by force that it is right." Allied sympathizers denounced Wilson's words, but the president's readiness to negotiate was generally approved.

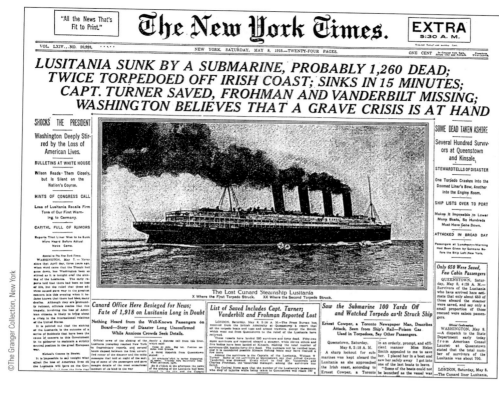

The destruction of the *Lusitania* was a shock to Americans who had not expected the war to touch their lives. The banner headlines in the *New York Times* convey something of the sense of amazement and surprise that accompanied the sinking of the passenger liner.

Wilson and the Submarine Crisis

Wilson combined firmness and flexibility in his demands on Germany. He sought an apology and a pledge to limit submarine warfare, but he did not threaten Germany with war if it did not comply. His diplomatic protest was strong enough, however, that Secretary of State William Jennings Bryan resigned in protest in June 1915. He was replaced by Robert Lansing, a pro-Allied diplomat. During the remainder of the summer, the Germans kept the negotiating process going without apologizing or yielding on any point.

Then, in August, the Germans torpedoed a British liner, the *Arabic,* wounding two Americans. Wilson told the Germans privately that the United States would break diplomatic relations with them if submarine warfare continued. Berlin offered a conditional pledge not to make unannounced attacks on passenger liners; this defused the situation briefly. Nevertheless, in the following year the Germans sank thirty-seven unarmed liners.

The United States and Its World Role

The neutrality issue forced Americans to consider the nation's future role in a warring world. Many groups wanted the United States to maintain its traditional posture of non-involvement. Progressive reformers regarded war and foreign commitments as the death of reform. In the Midwest and on the Pacific Coast, peace sentiments were widespread.

Other Americans did not see how the nation could escape participating in the fighting. Roosevelt and other northeastern Republicans called for military "preparedness" in the event of ultimate American entry into the war. Army and Navy officials knew that they would have to expand their forces greatly if they were to play any significant role. In late 1914 Wilson had blocked programs to strengthen the military defense. By the summer of 1915, however, he changed his position. He promised a Navy "second to none" and more troops for the regular Army. Many Democrats opposed Wilson on the issue of preparedness and the increased spending that it entailed. In early 1916 the president made a speaking tour to arouse popular support for his policy.

As the debate over preparedness intensified, some opinion leaders argued that a world organization should be formed to keep the peace once the fighting stopped. The League to Enforce Peace was created in June 1915, with William Howard Taft as its leader. Although he had earlier endorsed the idea of a league, Roosevelt now attacked it. As 1915 ended, Wilson had not yet thrown his influence behind the idea of a world organization.

Social Change during the Period of Neutrality

During 1915, despite their concern about the future, Americans flocked to theaters to see a new motion picture that vividly depicted sensational events in the nation's past. David Wark Griffith's ***The Birth of a Nation*** portrayed the Reconstruction period in the South as a time when ignorant African Americans terrorized whites and made a travesty of government. An artistic triumph because it used new techniques such as flashbacks and close-ups, the movie twisted history to glamorize the Ku Klux Klan and the white South. Efforts by African Americans to have the film banned were largely unsuccessful.

Inspired by the film's portrayal of the Klan, a group of white men burned a cross at Stone Mountain, Georgia, and used that episode to revive the hooded order. At first the revived Klan's membership remained under five thousand nationally, but the social tensions of the postwar era proved a fertile ground for organizing in the South and Midwest. The Klan's organizers exploited the fears about immigrants, Catholics, and African Americans that were pervasive among white Protestants during these years.

The political prospects for improved rights for blacks remained as bleak as they had been since the 1890s. The Wilson administration proved unsympathetic to any efforts to reduce racism. After protests from blacks and a few progressives, the White House retreated from efforts to enforce segregation in the federal government, but that was a minor victory. The Supreme Court did, however, rule in the case of *Guinn v. United States* (1915) that the grandfather clause Oklahoma used to exempt whites from a literacy test for voting was unconstitutional.

The Great Migration

For African Americans in the South, life was still painful and burdensome. Southern agriculture experienced crippling problems during the first fifteen years of the century. Natural disasters hit the region in the form of floods and droughts. The boll weevil, an insect that destroyed cotton, undermined the farm economy. Blacks began leaving the South for cities in the North. The **Great Migration** started slowly around 1910 and then accelerated between 1914 and 1920 when more than six hundred thousand African Americans left the South.

The outbreak of the war played a key role in this process. Immigration from Europe ended. The result was an expanding labor market for unskilled workers in the North. Now a southern black had a chance, as one said, to "elevate myself" in ways that their region could not offer them.

Those who came to the North found a better life, but not a paradise. They secured work in the coal mines of West Virginia, the stockyards of Chicago, and the steel mills of Pittsburgh. As their population in the North grew, blacks encountered discrimination in housing and public services. But the southern blacks continued to move north in a historic population shift that reshaped the politics and culture of the nation's largest cities.

The Rise of the Movies

In 1914 a young British comedian began appearing in films for the Keystone company, a filmmaking venture in Los Angeles. He made thirty-five movies in a single year. Although most of them were very short, one film, *Tillie's Punctured Romance,* ran for thirty minutes. As these movies reached audiences during the year, filmgoers began asking about the funny actor in the derby hat and little tramp costume. By 1915 the whole nation was talking about Charlie Chaplin. In January 1915 Chaplin signed with Essanay Pictures for the then-huge sum of $1,250 a week. Within twelve months Chaplin moved on to the Mu-

The Birth of a Nation
A twisted movie portrayal of the Reconstruction period in the South that depicted African Americans as ignorant and that glamorized the Ku Klux Klan.

Great Migration
A massive movement of blacks leaving the South for cities in the North that began slowly in 1910 and accelerated between 1914 and 1920. During this time, more than six hundred thousand African Americans left the South.

tual Film Corporation at $10,000 a week. Stardom had come quickly for the twenty-six-year-old actor.

After a shaky start at the beginning of the century, motion pictures had arrived as mass entertainment. There were more than ten thousand nickelodeon theaters by 1912, and up to twenty million Americans went to the movies on a regular basis. Soon movies became longer, and exhibitors began constructing motion picture theaters that could seat five thousand customers.

Although Chaplin was the most famous male performer of his time, he was not the only "star." Executives found that audiences wanted to know about the private lives of the people they saw on the flickering screens. Mary Pickford became "America's Sweetheart" in a series of roles that depicted a demure damsel in acute distress. Douglas Fairbanks used his athletic ability as the swashbuckling hero of such films as *American Aristocracy* (1916). Theda Bara became the "vamp" in *A Fool There Was* (1915). Advertisements described her as having "the most wickedly beautiful face in the world."

During the ensuing years, the business of making movies became concentrated in a few large studios. Because of its mild climate, Hollywood, California, emerged as the center of the picture industry. Studios like Vitagraph and Paramount dominated the making and marketing of films.

Most moviegoers lived in cities where the large theaters were located. Immigrants found that they could learn about American life at the movies. Parents worried when their children saw such films as *Women and Wine* or *Man and His Mate*. Reformers clamored for censorship boards to screen films for scenes that showed lustful images or suggested that criminals profited from their crimes. The mass media had begun to change American attitudes and social customs.

Shifting Attitudes toward Sex

The years around the beginning of World War I brought continued challenges to the nation's values. The divorce rate rose: in 1916 one of every nine marriages ended in the divorce courts. Meanwhile, family size was decreasing. By 1920 two or three children were born to the average mother; in 1860 the average had been five or six.

The most daring women of the decade were the **flappers.** They cut their hair short in the fashionable "bob," wore shorter skirts, and all seemed "lovely and expensive and about nineteen." Norms of sexual behavior slowly moved away from the restrictions of the Victorian era. For women born around 1900, the rate of sexual intercourse before marriage was twice as high as it had been for women born a decade earlier. Nevertheless, the overall incidence of premarital sexual behavior remained very low in comparison with the present. Hysterical fears about women being lured into prostitution spurred the enactment of the Mann Act (1910), which prohibited the movement of women across interstate lines for "immoral purposes" in what was referred to as the "white slave" traffic.

flappers
Young, single, middle-class women who wore their hair and dresses short, rolled their stockings down, used cosmetics, and smoked in public. Signaling a desire for independence and equality, flappers were self-reliant, outspoken, and had a new appreciation for the pleasures of life.

Birth Control

Despite the changes in actual sexual practices, the official attitudes of the nation remained restrictive. Homosexual relationships were outlawed. Laws governing the dissemination of information about birth control discouraged the use of contraception. A federal statute, the Comstock Law of 1873, barred the making, selling, distribution, or importation of contraceptives. The only ground on which abortions were permitted was to save the life of the mother.

Margaret Sanger, a thirty-two-year-old radical living in Greenwich Village, New York City, saw women suffering from disease and poverty because of the large number of children they bore. Often women had many babies because they lacked knowledge about ways to limit births. In 1914 Sanger coined the term *birth control* and began publishing a periodical called *Woman Rebel*. A year later she founded a clinic in a poor neighborhood of Brooklyn that distributed information about contraception to the female residents. The police soon closed the clinic down, and Sanger went to jail. When the case was appealed, a higher court affirmed the right of doctors to prescribe birth control devices. Sanger then

Margaret Sanger
Living in Greenwich Village, New York, she saw women suffering from disease and poverty because of the large number of children they bore. In 1914 she coined the term "birth control" and began publishing a periodical called *Woman Rebel*.

organized the Birth Control League to promote her cause. Sanger continued her efforts into the 1920s, and she was a significant figure in launching the movement for reproductive rights during the rest of the century.

The Persistence of Reform

Progressive reform campaigns pressed ahead despite the distractions of the European war. In fact, the impact of the fighting enhanced some of these campaigns. Prohibition capitalized on anti-German sentiment to reduce the political power of the brewing industry. Supporters of woman suffrage also used the war as a way of mobilizing women behind their cause.

Renewed Momentum for Woman Suffrage

Carrie Chapman Catt
A leader in the woman's suffrage campaign.

Woman suffrage gained strength after 1914 despite serious divisions among the movement's leaders. Alice Paul and the militant Congressional Union (see Chapter 21) pressed for a constitutional amendment to obtain votes for women. Their tactics included demonstrations and a direct challenge to the Democrats as the party in power. In contrast, the National American Woman Suffrage Association (NAWSA), led by **Carrie Chapman Catt** after 1915, emphasized nonpartisanship and state-by-state organization. This disagreement over tactics resulted in a split during the 1916 presidential election. Paul and her allies formed the National Woman's party to defeat Wilson and the Democrats. NAWSA, on the other hand, took a two-pronged approach. It continued its efforts to win the right to vote in individual states, but it now sought a constitutional amendment as well. As the election approached, the momentum for suffrage seemed to be building.

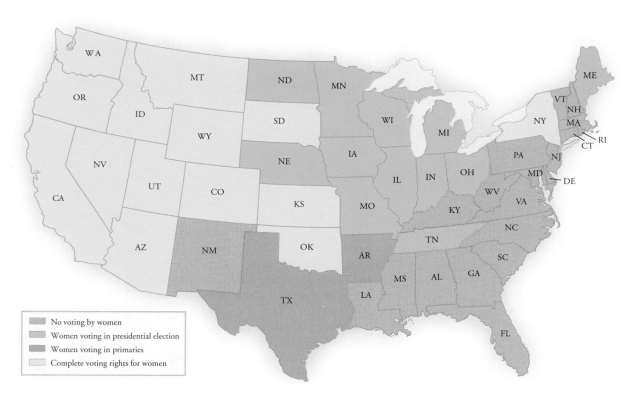

Legend:
- No voting by women
- Women voting in presidential election
- Women voting in primaries
- Complete voting rights for women

MAP 22.1 The March of Woman Suffrage
This map tracing the progress of woman suffrage gives an excellent sense of the sectional split over the issue with the West and Middle West in favor and the South and East in opposition.

The Drys on the Offensive

The drive for Prohibition also intensified. In 1914 the Anti-Saloon League decided to press for a constitutional amendment to ban the sale of alcohol. At the same time, the efforts to make the states liquor-free went forward. In 1913–1914 more than a dozen states adopted Prohibition legislation or held referenda in which the voters adopted Prohibition. Nine more states adopted Prohibition in 1915. The Anti-Saloon League hoped that in the 1916 election enough sympathizers would be elected to the House and Senate to assure passage of the Prohibition amendment.

Closing the Golden Door

The war in Europe shut off immigration to the United States from Eastern European countries. The reduced flow of newcomers did not stop the campaign to cut down on immigration. Proponents of immigration restriction contended that the eventual peace would open the door to an even greater influx of outsiders. In the 1916 election, neither major party wanted to alienate ethnic voters, although the Democrats denounced "all alliances and combinations of individuals in this country of whatever nationality or descent" who sought to embarrass or weaken the government in handling foreign policy.

The Enactment of Reform

In light of the results of the 1914 congressional elections, Wilson understood that he could not win reelection simply on the basis of the impressive achievements of his first two years in office. Putting aside his earlier reservations about the use of national power to achieve reforms, he shifted toward the progressive side of the political spectrum. Congressional Democrats wooed reform voters to retain the party's majority in Congress.

One notable step that Wilson took was to nominate Louis D. Brandeis to the U.S. Supreme Court in January 1916. Since Brandeis was a longtime champion of reform causes and a prominent Jew, his appointment aroused intense, often anti-Semitic, feelings among conservatives. In the end he was confirmed, and Wilson's strong endorsement of him convinced progressives that the president was on their side.

During the months before the election campaign began, Wilson came out for laws to restrict child labor, promote federal loans to farmers (known as agricultural credits), and cover federal employees with workers' compensation laws. When a national railroad strike threatened in August 1916, Wilson compelled Congress to pass the Adamson Act, which mandated an eight-hour working day for railroad employees. Labor responded with strong support for Wilson's reelection bid. Meanwhile, the improving economy gave the president the opportunity, as one Republican put it, to "make an appeal to the stomach of the nation."

Foreign Policy and the 1916 Election

The key to Wilson's reelection chances, however, was foreign policy. Wilson's success hinged on perpetuating the uneasy neutrality he had maintained toward the Germans and the British throughout 1916. The Republicans seemed divided between those who wished to do more for the Allies and those who either disliked overseas involvement or wished to help Germany. Wilson would benefit politically if he could find a middle position that combined defense of American rights with preservation of neutrality.

The president dealt with several related wartime issues during the first half of 1916. The main problem remained the submarine. By the end of 1915 Wilson had obtained a German apology and indemnity for the Americans who had died on the *Lusitania*. After the sinking of the *Arabic*, the Germans had also pledged not to attack passenger liners without warning. Then the United States suggested an arrangement in which the Germans would limit submarine warfare and the Allies would not arm merchant ships. When this proposal (or *modus vivendi*) collapsed because of British and German opposition, Germany resumed submarine attacks on *armed* shipping, whether belligerent or neutral in February 1916.

The *Sussex* Pledge

A few weeks later, on March 24, a German submarine attacked an unarmed steamer, the *Sussex,* in the English Channel. American passengers on board were injured, and another diplomatic crisis ensued. Wilson sent an ultimatum to Berlin stating that continued attacks on unarmed merchant vessels without warning would lead to a breaking of diplomatic ties. The Germans again faced the question of whether the submarine alone could win the war. At the time, they did not have enough undersea vessels to do so. With hopes of a victory on land still glimmering before them, the Germans pledged that they would not conduct attacks on merchant vessels without warning them. Their statement left open the right to resume unrestricted submarine warfare. For the moment, however, the so-called *Sussex* Pledge seemed like a major diplomatic success for Woodrow Wilson.

Seeking a Negotiated Peace

During these same months, Wilson also tried to arrange for a negotiated settlement of the war. In December 1915 he sent his close friend, Edward M. House, to discuss peace terms with the British, French, and Germans. House's talks led to an agreement with the British foreign minister, Edward Grey, for Anglo-American mediation of the war; if the Germans rebuffed the idea, the United States would enter the war on the side of the Allies. The House-Grey Memorandum, as the agreement was called, never took effect because Wilson watered it down and the British ignored it. The episode showed, however, how much effort Wilson invested in seeking a diplomatic end to the war.

During the first half of 1916, Wilson emerged as a forceful national leader. When Congress sought to assert itself through resolutions warning Americans not to travel on the ships of the warring powers, the president pressured Congress to have the resolutions defeated on the grounds that they interfered with his power to conduct foreign policy. In May 1916 the president argued, in a speech to the League to Enforce Peace, that the major nations of the world should find "some feasible method of acting in concert when any nation or group of nations" endangered world peace.

The Mexican Problem

The Mexican civil war had continued after the American intervention at Vera Cruz in 1914 (see Chapter 21). Although Wilson did not like the regime of Venustiano Carranza, he extended diplomatic recognition to it when it became clear that Carranza had emerged as the nation's effective leader.

When a rebel named Pancho Villa raided towns in New Mexico and Texas in 1916, the U.S. Army under General John J. Pershing pursued him across the Rio Grande. Tensions rose on both sides of the border. Heedless of Mexicans' feelings about this intrusion on their sovereignty, the United States seemed to be headed for a war with Mexico. Wilson negotiated a diplomatic settlement, however. Nevertheless, American troops remained in Mexico for two years, placing a continued strain on relations between the two nations.

The 1916 Elections

The Democrats approached the election of 1916 with a high degree of confidence. The president's program of progressive domestic legislation was moving through Congress; the international situation appeared to have vindicated Wilson's leadership; and the economy was prosperous. The Republicans were divided by the foreign policy issue. Eastern Republicans wanted the United States to intervene on the side of the Allies. In the Midwest, progressive Republicans and German Americans opposed a pro-Allied policy. The party had to find a candidate who could persuade these diverse factions to work together in the fall campaign.

The Republicans Select Hughes

Theodore Roosevelt hoped to be the Republican nominee, but on matters of foreign policy, Roosevelt was identified with the Allies, and a commitment to help them would have soon had the nation at war. The Republicans therefore avoided Roosevelt and turned to Supreme Court Justice **Charles Evans Hughes.** He had been a progressive governor of New York and

Charles Evans Hughes
A Supreme Court justice, he was the Republican candidate for president in the 1916 election. He had been a progressive governor of New York and said little about foreign policy.

had said little about foreign policy. The Republicans nominated him on the third ballot. A remnant of the Progressive party nominated Roosevelt, but he declined and the party soon disappeared. The Republicans offered assurances that they favored some domestic reforms and carefully straddled the more controversial questions of preparedness and neutrality.

"He Kept Us Out of War"

For the Democrats, Wilson's nomination was never in question. The excitement occurred over the party's platform. In his keynote address to the Democratic delegates, a former governor of New York, Martin Glynn, noted that Wilson had maintained neutrality. Each time he referred to this fact the audience exclaimed: "What did we do? What did we do?" and he shouted back: "We didn't go to war! We didn't go to war!" The Democrats had a campaign theme in the phrase "He kept us out of war."

In the campaign that followed, Wilson skillfully employed the themes of peace, progressivism, and prosperity in his speeches. Meanwhile, Hughes had difficulty finding a way to appeal to Republicans who shared Roosevelt's position and to the German-American voters who wanted the nation to stay out of the conflict. Hughes did have the benefit of a party that still attracted a majority of voters outside the South. To win, the Democrats assembled a coalition of voters in the South and West, the peace vote, women (who could vote in western states), and midwestern farmers who were happy with wartime prosperity.

The Outcome

Wilson won one of the closest elections in the nation's history. He gained 277 electoral votes from thirty states, whereas Hughes won 254 electoral votes from eighteen states. Although the president's winning margin in some states was very small (3,773 in the key state of California), he and the Democrats had won another victory.

Wilson's Attempts to Mediate

Wilson now believed that the time had come to press for a negotiated settlement among the warring powers. Relations with the British had soured during 1916 because of the way the Royal Navy and the British Foreign Office interfered with American shipping in enforcing their blockade against Germany. Meanwhile, the British were more dependent on American loans and credits to pay for supplies. Under the circumstances, the president believed, London might be receptive to an American mediation effort.

On December 18, 1916, Wilson sent a diplomatic message to the warring countries asking them to state their terms for a negotiated peace. Both the British and the Germans rejected the president's offer. In response, Wilson addressed the U.S. Senate on January 22, 1917, in a speech that called for a "Peace Without Victory" and set out a program that included plans to create a league of nations. The response of the warring powers was skeptical. The idea of a league of nations also aroused opposition in the Senate. Wilson's failure to consult with his political enemies on this matter was an error that would plague him throughout the war.

American Intervention in the War

Events now led the United States toward intervention in the war. The German military decided on January 9, 1917, that the submarine could win the war before the United States could move troops to Europe. Unrestricted submarine attacks would be resumed on February 1. Wilson learned of the German decision on January 31. He broke diplomatic relations on February 4 and waited for the "actual overt acts" from Germany that would mean war. The submarine campaign began as scheduled, and American lives were lost. On February 26 the president asked Congress for authority to arm U.S. merchant ships. With peace sentiment still strong on Capitol Hill, the administration faced a tough fight to get the bill passed.

An unexpected revelation about German war aims changed the legislative situation in the president's favor. British intelligence had intercepted and decoded a secret German diplomatic telegram to its ambassador in Mexico. The **Zimmermann Telegram,** named after the German foreign minister Arthur Zimmermann, dangled the return to Mexico of

Zimmermann Telegram
A secret German diplomatic telegram to the German ambassador in Mexico that was intercepted and decoded by the British. It dangled the return to Mexico of Arizona, New Mexico, and Texas as bait to entice the Mexicans to enter the war on the side of Germany.

Arizona, New Mexico, and Texas as bait to entice the Mexicans to enter the war on the German side. Wilson released this diplomatic bombshell to the public on March 1, and the House promptly passed the bill to arm merchant ships. Nevertheless, eleven senators, led by Robert M. La Follette of Wisconsin, filibustered against the bill until Congress adjourned on March 4. Wilson was outraged. "A little group of willful men, representing no opinion but their own, have rendered the Great Government of the United States helpless and contemptible," he complained. In fact, Wilson could arm the ships on his own authority, which he did on March 9.

The Outbreak of Hostilities

One stumbling block to American support for the Allied cause had always been the presence of Russia on the side of the British and French. Alliance with that autocratic monarchy seemed to mock the notion that the Allies were fighting for democratic values. However, the outbreak of revolution in Russia toppled the regime of Czar Nicholas II and offered some hope for reform. Meanwhile, the Germans sank three American ships on March 18 with large losses. Wilson decided to call Congress into special session on April 2. On a soft spring evening, the president asked for a declaration of war against Germany. "The world must be made safe for democracy," he told them.

Congress declared war on Germany on April 6, 1917. Although the votes were overwhelming (82 to 6 in the Senate; 373 to 50 in the House), the nation was divided about entering the conflict. In large parts of the South and West, peace sentiment was strong because the public felt no need to become involved in European quarrels. Opposition to the war remained high among German Americans and Irish Americans. Dedicated reformers and Socialists saw the war as a betrayal of reform ideals.

For Wilson himself, involvement in the war seemed to be the price the nation had to pay to influence the peace settlement. He did not put the issue that way to his fellow citi-

Wilson's War Message to Congress, April 2, 1917

In his message to Congress on April 2, 1917, Woodrow Wilson put the decision to go to war with Germany in a strongly moral context that helped make the American involvement in the conflict a war to make the world safe for democracy. The president's language in these concluding paragraphs of his message elevated a foreign policy decision to a national crusade.

. . . It will be all the easier for us to conduct ourselves as belligerents in a high spirit of right and fairness because we act without animus, not in enmity towards a people or with the desire to bring any injury or disadvantage upon them, but only in armed opposition to an irresponsible government which has thrown aside all considerations of humanity and of right and is running amuck. We are, let me say again, the sincere friends of the German people, and shall desire nothing so much as the early reëstablishment of intimate relations of mutual advantage between us,—however

hard it may be for them, for the time being, to believe that this is spoken from our hearts. We have borne with their present Government through all these bitter months because of that friendship,—exercising a patience and forbearance which would otherwise have been impossible. We shall, happily, still have an opportunity to prove that friendship in our daily attitude and actions towards the millions of men and women of German birth and native sympathy who live amongst us and share our life, and we shall be proud to prove it towards all who are in fact loyal to their neighbors and to the Government in the hour of test. They are, most of them, as true and loyal Americans as if they had never known any other fealty or allegiance. They will be prompt to stand with us in rebuking and restraining the few who may be of a different mind and purpose. If there should be disloyalty, it will be dealt with with a firm hand of stern repres-

zens. His lofty rhetoric encouraged Americans to believe that a better world could be obtained through the use of military force. In that sense the president paved the way for the later disillusion among Americans that frustrated his ambitious plans for world leadership.

A Nation at War

World War I produced significant changes in the way the United States functioned. The power of the federal government increased dramatically. Average citizens found that they had to respond to government programs and directives in strange and unfamiliar ways, such as accepting bureaucratic rules for their businesses, listening to government propaganda, and changing their eating habits. For Wilson, the war brought victory in 1918, followed by the loss of his dreams of world peace.

The State of the Conflict in 1917

Both the White House and Congress had initially assumed that the American contribution to the war would consist largely of furnishing money and supplies to the Allied cause. There was little sense of the extent to which the sacrifices of the preceding three years had weakened the ability of the British and French to wage war. It soon became apparent that American soldiers would have to go across the Atlantic and join in the fighting to achieve an Allied victory.

As of April 1917, the German army still occupied large portions of France that it had seized in 1914. On the "Western Front" the two sides fought in elaborate trenches from which soldiers fired at each other or mounted attacks against well-fortified positions. Dug-in artillery and machine guns gave the advantage to the defense. For three years the attacks went on. The Germans tried to break the will of the French at Verdun in 1916; both sides

sion; but, if it lifts its head at all, it will lift it only here and there and without countenance except from a lawless and malignant few.

It is a distressing and oppressive duty, Gentlemen of the Congress, which I have performed in thus addressing you. There are, it may be, many months of fiery trial and sacrifice ahead of us. It is a fearful thing to lead this great peaceful people into war, into the most terrible and disastrous of all wars, civilization itself seeming to be in the balance. But the right is more precious than peace, and we shall fight for the things which we have always carried nearest our hearts,—for democracy, for the right of those who submit to authority to have a voice in their own Governments, for the rights and liberties of small nations, for a universal dominion of right by such a concert of free peoples as shall bring peace and safety to all nations and make the world itself at last free. To such a task we can dedicate our lives and our fortunes, everything that we are and

everything that we have, with the pride of those who know that the day has come when America is privileged to spend her blood and her might for the principles that gave her birth and happiness and the peace which she has treasured. God helping her, she can do no other.

Questions to Consider

1. How does Wilson distinguish between the German government and the German people?

2. Why is he making this effort as he starts American involvement in the war?

3. What kind of peace does he envision coming out of the war?

4. How difficult will that kind of settlement be to achieve in light of the war aims of the European powers?

5. How realistic or idealistic is Wilson's statement?

Explore additional primary sources related to this chapter on the *American Passages* Web site: http://history.wadsworth.com/ayersbrief02.

lost more than three hundred thousand men in the ensuing struggle. The British attacked in northern France in 1916; sixty thousand men were killed or wounded in a single day's fighting. Similar carnage occurred when the British renewed their offensive on the Somme River in 1917. After the French went on the attack in 1917 with heavy casualties, their broken armies mutinied against further slaughter. To win the war, American troops would be needed in great numbers.

U.S. Armed Forces

The Wilson administration did not want to raise an army through volunteer methods. Experience in Europe had shown that a volunteer system was undependable and did not keep trained individuals at their jobs in key war industries. A draft seemed the fairest and most efficient method.

In May 1917 Congress adopted the Selective Service Act. Men between the ages of twenty-one and thirty had to register for the draft; local boards were set up to administer the program. By the end of the war, twenty-four million young men had been registered and about three million had been called into the armed forces. Another three hundred forty thousand men tried to evade the draft and became "slackers."

To command the American Expeditionary Force (AEF), Wilson selected General John J. "Black Jack" Pershing. The nation was ill prepared for war. The Army had no plans for a war with Germany in Western Europe, and it did not have the rifles and machine guns necessary for a modern conflict. Once Pershing got his troops to Europe, he would have much training to do to make them ready for combat.

Training the Army

Training the troops for warfare in Europe was not a simple process, and the indoctrination that the men received often reflected progressive ideals. The government endeavored to maintain the purity of troops with extensive programs to limit excessive drinking and venereal disease. Enlisted men also received intelligence tests. When the tests showed no significant difference in intelligence between black soldiers and white soldiers, the Army recalculated the results to conform with its prejudices.

While the Army was being raised, the Navy faced a more immediate challenge. During April 1917 German submarines sank almost 900,000 tons of Allied shipping. Ships were going down more quickly than they could be replaced, and the British had only six weeks' worth of food reserves. If the menace of the submarine could not be conquered, the war could be lost before Pershing and his men arrived in France.

The American naval commander in Europe, Admiral William S. Sims, called for the use of convoys to escort vulnerable merchant ships across the Atlantic. American destroyers on escort duty became a key part of the strategy that eventually ended the submarine threat. Troops began to move toward Europe. The Germans did not regard troopships as significant targets because of their belief that American soldiers lacked fighting ability. Two million men were shipped to France before the Armistice was signed, and they provided the margin for an Allied victory.

Financing the War

Drafted soldiers and submarine-dodging convoys were only part of the American experience of the war. At the movies where patriotic newsreels were shown, in the baseball stadiums where drives were held to sell war bonds, and at home tending their gardens to raise food, men, women, and children became part of the war effort.

Fighting a modern war required huge sums of money. The government raised a third of it, some $9 billion, through increased taxes. The remainder came from citizens who purchased

The government helped finance the war through the sale of war bonds. Celebrities such as movie star Douglas Fairbanks Sr. spoke to huge throngs and urged them to buy bonds. Fairbanks is seen here before a large crowd on Wall Street in New York City.

U.S. War Dept. General Staff photo no. 165-WW-2490D-1 in the National Archives

Liberty Bonds from the government. These interest-bearing securities brought in more than $15 billion. To persuade Americans to buy bonds, the government enlisted celebrities including Douglas Fairbanks and Charlie Chaplin to appear at rallies where bonds were sold. Children were taught to save their pennies and nickels for thrift stamps. Those who were unwilling to contribute were told that failure to buy bonds was unpatriotic and helped the Germans.

The total cost of the war exceeded $35 billion because the United States loaned more than $11.2 billion to the Allies. The loans proved to be vital to the Allied cause. President Wilson counted on the Allies' financial dependence on the United States as a weapon to use in achieving the goals of his postwar diplomacy.

Herbert Hoover and Food for the Allies

The Allies also desperately needed food. The British depended on supplies from their empire that took a long time to reach Europe by ship. Without American food, serious shortages would have impaired Allied ability to wage war. To mobilize the agricultural resources of the United States, Congress passed the Lever Act, which established a Food Administration. Wilson selected Herbert Hoover to head this new agency. A mining engineer from California, Hoover had gained international fame through his work to feed the starving people of Belgium after 1914.

Hoover's main weapon was publicity. He asked Americans to observe "wheatless days" and "meatless days" because "wheatless days in America make sleepless nights in Germany." Woodrow Wilson allowed sheep to graze on the White House lawn in order to produce wool. Women and children planted "war gardens" to raise more fruits and vegetables. Higher prices induced farmers to expand their production.

Prohibition and the War Effort

The campaign to conserve food provided a boost for the effort to restrict the sale and use of alcoholic beverages. Scarce grain supplies had to be reserved for soldiers in the field and Allied populations overseas. Prohibitionists also argued that drink impaired the fighting ability of the armed forces and those working in defense plants. The connection of the brewing industry with the German Americans also worked in favor of the prohibitionist cause.

Congress passed legislation to restrict the production of liquor and in December 1917 the lawmakers approved the Eighteenth Amendment, which banned the production, sale, and consumption of alcoholic beverages. All that remained was to ensure ratification of the amendment by the required number of states, a task that the Anti-Saloon League was well equipped to handle.

Managing the Wartime Economy

Coordination of the economy was not limited to the agricultural sector. The president used his power to wage the war to establish the expanded bureaucracy required to manage production of war supplies and oversee their shipment to the Allies. Wilson hoped that a business–government partnership would develop naturally. However, much government encouragement and direction were needed before the business community fully joined the war effort.

The eventual record of mobilization was a mixed one. The United States tried to build ships and planes under the direction of government agencies. Those efforts produced at least one British-designed plane that used American-built engines, and large numbers of merchant ships were constructed. On the other hand, Pershing's men used British and French artillery and equipment. The government had more success with expanding the production of coal through the Fuel Administration. Coal prices were raised to stimulate production, and "daylight savings time" was established to reduce the use of fuel for nonmilitary purposes.

Wartime Economic Problems

The nation's railroads became so confused during the first year of the war that immense and costly transportation snarls resulted. The armed forces insisted on immediate passage

Liberty Bonds
Thirty-year government bonds sold to individuals with an annual interest rate of 3.5 percent. They were offered in five issues between 1917 and 1920, and their purchase was equated with patriotic duty.

for railcars with war supplies; the result was tie-ups of rail traffic all over the East Coast. Finally the government simply took over the railroads in January 1918, placing the secretary of the treasury, William G. McAdoo, in charge of operations. McAdoo raised the wages of railroad workers, dropped inefficient routes, and allowed the lines to raise their rates. The tie-ups soon disappeared.

Even before U.S. entry into the war, the government had made plans for coordinating industrial production. The War Industries Board (WIB) was supposed to make sure that the purchasing and allocation of supplies for the armed forces followed rational programs. The WIB fell well short of this standard during 1917. In March 1918, Wilson placed Bernard Baruch, a Wall Street speculator and contributor to the Democratic party, at the head of the War Industries Board.

Bernard Baruch and the War Industries Board

Baruch used his political skills and business background to persuade industrialists to cooperate with the war mobilization effort. He and his aides standardized products, established priorities for the shipment of important goods, and set prices to encourage factories to turn out goods quickly. Simply by altering bicycle designs, the WIB saved two thousand tons of steel for war goods.

Not all industries cooperated willingly. Baruch had to compromise with both the automobile and the steel industries to induce them to abandon peacetime production. In the process, the industries made significant profits from their government contracts.

Labor and the War

The American Federation of Labor and its president, Samuel Gompers, threw their support behind the war effort. In return for the government's agreement to allow unions to participate in economic policy making, Gompers and the AFL promised not to strike or to press for union shops in factories. The short-run results were encouraging. Between 1917 and 1920 the AFL gained more than two million members.

Nonunion workers also benefited from the government's wartime policies. The National War Labor Board, headed by former President William Howard Taft, set standards for wages and hours that were far more generous and enlightened than those private industry had provided. A minimum wage was mandated, as were maximum hours and improved working conditions. The government also created housing for war workers and began a system of medical care and life insurance for federal employees.

Black Americans in the War

Most African American leaders agreed with W. E. B. Du Bois that they should "forget about special grievances and close our ranks shoulder to shoulder with our own fellow white citizens." Some three hundred sixty-seven thousand black soldiers served during the war. Most, however, were assigned to labor battalions and supply duties. The War Department moved very slowly to commission black officers; at the end of the war there were only twelve hundred. Several African American units fought bravely. Others were given inadequate training and equipment, but when they performed poorly in combat the blame was placed on their supposed inferiority. Blacks had little motivation to fight in the first place. Moreover, for some blacks in France, the experience of being in a country without a long tradition of racism made them long for greater freedom at home.

African American troops stationed in the United States faced familiar dangers. In August 1917 in Houston, Texas, black soldiers reacted to segregation and abuse by the police with attacks on the police and on white citizens that left sixteen whites and four soldiers dead. The Army indicted 118 soldiers, of whom 110 were convicted by courts-martial. Nineteen black soldiers were hanged.

Growing Racial Tension

Racial tensions intensified elsewhere in the nation. During the summer of 1917, race riots in East St. Louis, Illinois, resulted in the deaths of forty blacks and nine whites. Forty-eight lynchings occurred in 1917 and sixty-three in 1918. Facing discrimination and violence, blacks responded with a heightened sense of outrage. Marches were held to protest the race riots. Banners called upon President Wilson to "Bring Democracy to America Before You Carry It to Europe."

During the war the black migration to northern cities accelerated. As the African American communities in Chicago, New York, Philadelphia, and other northern cities grew, black newspapers began publishing articles about the **New Negro.** The repressive actions of the Wilson administration fed the new currents of militance among black Americans.

New Negro
African Americans after World War I who wanted their rights.

Women in Wartime

The great achievement of American women during World War I was winning the right of suffrage. Momentum had been building for a generation, but the demands of war brought success. The leaders of the National American Woman Suffrage Association decided that identification with the war offered the surest and fastest road to achieving their goal. Carrie Chapman Catt argued that giving women the vote would enable them to offset disloyal elements at home. Members of NAWSA appeared at rallies and proclaimed that suffrage should be a "war measure" that would repay women for their contributions to the war. The National Woman's party, on the other hand, picketed the White House and tried to embarrass Wilson for failing to support woman suffrage. The combined impact of these tactics led to the passage of the woman suffrage amendment in the House of Representatives in January 1918. The Senate still had to act, but the war had made possible the eventual victory of the campaign to give women the vote.

Beyond the success of woman suffrage, however, the war did not go on long enough to produce lasting changes in the condition of American women. Only about four hundred thousand more women joined the labor force. More than twenty thousand women served in the military. The Navy and the Marines enlisted thirteen thousand of them, largely in office jobs. The Army employed more than five thousand as nurses. Some agencies of the government added women workers. The National Railroad Administration, for example, created a Women's Service Section to lower barriers against female employment. In industry, women were hired as drivers, farm workers, and secretaries. As soon as the war ended, they were expected to relinquish these jobs to returning servicemen.

Militant proponents of woman suffrage picketed the White House in 1917–1918 to move President Wilson to support their cause. Their presence embarrassed the president, and several of the picketers went to jail for their beliefs.

Civil Liberties in Wartime

The Wilson administration believed that winning the war required mobilization of public opinion. As a result, the White House mounted a campaign of laws, agencies, and popular spirit to arouse support for the war and to quell dissent. To awaken national enthusiasm, the government created a propaganda agency to manage the news. The Committee on Public Information (CPI) was established on April 13, 1917, and President Wilson named George Creel, a former newspaperman, as its head. Creel saw his role as one of fusing Americans into "one white-hot mass . . . with fraternity, devotion, courage, and deathless determination." To spread its message, the CPI used every available instrument of public relations, from pamphlets and billboards to motion pictures. Seventy-five thousand speakers known as "Four-Minute Men" (because of the length of their talks) spoke to audiences throughout the nation.

The themes of the CPI's appeal were simple, patriotic, and strident. The great national goal was unity; the Germans were depraved animals; and the nation was engaged in a crusade to "make the world safe for democracy." Wilson's wartime speeches described the United States as "an instrument in the hands of God to see that liberty is made secure for mankind."

The Limits of Dissent

To guard against opposition to the war, the Wilson administration and Congress placed legislative limits on the ability of Americans to criticize the government or the war effort. The Espionage Act of 1917 curbed espionage and sabotage, but its definitions were so sweeping that they embraced even public criticism of the war and its conduct. A person who violated the law could be sentenced to twenty years in prison. The Trading with the Enemy Act, passed in October 1917, authorized the postmaster general to suspend the mailing privileges of foreign language periodicals and newspapers that he deemed offensive to the government. Postmaster General Albert S. Burleson used that law and the Espionage Act to bar from the mails publications that he considered treasonous or seditious. In 1918 Congress passed the Alien Act, which gave the government broad powers to deport any noncitizen who advocated revolution or anarchism. Most sweeping was the Sedition Act of 1918 that prohibited "uttering, printing, writing, or publishing any disloyal, profane, scurrilous, or abusive language" about either the government or the armed forces.

These laws were vigorously enforced. The Socialist magazine *The Masses* was barred from the mails for carrying articles claiming that "this is Woodrow Wilson's and Wall Street's War." People were sent to prison for saying that "Wilson is a wooden-headed son of a bitch" or remarking that this was "a rich man's war." Eugene V. Debs, the perennial Socialist candidate for president, received a ten-year prison sentence for opposing the draft and the war. The American Protective League, a volunteer organization designed to locate draft evaders, became a vigilante branch of the Justice Department that used wire-tapping, illegal searches, and other lawless techniques to find "slackers" and other opponents of the war.

Wartime Hysteria

The zeal of the government to stamp out dissent was matched by private hysteria toward Germans. Traces of German influence in American life were repressed. Sauerkraut became "liberty cabbage," hamburgers reemerged as "Salisbury steak," and some cities gave up pretzels. Speaking the German language in public was banned in half of the states by 1918, and German literary works vanished from libraries. Musicians with German names, such as the violinist Fritz Kreisler, found their careers crippled.

Some German Americans suffered more serious injuries. When they refused to buy war bonds, mobs beat them until they promised to contribute. Radicals, too, were the victims of mob violence. Frank Little, an organizer for the Industrial Workers of the World, was hanged from a railroad trestle in Montana for denouncing the war at a labor rally. State councils of defense used their power to attack allegedly disloyal individuals and to ensure national unity.

The Political Legacy of Repression

The government had a legitimate reason to be concerned about German espionage, but the repression of civil liberties during the war went far beyond any rational claim of national security. President Wilson did not directly order cabinet officials to engage in such conduct, but he failed to keep them in check. The government's campaign against radicals and progressives represented an attack on national freedom. It also undermined support for the president in domestic politics. In his eagerness to win the war, Wilson had allowed his government to destroy part of his own political base.

The Road to Victory

During the late winter of 1918, the Allies faced a dangerous military crisis. In November 1917 the Communist revolution in Russia had taken that nation out of the Allied coalition and enabled the Germans to concentrate on the British and French. The Germans moved troops to the Western Front in an attempt to achieve victory before the Americans could replenish the depleted ranks of Allied soldiers. The German attack came on March 21, 1918, against the junction of the British and French armies. The offensive made impressive gains before the German advance was halted. When further attacks were made against the French in April and May, American reinforcements were sent in to help

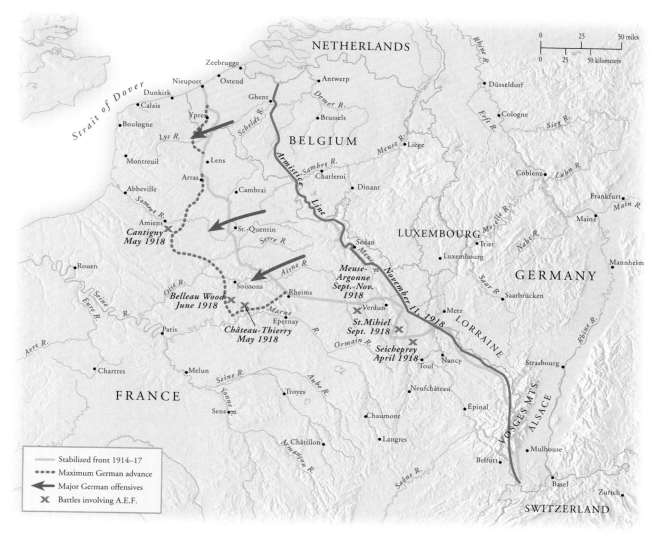

MAP 22.2 American Participation on the Western Front
This map indicates how the American Expeditionary Force helped to repel German offensives in 1918 and then pushed the enemy back toward the German border. View an animated version of this map or related maps at http://history.wadsworth.com/ayersbrief02.

stop the assault. At battles near Château-Thierry and in Belleau Wood in early June, the men of the AEF endured frightful losses but stopped the Germans.

The Germans made one more offensive thrust in mid-July, and the British, French, and Americans repelled it as well. Counterattacks moved the Germans backward, and German commanders warned their government that the fighting could not go on much longer. In September 1918 the American Army went on the offensive at the town of Saint-Mihiel near the southern end of the trenches. At the end of the month, Americans launched another thrust toward the Meuse River and the Argonne Forest and pierced the German defenses to threaten key supply routes.

Wilson's Peace Program

By October 1918 the German empire was crumbling. The issue now became the terms on which the war would end. Wilson set out his views in a major address to Congress on January 8, 1918. The Russian Communists had recently released secret treaties that the Allies had made before 1917 dividing up Europe and the Middle East once victory was achieved. These documents cast doubt on Allied claims that they were fighting for unselfish reasons. Wilson endeavored to shape the Allies' answer and regain the diplomatic initiative.

U.S. Army, American Image #11-SC-94980 in the National Archives

An American machine gun crew in action on the Western Front.

Fourteen Points
Wilson's peace program, which included freedom of the seas, free trade, and more open diplomacy.

To present the American cause in a better light, Wilson offered a peace program with fourteen specific elements that became known as the **Fourteen Points.** Among the key provisions were freedom of the seas, free trade, and more open diplomacy. The president also spoke of national self-determination for all nations. By this he meant that the borders of countries should reflect the national origins of the people who lived in a particular area. He also advocated an "association of nations" to keep the peace.

The End of the Fighting

The Fourteen Points would not be easy to achieve. After four years of slaughter, Britain and France wanted to punish Germany. They disliked Wilson's interference with European policies. For the desperate Germans, Wilson's Fourteen Points seemed much more appealing than did negotiations with London and Paris. In early October a civilian government in Germany asked Wilson to arrange an armistice based on the Fourteen Points. Working through Colonel House, the president negotiated an agreement for an end to the fighting. He also used the threat of a separate settlement with the Germans to induce the British and French to accept the Fourteen Points and attend the peace conference. The war came to end on November 11, 1918, at eleven o'clock in the morning.

Woodrow Wilson had achieved a diplomatic triumph with the conclusion of the armistice, but his success proved to be temporary. Even as he prepared to lead the American delegation to Paris, his domestic political base was eroding. During the war, partisan battles had continued with both Wilson and his enemies using the war for their own political purposes.

The 1918 Elections

During the war President Wilson kept the Republicans at arm's length. He did not bring Republicans into his government, and he made strong attacks on Republicans who opposed his policies. Meanwhile, his enemies capitalized on the unhappiness of farmers and workers over the administration's domestic programs. Midwestern farmers, for example, disliked the price controls that had been imposed on wheat. They complained that southerners in Congress had prevented similar price controls from being put on cotton. As a result, wheat farmers saw their profits held down while cotton producers did well. As the congressional elections in 1918 approached, the Republicans had a clear advantage. Wilson tried to stave off defeat with an appeal to the American people to elect a Democratic Congress. He asked the voters to show that he was "their unembarrassed spokesman in affairs at home and abroad." The statement was a serious political mistake because it allowed Wilson's enemies to claim that he had been decisively repudiated when the results showed that both the House and the Senate would have Republican majorities. For a president who needed bipartisan support in the Senate for any treaty he might write at the upcoming Peace Conference in Paris, it was a major blunder.

The Paris Peace Conference

Despite Republican criticism, Wilson believed that he needed to direct the negotiations himself. Moreover, his selection of delegates to accompany him showed his continuing insensitivity to bipartisanship. He chose Colonel House, Secretary of State Robert Lansing, General Tasker H. Bliss, and Henry White. White was a nominal Republican, but the selection of someone so far removed from the Republican mainstream did not impress the president's political enemies.

Wilson did not send any senators to Paris. Had he done so, he would surely have had to include Senator **Henry Cabot Lodge** of Massachusetts, the next chairman of the Foreign Relations Committee. Wilson and Lodge hated each other. That ruled out any lawmakers going with the president because, if he could not take Lodge, Wilson could not invite any other senators. Wilson also declined to select any other prominent Republicans.

The President in Europe

When Wilson arrived in Paris, two million people cheered him as he rode up the Champs-Élysées. They called him "Wilson *le Juste* [the Just]" and expected him to fulfill their desires for a peaceful world and for revenge against the Germans. Wilson came to believe that he could appeal to the peoples of the world over the heads of their leaders. It proved to be another miscalculation.

He faced a daunting task. The other major figures at the conference were David Lloyd George, the prime minister of Great Britain, and Georges Clemenceau, the premier of France. Both men were hard-headed realists. "God gave us the Ten Commandments, and we broke them," said Clemenceau. "Wilson gives us the Fourteen Points. We shall see." Along with the prime minister of Italy, Vittorio Orlando, Wilson, Clemenceau, and Lloyd George made up the "Big Four" who directed the peace conference toward a settlement of the issues that the war had raised.

Henry Cabot Lodge

A Massachusetts senator best remembered for spearheading Senate blockage of American membership in the League of Nations on the ground that its covenant threatened American sovereignty.

When Wilson arrived in Europe, he received a hero's welcome. As he disembarks in Great Britain and walks in with his British hosts, schoolgirls throw flowers in his path.

U.S. Signal Corps. Photo #111-SC-62979 in the National Archives

The Shadow of Bolshevism

Four years of war had left the world in disorder, and nations large and small came to Paris to have their fate decided. A striking omission was the Soviet Union, the Communist nation that the Russian Bolsheviks had established after their successful revolution. Civil war raged in Russia between the "Reds" of Communism and the "Whites," who wanted to block Bolshevik control of the nation. Meanwhile, the Bolsheviks' authoritarian leader, Vladimir Ilyich Lenin, and his colleagues wished to extend Communist rule beyond Russia's borders.

In 1919 national leaders worried that the infection of Communism might spread into Western Europe, and they had not recognized the government in Moscow. In fact, the French and British had tried to strangle the new regime by providing financial support for its enemies and intervening militarily in some areas of Russia. The United States had dispatched small detachments of troops to Siberia and Vladivostok in 1918 and 1919. The American presence in Russia became a long-standing grievance for the Soviet regime.

The Terms of Peace

The negotiations about the terms of peace with Germany produced both victories and defeats for Wilson. He had to accept the inclusion in the treaty of a clause that assigned Germany "guilt" for starting the war in 1914. The Germans were also assessed severe financial penalties in the form of reparations that eventually amounted to $33 billion. These provisions angered the Germans, fueling resentments that poisoned postwar international relations.

Wilson also achieved mixed success in his efforts to establish self-determination as a principle of the peace settlement. He accepted Italian desires for control of the city of Fiume on the Adriatic Coast, could not block Japan from territorial gains in China, and was unable to prevent several groups of ethnic and national minorities in Eastern Europe from being left under the dominance of other ruling groups, as in the case of Germans in the new nation of Czechoslovakia.

The League of Nations

The main achievement that Wilson sought was establishment of the League of Nations. The league consisted of a General Assembly of all member nations; a Council made up of Great Britain, France, Italy, Japan, and the United States, with four other countries that the Assembly selected; and an international court of justice. Article X required member nations to preserve each other's independence and take concerted action when any member of the league was attacked. Whether Article X bound the United States to go to war for the league became a key issue when the Senate considered the Treaty of Versailles in 1919.

In February 1919 Wilson returned to the United States for the end of the congressional session. Although popular opinion supported the idea of the league, the new Republican-dominated Senate was cool toward it. In early March Senator Lodge circulated a document that thirty-seven senators signed. It stated that the treaty must be amended or they would not vote for it. The president attacked his critics publicly, further intensifying partisan animosity.

Wilson and the Treaty of Versailles

To secure changes in the treaty, Wilson had to make concessions to the other nations at the Peace Conference. These included the imposition of reparations on Germany, the war guilt clause, and limits on Germany's ability to rearm. In return, Wilson obtained provisions that protected the Monroe Doctrine from league action, removed domestic issues from the league's proceedings, and allowed any nation to leave the world organization with two years' notice. The final version of the Treaty of Versailles was signed on June 28, 1919, in the Hall of Mirrors at the Palace of Versailles outside Paris. For all of its problems and weaknesses, the treaty was the closest thing to a reasonable settlement that Wilson could have obtained.

The Senate and the League

To get the treaty ratified and the League of Nations launched, Wilson faced the greatest political battle of his life. The Republicans now controlled the Senate forty-nine to forty-seven, so the president could not win the necessary two-thirds majority without the votes of some of his political opponents. Some Republicans were opposed to the treaty as an infringement upon American sovereignty. These were the fourteen "irreconcilables"; two Democrats were also part of this group. Wilson had to seek help from the twelve "mild reservationists" who wanted only changes in the wording, and the twenty-three "strong reservationists" who sought to limit the league's power over American actions. The president could count on about thirty-five of the forty-seven Democrats in the Senate. Assuming that some of the mild reservationists would support the treaty, the Democrats had to find twenty Republican votes to gain the necessary sixty-four votes to approve the treaty.

In the political battle that ensued, Senator Lodge focused on whether Congress should be able to approve American participation in the league's attempts to prevent international aggression. Lodge also played for time, hoping that public opinion would turn against the treaty. He had the lengthy treaty read aloud to the Senate. Meanwhile, Wilson insisted that the treaty be approved without changes or "reservations." However, the president was unable to win converts to his position.

Wilson's Tour and Collapse

By September 1919 the treaty was in trouble. Wilson decided to take his case to the American people themselves. His cross-country tour began slowly but gained in popularity when he reached the West Coast. The climax came in his address at Pueblo, Colorado, on September 25. A cheering crowd heard him warn of another world war if the treaty failed.

But Wilson's health broke under the strain. He was rushed back to Washington, where he suffered a massive stroke on October 2, 1919. His left side was paralyzed.

The president's wife and his doctors did not reveal how sick Wilson was. The First Lady screened his few visitors and decided what documents her husband would see. Mrs. Wilson did not become "the first woman president," as some people said at the time, but Wilson was only a shell of a president. As a result, the government drifted.

The Defeat of the League

The League of Nations was the first victim of Wilson's near-fatal illness. The Senate voted on the treaty on November 19, 1919, with reservations that Lodge had included in the document. The key change that Lodge demanded would have required Congress to approve any sanctions imposed by the league on an aggressor. When the Democratic leader in the Senate asked Wilson about possible compromises, he replied that changing Article X "cuts the very heart out of the Treaty." The Senate rejected the treaty with reservations by a vote of 39 to 55. Then the lawmakers voted on the treaty without reservations. It lost, 38 in favor and 53 against. In the end, the decision about a possible compromise with Lodge was Wilson's to make. He told Senate Democrats: "Let Lodge compromise."

From War to Peace

Meanwhile the nation experienced domestic upheaval. Foreign policy problems faded in importance. Citizens grappled with labor unrest, a **Red Scare** (fear of Communist or "Red" subversion), a surge in prices following the end of the war, and an influenza epidemic.

The influenza epidemic began with dramatic suddenness at the end of 1918 and spread rapidly through the population. No vaccines existed to combat it; no antibiotics were available to fight the secondary infections that resulted from it. More than six hundred fifty thousand Americans died of the disease in 1918 and 1919. The pandemic receded in 1920, leaving a worldwide total of twenty million people dead.

Red Scare
A label attached to the fear of many Americans that a radical movement existed within the United States that was determined to establish a Communist government here.

The Waning Spirit of Progressivism

By 1919 the spirit of progressive reform was waning. Much of what the reformers wanted had been achieved. Enough states had ratified the Prohibition amendment by January 1919 to make it part of the Constitution. In October 1919 Congress passed the Volstead Act to enforce Prohibition. Wilson vetoed the measure, but Congress passed it over his objection. The United States became "dry" on January 15, 1920.

After the House passed the woman suffrage amendment in 1918, it took the Senate another year to approve it. Suffrage advocates then lobbied the states to ratify the amendment. When the Tennessee legislature voted for ratification in August 1920, three-quarters of the states had approved woman suffrage. With these achievements came renewed attacks on reform measures as costly and intrusive, and a growing popular disillusionment with big government.

The Struggles of Labor

After the Armistice on November 11, 1918, the nation shifted from a wartime economy to peacetime pursuits with dizzying speed. The government declined to manage the changeover from a wartime to a peacetime economy. High inflation developed as prices were freed from wartime controls, and unemployment rose as returning soldiers sought jobs. The government's index of the cost of living rose nearly 80 percent above prewar levels in 1919, and it went up to 105 percent a year later. Unemployment reached nearly 12 percent by 1921.

Unions struck for higher wages. Seattle shipyard workers walked off their jobs, and the Industrial Workers of the World called for a general strike to support them. When sixty thousand laborers took part in the protest, the mayor of Seattle, Ole Hanson, responded with mobilization of police and soldiers. Newspapers depicted the strike as a prelude to a Communist revolution.

The Reaction against Strikes

The largest industrial strike of the year occurred in the steel industry. The American Federation of Labor tried to organize all steelworkers to end the seven-day week and the twelve-hour day. In September three hundred fifty thousand steelworkers left the mills. Led by the head of United States Steel, E. H. Gary, the steel manufacturers refused to recognize the union. The steel companies hired strikebreakers to keep their factories running while they waited for the strike to be broken through police harassment and internal divisions within the unions. Although the strikers remained united for several months, they could not withstand the accumulated financial and political pressure from management. This first effort at a strike by an entire workforce failed in early 1920.

Other strikes of the year included a strike by police in Boston. Inflation had hit the Boston police hard, and they struck late in 1919. When looting and other criminal acts occurred because of the absence of police, public opinion turned against the striking officers. The governor of Massachusetts, Calvin Coolidge, became a national celebrity when he said: "There is no right to strike against the public safety, by anybody, anywhere, any time."

An Upsurge of Racial Violence

Racial tensions also flared up after the war. There were frequent lynchings in the South, and in the North the tide of African American migration produced confrontations with angry whites. Rioting against blacks occurred in Washington, D.C. in June 1919. During the same summer a young black man was stoned and killed when whites found him on a Chicago beach from which African Americans had been excluded. Angry blacks attacked the police who had stood by while the killing occurred. Five days of violence followed in which thirty-eight people were killed and another five hundred were injured. Two dozen other cities saw violent episodes during what one black leader called "the red summer."

The Communist "Menace"

Searching for a cause of the social unrest that pervaded the nation, Americans looked to radicalism and Communism. The emotions aroused by the government's wartime propaganda fueled the "Red Scare" of 1919–1920. Only about seventy thousand people belonged to one of the two branches of the Communist party. However, the radicals' reliance on violence and terrorism inflamed popular fears. When several mail bombs exploded on May 1, 1919, the press and the public called for government action.

Attorney General A. Mitchell Palmer established a division in the Justice Department to hunt for radicals; the division was headed by J. Edgar Hoover who later became director of the Federal Bureau of Investigation. In November 1919 Palmer launched raids against suspected radicals, and a month later he deported three hundred aliens to the Soviet Union. Throughout the country, civil liberties came under assault. Communist parties were outlawed, antiradical legislation was adopted, and Socialists were expelled from the New York legislature. Suspected members of the IWW were subjected to vigilante violence and official repression.

The U.S. Supreme Court upheld the constitutionality of most of the laws that restricted civil liberties during the war and the Red Scare. Justice Oliver Wendell Holmes Jr. devised a means of testing whether the First Amendment had been violated. In *Schenck v. United States* (1919) he asked whether words or utterances posed "a clear and present danger" of interference with the government, the war effort, or civil order. The answer was that they had.

By 1920 the Red Scare had lost momentum. Palmer forecast a violent uprising on May 1, 1920, and when it did not occur, his credibility suffered. Some government officials opposed Palmer's deportation policies. Other public figures denounced New York's efforts against Socialist lawmakers. During this period, however, police in Massachusetts arrested two anarchists and Italian aliens, Nicola Sacco and Bartolomeo Vanzetti, for their alleged complicity in a robbery and murder at a shoe company in South Braintree, Massachusetts. Out of these events would come one of the most famous criminal cases of the 1920s.

lems of alcohol by an amendment to the Constitution restricting the sale and distribution of such beverages.

In the wake of World War I, the nation briefly contemplated a more active role in the world and then drew back. Woodrow Wilson's League of Nations, building on wartime idealism, seemed less attractive in the harsh light of the postwar disillusion with attempts to make the world safe for democracy. Though there was no going back to isolation, Americans for a season thought that they could let the Old World grapple with the consequences of its mistakes.

Later developments in the twentieth century, including the rise of Nazi Germany and the challenge from the Soviet Union, would make these judgments of the World War I period seem sadly mistaken. How could these men and women not see that in the errors of their great war lay the seeds of another greater conflict a generation later? What this chapter reveals is that in the setting of their time people buffeted by world war and profound social change embraced certainties of their past and pursued reassurance. Not knowing what their descendants would learn, they did their best in an era of upheaval and shock to deal with the world that had changed so much in just six short years.

Lend the way they Fight

Buy Bonds to your UTMOST

Gift of Henry Colgate, Picker Art Gallery, Colgate University

The government also employed advertising to sell bonds. This poster showing an American soldier at the Front was one of the ways that Washington sought to awaken public opinion to the need for bond sales.

National Archives #165-WW-269.c-7

The influenza epidemic of 1918–1919 affected every aspect of American life. This image of a policeman with a face mask, who directed traffic and sold Liberty Bonds at the same time, represented how much the threat of infection shaped popular attitudes.

Making Connections Across Chapters

LOOKING BACK

The problems that reformers encountered after 1914 had their roots in the record of the first years of the twentieth century. Looking back on the era of Theodore Roosevelt, William Howard Taft, and the early years of Woodrow Wilson's presidency, you can see the assumptions about human nature and the role of government that foreshadowed the later problems that weakened progressivism's hold on the American people.

1. How deeply rooted was the progressive spirit? What groups did it include, and which ones did it leave out?
2. How far did the presidents in this period want to go in changing American society?
3. Why did the First World War have such a devastating effect on progressive assumptions about the world?

LOOKING AHEAD

In the 1920s Americans would reject many of the accomplishments of the progressive era and repudiate much of what reformers had contributed to government and politics. In the next chapter discover whether these conservative trends went too far and what remained of value in the progressive movement.

1. Why did the United States adopt Prohibition as an answer to the problem of alcohol?
2. Why did woman suffrage not change the essential basis of national politics?
3. How did Americans feel about their place in the world after the experience of World War I and the battle over the League of Nations?

RECOMMENDED READINGS

Auchincloss, Louis. *Woodrow Wilson* (2000). A brief, readable life story of this important president.

Chambers, John Whiteclay. *The Tyranny of Change: America in the Progressive Era, 1890–1920* (2000). A helpful synthesis of this whole period.

Clements, Kendrick. *The Presidency of Woodrow Wilson* (1992). Offers a thorough guide to the accomplishments of Wilson in office.

Cooper, John Milton. *Breaking the Heart of the World* (2002). An excellent examination of the fight over the League of Nations.

Davis, Donald E., and Trani, Eugene P. *The First Cold War: The Legacy of Woodrow Wilson in U.S.-Soviet Relations* (2002). Considers the impact of Wilson's policies on these two nations.

Graham, Sara Hunter. *Woman Suffrage and the New Democracy* (1996). Describes how women obtained the vote during World War I and afterward.

Levin, Phyllis Lee. *Edith and Woodrow: The Wilson White House* (2001). Looks at the effect of Wilson's illness on his presidency.

Saunders, Ronald M. *In Search of Woodrow Wilson: Beliefs and Behavior* (1998). A very critical account of the president and his record.

Schaffer, Ronald. *America in the Great War: The Rise of the War Welfare State* (1991). An informative text about woman suffrage and race.

Trotter, Joe William, ed. *The Great Migration in Historical Perspective* (1991). An excellent collection of essays about the movement of African Americans to northern cities.

AMERICAN JOURNEY ONLINE AND *Ϙ* INFOTRAC COLLEGE EDITION

Visit the source collections at http://ajaccess.wadsworth .com and infotrac.thomsonlearning.com and use the Search function with the following key terms to explore documents, images, audio and video clips, articles, and commentary related to the material in this chapter.

Lusitania

Great Migration

Woodrow Wilson

Fourteen Points

Margaret Sanger

Carrie Chapman Catt

W. E. B. Du Bois

New Negro

ONLINE PRIMARY SOURCES

Here are some examples of the many primary sources related to this chapter that you will find on the *American Passages* Web site: http://history.wadsworth.com/ayersbrief02.

Letters of Black Migrants in the Chicago *Defender,* 1916–1918

Eugene V. Debs's Canton Speech, 1918

"I'm a Bolshevist from the Bottom of My Feet to the Top of My Head," Mother Jones, 1919

The site also offers self-quizzes, exercises, and many additional resources to help you study.

CHAPTER 23

The Age of Jazz and Mass Culture

1921–1927

DURING THE 1920S THE UNITED STATES BECAME MODERN AS THE automobile and other technological developments changed society. As the country became more uniform, the shared experiences of Americans made the nation more cohesive. Social attitudes toward sex and family life moved away from the restraints of the late nineteenth century. Movies, radio, and big-time sports became a part of everyday existence. Advertising made public relations a significant characteristic of the period.

After a postwar depression, the economy rebounded from 1922 to 1927. The Republican administrations of Warren G. Harding and Calvin Coolidge lowered income taxes and encouraged private enterprise. Issues of culture and morality shaped politics more than questions of economic reform.

In foreign affairs, the decade was officially a time of isolation. Although involvement in world affairs increased more slowly after 1921, the United States maintained a significant stake in the postwar European and Asian economies. However, the nation's stated policies and the actual course of events often moved in contradictory directions.

The Aftermath of War

When Warren G. Harding took the oath of office as president on March 4, 1921, the United States had passed through two and a half difficult years since the end of the First World War. Harding's calls for "normalcy" and healing proved effective during the 1920 election because they tapped voters' anxiety about the widespread rejection of older values and customs that had occurred in the postwar years.

A More Urban Nation

The Census of 1920 gave one important indicator of the country's new course. For the first time, the government reported that more Americans lived in towns and cities with 2,500 or more residents than in the countryside. More than ten million Americans resided in cities with a million people or more in 1920; that figure rose to more than fifteen million by 1930. Some nineteen million people left the country for the city over these ten years, and the migration of African Americans from the South to the North continued unabated during this period.

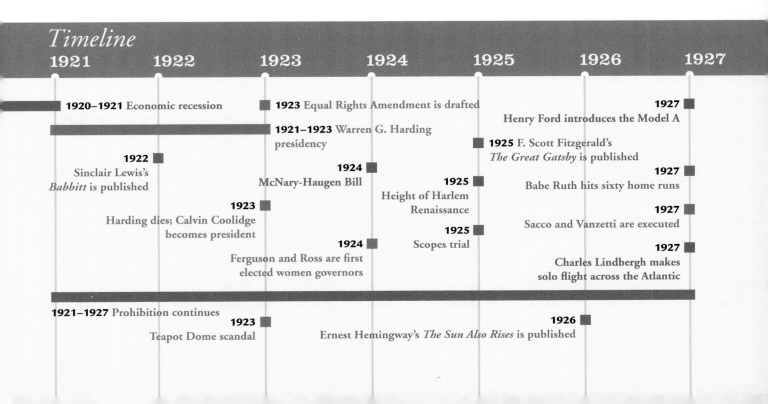

Timeline

| 1921 | 1922 | 1923 | 1924 | 1925 | 1926 | 1927 |

1920–1921 Economic recession

1923 Equal Rights Amendment is drafted

1927 Henry Ford introduces the Model A

1921–1923 Warren G. Harding presidency

1922 Sinclair Lewis's *Babbitt* is published

1924 McNary-Haugen Bill

1925 F. Scott Fitzgerald's *The Great Gatsby* is published

1927 Babe Ruth hits sixty home runs

1925 Height of Harlem Renaissance

1923 Harding dies; Calvin Coolidge becomes president

1927 Sacco and Vanzetti are executed

1925 Scopes trial

1924 Ferguson and Ross are first elected women governors

1927 Charles Lindbergh makes solo flight across the Atlantic

1921–1927 Prohibition continues

1923 Teapot Dome scandal

1926 Ernest Hemingway's *The Sun Also Rises* is published

For the young people who flocked to Chicago, New York, and Los Angeles, the city offered a degree of excitement and energy that the sedate farm could not match. Within the concrete canyons and electric avenues, visitors patronized theaters and dance halls and applauded vaudeville artists they could never hope to see in a small town. Many Americans resented the temptations of the city and associated them with foreign influences and assaults on traditional values. One flashpoint was the impact of a renewed surge of immigration.

Immigration Restricted

After the war, immigration returned to its former pattern. More than four hundred thirty thousand people sought entry to the United States in 1920, and another eight hundred five thousand arrived in 1921. In response, advocates of immigration restriction (see Chapter 22) renewed their campaign to shut off the flow of entrants from Southern and Eastern Europe.

Proponents of restriction argued that the immigrants lacked the qualities needed to be successful American citizens. "These people have not the same ideals and aspirations of Northern peoples," wrote the president of a Kiwanis Club in Tennessee. Madison Grant, one of the leading advocates of immigration restriction, said that "these immigrants adopt the language of the [native-born] American, they wear his clothes, they steal his name, and they are beginning to take his women, but they seldom adopt his religion or understand his ideals."

Sacco and Vanzetti
Two immigrants tried for murder in Massachusetts in the 1920s whose trial attracted worldwide attention because of allegations that the men had been unjustly convicted.

The widespread tension about immigration played a significant part in the fate of **Nicola Sacco** and **Bartolomeo Vanzetti,** who in June 1921 were on trial for a murder and robbery committed in Braintree, Massachusetts, a year earlier. There were allegations that authorities framed two Italians who believed in anarchism. In July both men were found guilty. Numerous appeals for a new trial were made, and the case soon became a focus for liberals and intellectuals convinced that Sacco and Vanzetti had not received a fair trial because of their foreign origin.

Immigration Quotas

The pressure on Congress grew. The American Federation of Labor, which feared the use of aliens as strikebreakers, added its weight to the campaign for immigration restrictions. In 1921 Congress enacted an emergency quota law that limited immigration from Europe to six hundred thousand people annually, and Great Britain and Germany were given the highest quotas. Three years later the lawmakers passed the National Origins Quota Act, which reduced annual legal immigration from Europe to about one hundred fifty thousand people, gave preference to entrants from Northern European countries, and blocked Asian immigrants entirely. The quota of immigrants from each country was determined by the number of residents from these countries counted in the 1890 Census.

After 1924 the recorded number of immigrants totaled about three hundred thousand annually until the beginning of the Great Depression. However, the impact on people who wished to emigrate from Southern and Eastern Europe was dramatic. Some ninety-five thousand immigrants had come into the United States from Poland in 1921; the annual total from that country over the next three years was only about twenty-eight thousand.

Since the immigration law did not affect Mexicans, some half-million newcomers from that country crossed the border during the 1920s and swelled the ranks of Americans of Hispanic ancestry. Mexicans were concentrated in California and Texas.

The Ku Klux Klan

The pressures of immigration from abroad and the movement of Americans from the country to the city produced intense social strains. The most sensational and violent of these developments was the popularity of the Ku Klux Klan. Revitalized after 1915 in the South, the Klan gained followers slowly until the end of World War I. By 1920 the Klan had become a marketing device for some clever promoters who used the allure of the Klan's brew of racism, anti-Catholicism, and anti-immigrant views to acquire members at a rapid rate. The masks and sheets members of the order wore provided an anonymity that attracted recruits.

A secret ritual added to the mystique of the hooded movement. Members read the Kloran and dedicated themselves to "Karacter, Honor, Duty." In time they might rise to become a King Kleagle or a Grand Goblin of the Domain. Members asked each other "Ayak," for "Are you a Klansman?" The proper reply was "Akia," meaning "A Klansman I am."

The Klan's program embraced opposition to Catholics, Jews, blacks, violators of the Prohibition laws, and anyone else who displeased local Klansmen. Even more than the Klan of the Reconstruction era, the Klan of the 1920s based its appeal on the desire of many white Americans for a more tranquil and less confusing social order. The Klan's efforts to create such an order initially made it attractive to many citizens. But the Klan also contained an ugly strain of violence. In many states its members lynched people they disagreed with; tortured blacks, Catholics, and Jews; and made a mockery of law enforcement.

Soon the Klan went into politics. In 1922 its members elected a senator in Texas and became a powerful presence in the legislatures of that state and others in the Southwest. In Indiana, the Klan was sufficiently strong that members of the order dominated the police of the state's major cities. The Klan also wielded significant influence in the Rocky Mountain states and the Pacific Northwest.

For the Democrats, the Klan posed a difficult problem. The party was already divided. Southern members favored Prohibition and disliked large cities. In the North, Democrats were opposed to Prohibition and rooted in the new urban lifestyles. The Klan intensified these tensions. Some "dry" Democrats saw the Klan as a legitimate form of political protest. The "wets" in northern cities regarded the Klan as an expression of cultural and regional intolerance. The Republicans benefited from this friction.

The Rise of Black Militance

The resurgence of the Klan came at a time when African Americans were asserting their identity and independence with greater energy. In the wake of the race riots of 1919, a growing spirit of assertiveness and militancy appeared in the art and literature of black intellectuals. But for the African Americans who crowded into the large northern cities during the Great Migration, the promise of America seemed to be an illusion. They lived in substandard housing, paid higher rents for their apartments than whites did, and could obtain only menial jobs. The Harlem neighborhood of New York City might be "the greatest Negro city in the world," as author James Weldon Johnson called it, but it was also a place where every day blacks saw how white society marginalized them.

Marcus Garvey and Black Nationalism

In 1916 a Jamaican named **Marcus Garvey** immigrated to the United States. Garvey promised to "organize the 400,000,000 Negroes of the World into a vast organization to plant the banner of freedom in the great continent of Africa." He worked through the Universal Negro Improvement Association (UNIA) to establish societies that were not controlled by imperialist nations. He founded his campaign on international shipping lines and newspapers that would enable blacks to travel to Africa and communicate among themselves.

Garvey's business ventures failed. The shipping lines collapsed, and the investors, mostly African Americans, lost their money. Blacks were divided in their views of the charismatic Garvey. The National Association for the Advancement of Colored People bristled when Garvey attacked its political agenda. His criticisms of labor unions alienated key African American leaders. Black opponents sent damaging information about Garvey's finances to the Department of Justice, and the government indicted him for mail fraud. He was convicted and went to prison in 1925. The important legacy of Garvey and the UNIA was the idea that urban blacks could band together to wield economic and political power.

Marcus Garvey

A Jamaican immigrant who promised to "organize the 400 million Negroes of the World into a vast organization to plant the banner of freedom in the great continent of Africa."

Dry America: The First Phase

The initial impact of Prohibition on the lives of Americans achieved much of what its proponents had predicted. The national consumption of alcohol declined from about two gallons per capita annually to around three-fourths of a gallon in 1921 and 1922. Many hospitals closed their alcoholism wards because of a lack of patients. States with mainly rural populations witnessed a virtual disappearance of alcoholic beverages. Contrary to later legend, Prohibition did change drinking habits in the United States.

Yet opposition persisted. The extent of compliance with Prohibition was spotty from the time the Volstead Law was passed. Some people made their own liquor; instructions for doing so were easily obtained. In cities like San Francisco and Boston, the law was never enforced. Several states did not even ratify the Eighteenth Amendment. Others failed to pass state laws to support the federal legislation. Believing that compliance ought to be voluntary, Congress appropriated inadequate funds to the Treasury Department's Prohibition Bureau. Although some agents, such as Izzy Einstein and Moe Smith, gained fame for the clever disguises they used to trap violators, there were never enough federal agents to cover the nation adequately.

The upper classes expected the working poor to obey the Prohibition law, but they resisted any change in their own drinking practices. With a ready market for illegal liquor in the major cities, enterprising individuals moved alcohol across the border into the United States. These "rum runners" and **bootleggers** brought in shipments of alcohol from Canada and the Caribbean. Their wares were sold at illegal saloons or "speakeasies" where city dwellers congregated in the evenings.

Contrary to stereotypes, however, Prohibition did not create organized crime. The nation became more aware of crime as a social problem because of the well-publicized activities of gangsters like **Alphonse "Al" Capone** and Johnny Torrio in Chicago. Prohibition offered individuals already involved in crime another incentive to band together and tap the immense profits to be had from easing the thirst of upper-class Americans. Capone in particular devoted himself to gaining control of gambling, prostitution, and bootlegging in the Chicago area. In New York, other mobsters built up networks of criminal enterprises to provide the same services. These sensational cases undermined faith in the positive effects of Prohibition.

bootleggers
Enterprising individuals who moved alcohol across the border into the United States from Canada and the Caribbean during Prohibition. Their wares were sold at illegal saloons or "speakeasies" where city dwellers congregated in the evenings.

Alphonse "Al" Capone
A gangster devoted to gaining control of gambling, prostitution, and bootlegging in the Chicago area.

Harding as President

Because of the scandals associated with his administration, Warren G. Harding is often depicted as the worst president in American history. During his brief term, however, he was very popular. He came to the White House from Marion, Ohio, where he had been a newspaper publisher before being elected to the Senate in 1914. His kindly nature impelled him to issue pardons to those whom the government had imprisoned for their beliefs during the war.

Harding also displayed a strong ambitious streak. He positioned himself in 1920 as the logical second choice when other candidates deadlocked at the Republican National Convention. When he promised to restore older values of the nation, he evoked resentment against an intrusive, expensive federal government that the voters associated with Wilson and the Democrats.

Harding sought to surround himself with what he called the "Best Minds," and his selection of Charles Evans Hughes as his secretary of state, banker Andrew Mellon as secretary of the treasury, and Herbert Hoover as secretary of commerce were cited as evidence of that commitment. After years in which the presidency had seemed separated from the people, Harding and his wife Florence opened up the White House and greeted visitors with evident pleasure. Throughout the country, Harding was a well-regarded president whose speeches appealed to a desire for a calmer, less activist chief executive.

During its first two years, the administration pressed for a legislative program that combined some constructive reforms with a return to older Republican trade policies. The 1921 Budget and Accounting Act established an executive budget for the president, a General Accounting Office for Congress, and a Bureau of the Budget in the executive branch. The Republicans rebuilt tariff protection in an emergency law of 1921 and then wrote the Fordney-McCumber Tariff Law a year later. Reflecting the party's suspicion of a powerful national government, Treasury Secretary Mellon pushed for lower income tax rates.

Harding and the World

In foreign relations, the Harding administration stayed aloof from the League of Nations. A separate peace with Germany in 1921 officially ended the nation's role in World War I. Throughout the 1920s Washington withheld recognition from the new Soviet Union. American interests turned back toward Latin America. To reduce the nation's military role in the region, the administration withdrew Marines from Haiti, the Dominican Republic, and Nicaragua. Trade and investment expanded south of the border.

Relations with Japan claimed a large amount of attention. The United States wanted to restrain the Japanese influence in Asia. Military action against Japan was politically impossible. Instead, the White House relied on diplomacy and economic pressure as its main weapons. Both nations were, however, increasing the size of their navies at this time. Budget limitations in both countries made a negotiated agreement on naval power a wise alternative. Congress and the administration concluded that a conference in which representatives of Great Britain, Japan, and the United States would meet was a logical move. The United States and Great Britain arranged for such a meeting in Washington in November 1921.

The Washington Conference and Beyond

The Washington Naval Conference of 1921 began with a dramatic proposal by Secretary of State Hughes. He said that sixty battleships should be scrapped outright. Limits should also be placed on the number of battleships and aircraft carriers that Japan, the United States, and Britain could build in the future. Out of the conference came the Five Power Treaty, which provided a fixed ratio for warship construction. For every five ships the United States built, the British could also build five, and the Japanese could build three. In return the Japanese secured an American pledge not to construct defenses in such U.S. possessions as Guam and the Philippines.

The Washington Conference also resulted in two other pacts. The Four Power Treaty ended a long-standing alliance (since 1902) between Great Britain and France, and it committed the United States, France, Great Britain, and Japan to respect each country's territorial possessions. In the Nine Power Treaty, the various nations agreed to avoid interference with China's internal affairs. Thus, the United States achieved much without having to make commitments that entailed the risk of force or greater international involvement. The happy combination of events that led to this success, however, would fade at the end of the decade.

The New Economy

The continuing postwar recession dogged the first two years of the Harding administration. Hard times contributed to substantial Republican losses in the 1922 congressional elections, yet the long-range news proved beneficial for Republicans. The economy slowly picked up in 1922 and 1923, productive output returned to 1918 levels, and employment rose. As wages climbed, discontent ebbed.

Prosperity and Its Benefits

The improvement in the economy's performance during 1922 began a period of unprecedented prosperity. The gross national product soared almost 40 percent. The per capita income of Americans went up about 30 percent during the same period. Real earnings for wage workers rose more than 20 percent, and hours worked declined slightly. The unemployment rate fell from 12 percent of the labor force in 1922 to 4 percent in 1927.

The Car Culture

The growth of automobile manufacturing represented one of the most significant changes in the industrial sector (see Table 23.1). The use of cars became widespread during the postwar years. By 1927 there were more than twenty million cars on the roads along with more than three million trucks and buses.

The impact of the automobile rippled through the economy. Automobiles needed oil and gasoline to operate, steel for their frames, rubber for their tires, glass for windshields, and service businesses for dealers and drivers. For the traveler on the road, motels offered accommodations, billboards advertised attractions, and roadside restaurants provided food and diversion. The size of the road network grew from seven thousand miles at the end of

Table 23.1 Automobile Registrations, 1921–1929

Year	Registrations
1921	9,212,158
1922	10,704,076
1923	13,253,019
1924	15,436,102
1925	17,481,001
1926	19,267,967
1927	20,193,333
1928	21,362,240
1929	23,120,897

Source: *The Statistical History of the United States* (Stamford, CT: Fairfield Publishers, 1965), p. 462.

the war to fifty thousand miles in 1927. Gasoline taxes brought in revenues for the states, enabling them to build more roads, which, in turn, fostered the development of suburbs. Traffic lights, first used in New York City, eventually spread across the country.

The automobile had cultural effects too. No longer did young women and men have to carry on courtship within sight of parents and chaperones. Family excursions were tied to the availability of the car. Cars consumed a large chunk of the working family's income as Americans readily took to the practice of buying their cars on the installment plan. The enclosed car, initially a prestigious model, soon became standard on the road. Freedom and "automobility" were the watchwords of the day.

Henry Ford Gives Way to General Motors

As the decade began, Henry Ford was still the most famous carmaker in the nation. His showplace was the huge factory on the Rouge River near Detroit. Sprawling across two thousand acres, the Rouge plant eventually employed seventy-five thousand workers to turn out the reliable, familiar Model T car on which Ford based his automobile empire. In 1921, Ford made more than half of the automobiles produced in the United States. A car cost under $300. Visitors marveled at Ford's organizational genius. At the same time, however, the carmaker deployed his vast wealth to promote his own political ambitions and crude anti-Semitism.

The Model T was a popular car but not a very attractive one. The joke was that you could get a Model T in any color, so long as it was black. Ford's failure to develop different car models opened a competitive opportunity to General Motors (GM). The DuPont family acquired the firm in 1920 and brought in Alfred P. Sloan Jr. as chief assistant to the president. In 1923 he became president. Sloan set up a system of independent operating divisions that produced models of Chevrolets, Buicks, and other vehicles annually. The constant flow of new models induced customers to want a fresh vehicle every few years. The General Motors Acceptance Corporation made it easy to acquire a car on the installment plan.

By the middle of the 1920s, Ford's sales fell as those of General Motors rose. Henry Ford had revolutionized American transportation before 1920. Now he was losing out because of his resistance to marketing and manufacturing innovation.

Electrical America

Increased reliance on electricity was another key element in the nation's industrial growth during the 1920s. By 1928 electricity drove 70 percent of factory equipment. Two-thirds of the families in towns and cities had electricity in their homes as well. Homemakers bought some fifteen million electric irons and another seven million vacuum cleaners. Advertisers appealed to women with descriptions of the all-electric kitchen "Where Work is Easy!" Sales of consumer appliances were one of the major economic stimulants of the decade.

The diffusion of electricity facilitated the growth of radio. The first station, KDKA in Pittsburgh, went on the air in 1920. After that the number of stations grew rapidly. In 1923 a New York station, WBAY, began selling time to anyone who would pay for it. Commercial radio caught on quickly. Soon announcers and performers became popular attractions. In 1923, there were radios in four hundred thousand households.

Three years later the Radio Corporation of America (RCA), led by its president David Sarnoff, established the first national network of stations, the National Broadcasting Company (NBC). Telephone wires carried the broadcast signals to stations scattered across the country. Programming was diverse, and commercial sponsors oversaw the content of such programs as *The Maxwell House Hour* and the *Ipana Troubadours*. Radio further advanced the movement of the 1920s toward a standard culture for the whole nation.

Movies in the Silent Era

The motion picture quickly became the most celebrated form of popular entertainment during the decade. Each week one hundred million people went to see movies. Some movie houses were plain and functional; others featured expensive lobbies and plush furniture. The Roxy Theater in New York City was dubbed the "Cathedral of the Motion Picture." Ticket prices were relatively low and stable, usually about 50 cents. Pictures shaped how young people kissed on dates, what they wore, and what they said.

From their uncertain beginnings at the turn of the century, motion picture studios had developed into large enterprises employing hundreds of people. They worked in Hollywood, California, because of its mild climate and the proximity of deserts, seashores, and open spaces for location shooting. Studio heads Adolph Zukor of Paramount Pictures and Louis B. Mayer of Metro-Goldwyn-Mayer (MGM) controlled chains of theaters. To get a popular feature film, theater owners would have to accept the entire yearly production of a major studio.

Motion picture stars were the bedrock of the business. Charlie Chaplin's popularity rose to even greater heights during the early 1920s in such films as *The Gold Rush* (1925). Other box-office attractions included Rudolph Valentino, whose sudden death in 1926 brought thousands of weeping fans, in a line stretching for eight city blocks, to his New York funeral.

To maintain its hold on the popular mind, Hollywood reacted quickly when sexual scandals tarnished the industry's image early in the 1920s. Tales of wild parties and mysterious deaths tainted such stars as Roscoe "Fatty" Arbuckle. The studios recruited Will H. Hays, a prominent Republican, to serve as president of the Motion Pictures Producers and Distributors Association in 1922. Hays tried to persuade filmmakers to inject more moral content into films. He relied on a series of "Don'ts and Be Carefuls" to guide producers and directors. Skillful directors such as Cecil B. deMille circumvented these mild warnings. He argued that the sexual scenes in *The Ten Commandments* were based on biblical descriptions.

Advertising America

The economic growth of the 1920s rested on consumer spending. Advertisers developed new and effective ways to persuade Americans to acquire the products coming out of the nation's factories and workshops. The advertising business boomed. Radios brought advertising into the home; billboards attracted the attention of millions of motorists. Advertising, said one of its practitioners, "literally creates demand for the things of life that raise the standard of living, elevate the taste, changing luxuries into necessities."

Among the products that advertising promoted was Listerine, which was said to eliminate bad breath. Cigarettes such as Lucky Strike were marketed as a means of achieving a slimmer figure. Other consumers were urged to ingest yeast at least twice a day to fight constipation and skin problems. The ingenious advertising executive Albert Lasker succeeded in inducing Americans to drink orange juice daily at breakfast, breaking the taboo against advertising the sanitary napkin Kotex, and describing Kleenex as "the handkerchief you can throw away."

The most celebrated advertising man of the decade was Bruce Barton, who wrote a biography of Jesus Christ to demonstrate that advertising went back to biblical times. In *The Man Nobody Knows* (1925), Barton retold the New Testament in terms that Americans of the 1920s could easily grasp. Jesus, wrote Barton, "recognized the basic principle that all good advertising is news." The twelve disciples were a model of an efficient business organization, and Jesus himself was a master salesman. Barton's book became a national bestseller.

Those Left Behind

The success of the consumer-related industries lifted the economy to new levels of prosperity after 1922. However, not all segments of society shared equally in the return of good times. The postwar depression hit the farm sector with devastating force. For labor, also, this was a time of retreat.

In some areas farm life resembled that of the pioneers more than it did the city dwellers. Overproduction of crops drove down prices and led to massive harvests that could not be marketed. In the South, for

Mechanized tractors, like this one from North Dakota, made it possible for farmers to increase their production far beyond what had been done with horse-drawn equipment. The result was an increase in crops and a continuing farm problem.

©CORBIS

example, the price of cotton was 40 cents a pound in 1920 but slid to 10 cents a pound in 1921. The postwar recovery of agriculture in Europe meant that overseas markets were smaller as well. The per capita income of most farmers did not rise substantially after 1919.

To improve their lot, farmers sought higher tariff duties on imported products. They also revived the idea of farm cooperatives. In 1921 and 1922 farmers rallied behind the "Sapiro Plan," named after Aaron Sapiro, who wanted producers to hold goods off the market until prices rose. If it was to work, the scheme required close cooperation among farmers. When that did not occur, it collapsed. Federal legislation to regulate the trading of grain futures and extend more credit to farmers was marginally helpful, but the underlying problem of overproduction continued.

Another idea for dealing with the farm situation emerged in 1921. A plow manufacturer named George Peek proposed that American farmers ship surplus products overseas at whatever price they could obtain. The government would buy farm products at the market price and then sell them abroad. Taxes on the processing of crops would cover the cost to the government and the taxpayer. The chairs of the House and Senate Agriculture Committees introduced a bill to enact such a program in January 1924. Known as the McNary-Haugen Plan, it gained much support in the Midwest and soon commanded national attention.

Labor in Retreat

The 1920s were an era of gloom and despair for organized labor. The number of unionized laborers dropped from nearly 5 million in 1921 to fewer than 3.5 million eight years later. The American Federation of Labor (AFL), under its president William Green, presented only weak challenges to employers. It accepted what management called "business unionism," or the nonunion "open shop," which was labeled the "American Plan." Efforts to organize unskilled workers were abandoned.

Government and business threw up numerous obstacles to labor's interests. The U.S. Supreme Court struck down minimum wages for women in Washington, D.C. In the case of *Adkins v. Children's Hospital* (1923), the Court ruled that the law infringed on the right of workers to sell their labor for whatever they could obtain. This "liberty-of-contract" doctrine accordingly barred Congress from passing such a law. In addition to an unsympathetic Supreme Court, unions faced opposition from the White House. When strikes occurred in railroading during 1922, the Harding administration obtained harsh court orders that effectively ended the walkouts.

Some of the bigger and more enlightened firms provided what became known as *welfare capitalism.* They sought to appease workers with recreational facilities, benefit plans, and sometimes even profit-sharing opportunities. After the middle of the decade, however, these programs stalled as the lack of labor militancy removed the incentive to make concessions to workers.

The Harding Scandals

Warren G. Harding did not live to see the political benefits of the nation's better times. By early 1923 his presidency was mired in rumors of scandal. Harding had chosen the "best minds" for the more important positions in his cabinet. His other appointments, though, were mediocre or worse. Attorney General Harry Daugherty was a political ally of the president, but his loose direction of the Justice Department allowed corruption to flourish. Scandals also festered in the Veterans Bureau and the Office of the Alien Property Custodian.

Albert B. Fall

The secretary of the interior involved in the Teapot Dome scandal.

The most serious wrongdoing involved the secretary of the interior, **Albert B. Fall.** Federal oil reserves at Elk Hills, California, and Teapot Dome, Wyoming (where the rocks vaguely resembled a teapot), were leased to private oil companies. Fall received $400,000 in loans from friends in the industry in what many interpreted as payoffs for his leasing decisions. The Teapot Dome scandal emerged after Harding died, but it established his administration's reputation as one of the most corrupt in American history.

Harding was not implicated in any of these misdeeds. A weak president and a poor judge of people, he allowed cronies and crooks to infest his administration. By 1923 he knew about the ethical problems in the Veterans Bureau, and he suspected that scandals lurked in the Department of the Interior and the Justice Department. During the summer of that year, he told a friend that "It is my friends who are giving me trouble." During a tour of the Pacific Northwest in July 1923, the president fell ill. He died in San Francisco on August 2 of heart disease.

Keep Cool with Coolidge

Harding's successor was Calvin Coolidge, the former governor of Massachusetts who became Harding's running mate in 1920. Coolidge came to be viewed in Washington as a stereotypical New Englander, a man of few words. In fact, Coolidge was quite talkative in the regular press conferences that he held twice a week. Although he slept twelve hours a day, Coolidge was not a lazy man. He worked hard addressing the needs of those who told him their problems with the federal government. Because he was unwilling to consult with Congress, his relations with Capitol Hill were cool and distant. His wife Grace brought glamour and a sense of fun to the White House, offsetting her husband's dour personality.

Coolidge was much more committed to the conservative principles of the Republicans than Harding had been. He sincerely believed that "the business of America is business," and he endorsed policies designed to promote corporate enterprise. He extended the tax-cutting policies of Treasury Secretary Mellon. The president also appointed pro-business individuals to head the regulatory agencies and departments that the progressives had established a generation earlier.

Coolidge lost little time in gaining control of the Republican party and was easily nominated as the party's candidate at the national convention. The delegates selected Charles G. Dawes, an Illinois banker, as his running mate. The Republicans ran on a platform of conservative policies and popular approval of Coolidge. The president used modern public relations techniques to bolster his image as an embodiment of old-time virtues of morality and frugality. Movie stars came to the White House to endorse the president and sing the campaign theme song: "Keep Cool with Coolidge."

The Democrats hoped that the Teapot Dome scandal and other revelations of wrongdoing in the Harding years would be their ticket back to the White House. Unfortunately for them, the Teapot Dome scandal could not be linked to anyone in the White House. Without sensational disclosures, the investigations bored the public and eventually faded away.

WHAT A FRIEND WE HAVE IN COOLIDGE!

THE CASH REGISTER CHORUS.

©The Granger Collection, New York

President Calvin Coolidge said that business prosperity was the key to national success. The business community felt the same way. This satirical cartoon mocks the way in which the Republicans served corporate America.

The Discordant Democrats

The larger problem for the Democrats was the cultural divide that separated the two wings of the party. The issue of Prohibition had split the party between the "dry" faithful of the South and West and the anti-prohibitionist residents of the large cities of the North and Midwest. The two leading candidates for the Democratic party nomination reflected this regional tension. William G. McAdoo had been secretary of the treasury and Woodrow Wilson's son-in-law. He represented the progressive, prohibitionist Democrats of the nation's rural states. But his candidacy suffered when it became known that McAdoo had done legal work for some of the men involved in the Teapot Dome scandal. The other major contender was Governor Alfred E. Smith of New York. His administrations had proposed some social justice measures, but he opposed Prohibition. His Roman Catholicism evoked fear and bigotry in places where the Ku Klux Klan was still powerful.

Stalemate in New York

The Democratic National Convention at Madison Square Garden in New York City left the party with almost no chance of defeating President Coolidge. McAdoo and Smith were deadlocked. Finally, after 103 ballots, the exhausted delegates compromised and chose a former member of Congress and Wall Street lawyer named John W. Davis. The ticket was safe, dull, and had little chance of victory. "What Davis needs is a rabbit foot," wrote William Howard Taft.

A third candidate challenged the Republicans and Democrats. Senator Robert M. La Follette of Wisconsin became the champion of what remained of the progressive spirit of the midwestern farmers. Although he was nominated for president at a convention of the Progressive party, he did not attend the meeting or identify himself with the party. The American Federation of Labor and the railroad unions backed La Follette but with little money or enthusiasm.

The 1924 Election in Perspective

The Republicans ignored Davis and concentrated on the alleged radicalism of La Follette. The choice, they said, was "Coolidge or Chaos." It was a dull campaign, and the outcome was never in doubt. Coolidge polled more than 15,718,000 votes, more than the combined total of Davis's 8,385,000 and La Follette's 4,831,000. The Republicans retained firm control of both houses of Congress. For the moment, it looked as if political reform was in disarray.

Yet beneath the surface, electoral trends were moving toward the Democrats. In the northern cities the party's share of the vote grew during the 1920s. If a candidate appeared who could unite the traditionally Democratic South with the ethnic voters of the Northeast, the Republicans' supremacy might be in jeopardy.

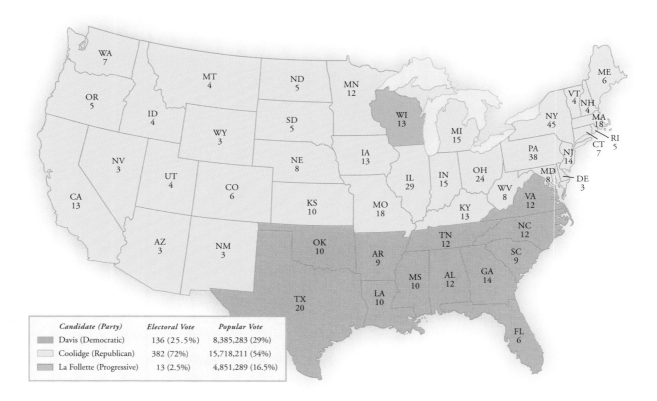

Candidate (Party)	Electoral Vote	Popular Vote
Davis (Democratic)	136 (25.5%)	8,385,283 (29%)
Coolidge (Republican)	382 (72%)	15,718,211 (54%)
La Follette (Progressive)	13 (2.5%)	4,851,289 (16.5%)

MAP 23.1 The Election of 1924

The election of 1924 was a landslide for Calvin Coolidge over John W. Davis and Robert M. La Follette. The divided Democratic party and the rebellious Progressives were no match for the united Republicans and the popular Coolidge.

A Blossoming in Art and Literature

During the 1920s, the nation's cultural life experienced a productivity and artistic success that would be unrivaled during the rest of the twentieth century. In music, drama, and literature, the decade brought forth a rare assembly of first-rate talents.

The Harlem Renaissance

Black writers made a notable contribution to this fruitful period. In the wake of the Great Migration, African American intellectual life had become centered in New York City. There, authors and poets lived in the black section known as Harlem. The "Harlem Renaissance" owed much to W. E. B. Du Bois's encouragement of African American writing in the *Crisis,* the journal of the National Association for the Advancement of Colored People (NAACP). In the New York of the early 1920s, the exciting nightlife, the relative absence of racial bigotry, and the interest of wealthy white patrons enabled a few black writers to pursue literary careers.

The Harlem Renaissance reached its peak in 1925, when **Alain Locke**'s book *The New Negro* was published. Locke argued that African Americans' "more immediate hope" depended on the ability of blacks and whites to evaluate "the Negro in terms of his artistic endowments and cultural contributions, past and prospective." Other major figures in the Renaissance were the poets Langston Hughes ("The Weary Blues"), Countee Cullen ("Do I Marvel"), **Zora Neale Hurston** (the play *Color Struck*), Claude McKay (*Harlem Shadows*), as well as the memoirist and songwriter James Weldon Johnson (*God's Trombones*). Although these writers' artistic merit was undeniable, the Harlem Renaissance did little to alter the segregationist laws and customs that restricted the lives of most African Americans.

Alain Locke
An African American poet and an important member of the Harlem Renaissance.

Zora Neale Hurston
An African American novelist who embodied the creative and artistic aspirations of the Harlem Renaissance in the 1920s.

The Sound of Jazz

The music that pulsed in the background of the Harlem Renaissance proved even more important for the development of American culture in the long run. After World War I, the improvised music that came to be called jazz brought together black musicians and a few white players in Kansas City, Chicago, and New York. At the rent parties where Harlem residents raised money to pay their landlords, in the nightclubs that organized crime controlled, and in the after-hours jam sessions, jazz became a unique American art form.

The major innovators of jazz included trumpeter **Louis Armstrong** and tenor sax player Coleman Hawkins, who took the new music beyond its roots in New Orleans toward a more sophisticated style. Blues artists such as Bessie Smith and Ma Rainey sold "race records" to black and white audiences. Edward Kennedy "Duke" Ellington and Fletcher Henderson led larger orchestras. White artists, including Benny Goodman and Jack Teagarden, moved the jazz that they heard toward acceptance by white audiences. The rhythms and sounds of jazz gave the 1920s its enduring title: the Jazz Age.

In the familiar bastions of artistic activity, the 1920s brought further disruption and change. Writers looked at the postwar world in a critical spirit. The most popular novelist of the early 1920s was Sinclair Lewis, whose books *Main Street* (1920) and *Babbitt* (1922) looked with unsparing honesty at small-town life in the Midwest. Lewis made a real estate agent (or "realtor") into the main figure of *Babbitt.* His portrait of Babbitt and his fellow townspeople was gently satirical and overwhelmingly factual. His novels *Arrowsmith* (1925) and *Elmer Gantry* (1927) enhanced his reputation.

Young people devoured the work of an acidic essayist and social critic, Henry L. Mencken, who wrote for the *American Mercury.* Mencken was a Baltimore newspaperman who had little time for the sacred cows of middle-class culture. He characterized democracy as "the worship of jackals by jackasses" and said that puritanism was "the haunting fear that somebody, somewhere may be happy." Aimed more at the middle-class audience was *Time,* started in March 1923 by Briton Hadden and Henry Luce. *Time* sought to present the week's news in readable and sprightly prose. *The New Yorker,* a sophisticated

Louis Armstrong
A trumpeter and a major innovator of jazz.

The Cotton Club in Harlem was the nightly center of the social scene of the Harlem Renaissance. The Cotton Club orchestra in 1925 entertained the white patrons who came up from lower Manhattan to share the excitement of black music and culture.

weekly, was headed by Harold Ross. The best American writers and poets strove to have their works published in *The New Yorker*.

The most influential fiction author of the decade was Ernest Hemingway. In *The Sun Also Rises* (1926) and *A Farewell to Arms* (1929), Hemingway expressed the anguish of young Americans who had lost faith in the moral customs of their parents. Hemingway's writing style was widely imitated, and he became an international celebrity.

Another serious novelist of the day was **F. Scott Fitzgerald.** Like Hemingway, he, along with his wife Zelda, captured attention as the embodiment of the free spirit of the Jazz Age. At the same time, Fitzgerald was a dedicated artist who sought to write a great novel that would ensure his fame. In *The Great Gatsby* (1925) he came as close to that goal as any author of the time. The book chronicled how a young man, Jay Gatsby, sought to recapture a lost love among the aristocracy of the Long Island shore. In Gatsby's failure to win his dream, Fitzgerald saw the inability of Americans to escape the burdens of their own pasts. He offered a deeply critical portrait of the newly rich Americans who had gained wealth during the 1920s.

An Age of Artistic Achievement

The list of important authors during the 1920s included such artistic innovators as T. S. Eliot, who lived in Great Britain and whose poems such as "The Waste Land" (1922) influenced a generation of poets on both sides of the Atlantic. Novelists John Dos Passos, Sherwood Anderson, Edith Wharton, Willa Cather, and William Faulkner produced a body of work that delved into the lives of aristocratic women (Wharton), prairie pioneers (Cather), the working poor and middle class (Dos Passos), the residents of small towns (Anderson), and the Deep South (Faulkner).

The theater witnessed the emergence of the Broadway musical in the work of Richard Rodgers and Lorenz Hart (*Garrick Gaieties*), George and Ira Gershwin (*Lady, Be Good*), Jerome Kern and Oscar Hammerstein II (*Showboat*), and Cole Porter (*Paris*). Serious drama drew upon the talents of the brooding and pessimistic Eugene O'Neill as well as Elmer Rice and Maxwell Anderson.

In architecture the innovative work of Frank Lloyd Wright had given him a reputation for artistic daring even before 1920, but commercial success eluded him. American architects designed planned suburban communities reminiscent of historical forms from England or the Southwest. Skyscrapers and city centers such as Rockefeller Center in New York City embodied a building style that emphasized light and air.

F. Scott Fitzgerald

A serious novelist of the day and author of *The Great Gatsby* who, along with his wife Zelda, captured attention as the embodiment of the free spirit of the Jazz Age.

Fundamentalism and Traditional Values

For most Americans the literary and artistic ferment of the 1920s was part of a broader set of challenges to older lifestyles. Residents of small towns and newcomers to the growing cities sought to find reassurance in the older ways. The currents of religious and social conservatism remained dominant. The Ku Klux Klan saw its political influence ebb because of popular disgust with its tactics, but an upsurge of evangelical Christianity underscored the cultural divisions within the nation.

The Klan in Decline

The Klan's influence peaked around 1923; after that its fortunes went into a slump. As it sought greater political power, the two major parties absorbed some of the Klan's appeal and weakened its hold on the public. In the key state of Indiana, parts of the Klan's program aroused fears that religious freedom might be at risk. Scandals also sapped the Klan's moral fervor. In Indiana the Klan leader, David Stephenson, went to prison for the death of a woman he had assaulted. Faced with jail, he revealed the bribes he had offered to state officials. The tawdry mess broke the Klan's hold on Indiana and hastened its decline elsewhere in the nation.

The Continuing Controversy over Sacco and Vanzetti

Meanwhile, the ordeal of Sacco and Vanzetti in the Massachusetts legal system continued as their attorneys filed a series of appeals. The lawyers challenged the conduct of the jury, attacked the quality of the evidence against the two men, and questioned the identifications of the defendants that various witnesses had made. Intellectuals became more convinced that the prosecution had either framed Sacco and Vanzetti or railroaded them into prison.

None of this changed the mind of the presiding judge, and by October 1924 all motions for another trial had been denied. The two defendants had hired a new attorney, and a campaign for a new trial and their eventual release gained greater national attention during 1925 and 1926. Within Massachusetts, where animosity against immigrants still ran strong, the state government did not waver in its belief that Sacco and Vanzetti were guilty.

The Fundamentalist Movement

Amid the social ferment of the 1920s, American Protestantism engaged in a passionate debate over the proper position of Christians toward science, the doctrine of evolution, and liberal ideas. Conservative church leaders spoke of the dangers to faith from a society that had moved away from the Bible and its teachings. In 1920 a minister called the movement "Fundamentalism" because it sought to reaffirm precepts of the Christian creed such as the literal truth of the Bible and the central place of Jesus Christ in saving humanity.

Fundamentalism had a political and social agenda as well as a religious message. On the local and state levels, believers sought to eradicate traces of modern ideas that contradicted biblical teachings. The doctrine of evolution became a special target of fundamentalist wrath. William Jennings Bryan emerged as a leading champion of the crusade. "It is better to trust the Rock of Ages," he said, "than to know the age of rocks." The Anti-Evolution League hoped to amend the Constitution to bar the teaching of evolution anywhere in the nation. In 1924 Tennessee passed a law that prohibited spending public money "to teach any theory that denies the story of the Divine Creation of man as taught in the Bible."

The Scopes Trial

In the following year a schoolteacher named John T. Scopes taught evolution in one of his classes in Dayton, Tennessee. The local authorities indicted Scopes, and his case came to trial. Bryan agreed to help prosecute Scopes, and the American Civil Liberties Union brought in the noted trial lawyer, Clarence Darrow, for the defense. The proceedings attracted national attention. The judge refused to let Darrow call in scientists to defend evolution. Stores in Dayton sold pins that said "Your Old Man's a Monkey."

Darrow called Bryan as an expert witness on the Bible. The two men sparred for several days. Bryan defended the literal interpretation of the Bible, but to the reporters covering the trial he seemed to wither under Darrow's cross-examination. Sophisticated Americans regarded Bryan as a joke, but in rural America he remained a hero. The jury found Scopes guilty and assessed him a small fine. Bryan died shortly after the trial.

To many Americans the **Scopes trial** seemed to signal the end of fundamentalism, and the political side of the movement did lose momentum during the late 1920s. But during the same period fundamentalism concentrated on creating a network of churches, schools, and colleges where its doctrines could be taught to future generations. The forces underlying fundamentalism during the 1920s would remain a potent element in American culture.

Prohibition in Retreat

By the middle of the 1920s the Prohibition experiment was faltering. The spread of bootlegging and its ties with organized crime meant that state and federal authorities faced an ever-growing challenge in attempting to stop movement of illegal liquor across the Canadian border or from ships that gathered near major U.S. ports. The brewing and liquor interests called for a campaign to repeal the Eighteenth Amendment. Newspapers published recipes for making illegal booze, and Congressman Fiorello LaGuardia of New York showed reporters how to turn "near beer," which had an alcohol content of less than .05 percent, into an alcoholic beverage.

Consumption of alcohol rose to over one gallon per capita annually by 1923 and reached almost one and one-quarter gallons three years later. With the national law on the books, the Anti-Saloon League lost some of its intensity during the 1920s. The consensus that had brought Prohibition into existence during World War I was crumbling as the 1928 presidential election approached.

Flaming Youth

During the 1920s, changes in the family gave youth more importance than they had enjoyed ever before. Women stopped having children at a younger age, and they thus had more time to devote to their own interests. Divorce gained favor as a way of ending unhappy marriages; the emphasis shifted to making marriages more fulfilling for both partners. Marriage counseling gained in popularity, as did manuals telling men and women how to achieve greater sexual gratification.

As the nature of marriage changed, the role of children in the household was also transformed. Parents were no longer regarded as the unquestioned rulers of the home. One major influence on how American children were raised was the work of the behavioral psychologist John B. Watson. He taught that by manipulating the stimuli that a child experienced, the parents could create the kind of adult they wanted. He instructed parents to follow a system of reward and punishment to shape the character of their offspring.

The ability of parents to decide what their children should read and think came under attack from the growing pervasiveness of the consumer culture. Young people were bombarded with alluring images of automobiles, makeup, motion pictures, and other attractions. Since children no longer were so important to the wage-earning power of the family, they were given greater freedom. A teenager might have four to six evenings a week to spend away from home. Adolescence came to be seen as a distinct phase in the development of young Americans. Dating became a ritualized form of courting behavior carried on at movies, dances, and athletic events, as well as in automobiles. Parents had much less influence on their children's decisions about clothes, hairstyles, and behavior.

More young Americans attended high school during the 1920s than ever before, and the percentage of those who went to college increased. Freed from parental supervision, college women could smoke in public, go out on dates, and engage in the latest trends in sexual activity, "necking and petting." Male students with enough income joined fraternities, drank heavily, and devoted endless amounts of time to athletic contests and dates.

Scopes trial
Local authorities indicted this Dayton, Tennessee, schoolteacher for teaching evolution in one of his classes. The jury found him guilty and assessed a small fine.

The college experience for students from lower-class families, different religious backgrounds, or minority groups was less comfortable. Informal quotas limited the numbers of Jewish students admitted to Yale, Columbia, or Harvard. In the South, African Americans of college age were forced to attend predominantly black institutions with fewer resources. Poorer students at state universities and private colleges worked their way through.

Big-Time Sports

On college campuses large and small, autumn was the football season. During the 1920s the college game grew into a national obsession as money was poured into the construction of stadiums, the coaching staffs, and in many instances, the players themselves. Institutions like Duke University, Stanford University, and the University of Texas built huge football arenas in pursuit of athletic greatness and profits. The business of football became the financial lifeblood at many institutions of higher learning.

The most famous football player of the era was Harold "Red" Grange of the University of Illinois. When he scored four touchdowns in twelve minutes against the University of Michigan in 1924, his picture appeared on the cover of the new *Time* magazine. After he left college, Grange joined the newly formed National Professional Football League and received some $12,000 per game at the start.

Boxing also attracted millions of followers. The first popular champion was William Harrison "Jack" Dempsey, who received $1 million for his fight against the Frenchman Georges Carpentier in 1921. To avoid confronting the leading African American contender, Henry Willis, Dempsey and his manager agreed to fight James Joseph Gene Tunney. Tunney defeated an overconfident Dempsey in 1927.

Other sports produced equally exciting heroes. The tennis stars of the decade included William "Big Bill" Tilden, who dominated the men's game from 1921 to 1925. Helen Wills Moody successfully challenged the reigning queen of tennis, the Frenchwoman Suzanne Lenglen. In golf, Robert "Bobby" Trent Jones won numerous tournaments as an amateur.

Baseball: The National Sport

Of all the American sports, however, baseball symbolized the excitement and passion of the 1920s. The game experienced a wounding scandal in 1919 when it was revealed that members of the Chicago White Sox had conspired to fix the World Series. Although the players were ultimately acquitted of any crime, the "Black Sox" scandal cast a shadow over the game. The owners hired a new commissioner, Kenesaw Mountain Landis, a former federal judge, and gave him sweeping authority over the operations of baseball. Landis exercised his power vigorously to keep baseball pure.

Baseball underwent even more dramatic changes because of the popularity of **George Herman "Babe" Ruth.** Ruth was a pitcher for the Boston Red Sox when they sold him to the New York Yankees for $400,000 in 1918. Ruth believed that he could hit home runs; he belted out fifty-four during the 1920 season. Fans flocked to see him perform. The Yankees decided to construct Yankee Stadium ("the House that Ruth built") to accommodate the customers who wanted to be there when Ruth connected. The Yankees won American League pennants from 1921 to 1923, and in 1923 they won the World Series. Batting averages rose in both leagues, as did attendance records. Professional baseball remained a white man's game, however; talented black players such as Josh Gibson labored in obscurity in the Negro leagues.

AP/Wide World Photos

Gertrude Ederle begins her swim of the English Channel.

George Herman "Babe" Ruth

This Boston Red Sox pitcher was sold to the New York Yankees in 1918 for $400,000. He belted out fifty-four home runs during the 1920 season, and fans flocked to see him play.

New Roles for Women

After the achievement of woman suffrage, most people expected the newly enfranchised voters to produce a genuine change in politics. It soon became apparent that women cast their votes much as men did. Yet while women did not change politics, they found that their place in society underwent significant transformations.

Elsie Hill on Why Women Should Have Full Legal Equality, 1922

In the wake of woman suffrage, the National Woman's party pressed forward with a feminist agenda that is well expressed in this statement of the movement's goals by Elsie Hill.

The removal of all forms of the subjection of women is the purpose to which the National Woman's party is dedicated. Its present campaign to remove the discriminations against women in the laws of the United States is but the beginning of its determined effort to secure the freedom of women, an integral part of the struggle for human liberty for which women are first of all responsible. Its interest lies in the final release of woman from the class of a dependent, subservient being to which early civilization committed her.

The laws of various States at present hold her in that class. They deny her a control of her children equal to the father's; they deny her, if married, the right to her own earnings; they punish her for offences for which men go unpunished; they exclude her from public office and from public institutions to the support of which her taxes contribute. These laws are not the creation of this age, but the fact that they are still tolerated on our statute books and that in some States their removal is vigorously resisted shows the hold of old traditions upon us. Since the passage of the Suffrage Amendment the incongruity of these laws, dating back many centuries, has become more than ever marked. . . .

The National Woman's party believes that it is a vital social need to do away with these discriminations against women and is devoting its energies to that end. The removal of the discriminations and not the method by which they are removed is the thing upon which the Woman's Party insists. It has under consideration an amendment to the Federal Constitution which, if adopted, would remove them at one stroke, but it is at present endeavoring to secure their removal in the individual States by a blanket bill, which is the most direct State method. For eighty-two years the piecemeal method has been tried, beginning with the married women's property act of 1839 in Mississippi, and no State, excepting Wisconsin, where the Woman's Party blanket bill was passed in June, 1921, has yet finished. . . .

The present program of the National Woman's party is to introduce its Woman's Equal Rights Bill, or bills attaining the same purpose, in all State legislatures as they convene. It is building up in Washington a great headquarters from which this campaign can be conducted, and it is acting in the faith that the removal of these discriminations from our laws will benefit every group of women in the country, and through them all society.

Questions to Consider

1. What arguments does Hill make for the Equal Rights Bill and for what became the Equal Rights Amendment?

2. What strategy is the National Woman's party pursuing to achieve their goal?

3. What obstacles does she believe her campaign faces?

4. Why would there be some resistance, even among women, to what Hill was proposing?

Explore additional primary sources related to this chapter on the *American Passages* Web site: http://history.wadsworth.com/ayersbrief02.

Women in Politics

National Woman's party
Created by Alice Paul, this organization pushed for the Equal Rights Amendment during the 1920s.

Contributing to the problems that women encountered were divisions among advocates of woman suffrage. After 1923, the more militant wing, identified with Alice Paul and the **National Woman's party,** advocated the Equal Rights Amendment (ERA). The amendment stated that "men and women shall have equal rights throughout the United States and every place subject to its jurisdiction." Other female reformers, such as Florence Kelley and Carrie Chapman Catt, regarded the ERA as a threat to the hard-won legislation that protected women in the workplace. These women favored an approach such as the Sheppard-Towner Act of 1921, which supplied federal matching funds to states that created programs in which mothers would be instructed on caring for their babies and safeguarding their own health.

Some women entered politics. Two states, Wyoming and Texas, elected female governors. Nellie Tayloe Ross of Wyoming was chosen to fill out the unexpired term of her husband after he died in office. Miriam Amanda Ferguson of Texas won election in 1924 because her husband, a former governor, had been impeached and barred from holding office in the state. Eleven women were elected to the House of Representatives, many of them as political heirs of their husbands. Many more won seats in state legislatures or held local offices.

Social causes enlisted women who had started their careers in public life years earlier. Margaret Sanger founded the American Birth Control League, which became Planned Parenthood in 1942. Sanger capitalized on a popular interest in "eugenics," a quasi-scientific movement to limit births among "unfit" elements of the population. She found increased support for birth control among doctors as the 1920s progressed. The greatest effect of the campaign was seen in middle-class women. The poor and minorities turned to older, less reliable methods of avoiding pregnancy.

The Flapper and the New Woman

Social feminism confronted a sense that young women were more interested in fun and diversion than in political movements. The "flapper," with her bobbed hair and short skirts, captivated the popular press. Older female reformers noted sadly that their younger counterparts were likely "to be bored" when the subject of feminism came up.

In their relations with men, young women of the 1920s practiced a new sexual freedom. Among women born after 1900, the rate of premarital intercourse, though still low by modern standards, was twice as high as it had been among women born a decade earlier. Although most young men and women did not sleep together, men and women engaged in more sexual play.

Women on the Job

Women joined the workforce in growing numbers. At the beginning of the decade, 8.3 million women were employed outside the home. Ten years later, the number stood at 10.6 million. A few occupations accounted for 85 percent of female jobs. One-third of these women worked in clerical positions, one-fifth labored as domestic servants, and another third were employed in factory jobs. The median wage for women usually stood at about 55 percent of what men earned for comparable jobs. At the same time women entered new professions and became celebrities. Amelia Earhart, for example, emerged as the most famous woman flier of the era.

For the majority of women, however, the barriers to advancement and opportunity remained high. Poor white women in the South often worked at dead-end jobs in textile mills or agricultural processing plants. Black women found it difficult to secure nondomestic jobs either in the North or the South. In the Southwest, Hispanic women picked crops, shelled pecans, or worked as domestic servants. Labor unions rarely addressed the situation of female workers. When strikes did occur, as in New Jersey and Massachusetts during the middle of the decade, employers sometimes granted concessions—and then moved their factories to the South where labor was cheaper and unions were weaker.

The Plight of the Career Woman

Career women faced formidable obstacles. When a woman schoolteacher married, many school districts compelled her to resign. College faculties, the medical profession, and the law made it difficult for women to advance in these careers. In government, men received favorable treatment. Although many women worked outside the home out of economic necessity, they were expected to juggle their careers and domestic responsibilities.

Coolidge in the White House

The inauguration of President Coolidge on March 4, 1925, was the first to be broadcast over the radio. The administration's policy goals were modest. In 1926 Coolidge asked Congress for a cut in taxes. The lawmakers responded with a measure that lowered the surtax on those people who made more than $100,000 annually, reduced the estate tax to 20 percent, and eliminated the gift tax. The changes in the law affected only the most affluent in society. The president also supported laws to oversee expansion of the new airline industry and to regulate the growing radio business. On the other hand, when Congress twice passed the McNary-Haugen Plan to assist agriculture, Coolidge vetoed it on the grounds that trying to raise crop prices through government intervention was both expensive and wrong.

Coolidge's Foreign Policy

Although the United States remained out of the League of Nations, it was not an isolationist country during the 1920s. The government encouraged the expansion of American business around the world, and Washington used corporate executives as ambassadors and in framing monetary policy. Americans applauded U.S. policy in Latin America, Asia, and Europe because it did not involve the use of force or the commitment of soldiers.

In Latin America, troubled relations with Mexico persisted. The administration sent an emissary, Dwight Morrow, who mediated an agreement to protect American oil companies from further expropriation. Marines were withdrawn from Nicaragua in 1925 but were sent back a year later when civil war erupted again. American efforts to instruct the Nicaraguans in what Washington said were democratic procedures did not produce the desired results.

Diplomacy and Finance in the 1920s

After the decision not to join the League of Nations, the U.S. interest in Europe became chiefly financial. American bankers and investors played a large part in providing the reparation payments required of Germany in the Treaty of Versailles (see Chapter 22). Because of the size of the sums they had to pay, the Germans were unable to meet their obligations without American help. In 1924 the Coolidge administration endorsed a plan that Charles G. Dawes, a Chicago banker, had developed. The proposal scaled back German reparations and loaned that country money to meet its debts. During the next four years Germany borrowed almost $1.5 million from the United States.

The Coolidge administration continued the policy of nonrecognition of the Soviet Union, but it did not object when business interests made substantial investments there. Americans also sent large amounts of aid and food when the Soviets faced famine during the early 1920s. In China the U.S. government watched apprehensively as revolution and civil war wracked that nation. Washington extended de facto recognition to the government of the Nationalist leader, Chiang Kai-shek.

Sentiment for peace remained strong. When the French foreign minister, Aristide Briand, proposed a mutual security agreement between his country and the United States, the State Department proposed instead a multilateral agreement to have signatory nations renounce war. Peace groups supported the idea, and the Kellogg-Briand Pact was signed and ratified in 1929.

Charles A. Lindbergh
His solo flight across the Atlantic Ocean in 1927 made him an international hero.

Charles Lindbergh's solo flight across the Atlantic Ocean in 1927 made him an international hero. The youthful Lindbergh stands stiffly in front of his plane, *The Spirit of St. Louis.*

©The Granger Collection, New York

1927: The Year of the Decade

The crosscurrents of the 1920s merged during 1927. The most striking individual achievement came in May, when **Charles A. Lindbergh** flew alone across the Atlantic Ocean from New York to Paris. Lindbergh did not make the first nonstop flight across the ocean. Two English aviators accomplished that feat eight years earlier, flying from Ireland to Newfoundland in 1919. By 1926, however, a $25,000 prize was offered for the first nonstop flight between New York and Paris, a distance of 3,600 miles.

Charles Lindbergh had been an army flier and was working as an airmail pilot for the government when he heard about the contest. He raised money from civic leaders in St. Louis and other cities. He called his monoplane *The Spirit of St. Louis.* On May 10, Lindbergh took off from Roosevelt Field in New York. When he landed in Paris thirty-six hours later, he was a worldwide celebrity. He received a ticker tape parade in New York City, medals from foreign nations, and a lifetime in the public eye. To the generation of the 1920s, Lindbergh's feat symbolized the ability of a single person to bend technology to his will.

It was a period of enthusiasm for science and technology. The achievements of Henry Ford and Frederick Winslow Taylor in industry captured worldwide attention. Sigmund Freud's psychological theories attracted popular notice. Universities and corporations supported scientific research. In this climate, a hero like Lindbergh found a ready audience.

A Heyday for Sports and a Big Change for Films

On athletic fields, stunning accomplishments marked 1927. The New York Yankees became known as "Murderers Row" because of their many hitters. Babe Ruth hit sixty home runs, a record that stood for thirty-four years. In boxing, Gene Tunney and Jack Dempsey had a rematch of their heavyweight championship fight. Dempsey knocked Tunney down in the seventh round but failed to go to a neutral corner quickly. The result was a "long count" that enabled Tunney to come off the canvas and win.

In the heyday of big-time sports, no one was more popular or well known than George Herman "Babe" Ruth of the New York Yankees. His prodigious home runs and gargantuan appetites made him a larger-than-life hero. This picture shows his powerful swing.

Chicago Historical Society

Motion pictures enjoyed strong popularity, but there was growing evidence that silent films were boring audiences. Fearful that they might lose their hold on the public, the major studios agreed that none of them would make talking pictures unless they all did. One of the smaller studios, Warner Brothers, was working on a sound picture called **The Jazz Singer.** Its star was Al Jolson, who specialized in blackface renditions of popular tunes. When he ad-libbed his catch phrase, "You Ain't Heard Nothing Yet," and sang several songs, the audience response was enthusiastic. Within two years silent pictures gave way to sound.

The Jazz Singer
One of the first motion pictures with sound, it starred Al Jolson who specialized in blackface renditions of popular tunes.

Ford Introduces the Model A

By the end of the 1920s, the simple Model T was no longer the car of choice for Americans. General Motors was offering Chevrolets that were only a little more expensive than Model Ts but had features and options that Ford did not. In addition, the annual models that Alfred P. Sloan had introduced promised consumers novelty and excitement as well as a better product. By 1926 the Model T had become an economic liability, and Ford's sales had slumped.

During the spring of 1927 Ford turned to the development of a new car. Soon the Model A was ready for consumers to sample, and interest in the product was high. Although it would be months before Ford could fill consumer demand for the automobile, on December 1, 1927, the company unveiled the Model A in cities around the country. Like its competitor General Motors, Ford marketed the Model A through a huge advertising campaign. By the end of the 1920s the major companies in the automotive business had adopted advertising and marketing techniques that became a fixture in American life.

The Execution of Sacco and Vanzetti

While the consumer culture of the 1920s flourished, the fate of Sacco and Vanzetti continued to attract international attention. By the spring of 1927 the appeals process had almost run its course. Despite strong evidence that the two men had not received a fair trial, the legal machinery moved them toward the electric chair. The date of their execution was set for July 1927. Important legal scholars such as Felix Frankfurter of the Harvard Law School argued for their innocence. The governor of Massachusetts appointed a special commission to review the case. After flawed and biased proceedings, the panel decided to affirm the convictions. Finally, the two men were electrocuted on August 23, 1927. The case convinced many radicals that more drastic measures would be necessary to reform American society.

"I Do Not Choose to Run"

Calvin Coolidge could easily have run for another term in 1928. His popularity was still high, and the nation's prosperity seemed to assure a Republican victory. However, the presidency had lost its appeal for Coolidge, and both the president and his wife were in uncertain health. Coolidge may also have sensed the weaknesses in the economy that would become evident two years later. While vacationing in the Black Hills of South Dakota during the summer of 1927, the president handed to reporters a simple statement: "I do not choose to run for President in 1928." This surprise announcement opened up the race for the Republican presidential nomination to other potential contenders such as the secretary of commerce, Herbert Hoover.

As 1927 ended, there were some signs that the economy was not as robust as it had been. Production slowed, and consumer spending also dropped. Despite these warning signs, the banking system continued to expand credit, and stock market speculation persisted.

Summary

Echoes of the Jazz Age

During the 1920s the United States became a modern, mass society in which a consumer culture and the emphasis on entertainment became a hallmark of national life. After World War I, the emergence of the motion picture, radio, and advertising industries in something like their modern form accelerated the shift from a rural lifestyle to an urban, cosmopolitan setting. Of course, these changes produced resistance from the regions of America that felt left behind. Religious fundamentalism, the Prohibition movement, and the Ku Klux Klan all provided various ways for the suspicion of modernism to manifest itself.

In politics, Progressivism ebbed and conservatism became ascendant. Three Republican presidents pushed the agenda that favored business and limited the power of labor unions and farmers. With the prosperity that accompanied the first seven years of the 1920s, the Democrats receded into minority status amid their own factional warfare. Most workers and their families had few of the protections such as unemployment insurance or old age pensions that are common in contemporary society. The rising tide of economic abundance was supposed to take care of such questions without government intervention.

The decade produced a cultural flowering in the arts that would reverberate through the rest of the century. In music, literature, and the arts, the 1920s were a time of creativity that has not been surpassed. Such names as F. Scott Fitzgerald, Duke Ellington. Frank Lloyd Wright, and Willa Cather captured the public's imagination. Big-time sports also dominated the columns of newspapers and the emerging airwaves of radio. The intense interest in celebrities reflected the way in which show business was setting priorities for the nation.

Beneath the prosperous surface, of course, inequities persisted. The farm sector remained depressed

The campaign to enforce Prohibition produced some results. Here police pour beer down a sewer.

Reproduced from the collections of the Library of Congress

The Scopes trial over the teaching of evolution resulted in a notorious legal confrontation between Clarence Darrow (*left*) and William Jennings Bryan. Many observers saw their duel as a symbol of the urban–rural tensions roiling the nation during the 1920s.

©The Granger Collection, New York

Reproduced from the collections of the Library of Congress

Automobile manufacturers competed for car buyers with advertising that stressed the mobility and freedom that these vehicles provided to Americans in the 1920s.

and never shared in the prosperity of the cities. Important parts of the economy were unregulated and subject to manipulation from speculators. Above all, the uneven distribution of income meant that the new consuming culture would be hard to sustain. By 1927 there were signs that the boom of the 1920s was showing signs of age. These developments did not reach a crisis point until after Herbert Hoover had defeated Al Smith in the presidential election of 1928.

In retrospect, these years would come to be seen as a time of isolation from the cares and problems of the postwar world. The United States was involved overseas with its destiny linked to the economies of Europe and Asia. The American people, however, did not yet believe that they would have to be militarily committed to the destinies of people beyond the two oceans that protected their continent. In the 1930s that confidence would decrease as dangerous new powers arose to challenge democracy in Western Europe and in the Pacific. Soon the 1920s would come to be regarded as a time of lost innocence.

Making Connections Across Chapters

LOOKING BACK

The 1920s owed much to the way that the economy made the transition from war to peace between 1918 and 1921. The political effects of the same period set the stage for Republican dominance during the decade. Unhappiness with the League of Nations also affected American foreign policy.

1. What problems did Warren G. Harding confront when he took office in March 1921?
2. How did the failure of the League of Nations affect foreign policy under Harding and Coolidge?
3. What were the roots of the cultural tensions of the 1920s that anti-immigration, the Ku Klux Klan, and the revolt against the city reflected?

LOOKING AHEAD

The key elements of the 1920s were economic prosperity, cultural change toward a more urban and cosmopolitan society, and the underlying problems that caused the Great Depression at the end of the decade. As you read, be alert for the ways in which these forces interacted to make the 1920s so important in shaping the rest of the century.

1. Although the 1920s were prosperous, not all sections of American life shared in the bounty. Why was the depressed state of agriculture so important?
2. How solidly based was the consumer culture of the decade in economic terms?
3. How was income distributed and what government policies affected this issue under Harding and Coolidge?
4. What accounted for the flowering of the arts and culture during this period? What traces of the 1920s can still be found in mass entertainment now?

RECOMMENDED READINGS

Brophy, Alfred I., and Kennedy, Randall. *Reconstructing the Dreamland: The Tulsa Race Riot of 1921* (2002). Looks at a case study of racial violence in the decade.

Coben, Stanley. *Rebellion against Victorianism: The Impetus for Cultural Change in 1920s America* (1991). Discusses how Americans in the 1920s reacted against the ideas and values of an earlier time.

Douglas, Ann. *Terrible Honesty: Mongrel Manhattan in the 1920s* (1995). A cultural history of the decade from the perspective of events in New York City.

Dumenil, Lynn. *The Modern Temper: American Culture and Society in the 1920s* (1995). An excellent analysis of the major trends of the period.

Ferrell, Robert H. *The Strange Deaths of President Harding* (1996). Explodes many of the sensational myths about Harding's career.

Ferrell, Robert H. *The Presidency of Calvin Coolidge* (1998). Provides a good survey of what Coolidge did as president.

Goldberg, David J. *Discontented America: The United States in the 1920s* (1999). Supplies a thoughtful narrative about the main currents of this period.

Larson, Edward J. *Summer for the Gods: The Scopes Trial and America's Continuing Debate over Science and Religion* (1997). A prize-winning look at the celebrated trial about evolution.

Leinwand, Gerald. *1927, High Tide of the Twenties* (2001). Considers the year that defined the spirit of the decade.

Parrish, Michael E. *Anxious Decades: America in Prosperity and Depression* (1992). A fascinating treatment of the interwar years.

 AMERICAN JOURNEY ONLINE AND 📞 INFOTRAC COLLEGE EDITION

Visit the source collections at http://ajaccess.wadsworth .com and infotrac.thomsonlearning.com and use the Search function with the following key terms to explore documents, images, audio and video clips, articles, and commentary related to the material in this chapter.

Warren G. Harding

Sinclair Lewis

Calvin Coolidge

Marcus Garvey

Charles Lindbergh

Zora Neale Hurston

Babe Ruth

flapper

Alain Locke

New Negro Renaissance

National Woman's party

woman suffrage

Sacco and Vanzetti

ONLINE PRIMARY SOURCES

Here are some examples of the many primary sources related to this chapter that you will find on the *American Passages* Web site: http://history.wadsworth.com/ayersbrief02.

Margaret Sanger, *Woman and the New Race,* 1921

Last Statement of Bartolomeo Vanzetti, 1929

"The Negro Speaks of Rivers" and "I Too" by Langston Hughes, 1920s

The site also offers self-quizzes, exercises, and many additional resources to help you study.

The Great Depression

1927–1933

I N ACCEPTING THE REPUBLICAN PRESIDENTIAL NOMINATION IN 1928, HERBERT Hoover proclaimed: "We in America today are nearer to the final triumph over poverty than ever before in the history of any land." Farmers would not have shared Hoover's optimism, nor would African Americans and the poor. Among those who had benefited from the boom of the 1920s, however, the prosperity and abundance enjoyed by the fortunate seemed destined to extend into the immediate future.

Then came the shocks, first the crash of the stock market in October 1929, then a severe economic depression that worsened during the early 1930s. The good times of the 1920s soon faded from memory. The administration of President Hoover took unprecedented actions to relieve the crisis, but nothing seemed to work. Resentment against the president, the economic system, and the wealthy grew. Pressures for political change led to the election of **Franklin D. Roosevelt** in 1932.

By 1933 the Great Depression, as it came to be called, affected almost everyone in American society. It worsened the already difficult situation of the nation's farmers. For African Americans, Hispanics, and the poor, it meant even more misery and suffering than they usually faced. A generation of Americans looked to the federal government for answers to the social and economic problems they confronted.

Franklin D. Roosevelt
The thirty-second president of the United States, he assumed the presidency at the depth of the Great Depression and helped the American people regain faith in themselves. He brought hope with his inaugural address in which he promised prompt, vigorous action and asserted that "the only thing we have to fear is fear itself."

The Election of 1928

President Calvin Coolidge's declaration that he would not run for reelection in 1928 set off a contest for the Republican presidential nomination (see Chapter 23). The front-runner was the secretary of commerce, Herbert Clark Hoover. Hoover seemed to represent a constructive blend of technology and reform devoted to public service.

The Engineer as Candidate: Herbert Hoover

Hoover had been reared as an orphan in a modest Quaker home in Iowa. He built a career as a mining engineer after graduation from Stanford University. He first gained world attention during World War I when he managed the campaign to bring food relief to the starving people of Belgium. After returning to the United States, he ran the Food Administration. Following the war, he sent relief and food to war-torn Russia. He served as commerce secretary under Warren G. Harding and Calvin Coolidge. During these years Hoover used the new technology of radio and motion pictures to spread his name and face to all corners of the United States.

Hoover had worked for the Wilson administration and had internationalist sympathies, so he was not popular among Republicans who wanted to limit foreign involvement. Nevertheless, Hoover was the most popular Republican hopeful in the race. As a result, he came

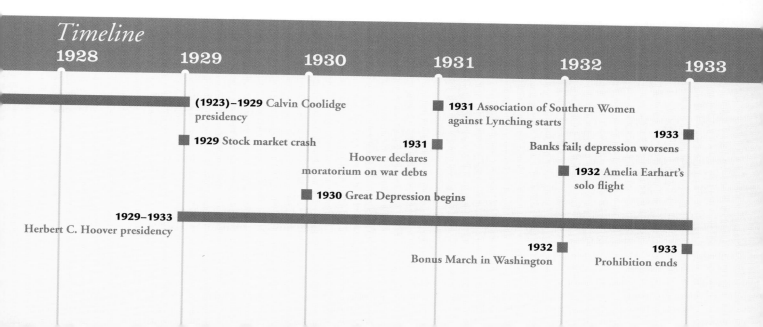

Timeline

| 1928 | 1929 | 1930 | 1931 | 1932 | 1933 |

(1923)–1929 Calvin Coolidge presidency

1931 Association of Southern Women against Lynching starts

1929 Stock market crash

1931 Hoover declares moratorium on war debts

1933 Banks fail; depression worsens

1932 Amelia Earhart's solo flight

1930 Great Depression begins

1929–1933 Herbert C. Hoover presidency

1932 Bonus March in Washington

1933 Prohibition ends

to the party's convention in Kansas City with more than enough support for the nomination. He received 837 votes on the first ballot and his selection was made unanimous.

Observing the tradition in which the party's nominee "accepted" the party's honor in a formal speech, Hoover waited two months to deliver his acceptance address. After forecasting the end of poverty, he announced that "the poorhouse is vanishing from among us." He promised "a job for every man" and "equality of opportunity for all irrespective of faith and color." Hoover read this address, as he did others, in a monotone, with little effort to arouse the enthusiasm of the audience. In 1928, however, sober and calm rhetoric impressed many voters as precisely what the times demanded.

From the Sidewalks of New York: Al Smith

The Democrats were divided along ideological lines. Liberals wanted a more activist government, whereas conservatives sought a return to the pro-business policies that predated the era of William Jennings Bryan and Woodrow Wilson. No one in the party, however, wished to repeat the mistakes of the 1924 convention, which had symbolized the bitter divisions among the Democrats over cultural and economic questions. This meant that the nomination of Alfred E. Smith, the governor of New York and the clear front-runner, was almost a certainty. Yet to nominate Smith was likely to release the passions and prejudices that had dogged the Democrats for twenty years. Whatever the party did in 1928, one of its factions was sure to be dissatisfied with the result.

Al Smith
A vigorous reformer as governor of New York, he became the first Roman Catholic to win the nomination of a major party for president of the United States.

Al Smith had grown up in New York City. He had a natural talent for politics and soon became identified with Tammany Hall, the Democratic party organization in Manhattan. Long notorious for its corrupt ways, the organization recognized in Smith a politician who could move beyond the older style of machine politics and deal with the voters who wanted relief from the injustices of an industrial society. Smith made his mark in the New York legislature and then was elected governor in 1918. Defeated in 1920, he was returned to office in 1922 and was reelected twice more. As governor, Smith championed moderate social welfare policies, administrative efficiency, and public works. Despite his reformist policies on the state level, however, Smith remained suspicious of arguments that the federal government should be deeply involved in regulating the economy and business.

Smith's Political Weaknesses

For all his political skills, Smith had some liabilities that alienated intolerant voters in 1928. A devout Roman Catholic, he confronted the currents of prejudice that limited presidential candidates to Protestant men. In his daily life, the governor pledged religious obedience to the Catholic clergy. As a public official, he defended separation of church and state.

The governor disliked Prohibition. He favored the right of an individual state to allow liquor to be sold within its borders. At the Democratic convention, he came out for "fundamental changes in the present provisions of national prohibition," a move that outraged southerners in his party. Despite reservations among his southern and western opponents, Smith's strength won him the nomination at the Democratic National Convention in Houston.

Hoover versus Smith: The 1928 Campaign

The campaign proved to be one of the most bitterly fought in history. Smith's religion and position on alcohol made him the focus of intense attacks on his character and record.

Most of the electoral advantages rested with Herbert Hoover. Many parts of the nation were prosperous, and

Courtesy of Herbert Hoover Presidential Library

Herbert Hoover talks with reporters covering his presidential campaign in 1928.

those who suffered from economic difficulties thought that they still had a chance to improve their lives. The Republicans made much of the issue of "business prosperity and sound economic principles and governmental practices" in their campaign literature. They took as their campaign slogan "a chicken in every pot and two cars in every garage." Hoover's strategists used large amounts of newsreel footage to bring their candidate to a national audience. Well financed and cohesive, the Republicans easily out-maneuvered the Democrats.

The Smith Response to Hoover

Smith did not campaign as a liberal alternative to Hoover. The men who directed his campaign were closely aligned with large corporations and opponents of Prohibition. The candidate, meanwhile, said little about economic distress, played down differences over the tariff and tax policy, and stressed his allegiance to a government that interfered "as little as possible with business."

Some devout Protestants saw in Smith's candidacy the specter of Catholic domination of the government. Even though Smith had announced his belief "in the absolute separation of Church and State," the forces of religious intolerance rallied against him. The manager of the *Fellowship Forum,* a Protestant publication that attacked Smith, said that "the real issue in this campaign was PROTESTANT AMERICANISM VERSUS RUM AND ROMANISM." When Smith campaigned in the South, he faced burning crosses and angry voters. Unlike John Kennedy a generation later, Al Smith made few efforts to allay the fears of more responsible voters about his own religious convictions.

A Landslide for Hoover

The election results were a landslide for Hoover. He received 21.4 million ballots to 15 million for Smith. In the electoral college, Hoover won the 444 electoral votes of forty states. Hoover carried five southern states, including Texas, and thus broke the "Solid South" that had provided the Democrats with an electoral foundation for so long.

Beneath the electoral wreckage, however, lay some modestly encouraging signs for the Democratic party. Smith carried the nation's largest cities and ran strongly in areas with large immigrant and Catholic populations. At the same time, however, the Democratic candidate did less well in his party's traditional areas of strength, the South and West. It remained to be seen whether the Democrats could become a majority party without some outside event transforming the political situation.

Hoover Takes Office

Herbert Hoover came to the presidency with a great fund of experience in business and government service. He worked long hours in the White House. He was the first president to have a telephone installed in the Oval Office and the last to dress formally for dinner with his wife each evening.

A problem left over from previous administrations was Prohibition. By 1929 enforcement of the policy took different forms across the nation. In regions where "dry" sentiment remained strong, penalties for violators could be harsh. In states with "wet" majorities, legislatures voted for repeal of the Eighteenth Amendment. Many Americans believed that Prohibition was becoming either a joke or a failure. Hoover had endorsed the amendment as "noble in motive and far-reaching in purpose," and he still hoped that it could succeed.

To address the problems, in May 1929 Hoover named a Commission on Law Enforcement, chaired by former Attorney General George Wickersham. The panel studied the impact of Prohibition for nearly two years. In January 1931 the Wickersham Commission issued its report, which said that enforcement was not working; a majority of the members favored revising the Eighteenth Amendment but did not call for repeal.

For the time being, President Hoover remained a strong backer of Prohibition. Lobbying efforts by organizations such as the Association against the Prohibition Amendment were beginning to take hold, however, and popular support for Prohibition was eroding. In the 1932 election campaign the Democrats came out strongly for repeal of the Eighteenth Amendment.

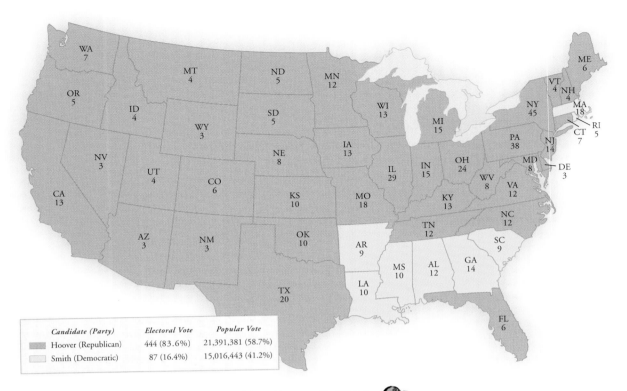

Candidate (Party)	Electoral Vote	Popular Vote
Hoover (Republican)	444 (83.6%)	21,391,381 (58.7%)
Smith (Democratic)	87 (16.4%)	15,016,443 (41.2%)

MAP 24.1 **The Election of 1928**

In the election of 1928, Herbert Hoover achieved an electoral landslide and cracked the "Solid South" for the first time since Republican successes in Reconstruction. Alfred E. Smith did carry Massachusetts and Rhode Island, whose heavily Roman Catholic populations supported him. Those victories anticipated Democratic gains in the 1930s. View an animated version of this map or related maps at http://history.wadsworth.com/ayersbrief02.

Despite his early successes in the White House, Hoover had certain political weaknesses. Reporters resented his insistence on saying little at news conferences and becoming upset with unfavorable press coverage. Hoover also stayed aloof from Congress and made little effort to persuade lawmakers to support his favorite programs. Above all, Hoover lacked the capacity to inspire public confidence in a crisis. His success depended on the national faith that he could carry on the prosperity of the Harding-Coolidge era. When that spirit evaporated, so did Hoover's presidency.

The Stock Market Crash of 1929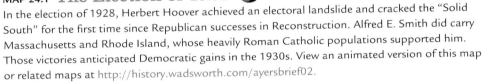

During the first six months of his administration Hoover pushed for reforms in the treatment of Native Americans and addressed a number of conservation issues. He also reduced American military commitments in Latin America and explored ways of achieving savings in military expenditures. The Great Engineer, as Hoover was known, seemed to be in charge of the nation's destiny.

To the average American, the economic signs during the summer of 1929 also seemed to be as encouraging as ever. The prices of stocks traded on the New York Stock Exchange were reaching ever-higher levels. At the beginning of 1928, for example, the industrial index of the *New York Times* was recorded at 245. It soared to 452 by September 1929. Individual stocks registered even more impressive increases. Radio Corporation of America stock shot up from $85 a share to $420 a share during 1928. President Coolidge said during 1928 that common stocks were "cheap at current prices."

The Crash Occurs

These rosy statistics and forecasts made the **stock market crash of October 1929** even more of a shock. The problem began in September as stock prices neared their record levels. Stock prices declined early in the month, regained some strength, and then drifted downward. Yet no abrupt collapse had occurred, and to many on Wall Street these events seemed to be another one of the temporary "corrections" that usually preceded upward surges. A few people warned of impending problems, but they were dismissed as chronic naysayers. A few shrewd investors, such as Joseph P. Kennedy (father of the future president), liquidated their stocks in anticipation of a decline. Even President Hoover told his financial broker to sell off some of his holdings. But most owners of stock simply waited for the rise in prices to begin again.

Then it happened. On October 24, 1929, which became known as **Black Thursday,** traders began selling stocks and quickly realized that there were few buyers for them. Prices collapsed, and the total number of shares traded that day reached thirteen million, an all-time record. Stockholders were estimated to have absorbed a $9 billion loss. During the afternoon, a banking syndicate led by J. P. Morgan Jr. and Co. urged investors to be calm. As the syndicate bought stocks, the market quieted.

Underlying forces, however, could not be stopped by symbolic gestures. On October 29, the selling of stocks resumed at an even more intense rate. More than sixteen million shares changed hands in a single day. The *New York Times* called it "the most disastrous day in Wall Street's history." Fistfights occurred on the trading floor, and rumors of suicides swept through the Exchange. It was a decisive moment in American financial history, one with important and enduring results.

Causes of the Stock Market Crash

What forces produced the stock market crash of 1929? The 1920s had been characterized by an investment fever that led people into risky ventures. In Florida, for example, there had been a land boom that saw prices for some lots rise to $15,000 or $20,000 a foot for coveted waterfront acreage. When the hysteria ended in 1926, after a devastating hurricane, land prices headed downward again. Willing investors then looked for other speculative opportunities.

By 1927 the stock market seemed to be just the place to make easy money. Corporations increasingly turned to the public through stock offerings to finance their business expansion. Stockbrokers sold their products with aggressive advertising techniques. Finally, during the Harding and Coolidge years, government tax policies enabled the wealthy to retain money to invest in securities. Five hundred families had incomes of more than $1 million in 1929. Many of these surplus funds fueled the rise in the stock market.

Playing the Market: Margin Buying and Investment Trusts

One tempting device for less well-off investors was to buy stocks in "margin" trading. An investor could purchase a stock on credit, putting up only 10 or 15 percent of the actual price, then sell the stock at a higher level, pay off the broker, and still pocket a substantial profit. Just as someone might acquire a house or a car on credit, so brokers urged their customers to invest $100 with the prospect of controlling $1,000 or more worth of stock. People borrowed money to buy on margin. Of course, the investor could be required to provide the full price of the stock at any time. But with the market headed ever upward, that risk seemed a small one.

Abuses of this trend soon followed. Investors with inside knowledge manipulated a stock's price up and down to fleece the unwary public. New companies often consisted of nothing more than schemes to issue stock based on the assumption that the market would rise. Government regulation of stock issues on both the state and federal levels was very

stock market crash of 1929
The collapse of stock prices that ended the speculative boom of the 1920s and is associated with the onset of the Great Depression.

Black Thursday
October 29, 1929, the day the spectacular New York stock market crash began.

©Bettmann /CORBIS

October 24, 1929, was the date when the stock market boom of the 1920s collapsed. Crowds milled around Wall Street trying to determine what was happening and what had gone wrong with the market.

lax, and the stock exchanges themselves had few requirements for revealing the true financial status of these companies. Some of the investment trusts, as they were called, were frauds; those who put money into them lost their entire investment.

The Impact of the Crash

The number of Americans who participated in the stock market in 1929 was between 1.5 and 2 million. Most of the corporate dividends in that year went to about 600,000 stockholders whose annual incomes were above $5,000. The crash of 1929 wiped out many of these investors. Others cut back on their stock holdings and trimmed their personal expenditures. The growing lack of confidence in the future of the economy would prove contagious.

The stock market collapse revealed serious underlying weaknesses in the economy. The well-to-do citizens who played the market were confident that other investors would buy their stocks at the higher price levels of the pre-crash period. However, there were not enough people in the upper brackets for that assumption to be realistic. Once the wealthy investors began to sell their stocks, there were no other potential buyers to keep security prices high.

The consequences of the stock market's decline were striking. The prices of individual stocks underwent a sustained downward slide. Within a few months such a high-flying issue as General Electric had dropped from $403 a share to $168. One index of stock prices had gone to 469.5 in September and was at 220.1 by November. During the next twelve months the gross national product went down from nearly $88 billion to $76 billion. Something had gone badly wrong with the American economy.

The Great Depression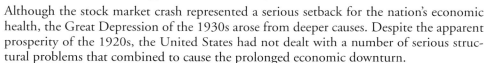

Although the stock market crash represented a serious setback for the nation's economic health, the Great Depression of the 1930s arose from deeper causes. Despite the apparent prosperity of the 1920s, the United States had not dealt with a number of serious structural problems that combined to cause the prolonged economic downturn.

The most pervasive dilemma had to do with the distribution of income. By 1929 the 5 percent of Americans at the top income level were receiving one-third of the total annual personal income. By comparison, those who made up the lowest 40 percent of the population received about one-eighth of the available income. For an economy that depended on the purchase of consumer goods for its expansion, this situation meant that there were simply not enough people with money to buy the products that industry was turning out.

Wealth was also concentrated in the hands of those with the highest incomes. About 2.3 percent of families with incomes above $10,000 a year possessed two-thirds of the available savings. Yet 80 percent of the population did not have any savings at all. A consumer society had emerged, but the bulk of the consumers were unable to participate fully in the economic process.

Instead of using the profits that their businesses gained from selling goods during the mid-1920s to invest in new factories or a better-paid workforce, industry leaders had put their gains into the stock market or speculative ventures. By 1927 the market for new cars and new houses began to weaken, indicating that demand for consumer goods was decreasing.

Other Economic Problems

Another chronic weakness of the economy was in agriculture. The problem of overproduction of farm goods had not been addressed successfully, and as prices fell at the beginning of the Depression, the farmers felt the effects most acutely. At the beginning of 1931, cotton stood at 9 cents to 10 cents per pound; when farmers brought in their crop in the fall, the price had skidded to under 6 cents a pound. Farmers could not pay off their mortgages, and rural banks soon failed. The ripple of banking failures strained a banking system that was already weakened by the effects of the stock market crash.

The International Situation

The world economy was also fragile. The settlement of World War I had imposed heavy reparation payments on the defeated Germans (see Chapter 22). Because the Germans could not pay these sums from their own economy, they borrowed from investors and banks in the United States. In that way Americans financed the Germans' debt payments to the victorious British and French. Those countries, in turn, could use the funds to pay off their war debts to the United States.

The Dawes Plan of 1924 had reduced the burden of German war debts, and in 1929 Owen D. Young proposed a plan that further cut back on the amount that Germany owed while extending the length of time for retiring the debt.

These concessions, in what became known as the Young Plan, alleviated the situation to some degree, but the basic problem persisted. The United States created tariff barriers that discouraged European imports and steered American capital toward internal economic development. When the European economies experienced difficulties themselves after 1929, the weakened structure of debts and loans soon collapsed, further damaging the economy of the United States. In fact, President Hoover would later argue that the entire Depression arose from causes beyond the borders of the United States.

A Worsening Economic Situation

In 1929–1930 there was no government insurance of bank deposits. The absence of that policy made individual banks vulnerable to sudden demands by depositors to withdraw their money. Such "runs" destroyed one institution after another. Many banks had invested in the stock market. Other prominent bankers had embezzled some of the funds under their control to finance their investing. Among banks in general, there was little cooperation when a crisis occurred. To save themselves, the stronger banks called in loans made to smaller banks.

For an individual employee thrown out of work, there was no unemployment insurance. Old age pensions were also rare. Many people believed that the natural forces of the economy must work themselves out without the government intruding into the process. Secretary of the Treasury Andrew Mellon told President Hoover that "a panic was not altogether a bad thing" because "it will purge the rottenness out of the system."

The President, Congress, and the Depression

For some months after the stock market crash, it seemed as though the economy might rebound without much assistance from Washington. President Hoover said in late 1929: "[T]he fundamental business of the country is sound." He conferred with leading business figures about measures to maintain public confidence, especially programs to bolster prices and wages. He asked the Federal Reserve System to facilitate business borrowing. For the moment, events seemed to be going Hoover's way. During the first several months of 1930, stock market prices recovered from their 1929 lows.

In 1930 Congress enacted the Smoot-Hawley Tariff, which raised customs duties to high levels. Republicans believed that tariff protection would enable American agriculture and industry to rebound. The Smoot-Hawley law has been blamed for the severity of the worldwide Depression because it made it more difficult for European business to sell goods in the United States. The negative impact of the Smoot-Hawley Tariff has probably been overstated, relative to the other, more severe causes of the Depression. In any case, by the middle of 1930, the effects of the downturn began to be felt in many areas of government activity.

Foreign Policy in the Depression

The onset of the Great Depression complicated President Hoover's management of foreign policy. He had come to the White House with well-formulated ideas about the national role in foreign affairs. Since future wars were unlikely, he believed, it was time to pursue disarmament. Secretary of State Henry L. Stimson did not share the president's optimism. The two men agreed, however, on the basic goals of diplomacy.

good neighbor policy
A new Latin American policy wherein Hoover withdrew the Marines from Nicaragua and Haiti, and in 1930 the State Department renounced the Roosevelt Corollary of 1904.

In Latin America the president announced the **good neighbor policy.** He withdrew Marines from Nicaragua and Haiti. In 1930, the State Department renounced the Roosevelt Corollary of 1904 (see Chapter 20). Despite outbreaks of revolutions in South America during his term, Hoover left Latin American nations alone.

Drawing upon his Quaker roots, Hoover thought that wars were senseless and sought disarmament as a key goal; however, the results were mixed. Hoover assembled the major naval powers—Great Britain, Japan, and the United States—in London for a conference on disarmament. They deliberated for three months before reaching an apparent understanding. The London Treaty of 1930 made only a modest contribution to peace, however. To reduce military spending, the provisions of the Washington Conference (see Chapter 23) were extended for five years. The United States won parity with Britain in all naval vessels, and the Japanese gained the same result for submarines. The London Treaty also contained language that allowed the signers to resume building ships if they were threatened with aggression. Meanwhile, popular opinion assumed that another world war was unthinkable.

The Effects of the Economic Crisis

As the United States economy deteriorated, however, the effects spread to Europe. Fewer American investors could lend money to European governments. The Smoot-Hawley Tariff made it more difficult for importers to sell their products in the United States. In 1931 Germany and Austria endeavored to set up a customs union to deal with their common problems, but the French objected to the plan and cut off payments to banks in the two countries. In the resulting turmoil, the Creditanstaldt, Austria's central bank, collapsed. The entire structure of international banking stood on the brink of disaster.

Hoover decided that the only answer was a moratorium on the payment of war debts. He declared on June 21, 1931, that the United States would observe an eighteen-month moratorium on the collection of its foreign debts. The French held back for two weeks, putting further strain on German banks. In the end, all the countries involved agreed to Hoover's initiative.

The moratorium came too late to stop the erosion of the international financial system. A few months later, Great Britain devalued the pound when it could no longer maintain the gold standard. This step reduced the price of British products and made them more competitive in world markets. Other nations soon followed this course. A series of obstacles to world trade arose, worsening the international Depression.

Domestic Issues for Hoover

At home President Hoover experienced problems in his dealings with Congress. Hoover named Charles Evans Hughes as chief justice of the U.S. Supreme Court early in 1930, but he had another Court vacancy to fill soon thereafter. He selected John J. Parker of North Carolina for the post. Organized labor opposed Parker's nomination because of Parker's issuance of anti-union injunctions in labor disputes. The National Association for the Advancement of Colored People assailed his racial views. The Senate rejected Parker's selection by a vote of 41 to 39 on May 7, 1930.

During the 1930s and afterward, many Americans would blame the Great Depression on President Hoover and his policies. That judgment was unfair. More than any previous chief executive, Hoover endeavored to use the power of his office to address the economic crisis. He favored reduction of taxes, easing of bank credits, and a modest program of public works to provide jobs. Some members of Congress opposed these ideas as too activist; others said that Hoover proposed too little. Meanwhile, the White House issued a series of confident statements to bolster public faith that the economic downturn would be brief.

The Deepening Depression

But as 1930 continued, it was clear that the Depression was not going away. Bank failures soared from 659 in 1929 to 1,350 a year later. Businesses were closing, investment was declining, and corporate profits were falling off. The number of Americans out of work kept rising. By October 1930 four million people were without jobs (almost 9 percent of the labor force). Within a year nearly 16 percent of the labor force was out of work.

Hoover exhorted businesses to keep prices up and employees at work. Conferences with industry leaders at the White House were designed to show the American people that the Depression was being addressed. The president lacked the power to make corporations retain workers or to prevent price-cutting. Despite any public pledges they might offer to Hoover, corporate executives trimmed payrolls and reduced costs when it seemed necessary. These actions further undercut Hoover's credibility.

Hoover's Programs to Fight the Depression

The president sought to apply his principles of voluntary action to keep the banking system afloat. In October 1931 he persuaded bankers to set up the National Credit Corporation, a private agency that would underwrite banks that had failed and safeguard their depositors. Unfortunately, the banks proved reluctant to acquire the assets of their failed competitors. The experiment was a disaster.

Despite his broadened use of the powers of his office, Herbert Hoover did not view government action as an appropriate way of responding to the Depression. Instead, he believed that the traditional self-reliance and volunteer spirit of the American people provided the most dependable means of ending the economic slump. He asked Americans who had jobs to invest more in their neighbors, to spend something extra to ensure that everyone could work. He set up presidential committees to coordinate volunteer relief efforts for the unemployed. One of those committees was the President's Organization of Unemployment Relief (or POUR).

The Persistence of Unemployment

These programs were inadequate to the size of the unemployment situation (see Table 24.1). By 1931 eight million people were on the jobless rolls. They overwhelmed the resources of existing charitable agencies that normally provided help to the blind, the deaf, and the physically impaired. Nor were the cities and states capable of providing relief at a time when the Depression reduced their tax revenues and increased the demand for services.

In this situation, the president's informal committees for dealing with unemployment proved ineffective. The POUR program coordinated relief agencies and urged people to help their neighbors. These efforts did little to deal with the mass unemployment that gripped the country. But when politicians clamored for action by the national government, Hoover remained resolutely opposed.

Table 24.1
Unemployment, 1927–1933

Year	Unemployment	% of Labor Force
1927	1,890,000	4.1
1928	2,080,000	4.4
1929	1,550,000	3.2
1930	4,340,000	8.7
1931	8,020,000	15.9
1932	12,060,000	23.6
1933	12,830,000	24.9

Source: *Historical Statistics of the United States* (1965/1985), p. 73.

A symbolic event underscored the president's political ineptitude in dealing with the Depression and its effects. When a drought struck the Midwest in 1930 and 1931, Congress proposed to appropriate $60 million to help the victims of the disaster buy fuel and food. Hoover accepted the idea of allocating money to feed animals, but he rejected the idea of feeding farmers and their families. One member of Congress said that the administration would give food to "jackasses . . . but not starving babies." The president accepted a compromise that spent the money without saying that some of it would be used for food. The image of a heartless chief executive remained in the public mind.

Everyday Life during the Depression

For most Americans, there was no single decisive moment when they knew that the economy was in trouble. Instead the problems came on slowly and at different rates. A husband might find his pay reduced or his hours of work cut back. Soon families were postponing purchases and sending children out to find jobs. When a person lost a job, savings helped tide the family over until another job could be found. As time passed and no jobs appeared, savings ran out and the family slipped into the ranks of the unemployed or the poor. In a trend that became a lasting image of the Depression, men selling apples appeared on the street corners in major cities.

For those who were at the bottom of the economy even during boom times, the Depression presented still greater challenges. In the South, whites seeking work took over the low-paying service jobs that African Americans had traditionally filled. Some black workers in the South encountered violence when whites compelled them to leave their jobs. Elsewhere, white laborers went on strike, insisting that African American workers be dismissed.

Women were told that they too should relinquish their jobs to men in order to end the unemployment crisis. Some corporations fired all their married women employees. Because women did the domestic and clerical tasks that men did not care to do even in hard times, the number of women employed did not decline as fast as the number of men.

For Native Americans, the hard times perpetuated a legacy of neglect that had endured for decades. The Bureau of Indian Affairs (BIA) did not address the many social problems that the people under its jurisdiction confronted. Poverty pervaded Indian society. Criticism of the BIA mounted, but despite a commitment to reform, the Hoover administration accomplished little to improve Native American life.

Crisis on the Farms

On the nation's farms, abundant crops could not find a market, so they rotted in the fields. Mortgages were foreclosed, and many former landowners fell into the status of tenant farmers. In 1929 President Hoover had persuaded Congress to pass an Agricultural Marketing Act that created a Federal Farm Board whose purpose was to stabilize farm prices. When farm surpluses around the world swamped grain markets in 1930, it proved impossible to prevent commodity prices from falling. Talk of strikes and protests was common among farmers. During the summer of 1932 Milo Reno, an Iowa farmer, created the Farmers' Holiday Association, which urged growers to hold their crops off the market until prices rose.

In the Southwest, the Hoover administration endeavored to reduce the people looking for jobs with a program to send Hispanic workers and their families back to Mexico and other Latin American countries. Some eighty-two thousand Mexicans were deported, and another half million immigrants crossed the border out of fear that they would be sent back under duress. For Hispanic Americans who stayed in the United States, relief from the government was often hard to find because of a belief that it should be limited to "Americans."

The shanty towns where the homeless and unemployed lived became known as "Hoovervilles." Their presence on the outskirts of the large cities became a common site as the Depression deepened.

©Bettmann /CORBIS

The Plight of the Homeless

As the Depression deepened, the homeless and unemployed took to the roads and rails, looking for work or better times. Migratory workers moved through the agricultural sections of California, picking figs and grapes for whatever they could earn. Others went from city to city, shuffling through a breadline in some cities, stealing or begging for food in others. The homeless lived in shantytowns outside of cities that were dubbed **Hoovervilles.** Soon derogatory references to the president spread throughout the nation. A pocket turned outward as a sign of distress was "a Hoover flag."

By 1931 a sense of despair and hopelessness pervaded many segments of society. People who had been out of work for a year or two had lost the energy and inner resources to rebound even if a job was available. Others began to question the nation's values and beliefs. The Communist party forecast that the system was toppling. A popular song caught the nation's angry, restless mood:

Hoovervilles
Makeshift "villages" usually at the edge of a city with "homes" made of cardboard, scrap metal, or whatever was cheap and available and named for President Hoover who was despised by the poor for his apparent refusal to help them.

> Once I built a railroad, made it run,
> Made it race against time.
> Once I built a railroad, now it's done
> Brother, can you spare a dime?

The Depression did not touch every American in the same way. Despite the economic disruptions, daily life in much of the nation went on as it always had. Families stayed together with the father holding a job, the mother running the home, and their children growing up and attending school. There might be less money to spend, but there was not extensive poverty. Nevertheless, the economic uncertainty that gripped so many people contributed to a general sense of unease and doubt.

Mass Culture during the Depression

Amid the hardships of the Depression, Americans found diversions and amusements in the mass media and popular entertainments that had emerged during the 1920s. Radio's popularity grew; the habit of listening for a favorite program became an integral part of the daily lives of many families. Americans told interviewers that the last appliance they would sell would be their radio.

Radio was becoming more commercial every year. Programming appealed to popular tastes and sought the largest available audience. Listeners preferred daytime dramas such as "One Man's Family," quickly dubbed "soap operas" after the detergent companies that sponsored them. With the increasing emphasis on profits and ratings, commercials became commonplace.

The most popular radio program of the Depression years was **Amos 'n' Andy,** which portrayed the lives of two African American men in Harlem as interpreted by two white entertainers, Freeman Gosden and Charles Correll. Performed in heavy dialect, the show captured a huge audience at seven o'clock each evening. The tales of black life appealed to white stereotypes about African Americans, but they also gained an audience among blacks because the characters' experiences were comparable to those of minority listeners.

Amos 'n' Andy
The most popular radio program of the Depression years, it portrayed the lives of two African American men in Harlem as interpreted by two white entertainers, Freeman Gosden and Charles Correll.

Off to the Movies

With ticket prices very low and audiences hungry for diversion, Hollywood presented a wide choice of films. Escapist entertainment dominated the movie screens. Audiences laughed at the Marx Brothers in *Cocoanuts* (1929) and *Monkey Business* (1931). Musicals found a ready audience, and there was a vogue for gangster films such as *Little Caesar* (1931) with Edward G. Robinson and *The Public Enemy* (1931) with James Cagney. Hollywood pressed the limits of tolerance for sexual innuendoes and bawdy themes with Mae West and other stars.

Despite the hardships of the economic downturn, the cultural flowering that had begun during the preceding decade continued. In Kansas City and other midwestern cities, African American musicians were developing a new jazz style that would become known as "swing" when white musicians smoothed its hard edges. The "golden age" of American popular song was in full sway. In 1932, one of the worst Depression years, listeners could hear such new songs as "Alone Together," "April in Paris," "Isn't It Romantic," and "The Song Is You."

A Darkening World

The worldwide Depression had calamitous effects on American foreign policy. With the economies of the democratic nations weakened and the structure of international relations tottering, authoritarian forces around the world asserted themselves. The first test came in the Far East.

In September 1931 Japanese troops detonated a weak explosive charge under a Japanese-owned railroad in Manchuria and blamed the episode on the Manchurians. The Japanese military had fabricated the incident as an excuse for attacking Chinese positions in Manchuria. During the weeks that followed, the Japanese army invaded Manchuria. The Japanese bombed Chinese cities to deter any opposition to their effort to occupy all of Manchuria.

Japan and its military wanted to establish their nation as the dominant force in Asia and expel the foreign countries that had achieved a political and economic presence in China and the Far East. Anger at the discriminatory racial policies of the United States,

Great Britain, and other European powers fed this ambition. Japan was also fearful that a resurgent China might pose a threat to Japanese ambitions and access to crucial materials for Tokyo's economy. Desire for political and economic supremacy in the Pacific completed the Japanese agenda.

A Challenge to the League of Nations

Japan's attack into Manchuria confronted the United States with the problem of what to do in response to a clear violation of policies and treaties to which Washington was a party, such as the Open Door and the Nine-Power Treaty. Yet the United States could not do much from a military standpoint. The American Army was no match for Japan's, and the administration had not maintained naval strength at the levels allowed in the various treaties that had been signed during the preceding decade. In addition, Congress would not have been sympathetic to U.S. intervention in a remote foreign quarrel. For the same reason, Washington could not look to European countries. The Hoover administration could only announce its dislike of events in Manchuria in vigorous words. Secretary of State Stimson issued statements to China and Japan that proclaimed the unwillingness of the United States to recognize territorial changes in China produced by aggressive actions. This policy of nonrecognition became known as the Stimson Doctrine. The Japanese pressed ahead with their campaign to occupy Manchuria and intimidate China despite the secretary's comments. In February 1932 Stimson wrote a prominent senator, warning him that the United States might strengthen its military readiness in the Pacific in response to Japanese actions. Japan knew that the United States could do nothing more than that, however, and Stimson's words had little impact.

The League of Nations criticized the Japanese policy, and Japan responded by withdrawing from the organization early in 1933. The United States and Japan were now embarked on a course that would lead to ever more bitter encounters and ultimately to all-out war.

Germany Moves toward the Nazis

The unhappy events in Manchuria foreshadowed what would happen in Europe soon thereafter. In Germany, where resentment about the Treaty of Versailles had grown during the Depression, the National Socialist party of Adolf Hitler was gaining support. Hitler's message of national revenge and hatred of the Jews proved intoxicating to the German people, and during 1932 he stood on the brink of obtaining power. Some Americans even admired the policies of Hitler and the Italian dictator Benito Mussolini because they apparently offered decisive action to deal with the economic crisis. The situation of democratic governments, on the other hand, was perilous.

A Political Opportunity for the Democrats

By the beginning of 1932, the Hoover presidency was in dire political trouble. Even his advisors were critical. Stimson said that a cabinet meeting was "like sitting in a bath of ink." Another official remarked that the president "has a childlike faith in statements."

By 1932 the limits of the president's voluntary approach had become evident even to him. During the winter he supported a congressional initiative to establish the Reconstruction Finance Corporation (RFC). Congress authorized this agency to loan up to $2 billion in tax money to save banks, insurance companies, and railroads from financial collapse. The law that set up the RFC put the federal government behind the effort to achieve economic recovery and signaled that Washington could no longer take a passive or hands-off role. The question was whether this action could reverse Hoover's worsening political fortunes.

Republican problems meant opportunity for the Democrats if they could seize the initiative. However, a deep split persisted within the party over the proper role of government in dealing with the Depression. The tradition of states' rights and limits on the national government remained strong among conservative party members. They would not look kindly on a candidate who wished to expand government's part in dealing with the Depression. Such conservatives controlled the official machinery of the party. It would be difficult for a candidate from the party's liberal wing to gain the nomination in 1932.

The Democrats in Congress

During the 1930 elections the Democrats picked up eight seats in the Senate. The Republicans retained control of the upper house by only a single vote. In the House, the Democratic gain was forty-nine seats, not enough to give them a majority. The Depression had hurt the Republicans, but it had not made the Democrats the majority party.

When Congress reassembled late in 1931, the Democrats had gained several other seats because of the death or retirement of four Republicans. As a result, **John Nance "Cactus Jack" Garner** of Texas became the new Speaker of the House. His answer to the growing budget deficit was to offer a national sales tax. Before the bill could pass the House, angry rebels in both parties killed the idea.

The Rise of Franklin D. Roosevelt

To win the White House in 1932, the Democrats needed a new face to run against Hoover. Among the hopefuls were Governor Albert Ritchie of Maryland, Newton D. Baker who had served in Woodrow Wilson's cabinet, and Speaker Garner. As the year began, however, everyone conceded that the front-runner was Governor Franklin D. Roosevelt of New York.

Roosevelt was fifty years old. He came from a wealthy branch of his family that lived on the Hudson River in Hyde Park, New York. After attending the aristocratic Groton School and Harvard University, he had studied law in New York City. In 1910 he won a seat in the New York State Senate, and three years later he became assistant secretary of the navy in the Wilson administration.

Although Franklin D. Roosevelt was only a distant cousin of Theodore, his wife Eleanor was the former president's niece. His connection to a famous name helped Roosevelt secure the Democratic vice presidential nomination in 1920. He proved to be an effective and popular campaigner, but he could not offset the Republican tide that swept Warren G. Harding into office.

Roosevelt's Illness and Political Comeback

Following that defeat, Roosevelt returned to private life. In 1921 he was stricken with polio and lost the use of his legs. Counted out of politics because of his illness, Roosevelt worked his way back into Democratic affairs during the mid-1920s and in 1928 was elected governor of New York by a narrow margin. Two years later he won reelection by a huge majority.

In public, Roosevelt, his wife, and their five children were the picture of a robust American family. But behind this façade lay personal difficulty. During 1918–1919 the Roosevelts' marriage had almost collapsed because of Franklin's affair with another woman. The Roosevelts stayed together, but theirs became a political partnership of convenience. During the 1920s, Mrs. Roosevelt played a greater role in politics herself.

Roosevelt shared many of the ideas of the mainstream of the Democratic party. He believed in balanced budgets, the gold standard, and capitalism. Yet he also had an instinctive rapport with people in all segments of society, and he relished the exercise of power. His progressive views on the role of government separated him from conservatives in his party. Roosevelt trusted no one completely, and many observers judged him to be superficial and shallow.

The Roosevelt Appeal

Roosevelt was one of the most gifted politicians in the nation's history. Earlier than most public leaders of his time, he recognized the power of radio to reach the American electorate. His jaunty manner and courage in the face of his disability conveyed a message of hope and optimism. Once nominated, he could appeal to all branches of the Democratic party. It remained to be seen, however, whether he could win his party's nomination in the face of the conservatives.

John Nance "Cactus Jack" Garner
Speaker of the House in 1931 whose answer to the growing budget deficit was to offer a national sales tax. He ran against Roosevelt for the Democratic nomination for president but released his delegates and was in turn rewarded with the vice presidential nomination.

Roosevelt's campaign got off to a strong start. His manager, James A. Farley, had mapped out a strategy to attract both big-city leaders, whose support for the Democrats had been growing, and the Solid South, a bastion of party strength since the end of Reconstruction. As a source of ideas for his campaign, Roosevelt turned to the academic community. He recruited several professors from Columbia University in New York to write speeches. Raymond Moley, Rexford G. Tugwell, and Adolf A. Berle were promptly named the **brain trust**. In his speeches, Roosevelt talked of "the forgotten man at the bottom of the economic pyramid" who was suffering from the effects of the Depression. The answer, Roosevelt said, was "bold, persistent experimentation."

brain trust
A group of prominent academics recruited as a source of ideas for the Roosevelt campaign to write speeches.

The Struggle for the Nomination

As Roosevelt's campaign gathered strength, other Democrats decided to challenge the front-runner. Al Smith wanted to stop Roosevelt and perhaps gain another chance at the White House. In February 1932 he indicated that he would accept a nomination if it came his way. He became a more active candidate as the weeks passed, and his strength in the Northeast made him a serious rival to Roosevelt. Roosevelt was clearly the choice of a majority of the Democrats, but party rules mandated that a nominee receive two-thirds of the votes of the convention delegates. If Garner and Smith teamed up against him and their delegates stood firm, Roosevelt could not win.

The Democratic National Convention opened in Chicago on June 20, 1932. The Roosevelt forces faced many difficulties during the days that followed, but when it came to the balloting, his opponents could not rally around anyone else. In the end Speaker Garner decided to release his delegates to Roosevelt; his reward would be the vice presidential nomination, which he said was "not worth a pitcher of warm piss." At the same time, the California delegation swung its support to Roosevelt on the fourth ballot.

A New Deal

In a dramatic break with the political tradition that barred candidates from appearing at a convention to accept a nomination, Roosevelt boarded a plane and flew to Chicago through stormy weather. There he spoke of the need to "resume the country's uninterrupted march along the path of real progress, real justice, of real equality, for all of our citizens great and small." As he concluded his speech, he used a phrase that would become the trademark of his presidency. "I pledge you, I pledge myself to a new deal for the American people." The convention band played the new Democratic theme: "Happy Days Are Here Again." For the first time since nominating Woodrow Wilson twenty years earlier, the Democrats sensed a decisive victory in the air.

The Republicans, on the other hand, recognized the defeat that awaited them. Gloom pervaded their national convention held in mid-June. Hoover and the administration had firm control of the proceedings, and their script was followed. Efforts to nominate anyone other than Hoover failed.

The Economy in Distress

While the two parties were choosing their candidates, the economy worsened. To deal with the growing budget deficit, Congress decided to impose new taxes. The sales tax idea had been dropped, but other levies on corporations, estates, and incomes made this the greatest peacetime increase in taxes in the nation's history. At a time when the economy needed fiscal stimulus, the tax measure drew funds out of the hands of consumers. Raising taxes in an election year added to Hoover's growing unpopularity with the voters.

The weakening of the Hoover administration led to an important change in labor policy during 1932. For many years employers had used friendly federal judges and the power of injunctions to cripple the ability of labor unions to win strikes. The Norris-LaGuardia Act of 1932, by contrast, extended to workers "full freedom of association" and labor representation, restricted the use of injunctions, and barred reliance on "yellow dog" contracts, which prevented workers from joining unions.

As the Depression worsened during its third year, the plight of unemployed Americans deteriorated well beyond the ability of cities and states to provide aid. Congress became restive as the Reconstruction Finance Corporation extended loans to large corporations, and the White House resisted legislation to help the needy and distressed. Bills were introduced to provide direct assistance to the unemployed, but a coalition of Republicans and southern Democrats blocked their passage. As news spread about how much money businesses had received from the RFC, pressure intensified for Congress to do something. The result was the Emergency Relief and Construction Act of 1932, which required states to attest that they could not raise any money themselves before federal funds were allocated to them.

The Bonus March

During the summer of 1932, desperate citizens sought immediate relief from the government in the form of cash. After World War I, Congress had promised war veterans cash bonuses in the form of paid-up life insurance to be disbursed in 1945. During the Hoover presidency, the needs of veterans as a group had been generously funded. As the Depression worsened, however, the veterans clamored for early access to their "bonus" money. During the spring of 1932, Congress decided not to authorize early payment of the bonuses.

To make their presence felt, thousands of veterans organized the Bonus Expeditionary Force, or the **Bonus Army,** which came to Washington during the summer of 1932 to listen to Congress debate the bonus proposal. They camped out in tarpaper dwellings and tents on the banks of the Anacostia River; some slept in government buildings. The authorities did what they could to provide them with food and shelter during their stay. Hoover ignored them. When it became clear that Congress was not going to help the Bonus Marchers and would adjourn in mid-July 1932, the Hoover administration urged the Bonus Army to leave Washington and even allocated $100,000 to pay for the cost of sending the men home. Some of the marchers took advantage of this offer and left Washington. Others stayed on, hoping for a change in government policy.

On July 28 Secretary of War Patrick J. Hurley ordered the police to remove marchers from government buildings. When the police moved in, the veterans resisted and fighting occurred. A police pistol went off; other officers began shooting; and soon two Bonus Marchers lay dead. The president ordered the federal troops in Washington, commanded by General Douglas MacArthur, to restore order. The general took his men, armed with tanks and machine guns, across the Anacostia River into the main camp of the Bonus Army. The veterans fled in terror as the soldiers approached. Tear gas canisters were hurled, tents were burned, and the crowd dispersed in a panic.

The Hoover administration laid the blame for the incident on the influence of Communists inside the veterans' camp. There were a few Communists among the veterans, but they had little influence on the protest. Law enforcement agencies found no evidence of an organized conspiracy among the marchers, and public opinion favored the veterans. "If the Army must be called out to make war on unarmed citizens," said a newspaper editor, "this is no longer America."

Bonus Army
Thousands of veterans, determined to collect promised cash bonuses early, came to Washington during the summer of 1932 to listen to Congress debate the bonus proposal.

©Bettmann /CORBIS

The Hoover administration sent in troops to disperse the Bonus Marchers after Congress refused to pay the veterans their bonuses early. The use of armed force against protesting citizens, especially the deployment of tear gas, made the episode a public relations disaster for the White House.

The 1932 Election

The economic devastation produced by the Great Depression offered groups outside the two-party system a promising chance to win votes for more radical solutions to the nation's problems. Socialists and other left-wing groups cooperated with the Communists in protest marches and petitions for relief. Efforts to organize sharecroppers and tenant farmers in the South also went forward under the sponsorship of the Communists during these years. The Communists wooed African American support when they defended the **Scottsboro boys,** a group of young black men who had been unjustly accused of raping two white women in Alabama in 1931. In 1932 some prominent intellectuals endorsed the Communist presidential campaign or supported the Socialist candidate, Norman Thomas.

Scottsboro boys
A group of black youths accused of raping a white woman in Alabama who became a source of controversy and the focus of civil rights activism in the early 1930s.

Franklin D. Roosevelt: Commonwealth Club Address

In the campaign of 1932, Franklin D. Roosevelt offered a vision of somewhat greater governmental action to meet the Depression. He did not, however, offer a radical program, as this excerpt from his speech to the Commonwealth Club of San Francisco on September 23, 1932, indicates.

. . . This implication is, briefly, that the responsible heads of finance and industry, instead of acting each for himself, must work together to achieve the common end. They must, where necessary, sacrifice this or that private advantage; and in reciprocal self-denial must seek a general advantage. It is here that formal government—political government, if you choose—comes in.

Whenever in the pursuit of this objective the lone wolf, the unethical competitor, the reckless promoter, the Ishmael or Insull whose hand is against every man's, declines to join in achieving an end recognized as being for the public welfare and threatens to drag the industry back to a state of anarchy, the government may properly be asked to apply restraint. Likewise, should the group ever use its collective power contrary to the public welfare, the government must be swift to enter and protect the public interest.

The government should assume the function of economic regulation only as a last resort, to be tried only when private initiative, inspired by high responsibility, with such assistance and balance as government can give, has finally failed. As yet there has been no final failure, because there has been no attempt; and I decline to assume that this nation is unable to meet the situation.

The final term of the high contract was for liberty and the pursuit of happiness. We have learned a great deal of both in the past century. We know that individual liberty and individual happiness mean nothing unless both are ordered in the sense that one man's meat is not another man's poison. We know that the old "rights of personal competency," the right to read, to think, to speak, to choose, and live a mode of life must be respected at all hazards. We know that liberty to do anything which deprives others of those elemental rights is outside the protection of any compact; and that government in this regard is the maintenance of a balance, within which

every individual may have a place if he will take it; in which every individual may find safety if he wishes it; in which every individual may attain such power as his ability permits, consistent with his assuming the accompanying responsibility.

All this is a long, slow task. Nothing is more striking than the simple innocence of the men who insist, whenever an objective is present, on the prompt production of a patent scheme guaranteed to produce a result. Human endeavor is not so simple as that. Government includes the art of formulating a policy and using the political technique to attain so much of that policy as will receive general support; persuading, leading, sacrificing, teaching always, because the greatest duty of a statesman is to educate. But in the matters of which I have spoken, we are learning rapidly, in a severe school. The lessons so learned must not be forgotten, even in the mental lethargy of a speculative upturn. We must build toward the time when a major depression cannot occur again; and if this means sacrificing the easy profits of inflationist booms, then let them go; and good riddance.

Faith in America, faith in our tradition of personal responsibility, faith in our institutions, faith in ourselves demand that we recognize the new terms of the old social contract. We shall fulfill them, as we fulfilled the obligation of the apparent utopia which Jefferson imagined for us in 1776, and which Jefferson, Roosevelt, and Wilson sought to bring to realization. We must do so, lest a rising tide of misery, engendered by our common failure, engulf us all. But failure is not an American habit; and in the strength of great hope we must all shoulder our common load. . . .

Questions to Consider

1. What view of government power does Roosevelt advance in these remarks?

2. How does Roosevelt's statement compare with Woodrow Wilson's inaugural address in 1913, which you read in Chapter 21?

3. What limits, if any, will Roosevelt be willing to place on personal freedom in this economic crisis?

Explore additional primary sources related to this chapter on the *American Passages* Web site: http://history.wadsworth.com/ayersbrief02

Source: *New York Times*, September 24, 1932.

For the majority of Americans, however, the only real choice lay between Roosevelt and Hoover. Many of Roosevelt's advisors told him that he did not have to campaign to win the race. Roosevelt saw the matter differently. If he ran a passive, traditional campaign, he would not persuade the voters who were looking for a change. A front-porch campaign would also have fed rumors that he could not withstand the physical rigors of the presidency. So Roosevelt crisscrossed the country, making speeches that assailed the Republican leadership and attacked Hoover's record.

Roosevelt's Campaign

Roosevelt wanted to occupy the political middle ground, and as a result his campaign speeches took a variety of contradictory positions. At times he seemed to be calling for a more activist federal government that would adapt "existing economic organizations to the service of the people." On other occasions he attacked Hoover's budget deficits and wasteful government spending. There were occasional hints of the New Deal ahead, but most of Roosevelt's appeal came down to hope, confidence, and the promise of political change.

The incumbent president knew he was going to lose, but he campaigned doggedly. He made nine major speeches, all of which he wrote himself in longhand. Hoover told the voters that the nation faced a choice between "two philosophies of government." He charged that the Democrats sought "to change our form of government and our social and our economic system."

Hoover Defeated

On Election Day, Roosevelt won overwhelmingly in the popular vote and scored a 472 to 59 triumph in the electoral college. His party made significant gains in Congress: ninety seats in the House and thirteen in the Senate. The election proved a major disappointment to both the Socialists and the Communists. Norman Thomas received fewer than a million votes. William Z. Foster, the Communist candidate, gained just over 100,000 ballots. Despite the Depression, the American people were willing to give the two-party system another chance.

Roosevelt and Hoover

By 1932 politicians realized that the four-month period between the time that a president was elected and the inauguration was too long. A constitutional amendment moving the date of the inauguration to January 20 was under consideration, but the **Twentieth Amendment** would not go into effect until 1937. Meanwhile, the country faced a worsening economic crisis with a repudiated lame-duck president and Congress that would remain in power until March 4, 1933.

During these four months, the Depression reached its lowest point. One-quarter of the workforce could not find jobs. The gross national product, which had stood at more than $103 billion in 1929, had slid to $58 billion by 1932. Farmers threatened more action to stop foreclosures of delinquent mortgages in their states. In December hunger marchers came to Washington to ask for government aid. The growing numbers of failing banks presented a dire threat: 1,458 banks shut their doors in 1932.

The defeated president believed that the cause of the Depression lay beyond the nation's borders. He wanted Roosevelt to support his policies. Wary of making commitments before taking office, Roosevelt dodged Hoover's efforts to obtain his backing. Hoover became convinced that Roosevelt cared little for the welfare of the country, whereas Roosevelt saw his defeated rival as a sore loser. The government drifted during these fateful months.

Roosevelt devoted most of his energy to forming a cabinet. He chose a diverse group, including Representative Cordell Hull as secretary of state, Progressive reformer Harold Ickes as secretary of the interior, and Frances Perkins, the first female cabinet member, as secretary of labor. Two weeks before the inauguration, at a speaking engagement in Miami, Roosevelt was talking with the mayor of Chicago, Anton Cermak, when a would-be assassin fired five shots at Roosevelt. None hit him, but one wounded Cermak, who died shortly afterward.

Twentieth Amendment
This amendment moved the presidential inauguration date from four months after the election to January 20.

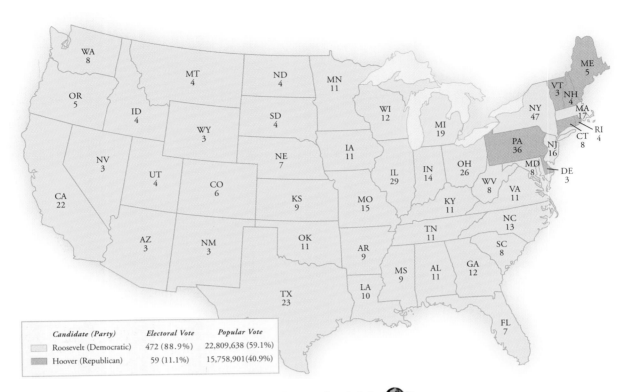

Candidate (Party)	Electoral Vote	Popular Vote
Roosevelt (Democratic)	472 (88.9%)	22,809,638 (59.1%)
Hoover (Republican)	59 (11.1%)	15,758,901 (40.9%)

MAP 24.2 The Election of 1932

As the Depression hit bottom in 1932, the voters rejected Herbert Hoover and the Republicans in favor of Franklin D. Roosevelt and the Democrats. The incumbent and his party did well only in the traditional Republican bastions of New England and two states in the Middle Atlantic region. View an animated version of this map or related maps at http://history.wadsworth.com/ ayersbrief02.

The Banking System Nears Collapse

As March 4 approached, a crisis of confidence in banks gripped the country. Alarm about the banking system had been spreading since October 1932. During that month the governor of Nevada proclaimed a twelve-day bank "holiday" to end depositor "runs" on banks in his state. The news spurred depositors in other states to remove funds from their local banks. In Michigan two banks in Detroit seemed about to fail by mid-February. Hoover tried to persuade business leaders, including Henry Ford, to place deposits in the troubled banks. Ford was willing, but others were not. The governor of Michigan intervened and declared a bank holiday on February 14. Depositors in other states, fearing that their deposits would be frozen, tried to withdraw their money from local banks. Governors in nine other states were forced to announce bank holidays. Hoover pressed the incoming president for immediate joint action, but Roosevelt was still reluctant to tie his own hands before he took office.

A Spreading Sense of Crisis

As the transition of power neared, general apprehension increased. By the morning of March 4, banks in New York City, the nation's financial capital, were shutting their doors. A weary Hoover concluded in a moment of personal despair: "We are at the end of our string." Shortly before eleven o'clock the outgoing president joined Franklin Roosevelt in a waiting limousine and the two men drove off toward the Capitol. Roosevelt waved to well-wishers in the crowd as Hoover sat in silence. A nation mired in the worst depression in its history waited to hear what the new president would say.

Summary

The Depression and Its Scars

In the period from 1927 to 1933, Americans experienced the onset of the Great Depression, the worst economic downturn in the nation's history. Almost a quarter of the work-force was unemployed, the relief rolls swelled, and the economy stagnated. The prosperity that seemed to be part of the dream for millions of citizens simply vanished amid doubts that it would ever return. By 1933 the economic system appeared to be on the verge of collapse (see Table 24.2).

President Herbert Hoover became associated with the Depression for his failure to relieve the problem during his term of office. While he took more vigorous action than had previous presidents who confronted similar situations, Hoover's inability to produce recovery, manage relief, and persuade people of his concern for their welfare doomed his presidency. By 1932 he was a rejected figure who lost in an overwhelming way to Franklin D. Roosevelt.

The exact causes of the Depression remain disputed. The stock market crash exposed the weaknesses in the economy and reversed the psychology of optimism that had raised

During the Great Depression, selling apples became one of the ways that poor people eked out an income. This satiric cartoon by Herbert Block (Herblock) from the early 1930s shows a rich man helping out a poor apple seller by buying and eating all the fruit that he can.

The farm sector felt the Depression with the most force. The auction of a farm and all its property became a typical scene for much of rural America during the early 1930s. Discontent and anger permeated the farm sector as a result of scenes such as this one.

Table 24.2 Bank Suspensions, 1927–1933

Year	Suspensions
1927	669
1928	499
1929	659
1930	1,352
1931	2,284
1932	1,458
1933	4,004

Source: *Historical Statistics of the United States,* 1985, p. 536.

As the financial system tottered, many banks failed in the Depression, taking with them the life savings of millions of people. The crowd of anxious people outside this bank in New York City was typical of the way depositors responded when they learned that they could lose everything in a bank failure.

©Bettmann / CORBIS

share prices. Why the failure in the market was followed by a more sustained economic slowdown has been attributed to a lack of consumer spending, poor government policies, international causes, and troubles in the banking system. For Americans of that time who watched their savings dwindle and their prospects darken, the inability of the political system to offer reassuring answers was one of the most dismaying parts of the Depression experience.

The erosion of confidence in democratic governments helped foster the rise of dictators in Europe and Asia. Adolf Hitler's emergence as the ruler of Germany, the consolidation of power by Joseph Stalin in the Soviet Union, and the dominance of militarists in Japan suggested authoritarian systems were gaining converts while democracies were under siege. The challenge of the 1930s would be in meeting these threats to societies that operated with the consent of the "governed.

Some trends of the 1920s continued even into the Depression years. Movies and radio still commanded large audiences as people sought diversions from their immediate problems. Show business and celebrity infused public life in ways that would not show up for another decade or so. Radicalism appealed to some of the discontented, and there were fears that Communism or Fascism might take root in the United States. Though the prospect for social disorder appeared to be real in the dark days of 1931 and 1932, most Americans still acted as if the traditional political parties could address their problems. That is why Franklin D. Roosevelt achieved such a popular mandate when in 1932 he promised a "New Deal" for the nation. By the time he took office in March 1933, the Depression had reached a low point. It was still in doubt whether a new president, even one with Roosevelt's optimism and confidence, could lift the nation out of the doldrums. Roosevelt promised to try, and for the moment that seemed to be enough.

The case of the African American men accused in the Scottsboro trial became another controversial episode in racial injustice in the early 1930s. Guarded by state troopers, the defendants in the case consult with their attorney.

©The Granger Collection, New York

Making Connections Across Chapters

LOOKING BACK

Causes of the Depression were rooted back in the period of World War I and projected forward into the developing economy in the 1920s. When reviewing the causes of the economic collapse, look for signs of problems that were discussed in the preceding chapter.

1. Why was the stock market crash of 1929 both an important element in the nation's economic problems and yet not a decisive cause of the Depression?

2. Why was more not done to prevent the weaknesses in the economy that became apparent after 1929?

3. Why was Herbert Hoover elected in 1928? What assets did he have that became liabilities once the Depression began?

LOOKING AHEAD

Nothing had prepared Americans for the Great Depression, and the effects proved to be long-lasting in all phases of life. Debate still continues over what caused the downturn and why it lasted so long. The next chapter focuses on what made this period so traumatic for so many citizens.

1. Why would the Depression prove to be so hard to end?
2. What structural weaknesses in the American economy did it reveal?
3. Herbert Hoover said that the 1932 election presented the United States with a fundamental choice between liberty and regimentation. What did he mean by that?
4. Why was Hoover, who was so successful in bringing relief to millions in Belgium and the Soviet Union, unable to do the same thing in the United States?
5. Which beliefs that Hoover deeply held did the Depression challenge?

Making Connections Across Chapters

RECOMMENDED READINGS

Clements, Kendrick. *Hoover. Conservation and Consumerism: Engineering the Good Life* (2000). Offers a probing study of the president's attitude toward nature and society.

Cook, Blanche Wiesen. *Eleanor Roosevelt, 1884–1933* (1992). The first volume of a biography of this important first lady.

Doherty, Thomas. *Pre-Code Hollywood: Sex, Immorality, and Insurrection in American Cinema, 1930–1934* (1994). Considers the role of popular entertainment during the Depression.

Finan, Christopher M. *Alfred E. Smith: The Happy Warrior* (2002). An engaging biography of the Democratic candidate in 1928.

Houck, Davis W. *Rhetoric as Currency: Hoover, Roosevelt, and the Great Depression* (2001). Examines how Hoover's speaking style affected his presidency.

Kennedy, David M. *Freedom from Fear: The American People in Depression and War, 1929–1945* (1999). Provides a prize-winning discussion of the Depression and its impact.

Liebovich, Louis. *Bylines in Despair: Herbert Hoover, the Great Depression, and the U.S. News Media* (1994). Looks at the troubled relations between Hoover and the press.

McElvaine, Robert S. *The Depression and the New Deal: A History in Documents* (2000). A well-chosen collection of revealing documents about the economic crisis.

Parrish, Michael E. *Anxious Decades: America in Prosperity and Depression, 1920–1941* (1992). An excellent synthesis of the interwar period.

Watkins, T. H. *The Great Depression: America in the 1930s* (1993). Offers a popular account of the events of the Depression decade.

AMERICAN JOURNEY ONLINE AND INFOTRAC COLLEGE EDITION

Visit the source collections at http://ajaccess.wadsworth .com and infotrac.thomsonlearning.com and use the Search function with the following key terms to explore documents, images, audio and video clips, articles, and commentary related to the material in this chapter.

Hoovervilles

Scottsboro

Stock market crash of 1929

Herbert Hoover

Amelia Earhart

Alfred E. Smith

Marx brothers

ONLINE PRIMARY SOURCES

Here are some examples of the many primary sources related to this chapter that you will find on the *American Passages* Web site: http://history.wadsworth.com/ayersbrief02.

New York Campaign Speech by Herbert Hoover, 1928

Special Message to the Congress on the Economic Recovery Program, 1932

The Music of Woody Guthrie, 1940 (audio clips)

The site also offers self-quizzes, exercises, and many additional resources to help you study.

1933 *to* 1960

AMERICANS WHO GREW UP IN THE DEPRESSION, SERVED THEIR COUNTRY during World War II, and ushered in the enormous prosperity of the 1950s and beyond have been celebrated in recent books and movies as "the greatest generation." There are good reasons for such praise. In no other period except the Civil War and Reconstruction was America as severely tested, its direction as radically changed. The 1930s saw the worst economic catastrophe in modern history. Banks collapsed, farms failed, factories closed, and bread lines formed in the cities. Yet what truly defined the nation in this decade was its passionate response to misfortune—the way Americans mixed

Following the former Soviet Union's spectacular launch of *Sputnik I,* the United States created the National Aeronautics and Space Administration (NASA) in 1958 to manage civilian space operations. Among its first tasks was the selection and training of astronauts (pictured) for Project Mercury, the human spaceflight program.

©Bettmann /CORBIS

protest, innovation, and reform. Dramatic changes occurred. The Great Depression not only increased the social responsibilities of government, it also opened the political process to millions of "forgotten Americans," who exercised power by joining labor unions, switching political parties, and migrating to places where they could vote and be represented. In contrast to the violent ideological struggles that gripped much of Europe in the 1930s, the United States witnessed a remarkable expansion of the democratic principles it held so dear.

Although the Great Depression would linger until World War II, the federal government provided Americans with food and employ-

Mar. 4, 1933   THE NEW YORKER   Price 15 cents

peter Arno

Franklin D. Roosevelt Library / The New Yorker

This *New Yorker* cartoon, sketched well before the inauguration, accurately predicted feelings of both men—the glum Hoover and the exuberant Roosevelt—as they rode down Pennsylvania Avenue together on March 4, 1933.

ment, optimism and hope. Furthermore, the vast public works projects of that era—the roads, dams, bridges, tunnels, schools, hospitals, post offices, airports, parks, and playgrounds—created a physical infrastructure that tied the nation together while it spurred its future success. World War II brought new challenges and opportunities. Battling on two fronts, the nation resolutely mobilized a superb U.S. fighting force and a masterful home front effort in which almost everyone took part. The war provided better employment for minorities and for women, although discrimination in wages and skilled jobs remained. So, too, did segregation in the armed forces—a hypocrisy that did not end till 1948. Nevertheless, Americans stood shoulder-to-shoulder against the villainy of fascism, Pearl Harbor, and Nazi genocide.

The enormous prosperity following World War II quickly pushed fears of economic depression aside. What remained in place, however, were the structural reforms that made banks safer, capitalism stronger, and people more secure. Postwar Americans strongly supported an active government role in domestic and foreign affairs. There was little opposition to expanding the social security system, increasing the defense budget, or providing hefty benefits to veterans of the war. Soldiers came home and picked up their lives. The marriage rate soared, a baby boom followed, and young families rushed to the suburbs. Peacetime consumption replaced wartime production as the key to national prosperity, with the sale of new homes, automobiles, and appliances reaching record heights.

The prosperity and good feelings generated by World War II were not equally shared, however. Employment opportunities for women fell dramatically after the veterans returned. Racial prejudice remained a national disgrace. The South still required segregation by law, and other regions discriminated more subtly in housing, education, and jobs. Furthermore, growing fears about Soviet expansion and domestic Communism dissolved the political unity, or bipartisanship, that had marked

American foreign policy throughout the war. The resulting Red Scare, fueled by opportunistic politicians such as Senator Joseph R. McCarthy, challenged America's most cherished ideals.

Still, the nation prospered and grew. The 1950s saw the spread of a powerful civil rights movement and the demise of Senator McCarthy. Breakthroughs in medicine

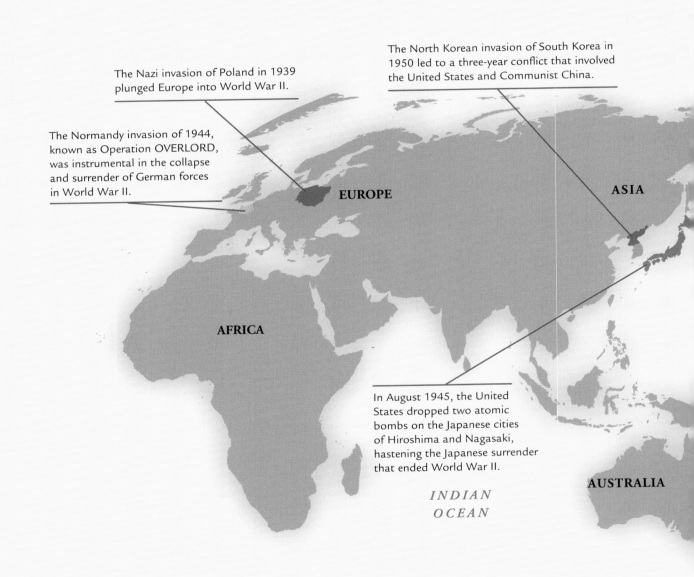

The Nazi invasion of Poland in 1939 plunged Europe into World War II.

The North Korean invasion of South Korea in 1950 led to a three-year conflict that involved the United States and Communist China.

The Normandy invasion of 1944, known as Operation OVERLORD, was instrumental in the collapse and surrender of German forces in World War II.

EUROPE

ASIA

AFRICA

In August 1945, the United States dropped two atomic bombs on the Japanese cities of Hiroshima and Nagasaki, hastening the Japanese surrender that ended World War II.

AUSTRALIA

INDIAN OCEAN

ANTARCTICA

and technology ended the nightmare of polio, fueled the space race, and brought the miracle of television into almost every American home. The economic boom continued, raising living standards and national confidence to even greater heights. As 1960 approached, the nation appeared content and comfortable—thanks in large part to the greatest generation, now approaching middle age.

America and the World: 1933–1960

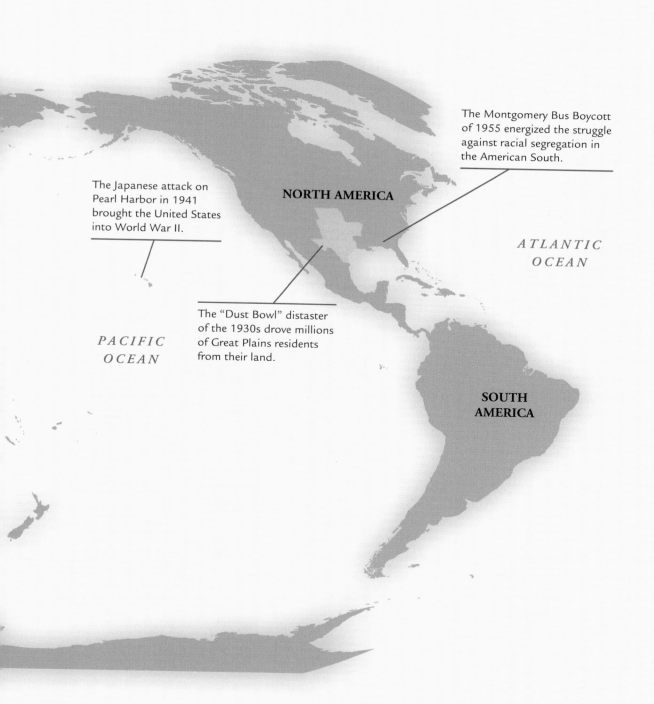

The Montgomery Bus Boycott of 1955 energized the struggle against racial segregation in the American South.

NORTH AMERICA

The Japanese attack on Pearl Harbor in 1941 brought the United States into World War II.

ATLANTIC OCEAN

The "Dust Bowl" distaster of the 1930s drove millions of Great Plains residents from their land.

PACIFIC OCEAN

SOUTH AMERICA

The New Deal

1933–1939

O N MARCH 4, 1933, FRANKLIN ROOSEVELT TOOK THE PRESIDENTIAL oath of office. "Only a foolish optimist can deny the dark realities of the moment," he told the huge crowd. Roosevelt's voice radiated confidence and concern. "This nation asks for action, and action now," he declared. Comparing the Depression to an all-out war of survival, he vowed to ask Congress for the "broad executive power . . . that would be given to me if we were in fact invaded by a foreign foe."

Roosevelt offered few specifics. His objective was to convince a dispirited people to have faith in him and in themselves. Standing erect in his cumbersome leg braces, Roosevelt stressed four major themes: sacrifice, discipline, compassion, and hope. "The only thing we have to fear," he assured the nation, "is fear itself."

Rock Bottom

This fear was understandable. The winter of 1932–1933 was a time of intense suffering. Unemployment reached a staggering 25 percent. Banks were failing everywhere. Food prices had collapsed, forcing farmers from their land. Roosevelt understood how deeply the Depression had shaken the country and sapped its confidence. His words reflected both his compassion for common people and his detachment from their lives. He would become a father figure to them in perilous times—bold and caring, yet distant and elusive.

Taking Charge

No peacetime president ever faced a tougher challenge. Respected commentators were predicting the end of capitalism if the Depression hung on much longer. At the very least, Americans were desperate for change—and that meant almost any initiative designed to revive the economy.

Roosevelt possessed neither a comprehensive plan to end the Depression nor a rigid set of economic beliefs. What he did have was the willingness to experiment, to act decisively, and to use the government as a powerful weapon in the struggle for economic recovery. He surrounded himself with men and women of talent, accomplishment, and wide-ranging progressive views. His closest advisors included agricultural theorists and urban planners, college professors and political pros. In addition, the **New Deal** attracted thousands of young people to Washington, drawn by the opportunity to do something meaningful— and perhaps historic—with their lives.

New Deal
The name given to the many domestic programs and reforms instituted by President Franklin D. Roosevelt and his administration in response to the Great Depression of the 1930s.

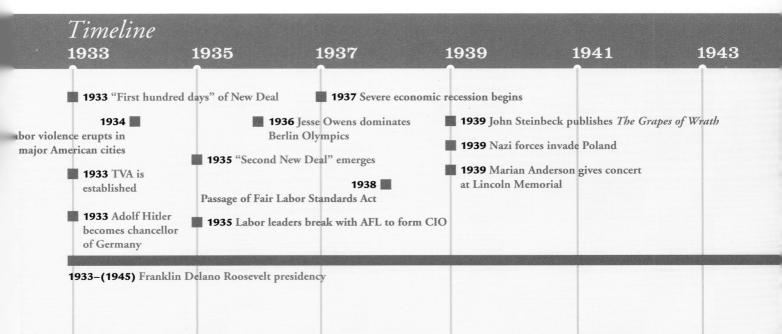

Timeline

| 1933 | 1935 | 1937 | 1939 | 1941 | 1943 |

1933 "First hundred days" of New Deal

1937 Severe economic recession begins

1934 ...bor violence erupts in major American cities

1936 Jesse Owens dominates Berlin Olympics

1939 John Steinbeck publishes *The Grapes of Wrath*

1935 "Second New Deal" emerges

1939 Nazi forces invade Poland

1933 TVA is established

1938 Passage of Fair Labor Standards Act

1939 Marian Anderson gives concert at Lincoln Memorial

1933 Adolf Hitler becomes chancellor of Germany

1935 Labor leaders break with AFL to form CIO

1933–(1945) Franklin Delano Roosevelt presidency

The Bank Crisis

More than five thousand banks had failed in the United States between 1930 and 1932, wiping out countless savings accounts. Panicked depositors, unable to tell a good bank from a bad one, lost faith in them all. An avalanche of withdrawals resulted. By the time Roosevelt took office, nineteen states had declared "bank holidays" (or closings) to head off a full-scale collapse.

On March 6, 1933, the president called Congress back into special session and proclaimed a national "bank holiday." Three days later, his emergency banking proposal was enacted. It provided for the federal inspection of all banks. Those with liquid assets would be allowed to reopen with a license from the Treasury Department; the others would be reorganized, if possible, or closed for good.

On March 12, Roosevelt addressed the nation in the first of his "fireside chats." His radio audience that Sunday evening was estimated at sixty million people. "I want to talk for a few minutes about banking," he began, assuring everyone that the system was now safe. The listeners believed him. In the following days, as the stronger banks reopened, deposits greatly exceeded withdrawals. By the end of March, almost $1 billion had been returned from mattresses to bank vaults.

Roosevelt's handling of the bank emergency revealed his essential pragmatism. He could easily have taken a more radical approach—by nationalizing the banks, for example, or by instituting much tighter controls. Instead, he demonstrated that his primary mission would be to preserve capitalism, and that meant reforming its institutions with substantial federal aid.

The president also showed himself to be a master of communication. His ability to reach people in the radio age was perhaps his greatest gift. He would use it often in the coming years as the nation faced the twin crises of economic hardship and global war.

Extending Relief

The special session of Congress lasted from March 9 to June 16, 1933, a period known as "the first hundred days." With both the House and the Senate now under firm Democratic control, Roosevelt had little trouble getting his legislation passed. As the banking crisis ended, he moved quickly to help those too desperate to help themselves.

The problem was daunting. By conservative estimates, more than thirty million Americans were now living in family units with no income at all. The wife of an Oklahoma oilfield worker said:

> There was thousands of people out of work . . . colored and white. Lost everything they had accumulated from their young days. . . . I knew one family, a man and a woman and seven children lived in a hole in the ground. . . . They had chairs and tables, and beds back in that hole. And they had the dirt all braced up there, just like a cave.

The Hoover administration had refused to consider federal payments to the jobless. As a result, state and local governments had been forced to ration what little relief they could muster. In 1932 the average weekly payment to an "out-of-work" family in New York City was $2.39. Some cities were forced to limit relief to families with three or more children; others offered free food and fuel.

Roosevelt believed that relief efforts should be a local responsibility. He, too, worried about the cost of funding such efforts. Yet there seemed to be no alternative. It was essential, said one of Roosevelt's advisors, to pursue "long-run" economic growth. The problem, he added, is that "people don't eat in the long run—they eat every day."

©Bettmann/CORBIS

One of the New Deal's most popular programs was the Civilian Conservation Corps, which took unemployed young men from the cities and put them to work on conservation projects in the country.

On March 21 the White House sent two major relief proposals to Capitol Hill. The first one created the **Civilian Conservation Corps (CCC).** The CCC provided government conservation jobs to "city boys," age seventeen to twenty-four, in isolated camps run by the U.S. Army. The pay was $30 a month, with $22 going directly to the worker's family.

The CCC was both popular and successful. It eased unemployment a bit, lowered crime rates in the cities, and kept countless families off relief. It also helped to protect and restore the nation's environment, while teaching young men about the discipline of hard work. More than half a million recruits cleaned beaches, built wildlife shelters, fought forest fires, and stocked rivers and streams.

Roosevelt's second relief proposal was the Federal Emergency Relief Administration (FERA), which had a budget of $500 million to be used to assist states in their efforts to help the unemployed. Hoping to spend the money as quickly and humanely as possible, Roosevelt chose **Harry Hopkins,** a former social worker who had directed New York's relief effort, to run FERA. With boundless energy and an ego to match, Hopkins personified the New Deal's activist, free-wheeling style. He became Roosevelt's closest advisor.

Most of the funding went to the jobless in the form of free food or a simple "dole." This troubled Hopkins, who understood both the need for such relief and the damage it could do. Real work "preserves a man's morale," he insisted. Knowing that Roosevelt felt the same way, he convinced the president to approve a federal work relief program.

With Hopkins in charge, the **Civil Works Administration (CWA)** hired more than four million people in a matter of months. Its aim was to create jobs and restore self-respect by handing out pay envelopes instead of relief checks. In reality, CWA workers sometimes performed worthless tasks, known as "boondoggles," such as raking leaves in huge circles or lugging shovelfuls of dirt to faraway piles.

But this was only part of the story. The CWA spent much of its $1 billion budget on projects of lasting value. Its workers built more than four hundred airports and two hundred thousand miles of roads. They ran nursery schools and taught more than a million adults to read and write. They immunized children, served hot school lunches, and took garbage off the streets. Yet Roosevelt ended the CWA experiment after only four months, citing its spiraling costs.

Conservation, Regional Planning, and Public Power

In the spring of 1933, FDR appeared to be governing the nation by himself. His proposals were so sweeping, and so easily enacted, that Congress seemed to have no independent function of its own. Never before had the White House taken such initiative on domestic legislation; never before had it been so successful.

At Roosevelt's behest, Congress created the Securities and Exchange Commission (SEC) to oversee the stock and bond markets. It established the Federal Deposit Insurance Corporation (FDIC) to insure bank deposits up to $5,000. It provided funds to refinance one-fifth of the nation's home and farm mortgages. And it effectively ended Prohibition by permitting the sale of beer and wine with an alcoholic content of 3.2 percent. (The Eighteenth Amendment would be repealed on December 5, 1933.)

Believing that poverty could be eradicated through the careful development of natural resources, Roosevelt turned the Tennessee Valley into a laboratory for his most cherished ideas. Covering seven states and forty thousand square miles, the Tennessee Valley was America's poorest region. Most of its four million people—mainly small farmers and sharecroppers—lived in isolated communities, without electricity, medical care, proper schooling, or paved roads. The **Tennessee Valley Authority (TVA),** created in May 1933, transformed this region in fundamental ways. Within a decade, sixteen huge dams and hydroelectric plants were in operation along the Tennessee River, providing flood control, cheap, abundant power, and thousands of jobs. Per capita income rose dramatically. Electric power gave local residents what millions of other Americans already took for granted: radios and refrigerators, plumbing, lights in houses and barns.

The TVA was widely viewed as one of the New Deal's greatest achievements. Yet its critics included many residents of the Tennessee Valley, whose complaints reflected the

Civilian Conservation Corps (CCC)
One of the New Deal's most popular programs, it took unemployed young men from the cities and put them to work on conservation projects in the country.

Harry Hopkins
Roosevelt's choice to run the Federal Emergency Relief Administration. He eventually became Roosevelt's closest advisor.

Civil Works Administration (CWA)
The agency tasked with creating jobs and restoring self-respect by handing out pay envelopes instead of relief checks. In reality, workers sometimes performed worthless tasks, known as "boondoggles," but much of the $1 billion budget was spent on projects of lasting value including airports and roads.

Tennessee Valley Authority (TVA)
Created in 1933 during the New Deal's first hundred days, it was a massive experiment in regional planning that focused on providing electricity, flood control, and soil conservation to one of the nation's poorest regions, covering seven states in the Tennessee Valley.

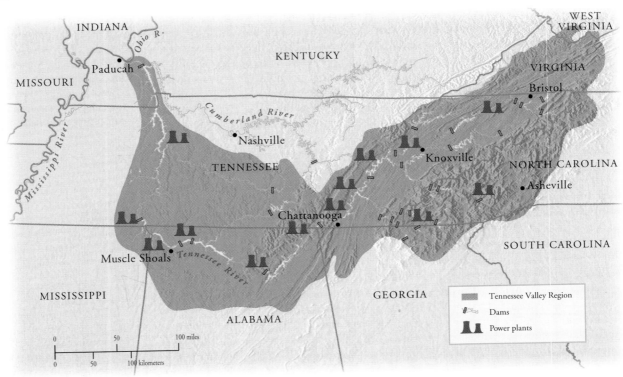

MAP 25.1 The Tennessee Valley
The Tennessee Valley Authority, acclaimed as the most visionary model of government planning in the New Deal era, brought electric power, flood control, and employment to one of the nation's most impoverished regions.

changing face of reform. To their thinking, the TVA displaced thousands of people, attracted low-wage factory jobs, and caused serious environmental damage. At best, they argued, it brought a measure of comfort and prosperity to a badly depressed region. At worst, it allowed distant bureaucrats to decide how local people should live.

Economic Recovery

With the bank crisis over and federal relief flowing to those most desperately in need, the Roosevelt administration turned to the long-term issue of providing a structure for the nation's economic recovery. In agriculture, the problems were severe. Most farmers had been slumping badly since the 1920s. The introduction of tractors and high-grade fertilizer had made them more productive than ever. Yet their share of the world market had declined because of high tariff walls and tough foreign competition.

If overproduction plagued American agriculture in this era, the problem facing American industry was quite the reverse. So many factories had closed their doors during the Depression that too little was being produced. The resulting unemployment caused a drop in purchasing power, which forced even more factories to shut down.

Trouble on the Land

The Roosevelt administration turned first to the agricultural problems. Farmers in 1932 were earning less than one-third of their meager 1929 incomes. As food prices collapsed, there was talk of open rebellion in the heartland. Farmers blocked roads, clashed with police, and threatened to lynch any official who foreclosed a family farm. Roosevelt was sympathetic. He believed that low farm income was a leading cause of the Depression, and he needed the support of rural legislators. The proposal he sent Congress, therefore, incorporated the ideas of the nation's major farm interest groups. Passed in May 1933, the

Agricultural Adjustment Act confronted the problems of overproduction and mounting surpluses that had conspired to erode farm income over the years. The act also created the Agricultural Adjustment Administration (AAA) to oversee this process.

The AAA had one clear goal in mind: to raise farm prices by encouraging farmers to produce less. The idea was no longer to win back world markets but rather to limit domestic output in order to achieve "parity," or fair price levels, within the United States. The original act compensated farmers who voluntarily removed acreage from production. And it funded these payments through a tax on farm processors, such as flour millers, meatpackers, and cotton gin operators.

Problems quickly arose. Because spring planting was already under way, the AAA encouraged farmers to plow under a large portion of their crops. Producing less food while millions were going hungry was difficult for people to understand, and destroying food seemed particularly senseless and cruel. Yet there seemed to be no other way to fix an economic system awash in idle workers and empty factories, hungry people and abundant food.

Within a year, more than three million farmers had signed individual contracts with the AAA. The early results were encouraging. Cotton, wheat, and corn production fell significantly. Farm income shot up almost 60 percent between 1932 and 1935—the result of rising food prices, generous mortgage assistance, and federal loans to those who stored their surpluses in government warehouses. Nature played a role as well. During the 1930s, the American farm belt experienced record highs in temperature and record lows in rainfall. The Great Plains was hardest hit. Terrifying dust storms swept through Kansas, Nebraska, Colorado, Oklahoma, Texas, and the Dakotas like a black blizzard, packing gale force winds and stripping nutrients from the soil. Cornfields were turned into sand dunes, and livestock were buried in their tracks.

©Bettmann/CORBIS

A farm family seeks shelter from a dust storm in 1937.

> ### Agricultural Adjustment Act
> Created under Roosevelt's New Deal program to help farmers, its purpose was to reduce production of staple crops, thereby raising farm prices and encouraging more diversified farming.

The **Dust Bowl** disaster triggered one of the largest internal migrations in the nation's history. More than three million people abandoned their Dust Bowl farms in the 1930s. By one account, "The people did not stop to shut the door—they just walked out, leaving behind them the wreckage of their labors: an ugly little shack with broken windows covered by cardboard, a sagging ridgepole, a barren, dusty yard, the windmill creaking in the wind."

Many set out for California, where the "fortunate" among them found work picking fruit, boxing vegetables, and baling hay. Living in hellish squatter camps, enduring disease and discrimination, they moved from field to orchard in the San Joaquin and Imperial valleys, earning pitiful wages and "going on relief."

> ### Dust Bowl
> The name given to areas of the prairie states that suffered ecological devastation in the 1930s and then again to a lesser extent in the mid-1950s.

Tenants and Landowners

The AAA helped countless farm families and ignored countless others. The large farmers got the biggest subsidies. Yet the system barely touched those at the bottom of the pile: the tenants and sharecroppers who comprised almost one-half of the nation's white farm families and three-quarters of the black farm families. Most of them lived in desperate poverty, working the cotton fields of the rural South. Under AAA regulations, these tenants were supposed to get a fair share of the acreage reduction payments. But few landlords obeyed the rules, and some evicted their tenants in order to take even more land out of production.

In response, tenants and sharecroppers formed their own organization, the Southern Tenant Farmers' Union (STFU). "The landlord is always betwixt us, beatin' us and starvin' us," complained a black sharecropper from Arkansas. "There ain't but one way for us to get him where he can't help himself and that's for us to get together and stay together."

This would not be easy. Despite the strong support of Norman Thomas and his Socialist party, the STFU could not match the power and resources of its opponents. Tenants who joined the union were evicted from their shacks, blacklisted by employers, and denied credit at banks and stores. Union organizers were beaten and jailed.

The president understood the racial implications of this struggle—most tenants were black; the landlords were white. But he did not want to jeopardize the AAA by offending powerful southern interests in Congress. "I know the South . . . ," he told Thomas, "and we've got to be patient." In the meantime, Roosevelt created the Resettlement Administration (RA), with modest funding, to assist evicted tenants and migrant farm workers. Headed by Rexford Tugwell, an outspoken civil rights advocate, the RA became a kind of "mini-AAA" for the rural poor.

Conditions were no better in the Southwest and Far West, where destitute Mexican farm workers struggled to survive. Many had been brought north by American ranchers and growers seeking cheap labor in better times. Now, as the demand for workers decreased, and job competition with poor whites intensified, their desperation grew. Since most of these farm workers were not U.S. citizens, local governments often denied them relief. Like the Tenant Farmers' Union in Arkansas, their attempts to unionize were crushed by local vigilantes and police. In 1936 John Steinbeck reported on a strike of Mexican lettuce workers near his home in Salinas, California. "The attitude of the employer," he wrote, "is one of hatred and suspicion, his method is the threat of the deputies' guns. The workers are herded about like animals."

The AAA revolutionized American agriculture. Never before had the federal government been as deeply involved in the affairs of the American farmer; never before had it encouraged its citizens to produce fewer goods, not more. Although key elements of the AAA would be struck down by the Supreme Court in *United States v. Butler* (1936), the concept of federal farm subsidies continues to dominate America's agricultural policy to the present day.

Centralized Economic Planning

National Industrial Recovery Act (NIRA)
Enacted on June 16, 1933, this emergency measure was designed to encourage industrial recovery and help combat widespread unemployment.

The Roosevelt administration had an equally ambitious plan to revive the economy, reopen idle factories, and put people back to work. In June 1933, Congress passed the **National Industrial Recovery Act (NIRA).** The NIRA was designed as a vehicle for centralized economic planning. Roosevelt himself viewed it as the primary weapon in his crusade against the Depression. The NIRA created two more federal agencies: the Public Works Administration (PWA) and the National Recovery Administration (NRA). The former, with a budget of $3.3 billion, was supposed to "prime the economic pump" by providing jobs for the unemployed and new orders for factories. What made the PWA so appealing was its emphasis on private employment. Workers were to be hired and paid by individual contractors, not by the federal government.

Roosevelt selected Secretary of the Interior Harold Ickes to run the PWA. It proved to be a controversial choice. Ickes scrutinized almost every construction contract himself, sometimes line by line. He wanted PWA projects to be free of graft, and he insisted that each one add something useful to a community's well-being. In the end, the PWA would spend only $2.8 billion of its budget. Nevertheless, under Ickes's leadership it constructed schools, hospitals, post offices, and sewage systems. It built the Golden Gate Bridge in San Francisco and the Triborough Bridge in New York City, the Grand Coulee Dam in Washington state and Boulder Dam in Colorado. No one brought more honest efficiency to government than Harold Ickes.

The key to Roosevelt's recovery program, however, was the NRA. Under the flamboyant leadership of General Hugh S. Johnson, the NRA encouraged representatives of business and labor to create codes of "fair practice" designed to stabilize the economy through planning and cooperation. Johnson's agency promised something to everyone, though not in equal amounts. Business leaders got the biggest gift of all: the suspension of antitrust laws.

In return for such generosity, these leaders agreed to significant labor reforms. Each NRA code featured a maximum hour and minimum wage provision (usually forty hours and twelve dollars per week). Child labor was forbidden, and yellow-dog contracts banned. Most important, Section 7 (a) of the NIRA guaranteed labor unions the right to organize and bargain collectively.

General Johnson barnstormed the country by airplane, giving speeches and lining up support. His tactics were the same ones he had used to mobilize Americans in the bond drives and mass rallies of World War I. With a patriotic symbol (the blue eagle) and a catchy slogan ("We Do Our Part"), Johnson organized the biggest public spectacles of the Depression era. In the summer of 1933, more than two hundred fifty thousand New Yorkers paraded down Fifth Avenue singing:

Join the good old N.R.A., Boys,
and we will end this awful strife.
Join it with the spirit
that will give the Eagle life.
Join in folks, then push and pull,
many millions strong.
While we go marching to Prosperity.

Johnson signed up the big industries—coal, steel, oil, autos, shipbuilding, chemicals, and clothing—before going after the others. By the end of 1933, the NRA had 746 different agreements in place. There was a code for the mop handle makers, another for the dog food industry, and even one for the burlesque houses that determined the number of strippers in each show. Before long, however, the NRA was in trouble. Small businessmen complained that the codes encouraged monopolies and drowned them in paperwork. Labor leaders charged that employers ignored the wage and hour provisions, while cracking down on union activity. And consumers blamed the NRA for raising prices at a time when their purchasing power was extremely low.

All of this was true. Because the codes were voluntary, they carried no legal weight. The large companies obeyed them when it was in their interest to do so, and ignored them when it wasn't. As a result, the codes became a device for fixing prices, stifling competition, and limiting production. This may have guaranteed a profit for some companies, but it was the wrong remedy for solving an economic crisis in which the revival of consumer spending was a key to recovery.

In 1934 General Johnson suffered a nervous breakdown, leading Roosevelt to replace him with a five-member executive board. The president seemed relieved when the Supreme Court, in *Schechter Poultry Company v. United States* (1935), struck down the NRA on the ground that Congress had delegated too much legislative authority to the executive branch. "It has been an awful headache," Roosevelt confided to an aide. "I think perhaps NRA has done all it can do."

New Deal Diplomacy

Foreign affairs were not high on President Roosevelt's agenda. The United States was in turmoil, struggling through the worst economic crisis in its history. Roosevelt's inaugural address devoted one sentence to foreign policy. "In the field of world policy," he declared, "I would dedicate this nation to the policy of the good neighbor"—a theme already sounded by outgoing President Herbert Hoover.

The Soviet Question

FDR was no isolationist. He believed deeply in the concepts of international cooperation and global security. One of his first diplomatic moves, in November 1933, was to extend formal recognition to the Soviet Union. The move was criticized by groups as varied as the American Legion and the American Federation of Labor, which viewed the Soviet Union as a godless, totalitarian society bent on exporting "Communist revolution" throughout the world. But Roosevelt believed that the United States could no longer afford to ignore the world's largest nation.

The move did not pay quick dividends to either side. Trade with the Soviet Union remained low. The Russians also ignored their promise not to spread "Communist propaganda" in the United States, and then refused to pay their $150 million war debt to

Washington. Yet for all of these problems, a major hurdle was cleared. Relations between the United States and the Soviet Union would slowly improve in the 1930s and early 1940s, as ominous world events drew them closer together.

The Good Neighbor

The Roosevelt administration showed a growing interest in Latin America, where U.S. companies had billions of dollars invested in the production of coffee and sugar and in raw materials such as copper and oil. Along with efforts to increase trade in this region, the United States extended the Good Neighbor Policy by affirming at the 1933 Pan-American Conference in Uruguay that no nation "has the right to intervene in the internal or external affairs of another." Shortly thereafter, the Roosevelt administration recalled several hundred U.S. Marines stationed in Haiti and signed a treaty with Panama recognizing the responsibility of both nations to operate and defend the Panama Canal.

There were exceptions, however. In 1934 the State Department used its considerable leverage to help bring an "acceptable" government to power in Cuba that was more sympathetic to North American business interests. With a friendly new regime in place, led by Sergeant Fulgencio Batista, the United States agreed to renounce direct intervention under the Platt Amendment in return for permission to keep its huge naval base at Guantánamo Bay.

The Good Neighbor Policy faced its sternest test even closer to home. In 1934 President Lázaro Cárdenas of Mexico began a national recovery program much like FDR's New Deal. Pledging "Mexico for the Mexicans," Cárdenas attempted to nationalize the agricultural and mining properties of all foreign corporations. Though Cárdenas promised "fair compensation" for these holdings, American and British companies demanded more than the Mexicans were willing to pay. Over the objections of many businessmen, the Roosevelt administration convinced Mexico to pay $40 million in compensation for foreign-owned lands it had seized, and another $29 million for the oil fields.

Roosevelt's caution was understandable. The president realized that better relations with Latin America required a new approach. Roosevelt's policy was also tied to larger world events. With fascism rising in Europe and Asia, the need for inter-American cooperation was essential.

Critics: Right and Left

By 1934 the Depression seemed to be easing. Though enormous problems remained, there was less talk about the dangers of economic collapse. The New Deal had injected a dose of hope and confidence into the body politic. Yet, as things got better, people inevitably wanted more. The spirit of unity began to dissolve.

The American Liberty League and the 1934 Election

The first rumblings came from the political right. In the summer of 1934, a group of conservative business leaders formed the American Liberty League to combat the alleged "radicalism" of the New Deal. They believed that Roosevelt was taking the country down "a foreign path" by attacking free enterprise, favoring workers over employers, and increasing the power of the federal government.

The league generously supported Roosevelt's political opponents in the 1934 congressional elections, but the results served only to reinforce the president's enormous popularity, or so it appeared. Instead of losing ground, the Democrats picked up nine seats in the Senate and nine in the House. Few pundits could recall a more lopsided election. As publisher William Allen White put it, Roosevelt had been "all but crowned by the people."

In reality, the election results were a mixed blessing for the Democrats. Most Americans approved of the New Deal. Their main criticism was that it had not gone far—or fast—enough to end the Depression. In Minnesota, for example, Governor Floyd Olsen was reelected on an independent "Farmer-Labor" ticket that advocated the state ownership

Huey P. Long Condemns FDR and the New Deal

During his first term in office, President Roosevelt was criticized by the political right for expanding the role of government to help end the Great Depression, and by the political left for not expanding that role even further. Among FDR's most vocal critics was Senator Huey P. Long of Louisiana, a self-styled "populist" with presidential aspirations. Shortly before his assassination, the flamboyant Long accused Roosevelt of reneging on earlier promises to help the poor, the hungry, and the unemployed.

I was the first man to say publicly—but Mr. Roosevelt followed in my tracks a few months later and said the same thing. We said that all of our trouble and woe was due to the fact that too few of our people owned too much of our wealth. We said that in our land, with too much to eat, and too much to wear, and too many houses to live in, too many automobiles to be sold, that the only trouble was that the people suffered in the land of abundance because too few controlled the money and the wealth and too many did not have money with which to buy the things they needed for life and comfort.

So I said to the people of the United States in my speeches which I delivered in the United States Senate in the early part of 1932 that the only way by which we could restore our people to reasonable life and comfort was to limit the size of the big man's fortune and guarantee some minimum to the fortune and comfort of the little man's family.

. . . So we convinced Mr. Franklin Delano Roosevelt that it was necessary that he announce and promise to the American people that in the event he were elected President of the United States he would pull down the size of the big man's fortune and guarantee something to every family—enough to do away with all poverty and to give employment to those who were able to work and education to the children born into the world.

Mr. Roosevelt made those promises; he made them before he was nominated in the Chicago convention. He made them again before he was elected in November, and he went so far as to remake those promises after he was inaugurated President of the United States. And I thought for a day or two after he took the oath as President, that maybe he was going through with his promises. No heart was ever so saddened; no person's ambition was ever so blighted, as was mine when I came to the realization that the President of the United States was not going to undertake what he had said he would do, and what I knew to be necessary if the people of America were ever [to be] saved from calamity and misery.

Questions to Consider

1. What made Huey Long's message so appealing to millions of Americans?

2. Was there truth to his criticism?

3. What impact did Long have on Roosevelt and his future New Deal agenda?

Explore additional primary sources related to this chapter on the *American Passages* Web site: http://history.wadsworth.com/ayersbrief02.

Source: *New York Times,* January 26, 1936.

---

of utilities and railroads. In neighboring Wisconsin, the sons of "Fighting Bob" La Follette formed a new Progressive party that endorsed the idea of a welfare state. And in California, Upton Sinclair, author of *The Jungle,* ran for governor on a program called EPIC (End Poverty in California), which promised to hand over idle factories and farmland to the poor and unemployed. Sinclair received almost nine hundred thousand votes in a bitter, losing effort—a sign of things to come.

"Every Man a King"

The most serious challenge to Roosevelt's leadership was offered by Louisiana's **Huey P. Long.** Known as the "Kingfish," Long combined a gift for showmanship with ruthless ambition. On the campaign trail he wore a white linen suit, orchid shirt, pink necktie, straw hat, and two-toned shoes. A superb orator and a master storyteller, he understood the

Huey P. Long

A Populist but dictatorial governor of Louisiana (1928–1932), he instituted major public works legislation, and as a U.S. senator (1932–1935), he proposed a national "Share-the-Wealth" program.

value of the spoken word in a state where few people owned radios, read newspapers, or traveled far from home.

As governor of Louisiana, Long pushed his unique brand of southern Populism. By revising the tax codes to make corporations and wealthy citizens pay more, he was able to construct new hospitals, bring paved roads and bridges to rural areas, and give free textbooks to the poor. At the same time, he built a political machine of almost totalitarian proportions. When Long vacated the governor's chair to enter the U.S. Senate in 1932, he controlled the legislature, the courts, and the civil service system of Louisiana.

"I came to the United States Senate," Long wrote, "to spread the wealth of the land among all of the people." As a Democrat, he campaigned hard for Roosevelt in 1932 and supported much of the early New Deal. But as time passed, he grew restless with the slow pace of reform. In 1934 Long proposed his own agenda for economic recovery.

Under Long's plan, no one would be allowed to earn more than $1.8 million per year or to keep a personal fortune in excess of $5 million. After confiscating this surplus, the government would provide each family with a house, a car, a radio, and an annual income of at least $2,500. Veterans would get their bonus, the elderly would receive pensions, and deserving students could attend college free of charge.

Most economists were appalled. They knew that there weren't nearly enough millionaires around to finance Long's proposal. According to one study, the government would have had to confiscate all yearly incomes above $3,000—not $1.8 million—to provide each family with $2,500. Yet by 1935 Long's "Share Our Wealth Society" claimed eight million members nationwide. It lured in people by promising them what the New Deal could not possibly deliver. At local meetings across the nation, his followers sang:

Every man a king, every man a king
For you can be a millionaire
But there's something belongs to others
There's enough for all to share.

The Radio Priest and the Pension Doctor

Long did not lack for competitors. In Royal Oak, Michigan, a working-class suburb of Detroit, Father Charles Edward Coughlin was busy leading a protest movement of his own. As the pastor of a small Catholic Church called the Shrine of the Little Flower, Coughlin became a towering figure in the 1930s by mixing prayer with politics.

Coughlin could be heard every Sunday on seventeen CBS radio outlets nationwide. An early Roosevelt supporter, he compared the New Deal to "Christ's Deal." Like Senator Long, Coughlin deplored the fact that too much wealth was concentrated in too few hands. Unlike Long, however, he blamed this evil on a tight money supply controlled by international bankers.

Coughlin believed that "free silver" would solve this problem and bring prosperity to all. His attacks on British bankers won him strong support in the Irish-Catholic community, and his call for monetary reform appealed to debt-ridden farmers and merchants in America's small towns. Before long, Coughlin's radio show, *Golden Hour of the Little Flower,* had more listeners than *Amos 'n' Andy* and *Gracie Allen.* He needed 150 clerks and four personal secretaries to handle the thousands of letters and donations that poured into his office. Some of this money was used to construct a new church of granite and marble, seven stories high, bathed in floodlights, with a huge Christ figure on top.

By 1934 the "Radio Priest" was souring on the New Deal. Angered by Roosevelt's disinterest in his "silver solution," he formed the National Union for Social Justice to challenge the president's leadership. "I glory in the fact that I am a simple Catholic priest," Coughlin declared, "endeavoring to inject Christianity into the fabric of an economic system woven upon the loom of the greedy."

A third protest movement, led by Francis E. Townsend, a retired physician living in California, offered yet another solution to the ills of the 1930s. Townsend had no desire to punish the rich, alter the money supply, or challenge the capitalist order. What disturbed him was the sight of elderly men and women sifting through garbage cans for food. In 1934 Townsend proposed a measure to revive the economy by meeting the specific needs of older Americans. It guaranteed a pension of $200 per month to those over sixty who promised to stay out of the job market and to spend the $200 by month's end. The pensions would be funded by a 2 percent sales tax on all "business transactions."

What Townsend didn't say was that his plan, known as Old Age Revolving Pensions Limited, was impossibly expensive. By most estimates, Townsend needed a sales tax approaching 70 percent to properly fund his proposal. When asked about this at a congressional hearing, the doctor replied: "I'm not in the least interested in the cost of the plan."

Neither were his followers. By 1935 more than ten million Americans had signed petitions supporting Townsend's idea, and public opinion polls showed strong support for a government-sponsored pension plan. Townsend had unleashed a powerful new interest group, the elderly, and American politics would never be the same.

The Second New Deal

The American Liberty League, the victories of Floyd Olsen and the La Follette brothers, the rumblings of Long, Coughlin, and Townsend— all raised nagging problems for Franklin Roosevelt and the New Deal. Though national income in 1935 was a full 25 percent above the 1933 level, millions were still living on handouts. In the spring of 1935, Roosevelt presented Congress with a "must" list of reforms, the so-called second New Deal. He requested—and received—$4.8 billion in work relief for the unemployed. After allocating generous shares to his favorite projects, such as the CCC, Roosevelt established yet another agency, the Works Progress Administration (WPA), with Hopkins in charge, to create "jobs, jobs, jobs!"

In that task, it was very successful. At its height in 1936, the WPA employed 25 percent of the nation's entire workforce. Many of these jobs, however, were low paying and temporary. Concentrating on small construction projects, the WPA built schools and playgrounds, repaired countless bridges and landing fields, and improved six hundred fifty thousand miles of roads. Its National Youth Administration provided part-time work to several million high school and college students.

The WPA also took advantage of the talents of jobless professionals. Under the WPA, the Federal Theater Project performed everything from Shakespeare to puppet shows for audiences that rarely, if ever, had

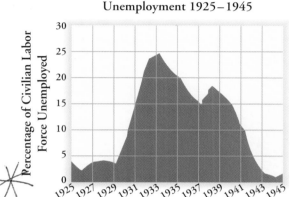

Unemployment 1925–1945

CHART 25.1 Unemployment 1925–1945

This chart shows the two great peaks of unemployment—the first in 1933 as FDR took office; the second (and smaller one) during the recession of 1938 when federal spending was reduced. The chart also shows the enormous impact of World War II in bringing unemployment—and the Great Depression itself—to an end.

WPA Mural; Coit Tower, San Francisco

Among the most controversial parts of FDR's New Deal was "Federal One," an experiment to provide government funding for the arts. Established under the huge Works Progress Administration, Federal One aimed to employ out-of-work professionals to help bring "culture" to the masses. It produced museum exhibits, murals for public buildings (like the one pictured here in San Francisco's Coit Tower), and painting classes for the poor.

seen a live show. The Federal Art Project produced museum exhibits, murals for public buildings, and painting classes for the poor. The Federal Writers Project published historical guidebooks for each state and collected oral histories of the "inarticulate," including three thousand former slaves. Playwright Arthur Miller worked for the WPA, as did actor Burt Lancaster, artists Jackson Pollock and Ben Shawn, and authors Saul Bellow, John Cheever, and Richard Wright.

Social Security

The president's "must" list included a social welfare plan that challenged the cherished concepts of voluntarism and individual responsibility. At the urging of Labor Secretary Frances Perkins, the nation's first woman cabinet member, Roosevelt proposed legislation (passed as the Social Security Act of 1935) to create a national pension fund, an unemployment insurance system, and public assistance programs for dependent mothers and children, the physically disabled, and those in chronic need. The pension was financed by a payroll tax to begin in 1937. Benefits were purposely modest—about $20 to $30 per month—because Roosevelt did not intend "Social Security" to be the main source of personal retirement income, as it has become for many people today.

The act had numerous defects. It excluded millions of vulnerable wage earners such as domestics, farm workers, and the self-employed. It taxed all participants at a fixed rate, forcing those with the lowest incomes to pay a far greater share of their wages into the system. Over time, the Social Security fund emerged as the country's most important and expensive domestic program.

"Class Warfare"

John L. Lewis
A labor leader who was president of the United Mine Workers of America (1920–1960) and the Congress of Industrial Organizations (1935–1940).

Roosevelt had never been a strong supporter of organized labor. He wanted to help workers through his own social programs rather than have them organize unions to help themselves. He felt uneasy about the tactics of labor leaders such as **John L. Lewis,** head of the United Mine Workers, who had tripled his membership with an aggressive organizing campaign that declared, "The president wants you to join a union!" Roosevelt worried that labor's militant new spirit would accelerate the violent confrontations of 1934, when pitched battles erupted between striking workers and police on the streets of Minneapolis, San Francisco, and Detroit.

In the wake of these disturbances, Senator Robert Wagner of New York authored a bill to protect the rights of workers to organize and bargain collectively. His legislation filled a dramatic void because the Supreme Court had just declared parts of the NIRA—including Section 7(a)—to be unconstitutional. Passed in 1935, the National Labor Relations (Wagner) Act prohibited employers from engaging in a wide range of "unfair labor practices," such as spying on their workers. The law also created the National Labor Relations Board (NLRB) to supervise union elections.

The Wagner Act revealed deep divisions within the union movement. At the American Federation of Labor's annual convention in 1935, John L. Lewis pleaded with fellow leaders to begin serious membership drives in the steel mills, automobile plants, and rubber factories. Lewis wanted these mass production workers to be organized by industry rather than by craft. Only then, he argued, could the power of big business be successfully confronted.

Most AFL leaders were unmoved. As representatives of skilled craftsmen, such as masons and carpenters, they had little interest in organizing industrial unions composed largely of African Americans and ethnic groups from Eastern and Southern Europe. Indeed, after Lewis finished his emotional plea to the AFL convention, Carpenters' President "Big Bill" Hutcheson called him a "bastard." Lewis floored Hutcheson with a solid right to the jaw and stormed out of the convention.

In November 1935 Lewis formed the Committee for Industrial Organization (CIO)—later the Congress of Industrial Organizations—to charter new unions in the mass production industries. He was joined by a handful of AFL leaders from the needle trades, including Sidney Hillman of the Amalgamated Clothing Workers and David Dubinsky of the International Ladies' Garment Workers. Although the AFL suspended these men and their unions for "fomenting insurrection," Lewis never looked back. His attention had turned to the CIO's organizing drives in the auto and steel industries. Labor's "civil war" had begun.

The Fascist Challenge

As the 1936 presidential election approached, Americans watched events in Europe with growing apprehension. From the Soviet Union came stories about a regime that was brutalizing its people in an attempt to "collectivize" the society and stamp out internal dissent. In Germany and Italy powerful dictators emerged, preaching race hatred and vowing to expand their nations' borders.

Hitler and Mussolini

Adolf Hitler became the German chancellor in January 1933. Born in Austria in 1889, Hitler had moved to Bavaria as a young man and fought in the German Army during World War I. Wounded and jobless, he helped form the National Socialist (Nazi) party, one of the many extremist groups that thrived in the economic chaos of war-battered Germany. In 1923 Hitler was arrested in Munich for staging an unsuccessful coup against the Weimar government. From his prison cell, he wrote *Mein Kampf* ("My Struggle"), a rambling account of his racial theories, his plans for Germany, and his hatred of Jews.

As the Weimar government collapsed in the Depression, the Nazis gained strength. Millions welcomed their promise to create jobs, restore German glory, and avenge the "humiliation" of Versailles. Nazi representation in the Reichstag (parliament) rose from 12 in 1928 to 230 by 1932. A year later, Hitler became chancellor of Germany. The results were alarming. Constitutional rights were suspended, and competing political parties were banned. Nazi supporters drove Jews from universities, boycotted their businesses, and attacked them in the streets. "Hitler is a madman," President Roosevelt told a French diplomat.

Under the Nazis, the state increased its control over industry. This allowed Hitler to begin a massive rearmament program, which produced badly needed jobs. By 1934 German factories were producing tanks and military aircraft. A year later Hitler proposed a five-hundred-thousand-man army and instituted the draft. In 1936 Nazi forces marched into the Rhineland—a clear violation of the Versailles Treaty—and reoccupied it without firing a shot.

Hitler had modeled himself, to some degree, after Italian dictator Benito Mussolini. Born in 1883, Mussolini had served in the Italian Army during World War I. Playing upon the social unrest of the postwar era, he seized national power in 1922 and proclaimed Fascismo, or fascism. As the supreme leader, or Duce, he preached national unity and state management of Italy's industrial base. Like Hitler, he destroyed labor unions, censored the press, abolished all political parties but his own, and relied on a secret police force to maintain order and silence his critics.

In 1935 Italian forces invaded Ethiopia from their neighboring colonies of Eritrea and Somaliland. The fighting in Ethiopia was brutal and one-sided, pitting Italian tanks and machine guns against local defenders armed with little more than spears and bows and arrows. At the League of Nations, Ethiopian Emperor Haile Selassie pleaded for support. The league responded by branding Italy the aggressor but sending no military help. After annexing Ethiopia in 1936, Mussolini signed a pact of friendship with Hitler, known as the Rome-Berlin Axis.

The Neutrality Acts

Americans were determined that American blood must not be shed again on foreign soil. There was only one way to avoid another war, most people believed, and that was to remain truly neutral in world affairs.

Although this sentiment had deep historical roots, the key to understanding America's anxiety in the early 1930s was the legacy of World War I—the belief that America had been lured into the conflict, against its vital interests, by a conspiracy of evil men. In 1934 the U.S. Senate set up a committee, chaired by isolationist Gerald P. Nye of North Dakota, to investigate the reasons for America's involvement in World War I. The Nye Committee highlighted a series of well-known facts. Large banks and corporations had made huge profits during World War I. It followed, therefore, that the United States had been led into this conflict by greedy bankers and businessmen determined to protect their investments. This explanation ignored the rather tangled reality of American intervention—from submarine warfare to the Zimmermann Telegram, from President Wilson's rigid morality to the defense of neutral rights. Yet the Nye Committee findings enjoyed wide popular support in a nation determined to avoid another war.

The isolationist impulse was particularly strong in the Great Plains and Upper Midwest. It attracted many Americans of German descent, who remembered their brutal treatment during World War I; those of Irish descent who opposed aid to Great Britain in any form; and those of Italian descent who viewed Mussolini as a hero in these years. Isolationism—in some cases combined with pacifism—also appealed to ministers, peace groups, and college students.

Congress responded to this public mood with legislation designed to avoid the "entanglements" that had led to American participation in World War I. The first Neutrality Act, passed after the Ethiopian invasion of 1935, empowered the president to determine when a state of war existed anywhere in the world. In that event, the president would declare an embargo on all combatants. American arms shipments would cease, and American citizens would be warned against traveling on the vessels of belligerents. In February 1936 Congress passed a second Neutrality Act, prohibiting American banks from extending loans or credit to any nation at war.

President Roosevelt did not like these bills. He believed that absolute neutrality favored powerful aggressor nations by forcing the United States to treat all sides equally. Yet FDR signed them into law for political reasons. He knew that a veto would give strong ammunition to the Republicans in the coming presidential campaign.

Mandate from the People

As the 1936 election approached, FDR had reason for concern. Although personal income and industrial production had risen dramatically since he took office, millions of Americans were still unemployed, labor violence was spreading, and the federal deficit continued to climb. In addition, more than 80 percent of the nation's newspapers, and most of the business community, remained loyal to the Republican party, meaning that Roosevelt's major presidential opponent could count on strong editorial and financial support.

The 1936 Election

In June the Republicans gathered in Cleveland to nominate their presidential ticket. Herbert Hoover received a thunderous ovation, but the convention delegates chose Kansas Governor Alfred M. Landon to head the Republican ticket and Frank Knox, a Chicago publisher, to be the vice presidential nominee.

Landon, a political moderate, promised "fewer radio talks, fewer experiments, and a lot more common sense." His problem was that he radiated little of the compassion and confidence that made Roosevelt so popular with the masses. Worse, Landon's bland pronouncements were overshadowed by the broadsides of more conservative Republican leaders, who denounced the New Deal as a radical plot to subvert free enterprise and individual rights.

Roosevelt also faced presidential challenges from the left. Both the Communists and the Socialists ran spirited campaigns in 1936, demanding more federal aid for the poor. But Roosevelt's most serious concern—a political merger involving Coughlin, Townsend, and Long—was effectively eliminated in September 1935 when an assassin's bullet killed the Louisiana senator in Baton Rouge. To replace the charismatic Long, these dissident forces nominated William "Liberty Bill" Lemke, an obscure North Dakota congressman, to be their presidential candidate on the new Union party ticket.

Roosevelt's political strategy differed markedly from 1932. In that campaign, he had stressed the common hopes and needs that bound people together; in 1936 he emphasized the class differences that separated those who supported the New Deal from those who opposed it. Time and again Roosevelt portrayed the election as a contest between common people and privileged people. In his final campaign speech at New York's Madison Square Garden, he declared that the "forces of selfishness" had "met their match" in the Roosevelt administration. "They are unanimous in their hatred of me," the president thundered, "and I welcome their hatred."

On November 3 FDR crushed Landon and Lemke in the most one-sided election since 1820. The final totals showed Roosevelt with 27,752,869 popular votes, Landon with 16,6674,665, and Lemke with 882,479. The Democratic party also added to its huge majorities in both houses of Congress.

African Americans and the New Deal

Roosevelt's landslide victory signaled a dramatic shift in American politics. A new majority coalition had emerged. In the farm belt, Roosevelt won over long-time Republicans with federal subsidies and price supports. In the cities, he attracted workers grateful for welfare benefits and WPA jobs. And he appealed to ethnic minorities by filling so many government posts with Catholics and Jews.

Adding to Roosevelt's strength was the support he received from the CIO. Describing Roosevelt as "the worker's best friend," CIO leaders campaigned tirelessly for him in key industrial states, and the effort paid off. Roosevelt captured the working-class vote in 1936 by a margin of 4 to 1.

The most striking political change, however, occurred within the nation's African American community. The steady migration of African Americans to northern cities, where they could vote, increased their political power. Historically, most blacks supported the Republican party, but with the New Deal a massive switch took place. In large part, African Americans became Democrats because the Roosevelt administration provided jobs and welfare benefits to all Americans, regardless of race. This federal assistance was especially welcome in black communities.

By 1933 black unemployment had reached a staggering 50 percent. Fortunately, the two New Deal administrators most responsible for creating jobs were sympathetic to minority needs. At the PWA, Harold Ickes insisted that blacks receive equal pay and minimum quotas on all construction projects. The PWA provided thousands of jobs for African Americans. At the WPA, Harry Hopkins set the same standards. Blacks received a generous share of WPA work in northern cities—a testimony to both their joblessness and political clout.

Many blacks viewed the New Deal as a progressive social force. They welcomed an administration that showed some interest in their struggle. And they particularly admired the efforts of First Lady **Eleanor Roosevelt,** who served as the White House conscience on matters pertaining to minority rights.

Mrs. Roosevelt had a passion for public service and a deep commitment to the poor. Her interest in civil rights had been fueled, in large measure, by her friendship with prominent African Americans such as **Mary McLeod Bethune,** founder of Bethune-Cookman College in Florida. Born in a sharecropper's shack, the fifteenth child of former slaves, Mrs. Bethune had acquainted the First Lady with the special problems facing African Americans. In 1936 Eleanor Roosevelt recommended Mrs. Bethune to head the National Youth Administration's Office of Negro Affairs.

As the New Deal's highest-ranking black appointee, Mrs. Bethune presided over the administration's "black cabinet," which advised the White House on minority issues. She helped to encourage—and monitor—the New Deal's racial progress. Much of it was symbolic. In an age of rigid segregation, Mrs. Roosevelt visited black colleges, spoke at black conferences, and socialized with black women. When the Daughters of the American Revolution refused to allow **Marian Anderson,** a gifted black contralto, to perform at Washington's Constitution Hall, Mrs. Roosevelt resigned from the organization. A few months later, Harold Ickes arranged for Miss

Eleanor Roosevelt
A diplomat, writer, and First Lady of the United States (1933–1945) as the wife of President Franklin D. Roosevelt. A delegate to the United Nations (1945–1953 and 1961–1962), she was an outspoken advocate for human rights. Her written works include *This I Remember* (1949).

Mary McLeod Bethune
An educator who sought improved racial relations and educational opportunities for black Americans, she was part of the U.S. delegation to the first United Nations meeting (1945).

Marian Anderson
An opera singer and human rights advocate, she performed on the steps of the Lincoln Memorial before a crowd of seventy-five thousand after being denied the use of Constitution Hall by the Daughters of the American Revolution. She helped focus national attention on the racial prejudice faced by African Americans in all facets of national life.

©Bettmann/CORBIS

Marian Anderson entertained a crowd of seventy-five thousand at the Lincoln Memorial on Easter Sunday 1939 after the Daughters of the American Revolution refused to allow her to perform at Washington's Constitution Hall.

Anderson to sing at the Lincoln Memorial on Easter Sunday 1939. An integrated audience of seventy-five thousand gathered to hear her.

Yet the good work of Eleanor Roosevelt and others could not mask larger New Deal failures in the field of civil rights. Throughout his presidency, for example, Franklin Roosevelt made no effort to break down segregation barriers or to enable blacks to vote. And he remained on the sidelines as federal antilynching bills were narrowly defeated in Congress. Roosevelt explained that he could not support civil rights legislation without alienating southern Democrats who controlled the most important committees in Congress. "They will block every bill I [need] to keep America from collapsing," Roosevelt said. "I just can't take that risk."

The president's position did not prevent blacks from supporting him in 1936. Roosevelt received 76 percent of their votes. On balance, African Americans viewed the New Deal as a clear improvement over the Republican past.

Popular Culture in the Depression

The economic struggles of the 1930s shaped not only the politics of American life but the culture as well. Hard times encouraged federal participation in the arts and triggered a leftward tilt among many intellectuals and writers. A flurry of "proletarian literature" emerged in the early Depression years, emphasizing the "class struggle" through stories about heroic workers resisting the exploitation of evil employers. Several important black writers—including Ralph Ellison, Richard Wright, and Langston Hughes—identified with the Communist party because it appeared to actively support civil rights. For most intellectuals, however, the fascination with Communism was fleeting. As free thinkers, they could not adjust to the party's rigid conformity.

The Depression era also witnessed the spread of a popular culture born in the preceding decades. Photojournalism came of age in the 1930s with the publication of magazines such as *Life* and *Look*. In the comics trade, "Superman" (1938) demonstrated that Americans were anxious to get beyond the tame characters from the newspaper strips. In popular music, the "swing era" brought the jazz of African American artists to a much broader public. In radio and in movies, the changes were most dramatic and profound.

The Big Screen

By the 1930s the motion picture was the leading form of popular culture in the United States. Theater owners attracted customers by offering inducements such as the "double feature," which dramatically increased the number of films produced during this decade. In the larger cities, movie theaters were transformed into fantasy palaces, with thick carpets, winding staircases, ushers in tuxedoes, and the twinkling lights of chandeliers. For millions, the theater became a temporary escape from the bleak realities of the Depression.

Hollywood mirrored the changing attitudes of the 1930s. It was no accident that the most popular movie of 1932 was Mervyn LeRoy's *I Am a Fugitive from a Chain Gang*, the story of a decent man, unjustly convicted of a crime, who escapes from a brutal southern penal farm. In the final scene, the hero meets his former girlfriend, who asks him how he survives. From the shadows of a dark alley—representing the Depression itself—he whispers, "I steal."

Other early films from this decade, such as *Little Caesar* (1930) and *Public Enemy* (1931), focused on big city mobsters who ruthlessly shot their way to the top. Although these "bad guys" were either killed or brought to justice on screen, the public's fascination with criminal activity reached a peak in these years with the romanticizing of bank robbers John Dillinger, Bonnie Parker and Clyde Barrow, Baby Face Nelson, and Ma Barker. All died in shootouts with local police or the FBI.

The evolving optimism of the 1930s was also apparent in Hollywood films. *Gold Diggers of 1933* was the first of several musical extravaganzas mixing escapism with hope. The 1930s saw Fred Astaire whirling Ginger Rogers across the nightclub dance floor; Mickey Rooney courting Judy Garland in the blissfully innocent "Andy Hardy" movies; and Walt Disney raising the animated cartoon to an art form in his feature film *Snow White and the Seven Dwarfs* (1937). Wildly popular in this decade (and beyond) were the Marx brothers—Groucho, Harpo, and Chico—whose classic comedies demolished upper-class snobbery, foolish tradition, and much of the English language.

More significant were the moral dramas of director Frank Capra, including *Mr. Deeds Goes to Town* (1936), starring Gary Cooper, and *Mr. Smith Goes to Washington* (1939), with Jimmy Stewart. Both the movies and the leading men represented the inherent virtues of heartland America, with its strong sense of decency and cooperation. Common people could be fooled by greedy bankers and selfish politicians, but not for long. Life got better when "good folks" followed their instincts.

The most memorable films of this era, *Gone with the Wind* and **The Grapes of Wrath,** showcased Hollywood's ability to transform best-selling fiction into successful movies. Both films related the epic struggle of families in crisis, trying desperately to survive. *The Grapes of Wrath,* set in the Depression, depicts the awful conditions faced by the Dust Bowl farmers who migrated to California. True to the 1930s, it is a story of marginal people confronting economic injustice. The hero, Tom Joad, promises his Ma that "wherever they's a fight so hungry people can eat, I'll be there." Ma Joad is a source of strength and common sense. "They ain't gonna wipe us out," she insists. "Why, we're the people—we go on."

The Grapes of Wrath
Written by John Steinbeck and published in 1939, this novel depicts the struggle of ordinary Americans in the Great Depression, following the plight of the Joad family as it migrated west from Oklahoma to California.

The Radio Age

Like the movie boom, the rapid growth of radio in the Depression encouraged the spread of popular culture. Politicians and public figures such as President Roosevelt and Father Coughlin used radio to great effect. So, too, did companies seeking to mass market their products. Organized along commercial lines in the 1920s, radio continued firmly down that path in the 1930s, with two giant firms—the National Broadcasting Company (NBC) and the Columbia Broadcasting System (CBS)—dominating the nation's airwaves.

In an odd way, the economic turmoil of the 1930s aided radio by weakening other forms of entertainment. As vaudeville failed, popular performers continued their careers on the radio. For morning and afternoon fare, the networks relied on domestic dramas such as *Ma Perkins* and *Helen Trent.* Often sponsored by soap and beauty companies, these "soap operas" doled out the story line in daily fifteen-minute installments. In the evenings, the entertainment broadened to include quiz shows, talent contests, and adventure programs. Surveys showed that the average American in the 1930s listened to more than four hours of radio each day.

Radio carried sporting events, political conventions, and the news. Millions followed the 1936 Berlin Olympics, where Jesse Owens, the African American track star, embarrassed Adolf Hitler by winning four gold medals. Two years later, the heavyweight title fight from Yankee Stadium between Joe Louis, the black champion, and Max Schmeling, the German challenger, was broadcast throughout the world. When Louis knocked out Schmeling in the first round, Americans celebrated in the streets.

Perhaps nothing better demonstrated the power of radio than the infamous "War of the Worlds" episode. On Halloween evening, 1938, actor Orson Welles did a powerful reading of the H. G. Wells novel, presenting it as a simulated newscast in which violent aliens from Mars land in the New Jersey town of Grovers Mills. "I can see the thing's body," sobbed a "roving reporter" at the scene. "It's large as a bear and it glistens like wet leather. That face . . . the black eyes and saliva dripping from its rimless lips." Although Welles repeatedly interrupted the program to explain what he was doing, a national panic ensued. Thousands fled their homes, believing that the Martians were advancing toward New York City. Traffic came to a halt in parts of the Northeast; bus and train stations were jammed; churches overflowed with weeping families. Newspaper headlines screamed: "Radio War Terrorizes U.S." and "Panic Grips Nation As Radio Announces 'Mars Attacks World.'" When the furor died down, President Roosevelt invited Welles to the White House. "You know, Orson," he joked, "you and I are the two best actors in America."

The Second Term

In his second inaugural address, FDR emphasized the New Deal's unfinished business. "I see one-third of a nation ill-housed, ill-clad, ill-nourished," he declared. The president was optimistic. The election had provided him with a stunning popular mandate and with huge Democratic majorities on Capitol Hill. To Roosevelt's thinking, only one roadblock lay in his path: the Supreme Court.

Challenging the Supreme Court's Power

The Supreme Court was dominated by elderly, conservative justices who despised the New Deal and worked zealously to subvert its legislation. In Roosevelt's first term, the Court had struck down the NRA, the AAA, and a series of social welfare laws. In the coming months, it would be reviewing—and likely overturning—the National Labor Relations Act and the Social Security Act.

Roosevelt struck first. In February 1937 he unveiled sweeping legislation to reorganize the federal court system. Under his plan, fifty new judgeships would be created by adding one judge for each sitting justice over the age of seventy who refused to retire. The Supreme Court would get a maximum of six new members, raising its total to fifteen.

The plan was legal. The Constitution sets no limits on the size of the Supreme Court; indeed, the number of justices, determined by Congress, had fluctuated between six and ten in the previous century. Roosevelt assumed that his overwhelming reelection in 1936 had given him the green light to crush all opposition to the New Deal, regardless of the source.

He was badly mistaken. His plan met quick and furious opposition. Many Americans were offended by Roosevelt's jab at the elderly. Others worried that his "Court-packing" plan would undermine judicial independence and threaten the balance of power among the three branches of government. As the opposition grew stronger, aides urged Roosevelt to withdraw the bill.

In the spring of 1937 the Supreme Court changed course. By votes of 5 to 4, with one moderate justice switching sides, it upheld both the Wagner Act and the Social Security Act. Then, one by one, the old conservatives decided to retire. This allowed Roosevelt to fill five vacancies in the next three years. The justices he chose—including Hugo Black, Felix Frankfurter, and William O. Douglas—would steer a more liberal course for decades to come.

Nevertheless, the Court battle wounded Roosevelt in significant ways. By refusing to withdraw his legislation, he subjected fellow Democrats to a bitter Senate debate—and to eventual defeat. The Court-packing incident also emboldened Roosevelt's opponents by proving that the president could be beaten.

Union Struggles

Away from Washington, new battles raged in the automobile plants of Michigan, the textile mills of North Carolina, and the coal fields of Kentucky as industrial workers demanded union recognition. In perhaps the most spectacular episode, autoworkers at a General Motors plant in Flint, Michigan, went on strike inside the factory, refusing to leave. Their spontaneous technique, known as the "sit-down," spread quickly to other sites. Though Roosevelt privately criticized these strikers for violating property rights, he declined to send in troops. In February 1937 GM recognized the CIO's United Automobile Workers (UAW) as the bargaining agent for its employees.

The victory at GM forced other employers into line. Firestone signed a contract with the CIO's Rubber Workers, General Electric and RCA with the Electrical Workers. Even U.S. Steel, an old enemy of organized labor, agreed to generous terms with the Steelworkers—union recognition, a forty-hour week, and a 10 percent wage increase.

There were some holdouts, however. Henry Ford hired an army of thugs to rough up union organizers and disrupt strikers on the picket lines. Republic Steel of Chicago stockpiled more weapons than the city police department. "I won't have a contract with an irresponsible, racketeering, violent communistic body like the CIO," fumed Republic President Tom C. Girdler. The worst violence occurred outside Republic's South Chicago mill on Memorial Day 1937. There heavily armed police battled rock-throwing strikers on the picket line. Before it ended, ten workers had been killed by gunfire, and dozens more had been injured.

In the following months, Ford and Republic Steel came to terms. Under pressure from the National Labor Relations Board, they gradually accepted industrial unionism as a legitimate force in American life. With a membership approaching three million, the CIO had come a long way since its break with the conservative, craft-oriented American Federation of Labor a few years before.

Losing Ground

The Court battle and the sit-down strikes slowed the political momentum that followed FDR's reelection landslide in 1936. Further problems loomed in Europe, where fascism continued to gain strength, and in the United States, where a serious recession in 1937 eroded public confidence in the New Deal.

Fascist Advances

Late in 1936 civil war broke out in Spain. A group of military officers, led by General Francisco Franco, attempted to overthrow the recently elected government. Because Franco represented the Falangist, or fascist elements in Spain, he received military aid from Hitler and Mussolini. On the other side, Joseph Stalin aided the government (or "loyalist") forces, which contained a large Socialist and Communist contingent. The war itself was brutal. Before it ended, more than six hundred thousand people were killed.

The Spanish Civil War triggered strong emotions in the United States. Some Americans praised Franco as a bastion against Communism; others condemned him as a fascist thug. Several thousand Americans went to Spain as part of the Abraham Lincoln Brigade, organized by the Communist party, to fight on the Loyalist side. As Ernest Hemingway said of Franco, "There is only one way to quell a bully and that is to thrash him."

Most Americans disagreed. In 1937 Congress passed a third neutrality bill that extended the arms embargo to include civil wars like the one raging in Spain. The bill also prohibited Americans from traveling on belligerent vessels. However, it did permit nations at war to purchase "nonmilitary" goods if they paid cash (no loans) and carried them away on their own ships.

The Rising Nazi Menace

In central Europe, meanwhile, Hitler marched boldly toward war. Vowing to unite all German-speaking people, he moved on Austria in 1938, adding six million "Germans" to the Third Reich. Then he demanded the Sudentenland, a region in western Czechoslovakia where three million ethnic Germans lived. The Czechs possessed both a well-trained army and a defense treaty with France. As central Europe's only remaining democracy, Czechoslovakia looked to the French and British for support against the Nazi threat.

That support never came. France had lost half of its male population between the ages of twenty and thirty-two during World War I. In Britain, Oxford students adopted a resolution in the 1930s declaring that they would not take up arms for their country under any circumstances. Antiwar feeling was so strong that a kind of diplomatic paralysis set in. The result was the Munich debacle of 1938.

At Munich, Prime Minister Neville Chamberlain of England and Premier Edouard Daladier of France agreed to Hitler's demand for the Sudetenland. In return the German leader promised not to take any more territory. Daladier then pressured the Czechs to accept this dismal bargain while Chamberlain congratulated everyone—Hitler included—for bringing "peace in our time."

The news from inside Germany was even worse. Early in 1938 the Nazis torched Munich's Great Synagogue and began the initial deportation of Jews to the infamous

In 1939 more than a thousand Jews fleeing from Germany aboard the ocean liner *St. Louis* were refused entry into the United States at the port of Miami and forced to return to Europe—and certain death.

©Bettmann/CORBIS

concentration camp at Buchenwald. On the evening of November 9—known as Kristallnacht, the "night of broken glass"—Nazi mobs burned synagogues, looted stores, and attacked Jews in cities throughout Germany. In addition, the Nazis passed new laws to confiscate Jewish property, bar Jews from meaningful employment, and deprive them of ordinary liberties such as attending school and driving a car.

When word of these events reached the United States, President Roosevelt was furious. He immediately called a conference of thirty-two nations to discuss plans for accepting desperate Jewish refugees from Germany, Austria, and Czechoslovakia. But only Holland showed a willingness to help. In the United States, a combination of anti-Semitism, isolationist sentiment, and hard times kept the "golden door" tightly shut.

The result was disastrous. At a time when many Jews had the ability to flee Hitler, there was almost no place for them to go. Between 1935 and 1941, the United States took in an average of eight thousand five hundred Jews per year. (Among those allowed to enter were "high profile" Jewish refugees such as Albert Einstein and composer Kurt Weill.) President Roosevelt refused to take additional steps against Hitler because he feared a political backlash.

An End to Reform

Until 1937 the American economy had been making steady, if uneven, progress. National income and production finally reached 1929 levels. Roosevelt now hoped to slow down government spending as the business picture improved. He wanted to balance the federal budget and cut the mounting national debt.

The president knew that national recovery had been fueled by the New Deal's farm subsidies, relief programs, and public works. He was familiar with the writings of British economist John Maynard Keynes, who advocated a policy of deficit spending in hard times to spur economic growth. Yet he feared that the growing national debt would generate inflation, and he worried about the effect of federal welfare programs upon the recipients' initiative and self-respect.

In 1937 Roosevelt slashed funding for both the PWA and WPA, cutting almost two million jobs. At the same time, the new Social Security payroll tax took effect, removing billions of dollars of purchasing power from the economy. The result was recession. As unemployment rose and production plummeted, the nation slipped back toward the nightmare of 1933.

In October Roosevelt called Congress into special session. Within weeks a $5 billion expenditure was approved for federal relief and public works. The economy responded, showing the impact of government spending once again. But the recession further weakened Roosevelt's image as a forceful leader in perilous times.

By 1938 the New Deal had clearly lost momentum. Harry Hopkins blamed it on six grinding years of Depression and reform. Facing a more combative Congress, Roosevelt decided to "tread water" for a while. Among his few legislative achievements that year was passage of the Fair Labor Standards Act, which abolished child labor in most industries and provided a minimum hourly wage (forty cents) and a maximum workweek (forty hours), to be phased in over time. Like Social Security, the act did not cover those who needed it most, such as farm workers and domestics. Yet almost a million Americans had their wages raised immediately by this law, and countless millions had their work hours shortened as well.

Summary

The New Deal in Retrospect

In responding to the enormous challenges of the Great Depression, Franklin Roosevelt's New Deal altered politics and society in fundamental ways. It forever changed the role of the federal government in American life. For the first time in our history, the government provided massive assistance to the poor and the unemployed. It stabilized the banking system, protected farmers with price supports, guaranteed the rights of organized labor, encouraged collective bargaining between workers and employers, and created a national pension plan. The New Deal also produced a more class-oriented Democratic party, appealing to industrial workers, hard-pressed farmers, and urban minorities. Under Roosevelt's leadership, a kind of broker state emerged in which diverse groups pushed their competing demands upon the federal government and received tangible rewards. Avoiding the political extremes that plagued other nations in the Depression era, Roosevelt steered a middle course between laissez faire and Socialism—a course that combined free enterprise and democracy with national planning and social reform.

During the New Deal years, the size and scope of the federal government increased dramatically. For most Americans, the question was no longer whether the federal government should forcefully intervene in their lives but rather the ways in which that intervention should occur. Facing a catastrophic depression, FDR used the presidential office, as never before in our

©Bettmann /CORBIS

Franklin Roosevelt contracted infantile paralysis, later known as polio, in 1921 at the age of thirty-nine. The disease permanently paralyzed him from the waist down. Though Americans, of course, were aware of his disability, it did not seem a part of the Roosevelt they knew. The photograph here typifies what Americans saw: FDR on his feet, leaning on a cane while grasping the arm of an aide.

Autoworkers celebrate the end of their "sit-down" strike at a General Motors plant in Flint, Michigan, in 1937.

©Bettmann /CORBIS

history, to extend needed relief, stimulate job growth, and regulate the economy. He became the first president to regularly fashion his own legislative agenda for Congress to consider, tilting the future balance of political power strongly in favor of the executive branch. At times Roosevelt badly overreached himself, as in his failed attempt to "pack" the Supreme Court in 1937. On the whole, though, he proved a remarkably popular and resourceful figure, using his ebullient personality, his courageous struggle with polio, and his understanding of the media, especially radio, to form a powerful bond with the people.

What the New Deal did best was to restore a sense of hope and purpose to a demoralized nation. Yet its overriding goal in these years—the promise of full economic recovery—remained elusive at best. Fearful of mounting budget deficits and ever-growing relief rolls, President Roosevelt never committed himself to the level of consistent federal spending urged by economists like John Maynard Keynes. When the New Deal ended in 1939, more than eight million Americans were still unemployed. It would take a world war, and the full mobilization that followed, to put them permanently back to work.

At the fateful Munich Conference in 1938, British Prime Minister Neville Chamberlain appeased Adolf Hitler's demands for territorial expansion, claiming the agreement would bring "peace in our time."

Making Connections Across Chapters

LOOKING BACK

Chapter 25 considers the impact of the Great Depression on the social, economic, and political structure of the United States. Among the key issues considered is the new relationship between the federal government and the average citizen.

1. What were the most pressing problems facing the Roosevelt administration when it came to power, and how did it address them?
2. Who were President Roosevelt's major critics, and how did they propose to deal with the Great Depression?
3. What impact did the Great Depression have on the realignment of the major political parties?
4. How did the American people view international relations in the 1930s, and what factors were responsible for the perceptions of America's role in the world?

LOOKING AHEAD

The next chapter examines the impact of World War II on American society. Following the Japanese attack on Pearl Harbor, isolationist sentiment would end, the nation would mobilize its defenses, and fifteen million men and women would serve in the armed forces against the Axis powers of Germany, Italy, and Japan.

1. What impact would the coming of World War II have on the economic problems facing Americans in the 1930s?
2. What would happen to the powerful isolationist movement of this era?
3. Given the darkening world situation, would President Roosevelt decide to break with political precedent and run for a third presidential term?

RECOMMENDED READINGS

Brinkley, Alan. *Voices of Protest: Huey Long, Father Coughlin, and the Great Depression* (1982). A revealing account of Depression era dissidents.

Cohen, Lizabeth. *Making a New Deal: Industrial Workers in Chicago* (1990). Examines working-class protest and culture during the Depression.

Cooke, Blanche Wiesen. *Eleanor Roosevelt* (1992). Follows the life of the nation's most active First Lady.

Fraser, Steve, and Gerstle, Gary, eds. *The Rise of the New Deal Order* (1989). Contains a series of original essays about the New Deal's impact on American life.

Goodman, James. *Stories of Scottsboro* (1994). Vividly recreates the most important civil rights trial of the 1930s.

Leuchtenburg, William. *The Supreme Court Reborn: The Constitutional Revolution in the Age of Roosevelt* (1995). Studies the conflicts and changes that altered the Supreme Court in the 1930s and beyond.

McElvaine, Robert S. *The Great Depression* (1984). An excellent survey of American life and politics during the New Deal era.

Terkel, Studs. *Hard Times* (1970). Views the Depression through the oral histories of those who lived through it.

Ware, Susan. *Holding Their Own: American Women in the 1930s* (1982). Explores the role of women in America's worst economic crisis.

Worster, Donald. *Dust Bowl: The Southern Plains in the 1930s* (1979). Examines the causes and the impact of this ecological disaster.

American Journey AMERICAN JOURNEY ONLINE AND INFOTRAC COLLEGE EDITION

Visit the source collections at http://ajaccess.wadsworth.com and infotrac.thomsonlearning.com and use the Search function with the following key terms to explore documents, images, audio and video clips, articles, and commentary related to the material in this chapter.

Franklin D. Roosevelt

New Deal

Civilian Conservation Corps

Tennessee Valley Authority

Dust Bowl

The Grapes of Wrath

Huey P. Long

Marian Anderson

Mary McLeod Bethune

ONLINE PRIMARY SOURCES

Here are some examples of the many primary sources related to this chapter that you will find on the *American Passages* Web site: http://history.wadsworth.com/ayersbrief02.

Roosevelt's Fireside Chat, 1933

Letters From the "Forgotten Man" to Mrs. Roosevelt, 1934

John L. Lewis on the NRA, 1934

The site also offers self-quizzes, exercises, and many additional resources to help you study.

CHAPTER 26

The Second World War

1939–1945

I N MARCH 1939 THE GERMANS MARCHED INTO CENTRAL CZECHOSLOVAKIA, MEETING no resistance at all. To the south, Franco's forces won a final victory in the Spanish Civil War, while Mussolini's army annexed neighboring Albania. Throughout the summer months, Nazi threats multiplied. "So long as Germans in Poland suffer grievously, so long as they are imprisoned away from the Fatherland," warned Hitler, "Europe can have no peace."

President Roosevelt declared neutrality. At the same time, he worked to mobilize the nation's defense effort and to shape public opinion steadily against the Axis powers. If possible, Roosevelt hoped to aid Great Britain and the Allies through "all measures short of war." If need be, however, he vowed to use military force to prevent a Nazi victory in Europe. Never in world history, Roosevelt believed, had the forces of evil been so determined.

War in Europe

In August 1939 Hitler and Stalin stunned the world by signing a "nonaggression" pact. Both dictators were buying time for an inevitable showdown between their armed forces, and both had designs on Polish territory, which they secretly divided in their agreement. On September 1, German ground troops and armored divisions stormed into Poland from the west, backed by their powerful air force (*Luftwaffe*). Two weeks later, Soviet troops attacked from the east, reclaiming the territory that Russia had lost to Poland after World War I. In the following months, Stalin moved against the Baltic states, subduing Estonia, Latvia, and Lithuania.

Blitzkrieg

Hitler's *Blitzkrieg* (lightning strike) into Poland shattered the lingering illusions of Munich. Having pledged themselves to guarantee Poland's borders, England and France reluctantly declared war on Germany. The British sent a small, ill-equipped army to defend Western Europe against further Nazi aggression. The French reinforced their "impregnable" Maginot Line facing Germany, while the Nazis fortified their Siegfried Line in the Rhineland facing France. An eerie calm settled over Europe.

That six-month calm, known as the "phony war," ended in April 1940 when the Nazis overran Denmark and Norway. In May they invaded Belgium, Holland, Luxembourg—and France itself. From the skies, the Luftwaffe strafed fleeing civilians and flattened cities. On the ground, German troops and armor swept through the Ardennes Forest, skirting the Maginot Line. Within weeks German units had reached the French coastline, trapping the British Army at Dunkirk. In early June a flotilla of small ships from England ferried

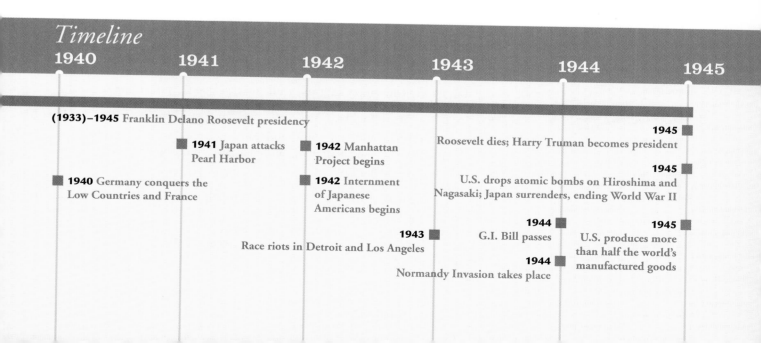

Timeline

| 1940 | 1941 | 1942 | 1943 | 1944 | 1945 |

(1933)–1945 Franklin Delano Roosevelt presidency

1945 Roosevelt dies; Harry Truman becomes president

1941 Japan attacks Pearl Harbor

1942 Manhattan Project begins

1945 U.S. drops atomic bombs on Hiroshima and Nagasaki; Japan surrenders, ending World War II

1940 Germany conquers the Low Countries and France

1942 Internment of Japanese Americans begins

1944 G.I. Bill passes

1945 U.S. produces more than half the world's manufactured goods

1943 Race riots in Detroit and Los Angeles

1944 Normandy Invasion takes place

330,000 soldiers to safety. It was both a defeat and a deliverance for the British forces, who had been badly mauled but rescued from disaster.

In mid-June Mussolini attacked France from the south. Following the French surrender on June 22, the German Luftwaffe attacked England in force. Day and night, German planes dropped their bombs on London, Coventry, and other cities in a murderous attempt to break civilian morale. Day and night, the British Royal Air Force rose up to meet the Luftwaffe, with devastating effect. By early fall Nazi air losses forced Hitler to abandon his invasion plans. "Never in the field of human conflict," said England's new Prime Minister **Winston Churchill** of the brave pilots who fought the Battle of Britain, "was so much owed by so many to so few."

A Third Term for FDR

Events in Europe shattered America's isolationist façade. The German invasions of Poland, France, and the Low Countries turned public opinion overwhelmingly against Hitler, though not in favor of participation in a European war. A national poll found 83 percent hoping for a British victory, 16 percent neutral, and only 1 percent supporting the Nazis.

The German Blitzkrieg increased American concerns about defense. In August 1940, as the Battle of Britain raged in the skies over England, President Roosevelt and Congress worked to fashion the first peacetime draft in American history, the Selective Service Act, as well as a $10.5 billion appropriation for defense. With factories now open round-the-clock to build tanks, war planes, and naval vessels, unemployment virtually disappeared.

As the 1940 election approached, there was no assurance that Roosevelt would run for another term. The loss of New Deal momentum and the Court-packing disaster pointed to his political retirement. Furthermore, though the Constitution set no limits on the number of terms a president could serve, George Washington, Thomas Jefferson, and James Madison had all retired after two full terms in office, setting an informal standard for the future. No president had ever served a third term, and opinion polls in 1938 showed Americans opposed to a third term by more than 2 to 1.

By 1940 the picture had changed. The idea of tested presidential leadership had taken on added appeal. Roosevelt expected to run again. Hoping to defuse the third-term issue, he allowed himself to be "drafted" by the Democratic National Convention in Chicago, thus appearing reluctant but dutiful in the public's mind. "The salvation of the nation rests in one man, because of his experience and great humanitarian thinking," declared Mayor Edward J. Kelly of the host city. Roosevelt selected the enigmatic Henry Wallace to be his vice presidential running mate.

The Republicans, meeting in Philadelphia, nominated **Wendell Willkie** of Indiana for president and Senator Charles McNary of Oregon for vice president. As a Wall Street lawyer and the head of a large utilities corporation, Willkie held two positions almost guaranteed to make the voters suspicious. He had never run for public office or held an appointive government position. His political ascent was due, in large part, to the public relations skills of his advisors.

The 1940 campaign was dominated by foreign affairs. Willkie attacked the president for moving too quickly on the European stage. Among Willkie's complaints was a controversial decision by FDR to supply England with "overage" destroyers. In the summer of 1940 Churchill had begged the United States for naval support to protect British sea lanes from Nazi submarine attacks. In September, without consulting Congress, the president sent fifty old but serviceable warships to England in return for long-term leases to British military bases in Newfoundland, Bermuda, and other parts of the Western Hemisphere. The agreement outraged isolationists.

Roosevelt defeated Willkie with ease—27 million votes to 22 million, 449 electoral votes to 82. He carried all of America's major cities, piling up impressive totals among blacks, Jews, ethnic minorities, and union members. New York Mayor Fiorello LaGuardia put it well: "Americans prefer Roosevelt with his known faults to Willkie with his unknown virtues." Still, the margin of FDR's popular victory made this the closest presidential election since 1916.

Winston Churchill
A British politician and writer, as prime minister (1940–1945 and 1951–1955) he led Great Britain through World War II. He published several books, including *The Second World War* (1948–1953), and won the 1953 Nobel Prize for literature.

Wendell Wilkie
A Wall Street lawyer who ran against Franklin D. Roosevelt in his bid for a third consecutive term, which Roosevelt won.

The End of Neutrality

Shortly after the election, Roosevelt learned that England could no longer afford the supplies it needed to fight the Nazi war machine. He responded by asking Congress for the authority to sell or lease "defense material" to any nation he judged "vital to the defense of the United States." Roosevelt compared his **Lend-Lease** proposal to the simple act of lending a garden hose to a neighbor whose house was on fire.

Lend-Lease

Lend-Lease set off a furious national debate. In 1940 FDR's opponents organized the America First Committee to keep the nation "neutral" by defeating Lend-Lease. Supported by Henry Ford, Charles Lindbergh, and Robert E. Wood, chairman of Sears, Roebuck, it appealed to the isolationist notion that the United States should be prepared to defend its own territory, leaving Europe's wars to the Europeans. At times, however, the committee's message became muddled and conspiratorial, as when Lindbergh described American Jews as the "principal war agitators" behind Lend-Lease.

By 1941 Roosevelt had gained the upper hand. Public opinion moved sharply against isolationism as Hitler became a more ominous threat. In March a $7 billion Lend-Lease bill sailed through Congress, assisted by powerful lobbying groups such as the Committee to Defend America by Aiding the Allies.

In June 1941 Hitler shattered the recent Nazi-Soviet Pact by invading Russia with more than two million troops. Roosevelt responded by offering Stalin immediate Lend-Lease support. The idea of aiding a Communist dictator was hard for Americans to accept. But Roosevelt stood firm, believing that wars made strange bedfellows, and that Hitler must be stopped at all costs.

With Lend-Lease in place, Roosevelt abandoned all pretense of neutrality. To ensure that American goods reached England, he instructed the Navy to protect merchant shipping in the North Atlantic sea lanes. In August 1941 Roosevelt and Churchill met aboard the USS *Augusta*, off the Newfoundland coast, to discuss their mutual aims and principles. The result was a communiqué known as the <u>Atlantic Charter</u>, which called for freedom of the seas, freedom from want and fear, and self-determination for all people in the postwar world.

At this meeting, Roosevelt secretly promised Churchill that the United States would try "to force an 'incident' that could lead to war" with Germany. In the fall of 1941, as Nazi submarines sank one Britain-bound freighter after another, the president armed America's merchant fleet and authorized U.S. destroyers to hunt these U-boats under a policy known as "active defense." In October a German submarine sank a U.S. destroyer off Iceland, with the loss of one hundred American lives. In his ballad to the men who died, Woody Guthrie asked:

> What were their names, tell me,
> what were their names?
> Did you have a friend
> on the good *Reuben James?*

War would come shortly, but not where Roosevelt expected.

The Road to Pearl Harbor

As Hitler swept relentlessly through Europe, another power was stirring halfway around the globe. Like Germany and Italy, Japan had become a militarist state controlled by leaders with expansionist ideas. In the 1930s the Japanese had invaded China, routing its army, terror-bombing cities, and brutalizing civilians in the infamous "rape of Nanking." The United States barely protested. Distracted by the Nazis, Roosevelt sought to avoid a crisis with Japan, even after its planes bombed an American gunboat, the *Panay,* on the Yangtze River in 1937.

In 1938 the Japanese unveiled their plan for empire, known as the "Greater East Asia Co-Prosperity Sphere." They aimed to rule their region by annexing European colonies in

Lend-Lease
Passed in 1941, this act forged the way for the United States to transfer military supplies to the Allies, primarily Great Britain and the Soviet Union.

Southeast Asia and the Western Pacific. Control of French Indochina, the Dutch East Indies, and British Malaya would provide the food and raw materials to make Japan self-sufficient and secure. Only one obstacle stood in the way—the United States.

Japan purchased the bulk of its steel, oil, heavy equipment, and machine parts from U.S. suppliers. To help prevent further Japanese expansion, the Roosevelt administration placed an embargo on certain strategic goods to Japan and moved the Pacific fleet from San Diego to **Pearl Harbor.** The Japanese responded by negotiating a defense treaty (the so-called Tripartite Pact) with Germany and Italy. Relations steadily declined. When Japan moved against Indochina in April 1941, Roosevelt retaliated by freezing all Japanese assets in the United States and blocking shipments of scrap iron and aviation fuel to Japan. In September Japanese leaders requested a meeting with Roosevelt to end the deepening crisis. The president agreed—but with certain conditions. Before sitting down together, he said, the Japanese must withdraw from both China and Indochina.

The Japanese refused, and both sides prepared for war. Military analysts expected Japan to move southwest, toward the Dutch East Indies and British Malaya, in search of needed rubber and oil. Instead, on November 26, 1941, a huge Japanese naval fleet, led by Admiral Chuichi Nagumo, left the Kurile Islands, just north of mainland Japan, and headed due east. The armada included six aircraft carriers with four hundred warplanes, two battleships, two cruisers, nine destroyers, and dozens of support vessels. Traveling under complete radio silence, the fleet was destined for Pearl Harbor, Hawaii.

On Sunday morning, December 7, 1941, Admiral Nagumo's fleet reached its takeoff point, 220 miles north of Pearl Harbor. At 7:40 a.m. the first wave of Japanese warplanes appeared. The wing commander radioed back the words, "Tora (tiger), Tora, Tora," meaning that surprise had been complete. The battleship *Arizona* suffered a direct hit and went up in flames. More than twelve hundred of her crew were killed. The *Oklahoma* capsized after taking three torpedoes, trapping four hundred men below deck. A second Japanese assault at nine o'clock completed the carnage. All told, eighteen warships had been sunk or were badly damaged, three hundred planes had been lost, and twenty-four hundred Americans had died.

Pearl Harbor

The site of a U.S. naval base on the southern coast of Oahu, Hawaii, which the Japanese attacked on Sunday, December 7, 1941; the United States entered World War II the following day.

©Bettmann/CORBIS

The Japanese attack on Pearl Harbor—December 7, 1941—destroyed eighteen warships, killed twenty-four hundred Americans, and plunged the nation into World War II.

Why was Pearl Harbor so woefully unprepared? By the fall of 1941, the United States had broken the Japanese diplomatic code, known as MAGIC. American planners knew that war was coming. On November 27, Army Chief of Staff George C. Marshall sent a warning to all American military outposts in the Pacific. "Negotiations with Japan appear to be terminated to all practical purposes," it said. "Japanese future action unpredictable, but hostile action possible at any moment."

Yet Pearl Harbor was not viewed as the likely point of attack. It was thousands of miles from Japan, and supposedly well defended. At Pearl Harbor, the commanders most feared sabotage from the large Japanese population living in Hawaii. Though some Americans believed that Roosevelt secretly encouraged the Japanese attack in order to bring the United States into World War II, the truth is more mundane. The debacle at Pearl Harbor was caused by negligence and errors in judgment, not by a backroom conspiracy at the White House.

On December 8 Congress declared war against Japan. Only Montana's Representative Jeanette Rankin dissented. (A long-time peace activist, she also had voted against President Wilson's war message in 1917.) On December 11 Germany and Italy honored the Tripartite Pact by declaring war on the United States. Almost instantly, Americans closed ranks. The foreign policy battles were over.

Early Defeats

The attack on Pearl Harbor began one of the bleakest years in American military history. In the North Atlantic, Allied shipping losses reached almost a million tons per month. On the Eastern Front, Nazi forces approached the outskirts of Moscow, where Soviet resistance was fierce. In Egypt, German General Erwin Rommel's elite Afrika Korps threatened the Suez Canal.

The news from Asia was grimmer still. Following Pearl Harbor, Japan moved quickly against American possessions in the Pacific, overrunning Guam, Wake Island, and eventually the Philippines. On December 10, 1941, the Japanese attacked the British fleet off Malaya, sinking the battleship *Prince of Wales* and the cruiser *Repulse*. In the following weeks, Burma, Hong Kong, Singapore, Malaya, and the Dutch East Indies fell like dominoes. Japan now had the resources—the oil, tin, rubber, and foodstuffs—to match its appetite for empire.

For Americans, the most galling defeat occurred in the Philippines, where a hundred thousand U.S. and Filipino troops surrendered to the Japanese after a bloody six-month struggle. The military campaign had actually been lost on December 8, 1941, when the Japanese successfully bombed Clark Field, destroying many of the planes based there to defend the islands. Lacking air cover, the defenders retreated to the jungles of the **Bataan Peninsula,** just north of Manila. As food ran out, they ate snakes, monkeys, cavalry horses, plants, and grass.

In March 1942 President Roosevelt ordered commanding **General Douglas MacArthur** to slip out of the Philippines, leaving his troops behind. The trapped defenders made their stand at Corregidor, a fortress-like island in Manila Bay. After two months of constant bombardment, General Jonathan Wainwright surrendered to the Japanese. His diseased and starving men were brutalized by their captors on the infamous Bataan Death March.

Despite these disasters, the nation remained united and confident of victory. The road ahead would be long, the challenges immense. As *Time* magazine reminded its readers,

> At the end of six months of war, the U.S. has:
> Not yet taken a single inch of enemy territory,
> Not yet beaten the enemy in a single major battle . . .
> Not yet opened an offensive campaign.
> The war, in short, has still to be fought.

Bataan Peninsula

U.S. and Philippine World War II troops surrendered this peninsula in western Luzon, Philippines, to the Japanese in April 1942 after an extended siege; U.S. forces recaptured the peninsula in February 1945.

General Douglas MacArthur

He served as chief of staff (1930–1935) and commanded the Allied forces in the South Pacific during World War II. Initially losing the Philippines to the Japanese in 1942, he regained the islands and accepted the surrender of Japan in 1945. He commanded the UN forces in Korea (1950–1951) until a conflict in strategies led to his dismissal by President Truman.

©Bettmann /CORBIS

The Bataan Death March, following the surrender of U.S. troops in the Philippines, further fueled America's boiling hatred of Japan.

The Home Front

The United States had begun to mobilize for World War II before the attack on Pearl Harbor. The draft was already in place, and defense plants were hiring new workers in the mad scramble to keep England, then the Soviet Union, and now America fully supplied. Furthermore, the positive feelings about this conflict—a "good fight" against Nazi and Japanese aggression—eased many of the problems associated with a democratic nation going to war. Few men refused to register for military service, and millions rushed to enlist. On the home front, Americans vowed to outproduce their enemies and to sacrifice for the "boys" at the front.

War Production

FDR named Donald Nelson of Sears, Roebuck to run the newly created War Production Board (WPB). Nelson's main job was to get companies such as Ford and General Motors to make tanks and warplanes instead of automobiles. To accomplish this, the federal government offered generous incentives. Antitrust laws were suspended so military orders could be filled quickly without competitive bidding. Companies were given low-interest loans to retool, and "cost-plus" contracts that guaranteed them a profit. Not surprisingly, the industrial giants made out best. Ford, for example, began construction of a huge new factory in 1941, named Willow Run, to build B-24 Liberator bombers. In the next four years, it turned out 8,685 airplanes—one every sixty-three minutes. When questioned about these enormous profits and market shares, Secretary of War Henry Stimson replied that "in a capitalist country, you have to let business make money out of the process or business won't work."

Between 1940 and 1945, the nation's gross national product doubled, and the federal budget reached $95 billion, a tenfold increase. In the first half of 1942, the government placed more than $100 billion in war orders, requesting more goods than American factories had ever produced in a single year. The list included sixty thousand planes, forty-five thousand tanks, twenty thousand anti-aircraft guns, and eight million tons of merchant shipping. The orders for 1943 were even larger. By war's end, military spending exceeded $300 billion.

Roosevelt hoped to finance this effort without dramatically raising the national debt. That meant taxation over borrowing, a policy Congress strongly opposed. The result was a compromise that combined both of these elements. The Revenue Act of 1942 added millions of new taxpayers to the federal rolls and dramatically raised the rates paid by Americans in higher income brackets. Along with increases in corporate and inheritance rates, taxation provided about 45 percent of the war's total cost.

Borrowing accounted for the rest. The government relied on banks and brokerage houses for loans, but common people did their share. "There are millions who ask, 'What can we do to help?'" said Treasury Secretary Henry Morgenthau in 1942. "Right now, other than going into the Army and Navy or working in a munitions plant, there isn't anything to do. . . . The reason I want a [war bond campaign] is to give people an opportunity to do something."

Morgenthau sold bonds in inventive ways. Hollywood stars organized "victory tours" through three hundred communities. Hedy Lamarr promised to kiss anyone who bought a $25,000 bond. Factory workers participated in payroll savings plans by putting a percentage of their earnings into government bonds. The Girl and Boy Scouts raised $8 billion in bond pledges.

By 1942 the problem was no longer finding enough work for the people, it was finding enough people for the work to be done. Factories stayed open around the clock, providing new opportunities to underemployed groups such as women, blacks, and the elderly. Seventeen million new jobs were created during World War II. Wages and salaries more than doubled, due in large part to the overtime that people put in. Per capita income rose from $373 in 1940 to just over $1,000 by 1945.

Making Do

In 1942 Congress created the Office of Price Administration (OPA) to ration vital goods, preach self-sacrifice to the public, and control the inflation caused by too much money chasing too few goods. Gas, tires, sugar, coffee, meat, butter, alcohol—all became scarce. Most car owners were issued coupon books limiting them to three gallons of gasoline per week. Pleasure driving virtually ended, causing thousands of restaurants and drive-in businesses to close. As manufacturers cut back on cloth and wool, women's skirts got shorter, two-piece swimsuits (midriff exposed) became the rage, and men's suits no longer had cuffs.

Changes on the home front could be seen through the prism of baseball. Many wanted Major League baseball suspended during the war, but Roosevelt disagreed, claiming that it united Americans and built up their morale. The 1941 season had been one of the best ever, with Ted Williams batting over .400 and Joe DiMaggio's fifty-six-game hitting streak. The next year was very different indeed. Night games were banned because of air-raid "blackouts." Spring training took place in the northern cities, rather than in Florida, to cut back on travel and save fuel. Ballparks held blood drives and bond drives, and soldiers in uniform were admitted free of charge. In 1942 Detroit Tigers slugger Hank Greenberg became the first major leaguer to be drafted into the armed forces. By 1943 most of the stars were gone, replaced by men who were too old or physically unfit for duty, such as Pete Gray, a one-armed outfielder for the St. Louis Browns.

Opportunity and Discrimination

In many respects World War II produced a social revolution in the United States. The severe labor shortage caused an enormous migration of people from rural areas to cities, from South to North, and especially to the West Coast, where so many war industries were located. With defense factories booming and fifteen million people in the armed forces, Americans were forced to reexamine long-held stereotypes about women and minorities in the workplace and on the battlefield.

Women and the War Effort

The war brought new responsibilities and opportunities for American women. During the Depression, for example, women were expected to step aside in the job market to make way for unemployed men. A national poll in 1936 showed an overwhelming percentage of both sexes agreeing that wives with employed husbands should not work. Furthermore, the majority of employed women held poorly paid jobs as clerks and "salesgirls," or as low-end industrial workers in textile and clothing factories. The war brought instant changes. More than six million women took defense jobs. They worked as welders and electricians, on assembly lines and in munitions plants. More than three-quarters of these women were married, and most were over thirty-five. Some had husbands in the armed forces. Young mothers were not expected to work, although a sizable number did.

The symbol of America's new working woman was **Rosie the Riveter,** memorialized by Norman Rockwell in *The Saturday Evening Post* with her overalls, her work tools, and her foot planted on a copy of *Mein Kampf,* helping to grind fascism to dust.

Rosie was trim and beautiful, signifying that a woman could do a man's job—temporarily—without losing her feminine charm. Advertisers played heavily on this theme. A hand-cream company praised the "flower-like skin of today's American Girl, energetically at work six days a week in a big war plant." A cosmetics ad went even further: "Our lipstick can't win the war, but it symbolizes one of the reasons why we are fighting . . . the precious right of women to be feminine and lovely."

Although these jobs paid very well, wage discrimination was rampant in the defense industries, where women earned far less than men in the same jobs. Employers and labor unions rationalized such inequities by noting that men had seniority, put in more overtime, and did the really "skilled" work. In 1945 female factory workers averaged $32 per week, compared to $55 for men.

Women also were told that their work would end with the war's completion. Many women welcomed a return to domesticity after four years of struggle, sacrifice, and separation from a husband overseas. But a survey of female defense workers in 1944 showed that most of them hoped to continue in their present jobs.

This was not to be. Though more women than ever remained in the labor force following World War II, the bulk of them were pushed back into lower-paying "feminized" work. Still, a foundation had been laid. As a riveter from Los Angeles recalled, "Yeah, going to work during the war changed me—made me grow up and realize I could do things."

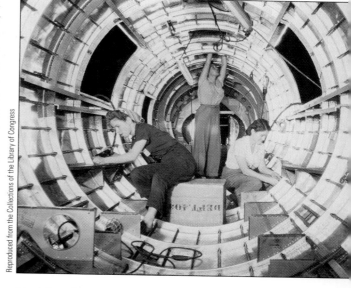

Reproduced from the Collections of the Library of Congress

The labor shortages of World War II created new employment opportunities for women, most of whom were married and over thirty-five. More than six million women worked in defense industries across the country, including shipyards, munitions plants, and aircraft factories.

Rosie the Riveter
A symbol of the new breed of working women during World War II.

The "Double V" Campaign

For millions of American blacks, the war against racist Germany and Japan could not be separated from the ongoing struggle to achieve equal rights. The *Pittsburgh Courier,* an influential African American newspaper, demanded a "Double V" campaign from the Negro community—"victory over our enemies at home and victory over our enemies on the battlefields abroad." To the cynical suggestion that minorities secretly wished for an

American defeat, black heavyweight champion Joe Louis responded: "America's got lots of problems, but Hitler won't fix them."

One obvious problem was the small number of blacks employed in high-paying factory jobs. In 1941 A. Philip Randolph, president of the Brotherhood of Sleeping Car Porters, an all-Negro labor union, proposed a "March on Washington" to protest job discrimination in the defense industries and segregation of the armed forces. "We loyal Americans," he said, "demand the right to work and fight for our country." Fearing the negative publicity, President Roosevelt convinced the organizers to call off their march in return for an Executive Order (8802) declaring that "there shall be no discrimination in the employment of workers because of race, creed, or national origin." To facilitate the order, Roosevelt appointed a Fair Employment Practices Committee (FEPC) to "investigate complaints" and "redress grievances." With a tiny budget and no enforcement powers, the FEPC held public hearings, preached equality in the workplace—and was largely ignored.

Still, the desperate need for labor provided new opportunities for minorities. More than a million blacks migrated to the North and West during World War II. Most were attracted by the higher wages and the chance to escape stifling oppression; many came from the Deep South, where the invention of the mechanical cotton-picker forced them from the land. The number of African Americans employed in the war industries reached 7.5 percent by 1944.

Black workers had little access to the skilled, high-paying jobs because powerful craft unions, like the Machinists and the Carpenters, remained lily-white. But thousands of African Americans took semiskilled positions on the assembly line. For black working women, the changes were more dramatic. On the eve of World War II about 70 percent of them labored as servants in private homes. By war's end, that figure had fallen below 50 percent.

Where racial barriers were crossed, however, violence often followed. In Mobile, Alabama, the promotion of eleven black welders led white shipyard workers to go on a rampage through the African American community. In Philadelphia white transit workers walked off their jobs to protest the elevation of eight blacks to the rank of motorman. Their stoppage brought the city to a halt. Moving quickly, federal officials sent eight thousand fully armed soldiers to run the buses and streetcars while threatening to fire the strikers and draft them into the armed forces. The walkout collapsed two days later.

The worst racial violence flared in Detroit, the nation's leading war production center. Detroit's areawide labor force grew from four hundred thousand in 1940 to almost nine hundred thousand by 1943. With the war effort receiving the government's full attention, little thought was given to building new homes, schools, and hospitals. Those who arrived in Detroit, mainly poor, rural people of both races, found themselves competing for living space and social services with Detroit's established blue-collar labor force—and with each other. One-half of Detroit's wartime black population lived in miserable, substandard housing, often one family to a room, with no indoor toilets or running water. Infant mortality rates skyrocketed, and tuberculosis reached epidemic proportions.

In 1942 an angry mob in Detroit kept several black families from moving into a public housing project in a white neighborhood. The following year a fight between whites and blacks at a municipal park sparked a race riot involving huge mobs with guns, knives, and clubs. Detroit's poorly trained police force, weakened by the departure of its best men to the armed forces, did little to stop the carnage. By the time federal troops established calm in the city, thirty-five people were dead, and more than seven hundred were wounded.

Mob violence on the West Coast involved other victims. In California a hate campaign led by local politicians and the press blamed Mexican Americans for an alleged rise in drugs, crime, and gang warfare. In June 1943 white sailors from surrounding naval bases roamed the Mexican districts of Los Angeles, Long Beach, Pasadena, and other cities looking for "zooters"—young Mexican Americans in ducktail haircuts, wearing long jackets with wide pleated pants, pegged at the cuff. Cheered on by white crowds, the sailors became a vigilante mob—stripping the young men of their "zoot suits," cutting their hair, and beating them senseless.

The zoot-suit violence had other roots as well. Unlike the Depression era, when jobs were scarce, the United States now needed all the labor it could get. In 1942 the American and Mexican governments agreed to a so-called bracero (contract labor) program in which several hundred thousand Mexicans were brought to the United States to plant and harvest crops. In addition, the shortage of factory labor during World War II led to an influx of Hispanic workers in the shipyards and defense plants of southern California. In cities like Los Angeles, crowding and competition bred resentment and fear.

To many residents of southern California, the "zooters" came to represent the Hispanic community as a whole. Rumors flew that Mexican Americans were hindering the war effort by evading the draft. In fact, the reverse was true. Mexican Americans served in numbers far greater than their percentage of the general population—350,000 out of 1.4 million—and seventeen were awarded the Congressional Medal of Honor.

Mexican Americans were integrated in the armed forces during World War II; African Americans were not. The Marines did not take blacks until 1943, when twenty thousand were recruited to unload supplies and munitions during the amphibious Pacific landings. The Navy segregated blacks by occupation, with most working as food handlers, stevedores, and "messboys." In July 1944 a huge explosion at an ammunition depot in Port Chicago, California, killed two hundred fifty black sailors from a segregated work unit. When fifty survivors refused an order to return to work, claiming they had been singled out for these dangerous jobs on account of race, they were court-martialed, convicted of mutiny, and sentenced to prison. Following an intense publicity campaign in the Negro press, the black sailors were returned to duty.

African Americans were rigidly segregated in the armed forces during World War II. One of the most celebrated black units was the 99th Air Force Fighter squadron, known as the Tuskeegee Airmen.

More than five hundred thousand African Americans served in the Army, which placed them in segregated divisions commanded by white officers. Since most training facilities were located in the Deep South, black recruits faced hostile surroundings. Racial clashes at military posts were regularly reported in the Negro press.

Only one black Army division saw significant combat—the 92nd Infantry in Italy. When questioned about this, Secretary of War Henry Stimson claimed that "Negroes have been unable to master efficiently the techniques of modern weapons." The truth, however, was that racial prejudice dominated the military chain of command. When given the opportunity, black units performed superbly. The 99th Air Force Fighter squadron, known as the Tuskeegee Airmen, earned two Distinguished Unit Citations and shot down a dozen Nazi planes during the Anzio invasion of 1943.

Such treatment fueled anger, protest, and pride. America's leading black organization, the National Association for the Advancement of Colored People (NAACP), increased its wartime membership from seventy thousand to five hundred thousand. In 1942 young activists, black and white, formed the Congress of Racial Equality to challenge segregated restaurants in Washington and Baltimore, chanting, "We die together. Let's eat together." A powerful civil rights movement was slowly taking shape.

Internment of Japanese Americans

President Roosevelt was determined to avoid a recurrence of the federal repression that had marred the home front during World War I. Yet the years between 1942 and 1945 witnessed the most glaring denial of civil liberties in American history. The victims included people of Japanese ancestry living mainly on the West Coast of the United States.

On December 8, 1941, Roosevelt issued a standard executive order requiring enemy aliens to register with local police. Before long, however, the president lifted the enemy alien designation for Italians and Germans in the United States, but not for the Japanese. The attack on Pearl Harbor, the Bataan Death March, the fall of Hong Kong and Singapore, Wake

Japanese Relocation Order February 19, 1942 (*Federal Register*, Vol. VII, No. 38) Issued by Franklin D. Roosevelt

On February 19, 1942, President Roosevelt issued Executive Order 9066, authorizing the evacuation of more than a hundred thousand people of Japanese ancestry—most of whom were American citizens—from the West Coast. Although Roosevelt framed the order as a measure to protect national security, other factors, including war hysteria and racism, played a major role.

Executive Order Authorizing the Secretary of War to Prescribe Military Areas

Whereas the successful prosecution of the war requires every possible protection against espionage and against sabotage to national-defense materials, national-defense premises, and national-defense utilities. . . .

Now, therefore, by virtue of the authority vested in me as President of the United States, and Commander in Chief of the Army and Navy, I hereby authorize and direct the Secretary of War, and the Military Commanders whom he may from time to time designate, whenever he or any designated Commander deems such action necessary or desirable, to prescribe military areas in such places and of such extent as he or the appropriate Military Commander may determine, from which any or all persons may be excluded, and with respect to which, the right of any person to enter, remain in, or leave shall be subject to whatever restrictions the Secretary of War or the appropriate Military Commander may impose in his discretion. The Secretary of War is hereby authorized to provide for residents of any such area who are excluded therefrom, such transportation, food, shelter, and other accommodations as may be necessary, in the judgment of the Secretary of War or the said Military Commander, and until other arrangements are made, to accomplish the purpose of this order. The designation of military areas in any region or locality shall supersede designa-

tions of prohibited and restricted areas by the Attorney General under the Proclamations of December 7 and 8, 1941,[1] and shall supersede the responsibility and authority of the Attorney General under the said Proclamations in respect of such prohibited and restricted areas.

I hereby further authorize and direct the Secretary of War and the said Military Commanders to take such other steps as he or the appropriate Military Commander may deem advisable to enforce compliance with the restrictions applicable to each Military area hereinabove authorized to be designated, including the use of Federal troops and other Federal Agencies, with authority to accept assistance of state and local agencies.

I hereby further authorize and direct all Executive Departments, independent establishments and other Federal Agencies, to assist the Secretary of War or the said Military Commanders in carrying out this Executive Order, including the furnishing of medical aid, hospitalization, food, clothing, transportation, use of land, shelter, and other supplies, equipment, utilities, facilities, and services. . . .

[1] 6 F.R. 6420.

Questions to Consider

1. Was the Japanese internment due to military necessity or racism?

2. Why was there so little opposition in the United States to the internment?

3. Why didn't the president, the Justice Department, or the Supreme Court step in to prevent it from happening?

4. Why were Japanese aliens and Japanese Americans singled out for special attention?

Explore additional primary sources related to this chapter on the *American Passages* Web site: http://history.wadsworth.com/ ayersbrief02.

Island, and the Philippines—all sent shock waves across the United States. Though J. Edgar Hoover saw no evidence of a Japanese "threat" to American security, the public thought otherwise. *Time* magazine published an article after Pearl Harbor entitled "How to Tell Your Friends from the Japs," which included such tips as "Japanese are likely to be stockier and broader-hipped than Chinese." More ominous were the words of Henry McLemore, a columnist for the *San Francisco Examiner*. "I am for the immediate removal of every Japanese on the West Coast to a point in the interior," he wrote. "Personally, I hate the Japanese. And that goes for all of them."

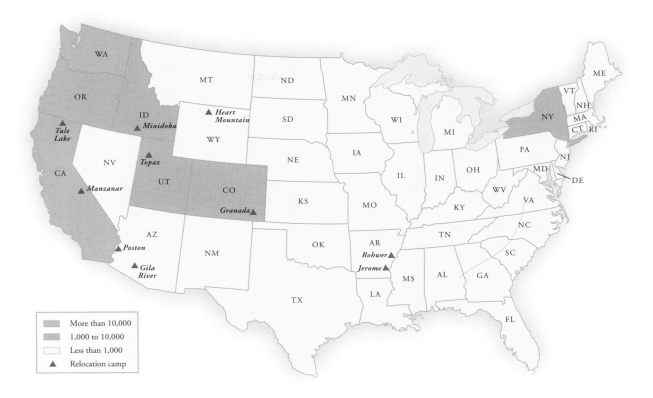

MAP 26.1 Japanese American Relocation
The one hundred twenty thousand Japanese Americans removed from the West Coast during World War II were sent to internment camps in six states, run by the newly established War Relocation Authority. The relocation order did not affect the small number of Japanese Americans living elsewhere in the United States or the large Japanese population living in Hawaii.

More than 90 percent of the one hundred twenty-five thousand Japanese Americans lived in California, Oregon, and Washington. (Two-thirds were citizens, or **Nisei,** born in the United States; the rest were noncitizens, or Issei, born in Japan.) Few in number and politically powerless, the Japanese in America made perfect targets. Military leaders raised the dangers of allowing them to live so close to aircraft plants and naval bases. Local farmers and fishermen resented the economic success of these hard-working people. All wanted their removal from the West Coast.

President Roosevelt capitulated. In February 1942 he issued **Executive Order 9066,** giving Secretary of War Stimson the authority to designate military zones inside the United States "from which any or all persons may be excluded." A few days later, the Army interpreted that order to include the entire West Coast and all people of Japanese extraction.

Roosevelt preferred a "voluntary" removal and resettlement to rural parts of the West. The problem, however, was that the Japanese Americans were unlikely to leave their homes and businesses voluntarily, and the western states were unwilling to take them. As the governor of Idaho said, "If you send them here, they'll be hanging from every tree in the state. Why not send them back to Japan?"

In March the president issued Executive Order 9102, establishing the War Relocation Authority. Internment camps were set up in the deserts of California and Arizona, the mountains of Wyoming, and the scrublands of Utah and Colorado. Japanese Americans on the West Coast were given a few weeks to sell their belongings, get their affairs in order, and report to "processing centers" at converted race tracks, ballparks, and fairgrounds. By June one hundred twenty thousand men, women, and children—most of them American citizens—reached the internment camps.

Conditions there were harsh, but not brutal. Families lived together in Spartan army barracks with little privacy and poor sanitation. Most worked as farm laborers. "All of

Nisei
A person born in the United States of parents who emigrated from Japan.

Executive Order 9066
Issued by President Roosevelt on February 19, 1942, it designated certain parts of the country as sensitive military areas from which "any or all persons may be excluded," which led to the forced evacuation of more than one hundred twenty thousand people of Japanese ancestry from the West Coast of the United States.

Manzanar was a stockade, actually—a prison," wrote a young Japanese American woman of her California camp. "We were in jail. There was barbed wire all around, there were great big watch towers in the corners, and there were spotlights turned on during the night."

The Supreme Court did not intervene. In *Hirabayashi v. United States* (1943) it upheld a curfew ordinance against Japanese Americans in Seattle on the ground that wartime conditions sometimes justified measures that "place citizens of one ancestry in a different category from others." The Court also ruled (*Korematsu v. United States,* 1944) that the evacuation of Japanese Americans was appropriate, but added (*Endo v. United States,* 1944) that the War Relocation Authority should attempt to separate "loyal" internees from "disloyal" ones," and set the loyal free.

It took almost forty years for a measure of justice to prevail. In 1981 a congressional panel concluded that the internment program had resulted from a combination of race prejudice, war hysteria, and the failure of political leadership. It had nothing to do with "military necessity," as its supporters had claimed. In 1988 Congress awarded each survivor of the internment camps $20,000 in "reparations" for the terrible wrong that had been done.

The Grand Alliance

Most Americans saw Japan as the primary villain of World War II. Opinion polls showed the public overwhelmingly in favor of concentrating the war effort in the Pacific. Yet President Roosevelt and his military advisors felt otherwise. To their thinking, American power should be directed against the stronger enemy—Germany. Roosevelt viewed the Nazis as the real threat to world peace, and Europe as the key battleground.

North Africa, Stalingrad, and the Second Front

The British did not believe in confronting Hitler with immediate, massive force. They remembered their staggering losses to the Germans during World War I, and they had felt the power of the Nazis at Dunkirk and in the London air raids. The British, moreover, had a far-flung empire to defend. Their strategy was to strike at "the soft underbelly" of the Axis in North Africa and the Mediterranean.

The Russians strongly disagreed. Already facing a huge Nazi force deep inside their territory, they wanted the United States and Britain to open a "second front" in Western Europe to relieve German pressure on them in the east. That meant a major Allied invasion of France.

Though the top U.S. military advisors leaned toward the Russian strategy, President Roosevelt favored the British approach. At present, he realized, the United States was unprepared for a full-scale invasion of Europe. But a smaller operation against Nazi forces in North Africa had the benefit of getting the United States into the war quickly on the proper scale.

To make this possible, the United States had to gain control of the ocean. In the first three months of 1942, German submarines sank almost one million tons of Allied shipping. By 1943, however, the use of sonar and powerful depth charges made German U-boats more vulnerable underwater, and the development of long-range attack planes and sophisticated radar allowed U.S. aircraft to spot and destroy them as they surfaced to recharge their batteries. The toll was enormous. More than 900 of the 1,162 German submarines commissioned during World War II were sunk or captured.

General Dwight D. Eisenhower

The thirty-fourth president of United States and supreme commander of the Allied Expeditionary Force during World War II. He launched the invasion of Normandy (June 6, 1944) and oversaw the final defeat of Germany in 1945.

In November 1942 American troops under the command of **General Dwight D. Eisenhower** invaded the French North African colonies of Morocco and Algeria in an operation code-named TORCH. At virtually the same moment, British forces badly mauled General Rommel's army at El Alamein in Egypt, ending Nazi hopes of taking the Suez Canal. Though Hitler rushed reinforcements to North Africa, the Allies prevailed.

In North Africa, the Allies fought and defeated twelve Nazi divisions. In the Soviet Union, the Russians were fighting two hundred German divisions along an enormous two-thousand-mile front. The pivotal battle occurred at Stalingrad, a vital transportation hub on the Volga River, in the bitter winter of 1942–1943. As the Germans advanced, Stalin ordered his namesake city held at all costs. The fighting was block-to-block, house-to-house, and finally hand-to-hand. Hitler would not let his forces retreat, even after they ran out of fuel and food. Surrounded by Russian forces, overwhelmed by starvation, exposure, and suicide, the German commander surrendered on February 2, 1943.

Stalingrad marked the turning point of the European war. The Russians were advancing steadily in the east, aided by a stream of tanks, planes, food, and clothing from the United States under Lend-Lease. Now Stalin expected an Allied thrust from the west—the long-promised second front.

Churchill had other ideas. At a meeting with Roosevelt in Casablanca, he convinced the president to put off a cross-channel invasion in favor of an assault on Axis troops across the Mediterranean in Italy. Roosevelt attempted to pacify Stalin by promising to open a second front the following year. But the Soviets, having sacrificed more troops at Stalingrad than the United States would lose in the entire war, were suspicious and displeased.

The Italian campaign began in the summer of 1943. Sicily fell in a month, and Mussolini along with it. Overthrown by antifascist Italians, the Duce fled to Nazi lines in the north. The new Italian government then declared war on Germany and was recognized as a "co-belligerent" by England and the United States. The battle for Italy was intense. Waging a brilliant defensive struggle in mountainous terrain, the Germans stubbornly blocked the Allied advance north to Rome.

The Italian campaign dragged on for almost two years, draining troops and resources for the planned invasion of France. Suspicions between Stalin and his wartime allies deepened as Roosevelt and Churchill set the terms of Italy's surrender without consulting the Soviet leader. In addition, postponement of the second front gave Stalin the opportunity to gobble up much of central Europe as his troops pushed toward Germany from the east.

The three Allied leaders met together for the first time in November 1943 at the Tehran Conference in Iran. Roosevelt and Churchill promised to launch their cross-channel invasion the following spring. The future of Poland, the partition of Germany, and need for a United Nations were also discussed. In public, at least, Allied unity was restored.

The Normandy Invasion

By 1944 the Allies were in complete control of the skies over Western Europe and in command of the seas. Their amphibious landings in North Africa and Italy had provided valuable experience for the job that lay ahead. In April and May General Eisenhower assembled his huge invasion force in England. Meanwhile, Allied aircraft pounded the Atlantic Wall, a line of German fortifications stretching hundreds of miles along the coast of France and the Low Countries.

Despite meticulous preparation, Eisenhower faced enormous risks. The Nazis had fifty-five divisions in France. To keep them dispersed and guessing, Allied intelligence spread false information about the planned invasion sites. The deceptions worked. Hitler and his generals put their strongest defense at Pas de Calais, the English Channel's narrowest point.

The massive D-Day invasion—**Operation OVERLORD**—began on the morning of June 6, 1944. Eisenhower's biggest worry was the weather. A channel storm had postponed one attempt, and another storm was predicted. Before the men left, he told them: "You are about to embark upon the Great Crusade, toward which we have striven these many months. The eyes of the world are upon you."

The invasion succeeded. With overwhelming air cover, Allied forces assaulted Normandy and dropped paratroopers behind enemy lines. The heaviest fighting took place at Omaha Beach, where U.S. Rangers scaled sheer cliffs under withering fire to silence Nazi gunners. By nightfall one hundred fifty thousand men were ashore.

Others quickly followed. Within two months, more than a million Allied troops were in France—liberating Paris in August, reaching the German border by September. With the Soviets pressing from the east, a Nazi surrender seemed only weeks away. But the Germans counterattacked in December 1944, taking British and American forces by surprise. The Battle of the Bulge was Hitler's last gasp. U.S. troops took heavy casualties, but stood firm. Germany lost a hundred thousand men and the will to fight on. Hitler committed suicide in his Berlin bunker on April 30, 1945, with Russian soldiers a few miles away. Germany surrendered a week later. The Thousand-Year Reich had lasted a dozen murderous years.

Operation OVERLORD
The name given to the Allied invasion of the European continent through Normandy.

MAP 26.2 The War in Europe

The U.S. military effort against German and Italian forces in World War II began in North Africa, moved to Italy, and culminated in the D-Day invasion of France in 1944. With the aid of England and other nations, the Allied forces reached Germany from the west in 1945. Meanwhile, following a tenacious defense of their homeland, Russian troops pushed deep into Germany from the east, destroying the bulk of Nazi fighting forces and playing a key role in the German surrender.

Facing the Holocaust

In the spring of 1945, Allied troops liberated the Nazi concentration camps in Poland and Germany. Ghastly pictures of starving survivors and rotting corpses flashed around the world, recording the almost inconceivable horror in which six million European Jews and four million others (including Poles, Gypsies, homosexuals, political dissidents) were exterminated during World War II.

To American leaders, these photos of the Holocaust produced shock, but hardly surprise. Evidence of the death camps had reached the United States in 1942, yet the government paid scant attention to the consequences. The State Department, well known for its anti-Semitism in that era, made it virtually impossible for refugees fleeing the Nazis to enter the United States. President Roosevelt did not seriously intervene, insisting that the best way to aid the victims of Nazism was to defeat Hitler's armies as quickly as possible. His only acknowledgment of the impending disaster came in 1944 when he created the War Refugee Board, which helped finance the activities of Raoul Wallenberg, the courageous Swedish diplomat who prevented thousands of Hungarian Jews from being deported to the death camps. Had it been formed earlier, the War Refugee Board might have played a major role in the saving of innocent lives.

The United States had other options as well. Its bombers could have attacked the rail lines leading to the death camps, as well as the gas chambers and crematoria that lay inside. The War Department avoided these targets, claiming they were too dangerous and too far away. This clearly was not true.

When liberation came to the concentration camps, the vast majority of prisoners were dead. One survivor at Dachau recalled the very moment the American troops arrived. "We were free. We broke into weeping, kissed the tank. A Negro soldier gave us a tin of meat, bread, and chocolate. We sat down on the ground and ate up all the food together. The Negro watched us, tears in his eyes."

The Pacific War

America's war against Japan would be fought differently from the war against Germany. In the Pacific, the United States would do the great bulk of the Allied fighting; in Europe that burden was shared by others, including Great Britain and, most important, the Soviet Union. The war against Japan would be waged largely at sea and from the air; though American Marines would meet fierce resistance in clearing Guadalcanal, Saipan, Iwo Jima, Okinawa, and other Japanese-held strongholds, there would be no massed land battles to match the Soviet defeat of German forces at Stalingrad or the Allied counterattack at the Bulge. In Europe, armor and artillery were essential to the Allied victory; in the Pacific, it would be aircraft carriers and submarines. By war's end, the United States had lost 128 combatant vessels to Japanese warships and aircraft, but only 29 to German fire. The Japanese surrender in 1945 would end the largest naval war in history.

Turning the Tide

The Japanese hoped to create an impregnable defense line in the Pacific. Their strategy included new conquests, such as Australia, and a naval thrust against the U.S. carrier fleet. Yet two key engagements in the spring of 1942 shattered Admiral Yamamoto's illusion about American willpower and naval strength. On May 7 a task force led by two American carriers—the *Lexington* and *Yorktown*—held its own against a larger Japanese force at the Battle of the Coral Sea, just north of Australia. Though the "Lady Lex" was sunk, heavy Japanese losses saved Australia from invasion or certain blockade.

A month later the two sides clashed again. Admiral Yamamoto brought a huge fleet to **Midway Island,** a thousand miles west of Hawaii, to flush out and destroy the American carrier fleet. But the U.S. Navy, having broken the Japanese military code, was well aware of his intentions. In a three-day battle, brilliantly commanded by Rear Admiral Raymond A. Spruance, the Americans sank four Japanese carriers (losing the *Yorktown*) and shot down 320 planes. Japan would never fully recover from this beating.

Midway Island
A naval battle in World War II in which land and carrier-based U.S. planes decisively defeated a Japanese fleet on its way to invade the Midway Island.

MAP 26.3 The War in the Pacific
America's war against Japan was fought differently than the war against Germany. In the Pacific, the United States did the great bulk of the Allied fighting; in Europe, that burden was shared by others. As shown on the map, the war against Japan was waged largely at sea and from the air; though U.S. Marines met fierce resistance in clearing Guadalcanal, Saipan, Iwo Jima, Okinawa, and other Japanese-held strongholds, there were no massed land battles to match the Soviet defeat of German forces at Stalingrad or the Allied counterattack at the Bulge.

Closing in on Japan

After Midway, the United States followed a two-pronged plan of attack. Admiral Chester Nimitz was to move west from Hawaii toward Formosa, while General Douglas MacArthur came north from Australia toward the Philippines, with their forces combining for an eventual assault on Japan. The fighting would be sporadic but brutal, involving air attacks, naval duels, and amphibious landings by U.S. Marines on selected Japanese-held islands. It would be "a war without mercy," with bitter racial hatreds on both sides.

The first U.S. offensive occurred at Guadalcanal, a small tropical island in the Solomons, off New Guinea, in August 1942. For six months, American Marines waged a desperate campaign in swamps and jungles, battling intense heat, malaria, dysentery, infection, and leeches, as well as the Japanese. When the island was finally secured in February 1943, General MacArthur began a "leapfrog" campaign across New Guinea to the Philippines, attacking some islands while bypassing others.

In the central Pacific, Admiral Nimitz was moving west, ever closer to Japan. In November 1943, the Marines assaulted Tarawa, a tiny strip of beach in the Gilbert Islands, taking three thousand casualties in a successful three-day assault. Next came the Marshall Islands; the Marianas—Guam, Tinian, and Saipan—followed. The battle for Saipan raged through June and July of 1944. The Japanese defenders fought, quite literally, to the last man. Worse, thousands of Japanese civilians on the island committed suicide—a preview, some believed, of what lay ahead in Japan.

The end seemed near. In October 1944 MacArthur returned to the Philippines in triumph, while an American naval force destroyed four Japanese carriers at the Battle of Leyte Gulf, outside Manila. To the north, American troops took the island of Iwo Jima in brutal combat, and then attacked Okinawa. Admiral Nimitz assembled a huge force for the invasion—180,000 troops, most of his carriers, and eighteen battleships. The Japanese had an army of 110,000 on Okinawa, the final barrier to the homeland itself.

The battle took three months, from April through June of 1945. Waves of Japanese kamikaze (suicide) planes attacked the Allied fleet, inflicting terrible damage. U.S. troops suffered a casualty rate of 35 percent, the highest of the war. Seven thousand were killed on land, five thousand at sea, and forty thousand were wounded. The Japanese lost fifteen hundred kamikazes and virtually all of their soldiers. These appalling losses would be a factor in America's decision to use atomic weapons against Japan.

Table 26.1
Second World War Casualties

Country	Battle Deaths	Wounded
Canada	32,714	53,145
France	201,568	400,000
Germany	3,250,000	7,250,000
Italy	149,496	66,716
USSR	6,115,000	14,012,000
Australia	26,976	180,864
Japan	1,270,000	140,000
New Zealand	11,625	17,000
United Kingdom	357,116	369,267
United States	291,557	670,846

Source: *Information Please Almanac* (Boston: Houghton Mifflin Co., 1988).

A Change in Leadership

In November 1944 the American people reelected Franklin Roosevelt to an unprecedented fourth presidential term. Roosevelt defeated Republican Thomas Dewey, the moderate forty-two-year-old governor of New York. Dewey hammered away at problems on the home front, such as food shortages, gas rationing, squalid housing for war workers, and government "red tape." Roosevelt campaigned as the war leader, urging voters "not to change horses in midstream." To bolster his chances, Democratic party leaders removed the increasingly unpopular Vice President Henry Wallace from the ticket and replaced him with Senator **Harry S. Truman** of Missouri.

The Yalta Accords

In February 1945, with Germany near collapse, an exhausted FDR met with Churchill and Stalin at Yalta, in southern Russia, to lay the groundwork for peace and order in the postwar world. The Russians promised to enter the Pacific war after Germany's defeat in return for territorial concessions in the Far East. The three leaders also blessed the formation of a new international body, known as the United Nations. But agreement on the larger issues proved elusive. The Soviet Union had suffered staggering losses at German hands. From Stalin's perspective, the Soviets deserved more than simple gratitude for their role in defeating the great bulk of Hitler's army. They needed the means to rebuild their nation and to protect it from further attacks.

Stalin hoped to ensure Soviet security through the permanent partition of Germany. And he demanded huge reparations from the Germans—at least $20 billion—with Russia getting half. Furthermore, Stalin had no intention of removing Soviet troops from the lands they now controlled in Eastern Europe.

Harry S. Truman
The thirty-third president of the United States, he took office following the death of Franklin D. Roosevelt. Reelected in 1948 in a stunning political upset, Truman's controversial and historic decisions included the use of atomic weapons against Japan, desegregation of the U.S. military, and dismissal of General MacArthur as commander of U.S. forces during the Korean War.

Roosevelt and Churchill had other ideas. Both men viewed a healthy, "de-Nazified" Germany as essential to the reconstruction of postwar Europe, and both feared the expansion of Soviet power into the vacuum created by Hitler's defeat. The British also claimed a moral stake in Poland, having declared war on Germany in 1939 to help defend the Poles from the Nazi assault. To desert them now—to permit a victorious Stalin to replace a defeated Hitler—smacked of the very appeasement that had doomed Allied policy a decade before.

The Yalta Accords created a legacy of mistrust. The parties agreed to split Germany into four "zones of occupation"—American, Russian, British, and French. Berlin, deep inside the Soviet zone, also was divided among the Allies. Yet the vital issue of reparations was postponed, as were plans for Germany's eventual reunification. At Roosevelt's urging, Stalin accepted a "Declaration for a Liberated Europe" that promised "free and unfettered elections" in Poland and elsewhere at some unspecified date.

In the weeks following Yalta, Roosevelt's optimism about Soviet-American relations seemed to fade. Pledges of free elections in Europe were ignored. The Yalta Accords did not prevent Stalin from ordering the murder of political dissidents in Romania and Bulgaria and the arrest of anti-Communist leaders in Poland. His ruthlessness seemed to highlight the unpleasant truth that the United States had little or no influence in the nations now occupied by Soviet troops.

Truman in Charge

On April 12, 1945—less than two months into his fourth term—FDR died of a massive stroke. The nation was shocked. Roosevelt had been president for twelve years, leading the people through the Great Depression and World War II. "He was the one American who knew, or seemed to know, where the world was going," wrote *Life* magazine.

The new president was largely unknown. Born on a Missouri farm in 1884, Harry Truman had been elected to public office in the 1920s with the aid of Tom Pendergast, a crooked Democratic boss. Truman walked a fine line between efficient service to his constituents and partisan loyalty to a corrupt political machine. Fair and honest himself, Truman went about the business of building better roads and improving public services while ignoring the squalor of those who put him in office.

Working for the Pendergast machine sensitized Truman to the needs of different people, fueled his belief in a welfare state, and got him elected to the U.S. Senate in 1934. On the other hand, the label of "machine politician" would plague him for years. It was hard to earn respect as a legislator when the newspapers kept referring to him as "the senator from Pendergast."

Truman did not inspire immediate confidence in his ability to fill Roosevelt's giant shoes. Small in stature, he seemed thoroughly ordinary to all but those who knew him best. As vice president, he was largely excluded from the major discussions relating to foreign policy and the war. After taking the presidential oath of office, Truman turned to reporters and said, "Boys, if you ever pray, pray for me now."

As expected, Truman received conflicting advice. A number of FDR's confidantes, including Henry Wallace and Eleanor Roosevelt, urged him to keep the wartime alliance alive by accommodating Russia's economic needs and security demands. But others, including Averell Harriman, U.S. ambassador to the Soviet Union, prodded Truman to demand Russia's strict compliance with the Yalta Accords. The new president still hoped for Soviet help in ending the Pacific war and building a lasting peace. Yet the more Truman learned about events in Poland and Eastern Europe, the angrier he became. Ten days after taking office, he confronted Soviet Foreign Minister V. M. Molotov at the White House, claiming that Russia had ignored the Yalta Accords and warning him that economic aid to Russia would never get through Congress so long as this attitude persisted.

In July 1945 Truman left the United States aboard the USS *Augusta* for his first face-to-face meeting with Stalin and Churchill at Potsdam, near Berlin. The three leaders agreed on a number of important issues, including the terms of peace for defeated Germany and public trials for Nazi war criminals. "I can deal with Stalin," Truman wrote in his diary. "He is honest—but smart as hell."

His optimism didn't last long. The conference was halted for several days by the stunning defeat of Winston Churchill's Conservative party in the British parliamentary elections. Churchill returned to England, replaced by the new Labour prime minister, Clement Attlee. When the talks resumed, Stalin brushed aside Truman's concerns about Poland and Eastern Europe, and Truman rebuffed Stalin's attempt to claim reparations from the western zones of occupation in Germany. There seemed little doubt that Russia would remain in the lands it now controlled and that Germany would remain divided for some time to come.

The Atomic Bomb

One of Truman's first decisions concerned the use of atomic weapons. As the United States took control of the island chains east of Japan in 1944, a ferocious bombing campaign of the Japanese home islands took place. In March 1945, three hundred American B-29s led by Major General Curtis LeMay firebombed Tokyo, killing a hundred thousand people and destroying much of the city. In the following months, conventional (nonatomic) bombings pounded half of Japan's sixty-six major cities.

AP/Wide World

Winston Churchill, Harry Truman, and Joseph Stalin clasp hands at the Potsdam Conference in July 1945. The good feeling did not last long, as Churchill's ruling party was defeated at the polls in England and relations between the United States and the Soviet Union swiftly moved downhill.

Shortly after taking office, President Truman was told about the atomic bomb by Secretary of War Stimson, who called it "the most terrible weapon ever known in human history." The decision to build this bomb had been made by President Roosevelt in response to reports from refugee scientists that the Nazis were already at work on one. The American effort, known as the Manhattan Project, included top-secret facilities in Hanford, Washington, Oak Ridge, Tennessee, and Los Alamos, New Mexico, to design and construct this bomb and produce the fissionable material for an atomic explosion.

At President Truman's direction, an Interim Committee was formed to advise him about the bomb. Chaired by Henry Stimson, the committee recommended the use of atomic weapons against Japan, without warning, as soon as they became available. Another group, the Target Committee, chose four major cities—Hiroshima, Kokura, Niigata, and Nagasaki—based on their strategic importance. On July 16, 1945, the atomic bomb was successfully tested near Alamogordo, New Mexico. The explosion, equivalent to fifteen thousand tons of dynamite, was visible two hundred miles away. Truman learned of the test while attending the Allied Summit meeting in Potsdam. He immediately issued a public ultimatum to the Japanese, calling on them to surrender unconditionally or face "prompt and utter destruction."

A number of top scientists on the Manhattan Project objected. They were joined by several ranking civilian and military officials who argued that Japan was close to surrender, that the naval blockade was going well, and that use of the bomb would trigger a dangerous arms race with the Russians.

But Truman held firm, believing that the bomb would save American and Japanese lives by ending the war quickly. On the morning of August 6, 1945, a B-29 named *Enola Gay* dropped an atomic bomb over Hiroshima, incinerating the industrial city and killing at least a hundred thousand people. (Thousands more would die of radiation effects, a problem poorly understood by scientists at that time.) Three days later, a B-29 named *Bock's Car* dropped a second atomic bomb on Nagasaki, with much the same effect. On August 14 the Japanese asked for peace.

Though Americans overwhelmingly supported these bombings, the decision remains controversial to this day. Some believe that Truman dropped the bomb to scare the Russians in Europe and to keep them out of the Asian war. Others think the decision was based on racism and revenge. Still others argue that the United States should have provided a "demonstration" of the bomb's power for the Japanese. For all the controversy, however, one inescapable fact remains: Japanese leaders could not bring themselves to surrender until two atomic bombs had been dropped.

World War II formally ended on September 2, 1945, when the Japanese signed the document of surrender aboard the battleship *Missouri* in Tokyo Bay. More than twenty-five million soldiers and civilians died in the struggle. American losses were smaller—three hundred thousand killed, seven hundred thousand wounded—but American power had been decisive. Speaking from the deck of the *Missouri* that day, General MacArthur issued a warning for the new atomic age. "We have had our last chance," he said. "If we do not devise some greater and more equitable system, Armageddon will be at our door."

Enola Gay

The B-29 bomber, named after the mother of pilot Colonel Paul W. Tibbets, that dropped the first atomic bomb on the Japanese city of Hiroshima on August 6, 1945, killing more than one hundred thousand people.

Summary

World War and American Society

In many ways, World War II was to Americans of the mid-twentieth century what the Civil War had been to Americans of the mid-nineteenth: a watershed event, defining the course of our history for generations to come. When war erupted in Europe in 1939, there seemed little chance that the United States would become involved. Bitter memories of World War I and its aftermath still prevailed in the United States, where people worried more about the lingering effects of the Great Depression than they did about the growing menace posed by Germany, Italy, and Japan. Though events in Europe and Asia led to increasingly bitter debates in the United States over the need for military preparedness, as well as the consequences of abandoning neutrality toward the combatants, most Americans seemed relieved by President Roosevelt's campaign pledge in 1940 that "your boys are not going to be sent into any foreign war."

When war did come with the Japanese bombing of Pearl Harbor, the nation quickly came together. The United States had been attacked, and virtually everyone understood the evil of the enemies they now faced. The war shattered the illusion that Amer-

Franklin Roosevelt's decision to seek a third term in 1940 broke a longstanding precedent. Note the political poster here, which uses the authoritative, nonpartisan image of Uncle Sam to make this point. At that time, the Constitution set no limits on the number of terms a president could serve. Given the state of world affairs in 1940, the third term issue generated little interest; Americans were far more focused on the coming of war.

Franklin D. Roosevelt Library

American fighter planes roll off the assembly line during World War II.

©Bettmann/CORBIS

632

icans could remain separate from the world's problems. In leading the Grand Alliance against Nazi and Japanese aggression, the United States took on the full responsibilities of a global power—morally, economically, and militarily. In doing so, it served notice that America's influence on world affairs would be substantial in the postwar era, whether in containing the spread of Communism, constructing a nuclear arsenal, spending billions in foreign aid, or rebuilding the battered economies of Western Europe and Japan. The days of isolationism, of being a disinterested world observer protected from harm and engagement by the geographical buffer of two massive oceans, were gone for good.

World War II had an equally profound impact on domestic affairs. It ended the Great Depression, created full employment, and increased mean family income an astonishing 25 percent. It demonstrated the ability of an ethnically diverse nation to unite in a just cause, although racial segregation remained in place and basic civil liberties, in the case of Japanese Americans, were tragically denied. And it opened new opportunities for women and minorities in the workplace, although full economic and political equality in the United States remained a dream unfulfilled. In 1945 Americans looked to the future with cautious optimism—proud of their accomplishments and yearning for better times.

Japanese representatives signed the formal declaration of surrender aboard the battleship *Missouri* on September 2, 1945.

LOOKING BACK

Chapter 26 examines both the way in which the United States fought World War II and the great changes that occurred in domestic and international affairs.

1. How did America mobilize for war? What changes took place on the home front that aided the war production?
2. How lasting and substantial were the gains made by women and minorities during the war?
3. How well did the Grand Alliance work, what strategies were employed to keep it together, and what problems arose regarding the interests of the different parties?

LOOKING AHEAD

The next chapter looks at American society following World War II, tracing the impact of the war on foreign and domestic affairs, from the Cold War to the baby boom to the growth of suburbia.

1. What decisions were made, or avoided, during World War II that had a direct impact on the diplomatic problems facing the United States and the Soviet Union in the coming years?
2. How difficult would it be for America's fifteen million veterans to readjust to civilian life following the war?
3. Would the tremendous wartime prosperity in the United States be maintained once the conflict was over?

Making Connections Across Chapters

RECOMMENDED READINGS

Birdwell, Michael. *Celluloid Soldiers* (1999). Carefully examines Hollywood's war effort against the Nazis.

Dower, John. *War without Mercy: Race and Power in the Pacific War* (1986). Explores the racial attitudes of the United States and Japan in the brutal Asian conflict.

Hartmann, Susan. *The Homefront and Beyond: American Women in the 1940s* (1982). Documents the extraordinary impact of World War II on women at home and in the workplace.

Jeffries, John. *Wartime America* (1996). Concentrates on the home front during World War II.

Kennett, Lee. *G.I.: The American Soldier in World War II* (1997). Describes the day-to-day order of life of the average U.S. soldier in the training camps, in combat, and in victory.

O'Neill, William. *A Democracy at War: America's Fight at Home and Abroad in World War II* (1993). Examines both the military front and the home front in lively detail.

Robinson, Gregg. *By Order of the President: FDR and the Internment of Japanese Americans* (2001). Offers a sobering account of Roosevelt's personal role in the internment process.

Tuttle, William. *Daddy's Gone to War* (1993). Re-creates these years in generational terms through the eyes of America's wartime children.

Walker, J. Samuel. *Prompt and Utter Destruction: Truman and the Use of Atomic Bombs against Japan* (1997). Offers a balanced account of the factors leading to the president's fateful decision.

Wyman, David S. *The Abandonment of the Jews* (1984). Examines the failure of U.S. policy makers, the press, and the larger public to provide a sanctuary for victims of the Holocaust.

AMERICAN JOURNEY ONLINE AND INFOTRAC COLLEGE EDITION

Visit the source collections at http://ajaccess.wadsworth.com and infotrac.thomsonlearning.com and use the Search function with the following key terms to explore documents, images, audio and video clips, articles, and commentary related to the material in this chapter.

Franklin D. Roosevelt

Lend-Lease

Pearl Harbor

Executive Order 9066

Enola Gay

Harry S. Truman

ONLINE PRIMARY SOURCES

Here are some examples of the many primary sources related to this chapter that you will find on the *American Passages* Web site: http://history.wadsworth.com/ayersbrief02.

A. Philip Randolph, "Why Should We March?," 1942

Relocation Order, 1942 (photo)

Harry S. Truman on the Bombing of Hiroshima, 1945

The site also offers self-quizzes, exercises, and many additional resources to help you study.

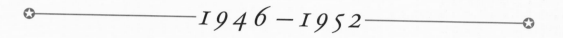

CHAPTER 27

Postwar America

1946–1952

HENRY R. LUCE WAS A MAN OF GRAND VISIONS. ONE RIVAL DUBBED HIM "Lord of the Press" because his publishing empire included *Time, Life,* and *Fortune.* In February 1941 Luce composed an editorial prodding the American people to accept their new role as citizens of "the strongest and most vital nation in the world." The time had come, he insisted, to exert "the full measure of our influence" in the dawning "American Century."

The belief in America's destiny was as old as the country itself. Yet the challenges of World War II had turned this rhetoric into reality. Only the United States seemed to possess the combination of military strength, economic resources, and political stability to rebuild a world battered by war. What worried Luce and others was the failure of American resolve. As columnist Dorothy Thompson put it, the United States "must lead now or take a back seat in history."

Reconversion

The United States faced two major problems. The first one concerned relations with the Soviet Union. Would the two nations be able to maintain the Grand Alliance, or would their obvious differences about the shape and direction of postwar Europe degenerate into conflict? The second problem related to the domestic economy. Many Americans feared that the Great Depression might return as defense spending dropped and factory jobs disappeared. In the months following Japan's surrender, the federal government canceled more than $30 billion in military contracts, forcing eight hundred thousand layoffs in the aircraft industry alone. Could the United States handle the difficult reconversion from a wartime to a peacetime economy?

The Veterans Return

President Truman's first job was to bring the soldiers home. Twelve million Americans were still in uniform in 1945. Their dream was to return home quickly and get on with their lives. Throughout Europe and the Pacific, GIs grumbled about the slow pace of demobilization while their loved ones barraged Congress and the White House with angry mail. This pressure brought results. Within a year, the number of men and women in the armed forces had dropped to three million.

For many GIs, however, these were anxious, difficult times. The divorce rate shot up dramatically in 1945, reflecting the tensions of readjustment to civilian life. A major hous-

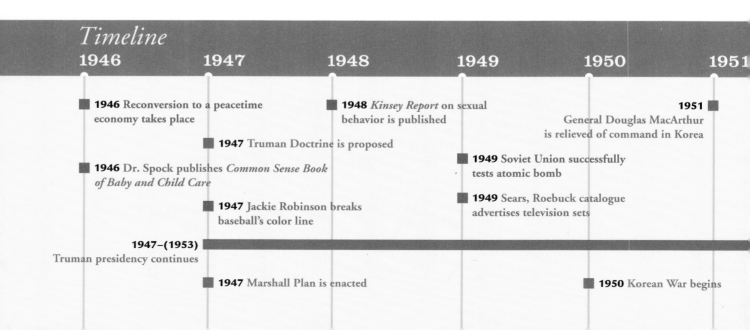

Timeline

| 1946 | 1947 | 1948 | 1949 | 1950 | 1951 |

1946 Reconversion to a peacetime economy takes place

1946 Dr. Spock publishes *Common Sense Book of Baby and Child Care*

1947 Truman Doctrine is proposed

1947 Jackie Robinson breaks baseball's color line

1947–(1953) Truman presidency continues

1947 Marshall Plan is enacted

1948 *Kinsey Report* on sexual behavior is published

1949 Soviet Union successfully tests atomic bomb

1949 Sears, Roebuck catalogue advertises television sets

1951 General Douglas MacArthur is relieved of command in Korea

1950 Korean War begins

ing shortage, brought on by the virtual absence of home building during World War II, made things even worse. Washington, D.C. reported twenty-five thousand homeless veterans, Chicago more than a hundred thousand. One serviceman complained: "You fight a damn war and you finally come home and everybody slaps you on the back and tells you what a wonderful job you did . . . but when it comes to really doing something, then nobody's home."

In fact, however, assistance for returning veterans had received careful attention from the wartime Congress, which passed the popular Servicemen's Readjustment Act in 1944. Known as the GI Bill, it provided almost $20 billion for various programs in the decade following World War II. The GI Bill fueled a nationwide construction boom by providing long-term, low-interest mortgages to veterans, plus a $2,000 bonus toward the purchase of a new home. Furthermore, it allowed former soldiers to fulfill the dream of a college degree, thereby expanding the system of higher education as never before. In 1947, for example, more than half of the thirty thousand students at the University of Minnesota were veterans of World War II. Older, more serious, and determined to make up for lost time, they formed the nucleus of America's expanding white-collar workforce in the prosperous years ahead.

Lurching toward Prosperity

The increase in federal spending for veterans helped to offset the decrease in defense spending. And for the past five years, Americans had worked overtime in offices and factories, banking their paychecks, buying savings bonds, and dreaming of the day when cars, appliances, prime beef, and nylon stockings would reappear in the nation's stores and showrooms. Between Pearl Harbor and the Japanese surrender, the public had accumulated an astonishing $140 billion in savings and liquid securities. "I'm tired of ration books and empty shelves," said one factory worker. "I'm ready to spend."

But factories could not change from fighter planes to automobiles overnight. With the demand for consumer goods far outracing the supply, President Truman hoped to keep inflation in line by extending wartime price controls. His plan met strong opposition from the business community, and in June 1946 Truman vetoed a compromise bill that extended the life of the Office of Price Administration (OPA) but effectively limited its power. The OPA was disbanded and price controls were lifted.

As controls ended, prices shot up. The cost of meat doubled in two weeks, leading the New York *Daily News* to quip:

Prices Soar, Buyers Sore
Steers Jump Over the Moon

Since higher prices meant a drop in real wages, the United Automobile Workers (UAW) demanded an average pay hike of 33 cents an hour from General Motors in 1946, from $1.12 to $1.45. When the corporation offered a 10-cent hourly raise, the union struck for 113 days, eventually settling for 18 cents. Shortly thereafter, the UAW and the auto companies agreed to a cost-of-living adjustment (COLA) clause in future contracts.

The country was soon plagued by a wave of strikes. In 1946 alone five million workers were involved in 4,630 work stoppages totaling 120 million days of lost labor. When two railroad brotherhoods threatened a national strike designed to shut down the country's rail service, President Truman signed an executive order seizing the railroads. "If you think I'm going to sit here and let you tie up this whole country," he told union leaders, "you're crazy as hell." A few weeks later, the United Mine Workers (UMW) went on strike, forcing power stations and factories to close for lack of fuel. This time, however, the union lost. President Truman went on radio to demand that the miners return to work at once. They did, coaxed along by a federal court injunction that led to $3.5 million in damages against the UMW.

For Truman, these victories came at a heavy cost. Not only did he offend large parts of the labor movement, he also appeared incapable of governing a nation wracked by consumer shortages, labor strife, soaring inflation, and an approaching cold war. In November 1946 the Democratic party suffered a crushing defeat at the polls. Campaigning against the ills of reconversion ("Had Enough?") and the president's alleged incompetence

("To Err Is Truman"), the Republicans gained control of the Senate and the House for the first time since 1928.

Affluence and Anxiety

The pain and sacrifice of the Great Depression and World War II led most Americans to yearn for both emotional security and material success. As expected, the family grew in importance, providing a sense of comfort and stability to people after years of separation and loss. Along with the focus on families came a changing middle-class culture, based on suburban living, a **baby boom,** an emphasis on more traditional sex roles, and an explosion of consumer goods. In the coming years, the nation's unprecedented prosperity would be measured by the increased size and abundant possessions of its thriving middle class.

baby boom
A sudden increase in births in the years after World War II.

The Postwar American Family

Beginning in 1946 the United States experienced a surge in marriage and birthrates, following record lows in the Depression decade. The young adults of this era (eighteen to thirty) became the most "marrying" generation in American history, with 97 percent of the women and 94 percent of the men taking marriage vows. By 1950 the age of marriage for American women had dropped below twenty, another record, while the percentage of divorces, initially high among returning veterans, reached an all-time low.

The baby boom was equally dramatic. The number of children per family in the United States jumped from 2.6 in 1940 to 3.2 by decade's end. Birthrates doubled for a third child and tripled for a fourth. At a time when access to birth control information was rapidly increasing, U.S. population growth rivaled not England's but rather India's.

These spiraling marriage and birth rates went hand in hand with a shift back to more traditional sex roles. Actress Ann Sothern exemplified the reordering of domestic priorities when she advised women, shortly before Japan's surrender, to begin "planning our house—our perfect house" and to think about the nursery. "I know a lot of men are dreaming of coming back not only to those girls who waved good-bye to them," she added. "They are dreaming of coming back to the mothers of their children and the least we can do as women is to try to live up to some of these expectations."

This emphasis on family life strengthened long-held prejudices against married women holding full-time jobs outside the home. As a result, the gains made in female employment during World War II largely disappeared. Returning veterans reclaimed millions of factory jobs held by women and minorities. The female labor force dropped from a wartime high of nineteen million in 1945 to less than seventeen million by 1947. Though many women gladly returned to their former domestic lives, the vast majority, according to postwar surveys, hoped to keep their jobs. "I'd stay if they wanted me to," said a female aircraft worker, "but without taking a man's place from him."

The social pressures on women were enormous. A host of "experts" asserted that women belonged in the home for their own good as well as the good of society. In their 1947 best-seller, *Modern Women: The Lost Sex,* Marynia Farnham and Ferdinand Lundberg noted that "all mature childless women are emotionally disturbed," and that "the pursuit of a career is essentially masculine." Furthermore, these experts claimed that returning veterans needed special love and attention after so many years away from home.

The concept of "mothering" as central to the postwar family was further popularized by Dr. Benjamin Spock, whose *Common Sense Book of Baby and Child Care* (1946) became the standard reference for parents of the "baby boom" generation. Although most review-

A trip to the suburban supermarket in postwar America.

ers noted Spock's relaxed, more permissive attitude toward child rearing, another message came through as well. Women must be the primary caregivers, Spock insisted. It was their role to shape the infant into a normal, happy adult. For Spock and countless others, a man's success was measured by his performance in the outside world, a woman's success by her skills in raising well-adjusted children.

The emphasis on traditional sex roles also affected female education. For the first time in history, women constituted a majority of the nation's college graduates. But the return of male veterans, combined with the educational benefits provided them by the GI Bill, reversed these temporary gains. Although the number of college women increased after World War II, the percentage of females in the college population declined dramatically. Worse, the percentage of college women who actually graduated fell from 40 percent during World War II to 25 percent by 1950.

The steepest declines occurred in professional education. Engineering colleges, which doubled their enrollments to more than two hundred thousand by 1946, accepted fewer than thirteen hundred women. Female enrollments in medical schools dropped from a high of 15 percent during World War II to 5 percent by 1950. A study of medical students in this era showed that the majority of men, believing they made better doctors, thought that women should face tougher admission standards. The majority of women, insisting that marriage was more important than a career, claimed they would cut back their hours, or even stop working, to meet their family obligations. On campuses across the nation, educators struggled to find the proper curriculum for female students. The ideal, said one college president, was to enable women "to foster the intellectual and emotional life of her family and community."

Before long, the postwar American woman became the nation's primary consumer. Between 1946 and 1950, Americans purchased twenty-one million automobiles, twenty million refrigerators, five and a half million electric stoves, and more than two million dishwashers. This consumer explosion resulted from a combination of factors: the baby boom, the huge savings accumulated during World War II, the availability of credit, and the effectiveness of mass advertising in creating consumer demand. In 1950, as consumer debt surpassed $100 billion, the Diner's Club introduced America's first credit card. The Depression age virtues of thrift and savings seemed as remote as the Depression itself.

Ironically, this new consumer society led millions of women back into the labor force. By 1950 more women were working outside the home than ever before. The difference, however, was that postwar American women returned to low-paying, often part-time employment in "feminine" jobs such as clerks, salespeople, secretaries, waitresses, telephone operators, and domestics. Working to supplement the family income, American women earned but 53 percent of the wages of American men in 1950—a drop of 10 percent since the heady years of "Rosie the Riveter" during World War II.

Suburbia

No possession was more prized by the postwar American family than the suburban home. In 1944 fewer than 120,000 new houses were built in the United States, a figure that rose to 900,000 by 1946, and 1.7 million by 1950. More than 80 percent of these new houses were built in suburban areas surrounding established cities. The rush to suburbia was accelerated by a flood of federal mortgage money and a revolution in the building of affordable, single-family homes.

The GI Bill provided the cash to bolster demand. Leading the way were builders like William Levitt, who purchased several thousand acres of farmland in Hempstead, New York, twenty-five miles east of Manhattan, for the mass production of private homes. Levitt modeled his operation after Henry Ford's automobile assembly plants. His building materials were produced and precut in Levitt factories, delivered by Levitt trucks, and assembled by Levitt work crews, each performing a single task. The typical dwelling—a solid, two-bedroom Cape Cod, with a kitchen-dining room, living room with fireplace, single bath, and expansion attic—sold for $7,900. When completed, **Levittown**, Long Island, contained 17,000 houses, plus dozens of parks, ball fields, swimming pools, churches, and shopping areas for the 53,286 residents. Levitt followed his Long Island venture with similar towns in Pennsylvania and New Jersey.

Levittown
An unincorporated community of 53,286 people in southeast New York on western Long Island, which was founded in 1947 as a low-cost housing development for World War II veterans.

City dwellers were attracted by Levittown's good schools, safe streets, and open space. The idea of owning one's home, moreover, was a central part of the American dream. And these suburban neighborhoods, filled with young families, provided a sense of shared experience and community that large cities sometimes lacked. What stood out to others, however, was the "sameness" of Levittown—a place where people lived in similar houses, accumulated similar possessions, and conformed to similar rules. Levitt salesmen restricted their communities to white applicants, who then signed pledges saying they would not resell their homes to blacks. As late as the 1960s, the percentage of African Americans living in the three Levittown developments was well below 1 percent, a figure that represented most suburban areas nationwide. Furthermore, Levittown appeared to reinforce the traditional family roles of postwar America, with mothers caring for their children while fathers commuted long distances to work.

The Soviet Threat

Relations between the United States and the Soviet Union were moving swiftly downhill. The failure to find common ground on a host of vital issues raised anger and suspicion on both sides. Soviet leaders now viewed the United States as largely indifferent to the security needs of the Russian people, and American leaders increasingly portrayed the Soviet Union as a belligerent force in the world, bent more on expanding its empire than on defending its territory. The Grand Alliance was over; the Cold War had begun.

Containment

Within hours of Germany's surrender, President Truman had signed an executive order ending Lend-Lease aid to the Allies. Though Truman reversed himself under a storm of criticism, Congress abolished Lend-Lease following Japan's surrender in August 1945. A few months later, the United States gave England a low-interest $3.75 billion loan, while ignoring a similar request from the Russians.

Stalin angrily viewed these moves as a sign of U.S. indifference to the suffering of his people. In February 1946 the Soviet leader delivered a major address predicting the collapse of capitalism and the dawn of a Communist world. The following month, with Truman at his side, former Prime Minister Churchill told an audience at Westminster College in Missouri that Russia had drawn an **iron curtain** across Europe. The West must unite against Soviet expansion, Churchill said.

A more compelling rebuttal to Stalin's speech came from a forty-two-year-old foreign service officer stationed at the U.S. Embassy in Moscow. In an eight-thousand-word telegram, George F. Kennan laid out the doctrine of "containment." According to Kennan, Russia was determined to expand its empire and to undermine Western democratic values. Serious negotiations were futile. America must define its vital interests and then be prepared to defend them through "the adroit and vigilant application of counterforce at a series of constantly shifting geographical and political points."

Kennan's "long telegram" arrived in Washington at the perfect time. Poland and Eastern Europe were now lost causes; there seemed little that the United States could do to change their dismal fate. The present objective, Truman believed, was to block Communist expansion into new areas vulnerable to Soviet influence and control.

The Truman Doctrine and the Marshall Plan

The new trouble spot appeared to be the Mediterranean, where Russia was demanding territorial concessions from Iran and Turkey, and where Communist-led guerrillas were battling the Greek government in a bloody civil war. Early in 1947, Great Britain, the traditional power in that area, informed the United States that it could no longer provide military and economic assistance to Greece and Turkey. It urged the United States to maintain that aid in order to prevent further Soviet expansion.

At a White House meeting six days later, **General George C. Marshall,** the new secretary of state, presented the case for U.S. aid to congressional leaders from both parties. When Marshall's soft-spoken approach failed to rally the meeting, his assistant, Dean

Iron Curtain
The military, political, and ideological barrier established between the Soviet bloc and Western Europe from 1945 to 1990.

General George C. Marshall
A soldier, diplomat, and politician who, as U.S. secretary of state (1947–1949), organized the European Recovery Plan, often called the Marshall Plan, for which he received the 1953 Nobel Peace Prize.

The Truman Doctrine, March 12, 1947

While recommending military aid for the anti-Communist governments of Greece and Turkey, President Harry Truman warned the American people about a grave new threat to world peace and democratic ideals. His graphic warnings about Soviet expansion, and the need to combat it, set a militant tone in foreign policy for decades to come.

AT THE present moment in world history nearly every nation must choose between alternative ways of life. The choice is too often not a free one.

One way of life is based upon the will of the majority, and is distinguished by free institutions, representative government, free elections, guarantees of individual liberty, freedom of speech and religion, and freedom from political oppression.

The second way of life is based upon the will of the minority forcibly imposed upon the majority. It relies upon terror and oppression, a controlled press and radio, fixed elections, and the suppression of personal freedoms.

I believe that it must be the policy of the United States to support free peoples who are resisting attempted subjugation by armed minorities or by outside pressures.

I believe that we must assist free peoples to work out their own destinies in their own way. . . .

Should we fail to aid Greece and Turkey in this fateful hour, the effect will be far reaching to the west as well as to the east. We must take immediate and resolute action.

I therefore ask the Congress to provide authority for assistance to Greece and Turkey in the amount of $400,000,000 for the period ending June 30, 1948. . . .

The seeds of totalitarian regimes are nurtured by misery and want. They spread and grow in the evil soil of poverty and strife. They reach their full growth when the hope of a people for a better life has died. We must keep that hope alive. The free peoples of the world look to us for support in maintaining their freedoms.

If we falter in our leadership, we may endanger the peace of the world—and we shall surely endanger the welfare of this nation.

Great responsibilities have been placed upon us by the swift movement of events. I am confident that the Congress will face these responsibilities squarely.

Questions to Consider

1. Why did President Truman feel the need to paint such a stark picture for the American people?

2. How did the Truman Doctrine differ in tone and substance from the Marshall Plan?

3. How did it fit into the overall strategy of containment?

Explore additional primary sources related to this chapter on the *American Passages* Web site: http://history.wadsworth.com/ayersbrief02.

Source: *Congressional Record,* March 12, 1947.

Acheson, took over. In sweeping terms, Acheson portrayed the future of Greece and Turkey as a test case of U.S. resolve against Soviet aggression. If Greece fell to the Communists, Acheson warned, other nations would follow "like apples in a barrel infected by one rotten one." When he finished, Republican Senator Arthur Vandenberg of Michigan summed up the feeling in the room. "Mr. President," he said, turning to Harry Truman, "if you will say that to Congress and the country, I will support you and I believe most members will do the same."

On March 12, 1947, the president offered his **Truman Doctrine** before a joint session of Congress and a national radio audience. In the present crisis, he began, "every nation must choose between alternative ways of life." One way guaranteed "individual liberty" and "political freedom," the other promoted "terror" and "oppression." In a world of good and evil, it "must be the policy of the United States to support free peoples who are resisting attempted subjugation by armed minorities or by outside pressures."

Some critics noted that the regimes in Greece and Turkey were a far cry from the democratic ideals that the president lauded in his speech. Others worried that the Truman Doctrine would lead the United States into an expensive, open-ended crusade against left-wing

Truman Doctrine
Reflecting a tougher approach to the Soviet Union following World War II, President Truman went before Congress in 1947 to request $400 million in military aid for Greece and Turkey, claiming the appropriation was vital to the containment of Communism and to the future of freedom everywhere.

Marshall Plan

Also known as the European Recovery Plan, this 1947 U.S. plan costing about $13 billion was credited with restoring economic confidence throughout Western Europe, raising living standards, curbing the influence of local Communist parties, and increasing U.S. trade and investment on the Continent.

forces around the globe. Yet most Americans supported Truman's position, and Congress allocated $400 million in military aid for Greece and Turkey.

On June 5, 1947, at the Harvard University commencement, Secretary of State Marshall unveiled a far more ambitious proposal known as the European Recovery Plan (ERP), or the **Marshall Plan.** The danger seemed clear: without massive economic aid, European governments might collapse, leaving chaos in their wake. "Our policy is not directed against any country or doctrine," Marshall said, "but against hunger, poverty, desperation, and fear."

Several weeks later, seventeen European nations met in Paris to assess their common needs. But the Russians walked out after a few sessions, forcing nations like Poland and Hungary to leave as well. The Soviets balked at the idea of divulging critical information about their economy to outsiders. And they surely feared that massive U.S. aid would tie them to a capitalist orbit that might undermine the Communist system.

Truman was not sorry to see them leave. He had been forced to invite all European nations to participate in order to avoid the appearance of worsening the Cold War. Yet he realized that Congress would not look favorably on the prospect of spending billions of dollars to reconstruct a nation that seemed so brutal to its neighbors. With the Russians and their satellites out of the picture, the remaining European nations prepared an agenda for economic recovery that came to $27 billion, a staggering sum. After six months of bitter debate, Congress reduced that figure by about one-half.

The Marshall Plan proved a tremendous success. By creating jobs and raising living standards, it restored economic confidence throughout Western Europe while curbing the influence of local Communist parties. Furthermore, it increased U.S. trade and investment in Europe, opening vast new markets for U.S. goods. As President Truman noted, "peace, freedom, and world trade are indivisible."

The rising prosperity in Western Europe was matched by growing repression in the East. Stalin moved first on Hungary, staging a rigged election. Opponents of the new Communist regime were silenced and imprisoned. Next came Czechoslovakia, where the Soviets toppled a coalition government led by Jan Masaryk. A few days later, Masaryk either jumped or was pushed to his death from an office window in Prague. Against this ominous background, President Truman proposed legislation to streamline the nation's military and diplomatic services. Passed as the National Security Act of 1947, it unified the armed forces under a single Department of Defense, created the National Security Council (NSC) to provide foreign policy information to the president, and established the Central Intelligence Agency (CIA) to coordinate intelligence gathering abroad. By 1948 the Cold War was in full swing.

The Marshall Plan at work in West Berlin. Billions of dollars in U.S. aid helped rebuild much of war-ravaged Europe.

Liberalism in Retreat

In foreign affairs President Truman could count on strong bipartisan support. But the president had no such luck on domestic issues. For one thing, the widening rift with Russia produced a growing concern about the influence of Communists and their "sympathizers" inside the federal government. For another, the president's attempt to extend the liberal agenda through ambitious social and economic legislation—known as the "Fair Deal"—met with stiff resistance in Congress after 1946.

The Cold War at Home

The Iron Curtain that descended on Europe had a tremendous psychological impact on the United States. The defeat of fascism had not made the world a safer place: one form of totalitarianism had been replaced by another. The result was an erosion of public tolerance for left-wing activity, spurred on by prominent government officials like Attorney General Tom Clark, who warned that Communists were "everywhere" in the United States—"in factories, offices, butcher shops, on street corners, in private businesses, and each carries with him the germs of death for society."

In fact, the American Communist party was far weaker in 1947 than it had been a decade before, and its numbers were dwindling by the day. Yet that did not stop President Truman from establishing a Federal Loyalty-Security Program that called for extensive background checks of all civilian workers in the federal bureaucracy. The criteria for disloyalty included everything from espionage to "sympathetic association" with groups deemed "subversive" by the attorney general. The Loyalty-Security Program provided minimal safeguards for the accused. Even worse, it frightened the country by conceding the possibility that a serious problem existed.

The congressional assault on domestic subversion was led by the **House Un-American Activities Committee (HUAC).** Formed in the 1930s to investigate Nazi propaganda in the United States, HUAC had been revived after World War II as a watchdog against Communist propaganda. Among its more visible members was a young congressman from southern California named Richard M. Nixon. In 1947 HUAC launched a spectacular investigation of the motion picture industry, alleging that "flagrant communist propaganda films" had been produced during World War II. The committee subpoenaed a number of pro-Communist writers and directors, who angrily refused to answer questions about their political beliefs and associations. Known as the "Hollywood Ten," these individuals were cited for contempt, sent to jail, and "blacklisted" from working in the entertainment industry. HUAC also heard from a host of "friendly" Hollywood witnesses, including movie stars Gary Cooper and Ronald Reagan.

The following year brought HUAC even more publicity. A witness named Whittaker Chambers, then a senior editor for *Time* magazine, claimed to have once been part of a "Communist cell" in Washington that included **Alger Hiss,** a former government official who had advised President Roosevelt in foreign affairs. Hiss denied Chambers's allegations in testimony before HUAC a few days later. When Chambers repeated the charge on a national radio broadcast, Hiss sued him for libel.

Chambers struck back hard, producing dozens of classified State Department documents from the 1930s which, he claimed, had been stolen by Hiss and passed on to the Russians. Suddenly the ground had shifted to espionage, a more serious charge. The evidence—known as the "Pumpkin Papers" because Chambers had briefly hidden them in a pumpkin patch on his Maryland farm—included five rolls of microfilm and summaries of confidential reports written by Hiss in longhand or typed on a Woodstock typewriter he once owned. In December 1948 a federal grand jury indicted Hiss for perjuring himself before HUAC. The first trial ended in a hung jury; the second one sent Hiss to jail.

The guilty verdict sent shock waves through the nation. Not only did it bolster Republican charges about the threat of Communists in government, it also served to undermine the liberal-internationalist philosophy that had guided the Democratic party since 1933. If Alger Hiss was a traitor, some wondered, how many just like him were still loose in the Truman administration, working secretly to help the Soviet Union win the Cold War?

The Domestic Agenda

The Republican landslide of 1946 appeared to signal the decline of American liberalism. In the following months, the Republican Congress brushed aside President Truman's proposals for national health insurance and federal aid to education while passing major legislation, known as the Taft-Hartley Act, to curb the power of organized labor. Republican leaders viewed the union movement as both an ally of the Democratic party and a threat to the employer's authority in the workplace. In 1947 organized labor was at the height of its influence, with fifteen million members nationwide. More than 35 percent of all nonagricultural workers belonged to a union, the highest total ever reached in the United States.

To counter the threats of powerful unions such as the United Mine Workers, Taft-Hartley gave the president authority to impose an eighty-day "cooling-off" period to prevent strikes that threatened the national interest. More important, the bill outlawed the

House Un-American Activities Committee (HUAC)
Formed in the 1930s as a watchdog against Nazi propaganda, HUAC was revived after World War II as a watchdog against Communist propaganda.

Alger Hiss
A U.S. public official accused of espionage at the height of the Cold War, he was convicted of perjury in 1950 in a controversial case.

closed shop, a device that forced workers to join a union at the time they were hired, and it encouraged the states to pass "right to work" laws that made union organizing more difficult. Though Truman strongly opposed Taft-Hartley, the Republican Congress easily overrode his veto.

Truman also confronted the issue of racial discrimination by forming a special task force on civil rights. Its final report included a series of bold recommendations, such as the desegregation of the armed forces and the creation of a special division within the Justice Department devoted solely to civil rights. Truman endorsed these recommendations, although his personal feelings about them were mixed. As a political leader, he had to balance the interests of two distinct Democratic party voting blocs: southern whites and northern blacks. As an individual, he believed that all citizens deserved political rights and equal opportunity, yet he felt uncomfortable with the notion of *social* equality for African Americans. Addressing the NAACP's national convention in 1947, Truman spoke out strongly against prejudice and hate. "The only limit to a [person's] achievement," he declared, "should be his ability, his industry, and his character."

Breaking the Color Line

Truman's statement seemed particularly appropriate in 1947. On April 15, Major League baseball broke its longstanding "color line" in an opening day game at Brooklyn's Ebbets Field. "History was made here Tuesday afternoon," reported the *Pittsburgh Courier*, an African American newspaper, "when smiling **Jackie Robinson** trotted out on the green-swept diamond with the rest of his Dodger teammates."

Baseball had been all white for generations. Blacks played in the so-called Negro Leagues. Poorly paid, they often barnstormed from town to town, taking on local teams in exhibitions that combined great baseball with crowd-pleasing entertainment. The top players—pitcher Leroy "Satchel" Paige, catcher Josh Gibson, infielder George "Cool Papa" Bell—were as good, if not better, than the top Major League stars. Yet the vast majority of Major League owners opposed integration.

Branch Rickey of the Brooklyn Dodgers was an exception. Mixing deep religious values with shrewd business sense, Rickey insisted that integration was good for America, for baseball, and for the Dodgers. To break the color line, Rickey selected Jack Roosevelt Robinson. The son of sharecroppers and the grandson of slaves, Robinson moved from rural Georgia to Pasadena, California, where his athletic skills earned him a scholarship to UCLA. A letterman in four different sports—baseball, football, basketball, and track—he also won tournaments in tennis and golf. Drafted into the Army during World War II, Robinson fought bigotry at every turn. As a second lieutenant in a segregated tank unit, he was court-martialed for insubordination, and acquitted, after refusing to move to the rear of an Army bus. Honorably discharged in 1944, he joined the Kansas City Monarchs, a Negro League team, as a shortstop at $400 a month.

Rickey met secretly with Robinson in the fall of 1945. Talent was not an issue; Robinson was hitting .385 for the Monarchs. What most concerned Rickey was Robinson's temper. For three hours, Rickey grilled Robinson about the need for absolute self-control. "Do you want a ballplayer who's afraid to fight back?" Robinson asked. "I want a ballplayer with enough guts *not* to fight back," Rickey answered. "You will symbolize a crucial cause. One incident, just one incident, can set it back twenty years." "Mr. Rickey," Robinson replied, "if you want to take this gamble, I will promise you there will be no incident."

Robinson kept his word, enduring segregated hotels, racial insults, even death threats against his family. His pioneering effort caught the public's fancy, and huge crowds followed him everywhere, with black fans leading the way. By season's end, Robinson had led the Dodgers to the National League pennant and won "Rookie of the Year."

Jackie Robinson
The first African American player in the Major Leagues in the twentieth century, he was a second baseman for the Brooklyn Dodgers, had a lifetime batting average of .311, and was inducted into the Baseball Hall of Fame in 1962.

Jackie Robinson, who broke Major League baseball's color line in 1947, led the Brooklyn Dodgers to six pennants and a World Series victory in his brilliant career.

AP/Wide World

It would be another decade before all Major League teams accepted integration. Yet the efforts begun by Branch Rickey and Jackie Robinson helped change the face of America by democratizing its "National Game." Looking back on the events of 1947, sportswriter Jimmy Cannon recalled a side of Robinson that captured both his courage and his pain. He was, said Cannon, "the loneliest man I have ever seen in sports."

Man of the People

As the 1948 presidential election approached, Harry Truman seemed a beaten man. His relations with Congress were stormy and unproductive. The press, remembering the elegant and fatherly FDR, portrayed Truman as too small for the job. Likely supporters deserted him in droves. In December 1947 a band of left-wing Democrats formed the Progressive Citizens of America. Their leader was Henry Wallace, the former vice president and secretary of commerce, who had been fired by Truman for criticizing the administration's firm stance toward the Soviet Union. Wallace opposed both the Truman Doctrine and the Marshall Plan. Though he had no hope of winning the presidential election in 1948, his Progressive party seemed likely to split the Democratic vote.

Some urged Truman not to run. A number of Democratic leaders suggested other presidential candidates, including General Dwight D. Eisenhower. *The New Republic,* a favorite of liberals, ran the front cover headline: "HARRY TRUMAN SHOULD QUIT." The Democrats convened in Philadelphia, where the heat was oppressive and tempers grew short. When word reached the convention that Eisenhower was unavailable, "Boss" Frank Hague of Jersey City threw down his cigar. "Truman," he mumbled. "Harry Truman, oh my God!"

Left with no alternative, the delegates nominated Truman for president and Alben Barkley, the Senate majority leader from Kentucky, for vice president. Barkley had strong ties to the South. Yet even he could not prevent the convention from dividing along sectional lines when northern liberals, led by Mayor Hubert Humphrey of Minneapolis, demanded the endorsement of Truman's civil rights initiatives. The passage of a strong civil rights plank led many southern Democrats to walk out of the convention. Two days later, waving Confederate flags and denouncing Harry Truman, they formed the States' Rights (Dixiecrat) party at a gathering in Birmingham, Alabama. The Dixiecrats chose governors Strom Thurmond of South Carolina and Fielding Wright of Mississippi to be their presidential and vice presidential candidates. Their platform demanded "complete segregation of the races."

Divided into three camps, the Democratic party appeared hopelessly overmatched. Not only did President Truman face Henry Wallace on his left and Strom Thurmond on his right, but the national Republican ticket of New York Governor Thomas E. Dewey for president and California Governor Earl Warren for vice president was the strongest in years. Truman's campaign strategy was to portray himself as a common people's president, protecting the voters and their hard-earned New Deal benefits from a heartless Republican assault. To highlight these differences, he called a special session of Congress to demand passage of an eight-point program that included civil rights, public housing, federal aid to education, a higher minimum wage, and storage facilities for farmers. When the Republican Congress refused to act, calling Truman's move a "publicity stunt," the president lambasted the Republicans as selfish politicians, interested only in the rich.

Truman also used his presidential power in significant ways. He showed support for the new state of Israel by offering it political recognition and economic assistance. He issued his promised executive order desegregating the armed forces. And he forcefully confronted Stalin in a showdown over Germany and Berlin.

In June 1948 Russian troops blockaded West Berlin to protest the merging of the French, British, and American occupation zones into the unified nation of West Germany. The city lay deep inside Soviet-controlled territory. Truman ruled out force to break the blockade because American troops were greatly outnumbered. Instead, he and his advisors decided to supply West Berlin from the air. In the coming months, Western pilots made close to three hundred thousand flights into the city, delivering food, fuel, and medical supplies. By the time the Russians called off their blockade, Berlin, the former Nazi capital, had become the symbol of resistance to Communist oppression.

AP/Wide World

A beaming Harry Truman holds up the mistaken *Chicago Daily Tribune* headline following his upset victory over Republican candidate Thomas Dewey in the 1948 presidential election.

Truman could see his fortunes rising as the 1948 campaign progressed. Crisscrossing the nation by train, he drew huge, friendly crowds at each whistle stop. To shouts of "Give 'em hell, Harry!" he ripped into the "do-nothing" Republican Congress and their "plans" to dismantle Franklin Roosevelt's work. "The Republican politicians don't like the New Deal. They want to get rid of it," Truman repeated. "This is a crusade of the people against the special interests, and if you back me up we're going to win."

The experts didn't think so. Opinion polls showed Dewey with a substantial lead. On election eve, the staunchly Republican *Chicago Tribune* carried the now-famous mistaken headline: "Dewey Defeats Truman."

In fact, Truman won the closest presidential contest since 1916, collecting 24.1 million votes to Dewey's 22 million, and 303 electoral votes to Dewey's 189. Strom Thurmond captured 1.1 million votes and four southern states under the Dixiecrat banner, while Henry Wallace won no states and barely a million votes. Ironically, the three-way Democratic split appeared to help Truman by allowing him to speak out forcefully against Soviet expansion and to aggressively court African American voters in the pivotal northern industrial states. In the end, the people chose Truman's frank, common appeal over Dewey's stiff, evasive demeanor.

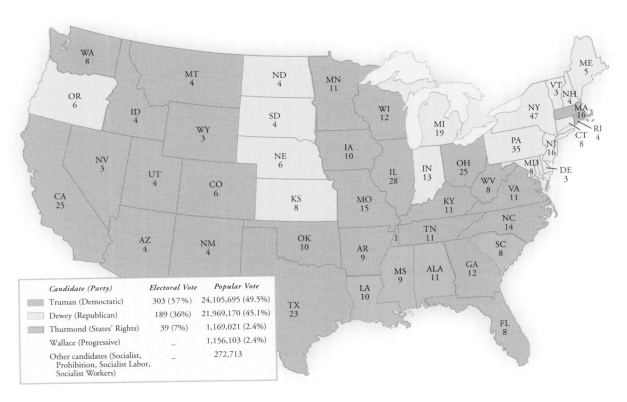

Candidate (Party)	Electoral Vote	Popular Vote
Truman (Democratic)	303 (57%)	24,105,695 (49.5%)
Dewey (Republican)	189 (36%)	21,969,170 (45.1%)
Thurmond (States' Rights)	39 (7%)	1,169,021 (2.4%)
Wallace (Progressive)	—	1,156,103 (2.4%)
Other candidates (Socialist, Prohibition, Socialist Labor, Socialist Workers)	—	272,713

MAP 27.1 The Election of 1948

The presidential election of 1948 is considered one of the greatest upsets in U.S. political history. Because there were four significant candidates, two running on third-party tickets, the victor, President Truman, captured a majority of the electoral votes without actually winning a majority of the popular vote.

Trouble in Asia

Truman had little time to savor his victory. In the summer of 1949, an American spy plane returned from a flight over the Soviet Union with photographs revealing strong traces of radioactive material. The conclusion was obvious: Russia had exploded an atomic device. Combined with alarming new developments in Asia, the loss of America's atomic monopoly served to heighten global tensions.

The Fall of China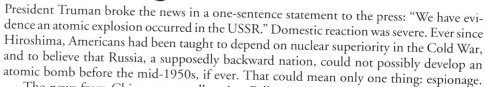

President Truman broke the news in a one-sentence statement to the press: "We have evidence an atomic explosion occurred in the USSR." Domestic reaction was severe. Ever since Hiroshima, Americans had been taught to depend on nuclear superiority in the Cold War, and to believe that Russia, a supposedly backward nation, could not possibly develop an atomic bomb before the mid-1950s, if ever. That could mean only one thing: espionage.

The news from China was equally grim. Following World War II, Chiang Kai-shek and his Nationalist (Kuomintang) forces had renewed their offensive against the Communist forces of Mao Tse-tung. Chiang counted heavily on American support. He believed that his powerful friends in Congress and his image as China's savior would force the Truman administration to back him at all costs.

Chiang was mistaken. The president and his advisors were far less interested in Asia than they were in Western Europe. They were not about to be trapped into an open-ended commitment in the Far East. From 1946 to 1949 the United States gave Chiang's government about $2 billion in military aid—enough, it was hoped, to satisfy Chiang's American friends without seriously affecting the more important buildup in Europe.

As civil war raged in China, Chiang's forces met defeat after defeat. Much of the American weaponry was discarded by fleeing Nationalist troops; it would end up in Communist hands. In August 1949 the State Department issued a 1,054-page "White Paper on China," conceding that the world's largest country was about to fall to the Communists. "The unfortunate but inescapable fact," said Dean Acheson, the new secretary of state, "is that the ominous result of the civil war in China was beyond [our] control." Though Acheson was correct, his White Paper sounded more like an excuse than an explanation. Americans were angered and bewildered by Chiang's demise. How well did "containment" really work, many wondered, when more than six hundred million people were "lost" to Communism?

This question was discussed in National Security Council (NSC) Paper Number 68, a secret document drafted by Acheson and Paul Nitze in 1950. According to NSC 68, Communist advances could and must be stopped by an abundance of military power. The United States should act in concert with other nations wherever possible, but alone if need be. The document called for an unprecedented peacetime increase in military spending and for the construction of a huge new "thermonuclear device," the hydrogen bomb. Though Truman never showed this document to Congress, it became, in Acheson's words, "the fundamental paper" governing America's defense policy in the coming years.

War in Korea

On June 25, 1950, troops from Communist North Korea invaded anti-Communist South Korea in a massive land assault. Korea had been arbitrarily divided by Russian and U.S. troops at the end of World War II. In 1948 an election to unify Korea had been canceled when the Soviets refused to allow UN observers north of the dividing line at the 38th parallel. A stalemate thus developed, with Kim Il Sung, the pro-Communist dictator of North Korea, and Syngman Rhee, the anti-Communist dictator of South Korea, making daily threats to "liberate" each other's land.

The North Korean attack put great pressure on President Truman. His administration had treated the Rhee government with indifference, removing U.S. combat troops from Korea in 1949. Yet here was a classic case of aggression, Truman believed. To ignore it was to encourage it elsewhere.

There were political considerations too. If the president did nothing, he would only reinforce the Republican charge that his administration was "soft" on Communism. Thus, Truman moved quickly, proposing a UN resolution that offered "such assistance to South

Korea as may be necessary to repel armed attack." A week later, without consulting Congress, Truman dispatched ground troops to South Korea.

Letters and telegrams of support poured into the White House, and the news from the front kept improving. After two months of backward movement, UN troops under the command of General Douglas MacArthur took the offensive. In September 1950 MacArthur outflanked the enemy with a brilliant amphibious landing at Inchon, on South Korea's west coast. By October UN troops had crossed the 38th parallel in pursuit of the routed North Korean Army.

There were ominous signs, however. First, by sending troops into North Korea, President Truman and the United Nations had gone beyond their original mandate to defend South Korea from outside aggression. Second, General MacArthur appeared oblivious to the possibility that Communist China might enter the war. As UN forces drove north, they captured scores of Chinese Communist troops near the Yalu River that divided North Korea and Manchuria. On November 5 the Chinese attacked, pushing MacArthur's startled Army back toward the 38th parallel. In the following weeks, U.S. Army and Marine units fought their way through mountain blizzards and a wall of Chinese infantry to form a defense line just south of the 38th parallel. Although disaster had been averted, the nation was shocked by what *Time* magazine described as "the worst military setback the United States has ever suffered."

By March 1951 the Communist offensive had stalled. UN forces pushed ahead to the 38th parallel, where the two sides faced each other in a bloody standoff. General MacArthur called for an escalation of the war, recommending a naval blockade of China's coast, massive bombing of its factories and power plants, and an invasion of the Chinese mainland by the forces of Chiang Kai-shek.

This plea for an expanded war was understandable. MacArthur, like most Americans, believed in the concept of total victory. His message, quite simply, was that the lands surrendered to the Communists by weak-kneed civilians like Truman and Acheson could be recaptured through the full exercise of U.S. military power.

The president saw things differently. Any attempt to widen the war, he realized, would alarm other UN participants. The Soviets might send troops to the Asian front or put pressure on Western Europe. Furthermore, Russia's involvement raised the threat of nuclear attack. As General Omar Bradley noted, MacArthur's strategy was the very opposite of the one proposed by President Truman and the Joint Chiefs of Staff. "So long as we regard the Soviet Union as the main antagonist and Western Europe as the main prize," he said, "it would involve us in the wrong war, at the wrong place, at the wrong time, and with the wrong enemy."

Despite repeated warnings from the president, MacArthur refused to keep his views to himself. The final blowup came in April 1951 when Republicans in Congress released a letter that MacArthur had sent them from the battlefield that criticized Truman's refusal to meet force "with maximum counterforce," and ended with the oft-

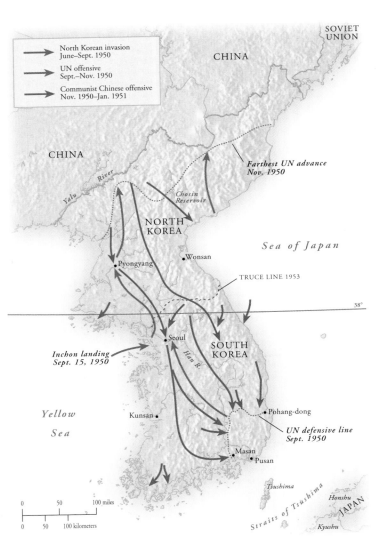

MAP 27.2 **The Korean War**

This map shows the main offensive thrusts: the North Korean attack into South Korea in June 1950; the Inchon landing of September 15, 1950; the UN offensive in the fall of 1950; and the Communist Chinese counteroffensive beginning in November of 1950. The war ended in stalemate, with the final truce line almost identical to the previous division of Korea into North and South at the 38th parallel.

quoted phrase: "There is no substitute for victory." Furious at such insubordination, the president relieved MacArthur of his command.

MacArthur returned to the United States a genuine folk hero, a man who symbolized old military values. Letters to the White House ran twenty to one against his firing. On Capitol Hill, angry representatives placed some of the telegrams they received into the *Congressional Record:* "Impeach the Imbecile" and "We Wish to Protest the Latest Outrage by the Pig in the White House." Harry Truman's old standard—"If you can't stand the heat, stay out of the kitchen"—had never been more strenuously tested.

McCarthyism and the Election of 1952

On a bleak February evening in 1950, a little-known politician delivered a speech about "Communist subversion" in the federal government to a Republican women's club in Wheeling, West Virginia. The topic was a common one, and large portions of the speech had been lifted word for word from a recent address by Congressman Richard Nixon. Only one explosive sentence had been added. "I have here in my hand," **Senator Joseph R. McCarthy** of Wisconsin told his audience, "a list of 205 Communists that were made known to the secretary of state and who are still working and shaping the policy of the State Department." The message was clear: America was losing the Cold War to the evil forces of Communism because the U.S. government was filled with "dupes" and "traitors" who *wanted* the Communists to win.

The Rise of Joe McCarthy

McCarthy held no list in his hand that night in Wheeling. He knew nothing about Communists in government or anywhere else. But the newspapers printed his charges, and the public was aroused. McCarthy had struck a nerve in the country, rubbed raw by Soviet aggression in Europe, the Communist victory in China, the Alger Hiss case, and the news of the Russian atomic bomb.

McCarthy's charges of treason in high places made him an instant celebrity. His face adorned the covers of *Newsweek* and *Time.* The *Washington Post* cartoonist Herblock coined a new word to describe his reckless behavior: "McCarthyism." But prominent Republicans, sensing the political benefits of the "Communist issue," rallied to his side.

President Truman viewed McCarthy as a shameless publicity hound who would say anything to make headlines. He was right about the senator, yet helpless to stop him. The fear of Communism kept growing, aided by the outbreak of war in Korea. Air raid drills became the order of the day. In school practice drills students were taught to dive under their desks and shield their eyes against atomic blasts. In New York City, school officials distributed metal "dog tags." "If a bomb gets me in the street," a first-grader explained, "people will know what my name is."

McCarthy's attacks grew bolder. As the 1952 presidential campaign approached, he called George C. Marshall a traitor, mocked Dean Acheson as the "Red Dean of fashion," and described President Truman as a drunkard, adding, "the son-of-a-bitch ought to be impeached." Yet party colleagues continued to encourage McCarthy, viewing him as the man who could turn public anxiety and distrust into Republican votes.

Joseph McCarthy
A U.S. senator from Wisconsin (1947–1957), he presided over the permanent subcommittee on investigations and held public hearings in which he accused Army officials, members of the media, and public figures of being Communists. These charges were never proved, and he was censured by the Senate in 1954.

The Korean War raised fears of a nuclear attack. Schoolchildren engaged in "take cover" drills by diving under their desks.

"I Like Ike"

By 1952 Harry Truman's public approval rating had dropped to 23 percent—the lowest ever recorded by a U.S. president. The *New Republic* called Truman "a spent force politically" and urged him to withdraw from the coming presidential campaign. In March Truman did just that.

He did not sulk on the sidelines, however. As the leader of his party, he wanted the Democratic nominee to defend the New Deal–Fair Deal philosophy. The most impressive candidate, Governor Adlai Stevenson of Illinois, had earned a reputation as a liberal reformer. Eloquent and witty, he appealed both to party regulars and to the liberal intelligentsia. Stevenson had his handicaps, including a recent divorce and a past friendship with Alger Hiss. The Democrats nominated him for president on the third convention ballot. Senator John Sparkman of Alabama, a Fair Dealer and a segregationist, was given the vice presidential nod.

The battle for the Republican presidential nomination was in many ways a battle for control of the Republican party. The moderate wing, represented by Governor Thomas Dewey of New York and Senator Henry Cabot Lodge Jr., of Massachusetts, was committed to internationalism and to many New Deal reforms. The conservative wing, led by Senator Robert Taft of Ohio, was suspicious of the New Deal and wary of America's expanding global commitments, especially the defense and reconstruction of Europe.

Senator Taft, the son of former President and Chief Justice William Howard Taft, had earned the respect of his colleagues and the plaudits of Washington reporters. On many domestic issues, Taft was more flexible than his conservative supporters. Yet he, too, feared that a powerful commitment to Western Europe could lead the United States into another world war.

Only one man stood between Taft and the Republican nomination. But he was a very powerful opponent. In 1948 the leaders of both major political parties had begged him, unsuccessfully, to enter their presidential primaries. "I don't believe a man should try to pass his historical peak," said General Dwight D. Eisenhower. "I think I pretty well hit mine when I accepted the German surrender in 1945." Yet his moderate Republican supporters, believing that Eisenhower alone could defeat Taft for the presidential nomination, convinced the general that people wanted him and that the country needed him.

Eisenhower, sixty-one, was raised in Abilene, Kansas, a prairie town west of Topeka. He attended schools with no lights or plumbing and earned his diploma while working the night shift in a dairy. In 1911 the young man—nicknamed Ike—won an appointment to the U.S. Military Academy at West Point. After graduating near the middle of his class, Eisenhower began his swift climb through the ranks. In the 1930s he served as chief aide to General Douglas MacArthur. In 1941 he moved to the War Department and helped plan the D-Day invasion of France. His work was so outstanding that President Roosevelt named him Commanding General, European Theater of Operations—a promotion that jumped him over hundreds of officers with greater seniority.

Eisenhower commanded history's most successful coalition force—American, British, French, Polish, and Canadian troops—with courage, diplomacy, and skill. He was brilliant at handling people and reconciling the most diverse points of view. In the following years, Eisenhower served as Army Chief of Staff, president of Columbia University, and commander of NATO forces.

The Republican convention nominated Eisenhower on the first ballot. He then defused the bitter feelings of conservatives by selecting Richard Nixon to be his running mate, and by accepting a party platform that accused the Democrats of lining their pockets, shielding traitors in high places, and bungling the Korean War.

On the campaign trail, General Eisenhower talked about leadership and morality. Traveling by train, he visited more than two hundred cities and towns. At every stop he praised America, bemoaned the "mess in Washington," and promised to clean it up. Then the whistle sounded and the train pulled away to the chants of "I Like Ike."

On September 28, 1952, the *New York Post,* a pro-Democratic newspaper, broke the biggest story of the campaign: "Secret Rich Men's Fund Keeps Nixon in Style Far Beyond His Salary." The Nixon fund (about $18,000) had never been a secret: it had been used for routine political expenses, and it was similar to those of other politicians. Nixon responded by blaming the "Reds" for his troubles. "The Communists, the left-wingers, have been fighting me with every smear," he declared.

Aboard the Eisenhower train, anxious advisors suggested that Nixon resign from the ticket. How could the general campaign against Democratic party corruption, they wondered, when his own running mate stood accused of taking secret gifts? On September 23 Nixon went on national television to explain his side of the story. He spoke about his boyhood, his family, his war record, his finances, and his admiration for General Eisenhower. He explained how the fund worked, asked the American people to support him, and then described the one gift he would never return. It was, said Nixon, "a little cocker spaniel dog and our little girl named it Checkers. And you know the kids love that dog and I just want to say that we're going to keep it."

The reaction was volcanic. More than two million phone calls and telegrams poured into Republican offices across the country. They were followed by millions of letters, running three hundred to one in Nixon's favor. Eisenhower had no choice but to keep his running mate on the ticket. The "Checkers Speech" saved Nixon's career.

It also demonstrated the emerging power of television in national affairs. In the campaign's final weeks, the Republican party ran dozens of twenty-second TV spots for Eisenhower, who used these ads to soothe voter anxiety about his views on popular New Deal welfare programs. "Social Security, housing, workmen's compensation, unemployment insurance—these are things that must be kept above politics and campaigns," he said. The general also vowed that if elected, he would visit Korea.

Stevenson tried to ridicule the announcement. "If elected," he replied, "I shall go to the White House." But on November 4, Eisenhower overwhelmed Stevenson—33.9 million votes to 27.3 million, and 442 electoral votes to 89. Eisenhower became the first Republican in decades to crack the solid South, winning four states and coming close in several others. He did well in cities, where ethnic voters, concerned about the rise of Communism in Europe, deserted the Democrats in droves.

Some observers spoke of a new Republican era, but this was not the case. Although the Republicans managed to gain a slim majority in Congress, they did so by riding the general's coattails to victory.

©Bettmann /CORBIS

Following charges that he kept a secret political slush fund, Republican vice presidential candidate Richard Nixon saved his political career in 1952 with a televised explanation that included his pet cocker spaniel, Checkers.

Summary

Alger Hiss is sworn in at a hearing of the House Un-American Activities Committee in 1948. Accused by Whittaker Chambers of being part of a Soviet espionage ring, Hiss went to federal prison in 1950 after a jury convicted him of perjury.

©Bettmann /CORBIS

Beyond Depression and War

Even before World War II ended, American planners, confident of victory, could sense the troubles that lay ahead. They saw big problems looming in foreign affairs, from the threat of Soviet expansion to the reconstruction of Western Europe and Japan. They feared that the United States might be overwhelmed by the return of fifteen million veterans to civilian life. And they worried about the impact of peace on the nation's wartime economic boom. What would happen, they wondered, when defense spending dropped and factory jobs disappeared? Was it possible, even likely, that the United States might slip back into the nightmare of the 1930s, when millions were hungry and unemployed?

The economic worries proved groundless. The war had created a near full-employment economy, though Americans at that time had little to buy. With consumer goods carefully rationed, people saved their money. By war's end, the public had a great pile of disposable income—and a powerful urge to spend. Congress, meanwhile, passed the Servicemen's Readjustment Act (or GI Bill), designed to help returning soldiers as well as to bolster the economy by encouraging veterans to get a college education and purchase a new home. The economy took off, fueled by a baby boom, a rush to suburbia, and an explosion of consumer goods. The postwar years were the most prosperous in United States history.

Things did not go as smoothly in foreign affairs. The reconstruction of Japan and Western Europe proved remarkably successful. In Japan, the U.S. occupation produced a stable, prosperous democracy; in Western Europe, demolished economies rebounded with billions of dollars of U.S. aid, much of it funneled through the Marshall Plan. At the same time, however, relations with the Soviet Union began a downward spiral, as the two re-

See for yourself!
All you want in your dream kitchen IS HERE!

Youngstown Kitchens

Peter Newark's American Pictures

An advertisement for the "dream kitchen." A surge of consumer spending after World War II quickly erased fears that the United States would slip back into economic depression.

maining superpowers of this era, suspicious of one another's intentions, entered into a Cold War punctuated by military threats and a growing arms race. One foreign policy crisis followed another: the Soviet takeover of Poland, the Iron Curtain descending over Eastern Europe, the Berlin Blockade, the fall of mainland China to Communism, and the North Korean invasion of South Korea. By 1950 the threat of international Communism seemed as ominous to the American people as the threat of Nazism had been a decade before.

Life in the postwar United States was marked by a combination of affluence and anxiety. Following two decades of depression and war, most Americans were finally enjoying the benefits of economic security, material comfort, and stable family lives. They wanted a political leader who would steer a moderate course in domestic and foreign affairs; a leader who would heal old wounds without turning back the clock; a leader who would stand up to the Russians without endorsing the conspiracy theories and smear tactics of Senator Joseph R. McCarthy; a leader who would end the present conflict in Korea without either widening it or compromising the nation's honor. In 1952 Dwight D. Eisenhower seemed to be the one.

©Bettmann /CORBIS

America liked Ike—who won a smashing victory at the polls in 1952, ending twenty years of Democratic party rule.

Making Connections Across Chapters

LOOKING BACK

Chapter 27 looks at the United States in the post–World War II years, following one of the defining moments in its history. Key points include the baby boom, the growth of suburbia, and the beginning of the Cold War.

1. What accounted for the worsening of relations between the Soviet Union and the United States?
2. Why did the wartime prosperity continue, and greatly increase, following World War II? What factors accounted for this?
3. Why did Harry Truman defeat Thomas Dewey for the presidency in 1948? Why did so many of the pundits think Dewey would win?
4. What impact did the case of Alger Hiss have on the rise of Senator Joseph R. McCarthy? What else was responsible for the popular support that McCarthy received?

LOOKING AHEAD

The next chapter examines the United States in the 1950s, a time of continued economic prosperity and material comfort, on one hand, and a time of enduring Cold War tensions and momentous racial stirrings, on the other.

1. What were the major problems Dwight Eisenhower would face in assuming the presidency?
2. Was it possible that a new administration in Washington would be better able to deal with international problems than the old one, especially problems relating to the Cold War?
3. Would the prosperity of the early postwar era last into the future, and would it expand to include the poorest groups in society?

RECOMMENDED READINGS

Ackerman, Marsha. *Cool Comfort* (2002). Describes how air-conditioning changed the way middle-class Americans lived and worked in this new age of affluence.

Bennett, Michael. *When Dreams Came True* (1996). Studies the impact of the GI Bill on the making of modern America.

Boyer, Paul. *By the Bomb's Early Light* (1985). Considers the impact of atomic weaponry on American society in the early Cold War years.

Grossman, Andrew. *Neither Dead Nor Red* (2001). Focuses on the often bizarre plans of U.S. officials to fight and survive a nuclear war.

Hamby, Alonso. *Man of the People* (1995). Examines the personal life and political career of President Harry Truman.

Jackson, Kenneth. *Crabgrass Frontier* (1985). Analyzes the suburbanization of the United States, especially after World War II.

Jones, James. *Alfred Kinsey: A Public/Private Life* (1997). The biography of the nation's leading sex researcher and his impact on American culture.

Spock, Dr. Benjamin. *Common Sense Book of Baby and Child Care* (1946). Had a lasting impact on child rearing and gender roles in the United States.

Tanenhaus, Sam. *Whittaker Chambers* (1997). Tells the absorbing story of the man who helped ignite the nation's anti-Communist crusade in the late 1940s.

Tygiel, Jules. *Baseball's Great Experiment* (1983). A fine account of Jackie Robinson and the integration of Major League baseball.

AMERICAN JOURNEY ONLINE AND INFOTRAC COLLEGE EDITION

Visit the source collections at http://ajaccess.wadsworth.com and infotrac.thomsonlearning.com and use the Search function with the following key terms to explore documents, images, audio and video clips, articles, and commentary related to the material in this chapter.

Harry S. Truman

Thomas Dewey

Marshall Plan

Truman Doctrine

Jackie Robinson

Alger Hiss

Joseph McCarthy

baby boom

HUAC

General Douglas MacArthur

ONLINE PRIMARY SOURCES

Here are some examples of the many primary sources related to this chapter that you will find on the *American Passages* Web site: http://history.wadsworth.com/ayersbrief02.

HUAC, Communism, and Hollywood, 1948 (video)

Russian Development of the Atomic Bomb, 1949

Senator Joseph McCarthy, Speech at Wheeling, West Virginia, 1950

The site also offers self-quizzes, exercises, and many additional resources to help you study.

CHAPTER 28

The Eisenhower Years

1953–1960

Cold War
War or rivalry conducted by all means available except open military action. Diplomatic relations are not commonly broken.

THE UNITED STATES IN THE 1950S WAS FAR DIFFERENT FROM THE NATION we live in today. The **Cold War** was at its height, U.S. soldiers were dying in Korea, and Communism seemed a formidable foe. The U.S. population of one hundred fifty-three million contained a small and declining number of foreign born, the result of strict immigration quotas installed in the 1920s. Most blacks still lived in the South where racial segregation was the law. Blue-collar workers outnumbered white-collar workers, and labor unions were at the height of their power. Major League baseball had only sixteen teams, none west of St. Louis. There were no supermarkets or shopping malls, no motel chains or ballpoint pens. Television was just beginning, rock music was still a few years away. It cost 3 cents to mail a letter and a nickel to buy a coke.

Marriage rates were at an all-time high, and divorce rates kept declining. In 1954 *McCall's* magazine used the term "togetherness" to describe American family life, with shared activities such as Little League, car rides, and backyard barbecues. Though more women worked outside the home in 1950 than at the height of World War II, they did so mainly to supplement the family income. In the growing cult of motherhood, fulfillment meant meeting the needs of others. Feminism was described in psychology books as a "deep illness."

America in the 1950s saw an acceleration of postwar trends: forty million people moved to the suburbs, and the large cities declined in population and quality of life. Racial lines remained rigid, with Census data showing the suburbs to be 98 percent white. Automobile sales skyrocketed, creating whole new industries to service the American traveler. Inventions poured forth, from the computer to the cure for polio, and a new president was elected to guide the country through these anxious, demanding times.

A New Direction

Dwight Eisenhower entered the White House in 1953 on a wave of good feeling. Americans trusted his judgment and admired his character. They believed that his enormous skills as a military leader would serve him equally well as president of the United States.

Modern Republicanism

Yet few Americans knew where Eisenhower stood on important domestic or international issues. His presidential campaign in 1952 had been intentionally vague. On the political spectrum, he stood somewhere between the Fair Deal Democrats of Harry Truman and

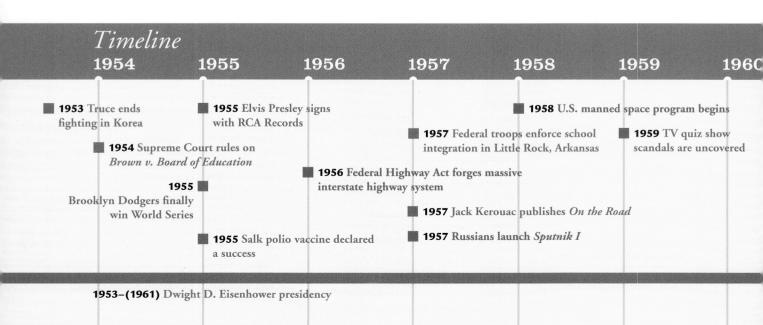

Timeline

| 1954 | 1955 | 1956 | 1957 | 1958 | 1959 | 1960 |

1953 Truce ends fighting in Korea

1954 Supreme Court rules on *Brown v. Board of Education*

1955 Brooklyn Dodgers finally win World Series

1955 Elvis Presley signs with RCA Records

1955 Salk polio vaccine declared a success

1956 Federal Highway Act forges massive interstate highway system

1957 Federal troops enforce school integration in Little Rock, Arkansas

1957 Jack Kerouac publishes *On the Road*

1957 Russians launch *Sputnik I*

1958 U.S. manned space program begins

1959 TV quiz show scandals are uncovered

1953–(1961) Dwight D. Eisenhower presidency

the conservative Republicans of Robert Taft. The new president described himself as a moderate.

Eisenhower filled his cabinet with prominent business leaders. For secretary of defense, he chose Charles E. ("Engine Charlie") Wilson, former president of General Motors. For secretary of the treasury, Eisenhower selected George Humphrey, a fiscal conservative. "We have to cut one-third out of the budget and you can't do that just by eliminating waste," Humphrey declared. "This means, whenever necessary, using a meat axe."

Eisenhower avoided such rhetoric. He had no intention of dismantling popular New Deal programs such as Social Security or unemployment insurance, and he supported a significant hike in the minimum hourly wage, from 75 cents to a dollar. Yet wherever possible, he worked to balance the budget, trim government expenditures, and stimulate private enterprise.

In his first year as president, federal spending and federal income taxes were both cut by 10 percent. Eisenhower also opposed expansion of such popular but expensive federal programs as price supports for farmers. In perhaps his most controversial early move, the president strongly supported passage of the Tidelands Oil Act, which transferred coastal oil land worth at least $40 billion from the federal government to the states. Critics, fearing the exploitation of these vital reserves by a few giant corporations, described "Tidelands" as the "most unjustified giveaway program" of the modern era.

Urban, Suburban, and Rural Americans 1940–1960

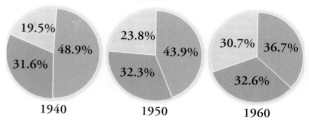

- Central-city dwellers
- Suburban dwellers
- Rural and small-town dwellers

1940: 19.5%, 31.6%, 48.9%
1950: 23.8%, 32.3%, 43.9%
1960: 30.7%, 32.6%, 36.7%

CHART 28.1 Urban, Suburban, and Rural Americans 1940–1960
These charts point to a number of important changes. First is the steady loss of population in small-town America. Second is the stagnation of the inner cities, reflecting both a loss of population in the older northern and midwestern cities and a growth in the sunbelt cities of the South and West. Third is the surge of population in the suburbs, which continues to this day.

A Truce in Korea

One member of Eisenhower's cabinet, Secretary of State John Foster Dulles, stood above the rest. The son of a minister and grandson of a former secretary of state, Dulles trained from his earliest days to serve God and country. Eisenhower respected his secretary as a tough, knowledgeable advisor who willingly took the heat for actions the president himself had formulated or approved.

The president's first priority in foreign affairs was to end the Korean conflict. Though willing to accept the same terms that Truman had proposed—two Koreas, North and South, divided at the 38th parallel—Eisenhower demanded a prompt resolution. To speed this process, Dulles apparently warned the Communist Chinese (through diplomatic channels in India) that the United States would not rule out the use of atomic weapons if the Korean stalemate dragged on.

The impact of this "nuclear threat" is difficult to gauge. The Chinese Communists probably viewed Eisenhower, a military leader, as a more dangerous foe than Harry Truman. Yet huge Communist battlefield losses, coupled with the sudden death of Joseph Stalin, helped spur the peace process. In July 1953 a truce was signed that stopped the fighting without formally ending the war. More than 50,000 Americans were killed and 103,000 were wounded in Korea. The Pentagon estimated that 2.4 million civilians died or were seriously injured in the three years of terrible fighting, along with 850,000 troops from South Korea, 520,000 from North Korea, and 950,000 from Communist China.

The Cold War at Home and Abroad

When Republicans took control of Congress and the White House in 1953, the "Communist issue" gained center stage. House Un-American Activities Committee Chairman Harold Velde of Illinois vowed to hunt down Communists like "rats." At the White House, President Eisenhower promised both a crackdown on "subversives" in government and a "New Look" in military affairs, designed to streamline U.S. forces for the continuing struggle against "worldwide Communist aggression."

The Hunt for "Subversives"

Shortly after taking office, President Eisenhower issued an executive order that extended the scope of the Federal Loyalty-Security Program. A few months later, he announced that 1,456 federal workers had been fired as "security risks." The most controversial security case involved J. Robert Oppenheimer, the distinguished physicist who directed the Manhattan Project during World War II. Oppenheimer's prewar association with left-wing radicals was widely known. He had been checked and rechecked by the FBI, cleared and recleared by the Atomic Energy Commission until 1953, when the Eisenhower administration suspended his top security clearance. Many believed that Oppenheimer's troubles resulted from his public opposition to the building of the hydrogen bomb—a charge the president vigorously denied.

Millions of Americans were riveted by the televised Army-McCarthy hearings, which lasted for thirty-six days in the spring of 1954.

In Congress, the Red-hunting fervor was even more intense. The Senate assault was led by Joseph McCarthy, newly appointed chairman of the Committee on Government Operations and its powerful Subcommittee on Investigations. Filling key staff positions with ex-FBI agents and former prosecutors, McCarthy looked for "Communist influence" in the State Department and other government agencies. His hearings didn't uncover any Communists. They did, however, ruin numerous careers, undermine worker morale, and make the United States look fearful in the eyes of the world. Not surprisingly, Republican criticism of McCarthy began to build.

Many expected Eisenhower to put the senator in his place. But the new president was slow to respond, believing that a brawl with McCarthy would divide Republicans into warring camps and seriously demean the presidential office. He changed his mind after McCarthy's subcommittee, spearheaded by Roy Cohn, an abrasive young attorney from New York, began to investigate charges that a "Communist spy ring" was operating at Fort Monmouth, New Jersey.

Army officials responded that Cohn was harassing the service in order to win preferential treatment for a close friend named G. David Schine, who had recently been drafted into the Army. Early in 1954 the Senate agreed to investigate these conflicting allegations. Eisenhower convinced Republican Senate leaders to televise the hearings. The president wanted the American people to see McCarthy in action, and it proved to be a very shrewd move. For thirty-six days, the nation watched the senator's frightening outbursts and crude personal attacks. The highlight of the hearings came on June 9, 1954, when Army counsel Joseph Welch sternly rebuked McCarthy for his menacing behavior, asking: "Have you no sense of decency, sir? Have you left *no sense of decency?*" The spectators burst into applause.

A few months later, the Senate censured McCarthy for bringing that body "into dishonor and disrepute." The vote was 67 to 22, with only conservative Republicans opposed. Many believed that McCarthy's censure was linked to the easing of Cold War tensions at home. The Korean War was over, Stalin was dead, and the radical right was in disarray. For McCarthy, things came apart at a wicked rate of speed. Reporters and colleagues ignored him, and his influence disappeared. Unable to get his message across, McCarthy spent his final days drinking in private and railing against those who had deserted his cause. He died of acute alcoholism in 1957, virtually alone, at the age of forty-eight.

Brinksmanship and Covert Action

Like Truman before him, President Eisenhower supported the containment of Communism through military, economic, and diplomatic means. What most worried him were the spiraling costs. "If we let defense spending run wild," he said, "we get inflation . . . then controls . . . then a garrison state . . . and *then* we've lost the very values we were trying to defend." Eisenhower called his solution the "New Look." In place of conventional forces, the United States must emphasize "the deterrent of massive retaliatory power." This meant using America's edge in nuclear weapons and long-range bombers to best advantage.

The "New Look" allowed Eisenhower to cut defense spending by 20 percent between 1953 and 1955. The number of men and women in uniform went down each year, while the production of atomic warheads dramatically increased. Secretary of State Dulles viewed the "New Look" as a way to intimidate potential enemies with the implied threat of atomic attack. He called this "brinksmanship."

Critics, however, saw brinksmanship as a dangerous game. Intimidation meant little, they warned, if the United States did not intend to back up its words. Was Eisenhower willing to consider atomic weapons as a viable option in every international crisis? If not, he undermined U.S. credibility; if so, he risked nuclear destruction.

In 1953 Eisenhower appointed Allen Dulles, younger brother of the secretary of state, to head the Central Intelligence Agency (CIA). Dulles emphasized "covert action" over intelligence gathering—a change the president fully endorsed. Most of the CIA's new work was cloaked in secrecy, and much of it was illegal. Covert action became one of Eisenhower's favorite foreign policy tools.

Iran was a case in point. In 1953 the new government of Mohammed Mossadegh nationalized the British-controlled oil fields and deposed the pro-Western Shah of Iran. The United States, believing Mossadegh's government to be pro-Communist, feared for its oil supplies in the Middle East. President Eisenhower thus approved a CIA operation that toppled Mossadegh and returned the young Shah to power. A few months later, Iran agreed to split its oil production among three Western nations, with U.S. companies getting 40 percent, British companies 40 percent, and Dutch companies 20 percent.

In 1954 the CIA struck again, forcing the overthrow of Guatemala's democratically elected president, Jacobo Arbenz Guzman. Guatemala was one of the world's poorest nations. Its largest employer and landholder, the U.S.-owned United Fruit Company, controlled much of the Guatemalan economy. After taking office, Arbenz Guzman supported a strike of banana workers on United Fruit plantations, who were seeking wages of $1.50 a day. Far more provocative, however, was a new law, known as Decree 900, which expropriated millions of acres of private property for the use of landless peasant families. Under this law, the Guatemalan government offered United Fruit $1.2 million for 234,000 acres of its land.

The company had powerful allies in the United States. Numerous government officials, including both Dulles brothers, were linked to United Fruit through their previous corporate positions. Defending the company's interests came naturally to them, whereas the idea of expropriating U.S. property smacked of "Communist thinking."

Eisenhower moved quickly, authorizing the overthrow of Arbenz Guzman by Guatemalan exiles trained at CIA bases in Honduras and Nicaragua. The small invasion force, backed by CIA pilots, tore through Guatemala's poorly equipped Army. The U.S. press, meanwhile, accepted the Eisenhower-Dulles account that Guatemalan liberators had ousted a dangerous, pro-Communist regime with minimal U.S. help. In the following months, the new government of General Carlos Castillo Armas established a military dictatorship and returned the expropriated lands to United Fruit.

Events in Indochina (or Vietnam) did not turn out as well. Following World War II, nationalist forces in that French colony, led by **Ho Chi Minh,** a popular Marxist leader, began an armed struggle for independence. The United States, viewing Ho (incorrectly) as a puppet of Moscow, supported French attempts to crush the Vietnamese resistance, known as the Vietminh. By 1953 U.S. military aid to France in the Indochina conflict totaled nearly $3 billion.

It failed to turn the tide. The Vietminh grew stronger. In 1954 Ho's forces surrounded twelve thousand elite French troops at an isolated garrison called Dien Bien Phu. Facing sure defeat, the French appealed to Eisenhower for help. When Secretary of State Dulles, Vice President Nixon, and several U.S. military officials suggested tactical nuclear weapons, Eisenhower was appalled. "You boys must be crazy," he said. "We can't use those awful things against Asians for the second time in ten years. My God!"

Eisenhower also refused to send U.S. ground troops to Indochina. And he rejected the use of conventional air strikes to save Dien Bien Phu unless the British took part—but Churchill sternly said no. On May 7, 1954, the battered garrison surrendered, effectively ending French rule in Vietnam.

Ho Chi Minh
Vietnamese leader and first president of North Vietnam. His army was victorious in the French Indochina War, and he later led North Vietnam's struggle to defeat the U.S.-supported government of South Vietnam. He died before the reunification of Vietnam.

At peace talks in Geneva, Switzerland, the two sides agreed to a cease-fire and a temporary partition of Vietnam at the 17th parallel. Free elections were scheduled for 1956. The United States refused to recognize the Geneva Accords. Eisenhower and Dulles were not about to acquiesce in a unified Vietnam under the leadership of Ho Chi Minh, the certain winner in the proposed election. The U.S. plan, therefore, was to prevent that election while creating a permanent anti-Communist government in South Vietnam.

domino theory
A theory that if one nation comes under Communist control, neighboring nations will soon follow.

To Eisenhower, the survival of South Vietnam became the key to containing Communism in Asia. He described the so-called **domino theory** at a press conference about Indochina in 1954. "You have a row of dominoes set up," he began. "You knock over the first one, and what will happen to the last one is a certainty that it will go over quickly. So the possible consequences of the loss [of Vietnam] are just incalculable to the free world."

The Civil Rights Movement

The 1950s witnessed enormous gains in the struggle for minority rights. In federal courts and in cities throughout the South, African Americans struggled to eradicate the system of racial segregation that denied them dignity, opportunity, and equal protection under the law. The movement for racial justice took on a power and a spirit that would transform the nation in the coming years.

Jim Crow was a way of life in the South, where theaters, restaurants, trains, buses, blood banks, hospitals, drinking fountains, waiting rooms, and cemeteries were all segregated by law.

Brown v. Board of Education 🌐

In September 1953 Chief Justice Fred Vinson died of a heart attack, requiring President Eisenhower to make his first appointment to the U.S. Supreme Court. Eisenhower offered the position to California Governor Earl Warren, who won prompt Senate approval. Far more liberal than Eisenhower on social issues, Warren would sometimes anger the president in the coming years, but rarely lose his respect.

The major issue facing the Supreme Court in 1953 was civil rights. For more than a decade, a group of talented African American attorneys had been filing legal challenges to segregated public facilities in the South, hoping to erode the "separate but equal" doctrine of *Plessy v. Ferguson.* Led by Thurgood Marshall and William Hastie of the NAACP's Legal Defense Fund, these attorneys targeted specific areas, such as professional education (law, medicine, teaching), to establish precedents for the larger fight.

This strategy worked well. In 1950 the Supreme Court stretched the *Plessy* doctrine to its limits in two lawsuits brought by the NAACP. In *Sweatt v. Painter,* the Court ruled that Texas authorities must admit a black applicant to the all-white state law school in Austin because they had failed to provide African Americans with a comparable facility, thereby violating the equal protection clause of the Fourteenth Amendment. And in *McLaurin v. Oklahoma,* the Court struck down a scheme that segregated a black student *within* that state's graduate school of education, forcing him to sit alone in the library and the lecture halls in a section marked "Reserved for Coloreds."

Brown v. Board of Education
The unanimous Supreme Court decision ruling that segregated facilities in public education were "inherently unequal" and violated the Fourteenth Amendment's guarantee of equal protection under the law. This decision overruled the longstanding "separate but equal" doctrine of *Plessy v. Ferguson.*

With these victories, the NAACP took on the larger challenge of racial segregation in the nation's public schools. The new cases touched millions of children in twenty-one states and the District of Columbia. By 1953 five separate lawsuits had reached the Supreme Court, including ***Brown v. Board of Education of Topeka.***

The case involved a Kansas law that permitted cities to segregate their public schools. With NAACP support, the Reverend Oliver Brown sued the Topeka school board, arguing that his eight-year-old daughter should not be forced to attend a Negro school a mile from her home when there was a white public school only three blocks away. Several justices supported the *Plessy* doctrine, whereas others argued that it fostered racial inequality. Believing racial segregation to be both unconstitutional and morally wrong, Chief Justice Earl Warren insisted that the Supreme Court speak in a powerful, united voice against this evil. Anything less, he reasoned, would encourage massive resistance in the South.

©Bern Keating/Black Star

Chief Justice Earl Warren, Opinion of the Court in *Brown v. Board of Education*, May 17, 1954

Ruling that racial segregation of the nation's public schools violated the Equal Protection Clause of the Fourteenth Amendment, a unanimous Supreme Court, led by Chief Justice Earl Warren, overturned the "separate but equal" doctrine set down fifty-eight years earlier in Plessy v. Ferguson.

THESE CASES come to us from the States of Kansas, South Carolina, Virginia, and Delaware. They are premised on different facts and different local conditions, but a common legal question justifies their consideration together in this consolidated opinion.

In each of the cases, minors of the Negro race, through their legal representatives, seek the aid of the courts in obtaining admission to the public schools of their community on a nonsegregated basis. In each instance, they had been denied admission to schools attended by white children under laws requiring or permitting segregation according to race. . . .

Today, education is perhaps the most important function of state and local governments. Compulsory school attendance laws and the great expenditures for education both demonstrate our recognition of the importance of education to our democratic society. It is required in the performance of our most basic public responsibilities, even service in the armed forces. It is the very foundation of good citizenship. Today it is a principal instrument in awakening the child to cultural values, in preparing him for later professional training, and in helping him to adjust normally to his environment. In these days, it is doubtful that any child may reasonably be expected to succeed in life if he is denied the opportunity of an education. Such an opportunity, where the state has undertaken to provide it, is a right which must be made available to all on equal terms.

We come then to the question presented: Does segregation of children in public schools solely on the basis of race, even though the physical facilities and other "tangible" factors may be equal, deprive the children of the minority group of equal educational opportunities? We believe that it does. . . .

To separate them from others of similar age and qualifications solely because of their race generates a feeling of inferiority as to their status in the community that may affect their hearts and minds in a way unlikely ever to be undone. The effect of this separation on their educational opportunities was well stated by a finding in the Kansas case by a court which nevertheless felt compelled to rule against the Negro plaintiffs:

Segregation of white and colored children in public schools has a detrimental effect upon the colored children. The impact is greater when it has the sanction of the law; for the policy of separating the races is usually interpreted as denoting the inferiority of the negro group. A sense of inferiority affects the motivation of a child to learn. Segregation with the sanction of law, therefore, has a tendency to [retard] the educational and mental development of negro children and to deprive them of some of the benefits they would receive in a racial[ly] integrated school system.

Whatever may have been the extent of psychological knowledge at the time of *Plessy v. Ferguson,* this finding is amply supported by modern authority. Any language in *Plessy v. Ferguson* contrary to this finding is rejected.

We conclude that in the field of public education the doctrine of "separate but equal" has no place. Separate educational facilities are inherently unequal. Therefore, we hold that the plaintiffs and others similarly situated for whom the actions have been brought are, by reason of the segregation complained of, deprived of the equal protection of the laws guaranteed by the Fourteenth Amendment. This disposition makes unnecessary any discussion whether such segregation also violates the Due Process Clause of the Fourteenth Amendment. . . .

Questions to Consider

1. What impact did *Brown* have on the civil rights movement, beyond the field of education?

2. Why did Chief Justice Earl Warren believe that the Supreme Court had to speak with one voice, unanimously, in this particular decision?

3. How did whites and blacks in the South respond to *Brown?*

4. Why did the Supreme Court wait a full year before issuing guidelines for its implementation?

Explore additional primary sources related to this chapter on the *American Passages* Web site: http://history.wadsworth.com/ayersbrief02.

Source: *Brown v. Board of Education,* 349 U.S. 294, 1954.

On May 17, 1954, the Supreme Court overturned *Plessy v. Ferguson* in a stunning 9–0 decision, written by Warren himself. Relying on the studies of social scientists such as Kenneth Clark, the chief justice claimed that racial segregation had a "detrimental effect" on black children by making them feel inferior to whites. "In the field of public education the doctrine of 'separate but equal' has no place," he stated. "Separate educational facilities are inherently unequal."

The Supreme Court put off its implementation guidelines (known as *Brown II*) for a full year, hoping to let passions cool in the South. *Brown II* required local school boards to draw up desegregation plans with the approval of a federal district judge. But the wording was intentionally vague. Integration should proceed, it said, "with all deliberate speed."

White southern reaction was intense. "You are not required to obey any court which passes out such a ruling," Senator James O. Eastland of Mississippi told his constituents. Violence flared across the South. "In one school district after another," wrote an observer, "segregationists staged the same drama: forcing young blacks to enter a school by passing rock-throwing white mobs and white pickets shouting 'Nigger,' 'Nigger,' 'Nigger.'" The Ku Klux Klan came alive in the 1950s, and new groups like the White Citizens' Council were formed to defend segregation and the "Southern way of life." In the summer of 1954, a black Chicago teenager named Emmett Till, visiting relatives in Mississippi, was murdered for allegedly flirting with a white woman at a country store. Two suspects—the woman's husband and his half-brother—were acquitted by an all-white jury in just over an hour.

Many Americans looked to the White House for guidance about civil rights. But when asked at a press conference if he had any advice for the South on how to handle the *Brown* decision, Eisenhower replied: "Not in the slightest. The Supreme Court has spoken and I am sworn to uphold the constitutional processes in this country; and I will obey."

The Montgomery Bus Boycott

The battle over public school integration was but one of many such struggles in the South during this era. Some involved ordinary men and women determined to challenge the indignities of racial segregation. "Nothing is quite as humiliating, so murderously angering," said one African American, "as to know that because you are black you may have to walk a half mile farther than whites to urinate; that because you are black you have to receive your food through a window in the back of a restaurant or sit in a garbage-littered yard."

The black people of Montgomery, Alabama, had experienced such treatment for years. Montgomery enforced segregation and racial etiquette in meticulous detail. Blacks always tipped their hats to whites, always stood in the presence of whites unless told to sit, and always addressed whites with a title of respect. Restrooms, drinking fountains, blood banks, movie theaters, cemeteries—all were separated by race. On the local buses, blacks paid their fares in the front, got off the vehicle, and entered the "colored section" through the rear door. They also had to relinquish their seats to white passengers when the front section filled up.

On December 1, 1955, a simple yet revolutionary act of resistance occurred on a crowded Montgomery bus. **Rosa Parks,** a forty-two-year-old black seamstress, refused to give up her seat to a white. The bus driver called the police. "They got on the bus," Mrs. Parks recalled, "and one of them asked me why I didn't stand up. I asked him, 'Why do you push us around?' He said, '. . . I don't know, but the law is the law and you're under arrest.'"

News of Mrs. Parks's defiance electrified the black community. Within days the **Montgomery bus boycott** was begun, organized by local clergymen and the Women's Political Council. Calling themselves the Montgomery Improvement Association (MIA), they chose a young minister named **Martin Luther King Jr.** to lead the struggle for open seating in public transportation.

King, twenty-six, was selected, in part, because his youth and vocation made him less vulnerable to economic and political pressure from whites. The son of a well-known Atlanta pastor, King earned his college degree at Morehouse and his doctorate at Boston University's School of Theology before heading south to serve as pastor of Montgomery's Dexter Avenue Baptist Church in 1954. Dr. King viewed mass action and nonviolent resistance as essential weapons in the war against racial injustice.

Rosa Parks
Her refusal to give up her seat on a bus to a white man in Montgomery, Alabama, resulted in a citywide boycott of the bus company and stirred the civil rights movement across the nation.

Montgomery bus boycott
Begun in December 1955 as a result of an act of protest by Rosa Parks against the segregated transportation facilities and humiliating treatment facing African Americans in the capital city of Alabama, the boycott soon became an international event.

Martin Luther King Jr.
An African American cleric whose eloquence and commitment to nonviolent tactics formed the foundation of the civil rights movement of the 1950s and 1960s. He led the 1963 march on Washington at which he delivered his now famous "I Have a Dream" speech. He was awarded the Nobel Peace Prize in 1964 and was assassinated four years later in Memphis, Tennessee.

King rallied the black community with the eloquent passion of his words. "There comes a time when people get tired," he told a packed rally after Rosa Parks's arrest. "We are here this evening to say to those who have mistreated us so long that we are tired—tired of being segregated and humiliated, tired of being kicked about by the brutal feet of oppression. We have no alternative but to protest."

King's reputation soared. Blacks in Montgomery formed car pools to get people to their destinations. The churches raised money for fuel, and black-owned garages did repair work free of charge. The boycott nearly bankrupted the city bus system and badly hurt the white merchants downtown.

In November 1956 the federal courts struck down the Alabama law requiring racial segregation in public transportation. A month later blacks sat in the front of the Montgomery buses without incident. The boycott, lasting 381 days, demonstrated both the power of collective action and the possibility of social change. In 1957 Dr. King joined with other black ministers to form the Southern Christian Leadership Conference (SCLC), an organization devoted to racial justice through peaceful means.

The Age of Television

In the 1950s social commentators analyzed a host of new issues in American life. Some worried about the struggle between individuals and organizations, the apparent quest for security over adventure, the monotony of modern work. A few focused on the supposed emptiness of suburban living, the growing cult of domesticity among women, the changing standards of success. Yet what struck virtually all critics and commentators in the 1950s was the impact of television on American life.

The Magic Box

In 1946 there were seventeen thousand TV sets in the United States. The late 1940s saw major changes in television technology, such as the use of coaxial cable and the introduction of color. In 1949 a TV set appeared for the first time in the Sears, Roebuck catalogue. A year later, Americans were buying twenty thousand television sets a day. The two most popular shows of that era were Milton Berle's *Texaco Star Theater* and Ed Sullivan's *Toast of the Town*.

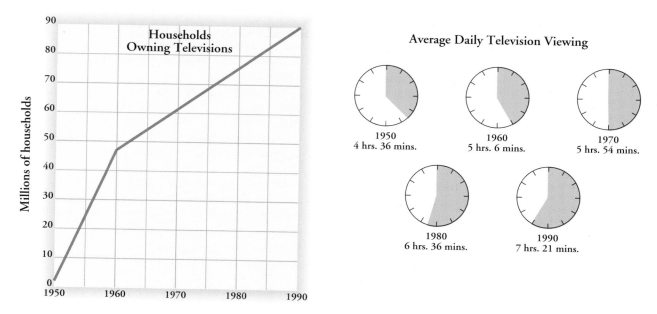

CHART 28.2 The Television Revolution 1950–1990

As television became commonplace in the 1950s, TV viewing altered the nature of U.S. politics and culture. Average daily television viewing has increased in each decade, with Americans now spending almost half their waking hours with their sets turned on. Source: Statistical Abstracts of the United States.

Berle, a physical comedian, seemed perfect for a visual medium like TV. His fast-paced humor relied on sight gags instead of verbal banter. The press called him "Mr. Television."

Sullivan, a former gossip columnist, was awkward and unsmiling on camera. What made him unique was his ability to provide fresh entertainment to Americans of all tastes and ages. Sullivan's Sunday night variety show ran for twenty-three years on CBS. His guests included Elvis Presley, Dean Martin and Jerry Lewis, pianist Van Cliburn, dancer Rudolf Nureyev, singer Lena Horne, and the Beatles.

Television's potential was impossible to ignore. In 1951 an obscure Tennessee politician named Estes Kefauver became a national figure by holding televised hearings into organized crime. Senator Kefauver grilled prominent mobsters like New York's Frank Costello as twenty-five million viewers watched in amazement. The TV cameras perfectly captured Costello's discomfort by focusing for several minutes on his jittery, sweat-soaked hands.

Nixon's "Checkers Speech" and the Army-McCarthy hearings further highlighted the impact of television in the political arena. Above all, however, TV possessed the power to sell. In 1950 local stations, desperate for programming, aired a series of old "Hopalong Cassidy" movies. Within months "Hopalong Cassidy" clothing and six-guns were in frantic demand. Walt Disney struck gold with his three-part series on Davy Crockett, which aired nationally in 1954. Millions of children wore coonskin caps to school. There were Davy Crockett shirts and blankets, toothbrushes and lunch boxes. One department store chain sold twenty thousand surplus pup tents in less than a week by printing "Davy Crockett" on the flap.

By 1954 three national networks were firmly in place: ABC, CBS, and NBC. They filled their early airtime by moving popular radio programs such as *Jack Benny, Burns & Allen,* and *Amos 'n' Andy,* over to TV. The faster television grew, the more its schedule expanded. Important advertisers signed on, sponsoring entire programs such as *Motorola Playhouse.* This, in turn, provided work for hundreds of performers at a time when the motion picture industry was losing ground to television. New York City, the early center of TV production, became a magnet for young actors and writers including Paul Newman, Sidney Poitier, Joanne Woodward, Rod Serling, Neil Simon, and Mel Brooks.

Some critics called this era the "golden age" of television. They pointed to the high quality of plays and dramas, the original comedy of Sid Caesar and Jackie Gleason, and the powerful documentaries of Edward R. Murrow on *See It Now.* Yet by 1955 this golden age was largely over. The networks abandoned most live broadcasts in favor of filmed episodes, with Hollywood quickly replacing Manhattan as television's capital. Popular new shows such as *Dragnet* and *I Love Lucy* showed the advantages of film over live TV. Production was less demanding, errors could be corrected, scenes could be shot at different locations, and episodes could be shown more than once.

Many television shows of the 1950s reflected both the yearnings and the stereotypes of American society. Popular situation comedies such as *Father Knows Best, Ozzie and Harriet,* and *Leave It to Beaver* portrayed the charmed lives (and minor problems) of middle-class white families in the suburbs. Mother was a housewife. Dad held a pressure-free white-collar job. The kids were well adjusted and witty. Money was never a problem. No one stayed angry for long.

Married women in TV "sit-coms" did not work outside the home. This rule even applied to childless couples like Ralph and Alice Kramden of *The Honeymooners,* one of television's rare programs about urban, working-class people. Furthermore, single women in sit-coms rarely took their jobs seriously. Like Eve Arden in *Our Miss Brooks,* they spent most of their time hunting for a husband.

Though racial minorities almost never appeared in these sit-coms, they did play major—if stereotypical—roles in two or three popular shows of the 1950s. There was "Beulah," the big-hearted domestic in a white suburban household, and "Rochester," the wise-cracking butler on the *Jack Benny Show.* Above all, there was *Amos 'n' Andy,* an adaptation of the popular radio show created by two white men, Freeman Gosden and Charles Correll, that featured an all-black cast. The NAACP angrily denounced *Amos 'n' Andy* for portraying blacks as "clowns" and "crooks," but others praised the performers for transforming racist stereotypes into "authentic black humor."

The Quiz Show Scandals

No event raised more concerns about the control and direction of commercial television in the 1950s than the quiz show scandals. Though quiz shows appeared early on television, they did not generate much interest until Revlon cosmetics produced a "big money" version in order to match the successful TV advertising campaign of rival Hazel Bishop. Named *The $64,000 Question,* it aired on CBS in June 1955.

Contestants Charles Van Doren and Vivian Nearing battle it out on the rigged quiz show *Twenty-One.*

The rules were simple. After choosing a topic such as science or baseball, the contestant fielded questions that began at $64 and doubled with each correct answer. At the $16,000 plateau, the contestant entered a glass "isolation booth." The tension was enormous, since a wrong answer wiped out all previous winnings. The show drew the highest ratings in TV history—a whopping 85 percent audience share—when contestants went for the $64,000 question.

Before long, the airwaves were flooded with imitations. In 1956 *The $64,000 Question* lost its top rating to NBC's *Twenty-One,* which pitted two competitors in a trivia contest structured like the blackjack card game. The stakes grew ever larger. Charles Van Doren, a handsome English instructor at Columbia University, won $129,000 on *Twenty-One* and became an instant national hero.

His good fortune did not last long. A grand jury investigation revealed that numerous quiz show contestants had been given the questions in advance. It turned out that both *The $64,000 Question* and *Twenty-One* were rigged, with players coached about every detail of their performance. The contestants blamed the producers, who then implicated the sponsors. Van Doren admitted the painful truth after first protesting his innocence.

The public was outraged. President Eisenhower condemned the "selfishness" and "greed" of the perpetrators. Yet there was nothing illegal about these shows. Indeed, some sponsors defended them as a form of *entertainment,* akin to professional wrestling or a "ghostwritten" book. As public anger mounted, however, Congress passed legislation to prevent the rigging of TV quiz shows, and the networks promised to regulate themselves.

The quality of television did not appear to improve. New programs became clones of each other—bland sit-coms or violent westerns and crime dramas. Advertising now consumed 20 percent of television airtime. "The feeling of high purpose that lit the industry when it was young," wrote the *New York Times,* "is long gone." Yet television's power kept expanding. One study in the 1950s estimated that an American youngster spent eleven thousand hours in the classroom through high school and fifteen thousand hours in front of the TV. There were complaints that television tended to isolate people and to shorten their attention span. Nobody needed to concentrate for more than a half-hour—and not very hard at that.

As television expanded, other media outlets declined. Mass circulation magazines such as *Look* and *Collier's* folded in the 1950s, and newspaper readership went way down. Movie attendance dropped and radio lost listeners, forcing both industries to experiment to survive. Hollywood tried Cinemascope, Technicolor, 3D glasses, drive-in movies, and big budget spectacles such as *The Ten Commandments* and *Ben Hur.* Radio moved from soap operas and big band music to "hip" disc jockeys spinning rock 'n' roll. Nevertheless, television was now king. America's popular culture, consumer needs, and general information—all came increasingly from TV.

Youth Culture

In the 1950s a distinctive "teenage culture" emerged. America's young people had not experienced the pain and sacrifice of economic depression and total war. Raised in relative affluence, surrounded by messages that undermined traditional values of thrift and self-denial, these new teenagers were perceived as a special group with a unique subculture. They rarely worked, yet their pockets were full. The typical adolescent spent as much on entertainment as did the average family in 1941.

A New Kind of Music

Nothing defined these thirteen million teenagers more clearly than the music they shared. In the 1940s popular music was dominated by the "big bands" of Glenn Miller and Tommy Dorsey, the Broadway show tunes of Rodgers and Hammerstein, and the mellow voices of Bing Crosby, Frank Sinatra, and the Andrews Sisters. These artists appealed to a broad white audience of all ages. Other forms of popular music—bluegrass, country, rhythm and blues—were limited by region and race.

But not for long. The huge migration of rural blacks and whites to industrial centers during World War II profoundly altered popular culture. The sounds of "race" music, "hillbilly" music, and gospel became readily available to mainstream America for the first time. Record sales tripled during the 1950s. The main consumers were young people.

In 1951 a Cleveland, Ohio, record dealer noticed that white teenagers at his store were "going crazy" over the songs of black rhythm and blues artists. He told a local disc jockey named **Alan Freed,** who decided to play these records on the air. Freed's new program, *The Moondog Party,* took Cleveland by storm. Soon Freed was hosting live shows at the local arena to overflow crowds. Pounding his fists to the rhythm, chanting "go man, go," Freed became the self-proclaimed father of rock 'n' roll.

Freed understood the defiant, sensual nature of rock 'n' roll, the way it separated the young from everyone else. It was their music, played by their heroes, set to their special beat. Indeed, rock's first national hit, "Rock Around the Clock," by Bill Haley and the Comets, became the theme song for *Blackboard Jungle,* a movie about rebellious high school students set to the throbbing rhythms of rock 'n' roll.

The Rise of Elvis

Haley's success was fleeting; he did not generate the intense excitement or sexual spark that teenagers craved. As Haley faded, a twenty-one-year-old truck driver from Memphis exploded onto the popular music scene. His name was Elvis Presley; the year was 1955.

Born in rural Mississippi, Presley was surrounded by the sounds of country music, gospel, and blues. As a teenager in Memphis, he frequented the legendary blues clubs along Beale Street. The music moved him deeply, providing both spiritual force and physical release.

Memphis was also home to Sun Records. Owned by Sam Phillips, Sun recorded white country singers such as Johnny Cash and black bluesmen such as B. B. King. What Phillips most wanted, however, was an artist who combined these two sounds instinctively, without appearing artificial or forced.

Presley was that artist. Signing with Sun Records in 1954, he took the region by storm. The press described his unique style as "a cross between be-bop and country," and "a new hillbilly blues beat." It wasn't just the sound. Tall and handsome, with long sideburns and slicked-back hair, Presley was a riveting performer, combining little boy shyness with enormous sexual drive.

When Presley became too big to handle, Sun Records sold his contract to RCA for $35,000. Before long, he was a national sensation. His early hits topped the charts in popular music, country, and rhythm and blues—the first time that had ever occurred. In less than a year, Elvis recorded eight number-one songs and six of RCA's all-time top twenty-five records. When he appeared on *Ed Sullivan,* the cameras carefully shot him from the waist up. The ratings were extraordinary.

Young Elvis was modest and polite. He didn't smoke or drink or use drugs. He was so devoted to his parents that friends laughingly described him as a mama's boy. Yet his exaggerated sexuality on stage made him the target of those who believed that rock 'n' roll was a vulgar and dangerous assault on America's youth. "Popular music," wrote one television critic, "has reached its lowest depths in the grunt and groin antics of Mr. Presley."

Such criticism served only to enhance Presley's stature in the teenage world. And his success led the major record companies to experiment more aggressively with black rhythm and blues. At that time, white "cover artists" still were used to record toned-down versions of "race" music for white teenage audiences. In 1956 rock music reached a milestone when **Little Richard**'s sensual recordings of "Long Tall Sally" and "Rip It Up" outsold the "sanitized" versions of Pat Boone, America's leading white cover artist. Using

Alan Freed
The self-proclaimed father of rock 'n' roll, he was the first DJ to play black rhythm and blues artists on the radio.

Little Richard
An American rock 'n' roll singer noted for his flamboyant style, he influenced many artists including Elvis Presley and the Beatles.

words and illusions that would have been unthinkable in mainstream America a few years before, Little Richard cried:

> Well it's Saturday night
> and I just got paid,
> A fool about my money
> don't try to save.
> Gunna Rock it up,
> Gunna Rip it up,
> Gunna Shake it up,
> Gunna Ball it up,
> Gunna Rock it up,
> And Ball tonight.

There was more to rock 'n' roll, of course, than Elvis Presley and rhythm and blues. Teenagers adored the sweet sounds of the Everly Brothers, the lush harmony of the Platters, and the clean-cut innocence of Ricky Nelson. Furthermore, jazz and folk singing retained a healthy following, as did popular artists Frank Sinatra, Perry Como, and Nat "King" Cole. Nevertheless, the music that defined this era for most Americans, but for teenagers in particular, was hard-edged rock 'n' roll. It was the car radio blasting Presley's "Hound Dog," Chuck Berry's "Maybellene," and Little Richard's "Tutti Frutti" on a carefree Saturday night: *A wop bop a lu bop a lop bam boom!*

The Beat Generation

Whatever else might be said about Elvis Presley and other rock heroes, they loved the system that made them millionaires. Elvis spent lavishly. His first royalties were used to purchase three new homes and matching Cadillacs for his parents. Material rewards were the standard by which Presley, and countless others, measured their success.

The Beat movement was different. Composed of young writers and poets based mainly in San Francisco and New York, it blossomed in the mid-1950s as a reaction against mainstream standards and beliefs. The word "beat" described a feeling of emotional and physical exhaustion. The Beats despised politics, consumerism, and technology. Their leading poet, Allen Ginsberg, provided a bitter portrait of generational despair in *Howl* (1955).

> I saw the best minds of my generation
> destroyed by madness,
> starving hysterical naked,
> dragging themselves through the negro
> streets at dawn looking for an angry fix . . .

The Beats linked happiness and creativity with absolute freedom. Their model was Dean Moriarty, the hero of Jack Kerouac's *On the Road,* an autobiographical novel about the cross-country adventures of Kerouac and his friends, finding adventure and renewal beyond the confines of middle-class life. *On the Road* became both a national best seller and a cult book on America's college campuses.

Crises and Celebration

In September 1955 President Eisenhower suffered a heart attack while vacationing in Colorado. The news raised obvious questions about his present and future course. At sixty-five, Eisenhower was one of the oldest presidents in U.S. history. How quickly would he recover, if at all? Who would guide the nation in his absence?

Eisenhower spent the next four months recovering in the hospital and at his Gettysburg farm. Fortunately, the fall of 1955 was a time of political tranquility. The president stayed in close contact with his advisors as he slowly regained his health. Returning to the White House early in 1956, he announced his plan to seek reelection. The public was vastly relieved. As columnist James Reston noted, Eisenhower was more than a president; he was "a national phenomenon, like baseball."

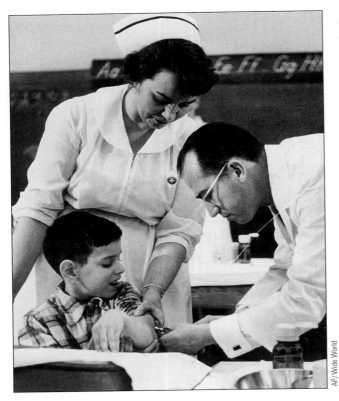

Dr. Jonas Salk, administering a polio vaccine he developed in 1954, helped eradicate a disease that terrorized Americans in the postwar era.

Conquering Polio

The president's full recovery was not the only positive "health news" of 1955. A medical research team led by Dr. Jonas Salk, a virologist at the University of Pittsburgh, announced the successful testing of a vaccine to combat poliomyelitis, the most frightening public health problem of the postwar era. More than fifty thousand polio cases were reported in 1954, mostly of children who took sick during the summer months. The disease produced flu-like symptoms in most cases, but a more virulent form, which entered the central nervous system, led to paralysis and sometimes death. Not surprisingly, the epidemic produced a national panic. Cities closed swimming pools and beaches; families canceled vacations, boiled their dishes, and avoided indoor crowds. The March of Dimes became America's favorite charity, raising millions to find a cure for polio and to finance the care of patients through therapy, leg braces, and iron lungs.

Determined to provide immediate protection against the disease, Dr. Salk began testing a "dead" polio virus vaccine on schoolchildren in 1954. (His critics, led by Dr. Alfred Sabin, insisted that only a "live" polio vaccine would trigger the immunities needed to provide a lasting solution.) Aided by the March of Dimes and an army of volunteers, Salk tested the vaccine—and a placebo—on several million youngsters nationwide. The testing proved extremely successful. The federal government approved the polio vaccine in 1955, touching off emotional public celebrations. Although the government did not provide the funds to immediately vaccinate all school-age children—in part because the American Medical Association objected to this "socialist" proposal—public opinion soon forced a more compassionate approach. In 1960 fewer than a thousand new polio cases were reported in the United States.

Interstate Highways

The nation's confidence soared even higher with passage of the Federal Highway Act of 1956, which authorized $25 billion in new taxes on cars, trucks, and gasoline for the construction of forty thousand miles of interstate roads over the next ten years. The huge highway network, linking all cities with more than fifty thousand people, allowed a driver to travel the continent uninterrupted, save stops for food and gas. Eisenhower viewed this project as both a convenience to motorists and a boost to the economy. The president also linked good highways to Cold War events, warning that cities must be evacuated quickly in the event of nuclear war.

The Highway Act spurred enormous economic growth. Improved roads meant higher oil revenues, soaring car sales, more business for truckers, and greater mobility for travelers. The so-called highway trade took off. Ray Kroc opened his first McDonald's in 1955 in Des Plaines, Illinois, a suburb of Chicago. In Memphis, Kemmons Wilson unveiled the first Holiday Inn, featuring a restaurant, a swimming pool, and clean, air-conditioned rooms with free TV. Before long McDonald's golden arches and Holiday Inn's green neon lettering were among the most recognizable logos in the United States.

Opposing the Highway Act of 1956 was akin to opposing prosperity, progress, and national defense. A few social critics, including Lewis Mumford, expressed concern about the deterioration of urban centers and the future of interstate rail service, but they were drowned out by the optimistic majority. As the prestigious *Architectural Forum* noted, America's new highway system was "the greatest man-made physical enterprise of all time with the exception of war."

Hungary and Suez

In the fall of 1956, foreign affairs took center stage. From Central Europe came a dangerous challenge to the Eisenhower-Dulles rhetoric about liberating nations from Commu-

[Alaska has no interstate highways]

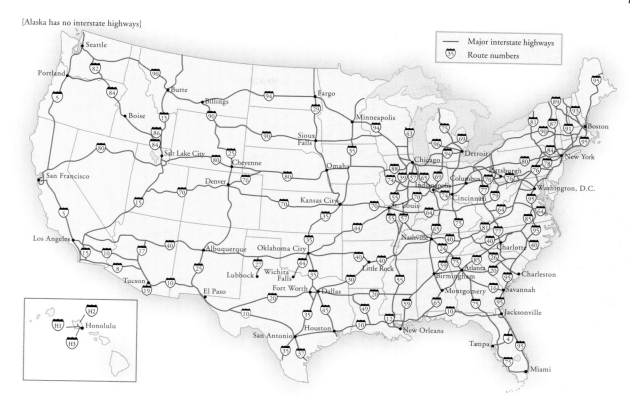

MAP 28.1 The National Highway System
The ability to drive almost anywhere in the continental United States on a superhighway transformed the nation's economy as well as its culture. Private transportation overwhelmed public transportation. Workers commuted longer distances between their homes and their jobs, spending more time on the road. Whole new industries arose to service the business traveler and vacationer, who no longer had to drive through the center of small towns or large cities to reach their destination.

nist oppression. From the Middle East came a crisis that pitted the United States against its most loyal allies—Israel, England, and France.

Following Stalin's death in 1953, Russian leaders called for "peaceful coexistence" between the Communist bloc and "differing political and social systems." In 1956 Soviet Premier **Nikita Khrushchev** stunned the Twentieth Communist Party Congress in Moscow by denouncing Stalin's brutality and hinting at a relaxation of the Soviet grip on Central and Eastern Europe. Protests flared throughout the Soviet bloc, demanding an end to Russian rule. In Warsaw, angry crowds sacked the Communist party headquarters, and in Budapest street battles escalated into full-scale civil war. Khrushchev was slow to respond. In the meantime, Hungarians overthrew the Communist government and installed the popular Imre Nagy as premier.

The Hungarian revolt put Eisenhower on the spot. In 1952 his campaign rhetoric had blasted the Democrats for being "soft" on Communism. From 1953 forward, his administration had vowed to "roll back" the Communist wave. Now the time had come to put words into action by supporting the anti-Communist freedom fighters in Hungary. Yet Eisenhower refused to send U.S. troops, or even to airlift supplies to the resisters, for fear of starting an all-out war with the Soviet Union. In October 1956 Russian tanks and troops stormed into Budapest to crush the revolt.

At the very moment of the Hungarian revolt, another crisis erupted in the Middle East. Though U.S. policy supported the new State of Israel, it also recognized the strategic importance and economic power of Israel's Arab neighbors. In 1952 a young Egyptian military officer named Gamal Abdel Nasser had dramatically altered Middle Eastern politics by overthrowing the corrupt regime of King Farouk. As an Arab nationalist, Nasser steered a middle course between the Cold War powers, hoping to play one side off against the other. To the

Nikita Khrushchev
A Soviet politician and Stalin loyalist in the 1930s, he was appointed first secretary of the Communist party in 1953. As Soviet premier, he denounced Stalin, thwarted the Hungarian Revolution of 1956, and improved his country's image abroad. He was deposed in 1964 for failing to establish missiles in Cuba or improve the Soviet economy.

Egyptian people, he promised both the destruction of Israel and an end to British control of the Suez Canal.

The United States tried to woo Nasser with economic aid. It even agreed to finance his pet project, the Aswan Dam, a huge hydroelectric plant on the Nile River. But trouble arose in 1956 when Secretary Dulles withdrew the Aswan offer to protest Egypt's recognition of Communist China. Unable to punish the United States directly, Nasser did the next best thing by seizing the Suez Canal.

The move could not be ignored. In 1955 Nasser had blockaded the Gulf of Aqaba, Israel's sole outlet to the Red Sea. Now he controlled the waterway that linked Western Europe to its oil supply in the Middle East. On October 29, 1956, Israeli armor poured into the Sinai, routing Egyptian forces. Two days later, French and British paratroopers landed near Alexandria and easily retook the Suez Canal.

Eisenhower immediately condemned this invasion. At the very least, he believed, the attack undermined Western interests in the Middle East by forcing Egypt and other Arab states closer to the Soviet bloc. Fearing the worst, Eisenhower placed U.S. armed forces on full alert. If the Russians "start something," he warned, "we may have to hit 'em—and, if necessary, with *everything* in the bucket."

Protesters in Budapest stand on a captured Soviet tank during the Hungarian uprising of 1956.

AP/Wide World

It never came to that. Privately, the White House pressured England, France, and Israel to withdraw. Publicly, the United States supported a UN resolution that denounced the invasion and called for negotiations regarding the canal. On November 6, a ceasefire was signed.

Events in Hungary and Suez came in the midst of Eisenhower's 1956 reelection campaign. Expecting an easy victory, the president worried most about picking the proper running mate. Eisenhower did not believe that Vice President Nixon was the best person to lead the nation in a crisis. He urged Nixon to trade in his vice presidential hat for a cabinet post. Yet when Nixon resisted, the president backed down, fearing a backlash within Republican ranks. In November 1956, Eisenhower and Nixon trounced the Democratic slate of Adlai Stevenson and Senator Estes Kefauver by almost ten million votes. Nevertheless, the Democrats easily retained their majorities in both houses of Congress, demonstrating that Eisenhower remained far more popular than the political party he led.

A Second Term

Eisenhower returned to office on an optimistic note. Events in Hungary and the Middle East faded momentarily from view. *Time* magazine even praised the president for his moderation "in time of crisis and threat of World War III." The nation seemed confident, prosperous, and secure.

Confrontation at Little Rock

Orval Faubus
Governor of Arkansas in 1957 who triggered a confrontation between national authority and states' rights by defying a federal court order to integrate the all-white Central High School.

These good feelings did not last long. Throughout the South, opposition to the *Brown* decision was spreading. In 1956 more than a hundred congressmen from the former Confederate states issued a "Southern Manifesto" that vowed to resist court-ordered integration "by all lawful means." A year later, in Little Rock, Arkansas, Governor **Orval Faubus** triggered the inevitable confrontation between national authority and "states' rights" by defying a federal court order to integrate the all-white Central High School. First the Arkansas National Guard, and then a crowd of angry whites, turned away the nine black students.

As televised scenes of mob violence in Little Rock flashed around the world, President Eisenhower finally, but firmly, took command. He nationalized the Arkansas Guard and dispatched a thousand fully equipped Army paratroopers to surround the high school and escort the black students to their classes. The soldiers remained for months, though peace was quickly restored.

Sputnik and Its Aftermath

On October 4, 1957, the Soviet Union launched **Sputnik I,** the first artificial satellite, weighing less than 200 pounds. The admiral in charge of the U.S. satellite program dismissed *Sputnik I* as "a hunk of iron almost anybody could launch." But one month later, the Russians orbited *Sputnik II,* a 1,100-pound capsule with a small dog inside.

The news provoked anger and dismay. Americans had always taken for granted their technological superiority. Even the Soviet atomic bomb was seen as an aberration, most likely built from stolen U.S. blueprints. But *Sputnik* was different; it shook the nation's confidence. The feeling grew that the United States had become complacent in its affluence. "The time has clearly come," said an alarmed senator, "to be less concerned with the depth of the pile of the new broadloom or the height of the tail fin of the new car and to be more prepared to shed blood, sweat, and tears."

The nation's educational system came under withering fire. Critics emerged from every corner, bemoaning the sorry state of America's schools. In an issue devoted to the "Crisis in Education," *Life* magazine followed a sixteen-year-old Russian student and his American counterpart through a typical high school day. Alexi took difficult courses in science and math. He spoke fluent English, played chess and the piano, exercised vigorously, and studied four hours after class. Stephen, meanwhile, spent his day lounging through basic geometry and learning how to type. The students around him read magazines like *Modern Romance* in their English class. No one seemed to study. The end result, warned the *Life* editors, was a generation of young Americans ill-equipped "to cope with the technicalities of the Space Age."

The embarrassments continued. In December 1957 millions watched on television as the U.S. Navy's much-publicized Vanguard rocket caught fire on takeoff and crashed to the ground. A month later, the Army launched a ten-pound satellite named *Explorer I* aboard its new Jupiter rocket. Determined to calm public fears, President Eisenhower insisted that the United States was well ahead of the Soviet Union in nuclear research and delivery systems. But the people thought otherwise, especially after the Russians orbited a third satellite weighing almost 3,000 pounds.

In fact, however, Eisenhower was correct. His own information, not available to the public, made two vital points. First, the Russians *needed* more powerful missiles because the warheads they carried were heavier and cruder. Second, the Soviets did not have enough intercontinental ballistic missiles (ICBMs) to counter America's huge lead in manned nuclear bombers.

Eisenhower got this information from the CIA's U-2 spy planes, which crossed the Soviet Union at seventy thousand feet. The U-2 flights were both secret and illegal, a clear violation of Russian airspace. But the cameras on board provided U.S. intelligence with a detailed picture of the Soviet war machine. Of course, the president could not speak candidly about Russian military power without also admitting the existence of these U-2 flights.

This was an awful dilemma. Critics now demanded expensive crash programs for weapons research, missile construction, and community "fall-out" shelters to protect against nuclear attack. Eisenhower vigorously opposed these programs, claiming that they undermined economic prosperity. Using his exalted stature as general and war hero, he battled hard—and successfully—to keep military budgets stable during these years.

Still, the impact of *Sputnik* did not quickly disappear. For the first time, Americans started to view their educational system in terms of national security. This meant greater emphasis on science, mathematics, and foreign language study. In 1958 Congress passed the National Defense Education Act, which funded high school programs in these fields and college scholarships for deserving students. That same year, Eisenhower reluctantly endorsed the creation of the National Aeronautical and Space Administration (NASA).

End of an Era

In November 1958 the Democrats won a smashing victory in the off-year elections, increasing their majorities in the House (282–153) and the Senate (62–34) to the largest level

Sputnik I

Launched by the Soviet Union in October 1957, it was the first artificial space satellite. News of its success provoked both anger and anxiety among the American people who had always taken their country's technological superiority for granted.

since 1936. *Sputnik* was partly responsible for this landslide, but so, too, was an economic recession in 1957 that lingered for the next two years. Determined to avoid the inflationary risks of increased federal spending, Eisenhower did little to counter a steady rise in unemployment and a sharp (if temporary) decline in the annual rate of economic growth.

There were optimistic signs, however. In the summer of 1959, Vice President Nixon visited Moscow at Khrushchev's invitation to open a trade show featuring consumer products from Russia and the United States. In a bizarre but friendly confrontation, the vice president and the Soviet premier stood nose-to-nose in a "model" American kitchen, arguing the merits of their nations' electrical appliances. Looking grumpily at a self-loading dishwasher, Khrushchev asked: "Don't you have a machine that puts food in your mouths and pushes it down?" When he bragged that Russia would soon "come alongside America, salute her, and move ahead," Nixon responded that it was "better to compete in the relative merits of washing machines than in the strength of rockets."

Several weeks later, Khrushchev accepted President Eisenhower's invitation to visit the United States. Khrushchev toured an Iowa farm and an IBM plant near San Francisco. At a Hollywood studio, he watched the filming of *Can-Can* and then, offended by the skimpy costumes, launched into a diatribe against capitalist "pornography." When his trip to Disneyland was canceled for security reasons, Khrushchev was furious. "What's wrong?" he yelled. "Do you have rocket launching pads there? Or have gangsters taken hold of the place?"

The trip ended on a hopeful note with a visit to the presidential retreat at Camp David, where Khrushchev and Eisenhower spent two days in leisurely conversation. They announced that Eisenhower would visit the Soviet Union in 1960 following a summit meeting of world leaders in Paris. The main issues, they agreed, were nuclear disarmament and the future of Berlin.

The summit meeting was a disaster. As he left for Paris in May 1960, Eisenhower learned that a U-2 spy plane was missing. A few days later, Khrushchev revealed that a U.S. aircraft had been shot down deep inside the Soviet Union. Assuming that the pilot was dead, Eisenhower falsely described the U-2 as a weather research plane that had veered off course. But Khrushchev then produced the pilot, **Francis Gary Powers,** frightened but very much alive.

Francis Gary Powers
Pilot of a U.S. U-2 high altitude reconnaissance aircraft shot down over the Soviet Union on May 1, 1960.

At the summit, Eisenhower took full responsibility for the incident, but refused to apologize. Indeed, he justified the U-2 flights by insisting that Soviet espionage inside the United States was rampant and that U-2 photographs were essential to U.S. defense, given the closed nature of Russian society. In response, Khrushchev turned the summit into a tirade against Western "banditry," adding that Eisenhower was no longer welcome on Soviet soil.

The failure at Paris deeply wounded the president. In his "farewell address" to the people, he warned that years of Cold War tensions were sapping U.S. strength and concentrating too much power in the hands of "a military-industrial complex." Speaking boldly, at times sadly, he urged the people to be on guard against militarism and greed, and to reject a "live for today" mentality. At risk, the president concluded, was "the loss of our political and spiritual heritage."

The Election of 1960

Who would lead the United States into the next decade? The election of 1960 generated drama from the start. Both major candidates were tough, hard-driving campaigners. Both were born in the twentieth century—a political first—and both entered Congress in 1946 after serving as junior naval officers during World War II. But the similarities ended there.

Richard Nixon, the forty-seven-year-old vice president, grew up in modest circumstances. His Quaker parents ran a small grocery store in Whittier, California, near Los Angeles, where Nixon worked as a boy. After graduating from Whittier College and Duke Law School, he married Patricia Ryan in 1940 and obtained his naval commission the following year.

Nixon's political rise was dramatic. As a new Republican congressman, he played a major role in the Alger Hiss case and then won a U.S. Senate seat in 1950 after accusing his Democratic opponent of being "soft on Communism." As vice president from 1953 to 1960, Nixon emerged as the Republican party's most aggressive defender.

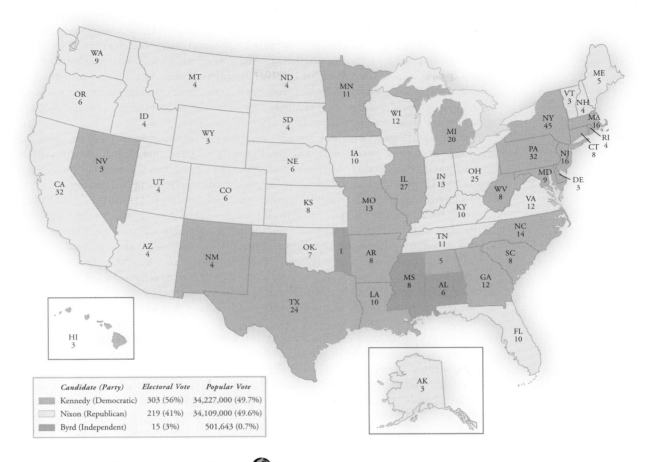

MAP 28.2 The Election of 1960

In winning one of the closest presidential contests in U.S. history, John F. Kennedy barely kept the Democratic New Deal coalition together. Several key factors were at work in this election, including the impact of the first televised presidential debates, the Catholic issue, and the suspicion of voter fraud in the key states of Texas and Illinois. View an animated version of this map or related maps at http://history.wadsworth.com/ayersbrief02.

John Kennedy took a different path to power. Born to wealth and privilege, he grew up in Boston, attended the finest private schools, and graduated from Harvard. His self-made millionaire father, Joseph P. Kennedy, served as ambassador to England under Franklin Roosevelt. He expected his oldest son, Joe Jr., to become the first Catholic president of the United States. When Joe Jr., died in combat during World War II, the torch was passed to John Kennedy, the next oldest son. In 1943 John barely escaped death himself when his PT boat was rammed by a Japanese warship in the South Pacific. Elected to Congress in 1946, and to the Senate in 1952, Kennedy did not excel as a legislator. In constant pain from his war wounds, he underwent delicate spinal surgery and then was diagnosed with Addison's disease, an adrenal malfunction that required daily doses of cortisone. While recuperating, Kennedy won the Pulitzer Prize for *Profiles in Courage,* an intriguing book, written almost entirely by his staff, about politicians who took brave but unpopular positions on the great issues of their time.

In 1956 Kennedy ran a close second to Estes Kefauver for the Democratic party's vice presidential nomination. "You know, if we work like hell the next four years," Kennedy told an aide, "we will pick up all the marbles." Healthy once again, he traveled the country with his glamorous wife, Jacqueline, to line up presidential support. The crowds they drew were so large and adoring that reporters used the Greek word *charisma* to describe the growing Kennedy mystique.

The Republican convention nominated Richard Nixon on the first ballot. As expected, Nixon chose a moderate easterner, Henry Cabot Lodge Jr., of Massachusetts, to be his vice presidential running mate. The Democratic convention was more dramatic. While also winning a first ballot victory, Kennedy surprised almost everyone by selecting Senator Lyndon Johnson, a long-time rival, for the vice presidential slot. As a Texan with liberal instincts, Johnson was expected to help Kennedy in the South without hurting him in the North. "The world is changing," Kennedy proclaimed in his acceptance speech. "We stand today on the edge of a New Frontier."

Nixon campaigned on the eight-year Eisenhower record, reminding Americans that their nation was prosperous and at peace. Kennedy attacked that record without criticizing the popular Eisenhower by name. Portraying the United States as stagnant in a changing world, he promised new leadership "to get the country moving once again."

Kennedy had two main hurdles to overcome: religion and inexperience. No Roman Catholic had ever been elected president. Religion became an open issue in the 1960 campaign after a group of Protestant ministers issued a statement questioning Kennedy's fitness to govern on the grounds that Roman Catholicism was "both a church and a temporal state." Kennedy confronted this issue in a powerful speech to a Baptist audience in Texas. Vowing to uphold the constitutional separation of church and state, he added: "If this election is decided on the basis that 40,000,000 Americans lost their chance of being president on the day they were baptized, then it is the whole nation that will be the loser in the eyes of history."

Kennedy's other hurdle—inexperience—was removed in a series of televised debates with Nixon that marked the beginning of modern presidential campaigns. The first debate had the greatest impact, as more than eighty million Americans watched on television or listened on radio. Though both candidates spoke well, the difference lay in cosmetics and style. The handsome, well-groomed Kennedy radiated confidence and charm. Nixon, by contrast, seemed awkward and pale. The hot TV lights made him sweat profusely, smudging his makeup. Those who heard the debate on radio scored it a draw. Those who saw it on television thought Kennedy the clear victor.

Kennedy won the election with 303 electoral votes to Nixon's 219. Yet the popular vote was the closest since 1888, with Kennedy getting 34,227,000 (49.7 percent) and Nixon 34,109,000 (49.6 percent). A swing of several thousand votes in Texas and Illinois, where suspicions of ballot fraud were rampant, would have given the election to Nixon. Kennedy did well among traditional Democrats (minorities, urban dwellers, the working class) and swept the Catholic vote, yet polls showed his religion costing him dearly in rural Protestant areas. Kennedy suspected that television won him the White House, and he may have been correct. The four debates, and a flood of prime-time advertisements, appeared to influence voters as never before.

Summary

The Ike Age

Americans look back nostalgically to the 1950s, and with good reason. These years were far more tranquil than the war-torn 1940s or the depression-scarred 1930s. The Korean War ended in 1953, and the Cold War thawed a bit with the death of Joseph Stalin, Russia's brutal dictator, that same year. There would be other foreign policy crises in the 1950s, in Suez and Hungary, in Guatemala and Lebanon, but U.S. soldiers would not be dying in faraway lands. The ugliness of McCarthyism—the partisan claims that the federal government was riddled with Communists—would recede as well with the Senate's condemnation of Joseph McCarthy in 1954. The political landscape after that would be marked by moderation and consensus. The Roosevelt-Truman years had come to a close, yet the New Deal legacy remained largely undisturbed. The American people in 1952 had voted for a new president, not a return to the days of Harding and Coolidge. Dwight Eisenhower accepted the idea that government must provide a safety net for its citizens in time of personal need and economic distress. And like Harry Truman, he intended to contain Communist expansion around the globe.

The 1950s saw an explosion of mass culture, from the coming of commercial television to the birth of rock 'n' roll. A national highway system was initiated, spurring the

Senator Joe McCarthy, America's premier Red-hunter, lectured Army counsel Joseph Welch (hand on head) about the Communist party during the celebrated Army-McCarthy hearings in 1954.

Rosa Parks rides a nearly empty but integrated Montgomery bus following the successful boycott she triggered in 1955.

Combining the sounds of black and white music with enormous sexual drive, Elvis Presley became the most successful recording star in history.

boom in automobiles and connecting the nation as never before. The widespread use of new wonder drugs such as penicillin and the successful testing of a vaccine against polio, a frightening paralytic disease that preyed on children, gave hope for a future in which laboratory science would provide cures for the worst medical afflictions of humankind.

The 1950s also witnessed *Brown v. Board of Education,* perhaps the most significant Supreme Court decision of the post–Civil War era. And there followed the mass protests that would awaken America to the long-standing injustice of racial segregation. The African American communities of Montgomery and Little Rock pointed the way, and new leaders emerged with innovative strategies to carry on the fight.

As the 1950s ended, however, nagging questions remained. Would prosperity and racial justice ever reach into the far corners of the land? Would the civil rights movement retain its momentum and nonviolent stance? Would the nation's expanding Cold War military commitment drain its economic strength—and moral authority? Would the lure of materialism and consumerism undermine precious national values? These questions would dominate the U.S. agenda in the tumultuous years ahead.

Making Connections Across Chapters

LOOKING BACK

Chapter 28 examines the promise and prosperity of the United States in the 1950s—a time of great medical and technological advances, the growth of commercial television, an exploding youth culture, and great legal advances and burgeoning movements in the struggle for equal rights.

1. What ideological principles and personal qualities defined the Eisenhower presidency? Why did this presidency seem to fit the national mood so well?
2. How did the spread of commercial television both define and reflect the cultural values of post–World War II America?
3. Why did the Soviet launching of *Sputnik* in 1957 have such a profound effect on U.S. society? Why did it cause so much national soul-searching and self-reflection?
4. How did the combination of legal victories and local protests combine to fuel the civil rights movement of the 1950s?

LOOKING AHEAD

The next chapter considers the turbulent times that followed the relative tranquility of the 1950s, showing the connections between these periods and following the political and cultural events that so badly divided the nation.

1. Did the razor-thin election victory of John F. Kennedy in the 1960 presidential election send a signal that Americans wanted a change of political course? If so, what sort of change did they have in mind?
2. Would it be possible to build on the major civil rights victories of the 1950s and fulfill the promises of Reconstruction almost a century before—the promises of voting rights, economic opportunity, and equal protection under the law?
3. Would the Cold War with the Soviet Union continue to dominate international relations, and would it expand into other areas of the world?

RECOMMENDED READINGS

Biskind, Peter. *Seeing Is Believing: How Hollywood Taught Us to Stop Worrying and Love the Fifties* (1983). Examines the way moviemaking shaped popular culture.

Dudziak, Mary. *Cold War, Civil Rights* (2000). Examines the impact of America's civil rights movement on the international scene.

Gilbert, James. *A Cycle of Outrage* (1986). Looks at the nation's reaction to juvenile delinquency in the 1950s.

Guralnick, Peter. *Last Train to Memphis: The Rise of Elvis Presley* (1994). Traces the early years of rock 'n' roll's most popular artist and the reasons for his extraordinary success.

Halberstam, David. *The Fifties* (1993). Offers an encyclopedic account of this decade, from McCarthyism to McDonald's.

Kahn, Roger. *The Boys of Summer* (1971). Recalls the glory days of Major League baseball in a simpler time.

Lewis, Tom. *Divided Highways* (1997). Shows how the building of the interstate highway system transformed American life.

Marling. Karal Ann. *As Seen on TV* (1994). Looks at the rise of visual culture in a new age of leisure.

May, Elaine. *Homeward Bound: American Families in the Cold War Era* (1988). Ties the anxieties associated with anti-Communism and the atomic bomb to the national quest for security and stability in the American home.

Oshinsky, David M. *A Conspiracy So Immense: The World of Joe McCarthy* (1983). Explores the life of America's great Red-hunter and the era that bears his name.

AMERICAN JOURNEY ONLINE AND ✆ INFOTRAC COLLEGE EDITION

Visit the source collections at http://ajaccess.wadsworth.com and infotrac.thomsonlearning.com and use the Search function with the following key terms to explore documents, images, audio and video clips, articles, and commentary related to the material in this chapter.

Dwight D. Eisenhower

Brown v. Board of Education

Sputnik

Montgomery Bus Boycott

Rosa Parks

ONLINE PRIMARY SOURCES

Here are some examples of the many primary sources related to this chapter that you will find on the *American Passages* Web site: http://history.wadsworth.com/ayersbrief02.

Polio Hysteria, 1953

Allen Ginsberg, "Howl," 1956

Lewis Mumford on Suburbs, 1961

The site also offers self-quizzes, exercises, and many additional resources to help you study.

WHO COULD HAVE PREDICTED THE TURMOIL AND TRAGEDY OF THE 1960s? The previous decade, after all, gave scant warning that trouble lay ahead. Filled with powerful milestones, such as the National Highway Act and *Brown v. Board of Education,* the 1950s seemed to reflect the optimism and stability of a confident nation—a place of widely shared values and little public complaint. All was well in prosperous postwar America, or so it appeared.

The tumult of the 1960s came suddenly, without letup or relief. It began with the jailings and beatings of civil rights workers in the South, which turned many activists against the philosophy of nonviolence. The civil rights movement, in turn, spawned a woman's movement, and then a student movement, which further challenged the status quo. Meanwhile, the escalating Vietnam War eroded the credibility of U.S. officials and divided the nation in dangerous ways. Against the backdrop of increasing bloodshed in Southeast Asia, the United States endured a horrifying cycle of homegrown violence in the 1960s, including inner-city riots, militant campus upheavals, and the assassination of prominent public figures President John F. Kennedy, his brother Robert, and the Reverend Martin Luther King Jr.

The 1970s brought little relief. A U.S. president resigned from office for the first time in the nation's history. The North Vietnamese Communists took over South Vietnam. Americans faced gas shortages, high unemployment, and staggering inflation. They watched with anger and embarrassment as their embassy in Iran was attacked and fifty-two Americans were held hostage for more than a year.

Republican Ronald Reagan won the 1980 presidential election by promising to reverse the nation's apparent decline. Mixing personal charm and optimism with the darker politics of resentment, he attracted mainstream voters by vowing to strengthen family values, reward hard work, and increase respect for the United States around the world. At the same time, he reinforced the notion among white working-class voters (known as "Reagan Democrats") that the party of Franklin Roosevelt had deserted their interests—that the real enemies of working people were no longer big business and the very rich but big government and the very poor. During the 1980s, the Reagan administration's policies regarding taxes, wages, unions,

In the oval office in 1963, a vigorous young president, with son John Jr., represented the hopes and dreams of a new generation.

©Bettmann /CORBIS

banking, and antitrust produced one of the most dramatic redistributions of wealth in U.S. history, with the top 1 percent seeing its yearly income rise by 75 percent while the rest of the nation experienced almost no gain at all. Nevertheless, Reagan remained a popular president, a politician who articulated the fears and dreams of Americans with extraordinary skill.

Through all the tumult of these decades, one certainty remained—the specter of international Communism, centered in Moscow. Although the fear of domestic subversion stirred up by Senator McCarthy had largely subsided by 1960, the anxieties generated by Soviet power and influence remained solidly in place. During the 1960s, the United States and Russia tangled over Berlin and Cuba, where the placement of offensive missiles, ninety miles from the Florida coast, led to the most dangerous confrontation of the entire Cold War. In Vietnam, meanwhile, U.S. officials defended the growing involvement as a test of will against Soviet-inspired aggression. The larger goals, they insisted, were to halt the spread of world Communism and to maintain U.S. credibility around the globe.

The 1970s brought an apparent thaw in U.S.-Soviet relations. The two sides signed a momentous agreement limiting nuclear weapons known as SALT 1. President Nixon also visited the Soviet Union as well as Communist China, raising hopes for serious dialogue, or détente. It didn't happen. As Nixon freely admitted, his visit to China was intended, in large part, to drive a wedge between the Russians and the Chinese, the world's two leading Communist powers. Furthermore, the very idea of negotiating with the Soviet Union over issues such as human rights and arms control offended hard-line anti-Communists who believed that U.S. military power must largely determine the outcome of the Cold War. In the 1980 presidential campaign, Ronald Reagan promised a much tougher stand against Communism in the future.

The Reagan administration dramatically increased the nation's defense budget. It also funded military campaigns against leftist rebels and Marxist governments in Africa, Asia, and Latin America. In one instance, it funneled money from a secret arms deal with Iran to illegally finance a right-wing guerrilla army in Nicaragua. President Reagan made no apologies for this activity. The Soviets had created an "Evil Empire," he declared, and it had to be destroyed.

The seven *Columbia* astronauts perished when their spacecraft burned up during reentry into the atmosphere in 2003.

In fact, that empire was already in trouble. Assuming power in 1985, Soviet Premier Mikhail Gorbachev well understood the problems his nation faced. Believing that Communism must become more democratic and market-oriented to survive, he encouraged the policies known as *glasnost* (openness) and *perestroika* (restructure). In trying to save Communism, however, Gorbachev set in motion the very forces that would bring it down. A wave of protest swept through Eastern Europe, with people demanding more freedom and closer contacts with the West. Unlike Hungary in 1956 and Czechoslovakia in 1968, the Soviet Union did not rush in troops to restore order. On a trip to West Berlin in 1987, President Reagan encouraged the protesters by demanding: "Mr. Gorbachev, tear down this wall." In 1989 the Communist governments in

Courtesy of NASA

Eastern Europe fell like dominoes—Hungary, Poland, Czechoslovakia, East Germany, Romania. It was one of those rare instances, noted *Time* magazine, "when the tectonic plates of history shift beneath men's feet, and nothing after is quite the same."

In 1991 the Soviet Union collapsed, and Russians began the painful transition to democratic politics and a free market economy. For the United States, meanwhile, a new set of challenges emerged. As the world's only remaining "superpower," it now faced a post–Cold War era marred by ethnic violence in the Balkans, tribal warfare in Africa, military aggression in the Middle East, nuclear proliferation in India and Pakistan, and continuing human rights violations from Latin America to China. In addition, a booming world birthrate and the specter of global warming raised serious environmental concerns, while the rapid spread of technology and information linked people together in truly remarkable ways. During the 1990s, the president who faced these issues, Bill Clinton, saw the economy achieve unprecedented levels of prosperity, and the lingering problem of the budget deficits eased dramatically.

Yet good times at home did not mean political calm. The Republicans regained control of the House of Representatives in 1994 for the first time in four decades and

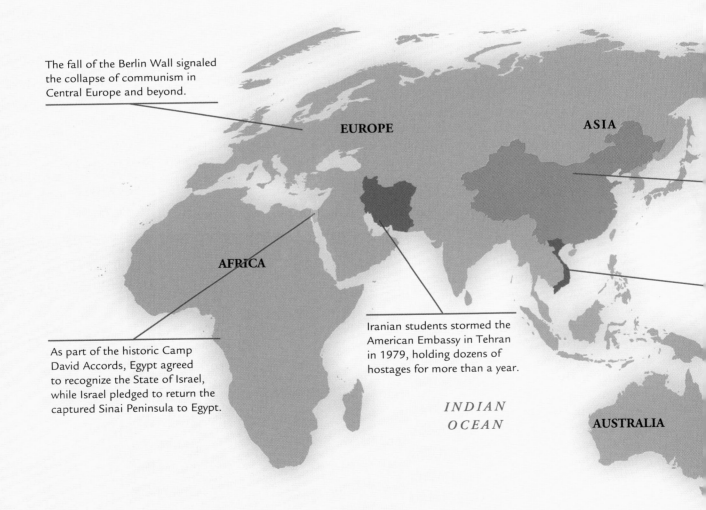

The fall of the Berlin Wall signaled the collapse of communism in Central Europe and beyond.

EUROPE

ASIA

AFRICA

As part of the historic Camp David Accords, Egypt agreed to recognize the State of Israel, while Israel pledged to return the captured Sinai Peninsula to Egypt.

Iranian students stormed the American Embassy in Tehran in 1979, holding dozens of hostages for more than a year.

INDIAN OCEAN

AUSTRALIA

ANTARCTICA

a second term for Clinton seemed doubtful. Yet he won again in 1996, only to face impeachment charges arising from a sex scandal in 1998. Despite his acquittal in 1999, his presidency ended under a cloud. His vice president, Al Gore, lost a close election to Republican George W. Bush in 2000.

On September 11, 2001, terrorist attacks on the United States stunned the American people and plunged the nation into war at home and in faraway Afghanistan. The Bush administration argued that Iraq was a major front in the war on terror and a source of danger because it possessed weapons of mass destruction. The United States and its allies invaded Iraq in March 2003. No weapons of mass destruction were found. After defeating the armies of Saddam Hussein, the coalition faced an insurgency against the occupation that continued into 2005 with mounting U.S. casualties. Following President Bush's reelection in November 2004, the nation confronted the threats of nuclear weapons programs in North Korea and Iran as well as escalating violence in Iraq. As the early years of the millennium unfolded, the menace of terrorism and its consequences tested the country's institutions in new and problematic ways.

America and the World: 1960–2005

The devastating attacks on the World Trade Center in Manhattan and the Pentagon in Washington, D.C. on September 11, 2001, brought the menace of foreign terrorism to American soil.

The attempt by the Soviet Union to deploy offensive missiles in Fidel Castro's Cuba in 1962 led to the most dangerous confrontation of the Cold War.

NORTH AMERICA

...sident Richard Nixon's dramatic visit to Communist ...na in 1972 opened the way for cultural and ...omatic exchange between the two former enemies.

PACIFIC OCEAN

ATLANTIC OCEAN

The Vietnam War dominated American politics in the late 1960s and early 1970s and bitterly divided the nation.

SOUTH AMERICA

The Turbulent Years

1960–1968

THE 1960S OPENED ON AN AMBIVALENT NOTE. THE GROSS NATIONAL PRODuct reached $500 billion for the first time, yet talk of economic recession was in the air. The darkest days of McCarthyism were over, but the fear of Communism remained. The development of new products and technologies bred optimism, while the spread of new weapons caused alarm.

Hints of protest and trouble had begun to appear. In Greensboro, North Carolina, four black college students sat down at a Woolworth lunch counter and were denied service, but refused to leave. Word of their defiance triggered "sit-in" protests across the South. Half a world away, supporters of North Vietnam's Communist ruler Ho Chi Minh announced the formation of a National Liberation Front to overthrow the anti-Communist government of **President Ngo Dinh Diem** in South Vietnam. President Diem did not seem concerned. With U.S. support, he boasted, his forces would quickly subdue these "Viet Cong" (or Vietnamese Communists).

Ngo Dinh Diem
A Vietnamese political leader who became president of South Vietnam in 1954. He was assassinated in a military coup d'état.

Early Tests

The 1960 election was a landmark event in American political history. At age forty-three, **John F. Kennedy** became the first Catholic president, the youngest candidate to win a presidential election, and the first president to be born in the twentieth century. His inauguration on January 20, 1961, seemed to herald a new era of idealism, commitment, and change. Kennedy declared that the "torch has been passed to a new generation of Americans," adding: "Ask not what your country can do for you; ask what you can do for your country."

John F. Kennedy
The thirty-fifth president of the United States, he was the first Catholic to win the White House and the first president born in the twentieth century. He was assassinated in 1963 during a trip to Dallas, Texas.

Idealism and Caution

The new administration appeared to mirror these words. Public service became a badge of honor. Kennedy's White House staff included fifteen Rhodes scholars and numerous Ivy League professors. The new secretary of state, Dean Rusk, came from the Rockefeller Foundation, and the new defense secretary, Robert McNamara, left the presidency of the Ford Motor Company to help "streamline" the nation's armed forces. Kennedy chose his younger brother Robert to become attorney general. Under Jacqueline Kennedy's

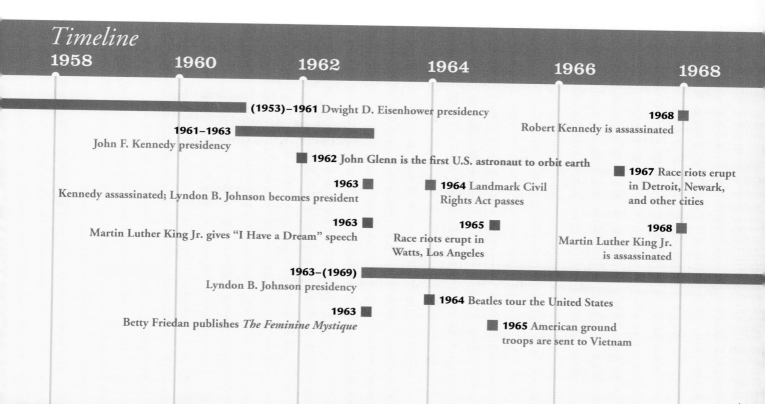

Timeline

| 1958 | 1960 | 1962 | 1964 | 1966 | 1968 |

(1953)–1961 Dwight D. Eisenhower presidency

1968 Robert Kennedy is assassinated

1961–1963 John F. Kennedy presidency

1962 John Glenn is the first U.S. astronaut to orbit earth

1963 Kennedy assassinated; Lyndon B. Johnson becomes president

1964 Landmark Civil Rights Act passes

1967 Race riots erupt in Detroit, Newark, and other cities

1963 Martin Luther King Jr. gives "I Have a Dream" speech

1965 Race riots erupt in Watts, Los Angeles

1968 Martin Luther King Jr. is assassinated

1963–(1969) Lyndon B. Johnson presidency

1964 Beatles tour the United States

1963 Betty Friedan publishes *The Feminine Mystique*

1965 American ground troops are sent to Vietnam

President Kennedy delivered a stirring inaugural address on a cloudless, bitter-cold afternoon in January 1961.

John Glenn

On February 20, 1962, aboard the *Friendship 7,* he was the first American to orbit the earth, and in 1998 he was the oldest person to participate in a space flight mission as a crew member of the space shuttle *Discovery*. From 1974 to 1998 he served as U.S. senator from Ohio.

Fidel Castro

Cuban revolutionary leader who overthrew the corrupt regime of dictator Fulgencio Batista in 1959 and soon after established a Communist state. Prime minister of Cuba from 1959 to 1976, he has been president of the government and First Secretary of the Communist party in Cuba since 1976.

Bay of Pigs

Fifteen hundred Cuban exiles, supported by the CIA, landed here on April 17, 1961, in an unsuccessful attempt to overthrow the new Communist government of Fidel Castro.

direction, the White House became a center for the arts. Cellist Pablo Casals performed at the Executive Mansion, as did the American Shakespeare Festival Theatre.

Despite the lofty rhetoric and the fanfare, Kennedy took a measured approach to his early presidential duties. For one thing, he lacked the huge popular mandate given to previous first-term presidents such as Franklin Roosevelt in 1932 and Dwight Eisenhower in 1952. For another, he worried about his relations with a Congress in which conservative Republicans and southern Democrats held the balance of power.

Several of Kennedy's early initiatives were in the New Deal tradition. He worked successfully to increase Social Security benefits and to raise the minimum wage from $1 to $1.25. Yet the Congress easily blocked his efforts to provide health insurance for the aged and to create a cabinet-level Department of Urban Affairs. Worse still was the defeat of Kennedy's $2.3 billion education bill for school construction and higher teachers' salaries, which raised nagging questions about the federal role in education. Would funds be given to racially segregated public schools or to private religious schools? Because of controversy over such questions, the education bill died in committee.

In other areas, the new administration achieved success. By executive order, Kennedy launched the Peace Corps in March 1961. Directed by the president's brother-in-law R. Sargent Shriver, the Peace Corps sent thousands of American volunteers to underdeveloped nations to provide educational and technical assistance. With a tiny budget, it became one of Kennedy's great triumphs, showcasing American idealism and know-how throughout the world.

Even more popular, though far more expensive, was the space program. Setting the goal of a manned moon landing "before this decade is out," Kennedy convinced a skeptical Congress to allocate billions of dollars for space research and rocketry, an astronauts training program, and a mission control center in Houston.

The "space race" captivated the world. In April 1961, Soviet Cosmonaut Yuri Gagarin orbited the globe in less than two hours. A month later, Commander Alan Shepard rocketed three hundred miles from Cape Canaveral in a suborbital flight, and in February 1962, Lieutenant Colonel **John Glenn** orbited the earth three times aboard *Friendship 7* before touching down in the Caribbean. Glenn became a national hero, with ticker tape parades and a televised address before a joint session of Congress.

The Bay of Pigs

Kennedy inherited his first crisis from the previous administration. As president-elect, he was told of a secret plan, personally approved by Eisenhower, to overthrow the new Marxist government of **Fidel Castro** in Cuba. The plan called for several hundred anti-Castro exiles, trained and equipped by the CIA, to invade Cuba and trigger an anti-Communist revolution.

Kennedy endorsed the plan. He believed that Castro set a dangerous example by aligning Cuba with the Soviet Union and by expropriating the property of U.S. corporations. Kennedy had promised to "get tough" with Castro during the 1960 campaign; he could not easily back down now.

On April 17, 1961, a brigade of fifteen hundred waded ashore at the **Bay of Pigs,** on Cuba's southern coast. Nothing went as planned. The landing site had sharp coral reefs and swampy terrain, making it hard to unload supplies and move out from the beaches. Local workers quickly spotted the invaders, and within twenty-four hours the brigade was surrounded by troops loyal to Castro. Kennedy refused to lend vital air and naval support to the brigade in a futile attempt to hide the role of the United States in this disaster. More than a hundred invaders were killed, and twelve hundred were captured.

The Bay of Pigs fiasco left a troubled legacy. On one hand, it angered other Latin American governments and drove Castro even closer to the Russian embrace. On the other, it fueled Kennedy's interest in covert operations and his desire to control them more directly. After removing long-time CIA Director Allen Dulles, the president approved a top-secret program, code-named Operation Mongoose, to topple the Cuban government

and assassinate its leaders. Its plans included the destruction of Cuba's vital sugar crop and a box of exploding cigars for Castro.

The Berlin Wall

In June 1961 Kennedy met with Soviet leader Nikita Khrushchev in Vienna. Khrushchev tried to bully the new president, threatening to give East Germany full control over road and rail access to West Berlin, in violation of previous guarantees. Berlin was both a danger and an embarrassment to Khrushchev. The prosperous Western sector stood as a model of democratic capitalism behind the Iron Curtain. Each day, more than a thousand refugees from the Communist side poured into West Berlin. At this rate, East Germany would lose most of its skilled workers to the West.

Kennedy was not intimidated. Calling West Berlin "the great testing place of courage and will," he declared that NATO forces would defend the city at all costs. To emphasize this point, the president tripled draft calls and requested $3 billion in additional defense appropriations, which Congress quickly granted.

The crisis ended in August 1961. As the world watched in amazement, workers in East Berlin constructed a wall of barbed wire and concrete around the western edge of their city, sealing off East Berlin, and eventually all of East Germany, from the non-Communist world. In a tactical sense, Khrushchev achieved his objective of stopping the East German exodus to the West. In a larger sense, however, the wall became an admission of failure.

The Freedom Riders

Kennedy's first domestic crisis occurred in the field of civil rights. The president wanted change to come slowly, without the mass protests and violent incidents that had previously made headlines. He worried, too, that White House support for *immediate* desegregation would cost him the goodwill of powerful southerners in Congress.

Yet, as Kennedy discovered, the real momentum for civil rights came from below. In 1961 the Congress of Racial Equality (CORE) announced plans to test a recent Supreme Court decision, *Boynton v. Virginia,* which prohibited racial segregation in bus terminals, train stations, and airports engaged in interstate transportation. CORE's objective, said its national director, was "to provoke the southern authorities into arresting us and thereby prod the Justice Department into enforcing the law of the land."

In May 1961 thirteen **freedom riders**—seven blacks and six whites—left Washington on a Greyhound bus bound for New Orleans. At each stop, they ignored the "white" and "colored" signs that hung by the toilets, lunch counters, and waiting rooms in defiance of federal law. Trouble erupted in Anniston, Alabama, when their bus was firebombed by a white mob. As the passengers struggled outside, they were beaten with fists and clubs. The violence continued in Montgomery and Birmingham, Alabama.

As new freedom riders arrived to replace the wounded, the Kennedy administration sent in federal marshals to protect them. It had no choice, given the violent scenes that flashed around the world. In September 1961 the federal government banned interstate carriers from using any terminal that segregated the races. After months of bloody struggle, the freedom riders prevailed.

freedom riders
Interracial groups who rode buses in the South so that a series of federal court decisions declaring segregation on buses and in waiting rooms unconstitutional would not be ignored by white officials.

The New Economics

Despite his increasing focus on civil rights, President Kennedy considered the economy to be his number-one domestic concern. Though real wages for an average family rose a remarkable 20 percent in the 1950s, a series of recessions toward the end of Eisenhower's second term prompted both a drop in factory production and a rise in unemployment. By the time Kennedy took office, more Americans were out of work than at any time since the end of World War II.

In 1962 Kennedy unveiled his economic program. He proposed a major tax cut for consumers and businesses, designed to stimulate purchasing power and encourage new investment. For Kennedy, the goal of full employment required sizable budget deficits in the short run as tax revenues declined. What worried him was the specter of inflation as the economy heated up.

To prevent this, Kennedy lobbied business and labor leaders to respect the wage-price guidelines his administration recommended. The Teamsters, Auto Workers, and Steel Workers all agreed to modest wage hikes in 1962 with the understanding that their employers would not raise prices. Two weeks later, U.S. Steel, the nation's third largest corporation, announced a whopping price increase of $6 a ton, leading other steel companies to do the same.

Calling the move an "irresponsible defiance of the public interest," Kennedy used his influence to roll back the price increase. Within days, the Justice Department threatened to investigate antitrust violations in the steel industry, and the Defense Department announced that it might not purchase steel from the "price-gouging" offenders.

Under enormous pressure, the steel companies gave in. The president had won a major victory in his battle against inflation, although his rough tactics aroused deep anger in the business community. Nevertheless, the economy prospered in the early 1960s, achieving low unemployment, stable prices, and steady growth.

The nation's great wealth and prosperity were not shared by all however, and this painful truth was the subject of a path-breaking book, *The Other America,* by socialist author Michael Harrington in 1962. Harrington exposed the grim face of poverty in urban slums and migrant labor camps, in Appalachian coalfields and dying rural towns. By his estimate, more than forty million people—one-quarter of the U.S. population—inhabited an "economic underworld" of joblessness, marginal wages, hunger, and despair.

President Kennedy believed that a strong economy, bolstered by government incentives, would provide most Americans with good jobs and material success. Yet Harrington's book, describing poverty as "a culture, an institution, a way of life" virtually immune to business cycles and overall prosperity, helped to change the president's mind. Kennedy directed Walter Heller, chairman of the Council of Economic Advisers, to prepare a memorandum on the root causes of poverty so that legislation could be framed to eliminate them.

Social and Political Challenges

Before long President Kennedy's political caution began to ease. A year of trial and error led him to take more confident stands. But as events unfolded in 1962, the president faced challenges in familiar places—the Deep South and the waters off Cuba. This time, the stakes were much higher.

The Battle for Ole Miss

In the fall of 1962, a federal court ordered the admission of James Meredith, a black Air Force veteran, to the all-white University of Mississippi, known as Ole Miss. Governor Ross Barnett led the opposition. A virulent racist, Barnett had kept a previous black applicant from entering Ole Miss by having him committed to a mental hospital. Now Barnett invoked the doctrine of interposition by warning that Mississippi would ignore all federal rulings in order to keep segregation in place.

Kennedy responded to Barnett's challenge by dispatching several hundred federal marshals to Ole Miss. They were met by a well-armed mob, more than two thousand strong. In the riot that followed, two people were killed and hundreds were injured. Kennedy rushed in troops and federalized the State Guard. With twenty-three thousand soldiers on campus—five times the student population—Meredith registered for classes under army bayonets. The battle at Ole Miss was over; the larger struggle for Mississippi lay ahead.

U-2
A U.S. spy plane. One piloted by Francis Gary Powers was shot down over the Soviet Union in 1960, which led to the angry breakup of a Summit meeting in Paris between President Eisenhower and Soviet Premier Nikita Khrushchev.

The Missiles of October

In October 1962 the world faced the most dangerous confrontation of the entire Cold War. It began with rumors, confirmed by **U-2** spy plane photos, that the Russians were deploying Intermediate-Range Ballistic Missiles (IRBMs) in Cuba. Speed was essential, for the missiles would become operational in less than a month. Kennedy convened an executive committee (known as ex-Comm) to provide a suitable response.

Castro's need for security was understandable. In addition to Operation Mongoose, the Kennedy administration had imposed an economic embargo on Cuba and engineered its expulsion from the Organization of American States. At Castro's urging, the Soviet Union sent thousands of military advisors to Cuba, as well as defensive missiles to shoot down invading planes. Yet the deployment of *offensive* weapons, capable of reaching Chicago or Washington with nuclear warheads, was an alarming escalation designed to tip the balance of terror in Moscow's favor.

Some ex-Comm members recommended immediate air strikes to take out the missile bases. Others, including **Robert Kennedy,** proposed a naval blockade of Cuba. The president carefully studied both options before choosing the latter. A blockade shifted the burden of responsibility to Khrushchev while allowing both sides to seek a solution short of war.

On October 22, 1962, Kennedy revealed the existence of the missiles in a nationally televised address. After describing the naval blockade, he demanded that Russia remove the IRBMs already in place. Any missile fired from Cuba, he warned, would be regarded "as an attack by the Soviet Union on the United States," requiring a "full retaliatory response." U.S. forces went on full alert. A U-2 plane over Cuba was shot down, and its pilot killed. The entire world watched anxiously as Russian vessels in the Caribbean inched closer to U.S. warships enforcing the blockade.

On October 26 Kennedy received an emotional note from Khrushchev suggesting a settlement: Russia would remove its missiles if the United States pledged never to invade Cuba. Before the president could respond, however, a second note arrived demanding that the United States also remove its Jupiter missiles along the Soviet border in Turkey. This new demand did not pose a security problem, since the Jupiter missiles were obsolete and about to be scrapped. Yet the president could not remove them without appearing to buckle under Soviet pressure.

Robert Kennedy provided the solution. Respond to the first note, he said, and ignore the second one. On October 27 the president vowed not to invade Cuba if the IRBMs were dismantled. In private, meanwhile, Robert Kennedy assured Soviet Ambassador Anatoly Dobrynin that the Jupiter missiles would be removed from Turkey in the near future. Kennedy also gave Dobrynin a deadline. If the Cuban missiles were not dismantled within forty-eight hours, the United States would destroy them.

Robert Kennedy

He served as attorney general during the presidency of his brother John F. Kennedy. Elected to the Senate in 1964, he was assassinated in Los Angeles while campaigning for the presidency.

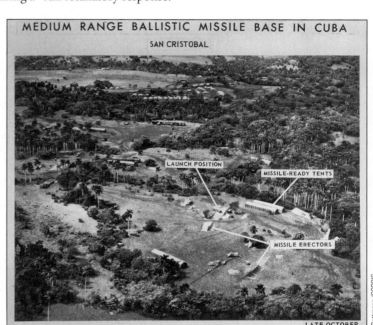

U-2 photos, such as this one, of missile bases being constructed in Cuba led to the most dangerous confrontation of the Cold War.

On October 28 Khrushchev accepted the deal. The Soviet premier had badly miscalculated the stern U.S. reaction to the placement of offensive missiles in Cuba. Khrushchev soon left office in disgrace, while Kennedy's reputation soared. For two weeks in October, the world seemed headed for nuclear war.

That fact alone seemed to sober both sides. In July 1963 a direct telephone link, known as the "hotline," was established between the White House and the Kremlin. In August the United States and Russia joined with ninety other nations to sign the "Treaty Banning Nuclear Weapons Tests in the Atmosphere, in Outer Space and Under Water." The treaty did not prevent underground testing or provide for onsite inspection, and several emerging atomic powers, such as France and China, refused to take part. Yet a first step had been taken to cleanse the environment of radioactivity—a symbolic step on the road to a safer world.

Trouble in Vietnam

President Kennedy came away from the missile crisis with greater confidence in his ability to manage foreign problems. His primary goal, in military terms, was to replace the Eisenhower-Dulles doctrine of "massive retaliation" with a "flexible response" policy that would maximize his options in any foreign crisis. The plan called for a buildup in nuclear missiles, conventional ground troops, and Special Forces such as the "Green Berets." Not surprisingly, the defense budget rose rapidly in the Kennedy years.

When Kennedy entered the White House, U.S. aid to South Vietnam topped $1 billion, and several hundred U.S. military advisors were in the field. Like Eisenhower, Kennedy hoped to formalize Vietnam's temporary partition at the 17th parallel by turning the South Vietnamese regime of Ngo Dinh Diem into a military and economic power capable of defending itself against attacks from Ho Chi Minh's Communist government in the north.

Kennedy welcomed the challenge. Under the doctrine of "flexible response," U.S. Special Forces were dispatched to train South Vietnam's army, along with CIA personnel to direct covert operations and economic experts to supervise the aid programs intended to stabilize Diem's regime. Among the worst problems, it turned out, was Diem himself. Educated in the United States, a Catholic in a largely Buddhist land, Diem had little in common with the people he ruled. The South Vietnam he envisioned did not include the vital measures, such as land reform and religious toleration, that were needed to keep him in power.

In 1963 protests erupted in Saigon and other South Vietnamese cities over Diem's autocratic rule. The Buddhists held mass demonstrations against religious oppression, with several monks setting fire to themselves. As the protests escalated, army units attacked Buddhist temples and arrested their priests, sparking even greater protests. Isolated in his presidential palace, Diem seemed oblivious to the crisis.

That fall, Diem was overthrown in a military coup. U.S. officials knew about the coup, but did nothing to stop it. To their surprise, however, the generals murdered Diem and his brother, Ngo Dinh Nhu, after taking them prisoner on the palace grounds.

By that time sixteen thousand U.S. troops were stationed in South Vietnam. For Kennedy and his advisors, the struggle had become a test of will against "Communist aggression." Yet the president also worried that the use of U.S. troops created a dangerous momentum of its own. "It's like taking a drink," he said. "The effect wears off and you have to take another."

The Rights Revolution: Early Steps

In the early 1960s, the fires of social and political protest slowly came alive. In 1962 a thirty-five-year-old Mexican American named **Cesar Chavez** moved to Delano, California, with his wife and eight children. A naval veteran of World War II, Chavez toiled in the plum orchards and strawberry fields of central California before turning to community organizing. With unshakable conviction, he aimed to better the lives of impoverished migrant farm laborers by uniting them under a single banner—the black Aztec eagle of the infant United Farm Workers Association.

The year 1962 also witnessed the publication of two path-breaking books: Harrington's *The Other America* and Rachel Carson's *Silent Spring*. Carson, a marine biologist, exposed the contamination of wildlife, water supplies, and farmland by pesticides such as DDT. Her book helped revive America's naturalist movement. In 1963 two more seminal works appeared: **Betty Friedan**'s *The Feminine Mystique,* which spurred the struggle for women's rights, and James Baldwin's *The Fire Next Time,* which warned of the growing racial divide. "To be a Negro in this country and to be relatively conscious," wrote Baldwin, "is to be in a rage all the time."

From Birmingham to Washington

By 1963 racial injustice in the United States was a central issue. Birmingham, Alabama, became the new battleground, as a coalition of civil rights groups, led by Martin Luther King's Southern Christian Leadership Conference, attempted to break down the walls of discrimination. Birmingham was so rigidly segregated that a book featuring black rabbits and white rabbits eating together was removed from city libraries.

Dr. King hoped to integrate Birmingham with a series of nonviolent protests codenamed "Project C," for confrontation. Using the local black churches as meetinghouses, he recruited hundreds of followers with his revivalist appeals. The demonstrations challenged segregation on many fronts. There were sit-ins at lunch counters, kneel-ins at white

Cesar Chavez
A labor organizer who founded the United Farm Workers Association in 1962.

Betty Friedan
A feminist who wrote *The Feminine Mystique* in 1963 and founded the National Organization for Women in 1966.

churches, and voter registration marches to city hall. Boycotts were organized to protest the all-white hiring practices of downtown department stores. Birmingham authorities cracked down hard. Led by Commissioner Eugene ("Bull") Connor, city police dispersed the protesters with attack dogs and high-pressure fire hoses.

Dr. King was among the hundreds arrested for violating local court orders against marching and picketing. From his jail cell, he defended the morality of civil disobedience, noting that "segregation statutes are unjust because segregation distorts the soul." President Kennedy offered firm support. After dispatching federal troops to Birmingham, he assisted in an agreement that integrated the city's lunch counters and department stores. At that very moment, however, Governor George C. Wallace vowed to block the admission of two black students to the University of Alabama by "standing in the schoolhouse door." When federal marshals arrived, Wallace dramatically stepped aside.

The president's decisive action in Alabama signaled a major change. Viewing civil rights for the first time as a *moral* issue, Kennedy delivered a moving appeal for justice on national television. "One hundred years have passed since President Lincoln freed the slaves," he said, "yet their heirs, their grandsons, are not fully free. . . . And this nation will not be fully free until all its citizens are free." Later that evening, civil rights activist Medgar Evers was assassinated outside his Jackson, Mississippi, home by a member of the Ku Klux Klan.

In June 1963 Kennedy sent Congress one of the most sweeping civil rights bills of the twentieth century. The bill, which prohibited discrimination in employment, federally assisted programs, and public accommodations such as restaurants and hotels, caused a furor on Capitol Hill. Southern legislators accused the president of "race-mixing," while others, including Senator Barry Goldwater of Arizona, criticized him for abusing the "property rights" of business owners. As the bill's momentum stalled, a number of civil rights groups led by A. Philip Randolph, long-time president of the Brotherhood of Sleeping Car Porters, announced a "March on Washington for Jobs and Freedom."

On August 28, 1963, more than two hundred thousand people gathered at the Lincoln Memorial. They listened to the spirituals of Mahalia Jackson, locked arms in solidarity as Joan Baez sang "We Shall Overcome," and rose in thunderous applause to the final words of Martin Luther King's now legendary address, "I Have a Dream":

From the steps of the Lincoln Memorial, Martin Luther King Jr. delivered his eloquent address "I Have a Dream" to a gathering of two hundred thousand people who had come to Washington to push for passage of a landmark civil rights bill in August 1963.

> When we let freedom ring, when we let it ring from every village and every hamlet, from every state and every city, we will be able to speed up that day when all God's children, black men and white men, Jews and Gentiles, Protestants and Catholics, will be able to join hands and sing in the words of that old Negro spiritual, "Free at last! Free at last! Thank God almighty, we are free at last!"

Feminist Stirrings

The civil rights movement always possessed a strong female strain. From Rosa Parks in Montgomery to **Fannie Lou Hamer** of the Mississippi Freedom Democratic party, women played a prominent role in the struggle for black equality. By 1963 the spirit of these protests created a sense of determination that sparked other movements, such as women's rights.

The revival of feminism in the 1960s seemed long overdue. More than four decades after winning the vote, American women played a minor role in government affairs. In 1963 there were no women governors, cabinet officers, or Supreme Court justices. The U.S. Senate contained one female member, Margaret Chase Smith of Maine. Women comprised 51 percent of the population, but only 3 percent of state legislators nationwide.

Discrimination also pervaded the workplace. Though more women were working outside the home in the early 1960s than ever before, they were increasingly concentrated in

Fannie Lou Hamer
Daughter of illiterate Mississippi sharecroppers, she helped lead the civil rights struggle in Mississippi, focusing on voting rights for African Americans and representation in the national Democratic party.

low-paying service and clerical jobs. Fewer than 4 percent of the nation's lawyers, and 1 percent of the top business executives, were female. As a result, full-time working women earned about 60 percent of the income of men.

These inequities were highlighted in 1963 by the final report of the Presidential Commission on the Status of Women. Led by Eleanor Roosevelt (who died in 1962) and Esther Peterson, an assistant secretary of labor, the commission detailed a wide range of problems, including job discrimination, unequal wages, lack of child care, and legal restrictions that prevented women, in some states, from sitting on juries or making wills. In direct response, President Kennedy issued an executive order banning sex discrimination in federal employment. A few months later, Congress passed the Equal Pay Act of 1963, requiring employers to provide equal wages to men and women who did the same work.

Even more important in terms of the emerging women's movement was the publication of *The Feminine Mystique.* In the opening chapters, Betty Friedan described "the problem that has no name," the emptiness felt by middle-class women who sacrificed their dreams and careers to become "happy homemakers." Blaming educators, advertisers, social scientists, and government officials for creating a climate in which femininity and domesticity went hand in hand, Friedan concluded that "we can no longer ignore that voice in women that says: 'I want something more than my husband and my children and my home.'"

The Feminine Mystique became an instant best-seller because it voiced the unspoken feelings of so many women. Their unhappiness was not caused by individual neuroses, Friedan argued, but rather by a set of cultural values that oppressed women while pretending to improve their lives. The message, she added, was that women must grasp their common problems in order to solve them.

Tragedy and Transition

By the fall of 1963, the fast pace and rapid changes of the new decade were leaving their mark. A growing economy, an emerging rights revolution, an expanding war in Southeast Asia, a frantic race to the moon—each would serve to reshape the fabric of American life in the years ahead. First, however, tragedy intervened.

Dallas

In late November 1963, John and Jacqueline Kennedy traveled to Texas. The 1964 presidential race was approaching, and Texas, which had narrowly supported the Kennedy-Johnson ticket three years before, could not be taken for granted. After greeting friendly crowds in Fort Worth, the Kennedys took a motorcade through Dallas, with the bubble top of their limousine removed. Along the route, people waved from office buildings and cheered from the sidewalks. As the procession reached Dealy Plaza, shots rang out from the window of a nearby book depository. President Kennedy grabbed his neck and slumped to the seat. Texas Governor John Connally was wounded in the back. The motorcade raced to Parkland Hospital, where the president was pronounced dead.

Lee Harvey Oswald
Alleged assassin of President John F. Kennedy, he was shot two days later while under arrest.

Within hours, the Dallas police arrested a twenty-four-year-old suspect named **Lee Harvey Oswald.** Two days later, Oswald was shot and killed in the basement of Dallas police headquarters by Jack Ruby, a local nightclub owner. These shocking events led many Americans to conclude that Oswald was innocent or that he did not act alone. Dozens of theories surfaced about the Kennedy assassination, blaming Fidel Castro and the Mafia, the Ku Klux Klan and the CIA. The most logical theory, that a deranged man had committed a senseless act of violence, did not seem compelling enough to explain the death of a president so young and full of life.

Few events in the nation's history produced so much bewilderment and grief. Charming and handsome, a war hero with a glamorous wife, Kennedy seemed the ideal president for the electronic political age. The media likened his administration to Camelot, a magical place that symbolized courage, chivalry, and hope. His tragic death added the further dimension of promise unfulfilled.

The reality was rather different, of course. Kennedy's 1,037 days in office were marked by failures as well as successes. Since his death, moreover, evidence of his extramarital affairs has raised legitimate questions about his character. Still, the president's final months were his most productive by far. The Test Ban Treaty offered hope for a safer world, and a new civil rights bill had been sent to Capitol Hill. There is also the suggestion—disputed by some—that Kennedy was rethinking his position on Vietnam. "If I tried to pull out completely now," he told Senator Mike Mansfield, "we would have another Joe McCarthy red scare on our hands, but I can do it after I'm reelected."

The trip to Dallas shattered those hopes and plans.

LBJ

Within hours of the assassination, Lyndon Johnson took the presidential oath of office aboard *Air Force One*. As the nation mourned its fallen leader, President Johnson vowed to continue the programs and policies of the Kennedy administration.

Lyndon Baines Johnson—known as LBJ—bore little resemblance to the president he replaced. Born in the Texas hill country in 1908, Johnson came from a lower social class and an older political generation. After graduating from a public college, he worked in the Washington office of a Texas congressman before returning home to become state director of the National Youth Administration, which provided work-study funds for needy students. Under Johnson's leadership, the Texas NYA became a model for the nation, providing employment in the construction of playgrounds and parks. The experience turned him into an avid New Dealer, with confidence in the government's ability to help people in need.

In the following years, Johnson won a seat in Congress, served as a naval officer during World War II, and became a U.S. senator in 1949. Elected Senate majority leader by his Democratic colleagues in the 1950s, Johnson worked efficiently with the Eisenhower White House to craft important legislation on defense spending, highway construction, and civil rights.

LBJ lacked the good looks and regal charm of John Kennedy. He seemed crude and plodding by comparison. Yet he understood the federal bureaucracy and recognized the true pockets of power. He knew when to flatter, when to bully, and when to bargain. Incredibly ambitious and hardworking, he entered the White House with three decades of political experience under his belt.

Lyndon Baines Johnson
The thirty-sixth president of the United States, he took over following President Kennedy's assassination in 1963 and was elected in a landslide the following year. He piloted a number of important initiatives through Congress, including the Civil Rights Act of 1964 and the Voting Rights Act of 1965.

Tax Cuts and Civil Rights

The new president moved quickly to restore public confidence. To calm mounting suspicion of conspiracy, he appointed a seven-member commission, headed by Chief Justice Earl Warren, to investigate the Kennedy assassination and issue a report. To provide stability in the executive branch, he convinced Secretary of State Dean Rusk, Secretary of Defense Robert McNamara, chief economic advisor Walter Heller, and other key officials to remain at their jobs.

One of his first acts as president was to work for the tax cut that Heller and Kennedy had supported. To please fiscal conservatives in Congress, Johnson agreed to slash the federal budget. He believed that lower taxes would spur economic growth and lower unemployment, thereby increasing federal revenues down the road. In February 1964 Johnson signed a measure that cut taxes by $10 billion over the next two years.

The economy responded. With more money available for investment and consumption, the gross national product shot up 7 percent in 1964 and 8 percent the following year, and unemployment fell below 5 percent for the first time since World War II. Furthermore, the economic boom generated even greater federal revenues—just as Johnson had predicted.

Within weeks after taking office, the president met with black leaders to assure them of his commitment to civil rights. This was essential, for Johnson's public record was mixed. As a young senator, he had opposed virtually all of President Truman's civil rights initiatives. Yet as majority leader, he had helped pass legislation giving the Justice Department more authority to enforce school integration and protect black voting rights. In his heart, Johnson considered segregation to be an immoral system that retarded an entire region's advancement. "He felt about the race question much as I did," a Texas friend recalled, "namely that it obsessed the South and diverted it from attending to its economic and educational problems."

The civil rights bill had strong public backing outside the South. In February the House of Representatives easily approved it by a vote of 290 to 130, but the bill hit a wall in the Senate, where southern opponents used the filibuster to prevent its passage. The bill's success depended on a vote for cloture, ending debate, which required the agreement of two-thirds of the Senate. Working together, Senators Hubert Humphrey (D-Minnesota) and Everett Dirksen (R-Illinois) gathered bipartisan support. The Senate voted for cloture on June 10, 1964, and passed the bill the following afternoon. Described by the *New York Times* as "the most far-reaching civil rights [legislation] since Reconstruction days," it withheld federal funds from segregated public programs, created an Equal Employment Opportunity Commission, and outlawed discrimination in public accommodations, such as theaters, restaurants, and hotels. Furthermore, a last-minute lobbying effort by Senator Margaret Chase Smith and other women's rights supporters added another category— "sex"—to the clause in Title VII that prohibited employment discrimination based on race, creed, or national origin. What seemed like a minor addition became a powerful asset to working women in the future.

President Johnson signed the bill into law on July 2, 1964. Though compliance came slowly, the Civil Rights Act marked a vital turning point in the struggle for equal rights.

Landslide in 1964

LBJ entered the 1964 presidential campaign on a tidal wave of popularity and goodwill. The nation prospered, Vietnam appeared as a distant blip on the screen, and the only war on Johnson's public agenda was the one against poverty, which he promised to wage—and win—after his expected victory at the polls.

The summer of 1964, however, offered signs of the trouble to come. In Mississippi an attempt to register black voters by local activists and northern college students met violent resistance from white mobs. On June 21 three volunteers—James Chaney, Andrew Goodman, and Michael Schwerner—disappeared after inspecting the ruins of a fire-bombed black church. Because Goodman and Schwerner were northern whites, the incident made the front pages of newspapers across the country. Five weeks later, FBI agents found three bodies buried in an earthen dam. The civil rights workers had been murdered by local Klansmen and police, seven of whom were eventually convicted and sent to jail.

Racial tensions that summer were not confined to the South. In July a confrontation between residents and police officers in Harlem led to several nights of arson and looting. The trouble was followed by disturbances in the black neighborhoods of Philadelphia, Pennsylvania; Paterson, New Jersey; and Rochester; New York. At the Democratic National Convention in Atlantic City, moreover, the race issue took center stage. Although the nomination of President Johnson and Senator Humphrey, his running mate, went smoothly, a floor fight erupted over the seating of two rival Mississippi delegations—one composed of state party segregationists; the other representing the biracial Mississippi Freedom Democratic party (MFDP). Led by Fannie Lou Hamer, the MFDP spoke for the disenfranchised black majority in Mississippi.

Johnson hoped to compromise. Acting through Senator Humphrey, he offered the Freedom party two voting delegates and the promise of a fully integrated Mississippi delegation at future national conventions. The compromise pleased no one. Hamer rejected it as a "token" gesture, and several white Mississippi delegates left Atlantic City in a huff.

At the GOP National Convention in San Francisco, the simmering feud between moderates and conservatives boiled over, with delegates shouting down opponents. After bitter debate, the convention chose Senator Barry Goldwater of Arizona for the presidential nomination, and Representative William Miller of New York for the vice presidential spot. In a defiant acceptance speech, Goldwater promised a "spiritual awakening" for America, adding: "Extremism in the defense of liberty is no vice. Moderation in the pursuit of justice is no virtue."

Goldwater opposed "big government" in domestic affairs but supported large military budgets to deter "Communist aggression." His Senate record included votes against Social Security increases, the Nuclear Test Ban Treaty of 1963, and the Civil Rights Act of 1964. In contrast to Goldwater, President Johnson came across as the candidate of all Americans, with promises galore. "We're in favor of a lot of things and we're against mighty few," he said.

Even in foreign affairs, Johnson appeared confident and controlled. In August 1964 two U.S. Navy destroyers, the *Maddox* and *C. Turner Joy,* engaged several North Vietnamese torpedo boats in the Gulf of Tonkin. The truth about this incident was overshadowed by Johnson's dramatic response. First he ordered U.S. planes to bomb military targets deep inside North Vietnam. Then he requested—and received—a congressional resolution authorizing the president to "take all necessary measures" to repel "further aggression."

The **Gulf of Tonkin Resolution** gave Johnson the authority he would need to escalate the Vietnam War. During the 1964 campaign, however, he assured voters that nothing could be further from his mind. "We don't want American boys to do the fighting for Asian boys," he declared. "We don't want to get tied down in a land war in Asia."

The election was never in doubt. Johnson projected optimism and energy, whereas Goldwater appeared defensive and out-of-touch. The president won 61 percent of the popular vote and forty-four of the fifty states. In addition, the Democrats increased their substantial majorities in both houses of Congress.

For Republicans, however, the news was not all bad. The election returns showed that a new coalition was forming in their ranks, with the party gaining strength among middle-class white voters in the South and Southwest. Furthermore, Goldwater attracted thousands of young recruits who were determined to reshape the Republican party along more conservative lines.

Gulf of Tonkin Resolution

Following reports of a confrontation with North Vietnamese in the Tonkin Gulf in 1964, President Johnson requested, and received, congressional authority to "take all necessary measures" to repel "further aggression" in Vietnam, giving the president formal authority to escalate the war.

The Great Society

President Johnson viewed his landslide victory as a mandate for change. Anxious to leave his mark on history, he spoke of creating "a great society" for Americans in which the "quality of our goals" exceeded the "quantity of our goods," a society in which poverty, ignorance, and discrimination no longer existed.

Declaring War on Poverty

The centerpiece of Johnson's expansive vision was his "war on poverty." Johnson named R. Sargent Shriver to coordinate the numerous programs created by the Economic Opportunity Act of 1964, including the Job Corps, the Neighborhood Youth Corps, and Volunteers in Service to America (VISTA), a domestic service program modeled on the Peace Corps. Though Congress allocated $3 billion for these programs in 1965 and 1966, this figure would decline as the Vietnam War expanded.

The most controversial aspect of the war on poverty was its emphasis on "community action," which encouraged neighborhood groups to play an active role in federally funded projects. Some initiatives, such as food stamps and Head Start, a preschool enrichment program, proved very successful. Others were cited for waste and fraud. Poverty did decline dramatically in this era—the result of an expanding economy as well as federal programs aimed directly at the poor. In 1960, more than forty million Americans (20 percent of the population) lived beneath the poverty line; by 1970 that figure had dropped to twenty-four million (12 percent).

Health Care and Immigration Reform

The Great Society's agenda included a mixture of original programs and borrowed ideas. A kind of infectious optimism gripped Washington. Nothing seemed politically impossible with Lyndon Johnson in charge.

Health care was a good example. When Johnson took office in 1963, a majority of older Americans were without health insurance, one-fifth of the nation's poor had never visited a doctor, and the infant mortality rate showed no signs of declining. Johnson believed that medical care for the poor and the elderly was an essential part of the Great Society. Yet the idea of federal involvement raised fundamental questions about the role of government in a free enterprise system. The American Medical Association (AMA) and private insurers strongly opposed such intervention, calling it "socialized medicine."

After months of intense lobbying, Congress passed the landmark legislation, known as Medicare and Medicaid, that Johnson requested. Medicare provided federal assistance to the elderly for hospital expenses and doctors' fees, while Medicaid extended medical coverage to welfare recipients through matching grants to the states. Both programs grew rapidly. Though supporters pointed with pride to statistics showing both an increase in life expectancy and a drop in infant mortality, critics noted the exploding federal costs and the inferior quality of health care to the poor. Few government programs proved more controversial and expensive to maintain than Medicare and Medicaid, and none would prove more difficult to reform.

The Great Society also included a new immigration law, passed in 1965. The Immigration Act removed the "national origins" quotas, as well as the ban on Asians, which dated back to 1924. While setting a ceiling of about three hundred thousand immigrants per year, the law permitted the family members of U.S. citizens (both naturalized and native-born) to enter the United States without limit.

The impact was dramatic. Prior to 1965, Europe accounted for 90 percent of the new arrivals to the United States; after 1965, only 10 percent. By the mid-1970s, a majority of legal immigrants came from seven Asian and Latin American countries: Korea, Taiwan, India, the Philippines, Cuba, the Dominican Republic, and Mexico.

The Expanding War

Nothing proved as important, or as damaging, to Johnson's presidency as the conflict in Vietnam. When Johnson assumed office, there were fewer than twenty thousand U.S. "advisors" in that divided country, training the soldiers and bureaucrats of anti-Communist South Vietnam. Within three years, that number had risen to almost five hundred thousand. Vietnam quickly became Johnson's war, and, ultimately, his nightmare.

Point of No Return

Vietnam was part of a larger "containment" effort that had guided U.S. foreign affairs since the end of World War II. Like Presidents Truman, Eisenhower, and Kennedy, LBJ based his commitment to Vietnam on a series of powerful assumptions, such as saving "democracy" in Asia, halting the spread of Communism, and maintaining America's credibility around the globe. It hardly mattered that South Vietnam was neither a democracy nor the victim of an international Communist plot. What did matter was the belief that a defeat for the United States anywhere would undermine its standing everywhere.

Johnson understood the political stakes. His plan was to pressure the Communist enemy in a measured fashion that would neither alarm the American public nor divert resources from his cherished domestic programs. The Gulf of Tonkin Resolution gave him the authority to move forward. The Viet Cong attack at Pleiku provided the motive.

Pleiku, a market town in the central highlands of South Vietnam, was home to a military airstrip guarded by U.S. Special Forces. In February 1965 a Viet Cong mortar barrage killed eight Americans and wounded more than a hundred. Several days later, U.S. warplanes began the massive bombing of North Vietnam. Known first as Operation Rolling Thunder, the air strikes hit targets checked personally by President Johnson. The problem, however, was that air power had little impact on North Vietnam's ability to wage war. The bombings killed thousands, flattened factories and power plants, and ravaged the economy; yet the flow of Communist troops and supplies into South Vietnam never stopped.

In March 1965 two Marine battalions arrived at the huge new U.S. Air Force base in Da Nang, raising the American troop total in South Vietnam above 100,000. In December, troop levels reached 184,000 and rose each month thereafter. Draft calls zoomed from 100,000 in 1964 to 340,000 by 1966, leading millions of young men to seek student deferments or to join the National Guard in the hope of avoiding combat in Vietnam.

By 1965 at least half of South Vietnam was controlled by Viet Cong or North Vietnamese troops. The new South Vietnamese government of General Nguyen Van Thieu appeared more stable than previous ones, but its army was no match for the well-disciplined Communist soldiers. As Johnson saw it, U.S. forces would defend South Vietnam until its people were ready to defend themselves.

The U.S. strategy in Vietnam had both a military and a political objective: to wear down the enemy with superior firepower, and to "win the hearts and minds" of the South Vietnamese people. Neither proved successful. North Vietnam, a nation of nineteen million, continued to field a large army despite enormous casualties, and the Viet Cong provided able support. Fighting on native soil, these soldiers waged relentless, often brutal war against a "foreign aggressor" and its "puppets" inside South Vietnam.

Americans fought bravely, and morale at this point remained high. Yet the very nature of the war alienated these soldiers from the people they had come to defend. Unfamiliar with the language and culture of Vietnam, Americans increasingly viewed everyone as the enemy. Each village appeared as "a dark room full of deadly spiders," a soldier recalled.

U.S. planners tried numerous strategies to isolate the Viet Cong and deprive them of their sanctuaries. Most included the movement of peasant populations from their ancestral lands to "strategic hamlets" or to cities unprepared for the arrival of thousands of homeless refugees. Between 1960 and 1970, the percentage of South Vietnamese living in urban areas jumped from 20 percent to 43 percent. In these bulging cities, jobs were scarce, prostitution flourished, and families split apart.

Those who remained in the countryside faced terror from all sides. There were North Vietnamese mortar attacks, Viet Cong assassination squads, and U.S. assaults from the ground and the air. U.S. planes and helicopters defoliated the fields and forests with chemical sprays and pounded suspected enemy strongholds with bombs and napalm (jellied gasoline). In one of the most telling remarks of the war, an American officer explained his mission bluntly: "We had to destroy this town in order to save it."

Early Protests

Even as President Johnson escalated the war in 1965, he expected the Great Society to move freely ahead. A "rich nation can afford to make progress at home while meeting its obligations abroad," he declared. For a time, his domestic agenda remained impressive. Fueled by the immense economic prosperity of 1965 and 1966, the Great Society added an Education Act, which extended federal aid to public and private schools, and a Model Cities Act, which provided funds to upgrade housing, health services, crime prevention, and parks. In addition, LBJ reaffirmed his commitment to civil rights by appointing the first African American Supreme Court justice, Thurgood Marshall, and the first African American cabinet member, Robert Weaver, to head the new Department of Housing and Urban Development (HUD).

The momentum didn't last. The decision to escalate in Vietnam divided the nation and sapped the president's strength. The first rumblings of antiwar protest came from the college campuses, where a new group, calling itself **Students for a Democratic Society (SDS),** was gaining ground. Formed in Port Huron, Michigan, in 1962, SDS issued a "Declaration of Principles" that denounced "racism" and "militarism," among other evils, and promised a new politics based on socialist ideals. Limited at first to "elite" colleges and major state universities, the organization expanded in direct proportion to the war itself.

The early student leaders called their movement the New Left. Some of them, known as "Red-diaper babies," were the children of "Old Left" radicals from the 1930s and 1940s. Others came from the burgeoning civil rights movement. Impatient and idealistic, these young radicals identified with the "revolutionary" movements of the emerging Third World. To their eyes, Fidel Castro and Ho Chi Minh were positive forces in history, representing a fundamental shift in power from the privileged elites to the struggling masses. Not surprisingly, Vietnam became the New Left's defining issue—a symbol of popular resistance to America's "imperialist" designs.

Early in 1965, antiwar students and faculty at the University of Michigan held the nation's first "teach-in" to discuss the consequences of escalation in Vietnam. The idea spread rapidly from campus to campus. On Easter Sunday, a crowd of thirty thousand attended the first major antiwar rally in Washington, sponsored by SDS. The speakers, including radical journalist I. F. Stone and folk singer Joan Baez, linked the Vietnam demonstrations to other issues that were percolating within the larger society, such as civil rights, women's rights, and the role of universities in fostering protest and dissent.

Students for a Democratic Society (SDS)

Formed in Port Huron, Michigan, in 1962, this group became one of the leading New Left antiwar organizations of the 1960s, exemplifying both the idealism and the excesses of radical student groups in the Vietnam era.

The Rights Revolution: Center Stage

The national mood of unity and reconciliation that followed President Kennedy's assassination in November 1963 did not last much beyond the landslide election of 1964. The war in Vietnam created divisions that grew wider by the year. Americans became more skeptical of their leaders and less likely to believe official explanations of events. Even a master consensus-builder like Lyndon Johnson faced an overwhelming task.

Table 29.1
Black Voter Registration

State	1960	1966	Percent Increase
Alabama	66,000	250,000	278.8
Arkansas	73,000	115,000	57.5
Florida	183,000	303,000	65.6
Georgia	180,000	300,000	66.7
Louisiana	159,000	243,000	52.8
Mississippi	22,000	175,000	695.4
North Carolina	210,000	282,000	34.3
South Carolina	58,000	191,000	229.3
Tennessee	185,000	225,000	21.6
Texas	227,000	400,000	76.2
Virginia	100,000	205,000	105.0

Source: U.S. Bureau of the Census, *Statistical Abstract of the United States: 1982–83* (103d edition) Washington, D.C., 1982.

Voting Rights

Following passage of the landmark Civil Rights Act of 1964, the struggle for racial justice moved to the next battleground: voting rights in the Deep South. The campaign was already under way in places like Selma, Alabama, where local activists, facing intense white resistance, asked Martin Luther King Jr. and his Southern Christian Leadership Conference for support.

The Selma demonstrations began early in 1965. Local blacks marched daily to the courthouse, where Sheriff Jim Clark used force to turn them away. Thousands were arrested, beaten with clubs, and shocked with cattle prods for attempting to register with the local election board. In March, Dr. King decided to lead a protest march from Selma to Montgomery, the state capital, fifty miles away.

On March 9—known as Bloody Sunday—a contingent of Sheriff Clark's deputies and Alabama state police attacked the marchers. Hundreds of civil rights leaders, entertainers, politicians, and clergy rushed to Selma to lend their support, but the violence continued. James Reeb, a Unitarian minister from Boston, was beaten to death by a gang of whites, and Viola Luizzo, a civil rights activist from Michigan, was shot and killed by the Klan.

On March 15, President Johnson made a special trip to Capitol Hill to urge passage of a new voting rights bill. In the most eloquent speech of his career, Johnson said:

> What happened in Selma is part of a larger movement which reaches into every section and state of America. It is the effort of Negroes to secure for themselves the full blessing of American life.
>
> Their cause must be our cause, too. Because it is not just Negroes, but really it is all of us who must overcome the crippling legacy of bigotry and injustice.
>
> And we shall overcome.

The Voting Rights Act, signed by President Johnson on August 6, abolished discriminatory practices such as the literacy test and authorized federal examiners to register voters in seven southern states. Within a year, almost five hundred thousand southern black voters signed up; within three years, a majority of African American adults in Mississippi and Alabama were registered to vote.

The Watts Explosion

Five days later, on August 11, a riot erupted in Watts, a black section of Los Angeles. The **Watts riot** began with the arrest of a black motorist by a white highway patrolman. A crowd gathered, police reinforcements arrived, and several arrests were made. As word of the incident spread, several thousand people—mostly young men—rampaged down Crenshaw Boulevard, looting stores, burning buildings, and overturning cars. The violence flared each evening for a week. It took fourteen thousand National Guardsmen to restore order. At least forty-one people were killed and a thousand were injured, with property damage estimated at $200 million.

News of the riot shocked President Johnson. "We simply hadn't seen the warnings," recalled Attorney General Ramsey Clark. "We had looked at [civil rights] as basically a

Watts riot
Among the most violent urban disturbances in U.S. history, it erupted in an African American neighborhood in Los Angeles following the arrest of a black motorist. By the time it ended, five days later, forty-one people were dead, hundreds were injured, property damage topped $200 million, and National Guardsmen had to be called in to restore order.

southern problem, but . . . in fact the problems of the urban ghettos exceeded any that we were dealing with in the South."

Times had changed. By 1965 almost half of America's black population lived outside the South, mostly in large cities. Good housing was scarce. As black neighborhoods became overcrowded, residents wishing to move elsewhere were trapped by racial discrimination. Inferior schools hampered upward mobility. Watts had the highest unemployment rate, and lowest income level, of any Los Angeles neighborhood except Skid Row. Crime was rampant, and public services poor. "The sewers stank in the summer, there was not enough water to flush toilets, not enough pressure to fight fires," said one Watts resident. "The social fabric just couldn't stand the strain."

Some rioters targeted white businesses in Watts for arson and looting. The Los Angeles police, suspecting a radical plot, stormed the Black Muslim Temple and arrested fifty-nine people. But the riot was a spontaneous event, not a planned act of destruction. In the next three years, hundreds of northern black neighborhoods would explode. The worst riots, in Newark and Detroit, would begin, as Watts did, with an incident between local blacks and white police.

Most African Americans deplored the riots. Yet a competing vision, far different from the one preached by Dr. King, was gathering strength in the black community. As he walked the streets of Watts after the riot, King met a group of youths shouting, "We won!" He asked how could anyone claim victory in the face of such violence and destruction? "We won," a young man answered, "because we made them pay attention to us."

Black Power

By the mid-1960s, Dr. King's leadership in the civil rights movement was increasingly under attack. At a 1966 rally in Mississippi, a recent Howard University graduate named Stokely Carmichael brought the issue to a head. Just released from jail for leading a peaceful civil rights protest, Carmichael vented his anger: "This is the twenty-seventh time I've been arrested," Carmichael shouted, "and I ain't going to jail no more. The only way we gonna stop them white men from whuppin' us is to take over. What we gonna start saying now is 'Black Power.'" The crowd took up the chant: "Black Power! Black Power! Black Power!"

Black Power became a symbol of African American unity in the mid-1960s. In local communities black activists lobbied school boards to add African American history and culture to the curriculum. On college campuses, black students pressed administrators to speed up minority recruitment, establish Black Studies programs, and provide separate living quarters. In the political arena, Carl Stokes of Cleveland and Richard Hatcher of Gary, Indiana, became the first African American mayors of northern cities. Across the nation, black men and women donned African clothing, took on African names, and wore their hair unstraightened in an "Afro" style. "Black is Beautiful" became a powerful slogan in this era.

To militants like Stokely Carmichael, Black Power meant a political separation of the races. His position reflected a generational split between "old" civil rights groups such as the NAACP, which viewed racial integration as the key to black advancement, and "new" movement groups such as Carmichael's Student Nonviolent Coordinating Committee (SNCC), which began to exclude whites. "Black people," said Carmichael, "must be seen in positions of power doing and articulating for themselves."

The separatist impulse had deep roots in the African American community. Its renewed strength in the 1960s was due, in large part, to a black nationalist movement that appealed to young people in the bleakest neighborhoods of urban America. "There is a different type of Negro emerging from the 18- to 25-year-old bracket," said a black leader in Watts. "They identify with Malcolm X's philosophy."

Malcolm X was the most popular and controversial Black Muslim leader of the 1960s. Born Malcolm Little, he joined the Nation of Islam while serving a prison term for robbery, and adopted the "X" to replace "the white slave-master name which had been imposed upon my paternal forebears by some blue-eyed devil." The Nation of Islam was a black nationalist group, organized in Detroit in 1931, that preached a doctrine of self-help, moral discipline, and complete separation of the races. Its code of behavior, based on the rejection

Black Power
Movement that developed in the mid-1960s calling for renewed racial pride in their African American heritage. They believed that to seek full integration into the existing white order would be to capitulate to the institutions of racism.

Malcolm X
A popular Black Muslim leader who advocated nationalism, self-defense, and racial separation. He split with the Black Muslim movement and formed the Organization of Afro-American Unity, which attracted thousands of young, urban blacks with its message of socialism and self-help. He was assassinated by a Black Muslim at a New York rally in 1965.

Malcolm X, the charismatic Black Muslim minister, preached a doctrine of black nationalism, self-help, and racial separation that held wide appeal for thousands of African Americans. He was assassinated by a rival Muslim group in 1965.

of racist stereotypes, stressed neatness, abstinence, and a firm division of male and female roles. Black Muslims were forbidden to smoke, drink alcohol, eat pork or cornbread, or have sex outside of marriage. "Wake up, clean up, and stand up," their motto declared.

Created by Elijah Poole, who renamed himself Elijah Muhammad, the Black Muslims were strongest in the urban ghettos, where their membership reached upwards of one hundred thousand. Assigned by Elijah Muhammad to a temple in Harlem, Malcolm X became a charismatic figure with his bold statements about the impact of white injustice on black behavior and self-esteem. "The worst crime the white man has committed," he said, "is to teach us to hate ourselves."

Malcolm also preached self-defense in language calculated to alarm moderates of all races, saying that blacks must protect themselves "by any means necessary," and that "killing is a two-way street." Such rhetoric made it easy to label the entire Black Muslim movement as extremist.

Malcolm created a public furor by describing the assassination of President Kennedy as an instance of "the chickens come home to roost." Expelled from the Nation of Islam by Elijah Muhammad, Malcolm traveled to Mecca on a spiritual pilgrimage and discovered, to his surprise, the insignificance of color in Islamic thought. This led him to form a rival Muslim group, the Organization of Afro-American Unity, which emphasized black nationalism in a manner that did not demonize whites. Assassinated in 1965 by followers of Elijah Muhammad, Malcolm became a martyr to millions of African Americans.

Occasionally Black Power became a vehicle of rage and racial revenge. SNCC Chairman H. Rap Brown, for example, urged a crowd in Cambridge, Maryland, to "burn this town down." Some went beyond rhetoric by forming terrorist groups such as the Black Panthers to take their grievances to the streets.

Founded in 1966 by an Oakland, California, ex-convict named Huey Newton, the Panthers provided a violent alternative to other black movements of this era. Portraying themselves as defenders of "oppressed" people against a "racist-capitalist police state," the Panthers demanded the release of all blacks from prison and the payment of "slave reparations" by whites.

Adept at self-promotion, the Panthers won modest support in black neighborhoods through their community work. They ran food banks, health clinics, and preschool programs in run-down city neighborhoods. At the same time, however, Newton and his aides routinely engaged in extortion, drug dealing, and other criminal acts. Heavily armed, wearing black clothing and dark sunglasses, the Panthers became a feared enemy—and primary target—of law enforcement, including the FBI.

"Sisterhood Is Powerful"

The rights revolution of the 1960s included demands for sexual, as well as racial, equality. Both the Equal Pay Act of 1963 and the Civil Rights Act of 1964 were important steps in the battle against gender discrimination, yet progress had been slow. In the fall of 1966, a band of activists formed the National Organization for Women (NOW) to speed the pace of change.

At NOW's first convention, the three hundred delegates elected Betty Friedan president and issued a statement endorsing "the world wide revolution for human rights taking place within and beyond our national borders." Never radical, NOW pursued its major goals—passage of an equal rights amendment and sexual equality in the workplace—through political means.

NOW grew slowly. Its membership in 1970 totaled fifteen thousand—mostly white, middle-aged, and middle class. Yet NOW's impact on the emerging women's movement was enormous. For many younger women, raised in the affluence of suburban America, the resurgence of feminism went beyond the fight for political and economic equality. What attracted them was the call for female solidarity—the power of sisterhood—in the larger struggle for sexual liberation.

Some of these women were veterans of the civil rights movement. Others worked for SDS and were active in the antiwar protests on college campuses. Although deeply committed to these causes, they discovered that sexism—the assumption of male superiority—also existed in organizations devoted to justice and equal rights. When asked what positions women filled in his organization, Stokely Carmichael brought roars of male laughter by noting, "The position of women in SNCC is prone."

Committed to equal rights, adept at organizing, and determined to confront sexism on all fronts, these "new feminists" developed strategies and communities of their own. As women's liberation emerged in the mid-1960s, feminist study groups appeared, along with feminist newspapers, health clinics, and bookstores. The more radical elements, viewing men as the enemy, opposed heterosexual relationships, denounced marriage as "legal whoredom," and regarded the nuclear family as a form of female slavery.

The new feminism met immediate resistance—and not only from men. Surveys of American women in the 1960s showed both a growing sensitivity to issues of sex discrimination and a strong distaste for "women's lib." Most housewives expressed pride in their values and experiences and resented the implication that outside employment was more fulfilling than housework, or that women degraded themselves by trying to appear attractive to men. As the country artist Tammy Wynette sang, "Don't Liberate Me, Love Me."

The Counterculture

The emerging radicalism of America's youth in the 1960s had both a cultural and political base. Bound together with civil rights, women's rights, and the antiwar protests was a diffuse new movement, known as the counterculture, which challenged traditional values on an unprecedented scale. The most powerful voice, perhaps, belonged to folksinger Bob Dylan, whose passionate lyrics and poetic images about nonconformity and political defiance, modeled to some extent on the songs of his hero Woody Guthrie, made him the reluctant spokesman for a generation. The old world of unchallenged adult authority was gone for good, Dylan believed: "For the times they are a-changin'."

In 1965 a San Francisco journalist used the term "hippie" to describe a new breed of rebel—passionate, spontaneous, and free. Like the Bohemians of the early 1900s and the Beats of the 1950s, the hippies defined themselves as opponents of the dominant culture, with its emphasis on competition, consumerism, and conformity. By rejecting such "empty values," they tapped into the youthful alienation so brilliantly portrayed in Mike Nichols's *The Graduate*. Unlike the "uptight" nine-to-five crowd, the hippies wore their hair long, dressed in jeans and sandals, and sought a "higher consciousness" through experimentation and uninhibited living.

The counterculture offered numerous attractions. Many young people embraced the chance to try out new arrangements and ideas. A few joined communes, explored ancient religions, studied astrology, or turned to the occult. Far more pervasive was the sexual freedom, the vital new music, and the illegal drug use that marked these turbulent times.

The counterculture did not begin the sexual revolution of the 1960s. That process was already under way, fueled by the introduction of oral contraceptives in 1960 and a series of Supreme Court decisions that widened public access to "sexually explicit" material. The counterculture played a different but equally important role by challenging conventional morality at every turn.

The results were dramatic. When the Beatles took the United States by storm in 1964, their chart-busting songs included "I Want to Hold Your Hand," "She Loves You," and "Please, Please Me." Marijuana use, a federal crime since 1937, was rare in middle-class society, and lysergic acid diethylamide (LSD) was largely unknown. By 1967, however, the Beatles were imagining "Lucy in the Sky with Diamonds" (LSD) and wailing, "Why Don't We Do It in the Road!"

The counterculture spread inward through the United States from the east and west coasts. In Cambridge, Massachusetts, a Harvard researcher named Timothy Leary became the nation's first psychedelic guru by promoting LSD as the pathway to heightened consciousness and sexual pleasure. In San Francisco author Ken Kesey (*One Flew over the Cuckoo's Nest*) and his Merry Pranksters staged a series of public LSD parties, known as Acid Tests, which drew thousands of participants in 1966.

To much of the public, San Francisco became synonymous with the counterculture. Acid rock flourished in local clubs such as the Fillmore West, where Jimi Hendrix ("Purple Haze"), Steppenwolf ("Magic Carpet Ride"), and the Jefferson Airplane ("White Rabbit") celebrated drug tripping in their songs. In 1967 more than seventy-five thousand young people migrated to San Francisco's Haight-Ashbury district to partake in a much publicized "summer of love." The majority of arrivals, studies showed, were runaways and school dropouts with no means of support. By summer's end, Haight-Ashbury was awash in drug overdoses, venereal disease, panhandling, and prostitution.

At first the national media embraced the counterculture as a "hip" challenge to the blandness of middle-class suburban life. Magazines as diverse as *Time* and *Playboy* doted on every aspect of the hippie existence, and the Levi-Strauss corporation used acid rockers to promote its new line of jeans. Hollywood celebrated the counterculture with films such as *Easy Rider,* about two footloose drug dealers on a motorcycle tour of self-discovery. The smash hit of the 1968 Broadway season was the rock musical *Hair,* depicting a draft evader's journey through the pleasure-filled Age of Aquarius.

Yet most young people of the 1960s experienced neither the nightmare of Haight-Ashbury nor the dream world of *Hair.* Millions of them remained on the margins of the counterculture. And millions more entered adulthood without the slightest sign of protest or alienation. Indeed, some commentators spoke of a serious *intra*generational split in this era, pitting young people who accepted, or aspired to, America's middle-class promise against more radical young people who did not.

A Divided Nation

General William Westmoreland

General who was the senior commander of U.S. troops in Vietnam from 1964 through 1968.

As 1968 began, **General William Westmoreland,** commander of U.S. forces in Southeast Asia, offered an optimistic assessment of the Vietnam War. In his view, U.S. and South Vietnamese (ARVN) troops were gaining strength and confidence as the fighting progressed. Their new vitality, he insisted, stood in direct contrast to the enemy's sagging morale.

The Tet Offensive

Four days later, seventy thousand Communist troops assaulted U.S. and ARVN positions throughout South Vietnam. Their lightning offensive, begun on the lunar New Year holiday of Tet, took Westmoreland by surprise. In Saigon, Viet Cong units reached the American Embassy before being driven back. After capturing Hue, one of South Vietnam's oldest cities, Communist soldiers murdered thousands of civilians and dumped their bodies into a mass grave.

Tet offensive

A major military operation by the North Vietnamese and Viet Cong in 1968. Though beaten back, there were tremendous casualties, and the enormity of the offensive served to undermine President Johnson's claim that steady progress was being made in Vietnam.

As a military operation, the **Tet offensive** clearly failed. Using their overwhelming firepower, U.S. and ARVN forces inflicted frightful casualties upon the enemy. In the three-week battle to recapture Hue, more than five thousand Communist soldiers were killed. Viet Cong losses were so severe that the brunt of the ground fighting after Tet would have to be shouldered by North Vietnamese troops.

In psychological terms, however, the Tet offensive marked a turning point in the war. The sheer size of the Communist attacks, their ability to strike so many targets in force, made a mockery of Westmoreland's optimistic claims. Reporting from Saigon after the Tet offensive, Walter Cronkite, America's most popular television journalist, claimed that a military victory was nowhere in sight. Opinion surveys after Tet showed dwindling support for Johnson's handling of the war. Johnson's approval rating dropped from 48 percent to 36 percent, with most Americans expressing skepticism about official claims of military progress in Vietnam. Columnist Art Buchwald compared LBJ to General Custer at the Little Big Horn, and the prestigious *Wall Street Journal* warned that "the whole war effort is likely doomed."

The President Steps Aside

In 1968 LBJ faced a spirited challenge from Senator Eugene McCarthy of Minnesota. McCarthy's presidential campaign reflected the deep divisions within Democratic party ranks. The "peace faction," led by younger activists such as Allard Lowenstein of New York, hoped to "dump Johnson" by mobilizing antiwar students to campaign against him in key primary states. Hundreds of college students arrived in New Hampshire to work for the McCarthy campaign. Long hair and beards were taboo, as well-scrubbed volunteers in sports coats and dresses ("be clean for Gene") ran phone banks, stuffed envelopes, and canvassed house to house.

The New Hampshire results sent shock waves through the political system. McCarthy came within a whisker of defeating President Johnson, who received less than 50 percent of the Democratic primary vote. Polls showed McCarthy winning the support of "hawks" who demanded victory in Vietnam as well as "doves" who wanted to pull out at once.

Four days later Robert Kennedy entered the presidential race. As the former attorney general and a current U.S. senator from New York, he was both a critic of the Vietnam War and a champion of minority causes, especially in the field of civil rights. Millions saw "Bobby" as the keeper of Camelot, the heir to his fallen brother's legacy.

On March 31 President Johnson announced his political retirement in a stunning televised address: "I shall not seek, and I will not accept, the nomination of my party for another term as your President." A few weeks later, Vice President Hubert Humphrey entered the presidential race as the "regular" Democratic candidate, endorsed by Johnson himself. Humphrey's strategy was to line up delegates for the presidential nomination without contesting Kennedy or McCarthy in the volatile state primaries, where his chances of winning were slim.

A Violent Spring

Early in April, Martin Luther King Jr. traveled to Memphis to support a strike of city garbage workers for better wages and conditions. His social vision was ever expanding, as he challenged Americans to confront the "interrelated" evils of racism, militarism, and poverty. In 1968, Dr. King's projects included a "Poor People's March on Washington" and a "moral crusade" to end the war in Vietnam.

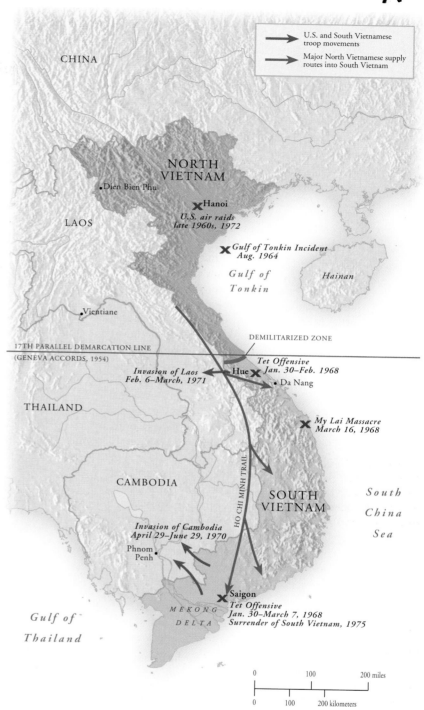

MAP 29.1 The Vietnam War

The map charts the evolution of U.S. military involvement from the Gulf of Tonkin incident in August 1964 to the surrender of South Vietnam in April 1975. In 1970 and 1971, U.S. and South Vietnamese troops briefly expanded the land war into Cambodia and Laos, stirring further antiwar sentiment inside the United States.

An Open Letter to the Grape Industry by Cesar Chavez

For years, Cesar Chavez had been struggling to earn better wages and livable working conditions for the men, women, and children who toiled in the fields and orchards of central California. In 1969, with the United Farm Workers on strike and a national boycott of table grapes gaining momentum, Chavez described the tactics and goals of his union in an open letter to E. L. Barr Jr., president of the California Grape & Tree Fruit League.

YOU MUST understand, I must make you understand, that our membership—and the hopes and aspirations of hundreds of thousands of the poor and dispossessed that have been raised on our account—are, above all, human beings, no better no worse than any other cross section of human society; we are not saints because we are poor but by the same measure neither are we immoral. We are men and women who have suffered and endured much and not only because of our abject poverty but because we have been kept poor. The color of our skins, the languages of our cultural and native origins, the lack of formal education, the exclusion from the democratic process, the numbers of our slain in recent wars—all these burdens generation after generation have sought to demoralize us, to break our human spirit. But God knows we are not beasts of burden, we are not agricultural implements or rented slaves, we are men. And mark this well, Mr. Barr, we are men locked in a death struggle against man's inhumanity to man in the industry that you represent. And this struggle itself gives meaning to our life and ennobles our dying.

As your industry has experienced, our strikers here in Delano and those who represent us throughout the world are well trained for this struggle. They have been under the gun, they have been kicked and beaten and herded by dogs, they have been cursed and ridiculed, they have been stripped and chained and jailed, they have been sprayed with the poisons used in the vineyards. They have been taught not to lie down and die or to flee in shame, but to resist with every ounce of human endurance and spirit. To resist not with retaliation in kind but to overcome with love and compassion, with ingenuity and creativity, with hard work and longer hours, with stamina and patient tenacity, with truth and public appeal, with friends and allies, with mobility and discipline, with politics and law, and with prayer and fasting. They were not trained in a month or even a year; after all, this new harvest season will mark our fourth full year of strike and even now we continue to plan and prepare for the years to come. Time accomplishes for the poor what money does for the rich.

This is not to pretend that we have everywhere been successful enough or that we have not made mistakes. And while we do not belittle or underestimate our adversaries, for they are the rich and powerful and possess the land, we are not afraid nor do we cringe from the confrontation. We welcome it! We have

On the evening of April 3, King delivered a passionate sermon at a Memphis church. Demanding justice for the poor and the powerless, he seemed to sense the danger he was in. "I've been to the mountaintop," he cried. "I may not get there with you, but I want you to know that we as a people will get to the promised land." The following night, King was shot by James Earl Ray, a white racist, as he stood on the balcony of the Lorraine Motel. He died instantly, at the age of thirty-nine.

News of Dr. King's death touched off riots in African American communities from Boston to San Francisco. At the White House, President Johnson proclaimed a day of national mourning for Dr. King against a backdrop of wailing police sirens and billowing smoke. Forty-five people died in these national riots, including twenty-four in Washington, D.C.

Among the presidential candidates, Robert Kennedy seemed closest to the message of Dr. King. Centering his campaign on the connection between domestic unrest and the Vietnam War, Kennedy visited migrant labor camps, American Indian reservations, and inner-city neighborhoods to highlight the problems of disadvantaged Americans, and the work to be done. He also supported the labor strike of Cesar Chavez and his United Farm

planned for it. We know that our cause is just, that history is a story of social revolution, and that the poor shall inherit the land.

Once again, I appeal to you as the representative of your industry and as a man. I ask you to recognize and bargain with our union before the economic pressure of the boycott and strike take an irrevocable toll; but if not, I ask you to at least sit down with us to discuss the safeguards necessary to keep our historical struggle free of violence. I make this appeal because as one of the leaders of our nonviolent movement, I know and accept my responsibility for preventing, if possible, the destruction of human life and property.

For these reasons and knowing of Gandhi's admonition that fasting is the last resort in place of the sword, during a most critical time in our movement last February, 1968, I undertook a 25-day fast. I repeat to you the principle enunciated to the membership at the start of the fast: if to build our union required the deliberate taking of life, either the life of a grower or his child, or the life of a farmworker or his child, then I choose not to see the union built.

MR. BARR, let me be painfully honest with you. You must understand these things. We advocate militant nonviolence as our means for social revolution and to achieve justice for our people, but we are not blind or deaf to the desperate and moody winds of human frustration, impatience, and rage that blow among us. Gandhi himself admitted that if his only choices were cowardice or violence, he would choose violence. Men are not angels and the time and tides wait for no man. Precisely because of these powerful human emotions, we have tried to involve masses of people in their own struggle. Participation and self-determination remain the best experience of freedom; and free men instinctively prefer democratic change and even protect the rights guaranteed to seek it. Only the enslaved in despair have need of violent overthrow.

This letter does not express all that is in my heart, Mr. Barr. But if it says nothing else, it says that we do not hate you or rejoice to see your industry destroyed; we hate the agribusiness system that seeks to keep us enslaved and we shall overcome and change it not by retaliation or bloodshed but by a determined nonviolent struggle carried on by those masses of farmworkers who intend to be free and human. Sincerely yours, CESAR E. CHAVEZ 1969

Questions to Consider

1. In choosing his words, his symbols, and his heroes, which other social movements is Cesar Chavez attempting to emulate and to identify with?

2. Are his words about the class struggle unique to the 1960s, or do they follow a long tradition of protest in the United States?

Explore additional primary sources related to this chapter on the *American Passages* Web site: http://history.wadsworth.com/ayersbrief02.

Source: Susan Ferriss and Ricardo Sandoval, *The Fight in the Fields: Cesar Chavez and the Farmworkers Movement,* 1997, pp. 150–151.

Workers Association against the grape growers in central California. As Kennedy campaigned in California, the grape strike was entering its third year. To protest the stalemate, and the growing violence on both sides, Chavez began a fast that continued for twenty-one days. He ended it, in poor health, by breaking bread with Senator Kennedy at a mass of thanksgiving.

In June 1968 Kennedy took a major step toward the Democratic presidential nomination by defeating Eugene McCarthy in the delegate-rich California primary. That night, after greeting

United Farm Workers' leader Cesar Chavez led a series of strikes and boycotts to win better wages and working conditions for union members. Behind him is the symbol of the organization, the black Aztec eagle.

©Bettmann/CORBIS

supporters at a Los Angeles hotel, Kennedy was shot and killed by a deranged Arab nationalist named Sirhan Sirhan. The nation went numb. Who could have imagined the horror of four national leaders—John F. Kennedy, Malcolm X, Martin Luther King Jr., and Robert F. Kennedy—all dead at the hands of assassins? "My dreams were smashed," a young man recalled. "I shared with a lot of other people these feelings of loss and despair and grim, grim days ahead."

The Chicago Convention

Throughout the spring of 1968, a coalition of antiwar groups prepared for a massive peace demonstration at the Democratic National Convention in Chicago. Mayor Daley made it clear that protesters were not welcome in his city, no matter how well they behaved. Fearing serious bloodshed at the Democratic convention, Senator McCarthy urged young demonstrators to stay away.

There was reason for concern. The continued military buildup in Vietnam had created a violent cycle of protest and response at home. That spring, thousands of young men burned their draft cards in public. Demonstrators tried to block troop trains and Army induction centers, leading to bloody clashes with police. At Columbia University, students from SDS took over several buildings and trashed them to protest "war-related" research on campus. Hundreds were arrested, a general strike followed, and the university closed down for the semester.

Chicago resembled a war zone in August 1968, with six thousand Army troops, five thousand National Guardsmen, and hundreds of Chicago riot police patrolling the streets. Denied permits to rally in public places, the protesters—perhaps four thousand strong—gathered in a park opposite the Hilton Hotel, where many Democratic party leaders were staying. Conflict was inevitable. Radical speakers from SDS and the Black Panthers harangued the crowd with calls for "guerrilla warfare," while Abbie Hoffman and Jerry Rubin, founders of the Youth International ("Yippie") party, held workshops on LSD production and then chose a pig as their candidate with the slogan: "They nominated a president and he eats the people. We nominate a president and the people eat him."

Chicago police wade into a crowd of protesters during the Democratic National Convention in 1968.

On the evening of August 28, the demonstrators tried to march to the convention arena. As millions watched on television, the police moved in with clubs and mace, and National Guardsmen fired tear gas at the crowd. Hundreds were badly beaten in what investigators later described as a "police riot." Even so, the blame did not rest entirely with one side. "We were not just innocent people who were victimized," Abbie Hoffman admitted. "We came to plan a confrontation."

News of the street violence shocked the Democratic convention. From the podium, Senator Abraham Ribicoff of Connecticut condemned "the Gestapo tactics on the streets of Chicago." Television cameras caught a furious Mayor Daley hurling ethnic insults at Ribicoff and telling the "lousy mother _____" to "go home."

The shaken delegates chose Hubert Humphrey and Senator Edmund Muskie of Maine to be their presidential and vice presidential nominees. A staunch liberal, Humphrey exemplified the New Deal Democratic tradition of Roosevelt, Truman, Kennedy, and LBJ. His great weakness in 1968 was his loyal (if reluctant) support for Johnson's handling of the war. To many Americans, Humphrey endorsed the very policies that had divided the nation and left the Democratic party in disarray.

Nixon's the One

Meeting in Miami, the Republicans faced a much simpler task. The Goldwater defeat of 1964 opened the door for candidates with broader political appeal, such as **Richard Nixon.** After choosing Nixon on the first ballot in 1968, the delegates selected Governor Spiro T. Agnew of Maryland to be his vice presidential running mate.

Richard Nixon
The thirty-seventh president of the United States. Known early in his career as a hard-line anti-Communist, he was the first U.S. president to visit Communist China. He also worked skillfully to ease tensions with the Soviet Union. He became the first president to resign from office, due to his involvement in the Watergate scandal.

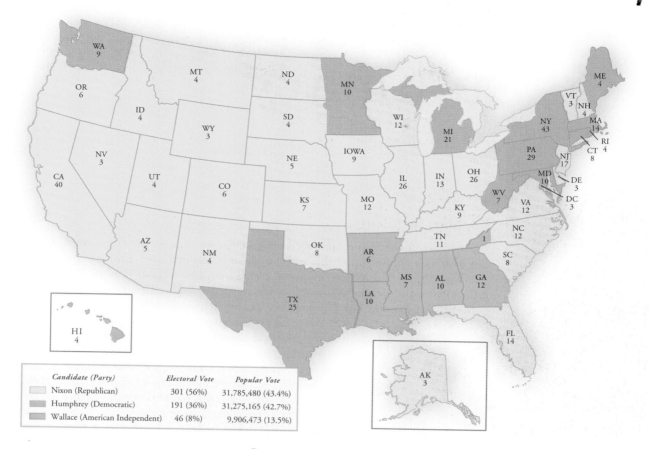

Candidate (Party)	Electoral Vote	Popular Vote
Nixon (Republican)	301 (56%)	31,785,480 (43.4%)
Humphrey (Democratic)	191 (36%)	31,275,165 (42.7%)
Wallace (American Independent)	46 (8%)	9,906,473 (13.5%)

MAP 29.2 The Election of 1968

In a bitterly fought three-way contest for the presidency, held against the backdrop of a nation badly split by the Vietnam War, Richard Nixon won a razor-thin victory with only 43 percent of the popular vote. View an animated version of this map or related maps at http://history .wadsworth.com/ayersbrief02.

Nixon campaigned as the spokesman for America's "silent majority"—the people who worked hard, paid their taxes, went to church, obeyed the law, and respected the flag. In a nation grown weary of urban riots and campus demonstrations, he vowed to make "law and order" his number-one domestic priority, while bringing "peace with honor" to Vietnam.

For the first time since 1948, the presidential campaign attracted a serious third-party candidate, Governor George Wallace of Alabama. An ardent segregationist, Wallace showed surprising strength in white working-class areas of the North and West, where issues such as rising crime rates, draft deferments for college students, and the court-ordered busing of schoolchildren to achieve racial integration were vital concerns. In blunt, sometimes explosive language, Wallace lashed out at "liberal judges," "welfare cheats," and "pot-smoking freaks in their beards and sandals."

Early opinion polls showed Nixon far ahead of Humphrey, with Wallace running a strong third. Yet the gap closed considerably in the campaign's final weeks when President Johnson ordered a temporary bombing halt in North Vietnam, and millions of Democratic voters, fearful of a Nixon presidency, returned to the party fold. On election day Nixon won 43.4 percent of the votes and 301 electoral votes, to 42.7 percent and 191 for Humphrey, and 13.5 percent and 46 for Wallace.

Summary

"A Nation Divided"

Few decades in U.S. history provided more drama and tragedy than the 1960s. What began with such hope and promise, with a popular young president, gave way to deep suspicion and despair by 1968, as Americans reeled from one crisis to another. Race riots, social protests, and generational conflict served to divide the country dangerously, while political assassinations and the escalating war in Vietnam combined to erode the public's trust and confidence in government itself.

Most Americans welcomed the vibrancy of President Kennedy as they had welcomed the steadiness of President Eisenhower eight years before. They applauded Kennedy's call for young people to get involved in public service, as well as his tough stance against international Communism, whether it be in Berlin, at the Bay of Pigs, or during the Cuban missile crisis. In truth, Kennedy's record in domestic affairs was relatively thin. Lacking a large electoral mandate and facing stiff congressional opposition, Kennedy moved cautiously in civil rights and federal spending for social programs, giving the impression that he would focus more heavily on such issues at some future time. His assassination in 1963 left a deeply grieving nation to ponder the legacy of a leader who died so young, with such enormous promise, and with so much left undone.

Lyndon Johnson claimed to understand the direction in which Kennedy had been heading. Using the memory of the fallen president, and retaining most of his key advisors, President Johnson pressed forward in both domestic and foreign affairs,

Led by Eugene ("Bull") Connor, Birmingham police used attack dogs and high-pressure fire hoses to disperse civil rights demonstrators.

Moving through the streets of Dallas, President Kennedy's limousine headed toward Dealy Plaza—and tragedy—on November 22, 1963.

©Robert Ellison/Black Star

crafting legislation that produced landmark advances in civil rights and the "war on poverty," while continuing the escalation of America's military commitment to an independent, anti-Communist South Vietnam. As Johnson soon discovered, however, the war in Vietnam cast a pall over the nation that would undermine his domestic programs and create deep skepticism about the truth of his claims that the war was being won—or was worth the cost. The shocks of 1968, beginning with Johnson's decision not to run for reelection, continuing with the assassinations of Dr. Martin Luther King Jr. and Robert F. Kennedy, and culminating in the riotous Democratic National Convention in Chicago, left Americans reeling and alarmed.

To a large degree, Richard Nixon rode the political whirlwind that swept America in 1968. His margin of victory against Hubert Humphrey was nearly as narrow as his margin of defeat against John Kennedy in 1960. Yet the combined total for Nixon and George Wallace in 1968—almost 57 percent—signaled a major swing to the right. The radical protests of the 1960s had fueled an inevitable backlash against the liberal party in power. The Great Society lay in ruins. The Nixon years had begun.

Although U.S. troops inflicted heavy casualties on the Viet Cong and the North Vietnamese during the Tet offensive of 1968, the intensity of the fighting shocked the American public and increased public criticism of the war.

LOOKING BACK

Chapter 29 examines the impact of the rights revolution, the Vietnam War, and the cultural struggles in the United States during the 1960s, one of the most challenging and bitterly divisive periods in recent history.

1. What accounts for the enduring popularity of President John F. Kennedy? Was it his policies, his vision, or were other factors at work as well?

2. In what ways did the assumptions of U.S. leaders regarding Communist expansion remain fixed in the 1960s, and it what ways did they change? Was Lyndon Johnson a prisoner to assumptions that went back to the early days of the Cold War?

3. What impact did the movement for racial equality have on other so-called rights movements in the 1960s? In what ways did the civil rights struggle itself change in this decade?

4. Is there a connection between the suburban baby boom of the late 1940s, the rise of a specific "teenage culture" in the 1950s, and the coming of the counterculture in the 1960s?

LOOKING AHEAD

The next chapter considers the consequences of the tumultuous events of the 1960s. The nation would wrestle with President Nixon's strategy to withdraw U.S. troops from Vietnam and, in an amazing turn of events, watch the president become embroiled in the greatest political scandal in U.S. history.

1. Would a nation as bitterly divided as the United States begin to heal its wounds with a new president at the helm, a president who vowed "to bring the American people together?"

2. Would the "rights revolution" of the 1960s continue to gain momentum in the coming years, and how would its impact be felt in the courts and in the political arena?

3. Was it possible to rekindle interest in the core programs of the Great Society, or would Americans move away from the ideas and proposals that had defined domestic liberalism since the New Deal era?

Making Connections Across Chapters

RECOMMENDED READINGS

Baughman, James. *The Republic of Mass Culture* (1992). Assesses the media's enormous impact on modern American culture.

Brennan, Mary. *Turning Right in the Sixties* (1995). Analyzes the impact of Goldwater conservatism on a changing Republican party.

Farber, David. *Age of Great Dreams* (1994). Provides an excellent synthesis of the political and cultural changes of the 1960s.

Friedan, Betty. *The Feminine Mystique* (1963). A path-breaking account of the domestic restrictions placed on women following World War II by those who shape American culture.

Harrington, Michael. *The Other America* (1962). Riveted national attention on the issue of poverty, leading to major government programs and reforms.

Horne, Gerald. *Fire This Time* (1995). Offers an interesting analysis of the Watts riot and the rise of black nationalism.

Karnow, Stanley. *Vietnam* (1983). Remains the best one-volume survey of U.S. involvement in our nation's longest war.

McDougall, Walter. *". . . The Heavens and the Earth": A Political History of the Space Age* (1985). Captures both the policy making and the drama behind the race to the moon.

Miller, James. *Democracy in the Streets: From Port Huron to the Siege of Chicago* (1987). A thorough history of the student movement that revolutionized U.S. culture and politics in the 1960s.

Munoz, Carlos, Jr. *Youth, Identity, Power* (rev. ed. 2000). Carefully examines the origins of the Chicano movement.

AMERICAN JOURNEY ONLINE AND INFOTRAC COLLEGE EDITION

Visit the source collections at http://ajaccess.wadsworth.com and infotrac.thomsonlearning.com and use the Search function with the following key terms to explore documents, images, audio and video clips, articles, and commentary related to the material in this chapter.

John F. Kennedy
Bay of Pigs
Students for a Democratic Society
Martin Luther King Jr.
U-2
Fannie Lou Hamer
The Feminine Mystique
Lyndon B. Johnson
Tonkin Resolution
Watts riots
Black Power
Malcolm X
Tet offensive
Cesar Chavez
Richard Nixon

ONLINE PRIMARY SOURCES

Here are some examples of the many primary sources related to this chapter that you will find on the *American Passages* Web site: http://history.wadsworth.com/ayersbrief02.

The Voting Rights Act, 1965
Special Purpose Telegram Blank No. 74/AG, 1966 (photo)
Rally against the Vietnam War at the Pentagon, 1967

The site also offers self-quizzes, exercises, and many additional resources to help you study.

CHAPTER 30

Crisis of Confidence

1969–1980

RICHARD NIXON HAD BEEN A CONGRESSMAN, A SENATOR, AND A VICE president. Bitter defeats in the presidential election of 1960 and the California gubernatorial race of 1962 did not diminish his ambition or ruin his dreams. On the morning after his presidential victory in 1968, Nixon addressed a nation battered by racial turmoil, urban violence, generational conflict, political assassinations, and continuing war. Vowing to unite the country and to restore confidence in its institutions, he recalled a campaign stop he had made in the little town of Deshler, Ohio. Near the back of the crowd a teenager held up a sign reading "Bring Us Together." That message, he assured his listeners, "will be the great objective of this administration . . . to bring the American people together."

America United and Divided

The new era began with optimistic signals and improbable events. For a time, the dark days of 1968 were pushed aside by the miracles of 1969. In January, the New York Jets, led by "Broadway" Joe Namath, won the football Super Bowl by crushing the heavily favored Baltimore Colts. In October, the New York Mets, once regarded as the worst team in Major League baseball history, defeated the Baltimore Orioles in a World Series that left millions of Americans screaming, "Ya gotta believe!" Sandwiched between these events were two enormous spectacles, each affecting the nation in a very different way.

The Miracles of 1969

In the summer of 1969, NASA fulfilled John F. Kennedy's bold promise to land a man on the moon "before this decade is out." On July 16 astronauts Neil Armstrong, Edwin "Buzz" Aldrin, and Michael Collins began their 286,000-mile lunar mission—*Apollo 11*—from Cape Kennedy aboard the command vessel *Columbia.* As they neared their destination, Armstrong and Aldrin entered the *Eagle,* a fragile moon module, for the final descent. On July 20, before a television audience of five hundred million people, Neil Armstrong put his foot on the lunar surface and said: "That's one small step for man, one giant leap for mankind."

Armstrong and Aldrin spent twenty-one hours on the moon. A television camera beamed back pictures of the men gathering samples, measuring temperature, and planting a small U.S. flag. What struck viewers was the sight of two space-suited figures leaping from place to place in the light gravity. As they rocketed back to earth, the astronauts provided breathtaking pictures of the world from 175,000 miles away.

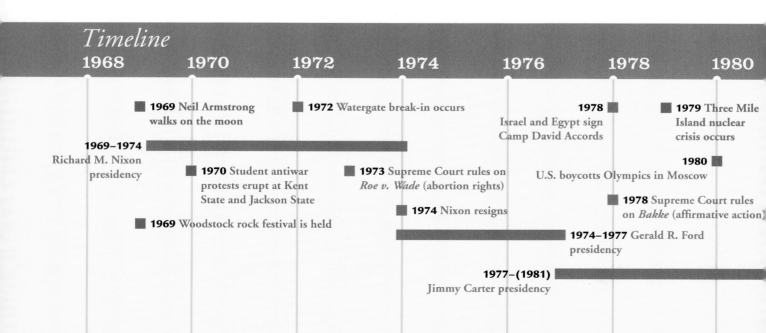

Timeline

1968 — 1970 — 1972 — 1974 — 1976 — 1978 — 1980

1969 Neil Armstrong walks on the moon

1972 Watergate break-in occurs

1978 Israel and Egypt sign Camp David Accords

1979 Three Mile Island nuclear crisis occurs

1969–1974 Richard M. Nixon presidency

1970 Student antiwar protests erupt at Kent State and Jackson State

1973 Supreme Court rules on *Roe v. Wade* (abortion rights)

1980 U.S. boycotts Olympics in Moscow

1969 Woodstock rock festival is held

1974 Nixon resigns

1978 Supreme Court rules on *Bakke* (affirmative action)

1974–1977 Gerald R. Ford presidency

1977–(1981) Jimmy Carter presidency

Other moon missions followed, including the dramatic rescue of *Apollo 13* in 1970. Americans marveled at the skill and bravery of these astronauts without fully understanding the scientific value of their missions. By studying lunar rocks and photographs, geologists learned that the earth and the moon were formed at the same time and that both had been pounded for millions of years by a hail of comets, asteroids, and meteorites that helped reshape their outer crust. The moon missions spurred the growth of computer technology and led to numerous product advancements, from fireproof clothing to better navigation systems for jetliners.

A month after the moon landing, national attention shifted to the **Woodstock Art and Music Fair** on a six-hundred-acre dairy farm in the Catskill Mountains northwest of New York City. Woodstock fused rock music, hard drugs, free love, and an antiwar protest. Expecting a crowd of perhaps a hundred thousand for a pageant that included Janis Joplin, Jimi Hendrix, Joan Baez, The Grateful Dead, and Jefferson Airplane, among others, the organizers were overwhelmed by the response. More than four hundred thousand people showed up, knocking down the fences and ticket windows, creating mammoth traffic jams, gobbling up the available food and water, and sharing marijuana and LSD.

Some news reports breathlessly portrayed the event as a cultural watershed. One magazine called Woodstock "an art form and social structure unique to our time." However, the vast majority at Woodstock were middle-class students and workers, not cultural dropouts or political revolutionaries. What survived Woodstock were the new attitudes of young people toward self-fulfillment, personal expression, political activism, and, in some cases, dangerous excess. These things did not die out in the 1970s, though they took rather different forms. The mellow portrait of Woodstock soon gave way to the ugly spectacle of Altamont, near San Francisco, where a rock concert featuring the Rolling Stones turned into a bloodbath, with one man beaten to death. In 1970 drug and alcohol addiction claimed the lives of Janis Joplin and Jimi Hendrix. For many young people, the age of innocence was over.

Vietnamization

To bring America together, Richard Nixon realized, he had to end its military involvement in Vietnam. The morning after his inauguration he was handed the weekly U.S. casualty figures from Vietnam: 85 killed, 1,237 wounded—a chilling reminder, he wrote, of the war's "tragic cost."

Within weeks Nixon unveiled a plan, known as **Vietnamization,** to end U.S. participation in the war. It called for the gradual replacement of U.S. troops by well-trained and supplied South Vietnamese soldiers—a process that included the deployment of U.S. air power and the intensification of peace efforts. From Nixon's perspective, Vietnamization represented the best solution to a dreadful dilemma. He refused to abandon Vietnam, yet he could not continue a conflict that cost 14,600 American lives and $30 billion in 1968 alone.

Vietnamization did not work well on the battlefield, as time would show. But it did have the advantage of substituting Asian casualties for U.S. ones, which made it popular in the United States. In June 1969 President Nixon announced that twenty-five thousand U.S. combat troops were being withdrawn from Vietnam—the first stage of a pullout to be completed by late 1972. At the same time, the U.S. Air Force stepped up its missions over North and South Vietnam, and Cambodia as well.

Confrontation at Home

Despite Vietnamization and troop withdrawals, the antiwar movement retained considerable force. On November 15, 1969—"Mobilization Day"—hundreds of thousands of people attended rallies in New York, Boston, San Francisco, Washington, and other cities to demand the immediate removal of all U.S. troops from Vietnam. Some considered the war immoral; others viewed it as a lost cause that was ripping the nation apart.

In March 1970 the White House announced the withdrawal of one hundred fifty thousand more combat troops over the coming year. The nation's leading antiwar group, the Vietnam Moratorium Committee, responded by closing its national office. But a

Woodstock Art and Music Fair
A fusion of rock music, hard drugs, free love, and an antiwar protest drawing four hundred thousand people in the summer of 1969.

Vietnamization
A policy whereby the South Vietnamese were to assume more of the military burdens of the war. This transfer of responsibility was expected to eventually allow the United States to withdraw.

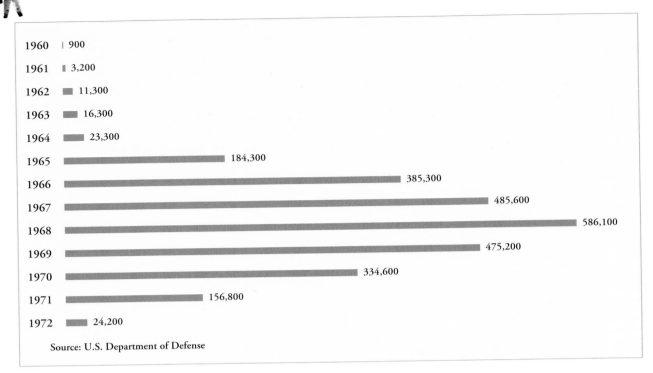

Year	Troops
1960	900
1961	3,200
1962	11,300
1963	16,300
1964	23,300
1965	184,300
1966	385,300
1967	485,600
1968	586,100
1969	475,200
1970	334,600
1971	156,800
1972	24,200

Source: U.S. Department of Defense

CHART 30.1 U.S. Troop Levels in Vietnam, 1960–1972

U.S. troop levels increased dramatically in 1965 following the Gulf of Tonkin incident and the Viet Cong attack on U.S. Marines at Pleiku. As the chart shows, troop levels began to decrease significantly in 1969 as newly elected President Richard Nixon began his policy of Vietnamization.

Source: U.S. Department of Defense.

month later, in a startling development, the president told the nation that U.S. troops had just invaded Cambodia to disrupt enemy supply lines that ran through that country along the so-called Ho Chi Minh Trail. The very success of Vietnamization depended on the elimination of these North Vietnamese sanctuaries, he declared.

The idea of expanding the war under any circumstances brought protesters back into the streets. At **Kent State University** in Ohio, several thousand students rampaged through the business district and clashed with local police. That evening, Kent State's ROTC building went up in flames, leading the governor to send in the National Guard. The troops were ordered to prevent students from gathering in large blocs—an ironic twist, since a noontime rally was planned to protest the Guard's presence. On May 4 the guardsmen confronted five hundred students at the rally, where rocks and bottles were thrown from a distance and tear gas was lobbed in return. Suddenly, without warning, a group of guardsmen fired their rifles at the crowd, killing four and wounding nine others.

Word of the shootings touched off campus protests nationwide. ROTC buildings were attacked, and governors in sixteen more states called out the National Guard. Many colleges simply shut down for the semester. At Jackson State in Mississippi, local police ended an altercation with black students by blasting their dormitory with machine guns and armor-piercing bullets, killing two and wounding several more. Although a presidential investigating commission described the Jackson State shootings as "an unjustified overreaction," a local grand jury warned that protesters "must expect to be injured or killed when law enforcement officers are required to reestablish order."

Both statements reflected the deep and bitter divisions in American society over political protest and social change. Surveys showed a clear majority supporting forceful measures against those who challenged government authority through unlawful, or even disrespectful, behavior. Many blue-collar Americans fumed at the sight of draft-deferred, middle-class students protesting the war from the safety of a college campus while their

Kent State University
National Guardsmen were sent to this Ohio campus to restore order following a series of tumultuous antiwar protests in May 1970. They fired into a crowd of students, killing four and wounding nine others.

own sons and brothers were slogging through the jungles of Vietnam. That rage turned to violence in New York City, when several hundred construction workers charged into an antiwar rally and severely beat the demonstrators and onlookers with hammers, pipes, and fists. A week later, President Nixon invited the leader of New York's construction workers' union to the White House, where the two men exchanged gifts and compliments.

The violence continued in fits and spurts. Left-wing radicals bombed the headquarters of Mobil Oil, IBM, and other pillars of the "imperialist war machine." In New York City, three radicals accidentally blew themselves to bits while mixing explosives. And in Chicago, a splinter group of the dormant Students for a Democratic Society attempted to "trash" the downtown business district in a final assault on the "ruling class." Three hundred looters and window-smashers were arrested.

My Lai and the Pentagon Papers

The news from Vietnam was equally grim. In 1968 reports surfaced about a massacre of civilians by U.S. troops at the village of My Lai, a suspected Vietcong stronghold. Encountering no resistance, an infantry unit led by Lieutenant William Calley methodically executed the villagers and dumped their bodies into a mass grave. A number of the women were raped; at least two hundred people, many of them children, were murdered. Evidence of these atrocities was ignored by field commanders until a soldier not connected with the incident sent letters to the Pentagon and the press.

Most Americans considered My Lai an aberration. Yet the public reaction to Lieutenant Calley's court-martial verdict (guilty) and sentence (life imprisonment) in 1971 raised the very issues that had divided Americans since the war began. Some believed that government policy in Vietnam made such tragedies inevitable. Others insisted that Calley acted out of frustration after seeing so many of his fellow soldiers killed. Still others blamed a society—as one GI put it—that "forced these kids to die in a foreign land for a cause it refused to defend at home." Congress and the White House were flooded with letters opposing the conviction. Following numerous appeals and a personal case review by President Nixon, Calley was paroled in 1974.

The My Lai incident raised nagging questions about the fitness of U.S. troops. By all accounts, U.S. soldiers had fought superbly under trying circumstances until 1969. But the process of Vietnamization, the stepped-up troop withdrawals, the rising antiwar protests—all served to isolate those who remained in Vietnam. Drug use increased dangerously. Racial tensions flared, as did violent attacks on officers, known as "fraggings," in which disgruntled soldiers used hand grenades as weapons. Some men ignored direct orders to fight.

Within weeks of Calley's court-martial, another crisis appeared with publication of the *Pentagon Papers,* a secret report of the decision-making process that led to U.S. involvement in Vietnam. Commissioned in 1967, and containing numerous classified documents within its seven thousand pages, the report was made public by Daniel Ellsberg, a former intelligence officer who had turned against the war. Ellsberg gave a copy to the *New York Times,* which printed the first installment on June 13, 1971.

The report focused mainly on the Kennedy-Johnson years. From a political standpoint, President Nixon welcomed the embarrassment it caused his Democratic opponents. Yet Nixon soon viewed Ellsberg's behavior as a threat to his own presidency as well. He feared that continued leaks of classified material might reveal damaging information about current policies. As a result, the White House sought a court injunction to halt further publication of the *Pentagon Papers* on grounds that national security was at stake. The Supreme Court rejected this argument, however, ruling 6 to 3 that suppression violated First Amendment guarantees.

Nixon did not give up the fight. Obsessed by the Ellsberg incident, he authorized the creation of a special White House unit, known as the "Plumbers," to "stop security leaks and investigate other sensitive matters." In a tape-recorded conversation on September 18, 1971, Nixon demanded that "the roughest, toughest people [get] to work on this." A few weeks later, the Plumbers carried out their first assignment, burglarizing the office of Ellsberg's psychiatrist in an attempt to gather embarrassing information.

Activism, Rights, and Reform

Political and social activism did not end with the 1960s. Although the angry, media-centered radicalism of groups like SDS and the Black Panthers largely disappeared, the movements for women's rights and minority rights remained very much alive, bringing progress and backlash in their wake.

Expanding Women's Rights

On August 26, 1970, feminist leaders organized a nationwide rally to mark the fiftieth anniversary of the Nineteenth Amendment, which had given women the right to vote. Thousands showed up with signs ranging from "Sisterhood Is Powerful" to "Don't Cook Dinner—Starve a Rat Today." The speeches focused on equality for women in education and employment, the need for reproductive freedom, and passage of the **Equal Rights Amendment (ERA).**

Equal Rights Amendment (ERA)
Congress overwhelmingly passed the Equal Rights Amendment in 1972, but by the mid-1970s conservative groups had managed to stall its confirmation by the states.

The revived women's movement was already making strides. In 1969 feminist protests forced a number of the nation's best colleges, including Yale and Princeton, to end their all-male admissions policy, and the military academies soon followed suit. Between 1970 and 1974, the number of women attending law school and medical school more than doubled. During the 1970s as a whole, female graduates from the nation's law schools rose from 5 to 30 percent of each class; and at medical schools from 8 to 23 percent. Yet the number of women elected to public office or promoted to high management positions lagged far behind, and the wages of full-time working women remained well below those of men.

MAP 30.1 The Struggle for the Equal Rights Amendment
Few issues proved more divisive in the 1970s than the Equal Rights Amendment. Written by feminist Alice Paul (see Chapter 21) a half century earlier, it declared that "equality of rights under the law shall not be denied or abridged . . . on account of sex." The map clearly shows the regional and cultural divisions over the ERA, with much of the opposition coming from rural and southern states. Only thirty of the needed thirty-eight states voted in the end for ratification, and the amendment died.

The women's movement had many voices and a wide range of ideas. Nothing better illustrated this diversity than the outpouring of books and magazines that provided an alternative to older publications such as *Good Housekeeping* and *Ladies' Home Journal.* Handbooks like *Our Bodies, Ourselves* (1971) and *The New Woman's Survival Catalogue* (1972) sold millions of copies by combining a new feminist ideology, based on professional achievement and personal freedom, with medical and psychological strategies for good health. A flood of best-sellers emerged—Kate Millett's *Sexual Politics* (1969), Shulamith Firestone's *The Dialectic of Sex* (1970), and Germaine Greer's *The Female Eunuch* (1970) among them—contending that women could never experience fulfillment within the traditional confines of marriage and family life. In 1972 three scholarly journals devoted to women's studies appeared. That same year marked the publication of *Ms,* the first feminist magazine to attract a mass circulation. A sampling of its articles showed how dramatically times had changed: "Raising Kids Without Sex Roles," "Women Tell the Truth About Their Abortions," and "Do Feminists Do It Better?"

"Women's March for Equality" moves down New York's Fifth Avenue.

In 1972, following a powerful lobbying effort by women's groups, Congress overwhelmingly passed the ERA. The amendment, stating that "equality of rights under the law shall not be denied or abridged by the United States or by any State on account of sex," was ratified that year by twenty-two of the thirty-five states needed for passage. Success seemed certain. As Congresswoman Bella Abzug of New York asked, "Who'd be against equal rights for women?"

The answer came quickly. As the women's movement gained strength and attention in the early 1970s, a countermovement rose up to contest it. Led by Phyllis Schlafly, a conservative activist, the countermovement won the support of those who viewed feminism as an affront to God's plan for the sexes, and others who resented the portrayal of housework and motherhood as trivial, slavish work. By the mid-1970s, the backlash against feminism had stalled ratification of the ERA and turned the debate over abortion into an increasingly angry—and violent—struggle.

Minority Power

The political and cultural upheavals of the 1960s had produced a "rights consciousness" that spread as the decade progressed. For many groups 1969 was a pivotal year, marking their emergence on the national scene. That summer, for example, a routine police assault against homosexuals at the Stonewall Inn in Manhattan's Greenwich Village produced a most uncommon response. For the first time the patrons fought back, triggering several days of rioting and protest against the harassment of homosexuals. The "Stonewall Riot" led to the formation of the Gay Liberation Front, which, in turn, began the movement to encourage group solidarity within the homosexual community. "We reject society's attempt to impose sexual roles and definitions of our nature," announced the Gay Liberation Front. "We are stepping outside these roles and simplistic myths. We are going to be who we are."

In 1969 Mexican American activists in Texas formed **La Raza Unida,** a political party devoted to furthering "Chicano" causes and candidates through the ballot. This new party, which spread to several southwestern states, reflected the growing demand for political power and cultural self-determination within the Hispanic community, which had grown from three million in 1960 to more than nine million a decade later. The increase, consisting mainly of Cuban Americans and Puerto Ricans on the nation's East Coast, and Mexican Americans throughout the West, provided unique opportunities for change.

On September 16, 1969, Mexican American students across the Southwest boycotted classes to celebrate ethnic pride (or "Chicanismo") on Mexico's Independence Day, and a

La Raza Unida
Formed in 1969 by Mexican American activists, it reflected the growing demand for political and cultural recognition of "Chicano" causes, especially in the Southwest.

group at Cal-Berkeley shouting "Brown Power" staged a sit-in to demand a program in Chicano Studies. Furthermore, political leverage by Hispanic groups spurred Congress to improve conditions for migrant farm workers, many of whom were Mexican American, and to provide federal funding for bilingual education. Mexican Americans were also elected to the U.S. House of Representatives in Texas and California, to the U.S. Senate in New Mexico, and to the governorships of Arizona and New Mexico.

©Bettmann /CORBIS

Seventy-eight American Indians occupied Alcatraz Island, site of an abandoned federal prison, in 1969.

In the fall of 1969 several dozen Native Americans took over Alcatraz Island, an unoccupied former federal penitentiary in San Francisco Bay, to publicize the claims and grievances of a younger, more militant generation. "It has no running water; it has inadequate sanitation facilities; there is no industry; there are no health care facilities," said one protest leader, comparing the rocky island to a typical Indian reservation. The protest signaled a change in the American Indian community. By any measure, Native Americans were the most deprived single group in the United States, with an unemployment rate ten times higher, and a life expectancy twenty years lower, than the national average. Belonging to the American Indian Movement (AIM), a new group inspired by the black freedom struggles of the 1960s, the Alcatraz demonstrators preached a "Red Power" that rejected the "assimilationist" policies of their elders.

In 1972 AIM led a march on Washington—named the "Trail of Broken Treaties"—that ended with a group of protesters barricading themselves inside the Bureau of Indian Affairs and wrecking much of the building. A year later AIM militants seized the South Dakota village of Wounded Knee on the Pine Ridge Sioux Reservation, site of an infamous massacre by federal troops in 1890. Two American Indians were killed in a seventy-one-day standoff with federal agents.

This militant pressure did result in minor change. In 1970 the federal government returned forty-eight thousand acres of sacred land to the Taos Pueblo of New Mexico, beginning a cautious policy of negotiation that grew significantly in the coming years. In addition, the Nixon administration targeted minority aid programs for Native Americans living in urban areas, and Congress added funding through the Indian Education Act of 1972. Nevertheless, the alarming rates of suicide, alcoholism, and illiteracy among Native American children continued throughout the 1970s and beyond—a clear warning of how much remained to be done.

Black Capitalism and Civil Rights

Richard Nixon took office at a crucial juncture in the campaign for civil rights. The epic struggles of the 1950s and early 1960s had formally abolished *de jure* (legal) segregation, yet serious problems remained. The vast majority of southern children still attended all-white or all-black schools, and the situation was little better in the North and West, where de facto segregation in housing and employment kept most neighborhood schools rigidly segregated by race. Furthermore, while the percentage of "middle-class" African Americans increased substantially in the 1960s, the rate of black unemployment remained twice the national average. This meant a deepening economic split within the African American community, with almost half the black families enjoying middle-class status, and an equal percentage living below the poverty line in run-down, unsafe, segregated neighborhoods.

Civil rights did not rank high on Nixon's domestic agenda. Because most blacks voted Democratic, the president owed them no political debt. On the contrary, he hoped to create a "new Republican majority" by winning over white working-class Democrats who feared that minorities were getting too much attention from the federal government. Choosing his words carefully, Nixon described racial integration as a process that demanded a slow but steady pace.

Nixon's boldest civil rights initiatives related to business and employment. In 1969 he created the Office of Minority Business Enterprise. Over the next three years, the federal government tripled its assistance to minority enterprises through grants and low-interest loans. More controversial was the administration's proposal to bring black workers into the high-wage, "lily-white" construction industry. Known as the Philadelphia Plan, it required the construction unions—carpenters, masons, electricians, and the like—to set up "goals" and "timetables" for hiring black apprentices on government-sponsored projects. Some civil rights leaders praised the Philadelphia Plan as a major step toward economic equality; others condemned it as a cynical ploy to woo black voters away from the Democratic party.

On the emotional issue of public school integration, the president took a more cautious approach. Hoping to win white political converts in the South, he supported the efforts of Mississippi officials in 1969 to postpone court-ordered school integration, while firmly opposing efforts to deny federal funding to segregated schools. When told that Justice Department officials were planning to speed up school integration, the president said, "Do what the law allows you and not one bit more." As a result, the battle shifted back to the courts, especially the U.S. Supreme Court.

The Burger Court

In 1969 Chief Justice Earl Warren stepped down from the bench. The seventy-seven-year-old chief justice had submitted his resignation in 1968, expecting President Johnson to choose a suitably liberal replacement. But problems arose when Johnson nominated his close friend, Associate Supreme Court Justice Abe Fortas, to become the new chief justice. Senate conservatives, charging "cronyism," organized a filibuster to deny Fortas the post; then a brewing scandal over his finances forced Fortas to resign from the Court. This gave incoming President Nixon the luxury of appointing two Supreme Court justices at once.

The first choice went smoothly. The Senate quickly confirmed Judge Warren E. Burger, a moderate northern Republican, to replace Warren as chief justice. But Nixon's other nominee, Judge Clement Haynsworth, a conservative from South Carolina, ran into trouble when Senate liberals raised questions about his antagonism toward civil rights and organized labor. Fifteen Republicans joined forty Democrats to reject Haynsworth.

Stung by the vote, President Nixon nominated another southerner, Judge G. Harrold Carswell, whose general qualifications and civil rights record were far inferior to Haynsworth's. The Senate rejected him as well. A few weeks later, the Senate unanimously confirmed Nixon's third choice, Judge Harry Blackmun of Minnesota. Ironically, the president got to make two more Supreme Court nominations the following year when Justices Hugo Black and John Marshall Harlan retired. His selections—William Rehnquist, a prominent Arizona conservative, and Lewis Powell, a distinguished Virginia attorney—were easily confirmed.

The Burger Court proved more independent than most people, including Nixon, had expected. Among other decisions, it upheld publication of the *Pentagon Papers;* struck down "capricious" state laws imposing the death penalty for rape and murder, thereby halting capital punishment for almost two decades (*Furman v. Georgia,* 1972); and ruled against President Nixon's claims of executive privilege in the **Watergate** scandals. In addition, the Burger Court held that state laws prohibiting abortion were unconstitutional because they violated a woman's "right to privacy" under the Fourteenth Amendment (**Roe v. Wade,** 1973). Justice Blackmun's majority opinion permitted a state to outlaw abortion in the final three months of pregnancy, noting, however, that the life and health of the mother must be considered at all times.

The Burger Court also confronted segregation in the public schools. Its unanimous ruling in *Swann v. Charlotte–Mecklenburg Board of Education* (1971) served notice that controversial methods such as "forced" busing could be used as legal remedies to achieve racial balance. Though millions of youngsters rode buses to school each day, the idea of transporting children to different neighborhoods in the name of racial integration fueled parental anger and fear. Opinion polls showed that whites overwhelmingly opposed forced busing, and that African Americans, by a smaller margin, also disapproved. For many black parents, busing simply obscured the problems of neglect and underfunding that had plagued their school districts for years.

Violence sometimes followed. In Boston a court-ordered plan in 1974 to bus white schoolchildren to Roxbury, a poor black neighborhood, and black children to South Boston, a poor white neighborhood, led to mob action. Buses were stoned, black students

Watergate
The Democratic National Headquarters at the Watergate complex in Washington, D.C. was burglarized in 1972, which led to criminal convictions for several top government officials and forced President Nixon to resign from office in 1974.

Roe v. Wade
Decided by the Supreme Court in 1973, this case along with *Doe v. Bolton* legalized abortion in the first trimester.

Roe v. Wade, 1973

In 1973 the Supreme Court heard the case of Jane Roe (pseudonym for an unmarried, pregnant Texas woman) who challenged the state's century-old criminal abortion law. Writing for the majority, Justice Harry J. Blackmun struck down state statutes banning abortion in the first and second trimesters of a pregnancy on the ground that they violated a woman's right to privacy under the Due Process Clause of the Fourteenth Amendment. Hailed by "pro-choice" advocates and condemned by "pro-life" groups, the decision remains controversial to this day.

The principal thrust of appellant's attack on the Texas statutes is that they improperly invade a right, said to be possessed by the pregnant woman, to choose to terminate her pregnancy. Appellant would discover this right in the concept of personal "liberty" embodied in the Fourteenth Amendment's Due Process Clause; or in personal, marital, familial, and sexual privacy said to be protected by the Bill of Rights. . . .

This right of privacy, whether it be founded in the Fourteenth Amendment's concept of personal liberty and restrictions upon state action, as we feel it is, or, as the District Court determined, in the Ninth Amendment's reservation of rights to the people, is broad enough to encompass a woman's decision whether or not to terminate her pregnancy. The detriment that the State would impose upon the pregnant woman by denying this choice altogether is apparent. Specific and direct harm medically diagnosable even in early pregnancy may be involved. Maternity, or additional offspring, may force upon the woman a distressful life and future. Psychological harm may be imminent. Mental and physical health may be taxed by child care. There is also the distress, for all concerned, associated with the unwanted child, and there is the problem of bringing a child into a family already unable, psychologically and otherwise, to care for it. In other cases, as in this one, the additional difficulties and continuing stigma of unwed motherhood may be involved. All these are factors the woman and her responsible physician necessarily will consider in consultation. . . .

On the basis of elements such as these, appellants argue that the woman's right is absolute and that she is entitled to terminate her pregnancy at whatever time, in whatever way, and for whatever reason she alone chooses. With this we do not agree. Appellant's arguments that Texas either has no valid interest at all in regulating the abortion decision, or no interest strong enough to support any limitation upon the woman's sole determination, is unpersuasive. The Court's decisions recognizing a right of privacy also acknowledge that some state regulation in areas protected by that right is appropriate. As noted above, a State may

---

were beaten, and federal marshals rushed in to protect them. Ironically, the schools in both neighborhoods were in awful condition. All too often, forced busing became a class issue, involving poorer people of all races.

New Directions at Home and Abroad

Like John F. Kennedy, President Nixon cared more about foreign policy than about domestic affairs. As a moderate Republican in the Eisenhower mold, Nixon endorsed the basic outlines of the modern welfare state, which included Social Security, unemployment insurance, a minimum wage, the right to unionize, and health care for the elderly. Yet Nixon also understood—and exploited—the public's growing concern that the Great Society Era had tilted too far in favor of poor people and minority groups. He tried to find, in his words, a domestic "middle ground."

properly assert important interests in safe-guarding health, in maintaining medical standards, and in protecting potential life. At some point in pregnancy, these respective interests become sufficiently compelling to sustain regulation of the factors that govern the abortion decision. The privacy right involved, therefore, cannot be said to be absolute. In fact, it is not clear to us that the claim . . . that one has an unlimited right to do with one's body as one pleases bears a close relationship to the right of privacy previously articulated in the Court's decisions. The Court has refused to recognize an unlimited right of this kind in the past.

We therefore conclude that the right of personal privacy includes the abortion decision, but that this right is not unqualified and must be considered against state interests in regulation. . . .

Measured against these standards, the Texas Penal Code, in restricting legal abortions to those "procured or attempted by medical advice for the purpose of saving the life of the mother," sweeps too broadly.

To summarize and to repeat:

A state criminal abortion statute of the current Texas type, that excepts from criminality only a *life saving* procedure on behalf of the mother, without regard to pregnancy stage and without recognition of the other interests involved, is violative of the Due Process Clause of the Fourteenth Amendment.

(a) For the stage prior to approximately the end of the first trimester, the abortion decision and its effectuation must be left to the medical judgment of the pregnant woman's attending physician.

(b) For the stage subsequent to approximately the end of the first trimester, the State, in promoting its interest in the health of the mother, may, if it chooses, regulate the abortion procedure in ways that are reasonably related to maternal health.

(c) For the stage subsequent to viability the State, in promoting its interest in the potentiality of human life, may, if it chooses, regulate, and even prescribe, abortion except where it is necessary, in appropriate medical judgment, for the preservation of the life or health of the mother.

Questions to Consider

1. How did *Roe v. Wade* fit into the larger "rights revolution" of the 1960s and 1970s?

2. What arguments—legal, ethical, religious—have opposing sides used to justify their positions?

3. In what ways have the nation's courts and legislative bodies tried to fortify or modify *Roe v. Wade* in the years since the decision was announced in 1973?

Explore additional primary sources related to this chapter on the *American Passages* Web site: http://history.wadsworth.com/ayersbrief02.

Source: *Roe v. Wade*, 410 U.S. 113, 1973.

Rethinking Welfare

President Nixon moved cautiously on the domestic front. His immediate goals were to implement a revenue-sharing plan that sent more tax dollars back to the states and localities, and to simplify the welfare system. Revenue sharing, designed to limit the power of the national government, was a modest success. Congress passed legislation transferring $30 billion in federal revenue over five years—less than Nixon wanted, but more than state and local governments had received in the past. Welfare reform proved a much harder sell. Here the president looked to domestic advisor Daniel P. Moynihan, a social scientist whose controversial writings on poverty and family breakup in the African American community reflected a shifting emphasis from equal rights, which focused on constitutional guarantees, to equal opportunity, which stressed socioeconomic gains. Everyone agreed that the current welfare system—Aid to Families with Dependent Children (AFDC)—was seriously flawed. Its programs lacked accountability, and the payments varied widely from state to state. At Moynihan's urging, President Nixon offered an alternative to AFDC, known as the Family Assistance Plan (FAP).

The new plan proposed a national standard for welfare designed to reduce the number of recipients—and bureaucrats—over time. Instead of providing a host of costly welfare services, the government would guarantee a minimum annual income to the poor, beginning at $1,600 for a family of four, with additional funding for food stamps. The individual states were expected to subsidize this income, and able-bodied parents (excepting mothers of preschool children) were required to seek employment or job training. Not surprisingly, FAP ran into withering criticism from all sides. Liberals complained that $1,600 was unreasonably low, whereas conservatives opposed the very concept of a guaranteed annual income. The National Welfare Rights Organization resisted the work requirement for women with school-age children, and community leaders and social workers worried about the elimination of vital services (and perhaps their own jobs).

To his credit, Nixon did not trim needed programs as his own plan went down to defeat. On the contrary, he supported Democratic-sponsored measures in Congress to increase food stamp expenditures, ensure better medical care for low-income families, and provide automatic cost-of-living adjustments (COLAs) for Social Security recipients to help them keep up with inflation. Although Nixon did not care to publicize this achievement, he became the first president since Franklin Roosevelt to propose a federal budget with more spending for social services than for national defense.

Protecting the Environment

On April 22, 1970, millions of Americans gathered to celebrate Earth Day, an event sponsored by the Sierra Club and other environmental groups to educate people about the ecological problems afflicting the modern world. Begun a few years earlier, the environmental movement gained strength after a series of well-publicized disasters: a chemical fire that ignited Cleveland's Cuyahoga River, a giant oil spill that fouled the beaches of Santa Barbara, and the "death" of Lake Erie by farm runoff and factory waste. The dire predictions of scientists about population growth, poisoned food and water, endangered species, and air pollution added fuel to the cause.

At first President Nixon showed little interest in environmental problems. Yet he soon considered environmentalism to be a powerful force—one that cut across class, racial, and political lines. Unlike many other issues, it gave the appearance of uniting Americans against a common foe.

Moving quickly, the administration banned the use of DDT in the United States, though not its sale to foreign countries; and stopped production of chemical and biological weapons, though not the plant defoliants or napalm used in Vietnam. More significantly, the White House supported a bipartisan congressional effort to establish the Environmental Protection Agency (EPA) and to pass the Clean Air Act of 1970 and the Endangered Species Act of 1973.

The Clean Air Act set strict national guidelines for the reduction of automobile and factory emissions, with fines and jail sentences for polluters. The Endangered Species Act protected rare plants and animals from extinction. The list included hundreds of categories above the microscopic level, from the spotted owl to the snail-darter. Congress also passed the Water Pollution Control Act over Nixon's veto in 1972. The law, mandating $25 billion for the cleanup of America's neglected lakes and rivers, was too costly for the president, though it proved effective in bringing polluted waters back to life.

Although Americans readily agreed about the need for clean air, pure water, and protecting wildlife, the cost of doing these things did not fall equally on everyone's shoulders. Auto manufacturers warned that the expense of meeting the new emission standards would result in higher car prices and the layoff of production workers. Loggers in the Northwest angrily accused the EPA of being more interested in protecting a few forest birds than in allowing human beings to earn a living and feed their families. In response to pressure from labor unions and businesses about lost jobs, rising costs and endless paperwork, the EPA modified some of its goals and deadlines for compliance with these new laws. Could strategies be devised to protect jobs and the environment simultaneously? Could U.S. corporations effectively compete with foreign companies that did not face such restrictions? Protecting the environment raised serious questions for the future.

A New World Order

Determined to control foreign policy even more rigidly than previous presidents, Nixon bypassed the State Department in favor of the National Security Council, based in the White House itself. To direct the NSC, he chose **Henry Kissinger,** a German refugee and Harvard political scientist. In Kissinger the president found the perfect match for his "realistic" view of foreign affairs in which hard assessments of the national interest took precedence over moral and ideological concerns.

Both men agreed that America's bipolar approach, based on the "containment" of Soviet Communism, no longer made sense. They wanted a more flexible policy that recognized the growing strength of Western Europe, Communist China, and Japan. They believed that the United States could no longer afford to play the world's policeman in every skirmish, or to finance an arms race that grew more dangerous—and expensive—with each passing year. The Nixon-Kissinger approach meant talking with old enemies, finding common ground through negotiation, and encouraging a more widespread balance of world power.

This innovative thinking, however, did not extend to all parts of the globe. The president still viewed Fidel Castro as a mortal enemy, and openly encouraged the CIA to undermine the democratically elected, left-wing government of Chilean President Salvadore Allende, who was overthrown and apparently murdered by right-wing military forces in 1973. In Latin America, at least, the New World Order appeared strikingly similar to the old one.

Henry Kissinger

A German-born American diplomat, he was national security advisor and U.S. secretary of state under Presidents Nixon and Ford. He shared the 1973 Nobel Peace Prize for helping to negotiate the Vietnam ceasefire.

The China Opening

In one sense, Richard Nixon seemed an odd choice to strip away years of rigid Cold War thinking in foreign affairs. He was, after all, known for his bitter attacks on State Department officials during the McCarthy years. Yet that is what made his new initiatives all the more remarkable. One of his first moves was to take advantage of the widening rift between Communist China and the Soviet Union. The United States at this time did not even recognize Communist China. Since 1949, U.S. policy considered the anti-Communist regime on Taiwan the legitimate government of mainland China. There were some who believed that only a politician with Nixon's Red-hunting credentials would dare to change this policy after so many years. No one could seriously accuse this president—as he had accused so many others—of being "soft on Communism."

Nixon wanted a new relationship with China for several reasons. The trade possibilities were enormous. Better relations also increased the chances of a peace settlement in Vietnam while strengthening America's bargaining position with the Soviet Union. Most of all, Nixon realized that China must now be recognized as a legitimate world power. The United States could no longer afford to ignore this reality.

Nixon worked behind the scenes, knowing that Americans considered China the "most dangerous" nation on earth. The first public breakthrough came in 1971, when an American table tennis team was invited to China for an exhibition tour. This "Ping-Pong diplomacy" led both nations to ease trade and travel restrictions. Meanwhile, Henry Kissinger secretly visited Beijing to plan a summit meeting between Chinese and American leaders.

Nixon arrived in China on February 22, 1972—the first U.S. president ever to set foot on Chinese soil. For the next eight days, the world watched in amazement as he walked along the Great Wall and strolled through the Forbidden City. "The Chinese Army band played 'America the Beautiful' and 'Home on the Range,'" wrote the *New York Times*. "President Nixon quoted Chairman Mao Zedong approvingly, used his chopsticks skillfully, and clinked glasses with every Chinese official in sight."

The trip ended with a joint statement, known as the Shanghai Communiqué, that promised closer relations between the two countries in trade, travel, and cultural exchange. Each nation agreed to open a legation (not an embassy) in the other's capital city, beginning the process of diplomatic recognition that would take seven more years to complete. The most important issues, such as human rights and nuclear proliferation, were tactfully ignored. And the most controversial issue—the future of Taiwan—demonstrated the deep rift that still existed. Communist China asserted its claim to the island, demanding that U.S. troops on Taiwan be removed. The United States called for a "peaceful solution" to the "Taiwan question" and promised to reduce its forces as "tensions" in the region declined. Still, the historic significance of Nixon's visit overshadowed the problems that lay ahead.

Détente

Three months later, the president traveled to Moscow for a summit meeting with Soviet leader Leonid Brezhnev. Nixon believed that his successful trip to China, coupled with a faltering Russian economy, would make the Soviets more likely to strike a serious deal with the United States. The key issues were arms control and increased trade. Both sides possessed huge atomic arsenals that cost billions of dollars and increased the chances of catastrophic war. The Russians desperately needed grain, heavy equipment, and technical assistance.

The Moscow Summit further enhanced the Nixon-Kissinger record in foreign affairs. On May 22, 1972, the United States and the Soviet Union signed a Strategic Arms Limitation Treaty (SALT) that limited the number of long-range offensive missiles (ICBMs), and an ABM agreement that froze the production of antiballistic missiles for the next five years. No one believed that the arms race was now over; both sides would continue to build long-range nuclear bombers and to develop the Multiple Independent Re-entry Vehicles (MIRVs), which permitted several warheads to be fired from a single missile. Yet these initial treaties represented a stunning breakthrough in Soviet-U.S. relations.

The economic agreements were less successful. Though U.S.-Soviet trade more than tripled over the next three years, the greatest increase came in a single wheat deal that caused a temporary shortage in the United States. American consumers fumed at the idea of shipping low-priced wheat to a foreign country while bread prices rose dramatically at home.

Nevertheless, the Moscow Summit provided a solid foundation for **détente.** As President Nixon left Moscow, he noted the differences between the Soviet leaders he faced in 1959, when he was vice president, and the ones who endorsed détente. The current leaders, he wrote, "do not have to brag about everything in Russia being better than anything anywhere else. But they still crave to be respected as equals, and on this point I think we made a good impression."

détente
An easing of tensions among countries, which usually leads to increased economic, diplomatic, and other types of contacts between former rivals.

Four More Years?

After a full term in office, Richard Nixon could look back on a record of notable achievement. Relations with Cold War opponents, the Soviet Union and Communist China, had dramatically improved as détente replaced confrontation. Although the Vietnam War continued, the steady withdrawal of U.S. troops meant fewer casualties and an end to the draft. Even the economy looked better.

The Landslide of 1972

Nixon's Democratic challengers faced an uphill battle. From the political right, Governor **George Wallace** of Alabama continued the presidential odyssey he began in 1968. Campaigning this time as a Democrat, Wallace won wide support among white working-class voters for his opposition to forced busing and his attacks on "welfare cheats." After winning the Democratic presidential primary in Florida, and running a close second in Wisconsin, Wallace was shot and paralyzed by a would-be assassin, ending his presidential quest.

A few weeks later, on June 17, 1972, five men were arrested while burglarizing the Democratic National Headquarters at the Watergate complex in Washington, D.C. They were led by James W. McCord, the security director for Richard Nixon's Committee to Re-Elect the President, known as CREEP. Supervising from a nearby hotel, and later arrested, were two presidential aides — Gordon Liddy and E. Howard Hunt — who belonged to the newly created "Plumbers" unit. Responding to the break-in, Nixon assured the public that no one "presently employed" in his administration was involved "in this very bizarre incident."

At the Republican National Convention in Miami, the delegates enthusiastically renominated the Nixon-Agnew team. The Democratic race, however, proved far more con-

George Wallace
A three-time governor of Alabama, he first came to national attention as an outspoken segregationist. Wallace ran unsuccessfully for the presidency in 1968 and 1972.

tentious. The candidates included Hubert Humphrey, the 1968 presidential nominee; Senator **George McGovern** of South Dakota, the favorite of younger, more liberal Democrats; and Representative Shirley Chisholm of New York, the first African American to seek the presidential nomination of a major political party.

The Democratic National Convention, meeting in Miami Beach, reflected the party reforms that followed the bloody "siege of Chicago" in 1968. The changes were dramatic, with the percentage of female delegates increasing from 13 to 38 percent, blacks from 5 to 15 percent, and those under thirty years of age from 3 to 23 percent. Moreover, these new delegates embraced the causes of numerous "out groups" in society, such as homosexuals, migrant workers, prisoners, and the urban poor. Deeply committed to the "rights revolution" of the 1960s, they proposed a major redistribution of political power and cultural authority in the United States.

The delegates chose George McGovern for president and Senator Thomas Eagleton of Missouri for vice president. But reporters learned that Senator Eagleton had been hospitalized in the past for mental depression and fatigue, twice undergoing electroshock therapy. At first McGovern stood by his running mate, offering him "1,000 percent" support. As criticism mounted, however, McGovern replaced Eagleton with former Peace Corps Director Sargent Shriver. Appearing weak and opportunistic, McGovern dropped further in the polls.

Far more damaging was the lack of unity within Democratic ranks. Many of McGovern's key positions, such as amnesty for draft resisters and greater welfare benefits for the poor, offended Democrats who believed their party had moved too far to the left. On election day Nixon overwhelmed McGovern, carrying every state but Massachusetts and winning 61 percent of the popular vote.

Yet Nixon's landslide victory was more limited than it appeared. Ticket splitting flourished in 1972, with the Democratic party easily retaining control of Congress. Furthermore, the percentage of eligible voters who cast ballots in presidential elections continued to fall, from 62 percent in 1964, to 61 percent in 1968, to 56 percent in 1972. This suggested a growing alienation from the political process.

Exit from Vietnam

The president's first task was to end the Vietnam conflict on honorable terms and secure the release of U.S. prisoners of war. But the key to any settlement, Nixon understood, was the future security of South Vietnam. What would happen after U.S. troops left that country?

In the spring of 1972, North Vietnam had mounted a major offensive in the South, gambling that Nixon's concern about the coming presidential election would prevent the United States from responding. The offensive failed miserably, however, when Nixon ordered massive bombing raids against North Vietnam. That fall, secret negotiations between Henry Kissinger and North Vietnam's Le Duc To produced a temporary ceasefire. The United States agreed to withdraw its remaining troops from Vietnam in return for the release of its POWs. President Thieu would continue to govern South Vietnam, and North Vietnamese troops were allowed to remain there until a final settlement was reached. A week before the 1972 presidential election, Kissinger declared that "peace is at hand."

The claim was premature. President Thieu opposed the ceasefire, demanding the removal of North Vietnamese troops from South Vietnam, and the North Vietnamese seemed intent on adding even more soldiers for a final assault. Following his reelection, President Nixon tried to force a settlement through a fierce air assault against North Vietnam. The damage done to North Vietnam was staggering: harbors, factories, railway lines, storage facilities, and sometimes adjoining neighborhoods were destroyed. North Vietnam's Communist allies did not strongly protest, even when a Soviet ship was damaged in Haiphong harbor. Interested above all in continuing the process of détente with the United States, the Russians signaled North Vietnam to return to the bargaining table. On January 27, 1973, the United States and North Vietnam signed an agreement quite similar to the one that had fallen apart a few months before. President Nixon got Thieu's reluctant support by vowing to "respond in full force" if North Vietnam renewed the fighting in the South. The United States, he proclaimed, had achieved "peace with honor" at last.

George McGovern
A U.S. senator from South Dakota, he opposed the Vietnam War and was defeated as the 1972 Democratic candidate for president.

What Nixon got, in reality, was an American exit from Vietnam that left the vulnerable Thieu government at the mercy of its Communist opponents. Despite his pledge, the United States could only respond to future treaty violations with air power; sending troops back into combat was now unthinkable. The agreement ended U.S. involvement without guaranteeing South Vietnam's long-term survival.

The American public expressed relief at the settlement, but little jubilation. The war had divided the country and drained billions of dollars from vital domestic programs. More than fifty thousand U.S. soldiers were killed in Vietnam and three hundred thousand were wounded. As the *New York Times* noted, "There is no dancing in the streets, no honking of horns, no champagne."

Public attention soon shifted to the return of 587 American POWs. Many had spent up to seven years in North Vietnamese jails, and some had been tortured. "We are honored to have the opportunity to serve our country under difficult circumstances," said their senior officer as his plane touched down on U.S. soil. That very day, ex-President Lyndon Johnson died in his sleep. "His tragedy—and ours," Senator Edmund Muskie stated, "was the war."

Watergate and the Abuse of Power

With Vietnam behind him, the president appeared ready to launch a successful second term. Yet all that ended in April when the Watergate burglars pleaded guilty to minor charges of theft and wiretapping to avoid a public trial. Suspecting a cover-up, federal judge John Sirica convinced the lead burglar, James McCord, to admit that high-ranking White House officials were involved in planning the break-in. This startling confession, combined with the investigative stories of *Washington Post* reporters Bob Woodward and Carl Bernstein, turned the Watergate affair into front-page news.

During the spring of 1973, President Nixon reluctantly appointed Harvard Law School professor Archibald Cox as an independent prosecutor in the Watergate case, and the Senate formed a special investigating committee chaired by seventy-three-year-old Sam Ervin of North Carolina. Under Ervin's careful direction, the committee heard sworn testimony from present and former Nixon aides about a "seamless web" of criminal activity designed to undermine the president's critics and political opponents. In meticulous detail, John Dean, the former White House counsel, implicated Nixon himself in a plan to ensure the silence of the imprisoned burglars by paying them "hush money."

Nixon, however, denied any involvement in Watergate. On national television, he took "responsibility" but no blame for the scandal, explaining that he had been too busy running the nation to bother with the day-to-day workings of his reelection campaign. Many Americans—and most Republican leaders—took Nixon at his word.

In July White House aide Alexander Butterfield stunned the Ervin Committee by revealing that Nixon had secretly recorded his Oval Office conversations since 1971. Judge Sirica, Special Prosecutor Cox, and Chairman Ervin all demanded to hear the relevant tapes. But Nixon refused to release them, citing executive privilege and the separation of powers. When Cox persisted, Nixon ordered Attorney General Elliot Richardson to fire him. Richardson and his top deputy refused, leading to their swift removal. These dramatic developments, known as the "Saturday Night Massacre," produced angry calls for Nixon's impeachment.

There was trouble for the vice president as well. In 1973 a Baltimore grand jury looked into allegations that Spiro Agnew, as governor of Maryland, had accepted illegal payoffs from building contractors. After first denying these charges, the vice president resigned his office and pleaded *nolo contendere* (no contest) to one count of income tax evasion. He received three years' probation plus a $10,000 fine.

Under the Twenty-fifth Amendment, adopted in 1967, the president is obligated to nominate a vice president "who shall take the office upon confirmation by a majority of both houses of Congress." To bolster his declining fortunes, Nixon chose the well-respected **Gerald Ford,** who was quickly confirmed. But the president ran into more trouble when the Internal Revenue Service (IRS) disclosed that Nixon owed $500,000 in back taxes from 1970 and 1971. Responding emotionally, Nixon told a press conference, "I am not a crook."

Gerald Ford
The thirty-eighth president of the United States, he was appointed vice president on the resignation of Spiro Agnew and became president when Richard Nixon resigned over the Watergate scandal. As president, Ford granted a full pardon to Nixon in 1974.

By this point, however, public confidence in Nixon had disappeared. The testimony of John Dean, the Saturday Night Massacre, the resignation of Spiro Agnew, the embarrassing IRS disclosures—all cast doubt on the president's morality and fitness to lead. In desperation, the president released transcripts of several Watergate-related conversations (but not the tapes themselves), claiming that they cleared him of wrongdoing. Many thought otherwise. The transcripts contained ethnic and racial slurs, vulgar language (with "expletives deleted"), and strong hints of presidential involvement in a cover-up.

Facing certain impeachment and removal from office, President Nixon resigned on August 9, 1974.

Nixon's refusal to release the tapes reached a climax in July 1974 when the House Judiciary Committee debated charges of presidential impeachment before a national television audience. The committee approved three charges—obstruction of justice, abuse of power, and contempt of Congress—at the very moment that a unanimous Supreme Court ordered Nixon to comply with Judge Sirica's subpoena for the Watergate tapes. On August 5 the president released the material that sealed his fate. Although providing no evidence that Nixon knew about the Watergate burglary in advance, the tapes showed him playing an active role in the attempt to cover up White House involvement in the crime.

Faced with certain impeachment and removal, Richard Nixon became the first president to resign from office. In a tearful farewell to his staff on August 9, he preached the very advice that he, himself, was incapable of following. "Never get discouraged. Never be petty," he said. "Always remember. . . . Those who hate you don't win unless you hate them. And then you destroy yourself."

OPEC and the Oil Embargo

In the midst of the Watergate scandal, a serious crisis erupted over the nation's energy needs. On October 6, 1973—the Jewish high holiday of Yom Kippur—Egypt and Syria attacked Israel from two sides. The United States backed Israel by airlifting vital military supplies. U.S. aid proved essential in helping Israel repel the attack, and the Organization of Petroleum Exporting Countries (OPEC) responded by halting oil shipments to the United States, Western Europe, and Japan.

The oil embargo created an immediate panic, though the problem had been building for years. As the U.S. economy flourished after World War II, its energy consumption soared. Americans, barely 6 percent of the world's population in 1974, used more than 30 percent of the world's energy. Furthermore, as the expense of exploring and drilling for domestic oil increased, the United States turned to foreign suppliers, especially in the Middle East. Between 1968 and 1973, U.S. consumption of imported oil tripled from 12 to 36 percent.

This reliance on foreign sources left the United States extremely vulnerable to the OPEC embargo. As the cold weather set in, President Nixon warned that "we are heading toward the most acute shortage of energy since World War II." In response, the government reduced highway speed limits to 55 miles per hour, lowered thermostats in office buildings to 68 degrees, eased environmental restrictions on coal mining, and pushed the development of nuclear power. Across the nation, stores and factories closed early, and northern colleges canceled their midwinter semesters. Long lines formed at the gas stations, which were closed on Sundays.

The oil embargo ended in April 1974, but the impact lingered on. Energy costs rose dramatically, even as supplies returned to normal, because OPEC tripled its price. Consumers faced soaring inflation, and manufacturers confronted higher production costs. Some regions, such as the automobile- and steel-producing Midwest, were particularly hard hit, while other areas, like the energy-producing Sunbelt, gained in population and political influence.

Above all, the energy crisis shook the foundations of the American dream. For three decades a booming economy had produced a standard of living unparalleled in terms of material comfort, home ownership, and access to higher education. American culture thrived on the assumption of upward mobility—that the nation's children would do better than their parents had done. After 1973 that assumption was in peril. Prosperity could no longer be taken for granted. Following the oil embargo, average weekly earnings in the United States (adjusted for inflation) stopped growing for the first time in thirty years. The increased cost of energy, combined with spiraling federal deficits and aggressive foreign competition in manufacturing and technology, made the U.S. economy more vulnerable than before. Some experts predicted a new age in which limits and sacrifice replaced abundance and expansion.

Gerald Ford in the White House

Vice President Gerald Ford, who had served for two decades in the U.S. House of Representatives, seemed like the ideal figure to restore public confidence in the presidency. Even his political opponents praised his decency, his integrity, and his humble, straightforward ways. After the charisma of John Kennedy, the explosive energy of Lyndon Johnson, and the divisive appeals of Richard Nixon, Americans were ready, it appeared, for a leader with common values and an ordinary touch.

The Watergate Legacy

Gerald Ford entered the White House at a pivotal time. He inherited a situation in which the legislative branch of government appeared anxious to restore its former authority by cutting the executive branch down to size. In 1973, for example, Congress passed the War Powers Act, which required the president to notify Congress within forty-eight hours about the foreign deployment of U.S. combat troops. If Congress did not formally endorse that action within sixty days, the troops would be withdrawn. In addition, Congress passed the Freedom of Information Act, which gave the American people unprecedented access to classified government material.

The Senate also held a series of spectacular hearings into the abuses, and criminal activity, of executive intelligence agencies such as the FBI and the CIA. The public learned that FBI agents had routinely harassed, blackmailed, and wiretapped prominent Americans such as Martin Luther King Jr., and that CIA operatives had engaged in illegal drug experiments, money laundering, and bungled assassinations of world leaders including Fidel Castro. These revelations led President Ford to create a monitoring device known as the Intelligence Oversight Board. But Congress, with fresh memories of the Watergate cover-up, formed a permanent watchdog committee to investigate such behavior on its own.

Ford, too, fell victim to the Watergate morass. During his vice presidential confirmation hearing in 1973, he had gone on record against a possible presidential pardon for Richard Nixon. Yet in September 1974 President Ford reversed his earlier position by granting Nixon a "full, free, and absolute pardon" for all crimes he "may have committed" during his term in office. Ford based his decision on a number of factors, including the impact of a criminal trial on Nixon's health. Above all, however, Ford hoped that a presidential pardon would finally put the "national nightmare" of Watergate to rest.

In fact, the opposite occurred. By appearing to place one man above the law, the pardon raised serious doubts about Gerald Ford's character. Within days the new president's public approval rating dropped from 72 percent to 49 percent. What bothered many Americans was the fact that Ford had granted the pardon without demanding contrition in return. Richard Nixon barely apologized for Watergate. He never admitted his crimes. For Gerald Ford, the pardon was an act of mercy, but others wanted justice as well.

The new president also tried to heal the internal wounds of the Vietnam War. Within days of taking office, he offered "conditional amnesty" to the three hundred fifty thousand Americans of draft age who had refused service in the armed forces by leaving the country. Under Ford's plan, a draft resister might be permitted to reenter the United States in return for alternative service in a hospital or a charitable institution. Not surprisingly, the program met stiff resistance. Many who left the country believed they had performed an act of conscience, whereas veterans' groups viewed them as military deserters who should serve their time in jail.

The Fall of South Vietnam

In October 1974, at a secret conclave outside Hanoi, the leaders of Communist North Vietnam prepared their final plans for the conquest of South Vietnam. Their main concern was the United States. Would it respond "in full force" to Communist violations of the 1973 peace accords? The North Vietnamese did not think so. "Having already withdrawn from the South," they reasoned, "the United States could hardly jump back in."

Their assessment was correct. The North Vietnamese launched a massive assault in March 1975, overwhelming South Vietnamese forces near the Demilitarized Zone (DMZ). As North Vietnamese troops advanced, a mixture of chaos and panic gripped South Vietnam, with thousands of soldiers deserting their units and masses of civilians clogging the highways in desperate flight. Ignoring a plea from President Ford, Congress refused to extend emergency aid to South Vietnam. On April 23 Ford acknowledged the obvious: the Vietnam War, he said, "is finished as far as America is concerned."

Saigon fell to the Communists on April 29. The televised images of Americans desperately boarding the last helicopters from the embassy grounds seemed a painful yet fitting conclusion to our nation's longest war. "What we need now in this country," said a solemn Henry Kissinger, "is to put Vietnam behind us and to concentrate on problems of the future."

This was easier said than done. The humiliating collapse of South Vietnam raised serious questions about the soundness of America's foreign policy and the limits of its military power. Furthermore, for those most deeply affected—the veterans of Vietnam—the collapse raised personal questions about the meaning of their sacrifice to the nation and to themselves. With the exception of the POWs, these veterans received no public tributes, no outpouring of thanks. Some Americans condemned the veterans for serving in an "immoral war," whereas others blamed them for participating in the nation's first military defeat.

The vast majority of Vietnam veterans expressed pride in their military service. Most of them adjusted well to civilian life, although a sizable minority suffered from posttraumatic stress disorder, substance abuse, and sometimes both. In addition, some veterans claimed that their exposure to Agent Orange, a toxic herbicide used to defoliate the jungles of Vietnam, had produced high rates of cancer, lung disease, and even birth defects in their children. After more than a decade of controversy, Congress passed legislation that extended benefits to Vietnam veterans with medical conditions linked to Agent Orange.

Public sentiment softened over time. Opinion polls by the late 1970s showed that most Americans considered the Vietnam veteran to be both a dutiful soldier and the victim of a tragic war. In 1982 the Vietnam Veterans Memorial, a dramatic wall of black granite with the names of fifty-eight thousand Americans who died or are missing in that war, was unveiled on the Mall in Washington, D.C.

Stumbling toward Defeat

The pardon of Richard Nixon and the fall of South Vietnam served to erode much of the goodwill that had accompanied Gerald Ford's early days in office. The president also faced a bleak economic picture in which unemployment and inflation reached their highest levels in years.

The president and the Congress disagreed about the best medicine for the economic slump. The Republican Ford, believing that a balanced federal budget was the key to cutting inflation, proposed sizable cuts in government programs and a voluntary citizen's campaign to curb rising prices, which he called "Whip Inflation Now" (WIN). The Democratic Congress called for increased federal spending to spur the economy and to lower unemployment by creating new jobs. Although Ford vetoed more than sixty bills during his brief tenure in office, Congress overrode the president to increase Social Security benefits, fund public works projects, and raise the minimum wage.

In foreign affairs Ford tried to maintain the policy of détente. But unlike Nixon, the new president worried conservatives with his alleged weaknesses as a negotiator. Of particular concern was the Helsinki Accord of 1975, which pledged the United States and the Soviet Union, among other nations, to recognize the Cold War boundaries dividing Eastern and Western Europe and to respect human rights within their borders. Many Americans were dismayed by the formal acceptance of Soviet domination over nations such as Poland and East Germany; and many more were skeptical about any Russian promise regarding human rights.

Even Ford's occasional successes left controversy in their wake. In 1975, for example, Communists in Cambodia seized the U.S. merchant ship *Mayaguez* in international waters off the Cambodian coast. The president responded with a daring rescue mission in which forty-one U.S. Marines were killed and forty-nine were wounded, although it turned out that the Cambodians had already released the *Mayaguez* and its crew. Although Ford received some criticism for not consulting Congress before sending troops into action, most Americans, recalling the *Pueblo* incident and the fall of South Vietnam, applauded his decisive action.

The Election of 1976

Gerald Ford dreamed of winning the White House in his own right. Yet unlike previous incumbents, who normally breezed through the presidential nominating process, Ford faced a serious challenge in 1976 from Ronald Reagan. Reagan's polished presence and outspoken conservatism played well against Ford's reserved manner and middle-of-the-road approach. Reagan portrayed Ford as a weak president, unable to tame a Democratic Congress or to confront the Russians at Helsinki. In his sharpest attack, Reagan blasted Ford for opening negotiations aimed at reducing U.S. control of the Panama Canal. "We built it, we paid for it, it's ours," Reagan thundered, "and we should tell [Panama] that we are going to keep it."

Though Reagan battled Ford to a draw in the state primaries, the president won a narrow victory at the Republican National Convention in Kansas City by agreeing to support a party platform sympathetic to the Reagan forces. The platform condemned both the Helsinki agreement and the Panama Canal negotiations, while endorsing constitutional amendments to legalize school prayer and prohibit abortions. For vice president, the Republican delegates selected Senator Bob Dole of Kansas, a tough campaigner with conservative views.

Because Ford appeared so vulnerable in 1976, the Democratic race for president attracted a very large field. Among the candidates was a little known ex-governor of Georgia named **James Earl ("Jimmy") Carter Jr.** Few observers took him seriously at the start, and the voters asked, "Jimmy who?" Yet Carter ran an effective, well-financed campaign, portraying himself as a political outsider, untainted by the arrogance and corruption of Washington.

Carter struck the right pose for the post-Watergate Era. A deeply religious man, he combined the virtues of small town America with the skills of the modern corporate world. Born in Plains, Georgia, in 1924, Carter graduated with distinction from the U.S. Naval Academy and spent seven years as a naval officer working on nuclear submarines. Following the death of his father in 1953, Carter returned to Plains to run the family's farm supply and peanut business. As the company prospered, he turned to politics, winning a state senate seat in 1962 and the Georgia governorship eight years later. Known as a "new South" politician, Carter supported progressive causes and reached out to black constituents.

Meeting in New York City, the Democratic National Convention chose Carter for president and Senator Walter Mondale of Minnesota for vice president. Carter ran a safe campaign that fall, avoiding controversial issues while claiming that America was no longer "strong" or "respected" in the world. The media, meanwhile, caught Ford in a series of bumbling accidents—banging his head on a car door, tripping on the steps of an airplane, falling down on the ski slopes—that made him look clownish and inept. Before long, the comedian Chevy Chase was beginning almost every episode of *Saturday Night Live* by taking a terrible tumble in the role of Gerald Ford. And the president only made things worse for himself with a series of embarrassing verbal blunders, such as his insistence during the televised debate with Carter that "there [was] no Soviet domination of Eastern Europe."

Still, the race was very close. Carter won 40.8 million votes, Ford 39.1 million. The electoral count was 297 to 240. Carter swept the entire South (except for Virginia) and the key industrial states of Ohio, Pennsylvania, and New York. Ford did well in the West, carrying every state but Texas. Polls showed Carter with large majorities among both minority voters and working-class whites who had rejected McGovern in 1972.

Jimmy Carter

The thirty-ninth president of the United States, his successes in office, including the Camp David Accords, were overshadowed by domestic worries and an international crisis involving the taking of American hostages at the U.S. Embassy in Iran. He was defeated by Ronald Reagan in the 1980 presidential election.

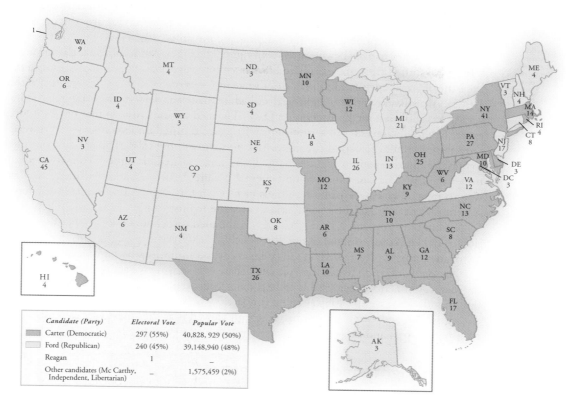

MAP 30.2 The Election of 1976

The 1976 presidential election, though one of the closest in history, was a major turnaround from the presidential election four years before when President Richard Nixon was reelected in a landslide, winning forty-nine states and more than 60 percent of the popular vote. Several factors worked to elect Democratic challenger Jimmy Carter in 1976, including the fall of South Vietnam, the stumbling economy, and President Ford's unpopular pardon for disgraced former President Nixon.

Jimmy Carter became the first president from the Deep South in more than a century. Furthermore, his election witnessed the growing importance of state primaries in the nominating process as well as the influence of the new Fair Campaign Practices Act of 1974. The law provided federal funds to the major candidates ($22 million each in this election), while establishing limits on personal contributions. The result was a longer, more expensive presidential campaign season, with television advertising playing an ever-larger role.

The Ford-Carter election continued the downward trend in voter turnout, from 55.7 percent in 1972 to 54.4 percent in 1976. Polls showed a growing sense of apathy and disillusionment among the American people. As one bumper sticker put it, "Don't Vote. It Only Encourages Them!"

The Carter Years

The new Democratic administration began with promise and hope. President-elect Carter took the oath of office as Jimmy (not James Earl) Carter before leading the inaugural parade on foot down Pennsylvania Avenue dressed in a simple business suit. Determined to be a "people's president," Carter surrounded himself with populist symbolism—giving fireside chats in a sweater and blue jeans, attending town meetings from New Hampshire to New Mexico, and staying overnight in the homes of ordinary Americans.

Civil Rights in a New Era

As governor of Georgia, Jimmy Carter had opened the doors of government to minorities. As president, he did much the same thing. Women, African Americans, and Hispanics were appointed to federal positions in record numbers. Women, for example, filled three of Carter's cabinet-level positions and numerous other policy-making roles. In addition, Carter's wife Rosalyn greatly expanded the role of First Lady by serving as a key advisor to the president and representing him on diplomatic missions.

Though Carter strongly supported civil rights, the momentum for racial change in the 1970s had shifted from the executive branch to the federal courts. During Carter's term, the issue of affirmative action took center stage in *University of California Regents v. Bakke* (1978). Allan Bakke, a thirty-eight-year-old white man, was denied admission to the University of California medical school at Davis. He sued on the grounds that his test scores exceeded those of several black applicants who were admitted under a policy that reserved sixteen of one hundred spots for minorities in each entering class. The policy amounted to "reverse discrimination," Bakke charged, and thus violated his right to equal protection under the law. The case raised a fundamental conflict between the government's obligation to treat all citizens equally regardless of race, and its responsibility to help the long-suffering victims of racial discrimination enter the mainstream of American society. In a 5–4 ruling, the Supreme Court struck down the medical school's quota policy as a violation of Bakke's constitutional rights. But it held that universities might consider race as a factor in admission "to remedy disadvantages cast on minorities by past racial prejudice."

The *Bakke* decision began a passionate debate over affirmative action that continues to this day. Opponents considered it to be a dangerous step away from the American tradition of individual rights. Why penalize innocent whites, they argued, for the sins of their ancestors? But supporters of affirmative action viewed it as the surest way to remedy discrimination, past and present.

Human Rights and Global Realities

President Carter knew little about foreign affairs. Yet he viewed his inexperience as an asset, believing that a fresh approach to foreign affairs would move the United States beyond the "big power" rivalries of the Cold War Era. What the United States needed, he thought, was a foreign policy that stressed democracy and human rights.

Carter chose a diverse foreign policy team. His UN ambassador, Andrew Young, was a black civil rights leader. His secretary of state, Cyrus Vance, was an experienced diplomat who worked tirelessly to keep détente alive. And his national security advisor, Zbigniew Brzezinski, was a Columbia University professor, born in Poland, who proposed a tough front against the Soviet Union. Their conflicting advice sometimes left the president confused.

Yet Carter scored some impressive foreign policy successes. Emphasizing human rights in Latin America, he withdrew U.S. support for Chile and cut off aid to the repressive Somoza regime in Nicaragua. Carter also presented the Senate with a treaty that relinquished U.S. control over the Panama Canal by the year 2000, and a second one that detailed U.S. rights in the Canal Zone thereafter. Both treaties provoked fierce national debate; both passed the Senate by a single vote.

Carter's greatest triumph occurred in the Middle East. In 1977 Egyptian President Anwar Sadat stunned the Arab world by visiting Israel to explore peace negotiations with Prime Minister Menachem Begin. Their discussions were cordial but fruitless. When the talks broke down, President Carter invited Sadat and Begin to his presidential retreat at Camp David in Maryland. For two full weeks in September 1978, Carter shuttled between the cabins of the two Middle Eastern leaders, patiently working out the details of a "peace process" between Egypt and Israel.

©Bettmann/CORBIS

Anwar Sadat (left) and Menachem Begin shake hands at Camp David, Maryland, as Jimmy Carter, who brought the men together, smiles in the background.

Camp David Accords
The historic treaty between Egypt and Israel, brokered by President Carter at Camp David in 1978, that returned the Sinai Peninsula to Egypt in return for Egypt's recognition of the State of Israel.

The **Camp David Accords** led to a historic treaty the following year. Egypt agreed to recognize the State of Israel, and Israel pledged to return the captured Sinai Peninsula to Egypt. Few could deny the enormity of what had transpired, or the pivotal role played by President Carter in bringing it about.

Economic Blues

Early success in foreign affairs, however, could not mask problems with the troubled economy. Carter's program to stimulate economic growth depended on a mixture of tax cuts, public works, and employment programs. The Democratic-controlled Congress responded sympathetically by funding large public works projects, reducing taxes by $30 billion, and raising the minimum wage from $2.30 to $3.35 over a five-year span. The good news was that unemployment dropped to 6 percent by 1978; the bad news was that inflation rose to 10 percent—and kept climbing.

Creating jobs now took a back seat to the problem of runaway inflation. Carter tried to attack inflation by tightening the money supply (through higher interest rates) and by controlling the federal deficit. This meant reduced government spending, a turnabout that alienated the Democratic Congress. Moreover, Carter's new policies appeared to increase unemployment without curbing inflation—the worst of both worlds.

This was not all Carter's fault, of course. The decline of U.S. productivity, the growth of foreign competition, and the surging cost of imported oil had plagued the nation for some time. In 1977 Carter offered a substantive plan for the energy crisis, which he described as "the moral equivalent of war." Based mainly on conservation—or reduced energy use—it ran into immediate opposition from oil companies, gas producers, the auto industry, and others who advocated the increased production of fossil fuels and the deregulation of prices.

The National Energy Act, passed in November 1978, did little to reduce America's energy consumption or its reliance on foreign oil. Carter's original plans to stimulate conservation efforts were overshadowed by incentives to increase domestic energy production through tax breaks for exploration, an emphasis on alternative sources (solar, nuclear, coal), and the deregulation of natural gas. The law did not address, much less solve, the nation's fundamental energy problems—as Americans would soon discover.

The Persian Gulf

In January 1979 a chain of events unfolded that shook the nation's confidence. The year began with the overthrow of America's dependable ally, Shah Riza Pahlavi of Iran. On a visit to Iran in 1977, President Carter had described it as "an island of stability in one of the most troubled areas in the world." Iran was vital to U.S. interests, both as an oil supplier and as a bastion against Soviet influence in the Middle East. Ironically, President Carter's concern for human rights did not extend to Iran, where the army and secret police used widespread torture and repression to keep the shah and his ruling elite in power.

The Iranian Revolution was led by Ayatollah Ruhollah Khomeini, an exiled cleric, and his devoted followers. Their aim was to form a fundamentalist Islamic state. When demonstrations paralyzed Iran, the shah fled his country, leaving the religious fundamentalists in control. One of Khomeini's first moves was to end oil shipments to "the Great Satan" America, thus allowing other OPEC countries to raise their prices even more. In the United States, long gas lines reappeared.

The news quickly got worse. In March 1979 an equipment problem at the Three Mile Island nuclear power plant near Harrisburg, Pennsylvania, overheated the radioactive core and threatened a meltdown. Coming at the same time as *The China Syndrome,* a hit movie with an almost identical storyline, the incident sent shock waves throughout the nation. For two weeks, technicians worked to contain the reactor, as thousands of residents fled their homes. The close call at Three Mile Island turned public opinion even further against nuclear power. The tremendous expense of building and servicing these

In a frightening scenario resembling *The China Syndrome,* an equipment failure at the Three Mile Island nuclear power plant near Harrisburg, Pennsylvania, in 1979 almost resulted in a meltdown. The close call increased public suspicion of atomic energy as a safe power supply for the future.

©Bettmann/CORBIS

reactors, combined with the potential nightmare of nuclear accidents, served to focus attention on the need for safe energy supplies in the future.

In June OPEC raised oil prices by another 50 percent. President Carter went on national television to speak partly about the energy crisis, but mostly about a "crisis of confidence" that struck "at the very heart and soul and spirit of our national will." His address was remarkably candid. Rather than assuring anxious Americans that they had nothing to fear, the president spoke of a nation in trouble, struggling with the values of its cherished past. In place of "hard work, strong families, and close-knit communities," he said, too many Americans "now worship self indulgence and consumption."

Having passionately diagnosed the illness, Carter provided no cure. The "crisis of confidence" deepened in the following weeks. In October the deposed shah of Iran, suffering from cancer, was allowed to enter the United States for medical treatment. This decision, which Carter viewed as a simple humanitarian gesture, produced an explosive backlash in Iran. On November 4 militant students stormed the U.S. embassy in Tehran, taking dozens of Americans hostage and parading them in blindfolds for the entire world to see. The militants demanded that the United States turn over the shah for trial in Iran. Otherwise, the Americans would remain as captives—and perhaps be tried, and executed, as spies.

Carter had almost no leverage with these militants. His attempts to settle the crisis through the United Nations were ignored by Iran. His orders to embargo Iranian oil and suspend arms sales were empty gestures because other nations refused to do the same. The remaining options—freezing Iran's assets in U.S. banks or threatening to deport Iranian students from the United States—did nothing to change the fate of the hostages in Tehran.

For a time, the American people rallied behind their president. Yet Carter grasped what many others did not: there was no easy solution to the hostage standoff. As the nation waited, public patience grew thin.

The year ended with yet another nasty surprise. In December Russian soldiers invaded neighboring Afghanistan to quell a revolt led by Muslim fundamentalists against the faltering pro-Soviet regime. The invasion ultimately backfired; fanatical resistance from Afghan peasant fighters turned the country into a graveyard for Russian troops. Determined to act boldly in light of the continuing Iran hostage crisis, Carter cut off grain shipments to the Soviet Union and canceled U.S. participation at the upcoming Summer Olympic Games in Moscow. More significantly, he announced a "Carter Doctrine" for the Persian Gulf, warning that "outside aggression" would "be repelled by any means necessary, including military force." For the first time since Vietnam, young men were ordered to register for the draft. In addition, Carter requested a major increase in defense spending, with $50 billion set aside for new weapons systems such as the multiple-warhead MX missile, which moved from place to place on secret railroad cars to prevent the enemy from tracking it. By 1980 the Cold War was heating up again.

Death in the Desert

As President Carter and the American people staggered through the repeated shocks of 1979, one issue dominated the national agenda: the fate of the hostages in Iran. The crisis took on symbolic importance as an example of America's declining power in the world. The television networks flashed nightly pictures of the hostages on humiliating public display in Tehran while frenzied crowds shouted "Death to Carter" and "Down with the United States." In Washington, meanwhile, the president worked tirelessly to find a diplomatic solution. But this seemed all but impossible because the Iranians, demanding both the shah and an American apology for supporting him, were not interested in a quick settlement. Reluctantly, Carter ordered a secret mission to free the hostages by force.

The result was disastrous. In April 1980 U.S. commandos reached the Iranian desert, where two of their helicopters were disabled by mechanical problems. Another hit a U.S. cargo plane, killing eight members of the rescue mission. The commandos departed without ever getting close to the hostages in Tehran. To make matters worse, the Iranians proudly displayed the burned corpses for television crews. Most Americans blamed the president for the debacle. What little remained of Jimmy Carter's credibility disappeared that fateful day in the Iranian desert.

Summary

Decade of Crises

The United States in 1980 was an uneasy land. The social upheavals of the 1960s and 1970s had fostered anxiety and doubt. America's innate faith in progress had been shaken. The movement for civil rights, so morally certain in the era of bus boycotts, lunch counter sit-ins, and voting rights marches, was now deeply divided over issues such as forced busing, affirmative action, and the use of violence, if need be, to achieve its ends. So, too, the struggle for women's rights generated fierce controversy over legalized abortion, appropriate sex roles, workplace equality, and the ERA. A step forward for one group meant a step backward for another.

On the economic front, Americans faced a world of new troubles—stagnant incomes, rising unemployment,

Mexican American activists formed La Raza Unida in 1969 to further "Chicano" causes. This poster advertises a benefit for striking grape workers in California.

"One giant leap for mankind." Neil Armstrong sets foot on the moon's surface July 20, 1969.

The OPEC oil embargo of 1973–1974 left Americans high and dry at the gas pumps.

mounting trade deficits, and skyrocketing inflation. No longer, it appeared, were young people guaranteed the prospect of moving a rung or two above their parents on the ladder of success. The American dream had always contained the assurance of upward mobility. To millions, at least, that dream was now on hold.

Above all, the nation seemed to lose confidence in its leaders and its goals. In 1973 the vice president of the United States pleaded no contest to a felony and resigned in disgrace. That same year, the president became embroiled in the worst scandal in U.S. history—a scandal, almost entirely of his own making, that would lead to his resignation under the threat of impeachment and send a number of his closest aides and advisors to prison. On one level, the scandal known as Watergate proved that the constitutional process worked well in times of extreme political crisis; on another level, it exhausted the nation and left many Americans bitter and disillusioned, especially after President Nixon received an "absolute pardon" from his successor.

One demoralizing crisis followed another in this star-crossed decade. The fall of South Vietnam signaled the end of a tragic endeavor in which more than fifty thousand U.S. soldiers gave their lives. The OPEC oil embargo added to America's growing economic woes. The near disaster at Three Mile Island further undermined faith in the future of nuclear power. The hostage crisis in Iran, and the bungled rescue attempt, raised serious doubts about the competence of the Carter administration. Taken together, these events reflected a loss of national purpose, authority, and prestige.

As the 1980 election approached, many Americans looked back into the past with a deep sense of nostalgia, hoping for someone to rescue the country and restore the American dream.

Making Connections Across Chapters

LOOKING BACK

Chapter 30 examines the political, economic, and psychological impact of the Watergate scandal, the OPEC oil embargo, the fall of South Vietnam, and other crises of the American people and their vision of the future.

1. What impact did the "rights revolution" of the 1960s have on political events in the 1970s? What role did the federal courts play in this process?
2. What were the defining features of the Watergate affair? Why is it considered to be the most significant, and potentially dangerous, political scandal in our history?
3. Though Americans most remember the Iran hostage crisis, the United States achieved some notable successes in foreign policy during the 1970s. What were these successes, and how were they achieved?

LOOKING AHEAD

The next chapter looks at the so-called Reagan Revolution, the attempt by a new president, with a different political philosophy, to restore national confidence and redirect the nation along more conservative lines.

1. How would President Reagan deal with the economic problems facing Americans in this era?
2. How would he differ from previous presidents in his dealings with the Soviet Union and in his personal view of international Communism and the Cold War?
3. Was it possible to narrow the social and cultural divisions that had plagued the United States in the 1960s and 1970s, or would they continue to widen over time?

RECOMMENDED READINGS

Carroll, Peter. *It Seemed Like Nothing Happened: America in the 1970s* (1982). A critical overview of American life in the new age of limits.

Chavez, Lydia. *The Color Bind* (1998). Analyzes the political battle surrounding affirmative action in California.

Hull, N. E. H., and Hoffer, Peter. *Roe v. Wade* (2001). Provides an excellent analysis of the abortion rights controversy in U.S. history.

Isaacson, Walter. *Kissinger* (1992). A comprehensive biography of the man who helped shape U.S. foreign policy in the 1970s and beyond.

Kutler, Stanley. *Abuse of Power: The New Nixon Tapes* (1997). The story of a president's demise told through the secret tapes that brought him down.

Lukas, J. Anthony. *Common Ground: A Turbulent Decade in the Lives of Three American Families* (1986). Examines the busing crisis in Boston from several perspectives.

Rudenstine, David. *The Day the Presses Stopped: A History of the Pentagon Papers Case* (1996). Looks at the legal and political issues surrounding the decade's most heralded First Amendment crisis.

Schoenwald, Jonathan. *A Time for Choosing* (2001). Describes the rise of modern conservatism leading to Ronald Reagan's election.

Shilts, Randy. *And the Band Played On* (1987). A superb account of the spreading AIDS epidemic in the homosexual community.

Wandersee, Winifred. *On the Move: American Women in the 1970s* (1988). Highlights the political struggle of women in this decade and the changes that occurred.

AMERICAN JOURNEY ONLINE AND ⵖ INFOTRAC COLLEGE EDITION

Visit the source collections at http://ajaccess.wadsworth.com and infotrac.thomsonlearning.com and use the Search function with the following key terms to explore documents, images, audio and video clips, articles, and commentary related to the material in this chapter.

Kent State

Watergate

Roe v. Wade

Gerald R. Ford

Jimmy Carter

Camp David Accords

La Raza Unida

Henry Kissinger

ONLINE PRIMARY SOURCES

Here are some examples of the many primary sources related to this chapter that you will find on the *American Passages* Web site: http://history.wadsworth.com/ayersbrief02.

The Evacuation of Saigon, 1975

Rejecting Gender-Free Equality, 1977

American Hostages in Iran, 1979

The site also offers self-quizzes, exercises, and many additional resources to help you study.

The Reagan-Bush Years

1981–1992

T HE PRESIDENCY OF **RONALD REAGAN** DEFINED THE DECADE OF THE 1980S. His election in 1980 brought to office the most conservative president since Herbert Hoover, and after two decades of "failed presidencies," his ability to serve for two consecutive presidential terms contributed to a mood of renewed optimism about the United States.

Ronald Reagan
The fortieth president of the United States, he represented the ascendancy of conservatism during the 1980s.

The actual achievements of Reagan and his successor, George H. W. Bush, remain in dispute. During these two administrations, the Cold War ended, the Berlin Wall toppled, and the Soviet Union collapsed. Yet victory in the Cold War did not result in a reduction of foreign policy issues and a safer world for the United States.

Although the economy boomed during the 1980s, the federal government's budget deficit increased dramatically. Rich Americans became richer, while the gulf between the affluent and the poor widened. Under the pressures of global economic change, U.S. businesses became more efficient and less unwieldy. The price, however, was a loss of jobs in many key industries as American workers faced the trauma of "downsizing." By the end of the 1980s, apprehension about the economic future of the average American had grown.

Uneasiness was particularly prevalent among young Americans. Would they enjoy a career or life as rewarding and prosperous as their parents and grandparents had experienced? Americans in their twenties doubted whether the "safety net" of Social Security and Medicare could survive when the baby boomers of the 1940s and 1950s began receiving their benefits after the year 2008. For all the ebullience and optimism of the Reagan-Bush period, critical social questions remained unanswered.

The Reagan Revolution

When Ronald Wilson Reagan took the oath as president of the United States on January 20, 1981, he was the oldest man to assume the nation's highest office. Born in Illinois in 1911, he had been an actor and television personality. Disillusioned with the political liberalism of his youth, he became a Republican. His good looks and pleasing personality made him extremely popular with conservative audiences. In 1966 friends pressed him to run for governor of California. He defeated the incumbent in a decisive victory. In 1968 he made an abortive run for the presidency, losing to Richard Nixon.

Reagan's record as governor of California was mixed. Instead of reducing spending and shrinking government as he had promised, taxes rose and the California government bureaucracy grew. Nevertheless, his blend of conservative rhetoric and a sunny disposition made him a natural advocate for what conservatives called "traditional values." As the nation became more conservative during the 1970s, Reagan's stock rose within the Republican party even though he lost the party's nomination in 1976 to President Gerald Ford.

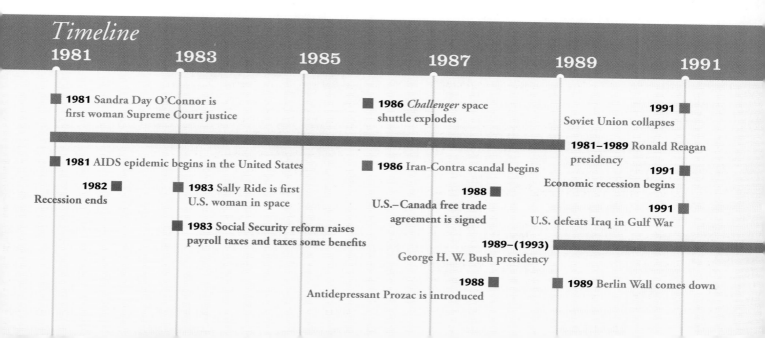

Timeline

| 1981 | 1983 | 1985 | 1987 | 1989 | 1991 |

1981 Sandra Day O'Connor is first woman Supreme Court justice

1986 *Challenger* space shuttle explodes

1991 Soviet Union collapses

1981–1989 Ronald Reagan presidency

1981 AIDS epidemic begins in the United States

1986 Iran-Contra scandal begins

1991 Economic recession begins

1982 Recession ends

1983 Sally Ride is first U.S. woman in space

1988 U.S.–Canada free trade agreement is signed

1991 U.S. defeats Iraq in Gulf War

1983 Social Security reform raises payroll taxes and taxes some benefits

1989–(1993) George H. W. Bush presidency

1988 Antidepressant Prozac is introduced

1989 Berlin Wall comes down

The problems of the Jimmy Carter administration gave Reagan his opportunity. He became the embodiment of the new national sentiment for lower taxes, restraints on government spending, and concern about inflation. At the same time, he promised increased spending on national defense and a stronger U.S. role overseas to meet the threat of Communism. As Americans faced spiraling inflation, rising interest rates, and gas lines at their service stations, their support for Jimmy Carter sagged.

Carter versus Reagan

The 1980 presidential election campaign took place in the shadow of the ongoing crisis involving the hostages who were being held in Iran. Nightly news broadcasts reminded audiences of how many days the hostages had been held in captivity. Initially the plight of the hostages helped Jimmy Carter fend off the challenge of Senator Edward M. Kennedy of Massachusetts for the Democratic presidential nomination. The failed military attempt to rescue the hostages in April 1980 undercut Carter's standing with the voters. Still, most Democrats believed that the president could defeat Reagan.

Reagan had emerged as the Republican front-runner after defeating Texan George Bush for the nomination. At the party's national convention he briefly considered asking Gerald Ford to be his running mate. After that initiative collapsed because Ford wanted a quasi-presidential role, Reagan invited Bush to run with him.

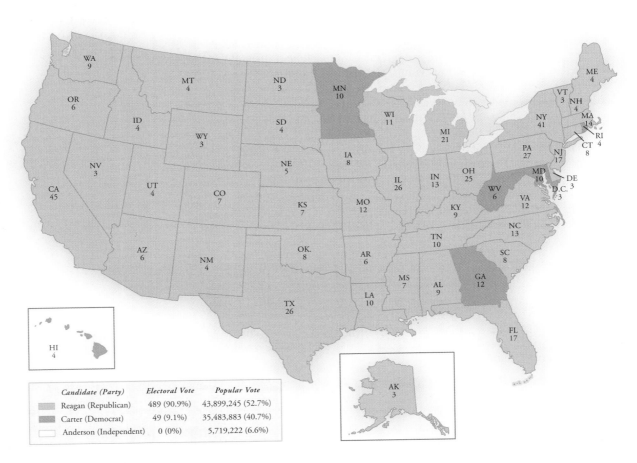

Candidate (Party)	Electoral Vote	Popular Vote
Reagan (Republican)	489 (90.9%)	43,899,245 (52.7%)
Carter (Democrat)	49 (9.1%)	35,483,883 (40.7%)
Anderson (Independent)	0 (0%)	5,719,222 (6.6%)

MAP 31.1 The Election of 1980

The election map reveals the repudiation of Jimmy Carter and his administration in 1980 and the swing to the right that put Ronald Reagan in the White House. Carter's economic record and the foreign policy problems of the late 1970s left him without an effective national political base.

"Are You Better Off?"

During the campaign, Reagan assailed Carter's record on the economy and national defense. The president fired back that Reagan was a dangerous and unreliable political extremist. The election came down to a televised debate between the two men in late October 1980. Polls indicated that the race was a dead heat. When Carter attacked Reagan's position on Medicare, the challenger responded with a wry remark: "There you go again," making Carter seem awkward and ill-informed. In winding up the debate, Reagan asked the American people "Are you better off?" than four years earlier. Poll results moved decisively toward Reagan.

Reagan and the Republicans won the election by a substantial margin in the popular vote: 44 million ballots for Reagan to 35 million for Carter. In the electoral college Reagan garnered 489 votes and Carter 49. The Republicans regained control of the Senate. Many wondered whether Reagan's victory signaled the arrival of a conservative coalition that would dominate national affairs for years to come.

The Rise of the Christian Right

A central element in Reagan's electoral victory was the votes of evangelical Christians. One manifestation of their political clout was the **Moral Majority,** an organization founded by the Reverend Jerry Falwell of Virginia in 1979. Moral Majority assailed "sinful" aspects of modern culture such as abortion, homosexuality, rock music, and drugs. It sought to have creationism rather than evolution taught in schools.

Throughout the 1980s evangelical Christianity permeated U.S. politics. On cable television, viewers tuned in to Pat Robertson's *700 Club* on the Christian Broadcasting Network. Other ministers such as Jim Bakker with his *PTL* ("Praise the Lord") program and the fiery evangelist Jimmy Swaggart commanded sizable audiences. Though both Bakker and Swaggart eventually ran afoul of the law for fraud (Bakker) and sexual misadventures (Swaggart), their message resonated in many areas of the nation. Ronald Reagan never implemented the evangelical agenda, but he gave it a sympathetic hearing.

The divisive issue of abortion helped fuel the rise of the Christian Right. Following the Supreme Court decision in *Roe v. Wade* (1973), the number of abortions in the United States stood at 1.5 million per year. Foes of abortion asserted that the unborn baby was a human being from the moment of conception and entitled to all the rights of a living person. To reduce the number of abortions and to overturn the *Roe* decision, the "right to life" forces, as they called themselves, pressured lawmakers to cut back on the right of abortion and to enact restrictive laws. The Hyde amendment, adopted in Congress in 1976, banned the use of Medicaid funds to pay for abortions to women on welfare.

The anti-abortion forces believed that more direct action was warranted. They conducted picketing and boycotts of abortion clinics in the 1980s. Their tactics became more violent as the decade progressed. Operation Rescue tried to prevent patients from entering abortion clinics. Other protesters turned to bombing buildings and assassinating doctors. The Republican party became largely anti-abortion in its policies and programs.

Reagan in Office

Reagan came to Washington determined to enact his conservative priorities. He set out his goals in a single sentence: "We must balance the budget, reduce tax rates, and restore our defenses."

Ronald Reagan brought striking political gifts to the White House. His long career in Hollywood had given him a skill in conveying his views that won him the title of **The Great Communicator.** His use of humor, especially when he stressed his own foibles, was deft; it reinforced his rapport with his fellow citizens. He exuded a degree of optimism about his country, sincerity about his positions, and confidence in the rightness of his views that made him a masterful politician.

Yet Reagan had significant weaknesses too. He knew very little about the actual operation of the federal government and read very few of the documents that crossed his desk. He did not inform the nation of the serious alternatives that had to be faced in reducing the deficits and curbing government spending.

Moral Majority
A political action group founded in 1979 and composed of conservative, fundamentalist Christians. Led by evangelist Rev. Jerry Falwell, the group played a significant role in the 1980 elections through its strong support of conservative candidates.

The Great Communicator
A nickname given to Ronald Reagan for his skill in conveying his views.

The Reagan Team

Part of the success that Reagan achieved during his first term came about because of the effective staff that managed his daily activities. His chief of staff was James Baker, a Texas politician. Baker proved to be an adroit player in the White House. Joining him were Michael Deaver, who directed media activities, and Edwin Meese—a longtime friend from California who tended to policy issues. These men "packaged" the president in settings that capitalized on his warm relationship with the American people. The gritty details of government went on out of the public's view.

Another important player in the Reagan presidency was his wife Nancy. Criticized for her opulent lifestyle during her early days as First Lady, she won over the Washington media with a deft blend of self-deprecating humor and commitment to a "Just Say No" campaign against drugs. She fretted about Reagan's place in history and urged the president privately to promote some degree of détente with the Soviet Union over nuclear weapons.

The Early Months

The situation that Ronald Reagan and the Republicans faced in the winter of 1981 seemed to warrant decisive action. The Republicans controlled the White House and the Senate, while Democrats remained the majority in the House of Representatives. The Reagan team believed that the nation was experiencing an economic crisis. In 1980 the inflation rate was over 12 percent, the unemployment rate was above 7 percent, and the prime interest rate had gone to almost 20 percent. The national debt had reached $908 billion. In Reagan's view, the responsibility for these ominous figures lay with the federal government.

To remedy the situation, the administration embraced a program that combined traditional Republican suspicion of government spending with an aggressive reduction in federal income taxes. The term "supply-side economics" became shorthand for what this program promised to do. The government should lower income and corporate tax rates to give private business and individual taxpayers more money to spend. The predicted surge in productive economic activity would result in an increase in tax revenues, which would prevent large budget deficits.

Defining the Reagan Presidency

In his first year Reagan benefited from an abundance of personal good fortune. He implemented his policy agenda as promised. The release of U.S. hostages in Iran on January 20, 1981, removed that troublesome issue from the public sphere. The president's confidence and self-assurance also drew a positive response from the American people. When Reagan was shot on March 30, 1981, the would-be assassin's bullet came closer to ending his life than the public knew. The president's courage and good humor in this moment of crisis increased his popularity.

The assassination attempt against Ronald Reagan on March 30, 1981, wounded the president more seriously than was revealed at the time. His optimism and high spirits in the face of his wounding added to his prestige. The picture shows an unidentified Secret Service agent yelling instructions after shots were fired.

A second event that raised Reagan even higher in the polls was his handling of a strike by the Professional Air Traffic Controllers Organization (PATCO). As government employees, the controllers could not legally strike, and the president fired them when they refused to heed a back-to-work order. The message for the nation was that the White House would be tough on organized labor.

The Economic Agenda

During the first half of 1981, the Reagan administration used its political muscle to enact its "economic recovery" program. A coalition of Republicans and "boll weevil Democrats" (southern and western conservatives) pushed through legislation that trimmed tax rates by 25 percent over three years. As the legislation went forward, a bidding war developed between the House Democratic leadership and the White House. Even more tax cuts for special interests were added.

In tandem with the tax measure, the administration sought budget cuts for a number of discretionary social programs. Although the budget act, passed in the House on June 25, 1981, promised future reductions in spending, during its first year it provided $16 billion in immediate cuts. That was $200 billion less than would have been required to achieve a real step toward a balanced budget.

The Limits of the Reagan Revolution

Two major policy commitments limited what the Reagan administration could accomplish. The president declined to make cuts in what he termed "the social safety net": Social Security, Medicare, veterans' benefits, Head Start, and school lunch programs. All of these spending policies had vocal and powerful supporters. The practical result was that almost half of the federal budget was placed beyond the reach of congressional budget-cutting efforts.

The other priority of the Reagan administration was a sharp increase in defense spending. Reagan believed that the nation's military establishment had been neglected during Carter's presidency. In 1979, however, the Democratic Congress and the administration had begun a long-range program to build up U.S. military power, and the Reagan White House expanded on that initiative. Under Reagan, the Pentagon budget rose to nearly $300 billion per year by 1985.

A Growing Deficit

The outcome of modest cuts in social programs and entitlements, sharp hikes in defense spending, and a reduction in tax rates was a growth in the government deficit to $128 billion by 1982. The ballooning federal deficits continued throughout the Reagan era, producing a surge in the national debt. The goal of a balanced budget in 1984 vanished quickly. The huge deficits drove economic policy for the decade that followed, and future generations were left with a massive debt to fund and pay off.

Reagan's Domestic Policies

As part of his response to a large, intrusive government, Reagan advocated an extensive program of deregulation of the private sector. The process of "getting government off the backs of the people," however, turned out to have significant consequences in banking and finance, telecommunications, and the environment.

The Reagan administration pursued a new course in environmental policy. Secretary of the Interior James G. Watt sought to open new areas for oil drilling, cut back on the acquisition of land for national parks, and put in place other bureaucrats eager to reduce environmental regulation. In late 1983 Watt left the administration under fire after commenting about an advisory panel that he had recently named: "We have every kind of mix you can have. I have a black, I have a woman, two Jews, and a cripple."

Table 31.1
Federal Government Deficits, 1980–1989 (in U.S. dollars)

Year	Deficit
1980	$73,808,000,000
1981	78,936,000,000
1982	127,940,000,000
1983	207,764,000,000
1984	185,324,000,000
1985	212,260,000,000
1986	221,140,000,000
1987	149,661,000,000
1988	155,151,000,000
1989	153,319,000,000

Source: *World Almanac, 1995*, p. 108.

The Savings and Loan Disaster

The most spectacular and disastrous example of deregulation occurred in 1982 when Congress and the White House agreed to lift restrictions from the savings and loan industry. During a time of high inflation and rising interest rates, savings and loan institutions, or "thrifts," had difficulty earning a profit because of the low rates of interest they were allowed by law to pay on their deposits. In 1980 Congress increased federal insurance coverage to $100,000 per account and allowed savings and loan companies to offer even higher interest rates. These measures did not, however, increase the savings and loan companies' profits on the money that they loaned. Partly in response to lobbying by the industry and the large campaign contributions that lawmakers received, Congress decided to deregulate the thrifts and allow them to invest in higher risk assets.

At the same time that lending practices were relaxed, the Reagan administration cut back on the number of banking and regulatory examiners. With federal deposit insurance guaranteeing that they would be bailed out, savings and loan operators plunged into ventures that were risky and often illegal. At first there seemed to be few problems, but by

1983 and 1984 troubling signs of weakness appeared in the banking and savings and loan businesses.

The Social Security Crisis

By the early 1980s Social Security had reached a funding crisis. During the 1970s Congress and the Nixon administration had established a system of cost-of-living-adjustments (COLAs) that raised benefits for Social Security recipients as the rate of inflation rose (known as indexing). Indexing of benefits caused the cost of Social Security to soar. But efforts to trim COLAs seemed futile because of the political fact that tinkering with Social Security benefits guaranteed electoral defeat for anyone who tried it.

President Reagan learned that lesson in the spring of 1981 when the administration proposed a cut in benefits for early retirees. When the initiative was announced, gleeful Democrats assailed it, and Republicans in Congress deserted Reagan. Social Security did not come up again until December 1981 when the president appointed a bipartisan panel to deal with long-range funding of the retirement program. The result was a 1983 compromise that raised payroll taxes to pay for Social Security, taxed some of the benefits of people over sixty-five who had high incomes, and put off providing for the long-term viability of the system. For the moment, the Social Security system seemed to be on solid ground once again.

Reagan and Foreign Policy: The First Phase

In foreign affairs, the new administration came into office with what seemed to be a clear, simple agenda. Reagan himself had little knowledge of foreign relations and was not curious about the subject. Secretary of State Alexander Haig sought to be the "vicar" of foreign policy, but he did not work well with the president's other advisors. Nor did Reagan make effective use of the National Security Council. Not until George Shultz became secretary of state in 1982 did some balance and stability characterize the administration's handling of foreign affairs.

Reagan operated from strong convictions about the relationship of the United States to its principal adversary. In 1983 he called the Soviet Union "an evil empire" and said that the Cold War was a struggle between "right and wrong and good and evil." In dealing with the Soviets, then, the president insisted arms agreements be based on the principle of "trust but verify." He was convinced that the United States could outspend the Soviet Union in an arms race. Faced with an aging and incompetent Soviet leadership between 1981 and 1985, the White House avoided any summit meetings during that period. As a result, Soviet-U.S. relations experienced a distinct chill during Reagan's first term.

This stern language did not rule out flexibility in some areas. Early in the new administration the president lifted the grain embargo that President Carter had established when the Soviet Union invaded Afghanistan in 1980. Reagan also reiterated his view that a nuclear war could not be won and should never be fought. Although the new White House team did not like the SALT II Treaty that Carter had negotiated, it largely observed the pact's provisions.

One area where the rivalry between the two superpowers flared up was Central America. The Reagan administration believed that the victory of the Sandinistas in Nicaragua in 1979 represented a serious threat to U.S. interests in the region. By late 1981 the United States was underwriting a rebellion against the Sandinista regime led by a faction called the **Contras.** Although President Reagan likened the anti-Sandinistas to the patriots of the American Revolution, in 1982 the Democratic House of Representatives adopted the Boland Amendment (named after Congressman Edward Boland of Massachusetts), which sought to block funds from being used to oust the Sandinistas.

Contras
A Nicaraguan military force trained and financed by the United States that opposed the socialist Nicaraguan government led by the Sandinista party.

The 1982 Elections

Reagan and his administration paid a political price for the policies of the first two years. A severe recession continued until almost the end of 1982. Although Reagan argued that the recession would soon end, the Republicans suffered a setback at the polls in the congressional elections. The Democrats gained twenty-seven seats in the House while the Republicans maintained their dominance in the Senate. Nevertheless, President Reagan again urged his fellow Republicans to "stay the course."

A Rebounding Economy and Foreign Policy Successes

Shortly after the election the economy picked up steam. As the recovery gained strength, so did Reagan and his party. Adding to the president's popularity was the U.S. invasion of the Caribbean island of Grenada in October 1983. Fearing that radicals close to Fidel Castro and Cuba were about to turn Grenada into a Soviet base, the administration launched a powerful invasion force that secured control of the island after a brief struggle.

In fact, the foreign policy scene was more complex than the victory in Grenada indicated. The war in Nicaragua was not going well for the Contras, and El Salvador was experiencing atrocities from right-wing death squads that murdered their opponents. In 1984 Congress adopted a second, more restrictive Boland Amendment to prevent the government from aiding the Contras.

In the Middle East Reagan's hopes of producing a lasting peace between Israel and its neighbors were also frustrated. The administration did not stop Israel from invading Lebanon in June 1982, and U.S. Marines were sent into the region as part of a multinational peacekeeping force. U.S. involvement in Lebanon's turbulent politics led to the death of 239 Marines when a terrorist bomb blew up a barracks in 1983. The Marines withdrew in early 1984, but the Reagan administration's diplomatic efforts in the region were unsuccessful.

Star Wars: The Strategic Defense Initiative

The most significant defense policy initiative of the first Reagan term came when the president announced in March 1983 what he called the **Strategic Defense Initiative (SDI).** Reagan envisioned a system of laser weapons, based in space, that would intercept and shoot down Soviet missiles before they could reach the United States. An appealing vision on the drawing board or in animated versions for television, SDI confronted immense technical problems that made it unlikely that it could be deployed for years. Critics promptly dubbed it "Star Wars" after the hit movie. For Reagan, the program represented an answer to the problem of relying on nuclear deterrence to stave off war between the superpowers. He pressed forward with SDI over the objections of his political opponents and the displeasure of the Soviet Union. Envisioned as a way to end the Cold War, the Strategic Defense Initiative complicated U.S.-Soviet relations during the last two years of Reagan's first term.

Strategic Defense Initiative (SDI)
A research and development program of the U.S. government tasked with developing a space-based system to defend the nation from attack by strategic ballistic missiles.

Social Tensions and Strains of the 1980s

The specter of nuclear war was not the only danger Americans faced in the early 1980s. In the early Reagan years Americans learned of a new and deadly disease. Scientists called it AIDS (acquired immune deficiency syndrome). The virus appeared in the United States first in 1981. It ravaged the immune system of its victims, and there was no known cure. Most of those infected were doomed to an inevitable and painful death.

The major process by which the virus spread within the population was through the exchange of bodily fluids. Mothers who were infected passed the condition on to their children; infected blood was transferred during transfusions. The most vulnerable groups were drug addicts, bisexuals, and homosexuals. During the first half of the decade, the spread of AIDS seemed to be confined to the homosexual community. Later, largely through sharing needles for drug injection and unsafe sexual practices, AIDS began to spread more rapidly among heterosexuals, especially in low-income communities.

The Intertwining of Technology and Culture

The sudden emergence of the AIDS epidemic was only one of a rash of new social and cultural developments that occurred during the early 1980s. The nation experienced the initial stages of a revolution in communications and culture that included the development of the personal computer and the ability of individuals to use the new technology to improve their lives. At the same time the spread of cable television and the emergence of alternatives to then major television networks allowed news and entertainment to be shared with ever-increasing speed. By the end of the 1980s, seeing movies at home on a video-cassette recorder (VCR) had become a major form of entertainment.

The Personal Computer

In 1981 International Business Machines (IBM) announced that it would market a computer for home use. Recognizing the potential impact of such a product, two young computer software writers proposed to develop the operating system for the new machine. Bill Gates and Paul Allen of Microsoft adapted an existing software program and transformed it into DOS (disk operating system), which ran the hardware created by IBM. Important changes followed throughout the decade, including the Lotus 1-2-3 spreadsheet program in 1982, Microsoft Windows in 1983, and the Apple Macintosh computer in 1984.

The computer revolution gathered momentum over the course of the 1980s. People found that they could publish books from their desktops, trace financial accounts, make travel reservations, and play a wide assortment of computer games. Growing out of the Advanced Research Projects Agency of the Pentagon was a network of computers founded in 1969. As computer users and researchers exchanged messages over this and other networks in the late 1970s and early 1980s, the National Science Foundation promoted the Internet as an overall network bulletin board. Usenet groups and e-mail became more common as the 1980s progressed.

The emergence of the personal computer transformed the U.S. economy in the 1980s. One of the most popular was the Macintosh, made by Apple Computer, shown here in its early version.

Courtesy of Apple Computer, Inc.

The Cable Generation

In 1981 a new network appeared on cable television aimed at a teenage audience. Music Television (MTV) presented round-the-clock videos of rock performers. At about the same time, Ted Turner launched the Cable News Network (CNN) and a related programming service, Headline News, which presented the news in half-hour segments twenty-four hours a day. As cable television expanded during the 1980s, the dominance of the three major broadcast networks (ABC, CBS, and NBC) gave way to a dizzying array of programming.

MTV offered the most intriguing cultural development of the period. Its audience was the middle- and upper-middle-class adolescent and preteen market for rock music. MTV featured major performers in video versions of their hits or potential hits mouthing (or "lip-synching") the words to a prerecorded soundtrack. So successful was MTV that in 1985 it spawned a second network, VideoHits1 (VH1), with a similar format.

Michael Jackson and Madonna: Media Stars of the 1980s

In December 1982 CBS Records released a new album by the twenty-four-year-old rock star Michael Jackson. At a time of lagging record sales for the industry as a whole, *Thriller* became a runaway hit, selling half a million copies a week. Then, in March 1983, Jackson gave a dazzling singing and dancing performance at the "Motown 25" reunion program that further accelerated sales of *Thriller*. Jackson's videos of hits from the album broke down the racial barriers that had kept black artists off the MTV and VH1 networks. Jackson became the most celebrated male artist of the decade, and his live appearances attained legendary status among the young people of the era.

Although her popularity did not reach the heights attained by Michael Jackson, Madonna (Madonna Louise Veronica Ciccone) combined records, video, cable television, and movie roles to achieve superstar status as a pop icon. Her first album, *Borderline*, was widely promoted through MTV, and in 1984 she used that venue to introduce two major hits: "Like a Virgin" and "Material Girl." She delved into controversial matters such as pregnancy among teenagers (in "Papa Don't Preach," 1986) and pushed the limits of sexual explicitness on television in subsequent songs and videos.

Like Jackson, Madonna capitalized on her fame to achieve larger-than-life status around the world. In a conservative era, sexual ambiguity and a lack of restraint commanded big returns from teenage consumers. By the end of the decade, conservatives clamored for record companies to engage in self-censorship of artists like Madonna.

The American Family in the 1980s

In 1981 the number of divorces stood at nearly 1.2 million annually, the highest rate ever, and the number of births to unmarried women rose dramatically during the 1970s. With these developments came a marked increase in single-parent families, which rose from 3.8 million in 1970 to 10.5 million by 1992. The impact of this trend was especially evident among African Americans: by the end of the 1980s more than 60 percent of all African American families were single-parent families, many living in poverty. In 1983 the Bureau of the Census reported that thirteen million children under age six were growing up in poverty.

One major area of concern for families was the state of the public schools. A series of high-profile national studies suggested that American education was "a disaster area." Students did not receive instruction in the skills needed if they were to succeed in a complex and competitive world. Parents complained that their children had to do little homework, were graded too easily, and often graduated without marketable skills. Conservatives blamed this state of affairs on government policies that "threw money" at schools. Liberals countered that government must spend even more to address the problems of the public schools. By 1983 another national survey, titled *A Nation at Risk,* said that the country faced dire consequences if public education did not undergo sweeping reform.

As families felt the effects of these economic and social changes, Americans responded with contradictory approaches. On one hand, sexual mores became more tolerant. On the other, efforts to recapture "traditional family values" animated many groups on the conservative end of the political spectrum. The boundaries that had governed the depiction of sexual behavior in the movies and on television relaxed in significant ways during the 1980s. On prime-time television viewers could hear language and see sexual intimacy depicted in a fashion that would have been unthinkable a few years earlier.

At the same time that some cultural taboos were relaxed, conservative groups struck back against what they saw as excessive permissiveness and laxity. The Coalition for Better Television, an offshoot of the Moral Majority, pressured the networks to promote programming of "that which lifts and inspires, not that which degrades and exploits." The group's organizers threatened nationwide boycotts of advertisers who did not follow its guidelines. The coalition attracted great media attention during the early part of the decade and was a source of concern for some sponsors of prime-time shows. When network profits remained high, the shows offered on television showed few effects of the boycott drive.

The 1984 Presidential Election

At the beginning of 1984 Reagan's popularity rating stood at 55 percent, and the electoral map seemed to favor the Republicans. The president had made substantial gains among what were known as "Reagan Democrats," people who shared the president's social conservatism. The Democrats experienced staggering problems in finding a plausible candidate to run against him.

In the initial stages the front-runner seemed to be former vice president **Walter Mondale** of Minnesota. Mondale had strong ties to the traditional elements of the Democratic party—labor, women, and environmentalists. He was not a good public speaker, yet it was widely expected that he would win the nomination.

Two challengers emerged to stop Mondale's bid for the nomination. The first was the Reverend **Jesse Jackson,** who combined powerful oratory with espousal of radical causes. He became the first credible African American candidate to seek the nomination of a major party, but he proved unable to reach beyond black voters in the primaries. The other Democratic hopeful was Senator Gary Hart of Colorado, who styled himself a "new Democrat,"

Walter Mondale
Vice president of the United States under Jimmy Carter, he earlier served as a U.S. senator from Minnesota and was the unsuccessful 1984 Democratic nominee for president.

Jesse Jackson
A Baptist minister and civil rights leader, he directed national antidiscrimination efforts in the mid-1960s and 1970s. His concern for the oppressed and his dramatic oratory attracted a large grassroots constituency.

which meant that he did not endorse the use of government power to regulate society to the extent that Mondale did. Hart won a surprise victory in the New Hampshire primary, but the front-runner countered with effective television ads and secured a majority of the convention delegates before the Democrats gathered in San Francisco in July.

Mondale's chances of winning the election against Reagan were slim at best. Under those circumstances, the choice of the vice presidential nominee became largely symbolic. Nominating Jesse Jackson would have been politically unwise. Gary Hart lost out because of his personal qualities, including rumors about his marital infidelities. Mondale came under intense pressure to select a woman as his running mate, and in the week before the convention opened he agreed to the selection of Representative Geraldine Ferraro of New York.

Ferraro was an intelligent, thoughtful politician, but her family's financial problems became a source of controversy when she refused to release her tax returns in a timely manner. For a campaign that needed help in the South and West, moreover, Ferraro did little.

The Republicans had all the best of the 1984 campaign. President Reagan's popularity crested during the celebrations of the fortieth anniversary of the D-Day invasions in June, and his appearance at the 1984 Olympic Games in Los Angeles identified him with an event in which U.S. athletes dominated the competition. In a time of patriotic enthusiasm, Reagan seemed more in tune with the optimism and confidence of the moment.

An earnest, dull man, Mondale addressed the serious issues that the country confronted. In the face of the huge budget deficits of the Reagan years, he warned that tax increases were necessary to pay for government programs that Americans wanted. For the Republicans, the chance to denounce the Democrats as big-spenders beholden to special interest groups was one that their skilled political strategists exploited to the full.

The only stumble for Reagan came in the first of two televised debates. He showed his age and lack of a clear grasp of many issues. Two weeks later, however, Reagan rebounded.

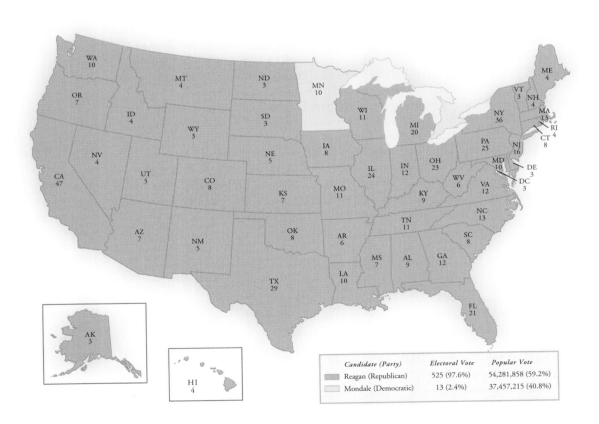

Candidate (Party)	Electoral Vote	Popular Vote
Reagan (Republican)	525 (97.6%)	54,281,858 (59.2%)
Mondale (Democratic)	13 (2.4%)	37,457,215 (40.8%)

MAP 31.2 The Election of 1984

In the 1984 race between Ronald Reagan and Walter Mondale, Reagan won reelection in a landslide victory where the incumbent carried forty-nine states, losing only Minnesota and the District of Columbia.

When a questioner asked him about his age, the president replied that he would not allow age to be an issue. "I am not going to exploit, for political purposes, my opponent's youth and inexperience," he said.

Reagan carried forty-nine of the fifty states; Mondale narrowly won his home state and swept the District of Columbia. The president collected 59 percent of the popular vote. The Republicans retained control of the Senate; the Democrats lost seats in the House but maintained their dominance of that chamber.

The 1984 election was largely an election about whether the American people liked Ronald Reagan's presidency. The Republicans offered no blueprint to guide the country. As the second term would demonstrate, the Reagan Revolution, as its partisans called it, had little that was new to offer the American people.

Reagan's Second Term

Changes in the president's staff marked the transition from one administration to the other. The White House chief of staff, James Baker, agreed to exchange jobs with the secretary of the treasury, Donald Regan. Regan, however, lacked political skill and did not know how to showcase the president's better qualities to advantage. Meanwhile, Reagan's media advisor Michael Deaver, and other key operatives, departed. The efficiency and smoothness of the White House eroded rapidly.

Tax Reform and Deficits

Despite Reagan's pledge to balance the federal budget by 1984, the combinations of tax cuts and increased spending on both defense and discretionary programs widened the budget deficit. Federal receipts reached $666 billion by 1984, but outlays stood at almost $852 billion, with a resulting deficit of $186 billion.

The administration did not have a strategy to trim the deficit, but the Senate devised a plan for doing so. Created by a new Republican senator, Phil Gramm of Texas, the measure required that federal spending programs be reduced by specified amounts or face across-the-board percentage reductions. Sponsored by Senator Warren Rudman of New Hampshire, one of Gramm's Republican colleagues, and Senator Ernest F. "Fritz" Hollings, a South Carolina Democrat, the scheme quickly became known as "Gramm-Rudman-Hollings." Congress embraced it enthusiastically.

The AIDS Crisis: The Second Phase

In October 1985 the public's perception of the threat of AIDS intensified when movie star Rock Hudson died of the disease. News of his illness, his long concealed homosexuality, and his death increased awareness of the dimensions of this mounting public health problem. More than 6,700 other Americans succumbed to AIDS in 1985, and the death toll shot up to 15,504 annually two years later.

The administration's response to AIDS reflected the division between those who wanted to deal with the virus as a public health issue and those who viewed it in ideological terms. In October Surgeon General C. Everett Koop issued a report that recommended three steps to control AIDS: "One, abstinence; two, monogamy; three, condoms." On the conservative side of the political spectrum, the mention of condoms aroused intense opposition that blocked further initiatives during the remainder of the president's second term.

Table 31.2
New AIDS Cases in the United States, 1988–1993

1988	30,648
1989	33,576
1990	41,642
1991	43,660
1992	45,883
1993	102,780

Source: *World Almanac, 1997,* p. 975.

The 1986 Tax Reform Battle

The administration did achieve one major domestic policy success. In 1986 Congress made significant reforms in the nation's tax laws. The reforms, originating with Democratic Senator Bill Bradley of New Jersey, were taken up by the Treasury Department early in Reagan's second term. The tax bill was passed by the House in late 1985 and went to the Senate. By April 1986 the Senate Finance Committee seemed likely to kill the bill, but at that point the chair of the committee, Senator Robert Packwood of Oregon, devised a bill with a much lower top rate for all taxpayers and an end to many time-honored deductions. The proposed law was quickly approved by the Finance Committee and sailed through the

Ronald Reagan's Second Inaugural Address, January 1985

This excerpt from Ronald Reagan's second inaugural address conveys the themes of optimism and smaller government that he advanced throughout the 1980s.

Four years ago I spoke to you of a new beginning, and we have accomplished that. But in another sense, our new beginning is a continuation of that beginning created two centuries ago when, for the first time in history, government, the people said, was not our master. It is our servant; its only power that which we, the people, allow it to have.

That system has never failed us. But for a time we failed the system. We asked things of government that government was not equipped to give. We yielded authority to the national government that properly belonged to states or to local governments or to the people themselves. We allowed taxes and inflation to rob us of our earnings and savings and watched the great industrial machine that had made us the most productive people on earth slow down and the number of unemployed increase.

By 1980 we knew it was time to renew our faith, to strive with all our strength toward the ultimate in individual freedom consistent with an orderly society.

We believed then and now there are no limits to growth and human progress when men and women are free to follow their dreams. And we were right. And we were right to believe that. Tax rates have been reduced, inflation cut dramatically and more people are employed than ever before in our history.

We are creating a nation once again vibrant, robust and alive. But there are many mountains yet to climb. We will not rest until every American enjoys the fullness of freedom, dignity, and opportunity as our birthright. It is our birthright as citizens of this great republic.

And if we meet this challenge, these will be years when Americans have restored their confidence and tradition of progress; when our values of faith, family, work, and neighborhood were restated for a modern age; when our economy was finally freed from government's grip; when we made sincere efforts at meaningful arms reductions by rebuilding our defenses, our economy, and developing new technologies helped preserve peace in a troubled world; when America courageously supported the struggle for individual liberty, self-government, and free enterprise throughout the world and turned the tide of history away from totalitarian darkness and into the warm sunlight of human freedom.

My fellow citizens, our nation is poised for greatness. We must do what we know is right and do it with all our might. Let history say of us, these were golden years—when the American Revolution was reborn, when freedom gained new life and America reached for her best.

Questions to Consider

1. What is President Reagan's judgment on the accomplishments of his first term? How well had he succeeded in implementing the promises of his campaign for the presidency?

2. What foreign policy initiatives of Reagan's second term are foreshadowed in his inaugural address in 1985?

3. Did the second Reagan term live up to the expectations of his January 1985 speech?

4. Have the 1980s become in historical memory "golden years" as President Reagan forecast?

Explore additional primary sources related to this chapter on the *American Passages* Web site: http://history.wadsworth.com/ayersbrief02.

Source: Official Website of the Ronald Reagan Presidential Library. Available at http://www.reagan.utexas.edu.

Senate by a vote of 97 to 3 in June 1986. After a difficult passage through a Senate–House conference committee, the tax reform law was approved and signed in September 1986. The bill simplified and reduced taxes, and it remained in effect for a decade before pressure for further tax changes emerged once again.

The Age of the Yuppy

The economic boom of the mid-1980s fostered an atmosphere of money-making and social acquisitiveness. Top executives received staggering annual salaries. Wall Street traders

Michael Millken and Ivan Boesky promoted lucrative corporate mergers through high-risk securities known as "junk bonds." Wall Street experienced a "merger mania" in which corporations acquired competitors through hostile takeovers. Manhattan real estate mogul Donald Trump became a celebrity. Business majors increased dramatically in American universities.

The youth culture reflected the spirit of materialism that permeated the 1980s. In the centers of technological change on the East and West Coasts, the press proclaimed the emergence of the "young urban professionals," dubbed "yuppies" by the media. These individuals had cosmetic surgery to retain a young look, took expensive vacations, and purchased costly sports equipment. Self-indulgence seemed to be a hallmark of young people.

The *Challenger* Disaster

A sobering moment in the frenetic decade came on January 28, 1986, when the space shuttle *Challenger* exploded. All seven crew members, one of them a schoolteacher (Christa McAuliffe) from New Hampshire, perished in the disaster. The event happened live before a shocked audience that watched the spacecraft lift off normally and then explode a few seconds later. Cable television replayed the events, including the faces of the schoolteacher's parents, over and over. A shocked nation grieved. For many young people, the accident became the most memorable event of their generation.

An official investigation revealed that the space program had grown overconfident about its procedures. Slipshod technology had contributed to the tragedy, but the incident did not undermine the public's faith in scientific progress and material abundance. By the end of the 1980s the shuttle program had resumed its regular series of flights.

The explosion of the *Challenger* space shuttle on January 28, 1986, was one of the dramatic moments of the decade. Seven astronauts perished when the rocket's O-rings failed and caused the shuttle to blow up.

AP/Wide World

Foreign Policy in the Second Reagan Term

Soviet-U.S. relations entered a new phase when **Mikhail Gorbachev** came to power in Moscow. Gorbachev pursued a more conciliatory policy toward the West while trying to implement a restructuring of Soviet society that came to be known as *perestroika*. He announced reductions in the deployment of Soviet missiles, and said that the Soviet Union wanted to be part of Europe, not an opposing ideology. He and Reagan agreed to hold a summit conference in Geneva in November 1985. Although not much was achieved at the meeting, the two leaders discovered that they liked each other. When they announced their joint communiqué, Reagan commented to Gorbachev: "I bet the hard-liners in both our countries are bleeding when we shake hands." The Russian leader agreed.

The two world leaders met again at Reykjavik, Iceland, in October 1986. There they attempted to outdo each other in calling for reductions in the number of nuclear weapons. Again there were no substantive results, but the experience indicated that a genuine arms agreement might be possible. Both the president and Mrs. Reagan hoped to crown his second term with an arms control treaty that would establish his historical reputation as a peacemaker. Before that goal could be achieved, however, the Reagan administration found itself caught in a major foreign policy scandal.

Mikhail Gorbachev
General secretary of the Soviet Communist party in the mid-1980s and president of the USSR from 1989 to 1991, he ushered in an era of unprecedented *glasnost* (openness) and *perestroika* (restructuring) and won the Nobel Peace Prize in 1990.

The Iran-Contra Affair

In November 1986 the American public first learned that the United States had sold arms to the Islamic regime in Iran that had sponsored terrorist activities against the United States for most of the 1980s. Within a month the revelation came that money obtained from the arms sales had been used to support the Nicaraguan Contras in violation of the Boland Amendments. The Reagan administration had deceived Congress, broken the law, and lied to the American people. A flood of news stories soon indicated the dimensions of what had occurred.

In 1985 members of the National Security Council (NSC) became convinced that the release of U.S. hostages held in Lebanon could be secured if the United States sold arms to Iran. National Security Advisor Robert McFarlane believed that "moderates" in Iran would use their political influence to free hostages if U.S. weapons were forthcoming. The Iranians could use the weapons in their bitter war with Iraq. Since disclosure of this new policy would have outraged Americans and provoked congressional investigations, the president's approval of arm sales was kept secret. The actual shipment of weapons to Iran was carried out by Israel with the United States replacing the transferred munitions. Unfortunately, the Iranians accepted the anti-tank and anti-aircraft missiles but released only three hostages.

In the course of the arms deals, a member of the NSC staff, Marine Colonel **Oliver North,** proposed that profits from the sale of weapons to Iran be used to support the Contras in Nicaragua. Although North maintained that his actions did not break the law, they were in clear violation of congressional directives barring the provision of aid to the Contras. Moreover, the use of funds without legislative approval was against the law. In addition, a privately financed, unaccountable, and clandestine foreign policy operation was well outside constitutional limits.

News of the scandal began to leak out in October 1986 when the Sandinistas shot down one of the planes taking weapons to the Contras. A captured crew member revealed the Central Intelligence Agency's links to the operation. Early in November news of the arms-for-hostages deal surfaced in the Middle East. Soon the press was in full pursuit of the sensational story.

For several weeks the Reagan White House tried to mislead Congress and the public about what had taken place. On November 13, 1986, the president told the American people: "We did not—repeat, did not—trade weapons or anything else for hostages, nor will we." He maintained this position even though it conflicted with the known facts. The public did not believe his assertions.

In late November conclusive proof of the diversion of money to the Contras came out. The president fired Oliver North and accepted the resignation of John Poindexter, McFarlane's successor as national security advisor and one of the central figures in the clandestine operation that the press was now calling the **Iran-Contra scandal.**

Three separate probes of the scandal began in early 1987. Reagan appointed the Tower Commission, named after its chair, former Senator John Tower of Texas, to look into the White House's role in the scheme. The House and Senate created a joint committee to examine the policy and its execution. The lawmakers soon decided to grant many of those individuals involved immunity in exchange for their testimony. That decision hampered the task of the special counsel, Lawrence Walsh, who was named to consider whether specific laws had been violated.

Although everyone concerned professed a desire to get to the bottom of the scandal, there was little inclination, even among Democrats, to see Ronald Reagan impeached for his role in it. Many Washington insiders questioned whether it would be good for the country to have another president driven from office in disgrace. As a result, much was revealed about the Iran-Contra affair, but most of the high-level participants were not subjected to serious legal penalties.

The Tower Commission, for its part, chastised the president for an inept "management style" that allowed his subordinates to lead him into the scandal. On March 4, 1987, Reagan said that he accepted the commission's findings while reiterating that he had not intended to trade arms for hostages.

For others involved in the scandal, the hearings brought a surge of notoriety that made North a subject of national debate. When North testified before the House-Senate Committee during the summer of 1987 in his Marine uniform, he proved a compelling presence on television. He exaggerated his closeness to Reagan and made some inaccurate or misleading statements. But his skill before the cameras deflected some of the blame from Reagan.

North and the other participants were indicted by Lawrence Walsh and convicted for some of their misdeeds, including perjury, mishandling government moneys, and other crimes. Because Congress had granted them immunity, however, higher courts overturned

Oliver North
A member of the NSC staff and a Marine colonel, he was a central figure in the Iran-Contra scandal.

Iran-Contra scandal
A major scandal of the second Reagan term that involved shipping arms to Iran and diverting money from the sale of these weapons to the Contra rebels in Nicaragua.

their convictions on the ground that the trials had been influenced by what had been heard in the congressional proceedings. The legal aspects of the Iran-Contra scandal dribbled away into inconclusive results during the early years of George Bush's presidency.

The Iran-Contra affair demonstrated the weaknesses of Reagan's handling of foreign policy. Reagan had failed to ask hard questions about the arms-for-hostages proposals, and he had allowed erratic subordinates like North to mishandle the nation's foreign policy. The outcome discredited the U.S. stance on terrorism and indicated that Reagan's command of his own government was weak and uncertain.

Remaking the Supreme Court: The Nomination of Robert Bork

One of the Reagan administration's major goals was to reshape the federal judiciary along conservative lines. The White House succeeded in doing so in the lower courts because, during eight years in office, Reagan nominated more than half the members of the federal judiciary.

The main focus of the effort to reshape the judiciary was the United States Supreme Court. In July 1981 Reagan named the first woman to be appointed to the Court, **Sandra Day O'Connor** of Arizona. The president did not have another opportunity to appoint a justice until Chief Justice Warren Burger resigned in 1986. Reagan elevated Justice William Rehnquist to replace Burger and named Antonin Scalia, a federal appeals court judge, to take the seat that Rehnquist vacated. Scalia was the first Italian American appointed to the court, and his intellectual brilliance appealed to conservatives.

In June 1987 Justice Lewis Powell resigned, and President Reagan named Robert Bork, another federal appeals court jurist to replace him. During a long career as a legal writer before becoming a judge, Bork had taken many controversial stands on divisive issues. He had opposed the decision in *Roe v. Wade* (1973) that established a woman's right to have an abortion, and he had questioned other decisions in the areas of privacy and civil rights. The nomination galvanized Democrats in the Senate, the civil rights movement, and women's groups in a campaign to defeat Bork.

The struggle that followed ultimately led to the rejection of Bork's nomination. The judge's admirers claimed that his enemies had distorted his record, but his foes were able to depict Bork as a conservative ideologue. The jurist's performance before the Senate Judiciary Committee failed to counteract the negative public opinion that his opposition had generated. In October 1987 Bork was defeated when fifty-eight senators voted against him. The president then named a law professor, Douglas Ginsburg, to the Court, but he had to withdraw when it was learned that he had used marijuana in law school. Finally Reagan nominated Judge Anthony Kennedy, whom the Senate confirmed in February 1988.

The battle over Bork's nomination put a decisive end to any illusions that Supreme Court nominations were not considered political events. Conservatives vowed to take revenge against the nominees of future Democratic presidents by "Borking" those selections.

Reagan and Gorbachev: The Road to Understanding

Although the Iran-Contra affair reduced Reagan's political standing, the resulting changes in his administration prepared the way for genuine foreign policy achievements. When Donald Regan left the government, the president named former Senator Howard Baker as his chief of staff, brought in Frank Carlucci as secretary of defense, and selected Lieutenant General **Colin Powell** to be the national security advisor. All three were prepared to take advantage of improved relations with the Soviet Union.

By late 1987 negotiators for the two sides had agreed to remove from Europe intermediate-range missiles with nuclear warheads. Gorbachev came to Washington in December 1987 for the formal signing of the pact. Seven months later Reagan went to Moscow to meet Gorbachev. Tensions between the two countries eased as the Soviets pulled out of Afghanistan. The improvement in the superpower rivalry helped Reagan regain some of his popularity with the American people.

Sandra Day O'Connor
Appointed during the presidency of Ronald Reagan, she was the first woman justice on the Supreme Court.

Colin Powell
He served as chairman of the Joint Chiefs of Staff from 1989 to 1996 and was influential in planning U.S. strategy during the Persian Gulf War.

George H. W. Bush won the Republican and the presidential election in 1988 on his promise to continue the legacy of Ronald Reagan and his pledge of "no new taxes."

The 1988 Presidential Election

With Ronald Reagan ineligible to seek a third term, the Republican party had to pick a successor to carry its banner against the Democrats. Vice President George Bush soon emerged as the front-runner. Bush had been a loyal subordinate, and Reagan proclaimed that he had given Bush an unprecedented role in the administration. So deferential had Bush been, however, that there were stories in the press that he had become too subservient.

George Bush came from an aristocratic New England background but had moved to Texas after combat service in the Navy during World War II. He became active in Republican politics and ran unsuccessfully for the U.S. Senate in 1964. Elected to the House of Representatives in 1966, he stayed for two terms and made another losing bid for the Senate in 1970. Service in the Ford administration as envoy to China and director of the Central Intelligence Agency added to his impressive résumé of government posts. He ran against Reagan for the Republican nomination in 1980 and became the vice presidential choice despite doubts among conservatives about his allegiance to their cause.

Bush's main rival for the Republican nomination was Robert Dole of Kansas, the Republican minority leader in the Senate. Dole defeated Bush in the Iowa caucuses and seemed to be on the verge of victory as the New Hampshire primary neared. With the help of Governor John Sununu, however, Bush made a dramatic comeback to win in New Hampshire and establish a momentum that carried him to the nomination.

At the Republican convention in New Orleans, Bush made two important decisions. For his running mate, he selected Senator J. Danforth Quayle of Indiana. Handsome and young, Quayle was generally regarded as a lightweight by his Senate colleagues, but he provided a contrast to Bush's age and experience. Quayle's candidacy got off to a shaky start when it was revealed that he had entered the Indiana National Guard at a time when enlistment there precluded active service in the Vietnam War.

Bush's other major decision involved the issue of deficits and taxes. In his acceptance speech, he predicted that Democrats in Congress would pressure him to raise taxes. He promised to reject all such proposals. "Read my lips," he said, "No new taxes!" Repeated and emphasized throughout the campaign, this pledge became identified with Bush as a solemn promise to the electorate.

The Democratic Choice

The Democrats approached the prospect of running against Bush with much eagerness. The prospective front-runner for the nomination was Senator Gary Hart, but his candidacy collapsed when it was revealed that his reputation for marital infidelity and sexual adventures was well deserved. Jesse Jackson ran again, but his strength remained concentrated among black voters. Out of the field of other candidates, Massachusetts Governor Michael Dukakis emerged as the best-financed and best-organized contender. He defeated Jackson in a series of primaries in the spring and came to the Democratic convention with the nomination virtually locked up.

Dukakis emphasized his family's Greek immigrant background and stressed his success in stimulating the Massachusetts economy during the 1980s. Democrats paid less attention to his tepid personality and lackluster abilities as a campaigner. At the convention, he selected Senator Lloyd M. Bentsen of Texas as his running mate.

The Campaign

The campaign that followed was a nasty one. The Republicans raised questions about Dukakis, the most penetrating of which had to do with prison furloughs that Massachusetts law granted to jailed criminals. In one case, a black convict named William "Willie" Horton who had been released on furlough had then fled the state and committed a rape in another state. The Republicans and their surrogates used the Horton case in powerful television commercials to demonstrate Dukakis's ineptitude as governor, but the racial dimensions of the incident were also evident.

The presidential debates produced two memorable images. In the debate between Bentsen and Quayle, the Republican compared his legislative record in the Senate with that of John F. Kennedy. Bentsen countered: "Senator, I served with Jack Kennedy, I knew

Jack Kennedy. Jack Kennedy was a friend of mine. Senator, you are no Jack Kennedy." When Bush and Dukakis debated for a second time, the Democratic nominee, an opponent of capital punishment, was asked how he would view the death penalty if his wife had been raped and murdered. Dukakis gave an unemotional answer that killed his remaining chances of winning the election.

Bush won the election with 53 percent of the vote to 46 percent for Dukakis. The margin in the electoral college was 426 to 112. Bush's victory was decisive, but the Democrats had done better than in any election since 1976. They retained control of both houses of Congress and had learned some valuable lessons about waging a competitive presidential election.

The Reagan Legacy

Even before Ronald Reagan left office on January 20, 1989, the debate about the impact of his presidency was under way. His partisans proclaimed the "Reagan Revolution" had transformed American attitudes toward government. They also assigned him a major role in winning the Cold War. Critics pointed to the huge federal budget deficits that persisted throughout the 1980s and blamed Reagan for policies that had widened the gap between rich and poor.

The impact of the 1980s on American life also became a source of contention. Conservatives applauded the economic growth that had occurred. Entrepreneurs and Wall Street traders such as Donald Trump, Michael Millken, and Ivan Boesky became cultural heroes for a time. When Boesky and Millken were convicted of insider trading, critics saw their sentences as retribution for the excesses of the period.

Both Reagan's admirers and his enemies overstated his influence on American history. By the mid-1990s the nation still seemed to want a smaller government in theory and more government services in practice. Reagan had halted the expansion of the welfare state, but that would probably have occurred in any event by the 1980s. Reagan certainly deserved some credit for the decline of the Soviet Union, though that nation's internal difficulties were more significant than the actions of the United States. Reagan's most enduring legacy was the federal budget deficit. Although Congress appropriated the money, he set national priorities, and his spending for defense went well beyond affordable levels.

Kinder, Gentler George H. W. Bush

George H. W. Bush came into office pledging to carry on Reagan's policies, but promising to do so in a more humane and judicious manner. He spoke of a "kinder, gentler" nation and government. He urged Americans to engage in charitable endeavors that would become "a thousand points of light" to inspire others to good works. Bush had no grand vision of what his administration should accomplish in the domestic arena.

Foreign affairs interested the new president much more than did shaping health care, environmental, or social policy. He had an effective foreign policy team. His secretary of state, James A. Baker, was a close friend and an adroit power broker; the national security advisor, Brent Scowcroft, and the chair of the Joint Chiefs of Staff, General Colin Powell, executed the president's policies with skill and efficiency. The collapse of Communism in 1989–1990, the challenge of Iraqi expansionism in the Middle East, and the shaping of a new role for the United States gave the Bush administration's foreign policy makers much to do.

The first half of the Bush administration went very well. The president approached his job by engaging in a frenzy of activity. His press conferences demonstrated his command of information in a way that Reagan never displayed. The public became used to seeing Bush jogging, entertaining numerous visitors to the White House, and rushing around the country from one event to another.

As time passed, however, questions arose about the purpose behind all this frenetic exertion. Bush spoke of the need to set larger goals for his presidency. He called it, in the abrupt shorthand that he often employed, "the vision thing." The phrase came into general use in discussions of whether Bush wanted to accomplish anything as president or simply wished to occupy the nation's highest office.

George H. W. Bush
The forty-first president of the United States, he was in office when the Soviet Union collapsed.

Bush's Domestic Policy

The president and his chief of staff, John Sununu, had no intention of breaking new ground in domestic affairs. They wanted to achieve whatever they could without violating the campaign pledge of "no new taxes." Much to the dismay of Republican conservatives, Bush went along with Democratic legislation such as the Clean Air Act and the Americans with Disabilities Act, which involved a growth in the federal bureaucracy and expanded regulations. Any legislation that he did not like, he vetoed. During the first three years of his presidency, Congress failed to override any of Bush's twenty-eight vetoes.

Bush's relations with Congress were not always successful. At the beginning of his administration he named former Senator John Tower to be secretary of defense. After a bitter struggle focusing on Tower's problems with alcoholism and other personal indiscretions, the Senate rejected its former colleague. To replace Tower, Bush picked Representative Richard Cheney.

On some domestic issues, Bush favored exhortation over government programs. He promised to be the "education president" but left most of the responsibility for changes in the system to the states and localities. The "war on drugs" was renewed, with emphasis on stopping the inflow of narcotics to the United States rather than reducing the demand for them among the population. An overall decline in drug use enabled the administration to claim victory for its strategy.

By 1989, however, the Bush administration had to deal with another major domestic issue. The deregulated savings and loan industry had a major collapse that left the taxpayers with a $500 billion cost to bail out depositors for the failed institutions. Congress established the Resolution Trust Corporation to sell off the assets of the failed banks and savings and loans and obtain as much money as possible from their sale.

The Continuing AIDS Crisis

Both funding for research on AIDS and public awareness of the disease increased during the Bush years. Congress created the National Commission on AIDS in 1989, and federal government funds for treatment and research rose to more than $2 billion by 1992. Still, the number of new cases continued to increase, reaching 45,603 in 1992 and 83,814 a year later. The announcement in 1991 that basketball star Earvin "Magic" Johnson had the HIV virus that causes AIDS shocked the public. However, opinions regarding what to do about the epidemic remained polarized. AIDS activists wanted more money for research and greater cultural tolerance for those afflicted with the disease. Conservatives such as Senator Jesse Helms of North Carolina contended that most AIDS victims were homosexuals who had brought their condition upon themselves through their own behavior. After some initial sympathy toward AIDS patients, the Bush administration's attitude cooled as the 1992 election approached.

Foreign Policy Successes, 1989–1990

At the end of 1988 Gorbachev had told the United Nations that the nations of Eastern Europe were free to determine their own destiny without Soviet interference. During 1989, the old order in Eastern Europe crumbled. Poland held free elections; Hungary opened its borders; and East Germany eased the barriers to travel to West Germany. By the end of 1989 the Cold War seemed to be over. In Nicaragua voters ousted the unpopular Sandinista government in 1990.

The trend in favor of the United States continued into 1990 as Gorbachev renounced the Communist party's monopoly over political power in February. The White House faced hard choices about which leader to support as rivals to Gorbachev emerged during 1990, particularly the new president of the Russian Republic, Boris Yeltsin.

One country where the administration's foreign policy encountered difficulty was China. Student protests during the spring of 1989 led to a brutal crackdown on demonstrators in Beijing's **Tiananmen Square.** The spectacle of students being killed and wounded produced an outcry in the United States. However, Bush believed that it was important to maintain good relations with the Chinese leaders, so the administration's response to the events of June 1989 was muted and cautious.

Tiananmen Square
Adjacent to the Forbidden City in Beijing, China, this large public square was the site of many festivals, rallies, and demonstrations. During a student demonstration there in 1989, Chinese troops fired on the demonstrators, killing an estimated two thousand or more.

Closer to home, however, the Bush administration took more decisive action toward Panama's strongman ruler Manuel Noriega. Corrupt and deeply involved in the international narcotics trade, Noriega had been on the U.S. payroll for many years as an informant on drug matters. In 1989 his dictatorial regime refused to adhere to the results of national elections. The White House sent additional troops to Panama and called for an uprising against Noriega.

In late December the United States launched an invasion that quickly overcame the Panamanian army. Noriega eluded capture for a few embarrassing days until he sought refuge in a Vatican Embassy. In early 1990 he surrendered to the United States and in 1992 was tried and convicted of drug trafficking in a federal court in Florida. The episode raised Bush's standings in the polls. It did not, however, slow the drug trade in Panama.

The End of No New Taxes

In the spring of 1990 President Bush made a fatal political blunder. His 1988 pledge of "no new taxes" had become ingrained in the minds of the American people. Conservative Republicans expected him to adhere to the commitment in spite of the desire of the Democratic majorities in Congress to raise taxes. In 1989 the president worked out a strategy with Congress that provided for budget savings. With the budget deficit growing, however, the Democrats did not see how spending cuts alone could reduce it. Having suffered setbacks in the 1988 elections, the Democrats were not going to propose tax increases unless President Bush agreed to them. Meanwhile, the Gramm-Rudman-Hollings law provided for substantial reductions in spending by the fall of 1990 if the president and Congress did not reach a viable budget agreement.

By early 1990 there were signs that the economy had begun to slow down. With a weakening economy, a budget stalemate posed dangers for both parties, and neither side really wanted to face the implications of the cuts that Gramm-Rudman-Hollings contemplated.

Negotiations between the president and congressional Democrats continued until, on June 26, 1990, Bush announced that dealing with the deficit problem might have to include "tax revenue increases." Republicans reacted with fury. Although the reversal of "no new taxes" may have made economic and political sense to those close to Bush, the president had squandered much of the trust that the American people had placed in him in 1988.

Iraq and Kuwait: Storm in the Desert

Foreign policy events soon overshadowed the political fallout from the broken tax pledge. On August 2, 1990, the Iraqi Army of Saddam Hussein invaded the oil-rich kingdom of Kuwait. Suddenly the oil supplies of the United States and the industrialized world faced a new and ominous threat from the Iraqi dictator. Bush's response and the war that followed temporarily restored his popularity.

During the 1980s, Iran and Iraq had fought a brutal and costly war. The United States had not taken sides in the conflict, hoping that the two countries, both of which were hostile toward the United States, would exhaust each other. Once the war ended, however, the Bush administration had pursued a conciliatory policy, allowing Iraq to purchase heavy machinery and paying little attention to its efforts to build a nuclear bomb and acquire weapons of mass destruction. During the spring of 1990, the American ambassador in Baghdad had informed Hussein that the United States took "no position" on Iraq's dispute with Kuwait.

When Iraqi military units rolled into Kuwait, Bush decided that the takeover must be resisted. Heavy economic sanctions were put into effect. More important, in Operation Desert Shield the United States deployed U.S. troops in Saudi Arabia to deter Hussein from attacking that country. The end of the Cold War meant that the United States had the support of the Soviet Union in isolating Iraq from the rest of the world and therefore had much greater freedom of action than would have been the case even two years earlier. Bush displayed impressive diplomatic skill in assembling and holding together an international coalition to oppose Iraq.

The Budget Battle

On the domestic side, the budget issue remained unsettled until the president and the Democratic leadership worked out a deficit reduction plan in September 1990. Republicans in

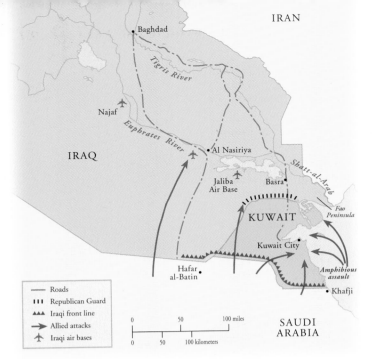

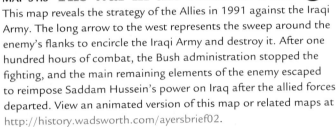

MAP 31.3 The War in the Persian Gulf

This map reveals the strategy of the Allies in 1991 against the Iraqi Army. The long arrow to the west represents the sweep around the enemy's flanks to encircle the Iraqi Army and destroy it. After one hundred hours of combat, the Bush administration stopped the fighting, and the main remaining elements of the enemy escaped to reimpose Saddam Hussein's power on Iraq after the allied forces departed. View an animated version of this map or related maps at http://history.wadsworth.com/ayersbrief02.

Burned out Iraqi vehicles mark the "Highway of Death" in the waning days of the Gulf War.

the House of Representatives lobbied against the plan, which was defeated a few days later. Intense negotiations between the White House and Capitol Hill produced a deficit reduction agreement at the end of October that involved both tax increases and spending cuts. The Republicans went into the fall elections in a divided and unhappy mood. Their losses were modest—eight seats in the House and one in the Senate—but the conservative faithful continued to smolder with anger against Bush.

War in the Persian Gulf

After the elections Bush stepped up the pressure on Saddam Hussein to leave Kuwait. The United Nations Security Council agreed to the use of armed force against Iraq if Kuwait had not been freed by January 15, 1991. As the diplomatic options faded, Congress insisted on a vote over whether U.S. troops should go into combat in the Middle East. The result on January 12, 1991, was a victory for the president, although the margin in the Senate was only five votes. Five days later, Operation Desert Storm began.

The military outcome was never in doubt. In a demoralizing series of strikes, the allied coalition bombed the Iraqi Army into submission. The most that Hussein could do in retaliation was to send Scud missiles against Israel in hopes of fracturing the coalition. The Iraqi ruler also set Kuwaiti oil wells on fire and dumped oil into the Persian Gulf. None of these actions, however, posed a serious threat to the buildup of the allied armies.

The second phase of Desert Storm began on February 24, 1991, with a huge assault of U.S. and allied troops against the weakened Iraqi defenders. A series of encircling maneuvers ousted the Iraqis from Kuwait with huge losses in troops and equipment. Within one hundred hours, the ground phase of the war ended in a complete victory on the battlefield for the anti-Iraq forces. President Bush decided not to press for Hussein's removal from power, a decision that was later criticized.

Victory in the Gulf War sent Bush's popularity soaring to record levels; he received approval ratings of nearly 90 percent in some polls. The chairman of the Joint Chiefs of Staff, General Colin Powell, became a nationally respected military figure. Bush's reelection seemed assured. Major figures in the Democratic party decided not to challenge Bush in 1992.

Yet the political dividends from Bush's military triumph did not last long. Hussein bounced back from his defeat to reassert his power in Iraq and, despite United Nations inspections, rebuilt his nation's economy and war-making capacity.

Other foreign policy problems troubled the White House during 1991. In the Soviet Union Gorbachev faced a coup designed to bring hard-liners back into power. A rival of Gorbachev, Boris Yeltsin, led demonstrations against the plotters in Moscow and their coup, which then failed. Thereupon the Soviet Union collapsed and its component nations broke apart. Yeltsin consolidated his power with promises of economic reform and put himself in a position to succeed Gorbachev. Champions of Ronald Reagan said that his policies had spent the Soviet Union into the ground. More significant in the breakup of the Soviet empire were the accumulated wounds of an inefficient economy, a bloated bureaucracy, and an inept leadership.

Another area of turmoil was Yugoslavia, where the Communist government had long suppressed historic rivalries among Serbs, Croats, Bosnians, and other nationalities. Tensions between Christians and Muslims added to the dangerous potential of the situation. Civil war broke out in 1991 as Serbs battled Croats, Slovenes, and Bosnians. The Bush administration recognized Bosnia as an independent nation and thus became involved in a Balkan struggle whose problems spilled over into the next presidency.

The Battle over the Thomas Nomination

Like Ronald Reagan, George Bush wanted to continue the conservative trend that the Supreme Court had been following since the 1970s. When the liberal Justice William Brennan retired in 1990, the president named David Souter of New Hampshire to succeed him. Confirmation by the Senate came easily.

The next nomination, in 1991, led to one of the most sensational confirmation struggles in the nation's history. When Justice Thurgood Marshall retired, the president selected **Clarence Thomas,** a Reagan appointee to the federal bench who had long opposed such programs as affirmative action. Thomas's qualifications for the Supreme Court were modest, but he seemed to be on the way to easy confirmation until it was revealed that a black law professor at the University of Oklahoma, **Anita Hill,** had accused Thomas of sexual harassment when she had worked for him at the Equal Employment Opportunity Commission during the early 1980s. Her charges led to dramatic hearings in which Hill laid out her allegations and Thomas denied them as a national television audience watched in fascination. In the end, the Senate voted 52 to 48 to confirm Thomas.

A Sense of Unease

When the controversy over the Thomas nomination ended, many observers believed that George Bush could expect easy reelection in 1992. No strong Democratic candidates had emerged to challenge him. Bush had the support of most Republicans, although there were rumblings of opposition among conservatives. It seemed probable, however, that Bush would be renominated and would then defeat whomever the Democrats put up against him.

When the Republicans made such optimistic assumptions, they failed to notice that the American people were anxious and fearful as the 1990s began. Major corporations had cut their payrolls to reduce costs in what became known as "downsizing." Other businesses moved production facilities overseas in search of lower labor costs. The economy created millions of jobs, but many of them were low-paying service jobs. Multinational corporations became a focus of voter anger, as did the specter of immigrants taking jobs away from native-born Americans.

In 1990 the press began commenting on "Generation X," the generation of Americans under age twenty-five, which accounted for some seventy-five million people. Generation Xers were derided as a "generation of self-centered know-nothings" in search of personal gratification and quick riches. The offspring of broken marriages and single-parent homes, they had raised themselves while their parents were at work, spent endless time before television sets and computer games, and were sexually active at ever-younger ages.

As 1992 began, there was a growing sense that the nation faced serious choices. One law student in North Carolina said, "For the first time I feel that a group of Americans is going to have to deal with the idea that they're not going to live as well as their parents." That fear of diminished possibility and reduced opportunity would seem odd later in the 1990s, but it was a genuine concern in the popular mind as the 1992 election approached.

Clarence Thomas
A Supreme Court justice appointed by President George H. W. Bush in 1991 whose confirmation became controversial due to allegations of sexual misconduct made against him.

Anita Hill
She brought charges of sexual misconduct against Clarence Thomas and herself became a very polarizing figure as a result.

Summary

One of the most hotly debated foreign policy issues of the 1980s had to do with the Reagan administration's support for the rebels against the Sandinista government in Nicaragua. The "Contras," as they were known, are shown here training in a remote area of their country.

©Bettmann/Reuters/CORBIS

Cold War Victories and New Challenges

For Americans the dozen years from 1981 to 1993 began in economic difficulties and ended the same way. In between, the nation experienced a revival of prosperity and a restoration of confidence that made for an ebullient period of expansion and optimism. The Republicans benefited politically from the good times, and Ronald Reagan enjoyed two terms with popularity and high approval ratings. These accomplishments came at some cost. The nation ran up large budget deficits that seemed likely to continue into the indefinite future. The problem of reconciling an expansion of government services, which most Americans wanted, with the smaller federal presence that the voters also like was never really attempted in these years.

Social and technological change dominated the period. Computers began to become a major presence in the economy and the culture. The first tentative steps toward the Internet began and laid the groundwork for its expansion during the 1990s. In popular culture, the increasing emphasis on sexuality and violence in the mass media ran up against the efforts of cultural conservatives to reinforce traditional family values. A more secular nation valued religious expression even as it applauded performers who emphasized sensuality in their appearances before large audiences.

The end of the Cold War seemed to promise a bright future for Americans as the United States emerged as the only superpower in the world. Prospects of a "peace dividend" glittered for a brief time amid the budgetary crises.

Yet the moment of optimism was very brief. In 1991 the Iraqi invasion of Kuwait and the ensuing Gulf War plunged the nation once again into the turbulent politics of the

AP/Wide World

The Iran-Contra scandal produced a congressional investigation at which the star witness was Marine Colonel Oliver North. His appearance in his winter uniform in midsummer and his aggressive tactics toward his questioners made him a national hero to conservatives.

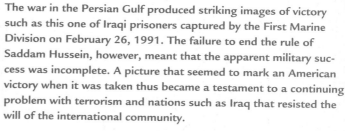

The war in the Persian Gulf produced striking images of victory such as this one of Iraqi prisoners captured by the First Marine Division on February 26, 1991. The failure to end the rule of Saddam Hussein, however, meant that the apparent military success was incomplete. A picture that seemed to mark an American victory when it was taken thus became a testament to a continuing problem with terrorism and nations such as Iraq that resisted the will of the international community.

A search for Soviet-U.S. understanding was a notable feature of Ronald Reagan's second term. His friendship with the Soviet leader Mikhail Gorbachev resulted in a marked lessening of Cold War tensions as the decade of the 1980s ended.

Middle East. Military victory did not oust Saddam Hussein, and the problem of his regime festered for the next decade. The Arab-Israeli conflict was still unresolved, and that dilemma led to other consequences. Little known to policy makers was the emergence of a shadowy terrorist group with the name al Qaeda, led by Osama bin Laden, that sought the ouster of the United States and the West from Muslim lands. As the country mastered the international environment of nation states, it was coming under assault from groups who moved from country to country with a radical anti-Western ideology. What this meant for international stability would not become apparent for another ten years.

In the 1980s and early 1990s, the United States saw old problems recede and newer ones not yet appear at the forefront of the national consciousness. The period now

President George H. W. Bush meets with General Colin Powell, chairman of the Joint Chiefs of Staff, and General Norman Schwartzkopf in the wake of the allied victory in the Gulf War.

seems more distant from the current predicament of the nation than mere chronology would suggest. Authors at the time wrote of "The End of History" as if Americans had escaped the boundaries of the past and could now make the world anew. As the dire events of the 1990s and early 2000s proved, human history would never be that simple or easily controlled. The age of Ronald Reagan and George H.W. Bush is likely to be seen as a kind of protracted pause before Americans turned to encounter the challenges and dangers of a world that terrorism had changed forever.

Making Connections Across Chapters

LOOKING BACK

Chapter 31 examines the impact of the Ronald Reagan and George H. W. Bush administrations in the context of the 1980s and early 1990s. A key point of the chapter is the nation's rightward shift in political terms and the consequences of that change for foreign policy and domestic priorities.

1. What problems confronted the new Reagan administration in 1981 as a result of the events of the Carter administration?
2. What was the international position of the United States relative to the Soviet Union in the early 1980s?
3. In what ways did Ronald Reagan change the role of the president? Which of his achievements have proved the most enduring and also the most controversial?
4. What were the most significant cultural and economic changes Americans experienced in the 1980s and early 1990s?
5. Was the first Iraq war as much of a victory as it was portrayed at the time?

LOOKING AHEAD

The concluding chapter of the book considers the administrations of Bill Clinton and George W. Bush. The problem of terrorism, which was barely on the national agenda as this chapter comes to an end, will arise as a central concern of domestic and foreign policy as we assess the current situation in the United States.

1. What problems did the first Bush administration leave on the national agenda for the Clinton presidency?
2. What economic choices did the people of the United States have to make in the mid-1990s as a result of the actions taken between 1981 and 1993?
3. Why were policy makers, the media, and the people generally slow to grasp the dangers of terrorism?
4. How did the legacy of Ronald Reagan affect the politics of the 1990s?

RECOMMENDED READINGS

Cannon, Lou. *President Reagan: The Role of a Lifetime* (1991). A biography of the president by a reporter who covered his entire career.

Draper, Theodore. *A Very Thin Line: The Iran-Contra Affair* (1991). A thorough review of the scandal and its effects.

Fitzgerald, Frances. *Way Out There in the Blue: Reagan, Star Wars, and the End of the Cold War* (2000). A critical look at the Strategic Defense Initiative.

Greene, John Robert. *The Presidency of George Bush* (2000). Covers the George H. W. Bush presidency thoroughly.

Johnson, Haynes. *Sleepwalking through History: America in the Reagan Years* (1991). Supplies the perspective of a Washington reporter on the 1980s.

Johnson, Haynes. *Divided We Fall: Gambling with History in the Nineties* (1994). Covers the Reagan-Bush transition and carries the story on to the beginning of the Clinton presidency.

Mervin, David. *George Bush and the Guardianship Presidency* (1998). Provides the perspective of a British scholar on the George H. W. Bush administration.

Parmet, Herbert. *George Bush: The Life of a Lone Star Yankee* (1997). The best biography of the forty-first president.

Pemberton, William E. *Exit with Honor: The Life and Presidency of Ronald Reagan* (1997). A sound one-volume study of the man and his impact on the nation.

Sloan, John W. *The Reagan Effect: Economics and Presidential Leadership* (2000). Looks at President Reagan's handling of the economy.

AMERICAN JOURNEY ONLINE AND INFOTRAC COLLEGE EDITION

Visit the source collections at http://ajaccess.wadsworth.com and infotrac.thomsonlearning.com and use the Search function with the following key terms to explore documents, images, audio and video clips, articles, and commentary related to the material in this chapter.

Ronald Reagan

Strategic Defense Initiative

Iran-Contra

Oliver North

Sandra Day O'Connor

Mikhail Gorbachev

George H. W. Bush

Tiananmen Square

Clarence Thomas

Anita Hill

ONLINE PRIMARY SOURCES

Here are some examples of the many primary sources related to this chapter that you will find on the *American Passages* Web site: http://history.wadsworth.com/ayersbrief02.

The Evil Empire, 1983

Rally for Gay Rights, 1984

George Bush on the Persian Gulf War, 1991

The site also offers self-quizzes, exercises, and many additional resources to help you study.

CHAPTER 32

From Prosperity to the Challenge of Terrorism

1992 – 2005

I N THE 1992 PRESIDENTIAL CONTEST, **WILLIAM JEFFERSON ("BILL") CLINTON** OF Arkansas defeated incumbent George H. W. Bush and billionaire independent candidate **Ross Perot** in a campaign that saw Americans campaigning and voting in greater numbers than had occurred in decades. Clinton's victory began a turbulent eight years. The new president stumbled during his first year in office, and in 1994 the Republicans regained control of both houses of Congress for the first time in four decades. Clinton rebounded in 1996 and became the first Democrat since Franklin D. Roosevelt in 1936 to be reelected to a second term.

Since the Republicans retained control of Congress, the nation lived through four more years of divided government during Clinton's second term. During 1997, the nation experienced a booming economy and a calm international scene. Personal scandals once again threatened Clinton's presidency in early 1999.

The Clinton years also witnessed continued debates within American society about the direction of the nation. Controversies about illegal and legal immigration affected politics, education, and the economy. Related to the diversifying population were arguments about multicultural values and the extent to which they should be pursued. The issue of race remained unresolved and potentially devastating. The 1990s began with the voters in a restless mood, and the decade came to an end with the future direction of the nation still in doubt.

William Jefferson "Bill" Clinton
The forty-second president of the United States.

Ross Perot
A businessman, he first came to national attention during the Iran hostage crisis when he funded an operation that rescued two of his employees from an Iranian prison. In 1992 he emerged as an independent candidate for president, expressing serious concern over the national debt.

An Angry Nation: 1992

The onset of the 1992 presidential election found Americans fretful and anxious. The economy had slipped into a recession by mid-1991 with unemployment rising, consumer confidence waning, and corporations laying off large numbers of employees. Outside Washington, unhappiness intensified about how officials in Congress and the White House conducted themselves. Speaker of the House of Representatives James Wright (D-Texas) had resigned under an ethical cloud in 1989 because he had accepted money from lobbyists and special interest groups. Other lawmakers had abused the procedures of the House bank to write checks for which there were not sufficient funds in their accounts. Campaign finance reform stalled as members continued to accept large contributions from corporations, labor unions, and special interest groups with a stake in the outcome of legislation. Voter anger surged during 1991.

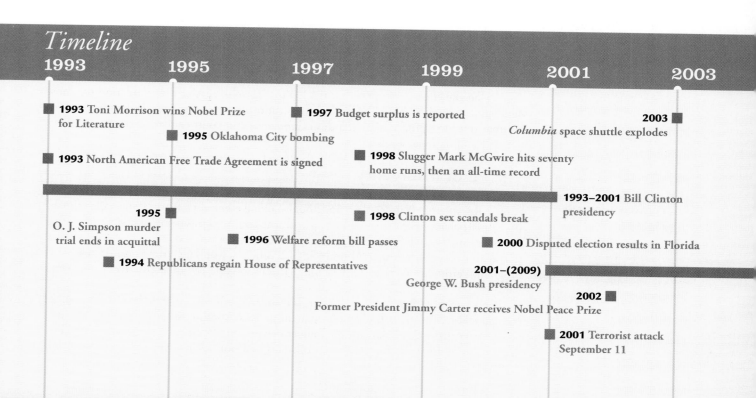

Timeline

1993   1995   1997   1999   2001   2003

1993 Toni Morrison wins Nobel Prize for Literature

1995 Oklahoma City bombing

1993 North American Free Trade Agreement is signed

1997 Budget surplus is reported

2003 *Columbia* space shuttle explodes

1998 Slugger Mark McGwire hits seventy home runs, then an all-time record

1993–2001 Bill Clinton presidency

1995 O. J. Simpson murder trial ends in acquittal

1998 Clinton sex scandals break

1996 Welfare reform bill passes

2000 Disputed election results in Florida

1994 Republicans regain House of Representatives

2001–(2009) George W. Bush presidency

Former President Jimmy Carter receives Nobel Peace Prize

2002

2001 Terrorist attack September 11

The Embattled Bush Presidency

Political pundits expected George H. W. Bush to win the presidency again. His success in the Gulf War seemed to assure his reelection. Still, the volatile nature of public opinion at the start of 1992 indicated that even Bush would not have an easy road back to the White House. The president seemed to many Americans to have little awareness of their problems and hopes.

President Bush soon had a challenger for the Republican nomination. Patrick J. Buchanan, a conservative commentator on cable television and former aide to Richard Nixon and Ronald Reagan, criticized the president for making the 1990 budget deal. The two men fought through the Republican primaries with Bush winning all of the contests. Still, the results showed that more than a quarter of the Republicans did not like Bush.

Among the Democrats, however, the major stars remained on the sidelines. New York Governor Mario Cuomo decided not to run as did Senator Lloyd Bentsen of Texas. Two other contenders, former Senator Paul Tsongas of Massachusetts and former Governor Jerry Brown of California, lacked a broad national base. Instead, Arkansas Governor William Jefferson ("Bill") Clinton built up a strong lead in delegate votes.

A New Democrat or "Slick Willie"?

From the outset Clinton aroused conflicting passions among Democrats. He was a young, attractive southern governor who campaigned as a "New Democrat" with a strong civil rights record. He had a solid record of supporting education and economic growth in Arkansas. On the negative side, however, critics charged that he had cheated on his wife Hillary Rodham Clinton with numerous women. During the Vietnam War, which he had opposed, he received special treatment to avoid the draft. There were also whispers about his business dealings, especially investments in a land development called **Whitewater.** An Arkansas columnist dubbed him "Slick Willie," and the tag stuck.

Whitewater
The popular name for a failed Arkansas real estate venture by the Whitewater Development Corporation in which then Governor Bill Clinton and his wife, Hillary, were partners.

Rodney King
The victim of a violent beating by Los Angeles police that was caught on videotape and became the central event of the 1992 riots.

Riots in Los Angeles

The tensions in the nation over racial issues burst into view in late April in Los Angeles. A year earlier policemen in that city had beaten a black motorist named **Rodney King** after stopping him for a traffic violation. The clubbing of King had been caught on videotape. After a lengthy trial, a white jury acquitted the four white officers. South Central Los Angeles, a black area, exploded into racial rioting. President Bush responded to the outbreak in a halting and indecisive manner.

The events in Los Angeles set off a national debate about race relations as they related to issues of crime, police brutality, and justice in the United States. Conservatives charged that the outbreaks of violence demonstrated the bankruptcy of the "Great Society" programs of the 1960s. Liberals responded that the nation had never committed itself in any serious way to alleviating racial strife. Attention focused on the policy of "affirmative action." Had the effort to assist minorities led to a form of reverse discrimination that now disadvantaged innocent white males? In California and elsewhere unhappiness with affirmative action produced referendum campaigns and court challenges to the policy on the state and national levels.

The Perot Insurgency

During the spring of 1992, the national spotlight turned to a Texas computer billionaire named Ross Perot. Plain-spoken and tough-talking, the feisty Perot argued that professional politicians lacked the will to deal with the country's problems. Faced with a losing football team, he said, "the best approach would be to get a new coach, a new quarterback, start with basics, clean it up." Announcing his candidacy on Larry King's call-in television program, Perot stirred enthusiasm among citizens looking for an alternative to Bush and Clinton.

Perot benefited from a grassroots movement that put his name on the ballot in all of the states. He soon led Bush and Clinton in the polls. Without specifying just what he would do, he promised to grapple with the budget deficit and clean up Washington. As the media investigated his previous record in business and politics, evidence of erratic and silly behavior surfaced. He monitored the private lives of his employees, and some called him "Inspector Perot." His poll numbers sank. Just before the Democratic National Convention, Perot withdrew from the race.

The 1992 Election Campaign

Bill Clinton received an electoral boost when Perot left the race, and the Arkansas governor swept the Democratic nomination. He selected Senator Albert Gore of Tennessee as his running mate. Although the presence of two southerners on the national ticket defied political wisdom, the Democratic team seemed youthful and energetic. A bus tour of the heartland of the country after the national convention attracted much favorable publicity.

The GOP delegates nominated Bush and Vice President Quayle amid an atmosphere in which the conservative social agenda dominated. In a fiery speech, Patrick Buchanan declared a cultural war to reclaim America from liberals, immigrants, and homosexuals. Much of the rhetoric from the podium focused on attacking Hillary Clinton and her alleged disregard for family values in her legal writings about children's rights. The spectacle added to Clinton's support, especially with women voters in the nation's suburbs.

In October 1992 Ross Perot changed his mind and reentered the presidential race. The three candidates then debated the issues before large national television audiences. Perot did not regain the levels of support that he had enjoyed in the spring, yet he retained a large and enthusiastic following. Bush closed the gap somewhat during the final weeks of the campaign, but the Perot candidacy split the Republican base in many states. The result was a Clinton-Gore victory. Clinton received 44,908,254 popular votes and 370 electoral ballots to Bush's 39,102,343 votes and 168 electoral votes. Perot made the best popular showing of any third party candidate in U.S. history with 19,741,065 votes, but he won no electoral votes. The Democrats continued their control of Congress, but the Republicans gained one Senate seat and picked up fourteen members in the House.

The Clinton Presidency: The First Two Years

As one of his first announced priorities, the president-elect indicated that he intended to lift the longstanding ban against declared homosexuals serving in the armed forces. After much debate within the military, the Clinton administration adopted a "Don't Ask, Don't Tell" approach in which gay personnel would not be asked about their sexual orientation and should not be openly homosexual. This stance contradicted Clinton's election appeal as a moderate rather than a liberal Democrat, and the religious right began an assault on the president and his wife that would continue throughout the next four years. After he was inaugurated, an armed confrontation between agents of the Bureau of Alcohol, Tobacco, and Firearms and members of the **Branch Davidian** religious sect outside Waco, Texas, in April 1993 led to the fiery deaths of many of the Davidians. Opponents of gun control and the federal government contended that the Clinton administration envisioned dictatorial rule. That fear on the far right further fed discontent with the new president.

Branch Davidians
A religious sect involved in a siege by government agents in Waco, Texas, in April 1993 that ended in deadly violence.

Clinton's Domestic Agenda

During his first two years, Bill Clinton achieved several domestic objectives at a high political cost. With the barest of voting margins in both the House and Senate, he secured adoption of an economic package that combined tax increases and spending cuts to lower the deficit for 1993 to $255 billion and for 1994 to $203 billion. Republicans depicted the president as returning to a traditional Democratic strategy of raising taxes and predicted economic calamity ahead. Clinton responded that the burden of higher levies fell only on the most wealthy Americans. Although the economy remained strong and the nation was prosperous throughout 1993 and 1994, the Republicans won the political argument.

Clinton pursued the cause of freer world trade when he advocated passage of the North American Free Trade Agreement (NAFTA), which cleared Congress in late 1993. The trade agreement split the Democrats, and approval came with the help of Republican

votes. In late 1994 the White House also secured congressional endorsement of the General Agreement on Tariffs and Trade (GATT) in a lame-duck session of the Democratic Congress. Again, Republican votes were central to this administration victory.

Reforming Health Care

The major goal of the new administration was reform of the nation's system of health care. In a dramatic expansion of the responsibilities for First Ladies, Clinton asked his wife to head the task force to prepare a health care plan within one hundred days. Working throughout 1993, Hillary Clinton's planners produced a health care blueprint in September. It envisioned health alliances to emphasize managed care, asked Americans to pay more to consult private physicians, and expanded coverage to include all citizens.

The plan soon became the target of attacks from Republicans and the insurance industry as too bureaucratic, complex, and costly. Despite the intense lobbying efforts that Mrs. Clinton expended, the "Clinton Health Plan," as it was known, had few friends in Congress. Republicans denied that any serious health care reform was needed and refused to present alternatives of their own. The drumbeat of opposition from the insurance industry took its toll on public opinion. By 1994 the health care issue had become a major liability for the Clinton White House.

Clinton's Political Troubles

Despite his domestic accomplishments, President Clinton's popular approval ratings remained low. From the political right, the president and his wife stirred dislike that bordered on outright hatred. Republicans charged that the Clintons were socialists bent on entrenching homosexuals, bureaucrats, and atheists in power in Washington. When an aide to the president, Vincent Foster, committed suicide during the summer of 1993, right-wing talk show hosts circulated wild and unfounded rumors that Foster had been murdered at the instructions of the president and his wife.

More serious were the charges of financial impropriety and ethical lapses that dogged the Clintons from their years in Arkansas. Investments that they had made in an Arkansas real estate venture on the Whitewater River became entangled with the failed savings and loan firm run by business associates of the Clintons, James and Susan McDougal. Federal regulators grew interested in these transactions, and in 1993 press reports disclosed that the Clintons could be named as potential witnesses and even targets of an investigation. Charges soon surfaced that an effort at a cover-up had been mounted from the White House. The all-purpose label for these and other related "scandals" was "Whitewater."

The charges against the Clintons led to the appointment of an independent counsel or special prosecutor in 1994. The first counsel was a Republican named Robert Fiske. When he concluded that Vincent Foster's death was a suicide, angry conservatives had him replaced with another counsel, **Kenneth Starr,** a former federal judge and solicitor general during the Bush administration. Starr's probe explored the Arkansas connections of the Clintons in a number of areas.

Kenneth Starr
Special prosecutor appointed to investigate the Whitewater affair. He expanded his investigation into other matters and eventually sent a report to the House of Representatives alleging that there were grounds for impeaching Clinton for lying under oath, obstruction of justice, abuse of power, and other offenses.

Personally embarrassing to President Clinton were allegations that he had sexually harassed an Arkansas state employee named Paula Corbin Jones in 1991. Jones filed a civil rights lawsuit in the spring of 1994 in which she claimed that then Governor Clinton had made unwanted sexual advances in a hotel room. The president's lawyers attempted to have the suit delayed until after the end of his administration. The issue of the president's right to have the lawsuit deferred until after he left office did not reach the Supreme Court until early 1997.

Clinton and the World

Bill Clinton came into office with his mind concentrated on domestic issues, and, as a result, his foreign policy got off to a shaky start. He faced a complex set of circumstances in the world in early 1993. The United States was heavily involved in a number of places around the globe—Haiti, Bosnia, and Somalia—but the previous administration had not linked these commitments to any kind of coherent structure.

Clinton's first year produced a number of foreign policy problems and disasters. In October 1993 eighteen U.S. servicemen died in a raid in Somalia that included television footage of crowds dragging the body of an U.S. pilot through the streets. The White House also suffered a setback in Haiti when a peacekeeping force was repulsed by angry inhabitants of the island threatening violence.

The main foreign policy problem of these initial months was in Bosnia. With United Nations peacekeeping troops, predominantly British and French, on the ground, the military options for Clinton were limited since the first targets of retaliation from the Serbs would be the Allied troops. Working through the United Nations also proved frustrating for the White House. Tensions rose between Washington and its allies throughout 1993 over the proper course of action in the Balkans.

In less publicized ways, the administration had some accomplishments. It succeeded in obtaining the withdrawal of Russian troops from the Baltic Republic of Estonia in 1994. Clinton also helped to broker peace negotiations among Ireland, Great Britain, and the Irish Republican Army's political arm Sinn Fein ("Ourselves Alone"). In the Middle East, State Department negotiators facilitated talks between Yasir Arafat of the Palestine Liberation Organization and Prime Minister Yitzhak Rabin of Israel. The United States also intervened in Haiti in 1994 and produced the ouster of the military rulers as a prelude to a more democratic government. Although he received little public credit for these accomplishments, Clinton became more adept on the world stage as his first term unfolded.

At the time, however, the perception that he was weak in foreign policy exacerbated his political troubles at home. During his first two years in office, Clinton's popularity ratings fell, his hold on the country remained weak, and there was speculation that he would be another one-term president.

The Republican Revolution: 1994

By 1994 the cumulative effect of the charges against the president and a Republican resurgence from the setback of 1992 transformed the political scene. Several elements fed the Republican offensive. In the House of Representatives, the Republicans chose as their next leader their ideological champion, Representative **Newton ("Newt") Gingrich** of Georgia. A former historian, Gingrich saw himself as the embodiment of a fundamental revolution in American values. An adroit political tactician, the burly, rumpled Gingrich used the television coverage of Congress that began in the late 1970s (called C-SPAN) to broadcast his ideas to a national constituency. His militancy contributed to a partisan intensity in the House, and he saw his greatest initial triumph when he forced Speaker Jim Wright from office for financial misconduct in 1989. Gingrich continued his abrasive tactics into the early 1990s, and conservative members in the House rallied to his banner.

Newt Gingrich
A congressman from Georgia first elected in 1978, he served as Speaker of the House from 1994 until he resigned from Congress in 1999.

The Republican Offensive

Aiding the Republican cause was the rise of conservative talk radio, embodied in its most militant exponent, Rush Limbaugh. A stocky, articulate performer, Limbaugh had millions of daily listeners over his "Excellence in Broadcasting" Network where he touted his "Talent on Loan from God." He and other conservatives on the radio assailed the Clintons and their program throughout 1993 and 1994. Their assaults mobilized the Republican electorate against the incumbent and his party.

To dramatize their appeal, Gingrich and the Republicans offered a **Contract with America** as their election platform. The Contract promised action on such items as a balanced budget amendment, term limits for Congress members, and making legislators obey the regulations they applied to society. All of these measures and others would be acted on within the first one hundred days of a Republican victory. As the elections began, the Republicans found their poll numbers rising, the Democrats in retreat, and the prospect of regaining control of Congress a real possibility.

Contract with America
The Republican election platform of the 1990s, promising action on such items as a balanced budget amendment, term limits for Congress members, and making legislators obey the regulations they applied to society.

The Democrats and President Clinton stumbled throughout the autumn of 1994. The failure to achieve reform of the health care system and a general weariness with big government underlined the apparent futility of the incumbents. Efforts to scare the voters about the prospect of a Republican takeover fell flat. On election night, the Republicans swept to victory. They had 235 seats in the House to 197 for the Democrats and they controlled the

Senate by a margin of 53 to 47. Newt Gingrich became Speaker of the House and Robert Dole was the Senate majority leader.

The Continuing Shadow of Race

The O. J. Simpson Trial

While Washington watched the 1994 elections with great intensity, Americans spent more time that autumn transfixed by what promised to be the last "Trial of the Century." In mid-June 1994 Nicole Brown Simpson, the estranged ex-wife of football star Orenthal James "O. J." Simpson, was brutally murdered at her home. Nearby lay the corpse of Ronald Goldman, an acquaintance and restaurant employee. Police suspicions soon focused on O. J. Simpson, whose Ford Bronco had blood that could be traced to the crime scene. The nation watched in fascination on a Friday evening a slow-speed chase through the Los Angeles freeway system as Simpson and a friend drove back to his home where he ultimately surrendered.

The murder trial of football star O. J. Simpson became one of the media events of the 1990s. Simpson stands with his lawyers F. Lee Bailey, Johnnie Cochran (middle), and Robert Shapiro as the jury announces his acquittal.

Although Simpson's playing career in the National Football League had ended some years earlier, he remained a national celebrity because of appearances in movies and television advertising. "The Juice," as he was known, was one of the small number of African Americans who had gained broad public acceptance among white Americans. Now he stood accused of a brutal double murder. It soon became evident that the nation was polarized about Simpson's guilt or innocence. Most white Americans believed that the strong evidence pointed to Simpson as the killer. Many black Americans talked of a police conspiracy to frame the former football star.

These opinions solidified during the protracted trial that began during the fall of 1994 and stretched on into much of 1995. Televised daily, the trial played out as a racially charged drama that dominated talk shows, tabloids, and popular opinion. The participants in turn became media figures on their own. As the months of testimony and controversy continued into 1995, the Simpson trial took on a life of its own as a forum where Americans confronted sensitive and explosive issues about how society dealt with minorities and race.

The Immigration Backlash

Adding to the social tensions of 1994 was the issue of immigration, both illegal and legal. Immigration into the United States had grown dramatically during the 1980s. By the early 1990s legal immigrants, most of whom were Hispanics and Asians, totaled almost six hundred thousand per year. Estimates of the number of illegal immigrants who had settled in the United States ranged from three hundred thousand to half a million. The Immigration and Naturalization Service (INS) forecast that there might be as many as thirteen million immigrants coming to the United States during the 1990s.

Critics of immigration charged that "the racial and ethnic balance of America is being radically altered through public policy." Studies demonstrated that immigrants, both legal and illegal, contributed more to society in taxes and productivity than they consumed from government services, but the mere increased presence of Hispanics and Asians produced political conflict, especially in California. During the riots after the Rodney King verdict in Los Angeles, for example, the stores of Korean and other Asian merchants became the targets of mob violence. In 1994 the rising discontent about immigration in California led to a landslide election victory for Proposition 187, which barred illegal immigrants from receiving state education and health benefits. After its adoption, court challenges delayed its implementation, but by 1996 the governor ordered many of its provisions into effect. On the national level Congress debated immigration restrictions as it decided what to do about reform of the welfare system.

The Republicans in Power

The new Republican majorities in Congress went to work in January 1995 with great energy to implement their "Contract with America." Laboring long hours at the start, they enacted a measure to make the regulations they imposed on Americans apply to Capitol Hill as well. The Republicans also pushed for a balanced budget amendment to the Constitution. Speaker of the House Newt Gingrich was an effective leader of his Republican troops in this early phase of the session, but his propensity for colorful attacks on his opponents made him a center of controversy. Confident Republicans looked toward ousting Clinton in two years.

The pace of the "Republican Revolution" remained hectic into the spring of 1995. Although the balanced budget amendment failed by a single vote in the Senate, Congress did pass a law to restrict itself from making the states enforce regulations without supplying the necessary funds to do so. Clinton approved the "unfunded mandates" measure on March 22, 1995. The Republicans failed, however, to pass a constitutional amendment imposing term limits on members of Congress. By April Republicans proclaimed that they had enacted most of the Contract within the one hundred days they had set for themselves.

Tragedy in Oklahoma City

A national tragedy shifted the political landscape. On April 19, 1995, the Alfred P. Murrah Federal Building in Oklahoma City blew up, killing 168 people inside. Two suspects, Timothy McVeigh and Terry Nichols, were quickly arrested and identified as having links with an extremist "militia" movement that sought the violent overthrow of the government of the United States. The public learned that small groups of militia met secretly in the countryside to practice guerrilla warfare tactics. The glare of publicity revealed that the militia movement, while violent and dangerous, commanded only a small cadre of followers. Still, the social tensions in the country intensified in the wake of the **Oklahoma City bombing.**

President Clinton went out to Oklahoma City in the wake of the tragedy and participated in the ceremony of national mourning for the victims. Clinton's speech on that occasion struck a resonant note of national healing and identified the president with the broad political center of the country. The two suspects, McVeigh and Nichols, were both tried and convicted for their roles in the bombing.

Oklahoma City bombing
Militant right-wing U.S. terrorists bombed the Alfred P. Murrah Federal Building in Oklahoma City in April 1995, causing the deaths of 168 people.

The Republicans Falter

Republican overreaching contributed to the president's rebound in the polls during the remainder of 1995. As the Republicans in Congress attacked environmental legislation and sought to remove government regulations on business, the White House assailed them for endangering the gains that the nation had made in clean air and clean water. Clinton threatened to veto legislation that cut back on environmental spending and money for education. He cast his first veto as president in June 1995 when he turned down a Republican spending measure that would have trimmed more than a billion dollars from education funding.

Troubles dogged Clinton during 1995, especially the long-running Whitewater saga. Despite the best efforts of Republican lawmakers, the inquiry did not turn up evidence that would incriminate the president or his wife in wrongdoing. The special prosecutor, Kenneth Starr, continued his investigations with indictments and convictions of several Arkansas political and business figures, but that effort also yielded nothing to embarrass the Clintons directly.

The Race for the Republican Nomination

The Republicans had an abundance of potential challengers for their nomination in 1996. The most formidable candidate would be General Colin Powell whose service as chairman of the Joint Chiefs of Staff in the Gulf War had made him a national military hero. As the first African American to be a serious contender for the Republican prize, Powell would be an asset to the party's ticket if he would agree to run as vice president. Throughout most of 1995, Powell hinted that he was a Republican and was thinking about running for president. He did not, however, make a firm declaration of his intentions.

Beyond Powell, the Republican field for 1996 included Senator Robert Dole, who began as the presumed front-runner. Since the party generally selected the leading candidate in the polls, Dole was likely to be nominated unless he stumbled badly. Waiting for him to falter were Senator Phil Gramm of Texas, former governor of Tennessee Lamar Alexander, and several long-shot aspirants. At seventy-two Dole had to overcome the age problem and his reputation as a strident partisan.

Dole endeavored to tap into the cultural fears of the right wing of his party in May 1995 when he assailed what he called "nightmares of depravity" that peppered audiences of adolescents with images of grotesque violence and sexual activity. The senator also went after the variant of pop music known as "gangsta" rap, which he labeled as degrading to women and in favor of crime. The speech attracted a great deal of attention and invigorated Dole's floundering candidacy during the summer of 1995.

Clinton Resurgent: Bosnia

The big political winner in the second half of 1995 continued to be President Clinton. Against all the critics who charged that his policy in Bosnia would lead to U.S. involvement and a military disaster, the president succeeded by the end of the year in producing a ceasefire in the conflict. The opportunity for a ceasefire emerged out of a complex series of events during the summer and fall of 1995. In July a Serb offensive imperiled several cities that were regarded as "safe havens" for refugees from the fighting. Helped by arms that had come in from Muslim countries, Croatian and Bosnian forces launched an offensive against the Serbs. At the end of August Clinton authorized air strikes against the Bosnian Serbs. Within a week, a tentative peace agreement was declared, and a month later a ceasefire was reached. The United States then brokered peace negotiations in Dayton, Ohio, that produced a settlement. U.S. troops were dispatched to help enforce the peace agreement. Fortunately for Clinton, the operation did not produce casualties that would have undercut the president's political standing.

The Politics of Race and Social Justice

The Simpson Verdict

While politics raged on during 1995, the O. J. Simpson trial plodded toward a conclusion. Popular interest in the proceedings remained high. The Simpson defense team associated their client with the oppression and injustice that blacks had received in the United States and put the Los Angeles Police Department on trial. Attention centered on one officer, Mark Fuhrmann, who had testified that he had not used racial slurs but was found to have lied under oath on that point. The case went to the jury in September 1995. After very brief deliberations, Simpson was acquitted on all counts.

Black audiences cheered the verdict as it was announced. Whites watching on television expressed dismay. The national debate over the case intensified as commentators divided along racial lines. Some Simpson partisans asserted that the jury's decision represented an effort to make up for decades of biased white verdicts toward black defendants. All of the participants in the case began to write books about the trial. Meanwhile, the families of Ron Goldman and Nicole Brown Simpson filed civil suits against Simpson that promised to keep the case in the headlines for years to come.

The Million Man March

Louis Farrakhan
Leader of the Nation of Islam who became controversial for his intense criticism of whites and their policies toward blacks.

Million Man March
A protest march in October 1995 in Washington, D.C. that was organized by Louis Farrakhan to draw attention to black grievances.

In October 1995 the Nation of Islam and its controversial leader, **Louis Farrakhan,** organized "a holy day of atonement and reconciliation" for black men. Designed to bring one million black men to the nation's capital, the event became known as the **Million Man March.** Commentators made comparisons with the March on Washington in August 1963 and the striking oratory of Martin Luther King Jr. Because of Farrakhan's espousal of anti-Semitic sentiments and his expressed dislike for white Americans, the 1995 march did not have the moral resonance of the earlier occasion, but it galvanized the participants. Within the black community, debate raged about Farrakhan's value as a spokesman for African American aspirations.

Culture Wars: Multiculturalism and Political Correctness

The Simpson trial and the Million Man March took place in the context of a national debate about what the United States should do regarding the continuing question of racial injustice. One source of debate and tension was the related issues of "multiculturalism" and what came to be called **political correctness.**

Multiculturalism had emerged in the 1980s in academic institutions. In gender, class, and racial concerns, multiculturalism sought to draw attention to such issues as the role of black soldiers in the Civil War, Japanese Americans in World War II internment camps, and women in the American Revolution, to pick among countless examples. In its positive aspects, multiculturalism was an effort to include groups, ideas, and experiences that had not been part of the mainstream. By the early 1990s, however, multiculturalism had come under attack from its enemies on the right who accused its adherents of enforcing what was called "political correctness." The critics of multiculturalism said that the academic left was using the movement to balkanize American society into warring ethnic groups, was limiting free speech on campuses, and was repudiating the whole tradition of Western culture.

Although some of the criticisms of multiculturalism did identify areas of exaggeration and overstatement from its proponents, the critics also overdramatized isolated incidents. What was significant about these cultural divisions was the polarization of American society in the 1990s that they revealed. In 1994–1995, for example, an exhibition at the Smithsonian Institution to mark the fiftieth anniversary of the atomic bombing of Hiroshima became a flashpoint when veterans groups charged that the organizers of the show were adopting an anti-American, pro-Japanese point of view. The curators who mounted the show responded that they were trying to reflect the diversity of scholarly opinion about the event. The protest triumphed and the exhibition was canceled. By the end of the decade, passions about multiculturalism had cooled somewhat, but tensions in other areas of society remained volatile.

> **political correctness**
> Of, relating to, or supporting broad social, political, and educational change, especially to redress historical injustices in matters such as race, class, gender, and sexual orientation.

The Battle over Gay Rights

The efforts of gays and lesbians to attain political and social equality within the United States were met with a strong counteroffensive from conservatives. In the 1990s homosexuals contended that they should have the right to marry (in what were called "same-sex" marriages) just as heterosexuals did. Identifying their campaign with the civil rights movement of the 1960s, gay groups wanted attacks on those who were openly homosexual to be classified as "hate crimes."

Conservative groups assailed homosexuality as a sin or a disease, in the words of Senate Majority Leader Trent Lott of Mississippi, "like alcoholism or kleptomania." Christian groups ran elaborate advertising campaigns to persuade homosexuals to abandon their lifestyle and seek religious treatment. The president of an anti-gay legal fund announced in 1998 that "Radical homosexuals are busy in the legislatures and are filing dozens of lawsuits across America to obtain custody of children, to gain the legal right to 'marry,' and to redefine the legal definition of a family." Periodic acts of violence directed against gays spurred calls for federal legislation to prevent such actions.

Affirmative Action and Civil Rights

Another issue that provoked serious divisions within society was the policy of affirmative action in industry, higher education, and government to provide minorities with greater opportunities for advancement. Although the Supreme Court had ruled in the late 1970s that race could be employed in university admissions when the goal was to achieve diversity in the student body, the justices scaled back on that commitment in a number of cases involving such policies as minority set-aside programs or congressional districts drawn to produce heavily minority-populated districts.

Unhappiness with affirmative action as a policy led some states such as California to adopt Proposition 209 in a referendum that abolished programs to assist minorities. In the *Hopwood v. Texas* case (1996), a federal circuit court invalidated the affirmative action plan of the University of Texas Law School, noting that any effort by universities to promote affirmative action was unconstitutional. The Supreme Court had not made a ruling on the question that affected the entire nation. In 1997 President Clinton appointed a President's Commission on Race to study these and other race-related issues. Its final report, issued a year later, satisfied neither the critics nor the proponents of affirmative action.

A President Reelected

As the budget negotiations between President Clinton and the Republican Congress produced no result toward the end of 1995, some of the more militant members of the GOP majority in the House called for a concerted effort to shut down the government as a way of pressuring the White House to agree to their position. They foresaw a humiliating cave-in from a president they distrusted and hated.

The Republican strategy backfired. Two government shutdowns occurred, a brief one in November and a second that lasted for twenty-one days from mid-December 1995 into early January 1996. Rather than blaming the president for the deadlock, the public put the responsibility on the Republicans for the government closures that affected tourists in Washington and at popular national parks.

Monica Lewinsky
An unpaid intern and later a paid staffer who had an affair with President Clinton in the White House.

An important personal development for President Clinton occurred during the crisis over the government shutdown. He began an extramarital sexual relationship with a White House intern named **Monica Lewinsky.** Clinton soon found himself involved in a sordid mess that could compromise his presidency if it became public. He and Lewinsky agreed that she would keep their activities a secret, but she told friends and her physician about it during 1996. Despite the dangers that it posed to his presidency, Clinton continued to see Lewinsky into 1997.

Clinton's Political Fortunes Improve

In November 1995, Israeli leader Yitzhak Rabin was assassinated. Gingrich flew with the president to the funeral, and then complained that he had not had a chance to talk with Clinton about the budget during the flight. He also had to leave *Air Force One* through the rear door, an action that the Speaker took as a personal insult. The ensuing flap left Gingrich looking petty and undercut his stature as a budget bargainer.

In early 1996 the Republicans realized that the prolonged shutdown was hurting their cause. Accordingly, they reached an accommodation with the White House that brought the crisis to an end. An interim measure to reopen the government passed both houses on January 5, and the government resumed official operations the next day. Budget negotiations went on, but Clinton had won the first major skirmish of the presidential campaign year decisively.

The First Lady Under Fire

While President Clinton had the upper hand in the national political arena, the long-running Whitewater saga took an ugly turn for Hillary Rodham Clinton in the early days of January. Billing records from Mrs. Clinton's former law firm in Arkansas, sought by the special prosecutor in 1994, turned up in the White House. Kenneth Starr, the Whitewater prosecutor, subpoenaed Mrs. Clinton to testify before his Washington grand jury. She spent four hours before the grand jury panel, but no results followed from her testimony. In mid-1997, press reports said that the jury had ended its life without issuing indictments against her.

Running parallel with Starr's probe were several congressional inquiries into the Whitewater story, the most notable being the one that Senator Alphonse D'Amato of New York conducted through the Senate Banking Committee. D'Amato's probe covered a wide range of issues relating to the economic activities of the Clintons in Arkansas, but the hearings yielded very little tangible evidence. The failure of D'Amato's inquiry to turn up sensational revelations helped defuse the Whitewater story as the 1996 election got under way.

The Republicans Pick Dole

Throughout 1995 the front-runner for the Republican nomination was Senate Majority Leader Robert Dole of Kansas (after Colin Powell decided not to run). A decorated World War II veteran and a gifted lawmaker, Dole had run in 1988 against George H. W. Bush for the GOP prize, but had lost badly. Yet Dole's weaknesses persisted. As in his attack on Hollywood, he often seemed out of touch with the culture and values of the 1990s electorate. He was not a good organizer, and friends worried about his ability to sustain a national presidential campaign.

A large number of challengers to Dole appeared. The best-financed was Phil Gramm of Texas, who used his connections in the Senate to assemble a large war chest as 1997 began. Gramm looked like the stereotype of the college professor he had once been. His campaign never caught fire. Lamar Alexander, the former governor of Tennessee, campaigned under the slogan of "ABC—Alexander Beats Clinton"—and wore a trademark checkered shirt. It was clever, but the electorate found little substance beneath the surface. Patrick Buchanan returned for another try at the Republican prize, and used his nationalistic, antiforeigner rhetoric to some effect in the early primaries. Millionaire publisher Steven Forbes entered the race late, and threw money into commercials that established him as a serious contender against Dole as the primary season began.

Dole as the Republican Candidate

Dole had problems in the early going and lost the New Hampshire primary to Buchanan. The key South Carolina primary went to Dole on March 2, and successive victories brought the Kansas senator within sight of the nomination by April 1996. The early victory left the Dole campaign broke and unable to counter Clinton's advertising until after the Republican National Convention in late summer when he received federal matching funds as the official Republican nominee. To jump-start his lagging candidacy, Dole resigned his Senate seat in June to campaign as a man without office or Washington power. None of these gimmicks did much to close the large gap in the polls that separated Clinton from his rival.

The spring of 1996 did not mean undiluted triumphs for President Clinton. In late May his onetime business partners James and Susan McDougal were found guilty of fraud and conspiracy in dealings in Whitewater-related transactions. One of the witnesses in the case alleged that then Governor Clinton had pressured him to make an illegal loan some years earlier. President Clinton denied the allegation under oath when he testified as a defense witness.

A month later another scandal broke. Congressional investigators learned that the White House had obtained the Federal Bureau of Investigation files for as many as six hundred individuals, among them prominent Republicans. Members of the GOP majority in Congress charged that the Clinton administration had abused its power and pressured the FBI to use the files against their enemies for political reasons. The White House blamed the episode on zealous subordinates.

An Uneasy Summer

On July 27, 1996, TWA Flight 800, en route from New York to Paris, exploded over the Atlantic Ocean off the coast of Long Island. There were 230 victims. Conspiracy theories soon surfaced that suggested the airplane had been the target of a terrorist missile, an errant government weapons test, or a domestic plot. Months dragged on with no resolution of the mystery, and skepticism about any official explanation mounted.

Ten days later, a bomb exploded at the Summer Olympics in Atlanta, Georgia, killing one spectator and wounding up to one hundred others. The explosive was in a knapsack, and the security guard who had pointed out its location soon was revealed as the ostensible suspect of the investigation. For weeks the unfortunate guard had media crews following him, and his indictment was predicted within a few days. Only months later did the FBI concede that the guard was not a suspect any longer. These events indicated how rapidly America gathered information in the mid-1990s and how the pervasiveness of news sometimes produced less social cohesion rather than more.

The Rise of the Internet

The powerful growth of the Internet and the World Wide Web in the 1990s transformed the way Americans got their news and communicated with each other. In 1996, eighteen million people, or about 9 percent of the population, accessed the Internet on a regular basis. A year later the figure stood at thirty million adults. By 1998, 20 percent of all American households had Internet access. Dominating the new field were such corporations as America Online, which provided connections for 30 percent of all Internet users in the country in 1996. Other businesses sought consumers on the Web through specific Web pages or by purchasing advertising space on popular Web sites. Popular movies such as *You've Got Mail* (1998) and the rise of news outlets on the Web underscored how the Internet had permeated American life.

So important had computers and the Internet become by 1998 that the prospect of a computer breakdown in the year 2000 emerged as a major social problem. Y2K, as it was known, stemmed from the inability of older computers to read the year 2000 correctly and remain functioning. Finding and fixing imbedded computer codes cost business and government hundreds of billions of dollars in 1998 and 1999. Some Americans hoarded food and weapons in preparation for what they forecast as a breakdown of civilization on January 1, 2000. More sober assessments predicted some disruption but not social chaos.

Welfare and Other Reforms in Congress

With the election approaching and polls showing their standing with the public in jeopardy, the Republican majority on Capitol Hill saw cooperation with the White House as a political necessity. As a result, the president and Congress found common ground on reform of the nation's welfare system in the summer of 1996. A compromise measure came out of Congress at the end of July. In place of the longstanding Aid for Dependent Children (AFDC) program, lawmakers established a system of block grants to the individual states. The measure also specified that legal immigrants into the United States would not be eligible for benefits during their first five years of residence. The legislation fulfilled Clinton's 1992 campaign promise to "end welfare as we know it," but it left many Democrats unhappy with the current direction of their party. For Clinton it represented a return to the "New Democrat" posture that had helped him win the election in 1992.

The waning days of the Congress saw other accomplishments. In August lawmakers enacted a rise in the minimum wage in two steps to $5.15 per hour. It was the first hike since 1991 and came after intense Republican opposition. Responding to the continuing public unhappiness with immigration problems, Congress included in its spending legislation funds for new personnel for the Immigration and Naturalization Service, the hiring of additional Border Patrol agents, and more severe penalties for bringing in illegal aliens. Republicans failed to get language that would have barred public education to the children of illegal immigrants. The achievements of Congress undercut Dole's argument that Clinton was not an effective leader.

The National Conventions

Both parties struggled for the political advantage in their national conventions. These gatherings had now become television spectacles. The major networks abandoned earlier policies of "gavel-to-gavel" coverage, with programming focused on key moments in the proceedings. Everything was carefully scripted and choreographed. The conventions were evaluated as if they were entertainment specials, which was what they had become by the summer of 1996.

Mindful of their public relations disaster in Houston in 1992, the Republicans sought to reassure voters that they were an acceptable and inclusive alternative to the Democrats. Their problem remained, however, one of making Senator Dole an exciting and charismatic figure who could compete with Clinton. Dole launched his preconvention offensive with the promise of a 15 percent tax cut over a three-year period. Reflecting the sentiment within the party for what was known as a "flat tax," an income tax at a low rate for all citizens, he advocated a "fairer, flatter tax." To Democratic charges that his proposal would "blow a hole in the deficit," Dole responded by saying that he would propose prudent spending cuts to find the $548 billion needed to offset his tax reductions.

The second daring maneuver came when Dole announced that he had asked former Congressman Jack Kemp of New York to be his running mate. A favorite of the conservatives, Kemp had long endorsed tax cuts and was popular among African American voters. In many respects, the choice was an odd one. Kemp brought little electoral strength to the ticket. Kemp was also an indifferent campaigner, but at the convention his selection lifted the spirits of the Republican delegates who saw Dole trailing badly in the polls to the incumbent president.

The convention was a well-scripted love feast for Dole that gave the senator a modest improvement (or "bounce") in the public opinion polls. Mrs. Elizabeth Dole was the hit of the conclave with a deft, informal speech outlining her husband's virtues. Dole's own acceptance speech was adequate but not spectacular.

Perot Again

Midway between the conventions of the major parties came the meeting of the **Reform party** that Ross Perot had established as the vehicle for his second presidential candidacy. Although there was an opposition candidate to Perot, former Governor Richard Lamm of Colorado, Perot won easily. Yet he had not captured the public's imagination as had happened in 1992. Perot's hope was to elbow his way into the presidential debates against Clinton and Dole, but neither of the major party candidates wanted to see the third party challenger in the event. Despite efforts to use the federal courts to gain access, Perot had to watch from the sidelines.

Reform party
A political party founded by Ross Perot in 1995 as an alternative to the Democratic and Republican parties.

Clinton Renominated

President Clinton enjoyed a harmonious convention when the Democrats met in Chicago in late August. The platform stressed centrist themes and spoke of a "New Democratic Party." Even bad news about one of Clinton's closest advisors did not disrupt the festivities. A tabloid newspaper revealed that Dick Morris, a campaign strategist and old friend of Clinton, had had a long-running affair with a prostitute. Morris resigned and the episode passed quickly. Clinton and Vice President Gore were renominated, and the president promised four more years of prosperity and moderate reform.

During September 1996, the campaign unfolded as though Clinton and the Democrats were certain winners. Despite some fluctuations, the lead over Dole in the polls remained strong. The two presidential debates did not attract the attention that had characterized the 1992 debates, and Dole failed to crack Clinton's armor with attacks on his character and administration scandals. By the middle of October, optimistic Democrats predicted a landslide for the president.

Campaign Scandals

Then newspaper reports appeared, and rapidly accelerated, about improprieties and possible crimes in the fund-raising for the Democratic party and the Clinton campaign. Money had flowed into the president's campaign war chest from Asian sources, and possible links to Communist China and Indonesian businesses emerged. A Democratic National Committee operative named John Huang soon became the focus of the press inquiries. Every day as the campaign wound down, new revelations of questionable campaign contributors and dubious funding sources followed. Rather than a triumphal march, the waning days of the 1996 election saw Clinton and his party staggering toward the finish line under a severe cloud of scandal.

Dole was not able to capitalize on this turn of events. His campaign manager asked Ross Perot to drop out to give Dole a chance against Clinton. Perot refused. In a last-minute blitz, Dole barnstormed the country nonstop to demonstrate that he was not too old to be president and that he had the energy to overtake Clinton. Nonetheless, although they retained doubts about Clinton as a candidate, the voters did not want to see Dole become president.

Clinton Wins a Second Term

Clinton's lead wavered a little as the election neared. Although most news organizations predicted a double-digit presidential win, that did not happen. The result over Dole was

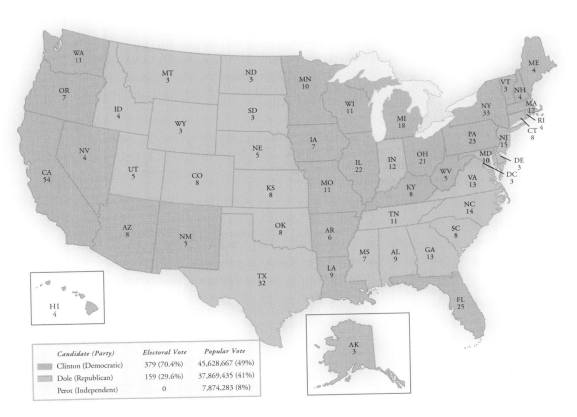

Candidate (Party)	Electoral Vote	Popular Vote
Clinton (Democratic)	379 (70.4%)	45,628,667 (49%)
Dole (Republican)	159 (29.6%)	37,869,435 (41%)
Perot (Independent)	0	7,874,283 (8%)

MAP 32.1 The Election of 1996

In the 1996 presidential election, Bill Clinton easily defeated Robert Dole. Since Clinton did not win a majority of the popular votes, however, doubts persisted about the legitimacy of his presidency.

never really in doubt on election night, but the triumph was more limited than had seemed possible when the campaign started.

On the other hand, Clinton's political obituary had been pronounced after the 1994 election, so his victory represented a substantial vindication. The Democratic ticket won 379 electoral votes and 49 percent of the popular vote to 41 percent (159 electoral votes) for Dole and Kemp. Ross Perot and the Reform party lagged with 8 percent of the popular vote and no electoral votes. Clinton's electoral coalition included California, New York, Illinois, Michigan, and Ohio. The president also carried two staunchly Republican states—Florida and Arizona. In all, Clinton won thirty-one states and the District of Columbia.

What made Clinton's success distinctive was his standing as the first Democratic president to secure consecutive terms since Franklin D. Roosevelt. During the 1990s, Clinton had gone a long way toward drawing the Democrats back to the political center and renewing them as a genuine electoral alternative to the Republicans. Whether the party's revival would outlast Clinton's second term remained to be seen.

Although Dole had lost badly, the Republicans retained control of both houses of Congress. They held onto the House but with a diminished majority of only ten seats. In the Senate, they picked up two seats for a fifty-five to forty-five margin over the Democrats. Since they needed sixty votes to block a Democratic filibuster, the Republicans would have to compromise with their opponents to get any legislation passed. The stage was set for another scenario of divided government.

A New Cabinet

For his second term President Clinton assembled a new cabinet. To succeed the outgoing secretary of state, Warren Christopher, the president selected the ambassador to the United Nations, Madeleine Albright. She became the first woman to serve as secretary of state, and she soon emerged as one of the most effective and popular members of the government. She brought a new tough tone and assertive style to the conduct of foreign policy.

In a gesture of bipartisanship, Clinton named former Maine Republican Senator William Cohen as his secretary of defense. Cohen was a moderate who could build coalitions with his former colleagues in the Senate while enjoying good relations with Democrats as well. More inclined to end the Bosnian commitment than Madeleine Albright, Cohen was a cautious voice in the Pentagon.

Modest Programs Modestly Advanced

For his second term President Clinton avoided large initiatives that might put him at odds with the Republican Congress. During the winter of 1997, he worked out a budget agreement that promised a balance within a few years. The U.S. economy proved so robust through the summer of 1997 that the deficit fell rapidly, and forecasters projected that a budget surplus might emerge by the end of the year. The stock market soared throughout this period. Clinton took credit for the impressive showing of the markets and the economy.

His goals for a second term seemed indistinct and modest well into 1997. Carrying forward the strategy of his reelection victory, he identified himself with small, incremental ideas such as a V-chip to enable parents to control the television programming that their children watched, a voluntary television ratings system, and greater computer training for schoolchildren.

An Ambitious Foreign Policy

For a president who had come into office promoting domestic issues, Clinton seemed to relish the international stage during his fifth year in office. He pushed hard for the North Atlantic Treaty Organization to add members from former Communist states in Eastern Europe and saw his vision fulfilled when Poland, Hungary, and the Czech Republic were added to the alliance. To overcome Russian opposition to the expansion of NATO, the United States and its allies told Moscow in May 1997 that neither nuclear weapons nor large numbers of combat forces would be placed on the soil of the new member states.

In other areas of foreign policy, the world's trouble spots remained volatile. The situation in Bosnia, while improved since the **Dayton Peace Accords,** still pitted Serbs, Croats, and Bosnians against each other. As for the Middle East, tensions between Palestinians and Israelis worsened amid sporadic terrorist violence. The Clinton administration pressed both sides for more movement to implement peace, but progress was elusive.

Dayton Peace Accords
A peace settlement involving Bosnia in 1995 that was worked out in Dayton, Ohio; it did not prove to be a permanent solution for the problems in the Balkans.

An Economic Boom

Throughout 1997 the U.S. economy went into high gear. Unemployment fell to 4.8 percent, and inflation no longer seemed a problem. With jobs plentiful and prices stable, a sense of economic optimism pervaded the nation.

Adding to the euphoria was the apparent end of the budget deficit problem that had shaped politics for so many years. Surging tax revenues meant that red ink started to disappear. The 1997 budget deficit was only $25 billion, the lowest since 1974, and 1998 promised the unheard of—a budget surplus. As a result of these trends, Congress and the president worked out a balanced budget agreement in May that was signed into law on August 5. Politicians could suddenly look forward to budget surpluses for years to come.

Clinton Embattled

The political result of these favorable economic events was a good year for President Clinton. The major setback of the year came when the Supreme Court ruled 9–0 on May 27, 1997, in *Clinton v. Jones* that the sexual harassment lawsuit against the president could go forward while he was in office. Other problems dogged Clinton. Congressional probes on the 1996 campaign scandal indicated that the president and Vice President Al Gore had played a larger role in raising money than they had earlier admitted. Kenneth Starr's Whitewater investigation moved along without major indictments but still posed a potential threat to the White House. Yet, for all these lingering concerns, it seemed to the chagrin of Clinton's most bitter political foes that "Slick Willie" would escape again.

You read the complete text and you begin to understand..

That the real problem of the Clinton Presidency is not that he lied under oath or obstructed justice...

The real problem is that there's a teen-ager living in the White House.

Clumsy, flirtatious, demanding, rejecting...

scared, shamed, dishonest, diffident.

No handcuffs, no whips and chains, just classic adolescent, guilt-ridden lust.

I don't think he should be impeached...

I think he should be grounded.

President Clinton's admissions of his sexual intimacy with Monica Lewinsky proved abundant source material for cartoonists. Jules Feiffer in the *New York Times* offers one interpretation of the president's misbehavior.

The Monica Lewinsky Scandal

Then, in mid-January 1998, a stunned nation learned that Monica Lewinsky had had a sexual relationship with President Clinton during her White House employment as an intern and low-level staffer. Once the news broke, Clinton asserted that he had not had sex with Lewinsky. For seven months he reiterated that version of events. Meanwhile, Kenneth Starr investigated whether Clinton had lied under oath in the Paula Jones case and whether he had asked others to lie on his behalf. This sordid spectacle absorbed vast amounts of television news coverage throughout 1998. It featured friends and enemies of Clinton debating his sexual drives, his honesty, and the future of his presidency.

Clinton's strategy of delay worked in the short run. His poll numbers remained high, and Starr's popularity sagged. In the end, however, abundant evidence emerged that Clinton and Lewinsky had been physically intimate. On August 17, 1998, Clinton acknowledged "inappropriate" conduct with Lewinsky when he testified before Starr's Washington grand jury from the White House. That night he told the nation the same thing in a four-and-a-half-minute speech that was widely regarded as a low point of his presidency.

A few weeks later Starr sent a report to the House of Representatives alleging that there were grounds for impeaching Clinton for lying under oath, obstruction of justice, abuse of power, and other offenses. The House Judiciary Committee recommended that an impeachment inquiry commence, and the House voted to authorize a probe after the 1998 elections.

The Monica Lewinsky scandal and its fallout left Clinton a wounded president. He retained the ability to achieve foreign policy successes such as a deal he brokered between Israelis and Palestinians in October 1998. With Clinton's resiliency as a politician, a rebound during his last two years was possible. But his tactics and conduct in handling the Lewinsky matter had cost him dearly. Whatever else would be said about his administration and record, his involvement with Monica Lewinsky would be the defining event of his historical reputation.

The 1998 Elections

The Republicans entered the 1998 election season with high ambitions. In the Senate, they hoped to reach a total of sixty Republicans, which would enable them to end Democratic filibusters. After Clinton's speech on August 17, it seemed as if a Republican rout was in the offing. Alienated Democrats were predicted to stay home, and energized Republicans would flock to the polls to rebuke Clinton. But the Republicans overplayed their hand. Their moves to impeach Clinton awakened the Democrats and produced a backlash. By the time the Republicans figured out what was going on, it was too late.

On November 3, 1998, the Democrats in the House actually gained five seats. Republican control of the House narrowed to 223–211, a very thin majority. In the Senate, the two parties battled to a draw, with the Republicans holding the same 55–45 edge that existed when Election Day dawned. The Democrats made gains in governors' races in the South as well. Two significant Republican victories came in Florida and Texas, where the two sons of former President George Bush, Jeb Bush in Florida and George W. Bush in Texas, were elected to a first and second term, respectively.

Despite the results of the congressional elections, Republican leaders in Congress pressed ahead with the impeachment of President Clinton. In December the House Judiciary Committee sent four articles of impeachment to the full house. That body adopted two articles of impeachment charging President Clinton with perjury in his grand jury testimony in August 1998, and with obstruction of justice in his relationship with Monica Lewinsky, members of his staff, and other individuals. The Senate opened its trial in mid-January. By the end of the month, it became evident that a two-thirds majority to convict and remove the president did not exist.

President Clinton's popularity with the public remained high, and his State of the Union address on January 19, 1999, drove his poll ratings still higher. Some conservatives, such as religious activist Pat Robertson, urged the Republicans to end the proceedings. The prosecution and impeachment trial in the Senate was hurting the Republicans' political posture with the American public. As January 1999 wound down, however, the impeachment trial continued.

President Clinton was acquitted on both counts when the Senate voted on February 12, 1999. On the perjury count, the total was 45 Republican senators voting to convict the president while all 45 Democrats and 10 Republicans voted for acquittal. On the second article involving obstruction of justice, the Senate split evenly with 50 Republican votes for conviction and 45 Democrats and 5 Republicans voting for acquittal.

The impeachment episode reflected the intense emotions that Clinton had provoked during his time in the White House. To the Republicans and Americans on the right, he was an illegitimate president who had committed crimes in office that warranted his removal. To the remainder of the country, some 65 percent according to most polls, he was a president who, while probably guilty of the offenses with which he was charged, was performing well in office and should not be removed.

In the weeks following the end of the impeachment trial, pundits forecast that Clinton's poll ratings would drop once the crisis was over. That did not happen as the economy remained prosperous and the Dow Jones Industrial Average hovered around 10,000. A possible danger for the president arose in late March 1999 when NATO began air strikes against the Serbian government to stop "ethnic cleansing" of Albanians near the city of Kosovo. Despite the warnings of critics of the Clinton administration, the air campaign in Serbia ended in success for the NATO forces.

The much feared Y2K crisis proved to be largely a nonevent. The government reportedly foiled several terrorist plots set for January 2000. More important, the changes made in computer systems in 1998 and 1999 reduced the disruptions to a minimum. Once the date had passed without major incident amid worldwide celebrations of the calendar change, Americans turned to the onset of the presidential election season.

The 2000 Presidential Campaign: Bush versus Gore

The Republican front-runner was Governor **George W. Bush** of Texas, the son of the former president. Elected governor in 1994 and reelected in 1998, the Texan announced for president in mid-1999 and soon amassed a campaign treasury that ultimately reached more than $100 million. Bush promised that he would be a "compassionate conservative" who would "change the tone" in Washington after the partisan discord of the Clinton era. He advocated a $1.6 trillion tax cut and promised to reform the educational system. Despite doubts about his ability to master the issues, Bush led all Republicans in the polls.

In the race for the nomination, Governor Bush lost the New Hampshire primary to Senator John McCain of Arizona, but then won a number of primaries to lock up the delegates needed to control the national convention in Philadelphia. For his running mate, Bush selected former Secretary of Defense Richard "Dick" Cheney, despite Cheney's history of heart disease. By the end of the convention, Bush had a double-digit lead in the opinion polls over his likely opponent, Vice President Al Gore.

Gore had experienced few problems in the Democratic primaries and easily bested former New Jersey Senator Bill Bradley. A lackluster campaigner, Gore had problems

George W. Bush
The forty-third president of the United States.

The three televised debates between George W. Bush and Albert Gore proved unusually important in deciding the outcome of the 2000 presidential election.

separating himself from the scandals of the Clinton years. He also faced a hostile press corps that focused on every personal and political lapse to paint Gore as indecisive and opportunistic. Gore emerged from the Democratic convention behind Bush but closed the gap during September 2000. The election then hinged on the results of three presidential debates.

The predictions were that Gore, a seasoned debater, would easily defeat Bush. Although neither candidate did well, Bush exceeded the low expectations that media pundits set for him. Gore, on the other hand, was better on substance but was labeled arrogant and condescending. The race remained tight down to the election. Most forecasters predicted a decisive Bush triumph in the popular vote with the electoral result too close to call.

As the results came in on election night, it was clear that a tight election had occurred. The Republicans retained control of the House of Representatives, but the Senate split evenly with 50 Democrats and 50 Republicans. The presidential race was a cliffhanger. Gore led in the popular vote, but the electoral vote produced a virtual dead heat. It became clear that the state of Florida would determine the result since its 25 electoral votes would push either of the two candidates past the 271 electoral votes needed. The networks called Florida for Gore based on exit polls, next assigned the state to Bush, and then deemed the outcome too close to call. State election officials put Florida in the Bush column by fewer than six hundred ballots after going over the official returns that came in during the week after the election. Gore's forces noted irregularities and flawed ballots in several Democratic counties and sought a recount in those areas.

The Bush camp insisted that the result favoring their man should be final, and charges of fraud, manipulation, and political pressure flashed back and forth throughout November. Lawsuits in state and federal courts dominated television coverage. Finally, the case of *Bush v. Gore* reached the United States Supreme Court in mid-December. On the key issue in dispute of whether a recount could occur, the Court ruled 5–4 in favor of Bush in a decision that many commentators dubbed both hasty and partisan. Gore accepted the outcome as final and conceded the election. The ruling wounded the prestige of the Court and left a cloud over the legitimacy of Bush's presidency.

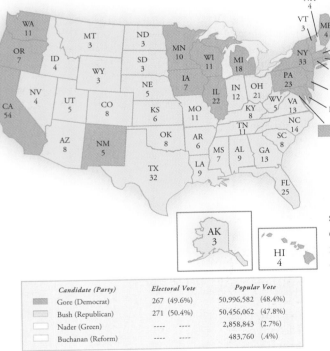

Candidate (Party)	Electoral Vote		Popular Vote	
Gore (Democrat)	267	(49.6%)	50,996,582	(48.4%)
Bush (Republican)	271	(50.4%)	50,456,062	(47.8%)
Nader (Green)	----	----	2,858,843	(2.7%)
Buchanan (Reform)	----	----	483,760	(.4%)

MAP 32.2 The Election of 2000

The map of the 2000 election reflects the closeness of the electoral vote. Note the extent to which the voters were distributed into a pro-Gore coalition on the coasts and a pro-Bush coalition in the interior of the nation, with some key exceptions in the Middle West and Far West. A comparison with the presidential election of 1896 (see Map 19.1) gives an interesting sense of how partisan alignments changed during the twentieth century.

The Presidency of George W. Bush

In office, Bush governed as a conservative who opposed abortion, rolled back environmental regulations, and pursued foreign policy initiatives that placed less reliance on working with the nation's overseas allies. The president advocated the immediate construction of a missile defense system, despite the opposition from Russia and many of the traditional friends of the United States. Congress enacted Bush's large tax cut, but the president saw control of the Senate slip out of Republican hands when Senator James Jeffords of Vermont left the GOP to become an independent. Throughout the summer of 2001, Republicans and Democrats braced themselves for legislative battles over education, the environment, and budget priorities. Meanwhile, the economy slowed and the stock market experienced substantial losses. Such corporations as Enron and WorldCom led a wave of corporate failures based on corrupt accounting.

One issue, international terrorism, had not been of central concern to most Americans during the waning years of the Clinton presidency and the early months of the Bush administration. Bombings of U.S. embassies in Africa in 1998 and a similar attack on the destroyer USS *Cole* in Yemen in October 2000 had not brought the issue home. The name of the leader of one terrorist group—Osama bin Laden—was largely unknown to the average citizen, even though bin Laden, a fundamentalist Muslim of Saudi Arabian origin, sought the violent end of American influence in the Middle East from his base in Afghanistan. Even a frightening report from a prestigious commission in February 2001 warning of a likely terrorist attack on American soil did little to shake the government and the mass media out of their indifference and lack of alertness.

On the morning of **September 11, 2001,** two hijacked jetliners slammed into the twin towers of the World Trade Center in New York City. Both buildings collapsed in flames and rubble, and an estimated four thousand people perished. A third airliner crashed into the Pentagon leaving another two hundred people dead. A fourth plane fell to the ground in rural Pennsylvania. All air traffic was grounded for several days, consumer spending slumped, and the weakened economy slipped into a recession.

This devastating attack on American soil, which was quickly linked to bin Laden and his terrorist network, al Queda, rattled the nation's morale as it became clear that the terrorists sought the removal of the United States from the Middle East entirely. President Bush launched a **war on terrorism** with air strikes and troops against Afghanistan and the Taliban regime there that harbored bin Laden. A new government emerged in Afghanistan, but bin Laden eluded capture.

The Bush administration's next priority was the regime of Saddam Hussein in Iraq, which the administration implied had ties to the September 11 events and was hiding weapons of mass destruction. A war with Iraq began in March 2003, and it resulted in the

September 11, 2001
On this date al Qaeda terrorists carried out a plan by Osama bin Laden that destroyed the World Trade Center towers and damaged the Pentagon in Washington, D.C.

war on terrorism
In response to the September 11 attacks, President George W. Bush declared war on the terrorists and sent U.S. troops to invade first Afghanistan and later Iraq.

The area in lower New York City where the World Trade Center towers collapsed in thousands of tons of rubble after the terrorist attack of September 11, 2001, became known as "Ground Zero."

President George W. Bush Responds to Terrorism

Following the terrorist attacks of September 11, 2001, President George W. Bush addressed a joint session of Congress on September 20. The well-received speech lifted President Bush in the polls and began a period of unprecedented, sustained popularity for the new chief executive. This excerpt from his speech focuses on the role of the Muslim religion in the crisis and what the stricken nation was prepared to do to win the war. In the immediate aftermath of the attacks, the issue of Iraq and Saddam Hussein, so important in the months to come, had not yet emerged as a central concern of foreign policy for the United States.

. . . I also want to speak tonight directly to Muslims throughout the world. We respect your faith. It's practiced freely by many millions of Americans, and by millions more in countries that America counts as friends. Its teachings are good and peaceful, and those who commit evil in the name of Allah blaspheme the name of Allah. The terrorists are traitors to their own faith, trying, in effect, to hijack Islam itself. The enemy of America is not our many Muslim friends; it is not our many Arab friends. Our enemy is a radical network of terrorists, and every government that supports them.

Our war on terror begins with al Qaeda, but it does not end there. It will not end until every terrorist group of global reach has been found, stopped and defeated.

Americans are asking, why do they hate us? They hate what we see right here in this chamber—a democratically elected government. Their leaders are self-appointed. They hate our freedoms—our freedom of religion, our freedom of speech, our freedom to vote and assemble and disagree with each other.

They want to overthrow existing governments in many Muslim countries, such as Egypt, Saudi Arabia, and Jordan. They want to drive Israel out of the Middle East. They want to drive Christians and Jews out of vast regions of Asia and Africa.

These terrorists kill not merely to end lives, but to disrupt and end a way of life. With every atrocity, they hope that America grows fearful, retreating from the world and forsaking our friends. They stand against us, because we stand in their way.

We are not deceived by their pretenses to piety. We have seen their kind before. They are the heirs of all the murderous ideologies of the 20th century. By sacrificing human life to

military defeat of the Hussein regime within a few weeks. No weapons of mass destruction were found in Iraq. An insurgency against the presence of the United States and its coalition soon appeared, however, and renewed fighting erupted that had cost more than 1,200 American lives and the lives of thousands of Iraqis by the end of 2004.

In the wake of the September 11 attacks, a moment of national unity occurred, and President Bush's popularity soared. The president chose to use this opportunity to push a conservative agenda at home and abroad. With the momentum the president and his party had achieved after September 11, they won substantial gains in the 2002 elections, and Republicans took control of the Senate and increased their margin in the House.

serve their radical visions—by abandoning every value except the will to power—they follow in the path of fascism, and Nazism, and totalitarianism. And they will follow that path all the way, to where it ends: in history's unmarked grave of discarded lies.

Americans are asking: How will we fight and win this war? We will direct every resource at our command—every means of diplomacy, every tool of intelligence, every instrument of law enforcement, every financial influence, and every necessary weapon of war—to the disruption and to the defeat of the global terror network.

This war will not be like the war against Iraq a decade ago, with a decisive liberation of territory and a swift conclusion. It will not look like the air war above Kosovo two years ago, where no ground troops were used and not a single American was lost in combat.

Our response involves far more than instant retaliation and isolated strikes. Americans should not expect one battle, but a lengthy campaign, unlike any other we have ever seen. It may include dramatic strikes, visible on TV, and covert operations, secret even in success. We will starve terrorists of funding, turn them one against another, drive them

from place to place, until there is no refuge or no rest. And we will pursue nations that provide aid or safe haven to terrorism. Every nation, in every region, now has a decision to make. Either you are with us, or you are with the terrorists. From this day forward, any nation that continues to harbor or support terrorism will be regarded by the United States as a hostile regime . . .

Questions to Consider

1. What case does Bush make for the causes of terrorism from al Qaeda and other groups in the Muslim world?

2. How long does he predict the war will last?

3. In what ways did the speech foreshadow the strategy that the Bush administration formed toward Iraq?

4. Has the United States continued to treat "any nation that continues to harbor or support terrorism" as "a hostile regime"?

Explore additional primary sources related to this chapter on the *American Passages* Web site: http://history.wadsworth.com/ayersbrief02.

Source: Excerpt from *Address to a Joint Session of Congress and the American People,* accessed February 11, 2003, on the White House Web site: www.whitehouse.gov/news/releases/2001/09/print/20010920-8.html.

Angry Democrats looked for a winning presidential candidate in 2004. That election pitted Senator John F. Kerry of Massachusetts against President Bush in a bitterly contested race that remained close until votes were cast on November 2, 2004. Bush won a majority of the popular vote and secured 286 electoral votes to 252 for Kerry. The Republicans picked up seats in both the House and the Senate and spoke of a mandate for their conservative philosophy during the four years to come. With large budget deficits projected into the future, an economy with substantial strains, and continuing polarization of the voters, the prospects for further political warfare seemed likely. Foreign policy issues in Iraq, Iran, and North Korea would also test the second term of George W. Bush.

Summary

The United States in the Twenty-First Century

This final chapter considers the 1990s and early years of the new millennium when the United States went from a period of prosperity to the challenge of terrorism after September 11, 2001. The decade began on a high note with the triumph in the Gulf War and the liberation of Kuwait. Despite that temporary success, President George H. W. Bush saw his popularity decline at home as the economy soured.

The election of Bill Clinton in 1992 opened a period of bitter political warfare as Republicans challenged a president they did not regard as a legitimate incumbent. The difficulties of the Clinton administration in its first two years led to Republican victories in the midterm elections. Newt Gingrich, the GOP leader in the House of Representatives, conceived the idea of a "Contract with America," which resonated with the American people. With control of the House and Senate, Gingrich, now Speaker of the House, and Senate leader Bob Dole sought to deny Clinton a second term. Investigations of the financial and personal affairs of Clinton and his wife Hillary Clinton ensued. Known as the Whitewater scandal after a real estate investment in Arkansas by that name, these charges against the president and his wife produced much heat but little evidence of wrongdoing. Despite these attacks, Clinton fought the Republicans to a stalemate and was able to defeat Dole in the 1996 presidential election. Republican resentment against the president intensified.

Investigations of Clinton's conduct by special prosecutor Kenneth Starr focused on sexual harassment charges against the president in 1997. Tips to that probe produced evidence of Clinton's relationship with a White House intern, Monica Lewinsky. The revelation of that sexual affair led to charges that the president had lied to prosecutors and obstructed justice. Starr sent his evidence to Congress in the fall of 1998, and the House voted two articles of impeachment in December. A trial in the Senate followed, and Clinton was acquitted.

In this intense atmosphere, Vice President Al Gore faced off against Texas governor George W. Bush in the 2000 presidential election. An electoral standoff ensued that was not decided until the Supreme Court in December 2000 in effect ruled that Bush had won the disputed electoral votes of Florida and thus the election. Bush took office in Janu-

The long-running Whitewater investigation brought Hillary Clinton to the federal courthouse in Washington, the only First Lady to be involved in a criminal proceeding as a possible target. No charges were ever filed against her, and she was elected to the United States Senate in 2000.

ary 2001 and pursued a conservative agenda that included large tax cuts. Revelations of corporate scandals, such as the one involving the giant energy firm Enron, marked Bush's initial months in office.

Then came the September 11, 2001, terrorist attacks. A shocked nation rallied behind the president, and the United States attacked the terrorist bases in Afghanistan. The administration's argument that Iraq was a major threat as well because of its weapons of mass destruction proved more divisive. Iraq was invaded in March 2003, but no such weapons were found. An insurgency against the Americans and their allies soon began and continued with mounting violence throughout 2004.

The Republicans won the elections of 2002, solidifying their control of the House and regaining control of the Senate. The election of 2004 pitted President Bush against Senator John Kerry of Massachusetts. Though the final result was close in the electoral college, Bush won the popular vote and reelection. As 2005 began, the nation was still involved in the war in Iraq, the economy was in a fragile state, and the threat of terrorism persisted. In response to these threats, the United States has expanded the power of the government to protect "homeland" security to an extent not previously seen in the nation's history. Twenty-first-century Americans now face the hard issues of whether the experiment in representative self-government, begun in the late eighteenth century, will endure beyond the early years of the new millennium.

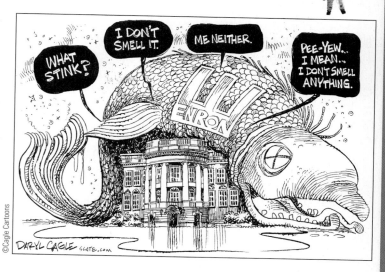

The scandal over the failed corporation Enron produced pain for its investors and employees but little public outrage.

LOOKING BACK

The 1990s and early 2000s have become contested terrain in the polarized politics of the modern United States. The two most recent presidents, Bill Clinton and George W. Bush, arouse intense feelings for and against them. The emphasis on personality and character that dominated politics also diverted attention from the serious problems that the nation faced as the threat of terrorism arose.

1. Where does Bill Clinton fit within the recent history of the Democratic party?
2. Why did terrorism receive so little attention as a threat during the 1990s?
3. What did George W. Bush mean by "compassionate conservatism," and how was that doctrine reflected in the policies of his administration?
4. What are the political strengths and weaknesses of American government as the twenty-first century begins?

LOOKING AHEAD

This is the last chapter of the book and so these questions are not for further reading. Think about these issues as you ponder the sweep of American history and what could occur during your lifetime as the national passage moves on.

1. What will it take to win the war on terrorism and defeat the ideology that justifies this strategy that has arisen in part of the Islamic world?
2. What should the United States do to resolve the conflict while at the same time preserving its democratic heritage?
3. How different will American society be in twenty-five years because of the developments in the 1990s and early twenty-first century?
4. Should optimism or pessimism be the dominant theme in evaluating the future of the United States in light of the history you have just finished reading?

Making Connections Across Chapters

RECOMMENDED READINGS

Benjamin, Daniel, and Simon, Steven. *The Age of Sacred Terror* (2002). An excellent look at the roots of terrorism and the U.S. response during the 1990s.

Clarke, Richard A. *Against All Enemies: Inside America's War on Terror* (2004). A critique of the war on terror under Presidents Bill Clinton and George W. Bush.

Conason, Joe, and Lyons, Gene. *The Hunting of the President* (2000). Looks at the anti-Clinton campaign and its development.

Drew, Elizabeth. *On the Edge: The Clinton Presidency* (1994). Provides a reporter's analysis of Clinton's first year in power.

Drew, Elizabeth. *Showdown: The Struggle Between the Gingrich Congress and the Clinton White House* (1996). Continues Drew's account of the internal politics of the Clinton White House in the struggle with Newt Gingrich and the Republicans.

Halberstam, David. *War in a Time of Peace: Bush, Clinton, and the Generals* (2001). Examines the nation's involvement in the Balkans.

Minutaglio, Bill. *First Son: George W. Bush and the Bush Family Dynasty* (1999). Offers biographical background on President Bush.

Toobin, Jeffrey. *Too Close to Call* (2001). Considers the events of the disputed presidential election of 2000 in Florida.

Walker, Martin. *The President We Deserve* (1996). A perceptive look at Clinton from a British perspective.

Woodward, Bob. *Plan of Attack* (2004). Provides an inside look at planning for the Iraq war.

AMERICAN JOURNEY ONLINE AND INFOTRAC COLLEGE EDITION

Visit the source collections at http://ajaccess.wadsworth.com and infotrac.thomsonlearning.com and use the Search function with the following key terms to explore documents, images, audio and video clips, articles, and commentary related to the material in this chapter.

William Jefferson Clinton

Branch Davidians

O. J. Simpson

Oklahoma City bombing

Dayton Peace Accords

Monica Lewinsky

Kenneth Starr

Contract with America

Million Man March

Whitewater Investigation

George W. Bush

September 11, 2001

War against terrorism

ONLINE PRIMARY SOURCES

Here are some examples of the many primary sources related to this chapter that you will find on the *American Passages* Web site: http://history.wadsworth.com/ayersbrief02.

Newt Gingrich, "Where We Go From Here," 1995

"The Era of Big Government is Over," 1996

A Brief History of the Internet, 1999

The site also offers self-quizzes, exercises, and many additional resources to help you study.

Appendices

The Declaration of Independence
The Unanimous Declaration of the Thirteen United States of America

When in the Course of human events it becomes necessary for one people to dissolve the political bands which have connected them with another, and to assume among the Powers of the earth, the separate and equal station to which the Laws of Nature and of Nature's God entitle them, a decent respect to the opinions of mankind requires that they should declare the causes which impel them to the separation.

We hold these truths to be self-evident, that all men are created equal, that they are endowed by their Creator with certain unalienable Rights, that among these are Life, Liberty and the pursuit of Happiness. That to secure these rights, Governments are instituted among Men, deriving their just Powers from the consent of the governed. That whenever any Form of Government becomes destructive of these ends, it is the Right of the People to alter or to abolish it, and to institute new Government, laying its foundation on such principles and organizing its Powers in such form, as to them shall seem most likely to effect their Safety and Happiness. Prudence, indeed, will dictate that Governments long established should not be changed for light and transient causes; and accordingly all experience hath shewn, that mankind are more disposed to suffer, while evils are sufferable, than to right themselves by abolishing the forms to which they are accustomed. But when a long train of abuses and usurpations, pursuing invariably the same Object evinces a design to reduce them under absolute Despotism, it is their right, it is their duty, to throw off such Government, and to provide new Guards for their future security. Such has been the patient sufferance of these Colonies; and such is now the necessity which constrains them to alter their former Systems of Government. The history of the present King of Great Britain is a history of repeated injuries and usurpations, all having in direct object the establishment of an absolute Tyranny over these States. To prove this, let Facts be submitted to a candid world.

He has refused his Assent to Laws, the most wholesome and necessary for the public good.

He has forbidden his Governors to pass Laws of immediate and pressing importance, unless suspended in their operation till his Assent should be obtained; and when so suspended, he has utterly neglected to attend to them.

He has refused to pass other Laws for the accommodation of large districts of people, unless those people would relinquish the right of Representation in the Legislature, a right inestimable to them and formidable to tyrants only.

He has called together legislative bodies at places unusual, uncomfortable, and distant from the depository of their Public Records, for the sole Purpose of fatiguing them into compliance with his measures.

He has dissolved Representative Houses repeatedly, for opposing with manly firmness his invasions on the rights of the People.

He has refused for a long time, after such dissolutions, to cause others to be elected; whereby the Legislative Powers, incapable of Annihilation, have returned to the People at large for their exercise; the State remaining in the mean time exposed to all the dangers of invasion from without, and convulsions within.

He has endeavoured to prevent the Population of these States; for that purpose obstructing the Laws for Naturalization of Foreigners; refusing to pass others to encourage their migrations hither, and raising the conditions of new Appropriations of Lands.

He has obstructed the Administration of Justice, by refusing his Assent to Laws for establishing Judiciary Powers.

He has made Judges dependent on his Will alone, for the tenure of their offices, and the amount and payment of their salaries.

He has erected a multitude of New Offices, and sent hither swarms of Officers to harass our People, and eat out their substance.

He has kept among us, in times of peace, Standing Armies without the Consent of our legislatures.

He has affected to render the Military independent of and superior to the Civil Power.

He has combined with others to subject us to a jurisdiction foreign to our constitution, and unacknowledged by our laws; giving his Assent to their Acts of pretended Legislation:

For Quartering large bodies of armed troops among us:

For protecting them, by a mock Trial, from Punishment for any Murders which they should commit on the Inhabitants of these States:

For cutting off our Trade with all parts of the world:

For imposing Taxes on us without our Consent:

For depriving us in many cases, of the benefits of Trial by Jury:

For transporting us beyond Seas to be tried for pretended offences:

For abolishing the free System of English Laws in a neighbouring Province, establishing therein an Arbitrary government, and enlarging its Boundaries so as to render it at once an example and fit instrument for introducing the same absolute rule into these Colonies:

For taking away our Charters, abolishing our most valuable Laws, and altering fundamentally the Forms of our Governments:

For suspending our own Legislatures, and declaring themselves invested with Power to legislate for us in all cases whatsoever.

He has abdicated Government here, by declaring us out of his Protection, and waging War against us.

He has plundered our seas, ravaged our Coasts, burnt our towns, and destroyed the lives of our people.

He is at this time transporting large Armies of foreign Mercenaries to compleat the works of death, desolation and tyranny, already begun with circumstances of Cruelty and perfidy scarcely paralleled in the most barbarous ages, and totally unworthy the Head of a civilized nation.

He has constrained our fellow Citizens taken Captive on the high Seas to bear Arms against their Country, to become the exe-

Text is reprinted from the facsimile of the engrossed copy in the National Archives. The original spelling, capitalization, and punctuation have been retained. Paragraphing has been added.

cutioners of their friends and Brethren, or to fall themselves by their Hands.

He has excited domestic insurrections amongst us, and has endeavoured to bring on the inhabitants of our frontiers, the merciless Indian Savages, whose known rule of warfare, is an undistinguished destruction of all ages, sexes and conditions.

In every stage of these Oppressions We have Petitioned for Redress in the most humble terms: Our repeated Petitions have been answered only by repeated injury. A Prince, whose character is thus marked by every act which may define a Tyrant, is unfit to be the ruler of a free People.

Nor have We been wanting in attentions to our British brethren. We have warned them from time to time of attempts by their legislature to extend an unwarrantable jurisdiction over us. We have reminded them of the circumstances of our emigration and settlement here. We have appealed to their native justice and magnanimity, and we have conjured them by the ties of our common kindred to disavow thee usurpations, which, would inevitably interrupt our connections and correspondence. They too have been deaf to the voice of justice and of consanguinity. We must, therefore, acquiesce in the necessity, which denounces our Separation, and hold them, as we hold the rest of mankind, Enemies in War, in Peace Friends.

WE, THEREFORE, the Representatives of the UNITED STATES OF AMERICA, in General Congress, Assembled, appealing to the Supreme Judge of the world for the rectitude of our intentions, do, in the Name, and by Authority of the good People of these Colonies, solemnly publish and declare, That these United Colonies are, and of Right ought to be FREE AND INDEPENDENT STATES; that they are Absolved from all Allegiance to the British Crown, and that all political connection between them and the State of Great Britain, is and ought to be totally dissolved; and that, as Free and Independent States, they have full Power to levy War, conclude Peace, contract Alliances, establish Commerce, and to do all other Acts and Things which Independent States may of right do. And for the support of this Declaration, with a firm reliance on the protection of divine Providence, we mutually pledge to each other our Lives, our Fortunes and our sacred Honor.

The Constitution of the United States of America

We the People of the United States, in Order to form a more perfect Union, establish Justice, insure domestic Tranquility, provide for the common defence, promote the general Welfare, and secure the Blessings of Liberty to ourselves and our Posterity, do ordain and establish this Constitution for the United States of America.

Article I.

Section 1. All legislative Powers herein granted shall be vested in a Congress of the United States, which shall consist of a Senate and House of Representatives.

Section 2. The House of Representatives shall be composed of Members chosen every second Year by the People of the several States, and the Electors in each State shall have the Qualifications requisite for Electors of the most numerous Branch of the State Legislature.

No Person shall be a Representative who shall not have attained to the Age of twenty five Years, and been seven Years a Citizen of the United States, and who shall not, when elected, be an Inhabitant of that State in which he shall be chosen.

Representatives and direct Taxes[1] shall be apportioned among the several States which may be included within this Union, according to their respective Numbers, which shall be determined by adding to the whole Number of free Persons, including those bound to Service for a Term of Years, and excluding Indians not taxed, three fifths of all other Persons.[2] The actual Enumeration shall be made within three Years after the first Meeting of the Congress of the United States, and within every subsequent Term of ten Years, in such Manner as they shall by Law direct. The Number of Representatives shall not exceed one for every thirty Thousand, but each State shall have at Least one Representative; and until such enumeration shall be made, the State of New Hampshire shall be entitled to chuse three; Massachusetts eight; Rhode Island and Providence Plantations one; Connecticut five; New York six; New Jersey four; Pennsylvania eight; Delaware one; Maryland six; Virginia ten; North Carolina five; South Carolina five; and Georgia three.

When vacancies happen in the Representation from any State, the Executive Authority thereof shall issue Writs of Election to fill such Vacancies.

The House of Representatives shall chuse their Speaker and other Officers; and shall have the sole Power of Impeachment.

Section 3. The Senate of the United States shall be composed of two Senators from each State, chosen by the Legislature thereof, for six Years; and each Senator shall have one Vote.[3]

Immediately after they shall be assembled in Consequence of the first Election, they shall be divided as equally as may be into three Classes. The Seats of the Senators of the first Class shall be vacated at the Expiration of the second Year, of the second Class at the Expiration of the fourth Year, and of the third Class at the Expiration of the sixth Year, so that one third may be chosen every second Year; and if Vacancies happen by Resignation, or otherwise, during the Recess of the Legislature of any State, the Executive thereof may make temporary Appointments until the next Meeting of the Legislature, which shall then fill such Vacancies.[4]

No Person shall be a Senator who shall not have attained to the Age of thirty Years, and been nine Years a Citizen of the United States, and who shall not, when elected, be an Inhabitant of that State for which he shall be chosen.

The Vice President of the United States shall be President of the Senate, but shall have no Vote, unless they be equally divided.

Text is from the engrossed copy in the National Archives. Original spelling, capitalization, and punctuation have been retained.

[1] Modified by the Sixteenth Amendment.
[2] Replaced by the Fourteenth Amendment.

[3] Superseded by the Seventeenth Amendment.
[4] Modified by the Seventeenth Amendment.

The Senate shall chuse their other Officers, and also a President pro tempore, in the Absence of the Vice President, or when he shall exercise the Office of President of the United States.

The Senate shall have the sole Power to try all Impeachments. When sitting for that Purpose, they shall be on Oath or Affirmation. When the President of the United States is tried, the Chief Justice shall preside: And no Person shall be convicted without the Concurrence of two thirds of the Members present.

Judgment in Cases of Impeachment shall not extend further than to removal from Office, and disqualification to hold and enjoy any Office of honor, Trust or Profit under the United States: but the Party convicted shall nevertheless be liable and subject to Indictment, Trial, Judgment and Punishment, according to Law.

Section 4. The Times, Places and Manner of holding Elections for Senators and Representatives, shall be prescribed in each State by the Legislature thereof, but the Congress may at any time by Law make or alter such Regulation, except as to the Places of chusing Senators.

The Congress shall assemble at least once in every Year, and such Meeting shall be on the first Monday in December, unless they shall by Law appoint a different Day.[5]

Section 5. Each House shall be the Judge of the Elections, Returns and Qualifications of its own Members, and a Majority of each shall constitute a Quorum to do Business; but a smaller Number may adjourn from day to day, and may be authorized to compel the Attendance of absent Members, in such Manner, and under such Penalties as each House may provide.

Each House may determine the Rules of its Proceedings, punish its Members for disorderly Behaviour, and, with the Concurrence of two thirds, expel a Member.

Each House shall keep a Journal of its Proceedings, and from time to time publish the same, excepting such Parts as may in their Judgment require Secrecy; and the Yeas and Nays of the Members of either House on any question shall, at the Desire of one fifth of those Present, be entered on the Journal.

Neither House, during the Session of Congress, shall, without the Consent of the other, adjourn for more than three days, nor to any other Place than that in which the two Houses shall be sitting.

Section 6. The Senators and Representatives shall receive a Compensation for their Services, to be ascertained by Law, and paid out of the Treasury of the United States. They shall in all Cases, except Treason, Felony and Breach of the Peace, be privileged from Arrest during their Attendance at the Session of their respective Houses, and in going to and returning from the same; and for any Speech or Debate in either House, they shall not be questioned in any other Place.

No Senator or Representative shall, during the Time for which he was elected, be appointed to any civil Office under the Authority of the United States, which shall have been created, or the Emoluments whereof shall have been encreased during such time; and no Person holding any Office under the United States, shall be a Member of either House during his Continuance in Office.

Section 7. All Bills for raising Revenue shall originate in the House of Representatives; but the Senate may propose or concur with Amendments as on other Bills.

Every Bill which shall have passed the House of Representatives and the Senate shall, before it become a Law, be presented to the President of the United States; If he approve he shall sign it, but if not he shall return it, with his Objections to that House in which it shall have originated, who shall enter the Objections at large on their Journal, and proceed to reconsider it. If after such Reconsideration two thirds of that House shall agree to pass the Bill, it shall be sent, together with the Objections, to the other House, by which it shall likewise be reconsidered, and if approved by two thirds of that House, it shall become a Law. But in all such Cases the Votes of both Houses shall be determined by yeas and Nays, and the Names of the Persons voting for and against the Bill shall be entered on the Journal of each House respectively. If any Bill shall not be returned by the President within ten Days (Sundays excepted) after it shall have been presented to him, the Same shall be a Law, in like Manner as if he had signed it, unless the Congress by their Adjournment prevent its Return, in which Case it shall not be a Law.

Every Order, Resolution, or Vote to which the Concurrence of the Senate and House of Representatives may be necessary (except on a question of Adjournment) shall be presented to the President of the United States; and before the Same shall take Effect, shall be approved by him, or being disapproved by him shall be repassed by two thirds of the Senate and House of Representatives, according to the Rules and Limitations prescribed in the Case of a Bill.

Section 8. The Congress shall have power To lay and collect Taxes, Duties, Imposts and Excises, to pay the Debts and provide for the common Defence and general Welfare of the United States; but all Duties, Imposts and Excises shall be uniform throughout the United States;

To borrow Money on the credit of the United States;

To regulate Commerce with foreign Nations, and among the several States, and with the Indian Tribes;

To establish an uniform Rule of Naturalization, and uniform Laws on the subject of Bankruptcies throughout the United States;

To coin Money, regulate the Value thereof, and of foreign Coin, and fix the Standard of Weights and Measures;

To provide for the Punishment of counterfeiting the Securities and current Coin of the United States;

To establish Post Offices and post Roads;

To promote the Progress of Science and useful Arts, by securing for limited Times to Authors and Inventors the exclusive Right to their respective Writings and Discoveries;

To constitute Tribunals inferior to the supreme Court;

To define and punish Piracies and Felonies committed on the high Seas, and Offences against the Law of Nations;

To declare War, grant Letters of Marque and Reprisal, and make Rules concerning Captures on Land and Water;

To raise and support Armies, but no Appropriation of Money to that Use shall be for a longer Term than two Years;

To provide and maintain a Navy;

To make Rules for the Government and Regulation of the land and naval Forces;

To provide for calling forth the Militia to execute the Laws of the Union, suppress Insurrections and repel Invasions;

To provide for organizing, arming, and disciplining, the Militia, and for governing such Part of them as may be employed in the Service of the United States, reserving to the States respectively, the Appointment of the Officers, and the Authority of training the Militia according to the discipline prescribed by Congress;

To exercise exclusive Legislation in all Cases whatsoever, over such District (not exceeding ten Miles square) as may, by Cession of

---

[5] Superseded by the Twentieth Amendment.

particular States, and the Acceptance of Congress, become the Seat of the Government of the United States, and to exercise like Authority over all Places purchased by the Consent of the Legislature of the State in which the Same shall be, for the Erection of Forts, Magazines, Arsenals, dock-Yards, and other needful Buildings;— And

To make all Laws which shall be necessary and proper for carrying into Execution the foregoing Powers, and all other Powers vested by this Constitution in the Government of the United States, or in any Department or Officer thereof.

Section 9. The Migration or Importation of such Persons as any of the States now existing shall think proper to admit, shall not be prohibited by the Congress prior to the Year one thousand eight hundred and eight, but a Tax or duty may be imposed on such Importation, not exceeding ten dollars for each Person.

The Privilege of the Writ of Habeas Corpus shall not be suspended, unless when in Cases of Rebellion or Invasion the public Safety may require it.

No Bill of Attainder or ex post facto Law shall be passed.

No Capitation, or other direct, Tax shall be laid, unless in Proportion to the Census or Enumeration herein before directed to be taken.

No Tax or Duty shall be laid on Articles exported from any State.

No Preference shall be given by any Regulation of Commerce or Revenue to the Ports of one State over those of another: nor shall Vessels bound to, or from, one State, be obliged to enter, clear, or pay Duties in another.

No Money shall be drawn from the Treasury, but in Consequence of Appropriations made by Law, and a regular Statement and Account of the Receipts and Expenditures of all public Money shall be published from time to time.

No Title of Nobility shall be granted by the United States: And no Person holding any Office of Profit or Trust under them, shall, without the Consent of the Congress, accept of any present, Emolument, Office, or Title, of any kind whatever, from any King, Prince, or foreign State.

Section 10. No State shall enter into any Treaty, Alliance, or Confederation; grant Letters of Marque and Reprisal; coin Money; emit Bills of Credit; make any Thing but gold and silver Coin a Tender in Payment of Debts; pass any Bill of Attainder, ex post facto Law, or Law impairing the Obligation of Contracts, or grant any Title of Nobility.

No State shall, without the Consent of the Congress, lay any Imposts or Duties on Imports or Exports, except what may be absolutely necessary for executing its inspection Laws: and the net Produce of all Duties and Imposts, laid by any State on Imports or Exports, shall be for the Use of the Treasury of the United States; and all such Laws shall be subject to the Revision and Controul of the Congress.

No State shall, without the Consent of Congress, lay any Duty of Tonnage, keep Troops, or Ships of War in time of Peace, enter into any Agreement or Compact with another State, or with a foreign Power, or engage in War, unless actually invaded, or in such imminent Danger as will not admit of delay.

Article II.

Section 1. The executive Power shall be vested in a President of the United States of America. He shall hold his Office during the Term of four Years, and, together with the Vice President, chosen for the same Term, be elected, as follows:

Each State shall appoint, in such Manner as the Legislature thereof may direct, a Number of Electors, equal to the whole Number of Senators and Representatives to which the State may be entitled in the Congress: but no Senator or Representative, or Person holding an Office of Trust or Profit under the United States, shall be appointed an Elector.

The Electors shall meet in their respective States, and vote by Ballot for two Persons, of whom one at least shall not be an Inhabitant of the same State with themselves. And they shall make a List of all the Persons voted for, and of the Number of Votes for each; which List they shall sign and certify, and transmit sealed to the Seat of the Government of the United States, directed to the President of the Senate. The President of the Senate shall, in the Presence of the Senate and House of Representatives, open all the Certificates, and the Votes shall then be counted. The Person having the greatest Number of Votes shall be the President, if such Number be a Majority of the whole Number of Electors appointed; and if there be more than one who have such Majority, and have an equal Number of Votes, then the House of Representatives shall immediately chuse by Ballot one of them for President; and if no Person have a Majority, then from the five highest on the List the said House shall in like Manner chuse the President. But in chusing the President, the Votes shall be taken by States, the Representation from each State having one Vote; A quorum for this Purpose shall consist of a Member or Members from two thirds of the States, and a Majority of all the States shall be necessary to a Choice. In every Case, after the Choice of the President, the Person having the greatest Number of Votes of the Electors shall be the Vice President. But if there should remain two or more who have equal Votes, the Senate shall chuse from them by Ballot the Vice President.[6]

The Congress may determine the Time of chusing the Electors, and the Day on which they shall give their Votes; which Day shall be the same throughout the United States.

No Person except a natural born Citizen, or a Citizen of the United States, at the time of the Adoption of this Constitution, shall be eligible to the Office of President, neither shall any Person be eligible to that Office who shall not have attained to the Age of thirty five Years, and been fourteen Years a Resident within the United States.

In Case of the Removal of the President from Office, or of his Death, Resignation, or Inability to discharge the Powers and Duties of the said Office, the Same shall devolve on the Vice President, and the Congress may by Law provide for the Case of Removal, Death, Resignation or Inability, both of the President and Vice President, declaring what Officer shall then act as President, and such Officer shall act accordingly, until the Disability be removed, or a President shall be elected.[7]

The President shall, at stated Times, receive for his Services, a Compensation, which shall neither be encreased nor diminished during the Period for which he shall have been elected, and he shall not receive within that Period any other Emolument from the United States, or any of them.

Before he enter on the Execution of his Office, he shall take the following Oath or Affirmation:—"I do solemnly swear (or affirm) that I will faithfully execute the Office of President of the United

---

[6] Superseded by the Twelfth Amendment.

[7] Modified by the Twenty-fifth Amendment.

States, and will to the best of my Ability, preserve, protect and defend the Constitution of the United States."

Section 2. The President shall be Commander in Chief of the Army and Navy of the United States, and of the Militia of the several States, when called into the actual Service of the United States; he may require the Opinion, in writing, of the principal Officer in each of the executive Departments, upon any Subject relating to the Duties of their respective Offices, and he shall have Power to grant Reprieves and Pardons for Offences against the United States, except in Cases of Impeachment.

He shall have Power, by and with the Advice and Consent of the Senate, to make Treaties, provided two thirds of the Senators present concur; and he shall nominate, and by and with the Advice and Consent of the Senate, shall appoint Ambassadors, other public Ministers and Consuls, Judges of the supreme Court, and all other Officers of the United States, whose Appointments are not herein otherwise provided for, and which shall be established by Law; but the Congress may by Law vest the Appointment of such inferior Officers, as they think proper, in the President alone, in the Courts of Law, or in the Heads of Departments.

The President shall have Power to fill up all Vacancies that may happen during the Recess of the Senate, by granting Commissions which shall expire at the End of their next Session.

Section 3. He shall from time to time give the Congress Information of the State of the Union, and recommend to their Consideration such Measures as he shall judge necessary and expedient; he may, on extraordinary Occasions, convene both Houses, or either of them, and in Case of Disagreement between them, with Respect to the Time of Adjournment, he may adjourn them to such Time as he shall think proper; he shall receive Ambassadors and other public Ministers; he shall take Care that the Laws be faithfully executed, and shall Commission all the Officers of the United States.

Section 4. The President, Vice President and all civil Officers of the United States, shall be removed from Office on Impeachment for, and Conviction of, Treason, Bribery, or other high Crimes and Misdemeanors.

Article III.

Section 1. The judicial Power of the United States, shall be vested in one supreme Court, and in such inferior Courts as the Congress may from time to time ordain and establish. The Judges, both of the supreme and inferior Courts, shall hold their Offices during good Behaviour, and shall, at stated Times, receive for their Services, a Compensation, which shall not be diminished during their Continuance in Office.

Section 2. The judicial Power shall extend to all Cases, in Law and Equity, arising under this Constitution, the Laws of the United States, and Treaties made, or which shall be made, under their Authority;—to all Cases affecting Ambassadors, other public Ministers and Consuls;—to all Cases of admiralty and maritime Jurisdiction;—to Controversies to which the United States shall be a Party;—to Controversies between two or more States;—between a State and Citizens of another State;[8]—between Citizens of different States,—between Citizens of the same State claiming Lands under Grants of different States, and between a State, or the Citizens thereof, and foreign States, Citizens or Subjects.

In all Cases affecting Ambassadors, other public Ministers and Consuls, and those in which a State shall be Party, the supreme Court shall have original Jurisdiction. In all the other Cases before mentioned, the supreme Court shall have appellate Jurisdiction, both as to Law and Fact, with such Exceptions, and under such Regulations as the Congress shall make.

The Trial of all Crimes, except in Cases of Impeachment, shall be by Jury; and such Trial shall be held in the State where the said Crimes shall have been committed; but when not committed within any State, the Trial shall be at such Place or Places as the Congress may by Law have directed.

Section 3. Treason against the United States, shall consist only in levying War against them, or in adhering to their Enemies, giving them Aid and Comfort. No Person shall be convicted of Treason unless on the Testimony of two Witnesses to the same overt Act, or on Confession in open Court.

The Congress shall have Power to declare the Punishment of Treason, but no Attainder of Treason shall work Corruption of Blood, or Forfeiture except during the Life of the Person attainted.

Article IV.

Section 1. Full Faith and Credit shall be given in each State to the public Acts, Records, and judicial Proceedings of every other State. And the Congress may by general Laws prescribe the Manner in which such Acts, Records and Proceedings shall be proved, and the Effect thereof.

Section 2. The Citizens of each State shall be entitled to all Privileges and Immunities of Citizens in the several States.

A Person charged in any State with Treason, Felony, or other Crime, who shall flee from Justice, and be found in another State, shall on Demand of the executive Authority of the State from which he fled, be delivered up, to be removed to the State having Jurisdiction of the Crime.

No Person held to Service or Labour in one State, under the Laws thereof, escaping into another, shall, in Consequence of any Law or Regulation therein, be discharged from such Service or Labour, but shall be delivered up on Claim of the Party to whom such Service or Labour may be due.

Section 3. New States may be admitted by the Congress into this Union; but no new State shall be formed or erected within the Jurisdiction of any other State, nor any State be formed by the Junction of two or more States, or Parts of States, without the Consent of the Legislatures of the States concerned as well as of the Congress.

The Congress shall have Power to dispose of and make all needful Rules and Regulations respecting the Territory or other Property belonging to the United States; and nothing in this Constitution shall be so construed as to Prejudice any Claims of the United States, or of any particular State.

Section 4. The United States shall guarantee to every State in this Union a Republican Form of Government, and shall protect each of them against Invasion; and on Application of the Legislature, or of the Executive (when the Legislature cannot be convened) against domestic Violence.

---

[8] Modified by the Eleventh Amendment.

Article V.

The Congress, whenever two thirds of both Houses shall deem it necessary, shall propose Amendments to this Constitution, or, on the Application of the Legislatures of two thirds of the several States, shall call a Convention for proposing Amendments, which, in either Case, shall be valid to all Intents and Purposes, as Part of this Constitution, when ratified by the Legislatures of three fourths of the several States, or by Conventions in three fourths thereof, as the one or the other Mode of Ratification may be proposed by the Congress; Provided that no Amendment which may be made prior to the Year One thousand eight hundred and eight shall in any Manner affect the first and fourth Clauses in the Ninth Section of the first Article; and that no State, without its Consent, shall be deprived of its equal Suffrage in the Senate.

Article VI.

All Debts contracted and Engagements entered into, before the Adoption of this Constitution, shall be as valid against the United States under this Constitution, as under the Confederation.

This Constitution, and the Laws of the United States which shall be made in Pursuance thereof; and all Treaties made, or which shall be made, under the Authority of the United States, shall be the supreme Law of the Land; and the Judges in every State shall be bound thereby, any Thing in the Constitution or Laws of any State to the Contrary notwithstanding.

The Senators and Representatives before mentioned, and the Members of the several State Legislatures, and all executive and judicial Officers, both of the United States and of the several States, shall be bound by Oath or Affirmation, to support this Constitution; but no religious Test shall ever be required as a Qualification to any Office or public Trust under the United States.

Article VII.

The Ratification of the Conventions of nine States, shall be sufficient for the Establishment of this Constitution between the States so ratifying the Same.

Done in Convention by the Unanimous Consent of the States present the Seventeenth Day of September in the Year of our Lord one thousand seven hundred and Eighty seven and of the Independence of the United States of America the Twelfth. In witness whereof We have hereunto subscribed our Names,

Articles in Addition to, and Amendment of, the Constitution of the United States of America, Proposed by Congress, and Ratified by the Legislatures of the Several States, Pursuant to the Fifth Article of the Original Constitution.

Amendment I [9]

Congress shall make no law respecting an establishment of religion, or prohibiting the free exercise there-of; or abridging the freedom of speech, or of the press; or the right of the people peaceably to assemble, and to petition the Government for a redress of grievances.

Amendment II

A well regulated Militia, being necessary to the security of a free State, the right of the people to keep and bear Arms shall not be infringed.

Amendment III

No Soldier shall, in time of peace, be quartered in any house, without the consent of the Owner, nor in time of war, but in a manner to be prescribed by law.

Amendment IV

The right of the people to be secure in their persons, houses, papers, and effects, against unreasonable searches and seiz-ures, shall not be violated, and no Warrants shall issue, but upon probable cause, supported by Oath or affirmation, and particularly describing the place to be searched, and the persons or things to be seized.

Amendment V

No person shall be held to answer for a capital or otherwise infamous crime, unless on a presentment or indictment of a Grand Jury, except in cases arising in the land or naval forces, or in the Militia, when in actual service in time of War or public danger; nor shall any person be subject for the same offence to be twice put in jeopardy of life or limb; nor shall be compelled in any criminal case to be a witness against himself, nor be deprived of life, liberty, or property, without due process of law; nor shall private property be taken for public use, without just compensation.

Amendment VI

In all criminal prosecutions, the accused shall enjoy the right to a speedy and public trial, by an impartial jury of the State and district wherein the crime shall have been committed, which district shall have been previously ascertained by law, and to be informed of the nature and cause of the accusation; to be confronted with the witnesses against him; to have compulsory process for obtaining witnesses in his favor, and to have the Assistance of Counsel for his defence.

Amendment VII

In suits at common law, where the value in controversy shall exceed twenty dollars, the right of trial by jury shall be preserved, and no fact tried by a jury, shall be otherwise reexamined in any Court of the United States, than according to the rules of the common law.

Amendment VIII

Excessive bail shall not be required, nor excessive fines imposed, nor cruel and unusual punishments inflicted.

Amendment IX

The enumeration in the Constitution, of certain rights, shall not be construed to deny or disparage others retained by the people.

---

[9] The first ten amendments were passed by Congress September 25, 1789. They were ratified by three-fourths of the states December 15, 1791.

Amendment X

The powers not delegated to the United States by the Constitution; nor prohibited by it to the States, are reserved to the States respectively, or to the people.

Amendment XI [10]

The Judicial power of the United States shall not be construed to extend to any suit in law or equity, commenced or prosecuted against one of the United States by Citizens of another State, or by Citizens or Subjects of any Foreign State.

Amendment XII [11]

The Electors shall meet in their respective States and vote by ballot for President and Vice-President, one of whom, at least, shall not be an inhabitant of the same State with themselves; they shall name in their ballots the person voted for as President, and in distinct ballots the person voted for as Vice-President, and they shall make distinct lists of all persons voted for as President, and of all persons voted for as Vice-President, and of the number of votes for each, which lists they shall sign and certify, and transmit sealed to the seat of the government of the United States, directed to the President of the Senate;—The President of the Senate shall, in the presence of the Senate and House of Representatives, open all the certificates and the votes shall then be counted;—The person having the greatest number of votes for President, shall be the President, if such number be a majority of the whole number of Electors appointed; and if no person have such majority, then from the persons having the highest numbers not exceeding three on the list of those voted for as President, the House of Representatives shall choose immediately, by ballot, the President. But in choosing the President, the votes shall be taken by states, the representation from each state having one vote; a quorum for this purpose shall consist of a member or members from two-thirds of the states, and a majority of all the states shall be necessary to a choice. And if the House of Representatives shall not choose a President whenever the right of choice shall devolve upon them, before the fourth day of March next following, then the Vice-President shall act as President, as in the case of the death or other constitutional disability of the President.—The person having the greatest number of votes as Vice-President, shall be the Vice-President, if such number be a majority of the whole number of Electors appointed, and if no person have a majority, then from the two highest numbers on the list, the Senate shall choose the Vice-President; a quorum for the purpose shall consist of two-thirds of the whole number of Senators, and a majority of the whole number shall be necessary to a choice. But no person constitutionally ineligible to the office of President shall be eligible to that of Vice-President of the United States.

Amendment XIII [12]

Section 1. Neither slavery nor involuntary servitude, except as a punishment for crime whereof the party shall have been duly convicted, shall exist within the United States, or any place subject to their jurisdiction.

Section 2. Congress shall have power to enforce this article by appropriate legislation.

Amendment XIV [13]

Section 1. All persons born or naturalized in the United States, and subject to the jurisdiction thereof, are citizens of the United States and of the State wherein they reside. No State shall make or enforce any law which shall abridge the privileges or immunities of citizens of the United States; nor shall any State deprive any person of life, liberty, or property, without due process of law; nor deny to any person within its jurisdiction the equal protection of the laws.

Section 2. Representatives shall be apportioned among the several States according to their respective numbers, counting the whole number of persons in each State, excluding Indians not taxed. But when the right to vote at any election for the choice of electors for President and Vice-President of the United States, Representatives in Congress, the Executive and Judicial officers of a State, or the members of the Legislature thereof, is denied to any of the male inhabitants of such State, being twenty-one years of age, and citizens of the United States, or in any way abridged, except for participation in rebellion, or other crime, the basis of representation therein shall be reduced in the proportion which the number of such male citizens shall bear to the whole number of male citizens twenty-one years of age in such State.

Section 3. No person shall be a Senator or Representative in Congress, or elector of President and Vice-President, or hold any office, civil or military, under the United States, or under any State, who, having previously taken an oath, as a member of Congress, or as an officer of the United States, or as a member of any State legislature, or as an executive or judicial officer of any State, to support the Constitution of the United States, shall have engaged in insurrection or rebellion against the same, or given aid or comfort to the enemies thereof. But Congress may by a vote of two-thirds of each House, remove such disability.

Section 4. The validity of the public debt of the United States, authorized by law, including debts incurred for payment of pensions and bounties for services in suppressing insurrection or rebellion, shall not be questioned. But neither the United States nor any State shall assume or pay any debt or obligation incurred in aid of insurrection or rebellion against the United States, or any claim for the loss or emancipation of any slave; but all such debts, obligations, and claims shall be held illegal and void.

Section 5. The Congress shall have the power to enforce, by appropriate legislation, the provisions of this article.

Amendment XV [14]

Section 1. The right of citizens of the United States to vote shall not be denied or abridged by the United States or by any State on account of race, color, or previous conditions of servitude—

Section 2. The Congress shall have power to enforce this article by appropriate legislation.

[10] Passed March 4, 1794. Ratified January 23, 1795.
[11] Passed December 9, 1803. Ratified June 15, 1804.
[12] Passed January 31, 1865. Ratified December 6, 1865.
[13] Passed June 13, 1866. Ratified July 9, 1868.
[14] Passed February 26, 1869. Ratified February 2, 1870.

Amendment XVI

The Congress shall have power to lay and collect taxes on incomes, from whatever source derived, without apportionment among the several States, and without regard to any census or enumeration.

Amendment XVII[15]

The Senate of the United States shall be composed of two Senators from each State, elected by the people thereof, for six years; and each Senator shall have one vote. The electors in each State shall have the qualifications requisite for electors of the most numerous branch of the State legislatures.

When vacancies happen in the representation of any State in the Senate, the executive authority of such State shall issue writs of election to fill such vacancies: *Provided,* That the legislature of any State may empower the executive thereof to make temporary appointments until the people fill the vacancies by election as the legislature may direct.

This amendment shall not be so construed as to affect the election or term of any Senator chosen before it becomes valid as part of the Constitution.

Amendment XVIII[16]

Section 1. After one year from the ratification of this article the manufacture, sale, or transportation of intoxicating liquors within, the importation thereof into, or the exportation thereof from the United States and all territory subject to the jurisdiction thereof for beverage purposes is hereby prohibited.

Section 2. The Congress and the several States shall have concurrent power to enforce this article by appropriate legislation.

Section 3. This article shall be inoperative unless it shall have been ratified as an amendment to the Constitution by the legislatures of the several States, as provided in the Constitution, within seven years from the date of the submission hereof to the States by the Congress.

Amendment XIX[17]

The right of citizens of the United States to vote shall not be denied or abridged by the United States or by any State on account of sex.

Congress shall have power to enforce this article by appropriate legislation.

Amendment XX[18]

Section 1. The terms of the President and Vice-President shall end at noon on the 20th day of January, and the terms of Senators and Representatives at noon on the 3d day of January, of the years in which such terms would have ended if this article had not been ratified; and the terms of their successors shall then begin.

Section 2. The Congress shall assemble at least once in every year, and such meeting shall begin at noon on the 3d day of January, unless they shall by law appoint a different day.

Section 3. If, at the time fixed for the beginning of the term of the President, the President elect shall have died, the Vice-President elect shall become President. If a President shall not have been chosen before the time fixed for the beginning of his term, or if the President elect shall have failed to qualify, then the Vice-President elect shall act as President until a President shall have qualified; and the Congress may by law provide for the case wherein neither a President elect nor a Vice-President elect shall have qualified, declaring who shall then act as President, or the manner in which one who is to act shall be selected, and such person shall act accordingly until a President or Vice-President shall have qualified.

Section 4. The Congress may by law provide for the case of the death of any of the persons from whom the House of Representatives may choose a President whenever the right of choice shall have devolved upon them, and for the case of the death of any of the persons from whom the Senate may choose a Vice-President whenever the right of choice shall have devolved upon them.

Section 5. Sections 1 and 2 shall take effect on the 15th day of October following the ratification of this article.

Section 6. This article shall be inoperative unless it shall have been ratified as an amendment to the Constitution by the legislatures of three-fourths of the several States within seven years from the date of its submission.

Amendment XXI[19]

Section 1. The eighteenth article of amendment to the Constitution of the United States is hereby repealed.

Section 2. The transportation or importation into any State, Territory, or possession of the United States for delivery or use therein of intoxicating liquors, in violation of the laws thereof, is hereby prohibited.

Section 3. This article shall be inoperative unless it shall have been ratified as an amendment to the Constitution by conventions in the several States, as provided in the Constitution, within seven years from the date of the submission hereof to the States by the Congress.

Amendment XXII[20]

No person shall be elected to the office of the President more than twice, and no person who has held the office of President, or acted as President, for more than two years of a term to which some other person was elected President shall be elected to the office of the President more than once.

But this Article shall not apply to any person holding the office of President when this Article was proposed by the Congress, and shall not prevent any person who may be holding the office of President, or acting as President, during the term within which this Article becomes operative from holding the office of President or acting as President during the remainder of such term.

[15] Passed May 13, 1912. Ratified April 8, 1913.
[16] Passed December 18, 1917. Ratified January 16, 1919.
[17] Passed June 4, 1919. Ratified August 18, 1920.
[18] Passed March 2, 1932. Ratified January 23, 1933.

[19] Passed February 20, 1933. Ratified December 5, 1933.
[20] Passed March 12, 1947. Ratified March 1, 1951.

Amendment XXIII [21]

Section 1. The District constituting the seat of Government of the United States shall appoint in such manner as the Congress may direct:

A number of electors of President and Vice President equal to the whole number of Senators and Representatives in Congress to which the District would be entitled if it were a State, but in no event more than the least populous State; they shall be in addition to those appointed by the States, but they shall be considered, for the purposes of the election of President and Vice President, to be electors appointed by the State; and they shall meet in the District and perform such duties as provided by the twelfth article of amendment.

Section 2. The Congress shall have power to enforce this article by appropriate legislation.

Amendment XXIV [22]

Section 1. The right of citizens of the United States to vote in any primary or other election for President or Vice President, or for Senator or Representative in Congress, shall not be denied or abridged by the United States or any State by reason of failure to pay any poll tax or other tax.

Section 2. The Congress shall have power to enforce this article by appropriate legislation.

Amendment XXV [23]

Section 1. In case of the removal of the President from office or of his death or resignation, the Vice President shall become President.

Section 2. Whenever there is a vacancy in the office of the Vice-President, the President shall nominate a Vice President who shall take office upon confirmation by a majority vote of both Houses of Congress.

Section 3. Whenever the President transmits to the President pro tempore of the Senate and the Speaker of the House of Representatives his written declaration that he is unable to discharge the powers and duties of his office, and until he transmits them a written declaration to the contrary, such powers and duties shall be discharged by the Vice President as Acting President.

Section 4. Whenever the Vice President and a majority of either the principal officers of the executive department or of such other body as Congress may by law provide, transmit to the President pro tempore of the Senate and the Speaker of the House of Representatives their written declaration that the President is unable to discharge the powers and duties of his office, the Vice President shall immediately assume the powers and duties of the office of Acting President

Thereafter, when the President transmits to the President pro tempore of the Senate and the Speaker of the House of Representatives his written declaration that no inability exists, he shall resume the powers and duties of his office unless the Vice President and a majority of either the principal officers of the executive department or of such other body as Congress may by law provide, transmit within four days to the President pro tempore of the Senate and the Speaker of the House of Representatives their written declaration that the President is unable to discharge the powers and duties of his office. Thereupon Congress shall decide the issue, assembling within forty-eight hours for that purpose if not in session. If the Congress, within twenty-one days after receipt of the latter written declaration, or, if Congress is not in session, within twenty-one days after Congress is required to assemble, determines by two-thirds vote of both Houses that the President is unable to discharge the powers and duties of his office, the Vice-President shall continue to discharge the same as Acting President; otherwise, the President shall resume the powers and duties of his office.

Amendment XXVI [24]

Section 1. The right of citizens of the United States, who are eighteen years of age or older, to vote shall not be denied or abridged by the United States or by any State on account of age.

Section 2. The Congress shall have power to enforce this article by appropriate legislation.

Amendment XXVII [25]

No law, varying the compensation for the service of the Senators and Representatives, shall take effect, until an election of Representatives shall have intervened.

---

[21] Passed June 16, 1960. Ratified April 3, 1961.
[22] Passed August 27, 1962. Ratified January 23, 1964.
[23] Passed July 6, 1965. Ratified February 11, 1967.

[24] Passed March 23, 1971. Ratified July 5, 1971.
[25] Passed September 25, 1789. Ratified May 7, 1992.

Glossary

abolitionism The movement that emerged in the 1830s in the United States dedicated to the immediate end of slavery.

Abraham Lincoln The sixteenth president (1861–1865), he led the United States throughout the Civil War.

African American soldiers Finally allowed to enlist in May 1863, African American soldiers accounted for more than one hundred eighty thousand troops and played a major role in the Union victory.

Agricultural Adjustment Act Created under Roosevelt's New Deal program to help farmers, its purpose was to reduce production of staple crops, thereby raising farm prices and encouraging more diversified farming.

Al Smith A vigorous reformer as governor of New York, he became the first Roman Catholic to win the nomination of a major party for president of the United States.

Alain Locke An African American poet and an important member of the Harlem Renaissance.

Alan Freed The self-proclaimed father of rock 'n' roll, he was the first DJ to play black rhythm and blues artists on the radio.

Albert B. Fall The secretary of the interior involved in the Teapot Dome scandal.

Alexander Graham Bell His invention of the telephone at the end of the nineteenth century changed the nature of life in the United States.

Alexander Hamilton The first U.S. secretary of the treasury (1789–1795), he established the national bank and public credit system. In 1804 Hamilton was mortally wounded in a duel with his political rival Aaron Burr.

Alger Hiss A U.S. public official accused of espionage at the height of the Cold War, he was convicted of perjury in 1950 in a controversial case.

Alice Paul A main figure in the radical wing of the woman's suffrage movement in the early twentieth century.

Alphonse "Al" Capone A gangster devoted to gaining control of gambling, prostitution, and bootlegging in the Chicago area.

Amistad A slave ship on which forty-nine Africans rebelled in 1839 off the coast of Cuba. The ship sailed to Long Island Sound where Spanish authorities demanded they be turned over for punishment. A group of American abolitionists, led by former President John Quincy Adams, fought for and won their freedom in 1841. The thirty-five who survived returned to Africa.

Amos 'n' Andy The most popular radio program of the Depression years, it portrayed the lives of two African American men in Harlem as interpreted by two white entertainers, Freeman Gosden and Charles Correll.

Anaconda Plan Term given to the strategy employed by the North during the Civil War in which the Confederacy would be slowly strangled by a blockade.

Andrew Carnegie A major business leader in the evolution of the steel industry.

Andrew Jackson The seventh president of the United States (1829–1837) who, as a general in the War of 1812, defeated the Red Sticks at Horseshoe Bend (1814) and the British at New Orleans (1815). As president he denied the right of individual states to nullify federal laws and increased presidential powers.

Andrew Johnson The seventeenth president of the United States (1865–1869); he succeeded the assassinated Abraham Lincoln.

Anita Hill She brought charges of sexual misconduct against Clarence Thomas and herself became a very polarizing figure as a result.

Anne Hutchinson English-born American colonist and religious leader who was banished from Boston (1637) for her religious beliefs, which included an emphasis on an individual's direct communication with God.

annexation To append or attach, especially to a larger or more significant thing.

Antietam The battle near Sharpsburg, Maryland, in September 1862 in which the Union Army stopped the Confederacy's drive into the North. With twenty-five thousand casualties, it was the bloodiest single-day battle of the Civil War.

anti-imperialists A league created during the last two years of McKinley's first term to unite the opposition against McKinley's foreign policy.

Antonio López de Santa Anna Leader of Mexico at the time of the battle at the Alamo. Taken prisoner when attacked at San Jacinto, he signed treaties removing Mexican troops from Texas, granting Texas its independence, and recognizing the Rio Grande as the boundary.

Appomattox The small Virginia village that served as the site of surrender of Confederate forces under Robert E. Lee to Ulysses S. Grant on April 9, 1865, generally recognized as bringing the Civil War to an end.

Articles of Confederation The compact first adopted by the original thirteen states of the United States in 1781 that remained the supreme law until 1789.

Atlanta Compromise A program for African American acceptance of white supremacy put forth by Booker T. Washington.

Atlantic slave trade In the 1440s Portugal initiated the trans-Atlantic trade that lasted four centuries. During that time, other European nations participated in a commerce that took more than ten million people from Africa.

Aztec Inhabitants of the Valley of Mexico who founded their capital, Tenochtitlán, in the early fourteenth century. Prior to the arrival of the Spanish, the Aztecs built a large empire in which they dominated many neighboring peoples. Their civilization included engineering, mathematics, art, and music.

baby boom A sudden increase in births in the years after World War II.

Bank of the United States The first bank was established in 1791 as part of the system proposed by Alexander Hamilton to launch the new government on a sound economic basis.

Bataan Peninsula U.S. and Philippine World War II troops surrendered this peninsula in western Luzon, Philippines, to the Japanese in April 1942 after an extended siege; U.S. forces recaptured the peninsula in February 1945.

Battle of Wounded Knee The last major chapter in the Indian wars, it was fought on the Pine Ridge Reservation in South Dakota.

Bay of Pigs Fifteen hundred Cuban exiles, supported by the CIA, landed here on April 17, 1961, in an unsuccessful attempt to overthrow the new Communist government of Fidel Castro.

Benjamin Franklin An American public official, writer, scientist, and printer. He proposed a plan for union at the Albany Congress (1754) and played a major part in the American Revolution. Franklin helped secure French support for the colonists, negotiated the Treaty of Paris (1783), and helped draft the Constitution (1787). His numerous scientific and practical innovations include the lightning rod, bifocal spectacles, and a stove.

Benjamin Harrison The twenty-third president of the United States, he lost the popular vote but gained a majority of the electoral college votes in the 1888 election.

Betty Friedan A feminist who wrote *The Feminist Mystique* in 1963 and founded the National Organization for Women in 1966.

bicameral legislature A legislature with two houses or chambers.

Bill Morris A black man burned at the stake in Balltown, Louisiana, for allegedly robbing and raping a white woman; no trial was held.

Bill of Rights The first ten amendments to the Constitution. These contain basic protection of the rights of individuals from abuses by the federal government, including freedom of speech, press, religion, and assembly.

Black Power Movement that developed in the mid-1960s calling for renewed racial pride in their African American heritage. They believed that to seek full integration into the existing white order would be to capitulate to the institutions of racism.

Black Thursday October 29, 1929, the day the spectacular New York stock market crash began.

Bleeding Kansas Nickname given to the Kansas Territory in the wake of a number of clashes between proslavery and antislavery supporters.

Bonus Army Thousands of veterans, determined to collect promised cash bonuses early, came to Washington during the summer of 1932 to listen to Congress debate the bonus proposal.

Booker T. Washington A spokesman for blacks in the 1890s who argued that African Americans should emphasize hard work and personal development rather than rebelling against their conditions.

bootleggers Enterprising individuals who moved alcohol across the border into the United States from Canada and the Caribbean during Prohibition. Their wares were sold at illegal saloons or "speakeasies" where city dwellers congregated in the evenings.

border ruffians Missouri settlers who crossed into Kansas to lend support for proslavery issues (1855).

Boss Politics An urban "political machine" that relied for its existence on the votes of the large inner-city population. The flow of money through the machine was often based on corruption.

Boston Massacre (1770) A pre-Revolutionary incident growing out of the resentment against the British troops sent to Boston to maintain order and to enforce the Townshend Act.

Boston Tea Party In 1773 Bostonians protested the Tea Act, which retained the Townshend duty on tea and granted a monopoly on tea sales in the colonies to the East India Company, by dumping chests of tea into Boston Harbor.

brain trust A group of prominent academics recruited as a source of ideas for the Roosevelt campaign to write speeches.

Branch Davidians A religious sect involved in a siege by government agents in Waco, Texas, in April 1993 that ended in deadly violence.

Brown v. Board of Education The unanimous Supreme Court decision ruling that segregated facilities in public education were "inherently unequal" and violated the Fourteenth Amendment's guarantee of equal protection under the law. This decision overruled the longstanding "separate but equal" doctrine of *Plessy v. Ferguson*.

Camp David Accords The historic treaty between Egypt and Israel, brokered by President Carter at Camp David in 1978, that returned the Sinai Peninsula to Egypt in return for Egypt's recognition of the State of Israel.

Carrie Chapman Catt A leader in the woman's suffrage campaign.

Cesar Chavez A labor organizer who founded the National Farm Workers Association in 1962.

Charles A. Lindbergh His solo flight across the Atlantic Ocean in 1927 made him an international hero.

Charles Evans Hughes A Supreme Court justice, he was the Republican candidate for president in the 1916 election. He had been a progressive governor of New York and said little about foreign policy.

Charles Grandison Finney An American evangelist, theologian, and educator (1792–1875). Licensed to the Presbyterian ministry in 1824, he had phenomenal success as a revivalist in the eastern states, converting many who became noted abolitionists.

Charles Sumner U.S. senator from Massachusetts (1851–1874), he was a noted orator with an uncompromising opposition to slavery.

Charlotte Perkins Gilman An ardent advocate of feminism.

Christopher Columbus An Italian mariner who sailed for Spain in 1492 in search of a western route to Asia. He located San Salvador in the West Indies, opening the Americas to European exploration and colonization.

Civil Works Administration (CWA) The agency tasked with creating jobs and restoring self-respect by handing out pay envelopes instead of relief checks. In reality, workers sometimes performed worthless tasks, known as "boondoggles," but much of the $1 billion budget was spent on projects of lasting value including airports and roads.

Civilian Conservation Corps (CCC) One of the New Deal's most popular programs, it took unem-

ployed young men from the cities and put them to work on conservation projects in the country.

Clarence Thomas A Supreme Court justice appointed by President George H. W. Bush in 1991 whose confirmation became controversial due to allegations of sexual misconduct made against him.

Cold War War or rivalry conducted by all means available except open military action. Diplomatic relations are not commonly broken.

Colin Powell He served as chairman of the Joint Chiefs of Staff from 1989 to 1996 and was influential in planning U.S. strategy during the Persian Gulf War.

Common Sense Published by Thomas Paine in January 1776, *Common Sense* convinced the American public of the need for independence.

Confederacy The Confederate States of America.

Constitutional Convention Fifty-five delegates met in Philadelphia in May 1787 to reform the U.S. government. They chose to draft a new constitution rather than revise the Articles of Confederation.

contrabands Term used by the Union for the black people who made their way to the Union ranks. This term usually applies to goods prohibited by law or treaty from being imported or exported.

Contract with America The Republican election platform of the 1990s, promising action on such items as a balanced budget amendment, term limits for Congress members, and making legislators obey the regulations they applied to society.

Contras A Nicaraguan military force trained and financed by the United States that opposed the socialist Nicaraguan government led by the Sandinista party.

Copperheads A term used by some Republicans to describe Peace Democrats. It implied that they were traitors to the Union. Peace Democrats thought that the war was a failure and should be abandoned.

Crazy Horse Native American Sioux leader who defeated George Custer in battle.

daguerreotypes An early photographic process with the image made on a light-sensitive, silver-coated metallic plate.

Dawes Act This act distributed land to the Indians so that it could be sold to whites.

Dayton Peace Accords A peace settlement involving Bosnia in 1995 that was worked out in Dayton, Ohio; it did not prove to be a permanent solution for the problems in the Balkans.

Declaration of Independence The document, drafted primarily by Thomas Jefferson, that declared the independence of the thirteen mainland colonies from Great Britain and enumerated their reasons for separating.

Denmark Vesey American insurrectionist. A freed slave in South Carolina, he was implicated in the planning of a large uprising of slaves and was hanged. The event led to more stringent slave codes in many southern states.

détente An easing of tensions among countries, which usually leads to increased economic, diplomatic, and other types of contacts between former rivals.

dollar diplomacy A phrase used to describe Secretary of State Philander C. Knox's foreign policy under President Taft, which focused on expanding American investments abroad, especially in Latin America and China.

Dominion of New England In an effort to centralize the colonies and create consistent laws and political structures, James II combined Massachusetts, New Hampshire, Maine, Plymouth, Rhode Island, Connecticut, New York, and New Jersey under the Dominion of New England.

domino theory A theory that if one nation comes under Communist control, neighboring nations will soon follow.

Dorothea Dix An American philanthropist, reformer, and educator who took charge of nurses for the U.S. in the Civil War.

Dred Scott **case** An enslaved man sued for his freedom in 1847, leading to a crucial Supreme Court decision in 1857 in which the Court ruled that African Americans held no rights as citizens and that the Missouri Compromise of 1820 was unconstitutional. The decision was widely denounced in the North and strengthened the new Republican party.

Dust Bowl The name given to areas of the prairie states that suffered ecological devastation in the 1930s and then again to a lesser extent in the mid-1950s.

Edmond Genêt French ambassador who enlisted American mercenaries to assist the French against the British. Genêt's move threatened relations between the United States and Britain.

Edward Bellamy The author of *Looking Backward* (1888), a major protest novel.

Eleanor Roosevelt A diplomat, writer, and First Lady of the United States (1933–1945) as the wife of President Franklin D. Roosevelt. A delegate to the United Nations (1945–1953 and 1961–1962), she was an outspoken advocate for human rights. Her written works include *This I Remember* (1949).

election of 1840 The election between Democrat Martin Van Buren and the Whig party's William Henry Harrison, won by Harrison.

electoral college The group that elects the president. Each state received as many electors as it had congressmen and senators combined.

Eli Whitney American inventor and manufacturer whose invention of the cotton gin (1793) revolutionized the cotton industry. He also established the first factory to assemble muskets with interchangeable parts.

Elizabeth Cady Stanton American feminist and social reformer who helped organize the first woman's rights convention, held in Seneca Falls, New York (1848), for which she wrote a Declaration of Sentiments calling for the reform of discriminatory practices that perpetuated sexual inequality.

Elizabeth I Queen of England (1558–1603) who succeeded the Catholic Mary I and reestablished Protestantism in England. Her reign was marked by several plots to overthrow her, the execution of Mary Queen of Scots (1587), the defeat of the Spanish Armada (1588), and domestic prosperity and literary achievement.

Ellis Island An immigration station opened in 1892 where new arrivals were passed through a medical examination and were questioned about their economic prospects.

emancipation The ending of slavery, initiated in the Emancipation Proclamation of 1863 but not accomplished in many places until the Confederate surrender in 1865.

Enlightenment A philosophical movement of the eighteenth century that emphasized the use of reason to scrutinize previously accepted doctrines and traditions and that brought about many humanitarian reforms.

Enola Gay The B-29 bomber, named after the mother of pilot Colonel Paul W. Tibbets, that dropped the first atomic bomb on the Japanese city of Hiroshima on August 6, 1945, killing more than one hundred thousand people.

Equal Rights Amendment (ERA) Congress overwhelmingly passed the Equal Rights Amendment in 1972, but by the mid-1970s conservative groups had managed to stall its confirmation by the states.

Era of Good Feelings Period in U.S. history (1817–1823) when, the Federalist party having declined, there was little open party feeling.

Erie Canal The first major American canal, stretching two hundred fifty miles from Lake Erie across the state of New York to Albany, where boats then traveled down the Hudson River to New York City. Begun in 1818, it was completed in 1825.

Eugene Debs Leader of the American Railway Union, which struck in sympathy with the workers at the Pullman Palace Car Company. This labor dispute experience helped persuade Debs to become a leader of the Socialist party.

Executive Order 9066 Issued by President Roosevelt on February 19, 1942, it designated certain parts of the country as sensitive military areas from which "any or all persons may be excluded," which led to the forced evacuation of more than one hundred twenty thousand people of Japanese ancestry from the West Coast of the United States.

F. Scott Fitzgerald A serious novelist of the day and author of *The Great Gatsby* who, along with his wife Zelda, captured attention as the embodiment of the free spirit of the Jazz Age.

Fannie Lou Hamer Daughter of illiterate Mississippi sharecroppers, she helped lead the civil rights struggle in Mississippi, focusing on voting rights for African Americans and representation in the national Democratic party.

Fidel Castro Cuban revolutionary leader who overthrew the corrupt regime of dictator Fulgencio Batista in 1959 and soon after established a Communist state. Prime minister of Cuba from 1959 to 1976, he has been president of the government and First Secretary of the Communist party in Cuba since 1976.

fire-eaters Southerners who were enthusiastic supporters of southern rights and later of secession.

flappers Young, single, middle-class women who wore their hair and dresses short, rolled their stockings down, used cosmetics, and smoked in public. Signaling a desire for independence and equality, flappers were self-reliant, outspoken, and had a new appreciation for the pleasures of life.

Fort Sumter The fort in the harbor of Charleston, South Carolina, that was fired on by the Confederacy on April 12, 1861, triggering the Civil War.

forty-niners Mostly men lured to California by the gold rush of 1849.

Fourteen Points Wilson's peace program, which included freedom of the seas, free trade, and more open diplomacy.

Francis Drake English naval hero and explorer who was the first Englishman to circumnavigate the world (1577–1580) and was vice admiral of the fleet that destroyed the Spanish Armada (1588).

Francis Gary Powers Pilot of a U.S. U-2 high altitude reconnaissance aircraft shot down over the Soviet Union on May 1, 1960.

Franklin D. Roosevelt The thirty-second president of the United States, he assumed the presidency at the depth of the Great Depression and helped the American people regain faith in themselves. He brought hope with his inaugural address in which he promised prompt, vigorous action and asserted that "the only thing we have to fear is fear itself."

Franz Ferdinand An Austrian archduke murdered along with his wife in Sarajevo, Bosnia. Austria's response to the dual murder led to the beginnings of World War I.

Frederick Douglass American abolitionist and journalist who escaped from slavery (1838) and became an influential lecturer in the North and abroad. He wrote *Narrative of the Life of Frederick Douglass* (1845) and cofounded and edited the *North Star* (1847–1860), an abolitionist newspaper.

free blacks The name often given to the hundreds of thousands of unenslaved African Americans who lived in the American South, especially in the Upper South states of Maryland and Virginia and in all the major cities of the region, during the days of slavery.

Freedmen's Bureau A federal agency created in 1865 to supervise newly freed people. It oversaw relations between whites and blacks in the South, issued food rations, and supervised labor contracts.

freedom riders Interracial groups who rode buses in the South so that a series of federal court decisions declaring segregation on buses and in waiting rooms unconstitutional would not be ignored by white officials.

Free-Soil party A U.S. political party formed in 1848 to oppose the extension of slavery into the territories; merged with the Liberty party in 1848.

French and Indian War The name often used for the Seven Years' War in North America. The conflict began in 1754 in the Ohio Valley between British colonists and the French and their Indian allies.

Fugitive Slave Act The federal act of 1850 providing for the return between states of escaped black slaves.

General Douglas MacArthur He served as chief of staff (1930–1935) and commanded the Allied forces in the South Pacific during World War II. Initially losing the Philippines to the Japanese in 1942, he regained the islands and accepted the surrender of Japan in 1945. He commanded the UN forces in Korea (1950–1951) until a conflict in strategies led to his dismissal by President Truman.

General Dwight D. Eisenhower The thirty-fourth president of the United States and supreme commander of the Allied Expeditionary Force during World War II. He launched the invasion of Normandy (June 6, 1944) and oversaw the final defeat of Germany in 1945.

General George C. Marshall A soldier, diplomat, and politician who, as U.S. secretary of state (1947–1949), organized the European Recovery Plan, often called the Marshall Plan, for which he received the 1953 Nobel Peace Prize.

General William Westmoreland General who was the senior commander of U.S. troops in Vietnam from 1964 through 1968.

George Armstrong Custer Colonel famous for his battle at Little Big Horn against the Sioux Indians.

George B. McClellan Major General of the United States Army who led forces in Virginia in 1861 and 1862. He was widely blamed for not taking advantage of his numerical superiority to defeat the Confederates around Richmond. McClellan ran against Abraham Lincoln for president in 1864 on the Democratic ticket.

George Dewey On May 1, 1898, he inflicted a decisive defeat on the Spanish Navy at Manila Bay in the Philippine Islands.

George H. W. Bush The forty-first president of the United States, he was in office when the Soviet Union collapsed.

George Herman "Babe" Ruth This Boston Red Sox pitcher was sold to the New York Yankees in 1918 for $400,000. He belted out fifty-four home runs during the 1920 season, and fans flocked to see him play.

George McGovern A U.S. senator from South Dakota, he opposed the Vietnam War and was defeated as the 1972 Democratic candidate for president.

George Pullman Developer of the railroad sleeping car and creator of a model town outside Chicago where his employees were to live.

George Rogers Clark American military leader and frontiersman who led raids on British troops and Native Americans in the West during the Revolutionary War.

George W. Bush The forty-third president of the United States.

George Wallace A three-time governor of Alabama, he first came to national attention as an outspoken segregationist. Wallace ran unsuccessfully for the presidency in 1968 and 1972.

George Washington Commander-in-chief of the Continental Army during the American Revolution, presiding officer at the Constitutional Convention, and the first president of the United States (1789–1797).

Gerald Ford The thirty-eighth president of the United States, he was appointed vice president on the resignation of Spiro Agnew and became president when Richard Nixon resigned over the Watergate scandal. As president, Ford granted a full pardon to Nixon in 1974.

Geronimo An Apache leader who resisted white incursions until his capture in 1886.

Gettysburg Address A brief speech given by President Lincoln at the dedication of the Gettysburg Cemetery in November 1863 that declared that the Civil War was dedicated to freedom.

Gifford Pinchot He worked closely with Roosevelt to formulate a conservation policy that involved managing natural resources, not locking them up for indefinite future use.

Glorious Revolution The English Revolution of 1688–1689 against the authoritarian policies and Catholicism of James II. James was forced into exile, and his daughter Mary and her husband William of Orange took the throne. The revolution secured the dominance of Parliament over royal power.

good neighbor policy A new Latin American policy wherein Hoover withdrew the Marines from Nicaragua and Haiti, and in 1930 the State Department renounced the Roosevelt Corollary of 1904.

Granville T. Woods A black inventor who devised the "third rail" to convey electric power to streetcars.

Great Awakening An immense religious revival that swept across the Protestant world.

great compromise A plan proposed by a delegation from Connecticut that established a bicameral

Congress with a House of Representatives, based on a state's population, and the Senate, in which each state would be represented equally.

Great Migration A massive movement of blacks leaving the South for cities in the North that began slowly in 1910 and accelerated between 1914 and 1920. During this time, more than six hundred thousand African Americans left the South.

Grimké sisters The first female abolitionist speakers; they were prominent figures in the antislavery movement of the late 1830s.

Grover Cleveland The twenty-second and twenty-fourth president of the United States, he was the first Democrat elected to the presidency after the Civil War.

Gulf of Tonkin Resolution Following reports of a confrontation with North Vietnamese in the Tonkin Gulf in 1964, President Johnson requested, and received, congressional authority to "take all necessary measures" to repel "further aggression" in Vietnam, giving the president formal authority to escalate the war.

Half-Way Covenant The Puritan practice whereby parents who had been baptized but had not yet experienced conversion could bring their children before the church and have them baptized.

Harpers Ferry A Virginia town that was the site of John Brown's raid in 1859, a failed attempt to lead a slave insurrection. It ignited public opinion in both the North and the South.

Harriet Beecher Stowe Author of *Uncle Tom's Cabin* (1852), the most important abolitionist novel.

Harriet Tubman An escaped slave who returned to the South and led hundreds of enslaved people to freedom in the North. Active throughout the 1850s, Tubman became famous as the most active member of the Underground Railroad.

Harry Hopkins Roosevelt's choice to run the Federal Emergency Relief Administration. He eventually became Roosevelt's closest advisor.

Harry S. Truman The thirty-third president of the United States, he took office following the death of Franklin D. Roosevelt. Reelected in 1948 in a stunning political upset, Truman's controversial and historic decisions included the use of atomic weapons against Japan, desegregation of the U.S. military, and dismissal of General MacArthur as commander of U.S. forces during the Korean War.

Hartford Convention A gathering of Federalists in 1814 that called for significant amendments to the Constitution and attempted to damage the Republican party. The Treaty of Ghent and Andrew Jackson's victory at New Orleans annulled any recommendation of the convention.

Haymarket Affair On May 4, 1886, workmen in Chicago gathered to protest police conduct during a strike at a factory of the McCormick Company.

Henry Cabot Lodge A Massachusetts senator best remembered for spearheading Senate blockage of American membership in the League of Nations on the ground that its covenant threatened American sovereignty.

Henry Clay American politician who pushed the Missouri Compromise through the U.S. House of Representatives (1820) in an effort to reconcile free and slave states.

Henry Ford An automaker who developed the assembly line and low-priced automobiles.

Henry Kissinger A German-born American diplomat, he was national security advisor and U.S. secretary of state under Presidents Nixon and Ford.

He shared the 1973 Nobel Peace Prize for helping to negotiate the Vietnam ceasefire.

Herman Melville Author of *Moby Dick* (1851), often considered to be the greatest American novel of the nineteenth century.

Hernán Cortés Spanish explorer who conquered the Aztecs initially in 1519, retreated when they rebelled, then defeated them again, aided by a smallpox epidemic, in 1521.

Ho Chi Minh Vietnamese leader and first president of North Vietnam. His army was victorious in the French Indochina War, and he later led North Vietnam's struggle to defeat the U.S.-supported government of South Vietnam. He died before the reunification of Vietnam.

Homer A. Plessy In a test of an 1890 law specifying that blacks must ride in separate railroad cars, this one-eighth-black man boarded a train and sat in the car reserved for whites. When the conductor instructed him to move, he refused and was arrested.

Homestead strike A labor uprising of workers at a steel plant in Homestead, Pennsylvania, in 1892 that was put down by military force.

Hoovervilles Makeshift "villages" usually at the edge of a city with "homes" made of cardboard, scrap metal, or whatever was cheap and available and named for President Hoover who was despised by the poor for his apparent refusal to help them.

Horace Greeley Grant's opponent in the 1872 election. Seen as a political oddball in the eyes of many Americans, the sixty-one-year-old editor favored the protective tariff and was indifferent to civil service reform. He was also passionate about ideas such as vegetarianism and the use of human manure in farming.

horizontal integration A procedure wherein a company takes over competitors to achieve control within an industry.

House Un-American Activities Committee (HUAC) Formed in the 1930s as a watchdog against Nazi propaganda, HUAC was revived after World War II as a watchdog against Communist propaganda.

Huey P. Long A Populist but dictatorial governor of Louisiana (1928–1932), he instituted major public works legislation, and as a U.S. senator (1932–1935), he proposed a national "Share-the-Wealth" program.

Hull House Founded in 1889 by Jane Addams and Ellen Gates Starr as a settlement home in a Chicago neighborhood to help solve the troubling problems of American city life.

Ida Tarbell A preeminent female crusading journalist.

Ida Wells Barnett An African American leader of an antilynching campaign.

impeachment The act of charging a public official with misconduct in office.

Indian Removal Act Passed in 1830, this act set aside land in the Oklahoma Territory for American Indians to be removed from the eastern United States. Over the next eight years, tens of thousands of Choctaw, Chickasaw, and Cherokee people were transported from their homes on what the Cherokees called the "Trail of Tears."

Interstate Commerce Act Passed by Congress in 1887, this act set up an Interstate Commerce Commission (ICC), which could investigate complaints of railroad misconduct or file suit against the companies.

Interstate Commerce Commission Passage of the Hepburn Act in 1906 gave this commission the power to establish maximum rates and to review the accounts and records of the railroads.

Iran-Contra scandal A major scandal of the second Reagan term that involved shipping arms to Iran and diverting money from the sale of these weapons to the Contra rebels in Nicaragua.

Iron Curtain The military, political, and ideological barrier established between the Soviet bloc and Western Europe from 1945 to 1990.

J. P. Morgan He purchased Carnegie Steel Company in 1901 for $480 million from Andrew Carnegie, creating United States Steel, which controlled 60 percent of the steel industry's productive capacity.

Jack Johnson The first African American heavyweight boxing champion, taking the title in 1908.

Jackie Robinson The first African American player in the Major Leagues in the twentieth century, he was a second baseman for the Brooklyn Dodgers, had a lifetime batting average of .311, and was inducted into the Baseball Hall of Fame in 1962.

James Buchanan The fifteenth president of the United States (1857–1861). He tried to maintain a balance between proslavery and antislavery factions, but his views angered radicals in both the North and South.

James Madison The fourth president of the United States (1809–1817). A member of the Continental Congress (1780–1783) and the Constitutional Convention (1787), he strongly supported ratification of the Constitution and was a contributor to *The Federalist Papers* (1787–1788), which argued the effectiveness of the proposed constitution.

James Monroe The fifth president of the United States (1817–1825), whose administration was marked by the acquisition of Florida (1819), the Missouri Compromise (1820) in which Missouri was declared a slave state, and the profession of the Monroe Doctrine (1823), declaring U.S. opposition to European interference in the Americas.

James Oglethorpe Along with John Viscount Percival, Oglethorpe sought a charter to colonize Georgia, the last of the British mainland colonies. Upon royal approval, he founded the colony with the intention of establishing a society of small farmers, without slavery or hard liquor.

James Wolfe British general in Canada. He defeated the French at Quebec (1759) but was mortally wounded in the battle.

Jamestown The first permanent English settlement in America (1607), it was located on the James River in Virginia.

Jane Addams Pioneer of settlement houses in Chicago and a major reform leader.

Jay Treaty Concluded in 1794 between the United States and Great Britain to settle difficulties arising mainly out of violations of the Treaty of Paris of 1783 and to regulate commerce and navigation.

Jefferson Davis United States senator, secretary of war and then president of the Confederacy (1861–1865). He was captured by Union soldiers in 1865 and imprisoned for two years. Although he was indicted for treason (1866), he was never prosecuted.

Jesse Jackson A Baptist minister and civil rights leader, he directed national antidiscrimination efforts in the mid-1960s and 1970s. His concern for the oppressed and his dramatic oratory attracted a large grassroots constituency.

Jimmy Carter The thirty-ninth president of the United States, his successes in office, including the Camp David Accords, were overshadowed by domestic worries and an international crisis involving the taking of American hostages at the U.S. Embassy in Iran. He was defeated by Ronald Reagan in the 1980 presidential election.

John Adams The first vice president (1789–1797) and second president (1797–1801) of the United States. He was a major figure during the American Revolution: he helped draft the Declaration of Independence and served on the commission to negotiate the Treaty of Paris (1783).

John Brown American abolitionist who, in 1859 with twenty-one followers, captured the U.S. arsenal at Harpers Ferry as part of an effort to liberate southern slaves. His group was defeated, and Brown was hanged after a trial in which he won sympathy as an abolitionist martyr.

John C. Calhoun Vice president of the United States (1825–1832) under John Quincy Adams and Andrew Jackson. In his political philosophy he maintained that the states had the right to nullify federal legislation that they deemed unconstitutional.

John Calvin French-born Swiss Protestant theologian who broke with the Roman Catholic Church (1533) and set forth the tenets of his theology, the Reformed tradition including Puritans, Huguenots, Presbyterians, and Dutch Reformed, in *Institutes of the Christian Religion* (1536).

John D. Rockefeller Key figure in the development of the oil industry and the growth of large corporations.

John F. Kennedy The thirty-fifth president of the United States, he was the first Catholic to win the White House and the first president born in the twentieth century. He was assassinated in 1963 during a trip to Dallas, Texas.

John Glenn On February 20, 1962, aboard the *Friendship 7*, he was the first American to orbit the earth, and in 1998 he was the oldest person to participate in a space flight mission as a crew member of the space shuttle *Discovery*. From 1974 to 1998 he served as U.S. Senator from Ohio.

John Jay American diplomat and jurist who served in the Continental Congress and helped negotiate the Treaty of Paris (1783). He was the first chief justice of the U.S. Supreme Court (1789–1795) and negotiated the agreement with Great Britain that became known as the Jay Treaty (1794–1795).

John L. Lewis A labor leader who was president of the United Mine Workers of America (1920–1960) and the Congress of Industrial Organizations (1935–1940).

John L. Sullivan A famous Irish American boxing champion of the late nineteenth century.

John Locke An English philosopher and author of *An Essay Concerning Human Understanding* (1690), which challenged the notion of innate knowledge, and *Two Treatises on Civil Government* (1690), which discussed the social contract.

John Marshall American jurist and politician who served as the chief justice of the U.S. Supreme Court (1801–1835) and helped establish the practice of judicial review.

John Nance "Cactus Jack" Garner Speaker of the House in 1931 whose answer to the growing budget deficit was to offer a national sales tax. He

ran against Roosevelt for the Democratic nomination for president but released his delegates and was in turn rewarded with the vice presidential nomination.

John Pemberton An Atlanta druggist who in 1886 developed a syrup from an extract of the cola nut that he mixed with carbonated water and called "Coca Cola."

John Smith English colonist, explorer, and writer whose maps and accounts of his explorations in Virginia and New England were invaluable to later explorers and colonists.

John Wilkes Booth An actor and southern sympathizer who assassinated Abraham Lincoln on April 14, 1865.

Joseph McCarthy A U.S. senator from Wisconsin (1947–1957), he presided over the permanent subcommittee on investigations and held public hearings in which he accused Army officials, members of the media, and public figures of being Communists. These charges were never proved, and he was censured by the Senate in 1954.

Joseph Smith An American religious leader who founded the Church of Jesus Christ of Latter-Day Saints (1830) and led his congregation westward from New York State to western Illinois, where he was murdered by an anti-Mormon mob.

Juan de Oñate Spanish explorer and conquistador who claimed New Mexico for Spain in 1598 and served as its governor until he was removed on charges of cruelty in 1607.

Kansas-Nebraska Act Written by Stephen A. Douglas, the act declared that people of new territories could decide for themselves whether or not their states would permit slaves and slaveholders.

Kenneth Starr Special prosecutor appointed to investigate the Whitewater affair. He expanded his investigation into other matters and eventually sent a report to the House of Representatives alleging that there were grounds for impeaching Clinton for lying under oath, obstruction of justice, abuse of power, and other offenses.

Kent State University National Guardsmen were sent to this Ohio campus to restore order following a series of tumultuous antiwar protests in May 1970. They fired into a crowd of students, killing four and wounding nine others.

Knights of Labor A labor organization that combined fraternal ritual, the language of Christianity, and a belief in the social equality of all citizens.

Know-Nothings The popular name for the American party, an anti-immigration party of the mid-1850s, derived from their response to any question about their activities: "I know nothing."

La Raza Unida Formed in 1969 by Mexican American activists, it reflected the growing demand for political and cultural recognition of "Chicano" causes, especially in the Southwest.

Lee Harvey Oswald Alleged assassin of President John F. Kennedy, he was shot two days later while under arrest.

Lend-Lease Passed in 1941, this act forged the way for the United States to transfer military supplies to the Allies, primarily Great Britain and the Soviet Union.

Levittown An unincorporated community of 53,286 people in southeast New York on western Long Island, which was founded in 1947 as a low-cost housing development for World War II veterans.

Lewis and Clark expedition From 1804 to 1806 Meriwether Lewis and William Clark led the Corps

of Discovery from St. Louis to the Pacific coast and back. They informed Native Americans that the United States had acquired the territory from France and recorded geographic and scientific data.

Liberal Republicans Organization formed in 1872 by Republicans discontented with the political corruption and the policies of President Grant's first administration.

Liberty Bonds Thirty-year government bonds sold to individuals with an annual interest rate of 3.5 percent. They were offered in five issues between 1917 and 1920, and their purchase was equated with patriotic duty.

Liberty party A U.S. political party formed in 1839 to oppose the practice of slavery; it merged with the Free-Soil party in 1848.

Lincoln-Douglas debates Seven debates between Stephen A. Douglas and Abraham Lincoln for the Illinois senatorial race of 1858.

Little Richard An American rock 'n' roll singer noted for his flamboyant style, he influenced many artists including Elvis Presley and the Beatles.

Louis Armstrong A trumpeter and a major innovator of jazz.

Louis Brandeis A prominent Boston lawyer and reformist thinker who was a consultant to Wilson during his campaign for election in 1912.

Louis Farrakhan Leader of the Nation of Islam who became controversial for his intense criticism of whites and their policies toward blacks.

Louisiana Purchase The acquisition in 1803 of the Louisiana Territory west of the Mississippi River and New Orleans by the United States from France for $15 million.

Lusitania A British liner hit by a German torpedo in May of 1915. Among the nearly twelve hundred passengers who died were 128 Americans.

Lyndon Baines Johnson The thirty-sixth president of the United States, he took over following President Kennedy's assassination in 1963 and was elected in a landslide the following year. He piloted a number of important initiatives through Congress, including the Civil Rights Act of 1964 and the Voting Rights Act of 1965.

Malcolm X A popular Black Muslim leader who advocated nationalism, self-defense, and racial separation. He split with the Black Muslim movement and formed the Organization of Afro-American Unity, which attracted thousands of young, urban blacks with its message of socialism and self-help. He was assassinated by a Black Muslim at a New York rally in 1965.

manifest destiny The belief that the United States was destined to grow from the Atlantic to the Pacific and from the Arctic to the tropics. Providence supposedly intended for Americans to have this area for a great experiment in liberty.

Marbury v. Madison The first decision by the Supreme Court to declare unconstitutional and void an act passed by Congress that the Court considered in violation of the Constitution. The decision established the doctrine of judicial review, which recognizes the authority of courts to declare statutes unconstitutional.

Marcus Garvey A Jamaican immigrant who promised to "organize the 400 million Negroes of the World into a vast organization to plant the banner of freedom in the great continent of Africa."

Margaret Sanger Living in Greenwich Village, New York, she saw women suffering from disease and poverty because of the large number of children they bore. In 1914 she coined the term "birth control" and began publishing a periodical called *Woman Rebel*.

Marian Anderson An opera singer and human rights advocate, she performed on the steps of the Lincoln Memorial before a crowd of seventy-five thousand after being denied the use of Constitution Hall by the Daughters of the American Revolution. She helped focus national attention on the racial prejudice faced by African Americans in all facets of national life.

Marshall Plan Also known as the European Recovery Plan, this 1947 U.S. plan costing about $13 billion was credited with restoring economic confidence throughout Western Europe, raising living standards, curbing the influence of local Communist parties, and increasing U.S. trade and investment on the Continent.

Martin Luther German theologian and leader of the Reformation. His opposition to the wealth and corruption of the papacy and his belief that salvation would be granted on the basis of faith alone rather than by works caused his excommunication from the Catholic Church (1521). Luther confirmed the Augsburg Confession in 1530, effectively establishing the Lutheran Church.

Martin Luther King Jr. An African American cleric whose eloquence and commitment to nonviolent tactics formed the foundation of the civil rights movement of the 1950s and 1960s. He led the 1963 march on Washington at which he delivered his now famous "I Have a Dream" speech. He was awarded the Nobel Peace Prize in 1964 and was assassinated four years later in Memphis, Tennessee.

Martin Van Buren The eighth president of the United States (1837–1841). A powerful Democrat from New York, he served in the U.S. Senate (1821–1828), as secretary of state (1829–1831), and as vice president (1833–1837) under Andrew Jackson before being elected president in 1836. He unsuccessfully sought reelection in 1840 and 1848.

Mary McLeod Bethune An educator who sought improved racial relations and educational opportunities for black Americans, she was part of the U.S. delegation to the first United Nations meeting (1945).

Massachusetts Bay colony Founded in 1630 by non-Separatist Puritans with the intention of creating a society in New England that would serve as a model for reforming the Anglican Church.

Maya Inhabitants of the Yucatan Peninsula whose civilization was at its height from AD 300 to 900. Their civilization included a unique system of writing, mathematics, architecture and sculpture, and astronomy.

Mayflower Compact When the *Mayflower* reached land at Cape Cod and the colonists decided to settle there, they lacked the legal basis to establish a government. Thus the adult males of the colony signed a mutual agreement for ordering their society later referred to as the Mayflower Compact.

Metacom Wampanoag leader who waged King Philip's War (1675–1676) with New England colonists who had encroached on Native American territory.

middle passage The transport of slaves across the Atlantic from Africa to North America.

midnight appointments Federal judicial officials appointed to office in the closing period of a presidential administration. The Republicans accused Adams of staying awake until midnight in order to sign the commissions for Federalist officeholders.

Midway Island A naval battle in World War II in which land and carrier-based U.S. planes decisively defeated a Japanese fleet on its way to invade Midway Island.

Mikhail Gorbachev General secretary of the Soviet Communist party in the mid-1980s and president of the USSR from 1989 to 1991, he ushered in an era of unprecedented *glasnost* (openness) and *perestroika* (restructuring) and won the Nobel Peace Prize in 1990.

Millard Fillmore The thirteenth president of the United States (1850–1853), who succeeded to office after the death of Zachary Taylor. He struggled to keep the nation unified but lost the support of his Whig party.

Million Man March A protest march in October 1995 in Washington, D.C. that was organized by Louis Farrakhan to draw attention to black grievances.

Missouri Compromise Measure passed by the U.S. Congress in 1820–1821 to end the first of a series of crises concerning the extension of slavery.

Monica Lewinsky An unpaid intern and later a paid staffer who had an affair with President Clinton in the White House.

Monroe Doctrine Authored by James Monroe, the doctrine declared U.S. opposition to European interference in the Americas.

Montgomery bus boycott Begun in December 1955 as a result of an act of protest by Rosa Parks against the segregated transportation facilities and humiliating treatment facing African Americans in the capital city of Alabama, the boycott soon became an international event.

Moral Majority A political action group founded in 1979 and composed of conservative, fundamentalist Christians. Led by evangelist Rev. Jerry Falwell, the group played a significant role in the 1980 elections through its strong support of conservative candidates.

muckraking The name given to investigative reporters in the early 1900s.

Muller v. Oregon Case in which the Supreme Court upheld limits on working hours for women.

Nat Turner American slave leader who organized about seventy followers and led a rebellion in Virginia, during which approximately fifty whites were killed (1831). He was then captured and executed.

Nathaniel Bacon American colonist who led Bacon's Rebellion (1676), in which a group of landless freemen attacked neighboring Indians and burned Jamestown in an attempt to gain land and greater participation in the government of Virginia.

Nathaniel Hawthorne Author of several important novels including *The Scarlet Letter* (1850) and *The House of Seven Gables* (1851).

National American Woman Suffrage Association This association was formed in 1890 through the efforts of Lucy Stone Blackwell, and its first president was Elizabeth Cady Stanton.

National Association for the Advancement of Colored People (NAACP) An organization that fights against racial injustice.

National Farmers' Alliance This group led to the emergence of the Populist party.

National Industrial Recovery Act (NIRA) Enacted on June 16, 1933, this emergency measure was designed to encourage industrial recovery and help combat widespread unemployment.

National Woman's party Created by Alice Paul, this organization pushed for the Equal Rights Amendment during the 1920s.

National Women's Trade Union League A feminist labor organization.

New Deal The name given to the many domestic programs and reforms instituted by President Franklin D. Roosevelt and his administration in response to the Great Depression of the 1930s.

New Jersey Plan Written by William Paterson, the New Jersey Plan proposed a one-house (unicameral) Congress in which states had equal representation.

New Nationalism Roosevelt's far-reaching program that called for a strong federal government to stabilize the economy, protect the weak, and restore social harmony.

New Negro African Americans after World War I who wanted their rights.

Newt Gingrich A congressman from Georgia first elected in 1978, he served as Speaker of the House from 1994 until he resigned from Congress in 1999.

Ngo Dinh Diem A Vietnamese political leader who became president of South Vietnam in 1954. He was assassinated in a military coup d'état.

Nikita Khrushchev A Soviet politician and Stalin loyalist in the 1930s, he was appointed first secretary of the Communist party in 1953. As Soviet premier, he denounced Stalin, thwarted the Hungarian Revolution of 1956, and improved his country's image abroad. He was deposed in 1964 for failing to establish missiles in Cuba or improve the Soviet economy.

Nisei A person born in the United States of parents who emigrated from Japan.

Northwest Ordinance Adopted by the Congress in 1787 to establish stricter control over the government of the Northwest territories ceded to the United States by the states. The ordinance was the most significant achievement of Congress under the Articles of Confederation.

Oklahoma City bombing Militant right-wing U.S. terrorists bombed the Alfred P. Murrah Federal Building in Oklahoma City in April 1995, causing the deaths of 168 people.

Oliver Evans American inventor who developed the first application of steam power in an industrial setting. He also developed a method of automating flour mills that a generation later was standard in U.S. mills.

Oliver North A member of the NSC staff and a Marine colonel, he was a central figure in the Iran-Contra scandal.

omnibus bill Grouping a number of items together in an attempt to get them passed; often used to enact controversial legislation.

Opechancanough Brother of Powhatan. In the 1620s Opechancanough organized a military offensive against English settlers.

Operation OVERLORD The name given to the Allied invasion of the European continent through Normandy.

Orval Faubus Governor of Arkansas in 1957 who triggered a confrontation between national authority and states' rights by defying a federal court order to integrate the all-white Central High School.

P. G. T. Beauregard American Confederate general known for his flamboyant personal style and dashing, but not always successful, strategic campaigns. He ordered the bombardment of Fort Sumter in April 1861.

panic of 1837 A financial crisis that began a major depression that lasted six years.

Paxton Boys To gain greater protection from Indian attacks in western Pennsylvania, the "Paxton Boys" of Lancaster County murdered a number of Christian Indians at Conestoga, then marched on Philadelphia.

Pearl Harbor The site of a U.S. naval base on the southern coast of Oahu, Hawaii, which the Japanese attacked on Sunday, December 7, 1941; the United States entered World War II the following day.

Peggy Eaton Wife of John Eaton and the central figure in a controversy that would divide President Jackson's cabinet into pro- and anti-Eaton factions.

Platt Amendment This amendment barred an independent Cuba from allying itself with another foreign power and gave the United States the right to intervene to preserve stability.

Plessy v. Ferguson The 1896 Supreme Court case that approved racial segregation.

Plymouth colony A colony established by the English Pilgrims, or Separatists, in 1620. The Separatists were Puritans who abandoned hope that the Anglican Church could be reformed. Plymouth became part of Massachusetts in 1691.

political correctness Of, relating to, or supporting broad social, political, and educational change, especially to redress historical injustices in matters such as race, class, gender, and sexual orientation.

popular sovereignty The concept that settlers of each territory would decide for themselves whether to allow slavery.

Populist party Also known as the People's party, they held their first national convention on July 4, 1892. The party platform took a stern view of the state of the nation, with planks endorsing the subtreasury, free coinage of silver, and other reform proposals.

Powhatan An Algonquian leader who founded the Powhatan confederacy and maintained peaceful relations with English colonists after the marriage of his daughter Pocahontas to John Rolfe (1614).

praying towns Established by John Eliot, praying towns were villages in which the Indians were supposed to adopt English customs and learn the fundamentals of Puritan religion.

predestination A theory that states that God has decreed who will be saved and who will be damned.

Prince Henry of Portugal Henry "the Navigator" (1394–1460) established a school for navigators and geographers. He sought to increase the power of Portugal by promoting exploration of trade routes to the East by way of Africa.

Proclamation of 1763 In an attempt to keep white settlers out of the Ohio Valley, the Proclamation of 1763 drew a line along the crest of the Appalachian Mountains from Maine to Georgia and required all colonists to move east of the line.

Prohibition An effort to ban the sale of alcohol; it was achieved in 1919.

Protestant Reformation The religious rebellion against the Roman Catholic Church that began in 1517 when Martin Luther posted his ninety-five theses on a church door in Wittenberg, Germany.

Pullman strike Strike by railway workers that led to nationwide unrest in 1894.

Puritanism The strain of English Calvinism that demanded purification of the Anglican Church, including elimination of rituals, vestments, statues, and bishops.

Ralph Waldo Emerson An American writer, philosopher, and central figure of American transcendentalism. His poems, orations, and especially his essays, such as *Nature* (1836), are regarded as landmarks in the development of American thought and literary expression.

Red Scare A label attached to the fear of many Americans that a radical movement existed within the United States that was determined to establish a Communist government here.

Reform party A political party founded by Ross Perot in 1995 as an alternative to the Democratic and Republican parties.

republican motherhood The idea of Dr. Benjamin Rush that nurturing incorruptible future leaders, or "republican motherhood," was women's principal responsibility under the new government.

Richard Nixon The thirty-seventh president of the United States. Known early in his career as a hard-line anti-Communist, he was the first U.S. president to visit Communist China. He also worked skillfully to ease tensions with the Soviet Union. He became the first president to resign from office, due to his involvement in the Watergate scandal.

Roanoke Island England's first attempt to establish a colony in North America was at Roanoke Island in 1585.

robber barons Railroad industry leaders such as Cornelius Vanderbilt and Jay Gould who became renowned for their ruthless methods against competitors.

Robert E. Lee American general who led the Army of Northern Virginia in the American Civil War.

Robert Kennedy He served as attorney general during the presidency of his brother John F. Kennedy. Elected to the Senate in 1964, he was assassinated in Los Angeles while campaigning for the presidency.

Robert La Follette Progressive governor and senator from Wisconsin.

Robert Morris American Revolutionary politician and financier. A signer of the Declaration of Independence, he raised money for the Continental Army, attended the Constitutional Convention (1787), and was financially ruined by land speculation.

Rodney King The victim of a violent beating by Los Angeles police that was caught on videotape and became the central event of the 1992 riots.

Roe v. Wade Decided by the Supreme Court in 1973, this case along with *Doe v. Bolton* legalized abortion in the first trimester.

Roger B. Taney American jurist who served as the chief justice of the U.S. Supreme Court (1836–1864). In the *Dred Scott* decision (1857) he ruled that slaves and their descendants had no rights as citizens.

Roger Williams English cleric in America who was expelled from Massachusetts for his criticism of Puritan policies. He founded Providence Plantation (1636), a community based on religious freedom, and obtained a charter for Rhode Island in 1644.

Ronald Reagan The fortieth president of the United States, he represented the ascendancy of conservatism during the 1980s.

Roosevelt Corollary Roosevelt's extension of the Monroe Doctrine to Latin American states and the right to supervise their behavior.

Rosa Parks Her refusal to give up her seat on a bus to a white man in Montgomery, Alabama, resulted in a citywide boycott of the bus company and stirred the civil rights movement across the nation.

Rosie the Riveter A symbol of the new breed of working women during World War II.

Ross Perot A businessman, he first came to national attention during the Iran hostage crisis when he funded an operation that rescued two of his employees from an Iranian prison. In 1992 he emerged as an independent candidate for president, expressing serious concern over the national debt.

royal fifth A tax on silver and gold of which one-fifth of its value went to the king of Spain.

Rutherford B. Hayes Nineteenth president of the United States, he was beneficiary of the most fiercely disputed election in American history.

Sacagawea Shoshone guide and interpreter who accompanied the Lewis and Clark expedition (1805–1806).

Sacco and Vanzetti Two immigrants tried for murder in Massachusetts in the 1920s whose trial attracted worldwide attention because of allegations that the men had been unjustly convicted.

Salem witch trials The prosecution in 1691 and 1692 of almost two hundred people in Salem, Massachusetts, and its environs on charges of practicing witchcraft. Twenty people were put to death before Governor William Phips halted the trials.

Samuel F. B. Morse American painter and inventor. He refined and patented the telegraph and developed the telegraphic code that bears his name.

Samuel J. Tilden Governor of New York selected to run as the Democratic candidate in the 1876 presidential election. He narrowly lost what has been considered the most controversial election in American history.

Samuel Slater British-born textile pioneer in America. He oversaw construction of the nation's first successful water-powered cotton mill (1790–1793).

Sandra Day O'Connor Appointed during the presidency of Ronald Reagan, she was the first woman justice on the Supreme Court.

Scopes trial Local authorities indicted this Dayton, Tennessee, schoolteacher for teaching evolution in one of his classes. The jury found him guilty and assessed a small fine.

Scottsboro boys A group of black youths accused of raping a white woman in Alabama who became a source of controversy and the focus of civil rights activism in the early 1930s.

Second Bank of the United States Created to prevent inflation and deflation of the American economy. Many prominent figures believed the Second Bank of the United States had too much power, one of whom was President Jackson, who vetoed the bank's attempt to recharter.

Second Great Awakening A series of Protestant religious revivals that began in 1797 and lasted into the 1830s.

Seminoles A Native American people made up of various primarily Creek groups who moved into northern Florida during the eighteenth and nineteenth centuries, later inhabiting the Everglades region as well.

Seneca Falls Convention The first major gathering of woman's rights advocates was held in Seneca Falls, New York, in 1848.

September 11, 2001 On this date al Qaeda terrorists carried out a plan by Osama bin Laden that destroyed the World Trade Center towers and damaged the Pentagon in Washington, D.C.

Seven Years' War The world conflict (1754–1763) fought in Europe, India, and North America between Great Britain, Hanover, and Prussia on one side and France, Austria, Spain, and other nations on the other side.

sharecropping Working land in return for a share of the crops produced instead of paying cash rent. A shortage of currency in the South made this a frequent form of land tenure, and African Americans endured it because it eliminated the labor gangs of the slavery period.

Shays's Rebellion The revolt by western Massachusetts farmers in 1786–1787 named after one of the leaders, Daniel Shays. Their demands included a more responsive state government, paper money, and tender laws that would enable them to settle debts and pay taxes with goods rather than with specie.

Sherman Antitrust Act This legislation was passed in 1890 to curb the growth of large monopolistic corporations.

Sieur de La Salle French explorer in North America who claimed Louisiana for France (1682).

Sir Edmund Andros English colonial administrator in America whose attempt to unify the New England colonies under his governorship (1686–1689) was met by revolt.

Sitting Bull Ally of Crazy Horse in the Custer battle.

Sixteenth Amendment Ratified in 1913, this amendment made an income tax constitutional.

Smoked Yankees The term used by Spanish troops to denote African American soldiers who fought in the war with Spain.

Social Darwinism A philosophy that allegedly showed how closely the social history of humans resembled Darwin's principle of "survival of the fittest." According to this theory, human social history could be understood as a struggle among races, with the strongest and the fittest invariably triumphing.

Sojourner Truth A former slave who became an advocate for abolitionism and for woman's rights.

Spanish-American War The conflict that brought the United States a world empire.

Special Field Order 15 Issued by William T. Sherman in January of 1865, this order reserved land in coastal South Carolina, Georgia, and Florida for former slaves. Those who settled on the land would receive forty-acre plots.

spoils system A system by which the victorious political party rewarded its supporters with government jobs.

Sputnik I Launched by the Soviet Union in October 1957, it was the first artificial space satellite. News of its success provoked both anger and anxiety among the American people who had always taken their country's technological superiority for granted.

Squanto A Patuxet Indian who helped the English colonists in Plymouth develop agricultural techniques and served as an interpreter between the colonists and the Wampanoags.

Square Deal Roosevelt's approach to treating capital and labor on an equal basis.

Stamp Act In 1765 the British Parliament passed a law requiring colonists to purchase a stamp for official documents and published papers, including wills, newspapers, and pamphlets.

Stephen A. Douglas American politician who served as U.S. representative (1843–1847) and senator (1847–1861) from Illinois. He proposed legislation that allowed individual territories to determine whether they would allow slavery (1854), and in the senatorial campaign of 1858 he engaged Abraham Lincoln in a famous series of debates.

Stephen Crane Author of *The Red Badge of Courage*.

stock market crash of 1929 The collapse of stock prices that ended the speculative boom of the 1920s and is associated with the onset of the Great Depression.

Stono Uprising A revolt of enslaved Africans against their owners near the Stono River in South Carolina.

Strategic Defense Initiative (SDI) A research and development program of the U.S. government tasked with developing a space-based system to defend the nation from attack by strategic ballistic missiles.

Students for a Democratic Society (SDS) Formed in Port Huron, Michigan, in 1962, this group became one of the leading New Left anti-war organizations of the 1960s, exemplifying both the idealism and the excesses of radical student groups in the Vietnam era.

suffrage The right to vote that was extended to African American males after the Civil War.

Susan B. Anthony Advocate of woman's suffrage and leader in the woman's rights movement along with Elizabeth Cady Stanton.

Tecumseh Shawnee leader who attempted to establish a confederacy to unify Native Americans against white encroachment. He sided with the British in the War of 1812 and was killed in the Battle of the Thames.

temperance Reducing the influence and the effect of alcoholic beverages in American life.

temperance movement The act of abstaining from partaking of alcoholic beverages.

Tennessee Valley Authority (TVA) Created in 1933 during the New Deal's first hundred days, it was a massive experiment in regional planning that focused on providing electricity, flood control, and soil conservation to one of the nation's poorest regions, covering seven states in the Tennessee Valley.

Tet offensive A major military operation by the North Vietnamese and Viet Cong in 1968. Though beaten back, there were tremendous casualties, and the enormity of the offensive served to undermine President Johnson's claim that steady progress was being made in Vietnam.

The Birth of a Nation A twisted movie portrayal of the Reconstruction period in the South that depicted African Americans as ignorant and that glamorized the Ku Klux Klan.

The Book of Mormon The holy book of the Church of Jesus Christ of Latter-Day Saints, or the Mormons.

The Federalist Papers James Madison, Alexander Hamilton, and John Jay wrote a series of eighty-five essays in support of the Constitution. First published in newspapers, they appeared in book form as *The Federalist* in the spring of 1788.

The Grapes of Wrath Written by John Steinbeck and published in 1939, this novel depicts the struggle of ordinary Americans in the Great Depression, following the plight of the Joad family as it migrated west from Oklahoma to California.

The Great Communicator A nickname given to Ronald Reagan for his skill in conveying his views.

The Jazz Singer One of the first motion pictures with sound, it starred Al Jolson who specialized in blackface renditions of popular tunes.

theocracy A government ruled by or subject to religious authority.

Theodore Roosevelt The twenty-sixth president of the United States, the youngest president in the nation's history. He brought new excitement and power to the presidency as he vigorously led Congress and the American people toward progressive reforms and a strong foreign policy.

Thirteenth Amendment Passed in 1865, this constitutional amendment abolished slavery.

Thomas Alva Edison The inventor of the phonograph, electric lights, and countless other products.

Thomas J. "Stonewall" Jackson American Confederate general who commanded troops at both battles of Bull Run (1861 and 1862) and directed the Shenandoah Valley campaign (1862). He was accidentally killed by his own troops at Chancellorsville (1863).

Thomas Jefferson The third president of the United States (1801–1809). A member of the second Continental Congress, he drafted the Declaration of Independence (1776). His presidency was marked by the purchase of the Louisiana Territory from France (1803) and the Embargo of 1807.

Thomas Paine Author of *Common Sense* (1776) and other pamphlets, Paine was a recent immigrant from England.

Tiananmen Square Adjacent to the Forbidden City in Beijing, China, this large public square was the site of many festivals, rallies, and demonstrations. During a student demonstration there in 1989, Chinese troops fired on the demonstrators, killing an estimated two thousand or more.

Tories The term referred to the followers of James II and became the name of a major political party in England. Americans who remained loyal to the British during the Revolution were called Tories.

Trail of Tears After determined efforts to move the Cherokee, the tribe was deported from Georgia to what is now Oklahoma; thousands died on the march known as the Trail of Tears.

transcendentalists Members of an intellectual and social movement of the 1830s and 1940s that emphasized the active role the mind plays in constructing what we think of as reality. A loose grouping of intellectuals in Massachusetts sought to "transcend" the limits of thought in conventional America, whether religious or philosophical.

Treaty of Paris Signed on September 3, 1783, the Treaty of Paris established the independence of the United States from Great Britain. It set specific land boundaries and called for the evacuation of British troops.

Treaty of Tordesillas The Treaty of Tordesillas (1494) located the Line of Demarcation 370 leagues (about 1,000 miles) west of the Azores and expanded the principle of "spheres of influence."

Treaty of Utrecht Ending Queen Anne's War between Great Britain and France, the Treaty of Utrecht ceded control of Nova Scotia, Newfoundland, and the Hudson Bay territory to the English.

Triangle Shirtwaist Fire A tragic fire at the Triangle Shirtwaist Company in which dozens of female workers perished.

Triple Alliance An alliance between Italy, Germany, and Austria-Hungary whose ties were frayed in 1914.

Truman Doctrine Reflecting a tougher approach to the Soviet Union following World War II, President Truman went before Congress in 1947 to request $400 million in military aid for Greece and Turkey, claiming the appropriation was vital to the containment of Communism and to the future of freedom everywhere.

trustbusters Term applied to Theodore Roosevelt's efforts to enforce the Sherman Act.

Tweed Ring The most celebrated example of political corruption in the Reconstruction Era, led by William Magear Tweed Jr.

Twentieth Amendment This amendment moved the presidential inauguration date from four months after the election to January 20.

U-2 A U.S. spy plane. One piloted by Francis Gary Powers was shot down over the Soviet Union in 1960, which led to the angry breakup of a Summit meeting in Paris between President Eisenhower and Soviet Premier Nikita Khrushchev.

Ulysses S. Grant The eighteenth president of the United States; commander of the Union Army in the American Civil War.

Uncle Tom's Cabin Novel by author Harriet Beecher Stowe that helped change white attitudes toward African Americans.

Upton Sinclair A writer whose novel *The Jungle* exposed abuses in the meat-packing industry.

vertical integration A procedure wherein a company gains control of all phases of production.

viceroy A man who is the governor of a country, province, or colony, ruling as the representative of a sovereign.

Vicksburg Mississippi battle site under siege by Grant's army for six weeks. Before falling it became the symbol of Confederate doggedness and Union frustration.

Victoriano Huerta The Mexican general who presented a problem for President Wilson.

Vietnamization A policy whereby the South Vietnamese were to assume more of the military burdens of the war. This transfer of responsibility was expected to eventually allow the United States to withdraw.

Virginia Company In 1606 King James I chartered the Virginia Company; one group was centered in London and founded Jamestown, a second group from Plymouth in western England founded the Plymouth colony.

Virginia Plan Written by James Madison, the Virginia Plan proposed a powerful central government dominated by a National Legislature of two houses (bicameral). It also favored a system of greater representation based on a state's population.

W. E. B. Du Bois Initially a supporter of Booker T. Washington's education policy, he later criticized Washington's methods as having "practically accepted the alleged inferiority of the Negro."

Walt Whitman A visionary poet who wrote *Leaves of Grass* (1855), inventing a new American idiom.

Walter Mondale Vice president of the United States under Jimmy Carter, he earlier served as a U.S. senator from Minnesota and was the unsuccessful 1984 Democratic nominee for president.

war on terrorism In response to the September 11 attacks, President George W. Bush declared war on the terrorists and sent U.S. troops to invade first Afghanistan and later Iraq.

Watergate The Democratic National Headquarters at the Watergate complex in Washington, D.C. was burglarized in 1972, which led to criminal convictions for several top government officials and forced President Nixon to resign from office in 1974.

Watts riots Among the most violent urban disturbances in U.S. history, it erupted in an African American neighborhood in Los Angeles following the arrest of a black motorist. By the time it ended, five days later, forty-one people were dead, hundreds were injured, property damage topped $200 million, and National Guardsmen had to be called in to restore order.

Wendell Wilkie A Wall Street lawyer who ran against Franklin D. Roosevelt in his bid for a third consecutive term, which Roosevelt won.

Whiskey Rebellion In the early 1790s western Pennsylvania farmers resisted the whiskey tax: they held protest meetings, tarred and feathered collaborators, and destroyed property. In 1794 the Washington administration sent thirteen thousand troops to restore order, but the revolt was over by the time they arrived.

Whitewater The popular name for a failed Arkansas real estate venture by the Whitewater Development Corporation in which then Governor Bill Clinton and his wife, Hillary, were partners.

William Henry Harrison While governor of the Indiana Territory, he attacked and burned Prophetstown in 1811. The ninth president of the United States (1841), he died of pneumonia after one month in office.

William Howard Taft The twenty-seventh president of the United States, who split with Theodore Roosevelt once in office.

William Jefferson "Bill" Clinton The forty-second president of the United States.

William Jennings Bryan Named secretary of state by Wilson, he pursued world peace through arbitration treaties.

William Lloyd Garrison American abolitionist leader who founded and published *The Liberator* (1831–1865), an antislavery journal.

William McKinley The twenty-fifth president of the United States, he won by the largest majority of popular votes since 1872.

William Penn An English Quaker leader who obtained a charter for Pennsylvania from Charles II in exchange for a debt owed to Penn's father. Penn in-

tended to establish a model society based on religious freedom and peaceful relations with Native Americans, in addition to benefiting financially from the sale of the land.

William Pitt A British political leader and orator who directed his country's military effort during the Seven Years' War.

William Randolph Hearst The most celebrated publisher of the yellow press.

William T. Sherman Union general under Ulysses S. Grant who took Atlanta and led the "March to the Sea."

William Walker A proslavery Tennessean who pushed for expansion of the American territory into Cuba or Central America, places where slavery could flourish.

Winston Churchill A British politician and writer, as prime minister (1940–1945 and 1951–1955) he led Great Britain through World War II. He published several books, including *The Second World War* (1948–1953), and won the 1953 Nobel Prize for literature.

woman suffrage Women achieved the right to vote in 1919–1920 after an intense struggle in Congress.

Woodrow Wilson The twenty-eighth president of the United States, he was an advocate for the New Freedom and the League of Nations.

Woodstock Art and Music Fair A fusion of rock music, hard drugs, free love, and an antiwar protest drawing four hundred thousand people in the summer of 1969.

writs of assistance General search warrants; a writ of assistance authorized customs officials to search for smuggled goods.

XYZ Affair Name given to the episode in which the French government (the Directory) demanded, through three agents known to the American public as X, Y, and Z, that the U.S. government pay a bribe and apologize for criticizing France.

yellow press (yellow journalism) A type of journalism that stressed lurid and sensational news to boost circulation.

Zachary Taylor The twelfth president (died in his first year in office in 1850), he became famous as a general in the war with Mexico. As Whig president, he tried to avoid entanglements of both party and region.

Zimmermann Telegram A secret German diplomatic telegram to the German ambassador in Mexico that was intercepted and decoded by the British. It dangled the return to Mexico of Arizona, New Mexico, and Texas as bait to entice the Mexicans to enter the war on the side of Germany.

Zora Neale Hurston An African American novelist who embodied the creative and artistic aspirations of the Harlem Renaissance in the 1920s.

Index